SEVENTY THOUSAND CAMELS

SEVENTY THOUSAND CAMELS

A Motivational Survivor's Memoir

ANGELICA A. BREWER

DoctorZed
Publishing
www.doctorzed.com

Second Edition published 2022 by DoctorZed Publishing.

DoctorZed Publishing books may be ordered through booksellers or by contacting:

DoctorZed Publishing
IDAHO
10 Vista Ave
Skye, South Australia 5072
www.doctorzed.com
info@doctorzed.com

ISBN: 978-0-6455442-7-5 (sc)
ISBN: 978-0-6455442-8-2 (e)

A CIP number for this book is available at the National Library of Australia.
This is a work of non-fiction. The views expressed in this work are solely those of the author and do not necessarily reflect the views of the publisher, and the publisher hereby disclaims any responsibility for them.

Printed in Australia, Uk & USA

DoctorZed Publishing rev. date: 07/07/2022

*I dedicate this book to my husband Adam Heath Brewer.
Without your wilful love or resilient patience, I'm not sure
I would have made it. Thank you for not giving up on me.*

'Life, it's no fun when you're hunted by the things that you feel.'

Lyrics from 'I hope I never' written by Tim Finn (*Split Enz*)

CONTENTS

———

INTRODUCTION

───

I do not recall my childhood beyond a certain age; perhaps as a six or seven-year-old. What I do recall are the things that were important to me emotionally and tangibly.

I didn't have much, and what I *did* have I treasured. A Cinderella handkerchief for example; it was almost transparent from overuse but I loved it. Disney films were my first introduction to fantastic escapism, and I was enamoured with all of Walt's heroes and heroines. I also revelled in old Hollywood films and their beautiful, translucent actresses.

My rollerskates spelt freedom from everything and everyone. Where other children received bicycles, our poverty afforded me only a pair of used skates, the type you strapped over your sneakers. I really loved rollerskating and when I wasn't zoning out on them, talking to my 'Invisible Friend', I'd readily take on the challenges of Castel Sant'Angelo's bituminised terrain.

My books; I had a thirst both for knowledge and for fantasy that has never dissolved. I cherished my Topolino comics and fairy tales, but sought out true life accounts as well – particularly those concerning crime and punishment. As well as reading, I would write my own stories as avidly and eloquently as I could recite poetry or illustrious quotations. My classroom comprehensions were always well received by my teachers, and my drawing skills were above my age group average. My peers lined up to have me decorate their homework pages. I could have been an artist someday.

Celebrations like Christmas and my birthday were to me hallowed days because it seemed that at long last I, as the only child in a miniscule family, might just receive *all* the attention. Ironic I know.

My imagination was boundless. Within my mind's eye, anywhere I found myself, I would create an adventure – with all of my quests bound by a common thread. I'd be rescued by a beautiful boy who'd fall in love with me at a glance and take me to magical heights such as I'd never before seen, and where no one would ever find me – especially not my mother.

Friendships were also important to me but, because of my upbringing, I was not always able to maintain or nurture them. I was a possessive, calculating child who needed to own someone in order to feel completely honoured. I was the same with my food, hiding goodies so that no one would ask to share them. I was happy to lend someone a book or a toy but beware if it was ruined or not returned.

I was the spirit of contradiction – as Mother dubbed me. If someone disliked something or someone I made it my mission to uncover why and proclaim the subject a hero. I developed this personality trait to defeat a narcissistic mother whose maternal warmth I could not have.

I was very tactile. I craved human touch and nurturing; it was rarely forthcoming but wherever possible I'd take it by force. At the same time, I found myself an excruciating empath, forever the champion of the underdog, and sporting greater insight than most of my peers. As I grew older this 'admirable' quality only intensified and was to cause me a great deal of personal grief. What I now realise of course is that I wasn't *really* saving others from circumstance or themselves, but was in fact projecting *my* inner trauma onto them, and attempting to save myself by proxy.

My fantasy world saw me the winner of titles, and the beguiling goddess who would blind all with her iridescent omnipotence and mystique. Inside my Olympic Universe I was the best runner, the best dancer, the smartest in the class, the one everyone wanted to know and be friends with, the most beautiful, the strongest, the queen of the Roll Arena, the wealthiest, the most generous, and a ruler of humankind. I was a prepubescent megalomaniac with too much empathy, who desperately needed to be loved and acknowledged, and was inherently afraid of loss.

I soon became obsessed with the unattainable and developed a morbid interest and admiration for cultures whose pre-eminent trait was to gain power via the subjugation of others: The Nazis, the Ancient Romans, and the Vikings. Yet I was not like these tyrants – I *cared* for people, especially the weak and helpless. I was extreme, dark, complex, excessive and antithetical, albeit kind, considerate, practical and logical.

These polar proclivities in my make-up were the same ones that would colour the rest of my life, creating opportunities and obstacles alike. For many years I thought I was somewhat mad, and this was compounded by tongue in cheek 'affectionate' remarks made by people close to me: "You're weird Angelica!", "You're just my crazy friend!" and that old chestnut, "What planet did *you* come from?"

The truth is I'm hypersensitive and open to everything. In my opinion I hail from *Planet Empath*, as do many others like me. I absorb all that surrounds me like a sponge, and have trouble cataloguing events and interpersonal interactions according not to reality, but to subjective expectation. I do not detach or regroup easily and I offer way too much without prior investigation. Life for me is often a simultaneous assault on all the senses, but I don't consider myself to be 'Asperger's'. I have a penchant for tautology both in the literal and metaphorical sense. I'm quite possibly borderline personality disordered, or something like that. Mystics would categorise me as an 'empath'.

Yet, at the end of the day I am simply *me* and cannot be anyone else no matter how hard I try. All my life I have made an attempt to adapt to how things should be and found myself wanting. One aspect of the complete liberation of the soul is accepting oneself's inimitable authenticity. One must then embrace it, fall in love with it, and to hell with public consensus! They are not the ones walking your path.

This story ends very differently from how it may be interpreted by run-of-the-mill perception or wishful thinking. I began life holding on to one steady view, but by the age of fifty that view had changed so dramatically, I felt left in contempt of my true self and make no apology for that.

And so folks, this is my weird and fantastical yet very true story. From 'Imperial' Rome, to notorious Cabramatta in New South Wales, to nondescript Tunkillo in South Australia and beyond. Enjoy a ride of a different kind and bless you all.

Namasthae)0(
(This is how it is written in Hindi)
Adel Angelica Brewer

PREFACE

——

A round 1980, I wrote my autobiography. I was fifteen years old. By that age I had already experienced a great deal of adversity, yet not in a context from which I, or most people, could learn.

In 1998, at the age of thirty-three, I rewrote my autobiography and sent the synopsis and manuscript to literary agents and publishers around the country and overseas. I received numerous appraisals but no publication offers. I knew instinctively that the journey was far from over, and I also knew that things do not happen until they benefit your Higher Purpose.

So in 2017 at the age of fifty-two I added to my prior attempts and finished the story. The journey is still far from over but I believe the messages are now ready for the public arena. I hope you my reader, derive something, anything, from this story. It's not a pretty story but, as one of my peer reviewers commented, it's a story offering hope and strength, and thank you for a most truthful appraisal *Sharon* and *Fred*.

Raised a Catholic, I discovered Metaphysics in 1990, aged twenty-five. I have not looked back since. For me religion, in the form of Catholicism, offered nothing, and when your entire life is fraught with painful, crushing experiences, one needs a little more than heaven and hell with purgatory in between.

Up until 1990 I continually asked myself *Why me? What did I do to deserve so much pain? Why am I such a shit magnet?* An understanding of Metaphysics helped solve the riddle, pointing me in the right direction. Let me add however that Metaphysics was neither an overnight solution for my troubles nor an immediate cure for my burnt out and twisted emotions. Like anything else worth changing in life, it was but another exercise to reach a fuller comprehension and acceptance of the Higher Self and its role in this, one of *many* incarnations.

The journey you are about to embark in will be raw and sometimes acrimonious; this is because I need to relate my experiences in an egoistic way to reach readers at an earthbound level. Nothing that happens to us is mere coincidence and we are all born carrying a life blueprint of our choosing prior to earthly incarnation.

As raw, acrimonious and earthy as my journey may appear, I am partially grateful to its antagonists, for they have brought me to this point of realisation and reformation. A cliché, yes – but true nonetheless. In *no way* do I state however that I have come to love, or have completely forgiven, some of the people who have hurt me at my deepest core. There are two people I still deeply resent and cannot bear to hear of or talk about. Cognition is a function separate from forgiveness, just as rationale differs from emotion.

As I age, I realise that forgiveness is indeed a 'key' to freedom from emotional pain just as our dear Buddhist teachers say, but it too has its time and place. At the end of the day before one can forgive others, they must forgive themselves for being human and making human errors in judgement. I think I'm more than halfway there.

The antagonists are real, the events and locations are real, but most importantly so are my feelings – they are 100 percent authentic: I have left nothing out. The names of the people I talk about have mostly been changed to protect their identity, and to guard myself from possible legal action. Not everyone is ready for the truth, alas, and in a society that thrives on travesty and lawsuits, pseudonyms are a necessity.

Nonetheless, I apologise in advance if 'you' who have contributed to my history, happen to recognise yourself and feel insulted or hard done by. I do mention the word truth, but in this book I speak only my own Truth and I humbly concede that truth or fiction is relative only to one's own interpretation, perception or judgement.

A Facebook meme I saw once puts the dilemma succinctly: 'I am responsible for what I say; I am not responsible for what you understand.'

Life is too short to harbour resentments, doubts or inner pain. The sooner we learn to understand why things happen to us, the sooner we are released from feelings of persecution, anguish, regret, and the conviction that sheer bad luck exists! My two favourite esoteric phrases are *Carl Jung's 'What you resist persists' and *James Redfield's 'Where Attention goes Energy flows; Where Intention goes Energy flows!' We are indeed captains of our own ship and masters of our own destiny.

Please do not say *Poor thing* about me as you continue reading. Say instead, *Wow, what a brave survivor,* and *Bless her for not giving up!* I am not about self-pity although occasionally I do enjoy having real friends and family rally around me for a little 'ear tickling'. Strength sometimes eludes us all and even Superman can be knocked out by kryptonite.

Cherish every day; do not look back, for the past is the past for a reason and the future is yet to be created and the type of creation you invoke depends entirely on how you think and behave *right now*, right this minute. And one last thing before I let you immerse yourself: choose your relationships *wisely* – not every one is real or meant to stay in your life. Listen to your gut – it is always right; your heart and mind are of the flesh and only there for the realisation of earthly desires.

Apna Khayal Rakhna)0(
(Take care of yourself – Hindi)

CHAPTER ONE

SSSSSSSSSSSS

———

The four choices were presented to me by *Source* and I knew the one I picked was not going to be easy. I also knew there was a possibility my mother may not carry me through to birth, but if I wanted to atone for all the bad I had done, this was the choice I had to take.

* * *

Fourteenth of May, 1965 circa 11.00 am. A little girl Snake is born barely alive inside a Roman hospital. Only medical staff and her grandmother are there to greet the blue-black blob with three foreheads.

The fragile infant had been choked by her own umbilical cord, which had wound itself three times around her tiny neck. An emergency caesarean was performed; the mother was bleeding profusely and in need of assistance herself. Forceps extracted the silent child – the marks of which were branded on her transparent temples. Both Mother and baby would be okay due to a miracle in the form of a doctor called away from theatre in order to deal with the situation. After some sculpting work the little girl was handed back to her mother who proclaimed her daughter *a little beauty*.

And this is how I came into the world, fiftyone years ago.

I was christened Adalgisa Angelica Domenica Edelmira, the *Fuck Child* of Gilda and Ettore – unmarried, emotionally absent parents.

Gilda, my mother, was a professional operatic soprano taught by Maria Callas's singing teacher, a fact I heard repeated ad nauseam. Born in Morocco to Spanish parents during a clandestine escapade, Gilda left Madrid when she was twenty-two years old to finish her conservatorium studies in Rome, closely followed by my grandmother, Letitia.

If the need called for it, Letitia would follow her daughter to the ends of the world. She was pathologically obsessed with the blonde, green-eyed beauty who was the little girl *she* was not allowed to be. This fixation was the beginning of the end for a promising career in opera simply because Letitia was the archetypal stage mother, and Gilda her fragile and impressionable child *artiste*.

Letitia, born and bred in Madrid, was the child of wealthy parents who could trace their roots to Spanish aristocracy. Letitia had seven brothers, her only sister dying in infancy. Letitia, perhaps predictably, became 'Daddy's girl' – self-indulgent, petulant and always 'up to no good'. Boasting she smoked from the age of ten and could beat any of her brothers in a fight or running race, this Sagittarian little minx was domineering and single-minded. When she was fifteen years old her nightgown caught fire, permanently disfiguring her back. I still remember, as a small child myself, seeing the tell-tale burn marks and trying hard to imagine the pain they must have caused her.

Letitia married Edmundo, my grandfather, who was named after his famous father and my great grandfather. Edmundo Senior was an influential magistrate, so renowned and revered that a street in central Madrid was renamed in his honour. Family legend states that during the Franco regime Letitia and Edmundo, staunch Republicans, conspired against the dictatorship by covertly harbouring and despatching activists. It is unclear which of them was the less faithful one in the relationship, but it was infidelity that led Edmundo into betraying his wife to the Franco authorities, resulting in an arrest and subsequent sentencing.

I wish I had asked my grandmother a thousand more questions about her life, as some of her stories were completely 'out there'. In relation to her revolutionary escapades, Letitia informed me she had *twice* been sentenced to death and evaded execution, and had spent five long years inside a Franco prison. My mother made suggestions that Letitia had led an unscrupulous life. She was of the firm opinion that Letitia had been 'sleeping with the right people' in order to obtain clemency.

Letitia's only child at the time, a boy known to us as Pepito, was sent to live with an aunt. Upon her release, five years later, Letitia tried to retrieve her son but Pepito had come to regard the aunt as his mother, so Letitia left him there.

My mother and her twin brothers Eduardo and Miguel have never met their older brother. It is painfully obvious that none of them ever tried to find him.

When she had been out of prison for a few years, Edmundo caught up with his estranged wife and, oddly enough, Letitia took him back. She spoke often of Edmundo's swashbuckling looks – *the most handsome man in Madrid*. The relationship did not survive, however, and Letitia took my mother to live with her rich mother in Benidorm. Where my uncles were at this time has never been disclosed and the only person who could possibly tell me anything today is my Uncle Eduardo, but, thoroughly honouring his mother, he refuses to discuss family issues. Unfortunately, my Uncle Miguel unceremoniously died in the early 1980s from cancer of the oesophagus.

Letitia would talk about Edmundo during our chats.

"The bastard, he wanted me back, but I struck him on the head with a stiletto. It got wedged into his skull and he never came looking for me again!"

Somehow, knowing the spirited Archer that was my grandmother, I did not doubt her version of events.

Neither my mother nor my uncles ever saw Edmundo again. I was thus robbed of not one but two potential grandfathers – but did it really matter?

My parents, during my life in Rome, effectively consisted of Gilda and Letitia. There were no male influences in my life; my biological father, Ettore, who I dubbed the *Sperm Incognito*, never showed his face to me – he simply did not exist. Even my Italian birth certificate noted him as Father Unknown.

When annoyed, my mother could be a very vicious woman so I rarely dared to 'rock her boat'. Though I needed to know about my father, I knew all too well the topic was off limits. Once, as we strolled along a *viale* to the *Radiotelevisione Italiana* (RAI) headquarters, I innocently mentioned that Ettore was my favourite man's name, and boy was I given a serve that day. Naturally I had no idea why I'd been scolded and I wasn't about to ask. Much later in life the penny dropped; but was my father really *that* bad, so bad that Mother could not tolerate the very mention of his name?

We were at the RAI that day for a preview of the televised broadcast of Piccinni's opera *La Buona Figliuola*, in which my mother played a starring role. I remember watching Gilda sweeping about the enormous stage trapped inside an equally enormous crinoline. The opera was performed at the sumptuous Teatro di San Carlo in Naples but, as the small child I was, I eventually fell asleep on Uncle Miguel's lap. Despite all the excitement of stardom, I found the opera as dull as a puddle.

Many years on, I found the 1969 recording of that production on YouTube and, much as I hate to admit it, Mother *was* an absolute star in every sense of the word.

Letitia delighted in the exhumation of family skeletons from our clan's tightly sealed vault. Whether the accounts are genuine or to what extent have been exaggerated, I'll never truly know. Our family, like so many others I suppose, kept a lot of things firmly under wraps.

As with my dramatic birth, I proved a tenacious child and never failed to deliver Letitia some well-planned prompting regarding the *Sperm Incognito*'s role in our lives. It went something like this. Ettore was just one of my mother's many boyfriends and suitors. She was a very beautiful and vivacious woman. Ettore, a native Roman public servant with a penchant for opera and mixing in intellectual circles, was tall, redheaded, befreckled, and had been raised by a psychologist mother and a university professor father. Both parents attended diligently to every one of their only child's whims, inadvertently turning Ettore into a narcissist and neo-sadist.

The relationship between Ettore and Gilda was, according to my grandmother, excruciating. When Mother found out she was pregnant with me, Ettore demanded she abort immediately. Gilda had had a number of previous terminations and flatly refused. Perhaps due to Catholic guilt, or a concern she might not get another chance at motherhood, another termination bothered her. In my twenties I discovered that Letitia, my grandmother, had actually supported terminating me; an inopportune child would only interfere with Gilda's career plans.

Once I was born, Letitia recounted, a thwarted and out of his mind Ettore attempted to kill both my grandmother and me by running over us with his car. He missed. What a shame! Imagine how much more productive my dear mother's life might have been, how much more glittering her career, without me in it.

By the age of one I had defied death *four* times. First by avoiding being terminated before I was born, then at my birth, and then the attempt on my life by my biological father. The fourth came when I tried to follow Eulalio (my cat) onto our apartment's window ledge up on the top floor. My mother saw my nappy-clad bottom disappearing behind the curtains and grabbed me by the ankles just before my lunge forward to catch up with my pet.

Cats have nine lives, yes, but how many lives do snakes have?

* * *

Snakes are the most demonised and misunderstood creatures on the face of the earth, when in fact they are placid and territorial creatures. The most likely reason for non-venomous snakes to bite is because they are afraid. When given a choice to bite or run away, the snake will choose the latter every time unless heavily pregnant. If a snake feels cornered or is unable to hide from perceived danger, she *will* strike out – more as a warning to leave her alone than to cause actual harm. Allow the snake to bask in the sun in peace. If she becomes interested in you, she may slither over. Don't ever force her to interact or her reaction will probably be either to fight you or take flight and, if she chooses to fight, expect to come out second best. According to the traditions of Chinese Astrology, May 1965 falls within the Year of the Snake.

CHAPTER TWO

ARRIVEDERCI ROMA!

———

Rome, the Eternal City, the birthplace of the Republican political system and, arguably, Western Civilisation. In spite of my Roman childhood I never truly felt Italian, perhaps because I am only *half* Italian and my Italian 'heritage' has more to do with birth location than genetic inheritance. Also, I never got to even *meet* my Italian father.

Our family lived in Via Pietro Cavallini 21, a street that runs by the Lungotevere dei Mellini, 3 kilometres from Vatican City, 9 kilometres from the Colosseum, and only one from the primary school I was enrolled in – Umberto Primo.

I shared a bedroom with my mother. My grandmother, Letitia, inhabited the smaller room which had a mini balcony with a partial view of Rome. We did not have the luxury of a bathroom, only a toilet, and this meant, if you wanted a wash, filling up a portable tub in the kitchen or taking a walk down to a nearby public bath in Via Crescenzio.

Letitia took care of the laundry, which she did by hand, but I was often sans knickers because I'd throw them under the bed at night, forgetting to give them to Letitia to wash. Once I walked to school in such a state of undress, oblivious to there being anything amiss; the lewd leering of the school janitor as I sat on a step, knees apart, served as a rude reminder. Sick of pulling out soiled undies from under my bed, my mother one day rubbed my nose into a pair and then shoved them into my mouth.

"Maybe *now* you will remember to put your filthy underpants into the wash basket!"

My bottom lip was left bleeding, such was the force she used.

Food and religious celebrations were important rituals in my family, though their lavishness or otherwise were dependent on Gilda's fortunes. Gilda was our breadwinner and whether we had a famine or a feast depended on Mother's work opportunities. I'm not sure if Letitia ever had a job as such, but I remember her saying she assisted in nursing Federico Fellini, the film director, having had 'the pleasure' of his derrière on more than one occasion. Letitia was more our homemaker. She took care of my immediate needs and acted more like a mother than Gilda could ever attempt. There was nothing Letitia could not do; she was a superb cook and knew everything about everything. To this day I still find myself referring to my grandmother about this, that, and the other.

Christmas and *Carnevale* were magical times for me. The entire city of Rome came to life. The streets were richly adorned, and everyone got into the spirit of things. The churches and cathedrals vied with one another to present the most lifelike Nativity scene, or *presepio*, complete with up-to-date machinations. We had our own Nativity scene at home, just like every other good Catholic family; this was exclusively 'Gilda's project'. I marvelled at the delicate diminutive figurines she purchased, and the way Mother would recreate the Bethlehem landscape out of such unlikely materials as glass from car accidents that she found on the road. With meticulous expertise and imagination Gilda would bring a pond or waterfall to life.

Our Christmas tree was also something else, complete with glass baubles and intermittent lights in all the colours of the rainbow. Whenever Uncle Eduardo came to stay, *he* was in charge of the tree and it was simply spectacular. Unlike with our *presepio*, though, Uncle Eduardo allowed me to help him. I would hold my favourite glass baubles up to the light in wonder. Even as a child I enjoyed a heightened sense of beauty.

Letitia compensated for the meagre Christmas gifts I received by taking me to Piazza Navona where the Christmas stalls were set up. Pedlars of roasted chestnuts occupied every corner. The richly sweet aroma of those roasting nuts was irresistible and Letitia would make sure I got my annual serve. Christmases in Rome gave me a fund of memories that cannot be erased, even if I wanted to.

In Italy *Carnevale* takes place between 12 February and 5 March and it's the last celebration before Ash Wednesday, the start of Lent. During this period everyone is encouraged to dress up in fancy dress – even at work. Bags of confetti or *coriandoli* are sold on the streets each year, the idea being to throw the *coriandoli* at passers-by in spirit of the *festa*. The streets become so littered with confetti that the scene appears sprinkled with snow. Once again, Letitia enriched my childhood by providing me with a great bag of the stuff to splash around as I pleased as I pranced happily in my Louisa May Alcott peach and navy silk costume that my mother had created for me, complete with parasol, bonnet and crinoline.

Although we were fairly poor, we ate well and always appeared to have more than enough, even during our 'famine' periods. I loved my *pastasciutta* – just as well because meat was expensive – with horse flesh or internal organs replacing beef and chicken. The majority of our meals were cooked on a budget but they were big serves, and oh so darn tasty. On cool nights Letitia made *sopa de ajos* which is basically a heavily garlic laden broth with stale pieces of crusty bread floating on it. My usual comfort food, that I received from Letitia (following a dose of punishment from Gilda), was a generous hunk of bread with a thick layer of unsalted butter topped with a generous sprinkle of sugar.

Our little family gathered daily around the table for meals, and this was a time for relating the day's events to one another. If Gilda was away or working, Letitia would set us up in front of the television, which I loved. Letitia would offer me forbidden items like a sip of wine from her glass, or a ristretto coffee. When I asked whether Mother would approve Letitia would just shrug her shoulders and assure me that "a little of anything" was never a problem. "Moderation is the key," she often reiterated, but it did not take long for me to connect food with a reward system, or to associate food with happiness and inner healing.

Not all my meals were heavenly, though. Gilda obsessed about iron and calcium in my diet and her favourite concoction for maximum iron intake consisted of a piece of raw liver mixed with spinach and sugar in a blender, and yes, *I had to drink all of it.* My other hates included manta ray, chicory, mallow soup, and my mother's more satanic creations like liquorice or beetroot ice cream. She even tried her hand at 'lentils' ice cream! Gilda delighted in reciting the offensive menu when I would storm into the kitchen after school asking excitedly, *what's for dinner?*

Porridge (or *pappone*) was another dreaded meal, one that nearly killed me. Mother was rushing out the door one morning leaving me with a big bowl of the foul, pasty gunk. Gingerly I threw it down the kitchen sink only to scoop it back up as fast as I could when I heard the key in the front door. Mother didn't come into the kitchen to check on me, though, just grabbed what she needed and dashed out again. I had only gulped a spoonful of the stuff when I felt the most atrocious burning sensation travel the length of my oesophagus. My eyes popped out of my skull and my throat felt like it was closing up. I staggered out into the foyer barely able to open the front door, and called out to Mother in a voice I did not know I still had. I felt like I had swallowed a blunt razor. Mother clambered back up and called an ambulance. That's all I remember.

I'd had an anaphylaxis attack and my throat and airways closed up. The night before my 'accident', Mother had treated our marble kitchen sink with caustic soda to remove its age-old stains, and the porridge I scooped up was coated with the lethal residue. Naturally I was later punished for being 'a sneaky little bitch' – as if extreme pain and near death were not punishment enough!

I *still* detest porridge, liver, liquorice, and beetroot.

My weekly routine was not unlike other kids living in the city of seven hills. I attended school in Via Cassiadoro from Monday through to Saturday. School hours were from 8.30 in the morning to 1 o'clock in the afternoon, with only a short recess during the day. Saturday was a sports and crafts day, and the rest of the week was devoted to serious topics like history, science, maths, grammar, and geography. I applied myself wholeheartedly to drawing and comprehension, with arithmetic my weakest subject.

After school I'd make my own way home, have lunch – or rather, the equivalent of dinner here in Australia, ('dinner' in Europe is more like what 'supper' is here, a light meal) then go and play with my school friends or anyone else who might want to join me, in nearby Piazza Cavour. After a couple of hours of unbridled horseplay, I'd return home to do my homework, eat supper, watch a bit of TV, and off to bed.

Following church services in the morning, Sundays were considered a family day, with Saturday afternoons our apartment's clean-up day. Personally I liked everything to be in its place, so my side of the room was often clean and well organised while Mother's side was a hovel. Letitia tried hard to cope with her daughter's messiness, understanding that Gilda was our provider and had little time at her disposal to clean and keep things nice, but it was painfully obvious that my mother really had *no* regard for anyone's efforts.

As a child I loved Disney cartoons and the *Golden Years of Hollywood*, and by the age of twelve I knew everything about the American stars, collecting all of their pictures and filmographies. I had a secret fetish for anything Anglo or Germanic, and desperately wanted to be either. As a grey-eyed blonde with fair skin I did not require much camouflage.

I was not an unhappy child but I was definitely a very lonely one, and when Gilda was around, I would become a defensive and frightened child. Fortunately for me I had Eulalio and my Invisible Friend to talk to and confide in during times of duress and they looked after me well. Letitia, too, always seemed good to me, and with her incessant stream of wise and practical advice, she was also good *for* me too. Between the three I had sufficient company at home to keep me sane. I yearned for a sister, though, a desire that never left me.

I was a friendly child, too, albeit a little bossy and demanding if ignored or undermined. The games I took part in or initiated greatly reflected these less than favourable personality traits. I simply *had* to be the leader and delegator of tasks, and because my imagination was versatile and expansive, my games were interesting if not often risqué; they drew in the local kids, who'd then stay and play for hours – even tolerating my pomposity.

Like my grandmother, I loved to climb and compete with the boys. I made it to the top of the bronze statue of Camillo Benso, Conte di Cavour only to slip down the granite pedestal, where I hit my head and cut it clean open. My blood soaked into the stone and was visible until the day I left Rome. To this day I still call Piazza Cavour, the *Blood Stain*.

My mother did not buy me a bicycle as it would cost too much; instead, I received a pair of second-hand rollerskates and learnt to love them. My favourite skating venue was in nearby Castel Sant'Angelo, only a stone throw away from St Peter's Square. I stacked it a dozen times but the grazed knees rarely worried me for I was a determined child who never gave up on anything I set my mind to – or that gave me pleasure and release. I eventually became a confident skater, spending hours on the pavement with my Invisible Friend; boy did we share some conversations! I solved most of my problems talking to him. Whether my imaginary friend was a faceless boy or a faceless father, I don't remember, but he was a reliable constant throughout my young life.

Back in Umberto Primo my best friend was a girl called Alessandra. I also had a male friend called Stefano, but the *real* object of my shady desire was a cute redheaded boy named Alfredo.

I liked school – it took me away from Gilda's screams and threats. I was also, in spite of my situation, a social person and a bit of a show off. A captive audience is after all a great tool for the development of ego. Intellectually I was pretty smart and had the ability to do well in class, but my acquired unruliness and indiscretion ensured my grades would remain average and sometimes below average. Arithmetic was my curse – I simply *could not* grasp it; I hated arithmetic almost as much as porridge, liver, and beetroot.

When I was in Year 2 one of the less tolerant teachers had me recite times tables in front of the class. I froze. The more I tried to remember the sequences, the more muddled my mind became. The teacher roared at me and I told her where to shove her times tables. I then felt a slap like concrete come down across my ear, so hard it left me partially deaf. At Letitia's insistence, the teacher was dismissed from her position but, together with a damaged left ear, I developed a pathological mental block for mathematics that lasted the rest of my school years.

As poorly as I performed at maths, I excelled in grammar and the arts – in fact I was at the top of my class in both subjects. Genetics played a part no doubt – my mother was a natural artist and could sing, write and draw consummately. I inherited a strong contralto voice from her too, but Gilda's obsession with opera put me off singing; I feared she would force me to follow in her footsteps. It took prolonged separation, both physical and emotional, from Mother, for me to appreciate *some* opera later in life.

At school I acted out the inner demons I had managed to suppress at home. Because my principal role model was a woman so authoritarian it verged on cruelty, I developed a hatred for females that in the school playground unleashed itself on some of my female classmates. It meant I was in gender denial, I suppose; I hated dressing up, I hated my long blonde hair, and I hated the sheer physical vulnerability of my female-hood. I decided I needed to be a boy in order to enjoy life and began copying everything boys did. I climbed, I broke things, I screeched, I punched, I terrorised, and I attempted to dominate whoever I could, just as Gilda dominated me.

Poor Alessandra said the wrong thing to me one lunchtime, something about my not having a father. She was loitering on a handrail above a descending staircase when I saw my opportunity to do some retributional damage. Completely indifferent to and possibly unaware of the consequences, I calmly walked up to Alessandra and just pushed the skinny kid off that handrail. Down she whirled, into the bottom of the staircase. Her head hit hard on the concrete floor and I got my first suspension from school. Alessandra suffered a serious injury and was gone for two weeks. I thank God I had not killed her, but it wasn't my fault I had no father and she should not have teased me about that.

Alfredo, though, was *so* cute. He collected plastic farm animals, and so *I* began to collect plastic farm animals.

I doubt Alfredo saw me – as in *really* saw me, the way I *wanted* to be seen. Very few people knew the authentic eight-year-old I was inside, a child who knew and felt far more than she showed. I decided Alfredo needed to find out who I was in spite of himself and I successfully lured him into my web by presenting him with my own collection of farm animals, one which did little to rival his.

"You don't have an armadillo Alfredo; here, have mine!" I was seizing a blissful day and dedicating it to gratuitous altruism.

Alfredo's dazzling blue eyes smiled, his freckles dancing gingerly across his nose and cheeks. I was in – *I think?*

Alfredo and I sat at the same desk in class now and, oh, how I loved our school desks! They had a lid that lifted up for storage – a perfect camouflage for inappropriate behaviour. I snuggled up next to the lovely Alfredo. Being the second tallest in my class Alfredo had nowhere to go and my first crush promised delicious abandon.

"Do you want to hold my hand Alfredo?" I smiled cheekily.

"No."

"Why not?"

"Because!"

Alfredo asked the teacher if he could sit elsewhere.

Well well well, Alfredo you unappreciative cad. I'll show you!

Revenge is sweet but not so sweet when you get home and your infernal mother is waiting to hang you from the highest point. I had duly corrected Alfredo's audacity by emptying a huge barrel of Lego over his head. How was I to know such little blocks, en masse, could damage skulls? My mother's wrath and another week's suspension were my rewards when Alfredo was sent home suffering from concussion and his mother summoned mine to talk about her 'problem child'. Fortunately, Mother had work to do, and Letitia fronted up instead.

My classroom conquests did not end with the frigid Alfredo though. In Year 3 I kissed Sabrina. She was the most beautiful little girl I had ever seen, an escapee from a fairy tale illustration. My prepubescent lesbian fling lasted just one day; I've not revisited that forbidden arena since.

School holidays in Rome are long, lasting almost three months. They were a torturous period for me as I had no fixed agenda and spent way too much time on my own or in Piazza Cavour loitering, until someone found me. For most of my classmates however, it was vacation time, with travels to other parts of Italy or even abroad. My out-of-home vacations depended heavily on Mother's work commitments or attempts at self-promotion, but one thing was certain – Gilda's reluctant career took me to some weird places.

Mother dabbled in religion in order to 'find herself' and if barbiturates count as an ethos, then Gilda was a true devotee. In between knocking herself out, Mother frittered her energy between belief systems that ranged from national Roman Catholicism to Freemasonry.

One of the weird places I remember her taking me to was known to me only as *Il pellegrinaggio*. To reach this venue we crossed pastoral fields on foot after alighting from an old bus. I can't even begin to tell you where these fields were but I have vivid flashbacks of having to climb over a sea of animal carcasses at a certain point in our journey. Their bleached bones terrified me and I cried all the way to the 'weird place', tugging at my mother's hand so we could turn back and away. The field must have been an abattoir's dumping ground.

Once past that horrific ossuary, we arrived at a homestead littered with cages housing exotic animals. I can recall some monkeys – their screeching faces still flash before my mind's eye, along with the way they clawed through their bars demanding food from the visitors. I think I heard someone say that the homestead was a private retreat of sorts, run by wealthy hippies dabbling in transcendental meditation. God knows what my mother got up to there. (I don't remember what *I* got up to, either.)

Mother loved the beach. If we couldn't get to the beach we went to the sulphur baths in Tivoli which was about 20 kilometres from Rome. I hated the rotten egg smell of the pools but once my olfactory senses adapted to them, I had lots of fun frolicking about in the water and I often met up with new children to play with. The closest beach was Ostia, about half an hour by bus. I too loved the beach and I was a proverbial water baby. As always I used my imagination to entertain myself, thus managing to stay out of Mother's hair for hours.

There was at least one occasion when I didn't enjoy the beach so much, though. I'd been left for the weekend with a distant relative by the name of Rita, someone I'd not met before, or since, and she had a daughter named Gea. Gea was angelic in appearance: pale and thin, with soft golden locks that fell like clouds across her face and uncannily translucent green eyes. But as far as personality went, Gea was more like Satan's spawn.

Most of my childhood memories are fragmented and recall occurs in flashback snapshots, or brief sequences and the Gea snapshots are not at all pleasant. First she decided to urinate on me in the bath, and then at the beach Gea challenged me to perform all sorts of nasty stuff. Back then I'd accept almost any task in order to earn the approval I did not receive at home. The main reason Gea and Rita remain firm fixtures in my memory bank are that they staged yet another of my near death experiences. Gea, Rita, and I went down to a beach only a few blocks from their apartment building. I was playing happily on the sand when, rather urgently, nature called. I advised Rita I really needed to go and she told me to do *it* inside the sand bucket and then throw the contents out to sea. I obeyed, but as I stopped in the shallows ready to dump my load, I heard Gea call out, "Not there you pig! Throw it *really far* into the ocean!"

I and the offensive bucket waded far, far into the blue stillness until I could no longer touch the sandy bottom with my toes, and suddenly I panicked. I couldn't swim and started thrashing about frantically, losing my bucket. Each time I came to the surface gasping for air, I'd scan the horizon for help. I could hear myself scream *Aiuto! Aiuto!* (Help! Help!) but this only helped me take in water and there wasn't a soul around who might save me.

Just as it dawned on me I was drowning, I felt strong arms around my torso. A man in his twenties had appeared out of nowhere to rescue me. I was dizzy and in shock but my memory is clear – just moments before there was absolutely *noone* in my vicinity.

Rita and Gea ran over to me and the man – my saviour – laid me gently onto the firm sand, checking me over. I was okay.

There was the inevitable commotion between Rita and Gea involving hows and whys, but I pushed past them to find my saviour so I could thank him personally – and he was nowhere to be seen. He had disappeared as quickly as that sandy sea floor. Where was he and *who* was he? Surely he'd stay a while to lap up the accolades. I asked myself whether he had even *saved* me, and how I may have very well just imagined the feat as one of my fantasy adventures. Much later in life, as I gathered knowledge on Scientific Metaphysics and Applied Spirituality, what happened that day became crystal clear to me. For now, however, it's time to move on to my next 'weird' holiday – in Assisi this time.

My mother had once again dumped me in the care of people I did not know. At age one she had left me for a year, then again at age two for six months, in the care of distant relatives in Düsseldorf, Germany. Mother was busy with operatic assignments in various parts of Europe and as Letitia followed her everywhere it seems the 'Düsseldorf option' was the only viable one for me.

Assisi is a small town in the region of Umbria, north of Rome. Its most famous natives, Giovanni 'Francesco' di Pietro di Bernardone (Saint Francis) and Chiara Offreduccio (Saint Clare), were born and lived here around the end of the twelfth century. The 1972 film by Franco Zefirelli, *Brother Sun Sister Moon*, is an artistic 'biopic' about the two saints' lives, and when eventually I saw the film I was excited about having walked their paths and visited their tombs. The family who billeted me had given me a little replica of the San Damiano cross, an important Assisi icon. I held onto this prized memento for many years. Saint Francis of Assisi is the protector and patron of all animals and possibly the only saint I paid homage to for this reason alone. My fondness for animals goes all the way back to Eulalio.

My onemonth 'holiday' in Assisi was a far less glamorous experience than Zeffirelli's beautiful film. I resided with a family I knew nothing about, and whose son succeeded in seriously traumatising me. I will call this godforsaken fiend 'Paolo' because my memory has suppressed his name.

The family appeared to be local farmers who lived on site and Paolo was a little older than me. Paolo turned out to be a sadist who delighted in all manner of unpleasant teasing. Paolo threw scorpions at me, planted a huge black spider in my bedroom, forced me to clean the pigsty because, apparently, it was *my* job, and he poked fun at me whenever and however he got the chance.

Paolo showed me his private parts and tried to touch mine. He taunted me, and chased me around the property throwing mud and stones. I counted the days until my mother would come for me. One night a suddenly congenial Paolo invited me into his bedroom; I was forced to surmise why and so suddenly, he wished to become my friend.

"Do you want to see something really cute?" He had a malicious glint in his eye.

Oh, here we go with his goddamn dick.

Paolo held out his hand and in his palm sat a big-eyed little dormouse known in Italian as a *ghiro*. Cooing and smiling I asked Paolo if I could hold it. Paolo replied:

"Sure, but only after I take off his coat." And in saying this, Paolo yanked off the little creature's skin with such skill and speed I knew he'd done it before.

Horrified, I turned away from the stunned pink mass and fled from Paolo's condemned room screaming. I could almost see the psychopath rolling around his bedroom floor, laughing his diabolical head off. At the close of my Assisi experience I vowed never to return to Paolo's farm and face this embryonic serial killer again.

Poor Saint Francis, the things he was forced to witness.

* * *

It appeared wherever I went trouble followed.

I was at a seaside trattoria with Mother, perhaps somewhere in Anzio – I think Mother had a gig there. One of her male friends, probably a boyfriend, decided it would be a blast to scoop me into his arms and dangle me over a balustrade overlooking a steep ravine leading to the sea. I screamed my head off but noone came to my rescue, not this time. Staring down at the crashing waves below me, one of my thongs came off. Frantic, I twisted and turned in the man's arms, begging to be pulled back to safety. The man kept laughing as he pulled me back over the balustrade. I jumped out of his vile grip, swearing at him, and ran out of harm's way, barefoot bar the remaining thong. I ran for Mother, who as always was nowhere to be found.

On another occasion I had my eyes focused firmly on the shiny coins that litter the bottom of the Trevi Fountain. Traditionally, people throw three coins into the fountain, hoping for true love to find them. Each time we'd pass by Via delle Muratte, I'd run ahead, ogling the statues and wishing all that loot could be mine. As a little girl on a mission, I decided I'd have some of that treasure, come hell or high water – but more likely the former.

Letitia left me to play by the fountain while she perused some nearby shops. There weren't too many people hanging about so I bided my time, waiting for the perfect moment. Kicking off my sandals I lifted my skirt up and waded into the cold water stashing as many coins as I could grab into my pockets, my knickers, and even inside my mouth. I then heard a voice call out from a window across from the famous landmark:

"*Ma chei stai faccendo cretina!*" (What are you doing you idiot!)

I looked up and a woman in her mid-forties was gesticulating furiously, clearly condemning my actions.

I jumped out of the pool and ran towards the shop where I thought Letitia might be. Coins fell out of my undies onto the cobblestone pavement, giving me away, but I dared not turn back to pick them up; Letitia hated thievery of any type. I sheepishly transferred the remaining coins into my little purse and continued looking for my grandmother. There she was, just finishing off her purchase.

As with food, money and possessions were weaknesses of mine and now that I had got away with stealing, I felt brave enough to try it again. Karma does not miss any perpetrator and so, as we retraced our steps home and past the apartments situated directly from the *Fontana*, something heavy came down from the sky and hit me square on the head. I dropped the ice cream Letitia had bought me and started wailing with pain. *That hurt!* Letitia looked up and saw a woman draw back from her window up on the third floor. The object that had hit me was an empty can and I was clearly its calculated target. I guessed it was the same woman who told me off about the coins a little earlier; had I perhaps interfered with her love wish? I hoped her 'beloved' would turn out to be the fat, ugly, sweaty greengrocer type you saw in comic films – a man who farted in bed, demanded food on the table the second he got home, and had his smelly feet rubbed till bedtime.

Gilda had many friends, mostly people from the arts world. I met so many I don't remember them all. A few of her contacts came from the theatre restaurant she worked in – Da Meo Patacca in Trastevere. The owner of the premises had scored himself a bit-part in the 1959 film *Ben Hur*, playing a centurion who whipped Jesus in the chain gang scene. In 1973, on my eighth birthday, I met this strange looking individual when Mother decided to take me to work with her.

Even though I sought and enjoyed attention from others, it always had to be on *my* terms. I was actually painfully shy and self-conscious. I *did* know what I wanted, but the exuberant, pushy and militant Adalgisa others often met was all bravado. Tonight, and on *my* birthday, exposure was definitely pushed to its limit.

Inside the vast performance hall, I was sitting at a table all on my own, watching Mother, in traditional costume, belting out tired renditions of 'Funiculi Funiculà', when I suddenly felt a spotlight's heat on me. Before I could figure out what was happening, one of the tenors jumped off the stage, skipping happily towards me. Falling on bended knee and with arms outstretched, the tenor began serenading me. I felt a rush of blood to my face – a rush to take the top of my head off. There were at least 150 people watching, cheering and clapping the over enthusiastic tenor along. Then, just as I thought I couldn't sit back into my chair any smaller, out came the proprietor carrying an enormous birthday cake bristling with candles burning almost as fiercely as my face. My ears rang, as well as burned, as the entire hall resonated with the birthday jingle – yet the only words I heard inside my head were *go away, go away, go away!*

Rome is an amazing city, one I never truly appreciated as a child. What kid does, though? Children take their immediate environment for granted, but in retrospect I was one of the luckiest girls in the world, able to claim the Eternal City as my very own. The greener grass is always on the other side, though, and I yearned for England or Germany, places that were home to calm and beautiful people, though my childhood memories of Rome and its remarkable locales stay with me like ageing snapshots …

The Colosseum was a place I was terrified of visiting. I believed wild animals still roamed beneath the decayed foundations of that infamous gladiatorial arena. Try as she might, Mother could not get me into this legendary landmark, and I chose her 'don't be such an imbecile' remarks over the deadly risks I would otherwise face.

The Villa Borghese, one of Rome's largest public parks, was one of my favourite places, with Letitia and I visiting here often. Villa Borghese was a beautifully converted sixteenth century vineyard, a project for the nephew of Pope Paul V, the Cardinal Scipione Borghese. In 1903 the park was opened to the public and it was absolute heaven for a fanciful little girl such as me, who loved collecting pine nuts and dreaming up scenarios in and around the many nooks and crannies found here. As Letitia read her religious texts on a park bench nearby, I was free to roam, dream and discover at will. Letitia seemed to have all the time in the world and I happily took every minute of it.

Castel Gandolfo, overlooking Lake Albano, is a medieval castle built in the eleventh century. I visited twice and it was this place that compounded my continuing love affair with castles and any manner of Gothic architecture.

My imagination was far reaching: places I cherished were in fact secret portals into fantasy worlds in which I reigned supreme. Castel Gandolfo was the city of wizards, witches, and dragons, a place fraught with danger, but also a place where the handsomest of princes would one day come for me. He'd fly in on his magnificent Pegasus and rescue me from the darkness of twisted beings, hungry lamenting creatures and jealous evil mistresses.

Beneath St Peter's Basilica in the Vatican, are the catacombs that hold the remains of popes, bishops and other ecclesiastical nobility. It is also where I was baptised a Roman Catholic. For me however, those saintly haunts were ghostly labyrinths where decaying zombies came to life as they reached out from the walls that interred them, shrieking for fresh meat and feral freedoms.

Castel Sant'Angelo, where I loved to rollerskate, was Roman Emperor Hadrian's mausoleum, and later a papal fortress; for me, though, it was the city of the damned. Tormented groans could be heard coming from shackled adulterers, blasphemers and insurgents. These pathetic creatures suffered unspeakable tortures inside the castle's subterranean prison dungeons. Above them in the sumptuous halls and corridors, the *true* criminals took up residence: incestuous nobility who committed the vilest of mortal sins without regret, their exaggerated gowns and fabricated beauty engulfing the senses of long suffering courtiers who had yearned for them but were denied a single glance into their world of debauchery. One thing I came to know well was debauchery.

The Roman Forum with all its stray cats and litter was simply *that*, the remnants of a glorious, long defunct era; an era of conquerors, statesmen, martyrs, heroes, murderers, villains, gods, goddesses, hedonist pomposity and peculiar cruelties. I could almost hear the ancient populace crying out by the torn feet of marble pillars – *legum servi sumus ut liberi esse possimus*: we are slaves of the law so that we may be free.

In Ridley Scott's epic *Gladiator*, Australian musician Lisa Gerrard, delivers a hauntingly beautiful ballad called *'Now We Are Free'. The words to this song are foreign to me(Lisa sings in her own idioglossia) but whatever they meant, I myself felt that noone born of the Eternal City could ever be truly free. I believe every place in our world holds within it a certain essence based on historical experience. A city painted with gratuitous murder and gluttony such as Rome could not possibly yield even the semblance of internal peace. I wondered how many people knew their beautiful *palazzi* were built on centuries old burial mounds that were layered one on top of the other. Back in ancient Rome life expectancy was twenty-five years on average. Rome is none other than a beautiful trap – like Odysseus's sirens. Strangely enough, Gladiator's protagonist is also a Hispano Roman like me.

I didn't know it at the time but either my birthplace or the lineage I was born into had paved my destiny with obstacles so insidious and insurmountable that even a character such as mine, forged from iron and encased in the hardest of diamonds, would find it almost impossible to overcome them.

CHAPTER THREE

THE SUFFERING OF THE CHILD

———

The beautiful Man in the long white woollen robe stood by the marble fountain, beaming down at me with an all-enveloping smile of pure love.

I skipped towards Him in my pristine little girl's dress, my eyes fixed on that famous smile and on His gentle blue eyes. I searched for the words I wanted to speak but could not find them. The experience was beyond words.

The garden was breathtaking for its sheer perfection, and a glow encompassed everything. The glow was not tangible and yet I felt it on my skin and inside my heart. Everything seemed to unfold in ethereal, surreal, slow motion. I found myself inside a magical place.

I *had* seen the Man's face before. The blue eyes and strawberry blond hair, that smile. I felt so warm, so loved, so safe. Then, so suddenly, I heard His voice inside my head. His lips did not move, did not disturb the smile, but I heard Him.

"Your mother loves you little one; she just does not know how to show it because she herself did not learn. She was not shown the way. You will not suffer all of your life; your pain will end and happiness will be yours."

I wanted the Man to hold me – he was peace and kindness personified. I held out my arms to Him so He would take me into His. It seemed as if an infinite corridor of distance had just materialised between us and it kept us from touching, but the Man stood there watching me, still smiling. A pure white lamb poked its little head from behind the Man's robe. It lingered for a moment, just looking at me, then, on spindly little legs, it skipped along out of my line of sight as suddenly as it had appeared. My gaze fixed itself onto His beautiful face once more.

"I want to stay here with you, don't send me back, please!" I begged Him.

With a deeper, more loving gaze He answered me.

"You have much to do little one. People are relying on you and you *will* be safe. Your mother does love you, and *I* love you."

And with this, the wonderful vision disappeared along with the magnificent garden and the peaceful loving glow. It was the most beautiful dream I'd ever experienced or would henceforth.

I woke up, and found myself in my bed. To gather my bearings, I looked over to my mother's side of the room. I followed her bed frame upward to the wall behind and there He was, the Man in my dream: Adolf Hyla's 1943 depiction of the Christ.

* * *

I was raised a Roman Catholic despite Mother's religious philanderings. Letitia was unmoved, remaining a staunch devotee and someone who made certain *I* did not stray too far from the faith either. I knew however that my special dream was not the fallout of religious proselytising; my dream was *real*, my Christ was *real*, I *had* been there where He was!

My beautiful Christ was wrong though, so very wrong. My mother did not love me, and even if she did I certainly did not feel it. Aside from the odd outing to Luna Park or the like, Mother was too busy, too tired, too poor, too angry, or too involved in her own affairs to pay me much attention.

Gilda had no clue about parenting. She teased me all the time and involved me in adult activities that left me scarred, like the time she took me to see the 1971 film *The Light at the Edge of the World* when I was only seven years old, a film about piracy that was violent and graphic even for its time. Later, when I was eight, we went to see *The Exorcist* and I did not sleep properly for months. My experience of *The Exorcist* was almost certainly the reason I became obsessed with the occult.

Perhaps due to her work, Mother was highly strung and neurotic. She was also a chronic insomniac. Whenever Gilda was about the apartment I needed to watch what I said, how I said it, and how loudly. Her working hours meant

Letitia and I needed to be deathly quiet as Mother rested through the day. To help her stay asleep, Gilda took barbiturates: I found the dark pills one day in her bedside drawer. Fortunately – and very much out of character for me – I was never tempted to pop one into my mouth.

Mother's insomnia brought out her inner demon. She would fly into demented rages over the smallest things. Sometimes, when she could, Letitia would rescue me from Mother's seething clutches, but more often than not I was left to bear the brunt of her ire. It was during moments like these that I developed a fighting spirit, the very survival mode that would see me through far worse times during the life to come. *Never give in. Never give up. Never let them win*, became my mantra. These were the words racing through my mind as I held my breath through yet another beating.

"*Tu sei lo spirito della contradizione!*" (You are the spirit of contradiction!) Gilda would yell, littering my face with spittle that I dared not wipe off.

Yes, Mother, I'd say to myself, I *am* the spirit of contradiction and you can go to hell. You can hurt me all you like but you will never break me. I grow stronger in your chains. I am tougher for your whip. I am defiance personified.

When Mother could not catch me she would self-harm by biting her forearms. She would pull at her hair, slap her own face, spit, stamp, and punch, whatever gave her relief. But I found her screams and curses to be far worse. They sliced through my very soul. Gilda's face would contort monstrously, her eyes bulging, her mouth frothing, and her skin crimson from complete and unstoppable rage.

"Die why don't you! You are a *nothing* Cicci; you will grow up and continue being a nothing, a little street whore perhaps or a drug addict, that's what you'll grow up to become! I should have got rid of you when I had the chance."

Gilda would then turn her rage to God.

"You pig, you son of a bitch, why do you allow me live like this? *I hate you,* I hate you!"

Like King Nimrod before her, Gilda spat at an imaginary deity, raising her shaking fist up to the ceiling to threaten 'God' with everything she had inside her.

I accidentally dropped a small bottle of mercurochrome in our bedroom once. I felt my body tense up the second I heard the glass hit the floorboards. It seemed like an eternity but I knew what was coming, that bloodcurdling screech: *Aaaaaaaaaaaaaahhhhh! Puttana! Mignotta! Assassinaaaaa!*

Frenzied, Gilda didn't know which part of me to violate first. She snatched at air each time I dodged her claws but then she got me – she always did. Mother pulled down my knickers with one quick yank and threw me on the bed. She then sank her teeth into one of my buttocks. She had bitten me so hard tears spurted from my eyes like blood from severed arteries.

"You careless bitch, you don't care about anything but yourself!"

I'd cower, scamper to a corner, or if I was lucky, Letitia would walk into the room and drag me away from her. I often couldn't remember how my escapes had occurred, only the internalised outrage and the pain that felt like crucibles.

Gilda was my mother. I depended on her and I was aware of that, but I'd be damned if I'd submit unconditionally to her petty cruelties. I could not get away from her permanently, I was too young to run away and social services were almost unheard of in 1960s Europe. I saw how homeless *scugnizzi* lived in Rome and I certainly did not fancy eating out of garbage cans or urinating on the roadside as they did. Just the same though, if I was able to deliver some form of payback, Mother *would* receive it – no matter how small. I refused to let her hurt me any more than was physically possible for me to endure. I wanted to cheat her out of whatever perverse pleasure she derived from beating a young child – *her* child, the child who had once loved her.

It was one thing for Gilda to swear at me constantly, but when I did it? Well …

"Come here! I'll teach you to swear!" she would gleam. "Open your mouth!"

I clamped my mouth shut; no way was I putting *that* in. A few slaps across the face and my mouth opened. In went a huge *pepperoncino* (hot chilli pepper).

"Chew it!" she'd command.

My mouth didn't move but the severe heat of the chilli started to spread across the roof of my palate.

"Chew it or I'll crack your head open!"

I swished the chilli around my mouth not daring to chew. I was already on fire.

"Now sit on that chair and don't move until I tell you to."

Fear of Mother's wrath was replaced with the blackest hatred and a desire to kill. *I'll get you Mother, one day I'll get you.* I learnt to hate so young. Sometimes, when I was alone, I'd flick through Gilda's crime magazines and feel an immediate attraction to what lay between those dark and seedy pages. Could children kill? What did it feel like to extinguish the life of a persecutor with your own bare hands?

I could see Eulalio watching me from the top of our earthen boiler where he always sat. I wondered if he knew what was happening for me. I had had many a solitary debrief with Eulalio, although he'd just lie there on my lap unperturbed as I sobbed, covertly divulging my woes. I guess Eulalio *did* take in my escape plans, but he never offered any *real* advice.

"Are you still chewing?" she'd call out from another room in that despised soprano voice.

Was I supposed to answer when all I wanted to do was chop my own head off? Bravado soon turned into submission as the pain and discomfort intensified to critical heights.

"I need a drink *Mamma, perfavore!*" I gasped.

"Ask me one more time and I'll give you another *pepperoncino, figlia di una gran puttana!*"

'Funny that,' I thought. *Had Mother just called herself a whore?*

When I couldn't bear that burning pain a second longer, I decided to act on a plan. Mother *had* to let me go to the toilet – surely. Following her merciful consent, I bolted the toilet door behind me, dived head first into the bowl and drank greedily. Sweeter than the relief this brought was that I had outsmarted the almighty Gilda, beating her at her own sadistic game.

I didn't have to swear to get punished; backchatting was another serious crime and Mother's modus operandi for *this* transgression was clever and unique.

At first glance I thought I was being rewarded with a bowl of ice cream. I skimmed the top of the scoops with gusto, but the next three spoonfuls weren't so delicious. As I swallowed, a burst of itchy soapy residue began to permeate my palate. Gilda had put Lux soap flakes inside my ice cream. My tender young throat burned for two days.

I was a glutton for punishment and far too rebellious for my own good. If I could just shut my big mouth and become transparent, I would have fared much better. Letitia, too, joked I was a motor mouth who couldn't give it a rest. Whenever Gilda was in one of her moods and I backchatted, Letitia would throw me that *shut your bloody mouth* stare, but I rarely took much notice; the defiance in me was cocky as hell and the bitter punishments continued.

Within myself I was like any other child. I loved the little things and the little things were after all, what we could afford. I was particularly attached to a little Cinderella handkerchief. I would lose myself into the image of the beautiful princess in her wondrous ball gown swirling about on tiny glass slippers as she gazed dreamily into her prince's eyes. I dreamed of Alfredo and wondered why he did not love me as I loved him. Would I ever find my Prince Charming, and would he rescue me from the operatic prison I lived in?

One thing I truly hated was my mother's vocal workouts. I'd mimic her *acuti* (high notes), scales, and arpeggios, pulling ugly faces and silently saying *vaffanculo* at the end of each. I wondered what my biological father would do had he remained with us. Would he have patted me on the head and said, 'there there, she's just doing what she knows'. Or would he have sided with Gilda and unleashed his own personal fury on me.

One day, as the perennial hero, I informed Gilda I was running away from home if ever she tried hitting me again. My mother lunged at me with a broom she was holding, grabbed me by my hair, threw me onto the kitchen floor and started beating me with the filthy thing. I tried to protect my vital parts by curling up into a ball, which only encouraged Gilda to swap weapons. She grabbed a knife and placed it against my throat. I stood *very* still.

"You want to walk the streets like the dirty little whore that you are, do you? Go get your things and get out then! Go on *get out* or I'll slit your throat from ear to ear you ungrateful little cunt!"

During this period my Uncle Eduardo and his new wife Gianna were staying with us. Auntie Gianna had been waiting in the wings, unsure of how she might help me. I then heard her voice break through the cacophony of Mother's profanities, interrupting the sound of my terrified little heart beating harder than drums.

"Here Gilda, let me help Cicci pack her things. You go and get some rest," Auntie Gianna said placidly.

"I don't give a damn what you do with her Gianna, but I want her *out!* I'm sick of her smart mouth."

When Gilda marched off into her bedroom, still ranting, Gianna pulled me up from the kitchen floor and into her ample Sicilian arms. Auntie Gianna always smiled, was always serene, always comforting and kind. She helped me with my homework after school with such patience. I still recall the smell of the crayons she bought for me once when I was learning to write in cursive. The crayons came with a writing book and Gianna sat down with me every afternoon, mixing the colours to make things fun, gently coaching me until I got things right.

It wasn't until many years later that I discovered Gianna had minimal literacy and numeracy, a common condition for many young Sicilian farm girls who left school early to help out at home. And yet Auntie Gianna always gave her everything, no matter how insignificant the task at hand.

Mother holding a knife to my throat had scared the hell out of me – I had seriously thought she would kill me this time. Could a mother do this – kill her own child? Gianna pulled out my little brown suitcase from the linen cupboard and handed it to me. Eyes liquid with compassion she said, "Just pretend you're leaving, it'll make her realise she doesn't want you to go. I'll talk to her afterwards. You just sit here quietly and everything will be alright."

During times such as these I'd hold my breath in, in case the very sound of my breathing upset Gilda some more. After hearing Mother's bedroom door slam shut and the ranting subside, I'd finally let go and come up for air. The tears and sobs would then spill out like waterfalls, with Gianna quickly closing the kitchen door to muffle the sounds of a little girl who was hurting beyond reason – for absolutely *no* reason.

Gianna hugged me and held me tightly against her, pressing my face into her warm chest, trying to subdue the endless avalanche of sobs.

"Shhhh Cicci, don't let her hear you," Gianna advised softly.

My auntie stroked my hair sympathetically, injecting some of her maternal nurturing into me, the kind only a *real* mother possesses.

"I don't want to leave home Zia Gianna," I pleaded between hiccups. "Where would I go?"

Gianna stroked my hair with added zeal, holding me a little tighter.

"Don't worry Cicci, she's just angry, she doesn't *really* want you to leave home." I jumped out of Auntie's arms.

"Yes she does! She *hates me!* She tried to kill me!"

Gianna pulled me back into her and began rocking me.

"She doesn't hate you Cicci; she's just tired from working so hard. She has a lot of responsibilities and is just lashing out. Just be good, don't answer back, be quiet and she'll forget all about today – you'll see, you'll see. Now shoosh up and stop crying, everything will be alright."

I circled Gianna's big round belly with warm gratitude – with *true* love. My watery grey-blue eyes with their red swollen hoods looked up into Gianna's bright blue ones and I heard myself think out loud.

"I love you Zia Gianna. I wish *you* were my mother."

* * *

The nickname Cicci sucked and I hated it. I was a rotund girl and I'm fairly certain 'Cicci' is a diminutive for the word *ciccia* or blubber (a nice thing to call your daughter). The other call I received from my mother when I was out of sight was a certain whistle. Put the two of these together and I was apparently, in my mother's eyes, a fat dog.

I'm not certain whether Letitia worked part time or had a casual boyfriend, but there wasn't someone at home all of the time, and so I was sometimes left with friends of the family. Most of these 'friends' I only ever met the one time.

L'ingeniere Trepiedi was one such friend. A chubby, balding man in his sixties, he began coming around *a lot*.

While Trepiedi was in our lives we enjoyed many luxuries we could not otherwise afford and it appeared this man never closed his wallet to us. Trepiedi gave me toys, clothes and outings, and Gilda was definitely less hard on me while he was around.

One evening Trepiedi and I were alone in my apartment. I assume he had been left to babysit me. I don't remember how it transpired, but I recall coming out of the toilet completely naked. Trepiedi sat in our foyer's divan waiting for me, a salacious smile across his face. I was seven and a half years old but I knew a strange look when I saw it.

Apparently, we were playing a game. The object of the game or why we played it are details I don't remember. What I *do* remember was me standing in front of this old man, wearing nothing, and his hands being all over my body. His caresses felt nice; I didn't get cuddles often and although I thought this situation was weird and *not* what a child should be involved in, I wouldn't pull away from the only nurturing I'd received in perhaps *never*.

Trepiedi assured me this was a *very good* game, and emphasised it would be *our* secret; *I* was not allowed to tell *anyone* – especially not Gilda or Letitia, as they might want to play too and it would totally spoil our fun. If I was able to keep our secret, Trepiedi promised to give me whatever I wanted.

"Really?" I exclaimed.

And so I told my new friend what I really wanted was a new pair of rollerskates.

This 'game' took place whenever I was alone with Trepiedi, and one day he let me touch his penis. It was the first time I saw an adult's one, and it was big and smooth and hard. On another occasion Trepiedi asked me to get under our dining table as our family gathered around for lunch. The round table was old and worn so Letitia had made a valance for it that went all the way down to the floor like a ball gown.

Mother and Letitia had absolutely *no* idea I was under there, sucking a sixty-seven-year-old man's penis, as they happily dined with their esteemed guest, laughing and praising him for being such a *great friend* to us all.

I began to ponder whether this game of ours was really something a girl my age should be engaging in. I never really thought of such things except what little I saw on television, in magazines, or on the film billboards about town. I knew that showing your 'rude bits' was naughty – only because a kid in my class, Stefano, made such a big deal about it. He had shown me 'his' behind our desk in class, and Alessandra often spoke of such things, but none of that was anything like what Trepiedi and I were doing.

Trepiedi was so very nice, though. He spoke in a soft, soothing voice and gave me lots of nice gifts, but best of all, Mother stopped getting angry with me. It was all too much to throw away.

Then one night, I was alone with him again. Straight after supper Trepiedi told me to get into my grandmother's bedroom and take off all my clothes as per usual. I liked Letitia's room; it had a double bed with a huge fluffy red quilt filled with feathers. When noone was around I'd jump on the quilt imagining it was one of Jesus' clouds up in Heaven. I often wondered how our body weight would withstand the porousness of a cloud. I once had a little duckling that Gilda bought for me as a pet. I thought the duckling would enjoy jumping on the bed as much as I did, so I threw him up into the air and watched him come down with his tiny fluffy wings outstretched. But then I threw him way too hard and he missed the mark landing on the hard slate floor. I watched my pet die slowly in my palms; he looked like he was gasping for air. I was inconsolable and cried the whole day and decided I was a horrible murderer, just like Paolo in Assisi.

Trepiedi came into Letitia's bedroom minus both trousers and underpants. He told me to fetch some cooking oil from the kitchen and I did. Trepiedi poured some on his hands and started rubbing his penis with it, then smeared some onto my privates. He then propped me on top of him and made me rock backwards and forwards. It felt very uncomfortable.

As he bore me down onto him, I began to feel sharp, ripping pains. I ordered Trepiedi to stop, I didn't like this part of the game at all. He didn't listen to me; he had a look on his face like he needed to go to the toilet. I screamed at him and tried to break free.

"Stop! Stop!"

Trepiedi did not listen to me. He continued to hold me firmly in place by my shoulders. I prised one arm free and slapped him as hard as I could across the face. It was an instinctive reaction and Trepiedi finally let go of me.

"It hurts! I hate it!" I yelled running out of Letitia's room almost in tears.

Still naked, I locked myself in the toilet. Trepiedi banged on the door pleading with me to come out.

"No, no! I'm not playing *anymore*! Go away or I'll tell my mother!"

Trepiedi promised me we would not play the game ever again if I came out. He would still buy me the rollerskates and anything else I wanted, but under no circumstance was I to tell my mother about this, or anyone else – did I understand him?

I think all I did understand then was that we were doing something terribly, horribly wrong.

After that terrible night Trepiedi stopped coming over as often. I was glad for it and certainly did not miss him. I spoke about this situation at length with my Invisible Friend and also about the *other* stuff we had done together. Neither of us could figure out what the 'game' was all about. I had liked it in the beginning, but then it got too crazy. I soon started to feel bad about myself the way someone might if they had maggots writhing all over their body or if they had been forced to eat their own poo. Something had changed inside me and I didn't understand what it was. I knew then I had to let *someone* know.

Letitia was sitting in the sewing room one afternoon when I returned home from school. I thought long and hard about disclosing what had been going on between our esteemed family friend and me. I worried about getting into trouble over it, but also about breaking the *big* promise I had made to Trepiedi – he had done so much for us after all. In the end, though, I decided that if there was anyone who could explain what all of this meant and keep my promise, it was my wise and open-hearted grandmother.

As I related my story I noticed Letitia's face change colour. Her jaw fell limp and her eyes suddenly seemed hollow. Oh my God, what had I done! I begged Letitia not to tell Mother in case all hell broke loose; it was *my* fault Trepiedi wasn't coming over now and I was going to get the beating of a lifetime for it.

Following that momentous afternoon in the sewing room, Trepiedi was never mentioned again but then, a week or so later, Letitia ordered me into the kitchen to help get dinner ready. Someone was coming over and everything had to be just perfect. She also mandated that I stay in the kitchen until asked to come out – no ifs or buts.

Finally, I heard a knock on the front door. Letitia looked at me with a concerned look on her face and reiterated, "Remember what I told you." She then turned and closed the kitchen door behind her.

As I busied myself with my chores I heard our friend's voice – *it was Trepiedi's!* I felt myself grow tense. Pricking up my ears to listen in on any conversation taking place, I muttered to myself: *Please God, please God, please God, don't let Letitia say anything.* I repeated this prayer in my head a dozen times as I grew hot, stuffy and feverish with nerves.

Gilda and Letitia sounded okay as they conversed normally with Trepiedi, and a sigh of relief made its way out of my body. As always, Trepiedi chatted and laughed freely back with them.

"Where's Cicci?" he asked.

Suddenly there was a massive uproar taking place in the lounge room. A scuffle filled with screams, whimpers, and bodies slamming into furniture left no clue that Trepiedi was being assaulted. Uttering my nickname must have been the trigger Letitia and Mother were waiting for. I so wanted to peer out from those glass doors but I didn't dare to. All of this was *my* fault and I was definitely going to be the one to cop it next.

One last desperate whimper and the front door slammed shut much harder than it ever had been before. My parents could be heard panting, as if they had just finished running a marathon. After what felt like an eternity, Letitia and Gilda walked into the kitchen red faced and dishevelled. Mother looked at me with great compassion in her eyes, something I saw only very rarely. She took me into her arms and hugged me for longer than I care to remember. Letitia looked on sadly.

Trepiedi was never mentioned again in our household, just like with my biological father, and I was cluey enough to do the same. In our family, it seemed, denial was an indispensable survival tool.

By this stage I knew what had happened to me was wrong – *very* wrong. What I wasn't so sure of, was whether I was to blame for not putting a stop to any of it. Was I responsible? Why couldn't anyone set me straight about what had really happened? One thing I *did* know for certain was, this sort of thing was *never* going to happen to me again. Yet there were others who tried.

A former Catholic priest – another friend of Mother's – came to the apartment for the first time. When Mother went into her bedroom to do something, the priest saw his chance and lunged at me like a cheetah, trying to pull off my knickers. I screamed at the top of my lungs and Mother ran out to see what was happening; I told her and the priest was chased out of our home.

Another guest of ours, a Hungarian film set designer called Janos, also had a go at me. Janos, I was told, had been the official set design sculptor for the 1963 film *Cleopatra*; I should add I have found no evidence of this in movie reference books or relevant websites.

Janos asked if he could draw my portrait. I was wearing plaits and a high necked sweater and I know this because his portrait still hangs on my wall today. As I was being drawn, Mother and Letitia prepared lunch. It seemed like forever before the drawing was finished and when Janos was finally done he showed me his work.

"Do you like it?" he asked.

I nodded. I looked prettier than even my perception of myself.

"So, what do I get for it?"

Janos had that look, the same one I'd seen so many times in Trepiedi's eyes. He leaned in towards me and planted a wet kiss onto my mouth, trying hard to force his slimy tongue inside. I shot out of my seat like an arrow from a bow and ran into my usual hiding spot, the toilet – the only room in this wretched apartment that had a lock. Janos stood at the door rapping his knuckles softly and nervously.

"I'm sorry, I'm sorry! Please come out!" he whispered.

I didn't want to. At first I thought Janos was nice because he wanted to draw me, but he wasn't. Janos was just another dirty man, like Trepiedi and *that* priest – and like another man who'd taught me how to swim at the sulphur baths but who'd been more interested in my vagina than the swimming lessons. What was wrong with me? Why did grown men want to do these filthy things to me?

I began feeling tears well up. If I told on Janos surely Gilda would think I was making up stories to grab attention and to play on one incident over and over. I bravely wiped away my tears and came out of the toilet. Janos breathed a sigh of relief. I kept the kiss to myself and, needless to say, we never saw Janos again. He was obviously a little more switched on than Trepiedi.

Our apartment block's caretaker at Via Pietro Cavallini 21 was a pleasant old man called Umberto. Umberto wore thick glasses which made his eyeballs look huge. Umberto seemed nice enough; he lived in special quarters outside in the courtyard, attached to the right hand stairwell.

The elevator on our building block was very small, but we lived on the top floor and it was a long way up the stairs. As I entered the elevator one afternoon after school, Umberto was inside cleaning it. I said hello to him and pressed the button for my floor. Once the door was closed Umberto took on 'the look', the one I had come to know so well. I held my breath and stood perfectly still. If you stand perfectly still you become invisible. It really *was* me who caused this behaviour in men and if I wasn't there, maybe these men would become different people.

When at last we reached my floor, Umberto moved past me and pulled back the safety screen. As he did so he rubbed the front of his trousers against my front. I could feel his hard penis poking through – my invisibility coat wasn't hiding me all that well after all. These predators could feel me, hear my breathing, even see me; *they* were a special breed.

Contrary to popular belief however, not all paedophiles are men. The estimated portion of female child molesters in substantiated assault cases is around 3 percent. So, I guess you can now guess that the next person to try and touch me up was a woman.

Mother billeted a small-time Bulgarian soprano who she had met during a working tour of Sofia. Cristina stayed with us for a few days, showering everyone with beautiful Bulgarian souvenirs. I received a set of *matryoshka* dolls, Letitia a jar of rose flavoured jam, and Mother a hand carved wooden flask filled with delicious smelling rose perfume. Cristina had really shiny red cheeks and seemed to smile all the time; I really loved her accent too.

Cristina longed for a proper bath; our little kitchen tub did not cut the mustard. She asked Mother for directions to the public bathhouse and if she could take me along. I could always do with a good wash but I wasn't at all that keen about Cristina seeing me naked; I had become very guarded with my body.

When Cristina and I arrived at the baths all the tubs were occupied bar one, which had been left in a disgusting condition. I'm sure a place such as this would be closed down nowadays as a health hazard. Cristina then opted for a shower cubicle. She announced we would be showering together and the alarm bells went off inside my head. I didn't want to shower with Cristina and vociferously refused. Cristina's permanent rosy smile disappeared.

"Take your clothes off right *now!*" she ordered in her broken Italian.

I felt scared but I really did *not* want to do this. I pushed past Cristina trying to shield my eyes from her nakedness. Cristina grabbed me by my arms. I swore at her and started screaming. Fed up, Cristina turned up the hot water and held me under it. Scalded and terrified I shut my mouth and began to play *nice*. Cristina regulated the hot water so it was no longer burning me and then began washing me, but not in the same way Letitia washed me. What choice did I have? I certainly didn't want to be scalded again.

* * *

Between 1973 and 1975 I was experiencing the most appalling and vivid nightmares, as a result of which I began to bed wet.

The images and beings I was seeing *had* to be nightmares because surely they couldn't be real? I was petrified of the dark but far more afraid of crossing the long corridor leading from our bedroom to the lounge room. Inside that damned corridor were faces protruding from the walls – *mean* faces, faces that reached out for me, one of the faces even called out my name. I was *so*, so afraid.

I'd lay immobile in bed, holding my breath until I could feel pins and needles and thought I was turning blue. I tried not to let 'them' know I was there. My bladder felt like it might burst at the seams as I lay wide awake in that condition for hours, blankets pulled firmly over my head. When I could no longer hold my urine in, I let it out in torrents that soaked right through everything. For me, lying in my own urine as it cooled until icy was far better than crossing that haunted corridor.

Letitia could save me from Mother's wrath only so many times and eventually my bedwetting was uncovered and I was seriously chastised. Late one-night Mother returned home from work and when she walked into our room, she switched on the light, with no regard for me being asleep. I woke up startled, then saw Mother hovering over me with a wild look in her eyes. Angrily, she pulled off my blankets and roared, "*Demon! Demon! Get out! Get out!*" as she poured a vial of water onto my face and chest. I guess she was attempting an 'exorcism' in order to resolve my bedwetting dramas.

Gilda – as I said earlier – shifted between various faiths and spiritual practices. For a while she participated in a shady group that performed regular séances. According to Gilda, Marilyn Monroe was one of the spirits that often 'showed up'. I recall seeing Marilyn in a movie on television and, smitten by her beauty and erotic poise, I mentioned her to Mother, who jumped like a cat on hot coals.

"Don't ever mention that woman's name in this house! She's a condemned soul."

It appears that during a séance session a member of the group asked Marilyn why she had taken her own life, on 5 August 1962. According to Gilda's version of events, Marilyn's anguished 'etheric essence' then took over the participant's body and started speaking through him. Mother explained how the young man let out a bloodcurdling scream and declared, "*I did not take my own life! I was murdered!*"

Mother saw the same young man on the street a few months later; he was sitting in a corner as if in a trance, wearing a blonde wig and a woman's dress, singing one of Marilyn's famous songs. Mother was now convinced Marilyn Monroe was an evil spirit who had possessed the innocent young man, and her stance was substantiated by the Catholic faith, which preaches that suicide is a mortal sin punishable by eternal damnation.

This ecclesiastical urban legend was the first thing that led me to question our faith in later years. Why *did* suicides have to go to hell? What if you were a kind, hardworking, law abiding, and humanitarian person who suddenly lost everything – who could not cope anymore and therefore chose to take his life in order to end perpetual suffering? Why should the wish to end emotional pain be punished by a suffering of a worse kind – and eternal at that? Was God really this cruel? And what of the iridescent Jesus I dreamed of? Did He agree with His Father too?

In retrospect, Gilda's spiritualist dabbling seemed to coincide with my nightmares. Could it be that it was my mother *herself* who brought home evil spirits from these séances?

I'd overheard Mother tell someone what a 'good child' I was – even as a baby. *She was no trouble at all*, Gilda reiterated. Why then, if I was 'no trouble at all' was I being treated so poorly all the time? A child cannot understand the pressures of life, including those she places upon herself. She cannot understand the stresses life's pressures create, so were Mother's stresses and responsibilities a valid excuse for inflicting filial abuse? The difficulties of being a single mother and struggling artist in Seventies Rome were far reaching, yes, but the only understanding I had of them came from a child's logic, so why didn't Mother just give me away to someone who might want me? Why did Mother choose her own life and then take her frustrations out on me? And why was Ettore not in the picture? Had I pushed him away somehow? Why wouldn't anyone tell me what happened there?

Eventually I came to believe my mother just enjoyed her petty cruelties – she must have for they happened far too frequently, and even when she appeared in a good mood beforehand. Take the following, for example: we went to see Disney's *Sleeping Beauty* in which a scene where Maleficent the Mistress of All Evil appears to Princess Aurora amid the flames of a fireplace. This image frankly scared the shit out of me, and the reason I felt so scared was that this scene correlated with some of the images I'd seen in the corridor back home. Mother noticed how frightened I'd been and when we returned home that night, she started to re-enact Maleficent's part, cornering me between the front door and the toilet alcove on my right. I was so afraid I instinctively hit Mother on the face to make her stop. I had never done anything like that before nor since – and although I paid a high price for my audacity, I went to bed feeling more than a little triumphant. It *was* in self-defence after all, right?

The strange occurrences in our apartment that pointed their eerie finger at me began affecting Letitia as well. One morning I woke up to a distinct kerfuffle taking place in the lounge room where, during my uncle and auntie's stay with us, Letitia slept on a pull-out bed. Gilda, always the loudest on the scene, could be heard exclaiming: "Oh my God, how can this be!" and "I need to take this to Pope Paul!"

Unlike Mother, Letitia did not deviate from Catholicism; she was a 100 percent devout and practising Christian. Letitia had read Maria Valtorta's *The Poem of the Man God* series at least three times over; she prayed with her rosary beads each night, and would fall asleep clutching them close to her chest.

Letitia related how the previous night she had a vivid dream in which Satan had spoken to her. When she awoke in the morning, she felt feverish and nauseous. Letitia then fumbled for her rosary looking for spiritual comfort only to find it lying in pieces under the bed covers. Each bead had been separated from the other with the link perfectly closed as if the beads had just melted away from one another. I had seen the beads myself and felt astounded. I *knew* there was a presence in our home all too well, and that it was *not* a friendly one.

Mother, who believed in demonic possession, became frantic. Gathering up the beads, she took them to the Vatican to be blessed and exonerated by Pope Paul VI himself – or so she hoped. I remember thinking one of those vaporous faces that tried grabbing me inside the corridor might grab my head from above my bedhead and strangle me in my sleep. I'd then lie with my head arched back so I could monitor the wall until I fell asleep; it meant waking up with a case of spasmodic stiff neck syndrome that would last for days. Unlike Mother, I did not believe these beings to be demons but rather, people who had 'crossed over' and were not happy with their afterlife. Even though I did not feel God was cruel and self-indulgent, I did not believe every one of us necessarily merited Heaven, not straight away anyway.

A second physical manifestation I witnessed, aside from the rosary beads, involved my room spinning around me like a centrifuge. As the atmosphere began to change, I remember lying in bed frozen and fearing the worst. I then felt like I was inside some sort of vacuum with my bed slowly levitating from the ground. This bizarre occurrence reminded me of *The Wizard of Oz*'s tornado scene with some of *The Exorcist*'s nastier aspects thrown in for good measure. Scientists and other sceptics would surely say that having watched both films, I was heavily influenced by their images – and that the hallucinations I experienced inside the corridor were directly related to past trauma, but I knew, *neither they nor this* were hallucinations. Yes, I was fanciful – what child isn't? – but even as a kid I was practical and logical, calling it as I saw it. I questioned absolutely everything, then and today, and have never accepted something on face value alone, knowing well the difference between fact and fiction – awake or asleep. Therefore, if I saw *it*, 'it' was most certainly there. I have a formidably strong will and there is very little that can influence me at length.

Eventually things settled down in the apartment and I stopped feeling or seeing things, but it did not mean I lost my fears. Fear had ingrained itself as my permanent companion just as it did with little Cole Sear (the protagonist of M. Night Shyamalan's *The Sixth Sense*). At least I stopped bedwetting and getting into trouble for it.

I distinctly remember the night the ambience in our house switched back to normal. I was in my room reading a *Topolino* comic. Mother walked in, saw a salamander sitting on the window shutter and screamed. Gilda hated reptiles, especially snakes. She grabbed a broom from the kitchen and frightened the poor creature back into the world outside. Catching her breath, Mother moved towards me holding a small package wrapped in white butcher's paper. Smiling, she unveiled its contents and said, "I bought you some mascarpone."

'Yummy,' I thought. I loved mascarpone and it was indeed a rare treat. I invited Mother to share the delicious cream cheese with me, but she gently declined.

"No Cicci, you enjoy it. I've been very hard on you lately and you are such a good girl. You have *always* been a good girl."

I looked up at my Mother and for a brief moment I saw the beautiful, loving, and kind face I hoped would stare back at me for the rest of my life.

How I wanted that fleeting sweet softness to remain etched into our existence. How I longed to be hugged warmly by her and never again beaten or punished. How I hoped she would say *I love you* just the once and *mean it*. Jesus was wrong about her. He was *wrong!* Mother simply did not know how to love or be loved, and even if she *did* tell me she loved me, I knew deep inside *I* could never say it back.

* * *

Around the age of eight, I began to display behaviours that are synonymous with the fallout of child abuse. The first of these I called 'rude art'.

I was a talented drawer, with the kids at school often asking me to draw things for them, something I did not mind as it offered me popularity, and I enjoyed creating or copying pictures. I particularly liked to draw beautiful girls – princesses and such; I think probably every little girl does. But following the experience with Trepiedi, I began to draw pornographic pictures in which the female subject was being 'hurt' by the male subject. Eventually my pictures became more and more sordid and 'snuff', like in nature.

Soon, I transferred this artistic morbidity onto my Barbie dolls, where I'd create a more 'lifelike' sense of brutality for myself. As I've mentioned, I had developed a bitter hatred for females *and* the female form alike. I guess it was a two-pronged symptom of the abuse I'd been subjected to in that I hated Gilda for hurting and frightening me, but also, in my formative years, Gilda represented the ultimate alpha female. Then there was the way I felt about myself and *my* female body following Trepiedi's gross sexual exploitation, of course.

With my poor Barbies, I'd sit in front of the heater slowly singeing their beautiful synthetic blonde hair until it had become a sticky, balding, grotesque mess. I'd stab their faces with scissors, try and cut out their breasts and privates, break their movable limbs, and anything else that had entered my angry, damaged mind. When I finally got my Ken doll one Christmas it was so that I could simulate rape on those plastic sluts. The *puttana* my mother always called *me*.

Pornographic imagery and subject material turned into a guilty obsession, and because my young body had been tampered with, I was acutely aware of my 'naughty bits' and the gratification they offered. I discovered that by holding my urine in for as long as possible, and by lying across a chair in a certain way, my engorged bladder would trigger off what I later realised was an orgasm. Needless to say I gave myself as many of these as I could, suffering terribly from regular bouts of cystitis as a consequence. I called my new found form of entertainment *pizzichino*, or 'tiny pinch'.

I'd also dress up in Gilda's clothes and perform stripteases in front of the mirror. The sexualised moves were copied from what I'd learnt from Trepiedi or found in adult references. I was a 'turned on' eight-year-old and although I'd not allow others to take advantage of me as Trepiedi did, I saw no harm in taking advantage of myself *on my own terms*.

My feline friend Eulalio and my Invisible Friend were the only sources of emotional release available to me, until I began to adopt a third pacifier – food.

I was very greedy with my food, but anything that gave me tactile pleasure was unsafe from me, and where food was concerned, I'd go to great lengths to obtain as much of it as I could, even if this meant retrieving discarded leftovers from the bin.

The patterns for future self-abuse had thus been set.

CHAPTER FOUR

GREAT SOUTHERN LAND

In 1972 Uncle Eduardo, Auntie Gianna and their new baby daughter Valeria left Italy for Australia and a new life.

Auntie Gianna had been pregnant twice but Valeria was the only child she took with her. Valeria was a very pretty baby: blonde, blue-eyed, and fair skinned, at last a little sister for a very lonely Adalgisa. But, sadly not to be; as seemed my destiny, everything I wanted would either leave or self-destruct.

From the moment my relatives left Rome, Letitia manipulated my mother into following suit, using the rationale that things weren't going well for her professionally in Europe and a new country like Australia would surely welcome an artist of her calibre. As much as I loved my cousin and her mother, I certainly did not want to leave. Rome was my *home*.

Gilda, though, was a one-eyed Spaniard who constantly insulted the Italians who gave her work, esteeming *España* as the seat of all things cultural and moral. In 1974 Letitia contracted a serious case of hepatitis A from a batch of contaminated mussels. Yellow as a lemon, she spent a substantial amount of time in hospital. Mother, meanwhile, took me to Spain to acquaint me with the different strands in my DNA. Once again we met up with the aunts who had taken care of me in Düsseldorf seven years earlier, as well as with my favourite uncle, Miguel.

Blanca, Berta, Alicia and Olga were aunties who had fussed over me like I was their own, and they now resided in Barcelona. Naturally I don't remember too much of my Spanish trip but, in Madrid, I do remember Uncle Miguel taking us on an impossible motorcycle ride around the city's landmarks like the Buen Retiro, the Puerta de Alcalá, the Plaza Mayor, the Palacio Real, the Puerta del Sol, and the Almudena Cathedral. Personally the place I enjoyed most was the Museo del Prado where my eyes did not drift from Francisco Goya's 'Black Paintings' – in particular *Saturn Devouring His Son* a picture that put me in mind of Gilda.

Uncle Miguel and his twin brother Eduardo were adventurous types, albeit reckless – typical Sagittarians, always up for the challenge. Eduardo was a decorated paratrooper in the German army, and when Letitia had effectively abandoned them in their late teens to follow Gilda and her career to Italy, both brothers had travelled Europe in search of themselves.

Letitia often said Eduardo was the dominant twin and that Miguel was shorter and less robust than his brother because Eduardo took over the womb – squashing his sibling into a corner. To me however, Miguel just came across as the meeker brother and thus my favourite. Eduardo, as well as being aggressive and arrogant, didn't seem to like me very much.

Bidding Miguel goodbye we ventured into Toledo, Valencia, and Mother's beloved childhood home in Benidorm. It was in Benidorm that Gilda had grown up with Letitia's mother while Letitia spent her conviction inside that Franco jail. Much later in life I discovered *all* four children were born prior to grandmother's imprisonment and not *just* Pepito, the eldest. This made it all the more difficult to understand why Pepito was the only child left behind.

Mother's life in Benidorm had been idyllic – a subject she rarely gave a rest. Her upbringing, although strict and pious, had most definitely been the 'correct way' to rear a child her age during this era. Apparently Mother's grandmother had been a grand lady who presided over the beautiful seaside villa, complete with hired help. The young Gilda spent five wonderful years here until Letitia, now released from prison, came to collect her, kicking and screaming, from that house of privilege, then flung her back into the squalor of post-war Madrid.

Prior to World War II, according to Gilda, the patriarchs of her family had owned a number of properties in Spain. Whether due to laziness, pride, or downright stupidity, all of them had been lost after the war. If these estates truly *did* exist, then *they* would have been my inheritance, rather than the handful of memories I was spoon-fed – as well as some highly *questionable* historical data.

* * *

I was not properly prepared for our relocation to the 'Great Southern Land'. One afternoon over lunch, Mother announced we were moving to Australia and that I needed to start packing my things. We could only take so much with us, so I was to sift through my possessions and choose *only* my favourite items. I was in shock. Where *was* Australia, for a start? Did they speak Italian there?

Saying goodbye to my Italian life brought many mixed feelings. On one hand I was excited to embark on a new adventure, but on the other I was not prepared to change anything at all on a personal level. I had established friendships at school and things had improved somewhat at home. I promised Ileana, my new best friend at Umberto Primo, I would write to her once a week the moment we arrived in this faraway, never before heard of country, a place where I knew not one word of its spoken language. Oh, let me rephrase that: Umberto Primo had just introduced English into its curriculum and so I *did* know one word – 'yes'.

As much as I'd dreamt of all that was Nordic, Australia was not England or Germany. The continent wasn't even 200 years old! There were no castles or dungeons there; I'd be surprised if they even had TV sets. I did *not* want to go there. (And fuck you Letitia for talking Mother into doing this!)

The mid-1970s saw many Europeans, fed up with pseudo-socialism and a lack of domestic opportunity on all fronts, looking towards new lives abroad. They left their maternal countries in droves to settle into the two countries open for immigration at the time – Canada and Australia. If you were a common labourer or farmer, Australia was the ideal place to relocate to, with an immigration program open to the disillusioned from 1945 to 1975, designed to backfill these job descriptions.

In December 1974 the three of us were booked onto the SS *Galileo Galilei*, bound for the *Terra Australis*. Alongside dozens of other female migrants, we stood in line, naked and self-conscious, to receive the mandatory inoculations and physical inspections required. It looked like a scene from an Auschwitz documentary.

The *Galileo Galilei*, launched in 1961, had been built specifically for transporting Italian migrants to Australia. We boarded the liner in January 1975 and the trip took close to a month to complete. There were frequent stopovers in interesting places like the Canary Islands and Cape Town, and I soon forgot the bitter farewell tears that were dropped on the shores of my birth city. As a methodical Taurean who appreciates the status quo and familiarity, some internal juices were now being stirred. A sense of adventure was being roused, and curiosity slowly began to set in.

The ship was just like any other cruise ship: plenty of food and entertainment, and, for me, an infinite playground where I could get up to my elbows in mischief. Mother ordered me to attend English classes while on board to prepare myself for school in Angelicaaide, but I preferred to sneak into the cinema to watch the adult features. Angelicaaide was South Australia's capital city and somewhere in the Adelaide suburbs Uncle Eduardo and Auntie Gianna had settled down with Valeria and their new daughter, Bianca. They had, with great kindness, agreed to let us stay with them until Mother found a place of our own.

Not so long before we left for Australia, Mother had hooked up with a colleague from Da Meo Patacca, a superb but untrained tenor named Alfonso. Gilda and Alfonso fell in love and Mother vowed she would return to Rome and collect him. Alfonso was seriously overweight, though, and a condition for migration to Australia was overall good personal health. Alfonso had not been allowed to leave with us in January because obesity was considered a health risk that could affect future employment.

I did not like Alfonso from the start. He tried hard to win me over with gifts and the like but my mind was firmly made up. *The fat Sicilian was not getting my mother!*

Mother's beauty, academic intelligence, and her public persona made her a prime target of male admiration so there was no doubt she had 'settled' in accepting Alfonso as her husband and my stepfather. There had been a multitude of eligible men she could have successfully paired with, men I would have preferred over the fat tenor. One of Gilda's many short-lived affairs was with an American artist who looked exactly like Charlton Heston. Another I had hoped might become my stepfather was Marco, the flute player on the Da Meo Patacca's entourage. Marco was tall and handsome, but the best thing about him was his daughter, a girl exactly my age who could easily have been the sister I craved for.

Once, in Rome, I walked into our bedroom and found an older gentleman on bended knee begging my mother's hand in marriage. Letitia told me he was a rich industrialist who would have changed our lives, but Mother had just not liked him enough. Years before, my mother was engaged to an influential Iranian, when Iran was still known as Persia. This wealthy Persian had subsequently annulled their engagement when Mother had publicly embarrassed him by getting drunk at a party he was hosting. Gilda was allowed to keep the expensive engagement bracelet he had given her *provided* she leave Persia immediately. Thank God for that too – imagine life as a woman under Sharia Law, courtesy of the Ayatollah Khomeini.

'A man can have sex with animals such as sheep, cows, camels and so on. However, he should kill the animal after he has his orgasm. He should not sell the meat to the people in his own village; however, selling the meat to the next door village should be fine.'

Such was one of the Ayatollah Khomeini's stated laws.

When we docked at Cape Town I was not allowed to leave our ugly steerage cabin because I had a massive throat infection that disabled me in every way. Letitia, essentially a racist, was not interested in checking out South Africa and remained on board with me. Mother on the other hand couldn't get out fast enough. Her penchant for the exotic was all pervasive, but in reality there was nothing exotic about Cape Town in 1975. South Africa's apartheid system was at its horrific height. Mother told us that each time she approached a non-white citizen, he'd recoil in fear, holding out closed fists: the threat of an arrest.

* * *

When we finally arrived at Adelaide, in February 1975, Uncle Eduardo greeted us at Outer Harbour and took us back to his home in Leslie Street, Woodville Park. Mother, Letitia and I could not believe our eyes: what a luxury, being able to rent a freestanding house complete with front and back yards. In crowded cities like Rome, single storey homes were only for the rich or famous.

The shipping cargo carriers, Brambles Limited, seemed to have lost our trunks, which meant most of our valuables and all of my toys were gone. Mother, of course, was beside herself with grief for all her *spartitos* (scores) were in those trunks ... but fuck my toys, my precious things, right? It had to be *always* about *her* and her opera.

Baby Valeria had grown into a big girl. She was now four years old and her little sister Bianca was eighteen months old. I then decided my cousins were the sisters my mother did not give me and hoped Valeria would never recall what I'd done to her in Italy when she was a baby.

It was Christmas Day and I was playing with a musical ornament, a favourite of mine. Little Valeria was in her pram, screaming at the top of her lungs for what seemed like hours. I couldn't hear the ornament's chime and I became so agitated I planted a lounge cushion over Valeria's little face to drown out her cries. Auntie Gianna then walked in to attend to Valeria and, realising I was in fact suffocating her, I yanked the cushion off her face. Valeria let out a choked sigh and collected her breath but her face was crimson. Had Auntie Gianna not walked in when she did, God knows I may have killed my little cousin. It was only many years later I gathered the courage to tell Valeria what I had done. I was expecting the worst, but Valeria just laughed in my face. It wouldn't be for first time – and for all the wrong reasons.

I was enrolled in a nearby primary school, Whitefriars, which was run by Catholic nuns. Because I had no English, I attended English as your Second Language classes. I think I was one of three kids in the class; our introduction to the language was a children's book, Roald Dahl's *Charlie and the Chocolate Factory*.

Up until my tenth birthday the Australian children gave me a really hard time. It made me determined to learn their language – and at lightning speed too. One dark rainy day after class, I found myself soaked to the bone and sitting in a pool of muddy water. I had been ambushed by the usual suspects and that was where they'd left me. I ran all the way to my uncle's house crying my eyes out and vowing to master the infernal language called English so that one day those bastards would rue the day they laid their hands on me. Whatever they were saying to me, my tentative 'yes' replies delivered the desired effect.

By September 1975 I was conversing in English. I graduated from the ESL class with honours and was placed in the year above instead of Year 3, which would have been appropriate for my age. Academically I was *too advanced* for that class, proof that the European education system was way ahead of the Australian one.

I was too kind to wreak my planned revenge on the kids who had tormented me; instead, I decided to entertain them. I became the clown – quick witted, sly, always begging for mischief. The kids loved me – the nuns, perhaps not quite so much. One of the kids who pursued me most was a blonde, freckly girl called Bernadette. Bernadette, or Bernie, wanted to become a detective when she grew up and together we engaged in pretend murder investigations. Bernie introduced me to *The Hardy Boys* and *Nancy Drew* series, and these paperbacks continued to pique my interest in crime and punishment.

Late in April, Mother returned to Rome to marry Alfonso. She couldn't even wait until May when I'd be turning ten. This self-serving urgency placed Alfonso in my bad books even more.

Marrying Alfonso meant that as the responsible immigrant, Mother was allowed to bring her husband into the country and would therefore take on any impositions he might incur on the state. To be honest I didn't really care that Gilda had left; I liked living with Auntie Gianna and her daughters. Uncle Eduardo was not as accommodating or congenial but I managed to dodge him more often than not. In sharp contrast, Auntie Gianna made little maternal distinction between me and her daughters. She was the consummate nurturer, a true earth mother, and Florence Nightingale. I loved Auntie Gianna's smile and blue eyes. I just *loved her*.

While Mother was away getting married I shared a room with my grandmother. One night I awoke from a horrible dream where a hoofed monster was chasing me. In the dream the beast told me he was Satan and that he would kill me and my entire family. The dream was followed by a tremendous thump against the bedroom door, loud enough to have woken the entire household. I looked over at Letitia, expecting to see her wide awake, as frightened as I was. My grandmother was sound asleep and snoring softly but there was *no* way she could not have heard *that*!

I crawled out of bed filled with trepidation. I prayed the old foes from the apartment in Rome had not returned to haunt me. Perhaps the commotion was Auntie Gianna and Uncle Eduardo; they fought a lot. I listened for sounds of bickering voices but there were none. My cousins weren't crying and the house was deathly still. I summoned the courage to walk out of our bedroom to investigate things further – it was exactly what Bernie would have done. I opened and peered through every bedroom door but all were fast asleep.

The next morning, I tried getting out of bed again to prepare for school, but instead I stumbled and collapsed into a heap on the floor. Auntie Gianna rushed in and began calling out my name, shaking me vigorously. She then told Letitia I was burning up with fever.

I stayed in bed sick for three days. The mysterious thump offered no explanation for my condition but I was convinced it had something to do with that 'demonic' dream. Although I was young and impressionable and a lot of bad things had happened to me, I *knew* I was not imagining things. I possessed *something* that enabled me to tune into things that were not of this world, but at that point in my life I had no name for it.

The old fears I thought I'd left in Rome returned and I started 'acting out' again. Uncle Eduardo made it perfectly clear I wasn't liked in his home and that I was considered a 'bad influence' on Valeria and Bianca.

"She's just like her mother that one, nothing but trouble," I'd hear him tell Letitia.

Where else does a sad child take out her frustrations but at school, where guardians don't see them. I had the distinction of being the only girl at Whitefriars to receive the cane. I taunted the nuns like the kids once taunted me, and a smart, well-meaning kid turned into an infamous intransigent. Bernie loved it. My bravado made for great unsolved mysteries. Once we even broke into the school hall, looking for murder most foul after reading an article about a monastery in Europe where the bodies of unborn foetuses and newborn babies had been uncovered beneath the courtyard pavers.

Eventually, Mother returned to Adelaide with her new husband, fat Alfonso, in tow. Together we rented a house in Edward Street in Woodville South, on the other side of busy Port Road. The house belonged to the relative of a rich Italian property developer, Guglielmo Rossi. I had a room to myself and our yard was huge, just made for adventure.

I walked to school on my own every day, wondering when I was going to get hit by a car on that insane Port Road. It was the era of Abba, the Bay City Rollers, John English and Sherbet, and to lighten the 2kilometre journey, I'd listen to these, my earliest musical heroes on the tiny transistor radio I had asked for and received for my birthday. My love affair with pop music had begun.

At home, Mother's singing practice, in the form of operatic scales day in and day out, were driving me mad. When Alfonso came on the scene the two of them started practising duets. Modern music, though, was banned from our house; Mother considered it the work of Satan.

"God created a perfect instrument, the human voice, and it must *not* be used as a trashcan!" she'd declare.

Because of Gilda's one-eyed hysteria, I dared not play my transistor aloud. At night I'd bury myself as deep as possible into my bed with the radio attached to my ear on the lowest volume, indulging in everything Seventies pop had to offer. It was a tiny luxury that made my otherwise abysmal home life just a little sweeter.

* * *

I was informed that my surname had changed. Alfonso had legally adopted me while in Rome, around the same time he married Gilda. I was not pleased: my new name sucked … and who the hell did this fat Sicilian think he was, waltzing into my life and pretending to be *my* father? He would have to go, of course.

So, I began plotting Alfonso's demise, which would naturally be deemed accidental. It began with a collection of red-back spiders I found in and around the old brick barbecue in the backyard. I placed the little killers inside a glass jar and the next day, when I returned from school, I released the spiders inside Mother and Alfonso's bed, aware that the fat slug took a solitary nap soon after supper. The spiders would kill Alfonso and he'd be out of my life forever – hurrah!

As if dealing with a neurotic mother wasn't enough, Alfonso was ordering me around like he owned the place, telling Gilda I wasn't to do this or that.

"In Sicilia, girls stay home and work for their family! None of this *can I go here or there* – and besides, Cicci is at an age where she could get pregnant."

Pregnant? I was eleven years old for Christ's sake! I hadn't even had a period – and who gives a shit what people did in *Sicilia*. We live in *Australia* now you asshole!

The only thing that had kept me sane back in Rome was the tiny amount of freedom I stole when Mother wasn't around, and if the slug thought he could now take this away from me, well did *I* have news for him!

When murder attempt number one did not work (the redbacks mysteriously vanished, or had maybe died), attempt number two – less imaginative yet more dramatic – was soon applied.

Late one night, I pretended to be sleepwalking. Reaching into the kitchen drawer I retrieved a large knife. Mother and Alfonso's bedroom door was jammed and wouldn't lock so my guardians pushed a heavy armchair against it for privacy. Very slowly, I pushed against the door listening carefully for sounds of bodies stirring. Once inside I raised my knife and just took a swing at my stepfather. My plan involved Mother realising I was a sleepwalker so that I couldn't be blamed for 'accidentally' killing her husband. How ambitious of me.

Fortunately, Alfonso was in the hypnogogic stage of sleep and, feeling me standing over him, he shrieked himself awake and grabbed my wrist. Mother leapt out of bed and pulled me out of the room by my nightgown. She pushed me inside my room and proceeded to give me the thrashing of a lifetime.

Ironically it was my nemesis who came to my rescue as he talked Gilda down, telling her exactly what I had hoped she would conclude for herself. Having Alfonso rescue me from Mother's diabolical hands did not endear him to me, though. I was on a mission and, come hell or high water, *it* was going to happen.

In August of 1975 Mother announced she was pregnant. To me it seemed obvious from the start that Mother and Alfonso were a match made in hell. They fought ceaselessly, which I of course lapped up with gusto. Discord between them meant they'd separate and divorce soon enough. Mother's self-harming became more brutal than I'd ever seen: she punched her pregnant belly, to relieve her anger but also to punish Alfonso. God only knew how my half sibling was faring in there. I had to ask myself if I was born black and blue as result of similar attacks, with the 'Ettore bashings' a convenient cover story.

Alfonso appeared to have both the patience of several saints and the tenacity of a giant clam. Gilda gave it to him worse than she ever gave it to me yet he rarely defended himself against her, and *never* threatened to leave. Mother was carrying his only child and, from what I could see and understand, Alfonso was deeply and hopelessly in love with his wife.

To allow my guardians some newlywed privacy, Letitia was staying at Leslie Street with my uncle and auntie, something she wasn't happy about. Letitia worshipped the ground Gilda walked on and it didn't take long for her to become an ally in the cause of removing Alfonso from our lives. She embarked on a most scathing smear campaign, labelling Alfonso a fraud and an opportunist. Letitia hated that not only did he not work, he did not even *try* to find a job. Alfonso had the voice of a great tenor but he was untrained and inexperienced; as far as Letitia was concerned a man without conservatorium qualifications had no right to demand the same kind of work as my mother, a trained singer. Alfonso should have been hitting the streets looking for an honest living instead of presenting himself at auditions and operatic agendas alongside her precious daughter.

Letitia was also as unimpressed with Gilda's pregnancy as she had been with me; her daughter may as well have swapped her concert gowns for aprons, for all the good another child would do for her career at the age of forty-one.

On 30 April 1976 my half-brother Piero was born and was pronounced the image of his father. Around the same time Auntie Gianna announced her own pregnancy and Mother decided Gianna must be jealous, wanting a son of her own. On 18 December that year Valeria and Bianca joyfully welcomed a little brother, my cousin Rodolfo, into the family.

Things plodded along for a while without too much drama. I had a new cat to love, a ginger called Kitty, who followed me and my family everywhere we went. Kitty was not so much a cat as a human in feline form; she knew when you were feeling down and would jump on your lap licking your hands, or rub herself on you to lighten the mood. I loved her *so* much. Each time I'd walk to school Kitty would follow me, stopping at Port Road and surveying the speeding traffic with cautious judgement. Regardless, I would shoo her away in case she negotiated a break in the traffic and attempted to cross that deadly thoroughfare with me.

Cats are supposed to have nine lives, but not Kitty. One day her judgement was not so sharp and she decided to do more than simply wish me a good day from the kerb. After I'd reached the other side of the road, Kitty crossed after me and an oncoming car clipped her. Kitty turned to hop away and received the full brunt of a second vehicle which killed her on impact, before my eyes. I watched helplessly as her little body flew across the road with vehicles running over her one after the other like she was nothing. I screamed and screamed. I wanted to run onto that infernal road but the cars were going too fast. There was nothing I could do to rescue my beloved Kitty, or even offer her the dignity of a less mutilated corpse. When finally, I caught a break, I ran across past Kitty's headless body and all the way home, screaming and sobbing. Mother wasn't home and Alfonso clearly didn't give a shit about me or Kitty; he appeared only mildly concerned, telling me this is what cats do, and that sometimes they lost all nine lives at once. He then insisted I go to school, to help me take my mind off what had just happened.

I didn't want to go to school! I was completely devastated and all I could do was cry and cry ... I had just lost my best friend!

The journey back to Whitefriars seemed endless as I pushed on through my tears. My bawling did not stop in class and all Miss McDonald could do was send me to the sick bay for the remainder of the day. My parents were notified by phone but they did not come and get me. What decent parent would send their child to school under such circumstances? Noone gave a damn about Kitty but me. Noone gave a damn about how *I* felt either. Noone gave a damn about *both of us*.

On the way back home that afternoon I braced myself for the inevitable. There she was, my little Kitty, now several pieces, all burned into the bitumen.

My best friend had become bloodied smears of nondescript roadkill. In a strip of South Australian road lay the remnants of a beautiful little soul, a creature who selflessly offered me hours of comfort noone else could or would. It should have been Alfonso ingrained into that bitumen, if the world had any justice.

Piero was a normal baby; he cried and fed, cried and slept, cried and pissed and shat. I didn't know how to look after a baby but Mother must have thought I did because Piero seemed always to be in *my* care. I hated it when a baby cried.

Gilda and Alfonso had a visitor, some Italian radio guy who might be putting them on the *Mamma Lena* program. Mum shooed me into Piero's room and told me to keep him quiet. Begrudgingly I picked up my screaming half-brother from his cot – *Shut up you little shit!* I furiously rocked Piero back and forth in my arms. It didn't help and he only screamed louder. If he kept this up it would *me*, not him, getting into trouble for disturbing the peace; I rocked him harder.

Suddenly, Piero flew out of my arms as I watched his flight in slow motion, frozen in time, anticipating the terrible result of my stupidity. Yet, somehow, God only knows how, my brother landed on the floor directly onto his well-padded bottom. His little frame stood completely upright with only the slightest possibility of a whiplash. Piero stopped crying then, and smiled at me; he appeared fine. I quickly gathered him back into my arms, checking him over for broken bits – nothing. How the hell could it be that there was nothing wrong with him? I couldn't believe what my eyes were telling me; it was as if an angel had caught him in mid-air and then gently placed him on the ground. I began wondering if it could be the same angel who rescued me from that near drowning a few years before in Italy.

We started frequenting Mother's real estate friends a lot. They were hugely rich and Mother boasted they owned half of Adelaide. Maria, the wife, was a lovely and elegant lady who could never do enough for us; nonetheless I was extremely wary of her husband, and of their son.

One afternoon I found myself inside the family's luxury bathroom, when suddenly I could see the door handle turn.

"I'm in here!" I called out.

The husband paid no attention to me and opened the door, heading straight for me with the 'Trepiedi look' and that familiar sickening grin dancing across his face. *Oh not again.*

I firmly commanded the husband to walk out at once. He stopped for a moment, weighing his options, and mercifully he did as I asked. My knees hurt from squeezing them shut so tightly. Following this incident, the husband maintained a polite distance, aside from the obligatory greeting hugs which I endured for the sake of familial harmony. I had witnessed the way he 'hugged' Valeria though, and it made me thoroughly sick. The son was the same, and so I stayed away from him, especially after he tried putting his grubby hand up my skirt during a game of musical chairs.

Adelaide, as it turned out, was a beautiful city: clean, tidy, and seemingly friendly. I missed Rome terribly but South Australia had its good points. I loved going out with my cousins to Semaphore, Henley Beach and Grange. I was still a water baby at heart and, despite that near drowning, going in deep did not frighten me.

Valeria and Bianca were indeed the sisters I had always craved for; they seemed to like me and I sure loved *them*. Valeria was a bit of a sook and seemed to have eating issues. Auntie Gianna gave her daily doses of emollient to open up her appetite but it didn't seem to help. Letitia had no time for Valeria but adored Bianca and Rodolfo. Rodolfo looked a lot like Uncle Eduardo and I couldn't help but wonder if he reminded Letitia of the son she gave away during the war.

My English was now fluent and the kids at school never again picked on me – in fact I became quite popular and amassed a lot of friends. My grades were okay too and life appeared for once to sail by on an even keel. Mother, being my mother, never stopped screaming, but it was mainly at Alfonso which I didn't mind one iota. I learnt to ignore them both, still hoping my mother's repulsive nature would eventually drive him away.

In September 1977 Mother dropped another bombshell. Life in Adelaide was not furthering her career and so we would be relocating to Sydney. *Fuck you!* I thought. Does life ever revolve around *anyone* but Gilda and her precious, cocksucking career? I had only *just* started settling in!

In late October then, aged twelve, I found myself in another Australian suburb, much less attractive than Woodville South; this ugly new neighbourhood's name was Cabramatta. I immediately hated it.

Fuck you Mother … and *fuck* you Sydney! Fuck the spineless Alfonso too … he could have made a stand and said *no we're staying right here!* Had he done so, I might have developed some respect for him.

CHAPTER FIVE

CABRAMATTA HIGH SCHOOL

———

Prior to our arrival in New South Wales, Alfonso, who had left before us, tried to negotiate the purchase of a three-bedroom terraced house in Paddington, an uptown, fashionable suburb in Sydney's Eastern Suburbs. My life might have turned out somewhat differently, had Alfonso been successful in obtaining the property, but it was not to be. Instead, we moved into an old, rat infested, fibro rental house in Cabramatta West, a blue collar, 'multicultural' suburb in Sydney's Outer West.

Letitia, refusing to be kept away from her daughter a second time, followed us here – much to Alfonso's disgust.

I was enrolled at Cabramatta West Primary School, where I finished Year 5. The first friend I made here was a skinny, fuzzy haired Italian girl named Annabella. Her best friend was a tall and robust blonde of Austrian origin, named Leisl. By the end of Year 5 I was also good friends with two other girls, Patricia and Susan.

Even though I had made some friends, I was being tested by some others in my year. In order not to lose face and be branded a 'chicken', I accepted all of the dumb schoolyard challenges, fronting up at the end of school for a fight or two. Holding my own gained me the respect I needed to survive yet another round of this stupid life of mine; it made me wonder how the weak and fearful fare in our world.

In Year 6 I dated for the first time; his name was Darren. Like most of the Geminis I'd met throughout my life, Darren was funny, confident, energetic, and outspoken. Our romance blossomed over a handball match which I famously won. For our first 'proper' date, Darren wanted to take me to the Rollarena in Fairfield. How was I going to convince Gilda and Alfonso to let me go? Yet I would definitely *be* going. I had to. My reputation depended on it.

If embarrassment is a disease, then on that evening I found myself on my death bed. My ridiculous guardians decided the only way I could go out with my new beau was with Letitia as chaperone. Naturally we weren't at the Rollarena for longer than an hour. Letitia announced she hated the loud music and demanded we leave. Darren, needless to say, was unimpressed and I was dumped the very next week for another Year 5 girl named Julie. He even made me return the Abba medallion he'd given me, thus rendering my heartbreak complete and irreversible.

In order to retrieve my honour, I summoned Darren to an after-school duel (actually a fist fight). Shortly after that, I fell in 'rebound love' with Robert, a redheaded, freckly boy who reminded me of Alfredo, my Roman first love. Redheaded Robert was out of my league, though, and already in love with someone else.

Unlike the other kids of Cabramatta West, I was not allowed to do anything. My peers went out with their friends and took trains to the city, plaza shopping, the movies, the beach – pretty much anywhere they fancied. *I* wasn't allowed to have more than two people over my place at the same time, let alone go to *theirs* for a 'sleepover'. It wasn't my mother who was stopping me, though, it was Alfonso; the slug was always in her ear. The freedom I'd enjoyed in Rome ended the day Alfonso took over my family. Once more, I decided to kill him.

Alfonso's peasant mentality, an anachronistic outlook in which women are little more than house servants and breeding mules, and where prepubescent boys leave school early to go to work, was in sharp contrast to everything my mother stood for. Alfonso had left school at the age of nine to provide for his large family and as a result his level of literacy was shameful. During those ferocious fights I so thrived on, Gilda loved to berate him about being 'analphabetic'. Just what the hell did she think she'd gained by marrying him? And to hell with *my* needs or wants, correct?

Australian girls seemed vastly different from Italian ones. Girls here appeared freer in the way they expressed themselves, loitering in the streets at night, going out with their friends as they liked, wearing short skirts and too much makeup. They followed football as avidly as the boys, watched

Countdown and had multiple boyfriends. Gilda and Alfonso had no clue how the restrictions they imposed on me affected my social life. I wasn't allowed to get my ears pierced or even to wear nail polish!

My skinny friend Annabella gave me a dress that was too big for her. It had a halter neck and was tight fitting. I loved it – my budding figure looked good in it, and I decided I was going to wear it to school on mufti day. When my guardians saw me in it I got, perhaps too predictably, *you look like a slut!* The dress disappeared from my wardrobe.

To maintain some form of social identity that would see me through the hardest part of my formative years I became a storyteller and class clown. The ridiculous BS I'd tell my friends in order to fit in became legendary, and I was always able to back it up with 'hard evidence'. I was fairly certain most of my friends did buy into the lies and antics as I was rarely questioned over anything I did or said.

At the top of the list of infamous lies I related to Annabella and Leisl was the one in which I'd qualified for, and been accepted into, the Bolshoi Ballet as a junior ballerina. I even brought in a pair of my grandmother's jiffy slippers modified to look like ballet shoes. In them I'd pirouette and bounce around on the grassy areas at lunchtime like a complete idiot. To anyone in the know I must have looked like a terminal loser. Surely there aren't too many overweight teenage girls in the Bolshoi?

Not knowing who my biological father was meant I could invent one. I decided my father was a German Count called Herr Schuschnembach. He was forced to leave my pregnant mother in Rome in order to flee back to Germany because post-Mussolini Italians had discovered that he'd harboured Nazi affiliations during the war. Never mind any chronological faux pas on my part, with 'Herr Schuschnembach' being only five years old in 1939 … Not to worry, kids know bugger all about history, especially those Aussie ones.

At times my lying got me into trouble but I'd get myself out of it by utilising higher fiction (i.e. telling even more elaborate lies). It dawned on me how dynamic and charismatic I really was, and that feeding people bullshit was more about carefully crafted communication and intonation than deviancy.

Early in 1979 I started at Cabramatta High School in Aladore Avenue, just a stone's throw from Cabramatta Road. My first day there was sheer agony.

Mother refused to buy a school uniform because it was *too expensive*, so she commissioned Letitia to make one for me. The slacks were oversized and had a drape reminiscent of Charlie Chaplin's in *The Tramp*. My schoolbag translated into one of Letitia's hessian shopping bags, and the white blouse sported distinctly old fashioned embossing. Walking through those front gates, the crucial question was – what do I play down more, the slacks or the handbag? Fortunately, things turned out okay. I wasn't the *only* 'stand out' girl there and with my colourful personality on hand I got by, as always.

I began to make more friends not only in my year, but from within the lower and higher years too. A great number of the students there were of different nationalities, with a variety of domestic backgrounds and academic levels. I rarely settled into the one group, flitting between various others during lunchtime and recess. I snubbed my nose at secondary school hierarchy or culture, and it was in high school that I obtained a term of endearment that diluted the sad, trapped, lonely child I really was. Here I became 'crazy Adalgisa' – but I wasn't at all crazy. I was a masked survivor and people watcher, one self-taught in 'street psychology', even at such a young age.

The teachers at Cabramatta High didn't know whether to love or hate me. I demonstrated the level of academic intelligence they looked for, but then shot it down with unabashed unruliness and gratuitous laziness. I was a natural at English, art, and history, and these were the classes I excelled in. For every other class I was a teacher's nightmare, especially in maths, which totalled my Year 7 report card for truancy.

By Year 9 I had worked my way up from English 5 to English 1, arriving second in my class – and therefore my entire year, for the top mark accolades. My English teacher, Mr David Morse, who I adored, wrote the following for my Year 10 report: 'The best writer I've ever taught; she has a love of words and literature. A very creative and original person. Will do well as a senior student.'

When it came to Sports, I entered all the long distance running races. I had never learnt to breathe properly, holding it in unnaturally, and this was a legacy of Mother's wrath throughout my childhood. Strangely I found that holding my breath accentuated a level of endurance, and I often came fourth or fifth during home run races which then positioned me inside district titles. Of course, I was not allowed to attend these out of school hours' events in case I 'fell pregnant'. All other sporting feats such as netball or cricket were pointless pursuits because training took place after school, and I was expected to be home, to get fat on pasta and perform my chores. So, on Tuesdays (Sports Day), I was forced to choose elective sports because these were held within school time. Ten pin bowling and the Rollarena cost $5, something I didn't have and was too scared to ask for. So, in order to attend, I started stealing from my guardians; I became a thief as well as a liar.

At Cabramatta High I was always in love with someone and *desperately* wanted a boyfriend. I found the boys liked and spoke to me but always as a friend; even the unattractive unpopular boys kept me at arm's length romantically. I *was* a bit chubby yes, but I'd decided I was also quite pretty and there were girls far chubbier and less pretty who had perfectly good boyfriends. I wasn't outwardly shy or backward in coming forward with my intentions either. Perhaps too much brazen bravado was the problem?

On the bus to school I would put on mascara and change my 'burqa' pants into a tight fitting skirt I had secretly made myself. Before returning home I would frantically rub the mascara off and change back into the dreadful pants. Gilda and the slug were controlling and irrational. Here I was, fifteen years old and forbidden to dress and act like a normal teenager. Gilda's behaviour had nothing to do with protection from exploitation, it seemed to me, and everything to do with personal jealousy. At forty-seven, Mother's looks were fading as fast as her career prospects.

For me home was now *Alcatraz*. From Years 7 to 10 my life consisted of school, homework, looking after Piero, embarrassing family excursions, and dreaded, duller than fog church services. The only escape for me other than school was time spent in my room expressing myself with drawing and writing. On these white sheets of paper, I created worlds that were almost tangible, and offered some comfort from the quicksand of reality that devoured me daily.

The school projects I completed for English, art and history were always the highest scorers, and the respective teachers would question me as to why the heck did I not apply myself holistically to the curriculum. The answer was that I simply wasn't *interested* in anything else – when it came to topics that failed to ignite my imagination I had the attention span of a drunken gnat. Books, though, helped me escape the doldrums of my sequestered life, with archaeology, mythology and literary classics my staples.

School holidays were both my death sentence and tomb. I hated Mother's 'must do' trips to Bondi or Manly. My family, with their smelly sandwiches, loud voices, and overstretched St Vinnie's swimwear, were the stereotyped, detested 'wog' entourage. Also, by this stage it had become painfully obvious that Piero had suffered neurological damage at birth, with severe mental delay his lifelong lot. I hoped the accidental fall I caused him as a baby was not to blame – he had not landed on his head, after all. I believed Mother's self-harming behaviour when pregnant was much more likely to be the cause, along with her age.

Piero's antics, due to his mental disability, caused a commotion in public and, of course, it was *my* responsibility to keep his behaviour in check. My resentment towards my half-brother grew monumentally, turning into antipathy towards his wellbeing. I took to beating him, the way Mother had beaten me. I had no understanding that his behaviour stemmed from a significant disability. To me Piero was just a pain, the direct result of a misguided marriage to a man I hated.

* * *

Cabramatta High's student body comprised seventyseven nationalities, with the so-called Asian invasion only just starting. Cabramatta often appeared on the news because the Serbs and Croats seemed to be at each other's throats, with frequent bombings of restaurants and stabbings. Much later, the trouble between the then Yugoslavs was superseded by Vietnamese gang warfare, making my suburb one of the most notorious in Sydney.

I'd skip a lot of classes with Annabella and Leisl, thoroughly enjoying the rebellious component truancy offered me. Even though they did not know about it, wagging off school was another way I was repaying Gilda and Alfonso for the stranglehold they placed on me.

The three of us would sneak out via the back oval into a large paddock, either at lunchtime or recess, and on to Annabella's place. With her parents at work we had the run of the place, and it was here that I discovered peanut butter, Vegemite and Tang! I had come to hate my garlicky 'wog' lunches that stank out my school bag. My family had no idea of the suffering they caused me on a daily basis. I flatly refused those options, eventually, taking only plain cheese sandwiches, which earned me the nicknames Adalcheesa and Cheesy Grins. 'Aussie' food was *the best*, so on top of stealing money for elective sport, I grabbed a little more for the odd school canteen pie or sausage roll. There is no describing the bliss of hot, chewy pie, smothered in runny gravy, sliding down my throat.

I was banned from Annabella's place, because not only did we smoke her parents' cigarettes, we also ran up a huge phone bill pranking random numbers in Sydney and abroad. But we did find a new truant leisure spot – Leisl's place, a few houses up! Here we'd listen to her vast collection of rock music, and I discovered artists like Kiss, Rod Stewart, Led Zeppelin, Jimi Hendrix and

Black Sabbath. It was during these illicit escapades that the sense of freedom I had relished so much in Rome returned. This bull was not going to be corralled by anyone – friend or foe!

I managed to intercept our mail most days, confiscating any letters of reprimand from the school, and forging ones that required parental consent for anything I was interested in, during school hours. To attend these places of interest however, I had to steal the money. I was not allowed to go on camps or dances for fear I might 'get pregnant' there. When all the other students were talking of little else but the upcoming school camp or disco, I'd just shrink into the background knowing I'd be the one to miss out.

I only had one birthday party, in Year 6. I was allowed to invite just *two* guests – Annabella and Leisl of course. I watched teenage life from the periphery, sadly begging God to give me a break and grant me the freedom I craved; either liberty or an early death, was my desire. This all sounds very melodramatic, given the life conditions of many other children living in this world, but I can only relate how my environment left *me* feeling, and the way I felt was completely hopeless.

Alfonso was my primary jailer. On the rare occasions Mother would say *Yes*, the slug would jump in with a firm *No!* One day after yet another *no*, I stood up to the slug and called him every name I could think of, hoping he'd give chase to me. I had planned to exert him into a heart attack. He chased me alright, but he had more stamina than I'd given him credit for, so nothing happened other than another hiding from Gilda

All of my 'adverse behaviours' were blamed on Cabramatta High School and those damned Anglo Saxons. Gilda was forever threatening to pull me out of Cabramatta High to have me home schooled, so I lived in fear of losing the only lifeline I clung to. It was around this time, to cope with this added stress, that I began cutting.

Mother was not getting anywhere with the Australian Opera. She had auditioned for Richard Bonynge, *La Stupenda's* husband, but nothing came of it and Gilda's vocational frustrations continued to be vented on those around her. The screaming, the profanities, the sheer misery that permeated our home had intensified the suicidal thoughts I was having, forcing me to find release in other ways. Tormenting my uncontrollable brother Piero came top of the list ... shit floats downhill, right? As a secondary measure, I began shoplifting.

Piero got into everything. Because he could not communicate normally he'd bang his foot against my bedroom door repeatedly when all I wanted was to do my homework in peace. He only wanted some attention, and I'd slap his face with my thong or across his open palm with a shoe horn. I decided that if it was okay for me to get in trouble for supposedly doing the wrong thing, then it was okay for him too. It was all so unfair: just because Mother wasn't coping, I had to? I was only a kid. *Leave me the fuck alone!*

I was now Piero's ghoul, just as Gilda and Alfonso had been mine. I didn't feel guilt, only vindication. Besides, Piero didn't seem to react to physical pain, something I could not understand. It didn't matter what I did to him, he didn't cry and barely even flinched.

In 1980 we relocated to Bishop Crescent, Bonnyrigg, west of Cabramatta, into a Housing Commission fibro home. Here I befriended my new next door neighbours' daughter Maria. Her parents were Spanish, from Madrid, and so my family and theirs became good friends in no time. Maria looked like she hated the world and I wondered if her parents were as fucked up as mine. The 'wog' mentality often kills off the identity of young people.

If Mother couldn't break into the Australian Opera, she'd be damned if she'd work in any other capacity. Gilda started organising a number of theatrical productions including an operatic rendition of *Little Red Riding Hood,* which was accepted by the respected Club Marconi, an Italian social club in Bossley Park. At the time I was cast as a fourteen-year-old grandmother. I really wanted to play the wolf, though, so I might experience what it felt like to devour my mother.

Following *Little Red Riding Hood,* which only attracted a small and select audience, Mother's second production, titled *Tiempos Para Vivir* ('A Time for Feeling Alive'), was all about the Spanish *zarzuela,* or operetta. The Spanish Club in the city helped Gilda out by lending her the upstairs function room for rehearsals free of charge. Besides me and Alfonso, Mother had involved Maria's entire family too. Mother wanted me to ask my school friends to play extras but I managed to find plausible excuses as to why they could not. The rest of my life had embarrassments enough.

It was through *Tiempos Para Vivir* that I got to know Maria a lot better; we played early nineteenth century maids who were also the best of friends. Maria was aloof and perpetually on the defensive because, as I later discovered, she was bullied at school on a daily basis. Maria did not fare much better at home. Her parents displayed no affection towards her and Claudio, her brother, teased her mercilessly. Her little sister Abril was the apple of her parents' eyes though and, like me with Piero, Maria deeply resented the favoured sibling.

Maria and I found much common ground in each other and we began spending every possible moment together. She'd whistle for me to come out and chat and I'd trip over myself to go to her. From the moment Maria allowed me into her world, she became the sister I had always wished for. Maria was bad news, though, in many ways: she introduced me to pot, masturbation and how to get away with murder. *I* then introduced Maria to shoplifting and we became an unofficial 'Thelma and Louise' duo. With a close friend nearby, I stopped cutting or contemplating suicide. We planned how we'd run away together to live our lives free and easy, *without* parental control. The dream sounded both blissful and 'do-able'.

In Year 10 I decided to put my name down for the school's annual Talent Quest. I had a strong contralto voice and my friends told me I'd win for sure. First prize was the students' net entry fee into the hall, minus $20 which would go to second place. I chose *Bette Midler's 'The Rose' and Mr Adams, a sympathetic maths teacher, was to be my accompanist on the piano.

When I stepped onto the stage I felt terrified, the school hall was packed to its rafters and here I was standing in front of each student and teacher present that day in my St Vinnie's silky peach skirt which made me look even fatter than I was. Mr Adams opened our act on the piano and I felt myself shaking uncontrollably; if that was what stage fright feels like, I doubted I'd ever become a public performer. Trying to stabilise myself, all I could do was open my mouth and just sing. I had people to impress.

Open my mouth and sing I did; these lyrics were personal.

When I finished I was astounded to receive a standing ovation. Wolf whistles came from everywhere. Our school magazine, *Thuruna*, wrote of my performance:

The somewhat exuberant audience was stunned into silence when Year 10's Adalgisa G sang The Rose beautifully. Mr Adams accompanied Adalgisa on the piano and the applause for this act nearly brought the hall down. Adalgisa earned second prize.

I did love to sing and dance. The moment my guardians left the house I'd bring out my well-hidden singles and play them on Mother's portable stereo and I'd sing and dance until I fell into a heap. The success of 'The Rose' had clearly paved the path to a future in music – *my type of music* and to hell with opera! 1981 was quickly becoming the greatest year of my life.

'The Rose' brought my powerful voice into the school's performing spotlight and I was asked to take part in that year's 2SM 'Rock 'n' Roll Eisteddfod', an absolute honour! The class clown, who ate cheese sandwiches every day and who took every stupid dare thrown at her to attract attention, was about to legitimately rub shoulders with the cool kids; not surprisingly however, Mother wouldn't hear of it. I thought of a hundred ways I could sneak out for rehearsals, but none were worth the risk. Here was an opportunity to finally do something of value, a possibility to *become* somebody, and all I could do was walk into the focus group head hung low and say, "Sorry guys, but my parents won't let me take part."

With my stage fright as it was, I was probably dodging a massive bullet anyway. What could I really offer them? The Eisteddfod was beyond me; it was going to be judged by singing legend Marcia Hines and radio personality Jonathon Coleman. I wasn't possibly good enough to impress *them*. I'd probably forget my lines and embarrass my school. Cabramatta High was selected from hundreds of schools around the state and the cool kids knew what they were doing, and they were far better than I was at doing it.

My school made it into the Rock Eisteddfod's final, held in the prestigious Capitol Theatre on 15 July 1981. The extravaganza, named *Hurricane*, was judged the winner, earning our school an excellent reputation, a colour video recorder, and a performance by the up and coming band INXS at our next school dance. INXS's only big hit at the time was 'Just Keep Walking' and Michael Hutchence was not the legend he is today. Because of the millstone around my neck that was Mother and my stepfather, I'd never be able to tell this story in the first person because, naturally, I was not allowed to attend the dance.

At this stage of my life the only thoughts dancing around inside my head had to do with escape – escape from an unjust home life, escape from the gnarled clutches of the two bastards bent on squeezing the life out of me, slowly and with malicious intent.

My performing career may have been thwarted by Gilda's narcissism and obsessions, but the one thing she could not deny me was the attention my writing abilities received at school. Our magazine, *Thuruna*, that year published five of my poems plus a short story. My poetry was political and even at fifteen I held strong opinions about social and environmental issues. Two poems that reflected my stances on the current climate were 'An Appeal from Aborigines' and 'Auto Disintegration in the 20th Century'. Both made it into *Thuruna*. A third, 'Facing the Headmaster', was a personal cry for help for my domestic situation. Here I tried to explain the poor concentration and behavioural issues I was picked up on in the classroom.

The end of 1981 saw another contest opportunity, a writing competition. I entered my most cherished *Thuruna* publication, the beautiful and melancholic love sonnet, 'Night and Day'.

My writing was considered highly advanced for my age, but 'Night and Day' was deemed 'plagiarised' by the judging panel because it appeared *too* advanced. To my astonishment First Prize went to Julie, the same girl Darren had dumped me for in Year 6, following the Rollarena fiasco.

In December of 1981, Year 10 was done and dusted. I was indecisive about continuing with Years 11 and 12. Home life was now unbearable. Annabella and Leisl had decided to keep going, but Patricia was leaving. I did not know whose footsteps to follow; the three were my very best friends in the world, although I *had* grown close to Maria. I could not see school as a means to a future, merely as an escape vehicle from home and a place where I obtained much needed attention and praise – a sanctuary. I knew that scholastically, senior years would be harder on me, and that with little self-esteem and waning ambition, the last thing I needed was *added* pressure.

Various couples had come together at school, and some of them are still together today. Aside from becoming *someone*, my other burning ambition was to *be with* someone. I scoured the playground, week in, week out, for a boy who might love me. There was one I grew obsessed with: Philip. This big nosed boy, who sat idly in all of the low classes, knew I liked him – each time he saw me coming he'd run and hide. His mates would then tease him about me, which certainly didn't help my cause.

In attempts to grab Philip's attention I tried ridiculous things like setting a bin on fire and rolling it down the maths block corridor. Only the year before, a student in my year had done serious 'juve time' because he'd set the admin block alight, completely gutting it. Desperate to deflect my bold advances, Philip dated a most unlikely senior student, a dwarfish looking girl, and not a looker. Looking at myself in the mirror I did not see an unattractive girl staring back. I had beautiful large grey-blue eyes and a bright smile with luscious lips, so why would anyone not want me, love me, including the boys no other girl wanted? What was so wrong with *me*?

There *was* a boy who loved me – not that I'd noticed. Coincidentally, he was another Gemini named Darren. Darren was bizarre: he would sit behind me in class, pulling out strands of my hair. By the end of term, he presented me with a clipboard covered in neatly combed hair, all mine. On other occasions, after speaking on the phone with him, I'd return a while later to call someone else only to find Darren still on the other end, chatting away to me as if I hadn't left.

Darren was very unattractive. Even though I wasn't after a Christopher Atkins type, I did have *some* standards. I was also still too young to understand that sometimes a great personality and good intentions far outweigh good looks.

At fifteen, *noone* is truly ready for love, are they?

CHAPTER SIX

THE FACE OF FREEDOM

———

Maria and I grew so close I lost interest in Annabella and Leisl; it appeared to me they were already paired, with me as third wheel in their relationship. As often happens among those of us who feel oppressed and hopeless, my bond with Maria, based on our abusive past, grew stronger. Maria disclosed that her brother may have tried to molest her when she was little, and I of course had Trepiedi under *my* belt.

Traumatised friends also teach one another bad things and Maria was now a consummate thief. We would plan shoplifting trips with me taking orders from my friends at school. Maria in turn, taught me how to smoke tobacco and I began smoking *a lot*, costing me money I didn't have. To continue financing my habit I'd steal something, take it back to the store, cry *poor me* for losing the receipt, and then talk the cashier into giving me a refund anyway. Stealing gave me feelings of euphoria and control and I justified my actions by blaming my guardians for not buying what I needed, and for not giving me pocket money like other parents did. Any consequences that might befall me in the future were, therefore, entirely *their* fault.

Maria was beautiful and she knew it, although she was always going on about her 'huge gut'. There was no *huge gut*; she had a figure I could only wish for. Maria was boy crazy like me, but whereas my methods of seduction verged on the comical, Maria was more the femme fatale.

Maria and I discussed every topic a girl would normally turn to *Dolly* magazine for, but Maria would add a new dimension to some of these that often left me shocked, yet mesmerised. Something inside me told me Maria might be a dangerous person and to tread softly with and around her. Regardless, having Maria by my side dimmed the lustre of Cabramatta High, and soon enough I began to disregard the girls I had considered my soul sisters there. Maria made life a lot more exciting.

The pop singer Jon English, known for hits like 'Hollywood Seven', 'Six Ribbons' and 'Camilla', had been a Cabramatta High School student in the 1960s. He'd been invited back to our school as an honorary guest and lucky me, I was chosen to be a part of the entertainment for this night of nights. I begged Letitia to cover for me for I simply *had* to be there! Letitia wasn't happy about it but agreed to chaperone me and my heart did cartwheels. Maybe I could become a professional singer after all.

I practised my songs each lunchtime accompanied by three Year 12 boys who had formed a band in Year 10: cute South American twins named Luis and Mario on drums and keyboard, and Enrico, a fellow 'Romano', on lead guitar. The songs I chose for Mr English were *Stevie Wonder's 'Lately' and *Barbra Streisand's 'Evergreen'. The boys liked my singing and were very encouraging. Mario in particular, appeared to like other aspects of me as well – something that did not bother me in the least as he had the most beautiful green eyes.

Maria was very unhappy at Bonnyrigg High and seriously wanted out. She was fighting kids almost weekly now, just to maintain some degree of dignity. When I told her how friendly and supportive the kids at Cabra High were, she begged me to introduce her to some of my friends. I was now in Year 11, Maria was in Year 10 and there was *no way* she was continuing on as a senior student. One lunchtime both of us wagged school and I snuck Maria through Cabra's front gates to make her known to the people who mattered – including my lovely Argentinian twins. Luis was immediately smitten with her.

On the night of the tribute, and with Jon English looking on, I managed to sing beautifully. I did repeat a verse during 'Lately' but I don't think anyone noticed and 'Evergreen' received another standing ovation. I was dancing on air – but not for long.

My grandmother appeared quite disgusted with me and repeated Rollarena history by insisting we leave immediately. Maria, who had accompanied us, began arguing with Letitia but to no avail. Any 'normal' parent would have been proud, but not my narrow-minded, obsessive, fucked up family. By performing 'Satan's music' I'd betrayed their operatic legacy. Emotionally and socially my clan was caught up in a time warp I would never escape, let alone reason with.

"What are you doing singing this crap? If your mother knew she'd give you a hiding," Letitia scolded.

'And exactly whose side are you on, you old bitch,' I thought disdainfully.

I was shuffling grudgingly out of the school hall when Mr Adams, who'd accompanied me with 'The Rose', stopped me in my tracks.

"Adalgisa wait! Jon English wants to meet you!"

I just wanted to die; a huge name in the Australian music industry wanted to speak to me – *me*, Adalgisa from a Housing Commission project! Naturally I could not go and meet Jon because my grandmother, who I had thought was my saviour, had now sided with my mother's arcane idolatry. This was the straw that broke this camel's back. It was time to abandon ship.

Maria was fuming. She had come along to meet Luis, but for the first time I caught a glimpse of an opportunistic nature which had absolutely nothing to do with supporting a friend. As was my nature back then, I discounted her moment of egotism and thought nothing more of it.

I couldn't sleep that night. Nasty emotions of every kind flooded my mind. I *was* a singer; I had the right to sing what *I* liked not what Mother expected of me. I wasn't Gilda and I hated opera, I hated Spain for releasing this side of my family, I hated the *Sperm Incognito* for leaving me, but most of all, I *hated Mother!*

The day after the Jon English gala Mr Adams approached me at recess and handed me a note. It was written by Jon.

> *Hi Adalgisa, you have a great voice. I really enjoyed the songs you sang. If you like I can help you record a demo at Now Studios in Rushcutters Bay where I am currently doing the soundtrack for Against the Wind. Let me know by leaving a message with the studio's reception. You have a bright future ahead of you. Jon English.*

* * *

Maria and I got stoned, and whereas she thrived on the experience I was less impressed – I thought it was shit. Still, I felt very cool for having tried pot.

My stepfather, the slug, used to hang out at the notorious Rainbow Bar opposite Cabramatta Railway Station, and I became convinced he was involved in the local mafia, which was renowned for selling drugs to minors. I heard that Alfonso had been seen going into a 'locale' known as one where men could be 'serviced' by Asian prostitutes, including some who were rumoured to be underage. Old habits die hard, and young Sicilian boys are introduced to sex this way back in the 'old country'. Maybe syphilis was the reason Piero was three sandwiches short of a picnic.

Drugs or alcohol held no appeal for me and prostitution was a disgraceful way to make a living. What wasn't immediately obvious, however, was Cabramatta's gradual metamorphosis into Australia's heroin capital, and that many of the prostitutes working here were addicts financing their habit.

Maria's parents and Gilda were such good friends now that I was trusted to go out with my new best friend. Getting on the city bound notorious 'red rattlers' was something other kids took for granted but for me it was a real taste of freedom and excitement. Maria and I went to the movies in George Street – my very first time here in Australia. The film playing was *Puberty Blues. I saw John Waters, the renowned Australian actor of stage and screen, waiting in line to watch another film. I was so excited I walked straight up to him to ask for an autograph. Puberty Blues really spoke to me. I envied the life Debbie and Sue led in the film; they appeared so free at first, but then so totally trapped. It wasn't going to be like this for *me*, though; I'd make *good* life choices once I left home, and losing my virginity – or what Trepiedi had left of it – would be a far more glamorous affair then how those Cronulla girls went about it.

In the phone book I found one of the authors of the *Puberty Blues novel, Kathy Lette. Dialling her number thoughts rushed through my head regarding what I might say to a famous writer. One thing I wanted to tell her was that I too was a writer, a writer with a *big* story to tell. Then a voice answered.

"Hi, can I speak to Kathy?" I asked.

"She's not home right now, can I tell her who's calling?"

"No it's okay, I'll try again another time."

Another time never came around; my bravado hadn't lasted that long. Of course nowadays Kathy Lette is huge, with fourteen successful books under her belt. No chance to get to speak with her now.

Maria and I were allies in mischief, plotting tirelessly against our tormentors. I'd hide her from her parents at my house, and she would do the same for me. We discussed sex more than any other topic and it was obvious Maria was ready to 'do it' as soon as the chance presented itself. She explained how she pleasured herself in the bath and told me to give it a try.

"When I whistle come out and tell me how it was for you," she ordered with a devilish glint in her eye.

The whistle came and I made up some story out of a movie I'd watched once. There was *no way* I was putting anything 'in there'! I almost died when Maria showed me a dildo she had found at the tip that existed directly behind her house.

"That's disgusting!" I shrieked.

"I washed it!" Maria defended, entirely missing my meaning.

Another school disco came up in June 1982. Mario, the Argentinian twin who had shown an interest in me, finally found the guts to ask me out as his date for the evening. I was overjoyed. Multi-coloured fireworks exploded inside my mind's eye and imperial orchestras filled my inner ears with euphoric anticipation. I was sweet sixteen and on the verge of having an older boyfriend – wow! I had to do whatever it took to attend this disco. I told my parents that Jacqui, another good friend from school, was holding a fancy dress party at her house and her parents would drop me back home once the last guest left. I had no idea how I'd get home, and I really did not care. Maybe Mario had his licence and would drive me home.

Alfonso *ummed* and *arred* as per usual, trying to find a legitimate reason to keep me at home, as the fucked up version of Cinderella that I had become. Mother too *as per usual* left the final decision up to the slug. I begged Alfonso to let me go, and to my surprise, he relented. I almost kissed him, then thought better of it. What most kids my age took for granted I had to jump through hoops to obtain; one day very soon I would beg not a soul for *anything*.

The next afternoon after school I made my way into the Cabramatta Woolworths to shoplift some hot heels that might impress Mario. The rest of my outfit was all figured out. I saw just the ones I needed, strappy six-inch heels of pure indigo. They went straight into my schoolbag. As always noone saw me and, feeling ten feet tall, I walked gingerly out of the store.

The disco's theme was Punk and Seventies Glamour; I mixed the two and looked pretty damn fine, I thought. I looked like Cindy Lauper meets Boy George. Flying through the door to catch the bus, I felt Alfonso's disapproving eyes on me but I couldn't care less: I was Cinderella going to the ball and my golden carriage was ready to collect me.

Everyone I knew who mattered was attending the dance, but my eyes scanned the room only for the one person, my green-eyed Mario. There he was sitting by the wall waiting for me. His eyes widened as he caught sight of me. Perhaps he liked what he saw – I certainly hoped so. Unsure of how to act, I instinctively gave Mario a hug then moved us onto the dance floor. I loved to dance and the rhythm knew how to utilise my body. Mario smiled knowingly and I knew the night would end in romance.

The night whirled around me like an intoxicating fun ride. Mario's body pressed against mine as we slow danced to a romantic song I cannot recall because I was too immersed in the sensations of budding love and eroticism. I felt his penis harden and I so wanted him to kiss me – even though I didn't know how to reciprocate for I'd never been kissed before.

Mario was shy and the kiss would not be delivered on this night. Suddenly and in the same way I imagine a tsunami might hit a sleeping shore, a teacher tapped me on the shoulder, his face troubled.

"Come with me for a moment please Adalgisa."

Reluctantly I followed the teacher outside the booming school hall. There was a distinct lump in my throat, and a certain foreboding began to wash over me. Outside two police officers stood by staring intently at me. Alfonso was beside them triumphantly puffing his chest out. The officers then informed me I was to return home immediately; my 'father' had been worried sick because I was not where I'd said I would be, and he thought I had run away. I argued my case with the visibly annoyed officers but was gruffly brushed off; they had *real* work to do.

Glaring at Alfonso and feeling a thousand stinging needles of hatred, I asked them if I could at least go back in for a moment and say goodbye to my friends. The officers agreed but asked the teacher to follow me inside. I ran straight to Mario and told him I wasn't able to explain why I was leaving right that moment but, that I'd find him the next day at lunchtime and we'd discuss it. I then boldly stole the kiss I so yearned for. The last memories I took home with me from that wonderful night were Mario's gorgeous eyes and his beaming smile.

Just like Cinderella, time elapsed, the magic evaporated, and I was returned to my special brand of hell.

* * *

Because of my 'diabolical treachery' I was now confined to the house, which included staying away from Maria's house and no visits to the local park with her. Under these circumstances I began to suffer major withdrawals from smoking, which translated into epic eating binges. Already chubby, I began to get downright fat.

Mother had an inbuilt radar for the smell of nicotine, and each time I went to the park for an 'ekoms' (Maria's code word for smoke), I needed to undergo an extensive cleansing routine before re-entering the house. Gilda claimed cigarette smoke destroyed her vocal cords and she would go apeshit if anyone dared to smoke near her. Once while travelling on the train, she saw a man puffing away in our carriage. Gilda confronted him, demanding he extinguish the cigarette immediately. Defiant the man told Gilda to 'get fucked' and pressed on with his smoke. Not to be subdued, Gilda pushed the emergency stop button, halting the train. When the station master entered the carriage to sort things out he was met with a hysterical woman spitting chips in broken English. Although the smoker *was* breaking the law, the station master shook his head in disbelief at Gilda's pettiness, before apologetically ushering the smoker off the carriage. I sank into my seat, hoping noone had seen me. As the train pulled away, I saw the smoker and station master sharing a laugh at my mother's expense.

Another time Mother caught my school bus, which also carried passengers from Cabramatta Railway Station. I swiftly moved to the very back and asked my friends to shield me from Mother's line of sight. To my horror Gilda was wearing a surgical mask, Michael Jackson style, and holding up a can of Glen 20. She began spraying the bus before sitting down for her trip.

Inside a rented hall in Cabramatta, *Tiempos Para Vivir* finally went on stage, after months of rehearsals, playing to an audience of mostly local South Americans. I was the character *Yo También*, a housemaid who would interrupt conversations with the affirmative, *me too!* I found acting before an audience less daunting than singing but felt unnatural and unconvincing. Acting was certainly not for me. Maria on the other hand thrived on the attention and was actually very good and 'typically Spanish' in her role.

In July 1982, straight after school, I went into the Cabramatta Woolworths and took a Kambrook power board worth $20, with a view to gaining one of my bogus refunds. I walked out of the store as I had done so many times before, but this time was halted at the lights by a security guard. A woman approached us – I recognised her as a shopper I'd seen while browsing. She verified I was indeed the person the guard needed to apprehend. I was then walked into the store manager's office where the police were called. Panicked, I begged the store manager not to call the police. He ignored me; I cried.

The police arrived and escorted me, still crying, out of the store via the docking area. Seating me between them, the officers spared me the back of their paddy wagon, but the short trip to Cabramatta Police Station was the longest in my life. A bitter end to any quality of life at home, I knew.

Following a short wait at the police station, I was allocated an officer who asked me for my parents' contact number. I shook my head and asked him to call my next door neighbours instead. I explained to the officer that my parents were abusive and would hurt me if they knew what I had done. In an attempt to gain clemency, I told the officer I had lost the $20 my stepfather gave me to buy the power board and, fearing a beating, I stole it instead. My supplications fell on deaf ears and I was subsequently fingerprinted, charged, and booked to attend the Minda Children's Court in Lidcombe. Right now though *someone* had to come to the police station and collect me.

I called Maria's father, Marcelo, begging him to keep from Mother what had transpired. I'd try and figure a way out of my predicament if only he would come and get me this once. Marcelo was not at all happy with this turn of events, but he came to the station all the same.

There was a deathly silence in Marcelo's Holden. We drove directly from the station to the city for another *Tiempos Para Vivir* rehearsal. Gilda was repeating the production at the Spanish Club, following its moderate success in Cabramatta. Maria looked at me, wanting more information, but my mind was a blur. What the hell was I going to do now?

When we returned home that night I stepped out of Marcelo's car and went straight to my room to pray for a miracle. Marcelo, Pilar (Maria's mother) and my parents remained in our backyard for a while talking. Suddenly there was a roar at my bedroom door. Mother flew in and started thrashing her arms about, spitting insults and accusations into my face. Noone came to my rescue, not Letitia or my neighbours, and certainly not Alfonso the slug, who was probably thoroughly enjoying himself. Had my parents given me an allowance, like other normal parents, I would *never* have resorted to stealing … couldn't anyone see this?

My home had been a prison; I was now in solitary confinement. Additionally, Mother confirmed she was taking me out of school once and for all and would contact the Principal the very next day. Gilda always blamed the school *and* the Australian lifestyle for how I was 'turning out'. From now on, though, I'd be brought up *correctly*. I knew I would not cope with any of it. This was the cue I needed to leave home and never look back. I thought of my friend Jacqui; her parents were always so nice to me, so they would take me in for a while, I was sure. I carefully whistled for Maria from my bedroom window and she discreetly climbed over the fence. I begged her complicity with my escape plans.

That night, my last night in hell, I did not sleep a wink. I spent it packing my few belongings into one suitcase and a garbage bag I snuck out from the kitchen. I timed every move by creaks I heard coming from the bedroom next to mine, which was Alfonso's and Gilda's. How I'd hated the disgusting sex noises they made when we first moved here. Nowadays, though, the creaks had more to do with the slug's obese body and tired bed springs.

At 6 o'clock sharp, Maria was dutifully at my bedroom window. Together we managed to pull me and my stuff out of the narrow rectangular window frame without making a sound. A taxi that Maria had arranged for me was waiting outside, a few houses up the street. I kissed Maria goodbye thanking her for her invaluable help, and assured her I would be in touch once I was settled in somewhere. My friend had tears in her eyes as she pushed a crumpled note into my hand to pay for the fare.

At 6.30 am I knocked on Jacqui's front door. The taxi scurried off and I stood there like a hobo hoping I would not be turned away. Jacqui's father opened the door and looked me over with a puzzled expression. *Why was I here so early?* Jacqui and I had discussed me staying with the family but she must have forgotten to mention it to her parents. Jacqui's father benignly invited me in and offered me breakfast. I blurted out my hopes with a single breath, preparing for a rejection with my next. The family was a refined Anglo-Indian household, hardly charity cases, and they kindly explained to me why I could not remain with them. My heart sank. Jacqui's father drove us all to school at 8.30 am, leaving my belongings at his house until I found alternative accommodation. It was the least he could do for me, but I *did* appreciate it.

The only recourse left for me now was to speak with the school counsellor and see what *she* could do for me. Our school counsellor *was* very understanding. She accepted that I was never returning home and dutifully called my parents to inform them of my decision. She suggested I try mediation with my grandmother before making any concrete move towards the only other option available, temporary supported living in a youth refuge. Grudgingly, I accepted her suggestion, but when Letitia arrived, furiously yelling at me, I knew option B *was* my only option.

That afternoon when the bell rang at 3.15 pm, I returned to the counsellor's office and she drove me to collect my belongings from Jacqui's house and then to the youth refuge in Fairfield West. A residential worker opened the crabby looking doors and greeted me warmly. It then dawned on me I was now both a criminal *and* a homeless runaway ... how the fuck did I get myself into this position, and was it all worth it? A District Officer was appointed to me and the court hearing was to take place at the end of two weeks; there'd be no singing career for me now, no Mario, no Maria whistling over the fence for 'ekoms', no Year 12 graduation, nothing. I had wished to continue with school but, as the youth workers explained, I had accommodation at the refuge for only three months; at the end of those three months I needed to find elsewhere to live.

I felt afraid and bewildered yet simultaneously liberated and light; for a few fleeting moments, freedom tasted so very *very* sweet.

CHAPTER SEVEN

HOMELESSNESS AND OTHER DRUGS

———

The youth refuge held twelve young people, six boys and six girls, who were placed in separate quarters but were permitted to share common areas.

Immediately, I found myself a fish out of water. I was not a drug addict, not a teenage prostitute, not even a horribly abused person – or so I thought. The young people I met at that refuge seemed far worse off than me on so many levels and their stories were mindboggling, albeit fascinating. Compared with these guys I still had a good, functioning mind to reason and make cautious decisions with. Even with my abused young life, my self-esteem was in far better shape than it was for these damaged youths. I still had ambitions, dreams of grandeur … the kind of aspirations that won't let you sink below certain standards.

There was a period of settling in. The kids began testing me the moment I arrived, just as they had at Whitefriars in Adelaide. Bravado, a sense of humour, and my ability to draw well saved the day, and I wasn't heckled for long. I began drawing portraits of the kids and their idols and by week two, they couldn't get enough of me. The residential carers at that refuge were people genuinely committed to improving the young people's lives and I admired them.

There were five kids that I will never forget, although the real names of three have escaped me. 'James' never uttered a word; he was so drug-addled and hell-bent on ending his life he had given up contact with our world, keeping to himself as much as possible. Lydia had been raped by every male member in her family. She acted out her inner pain by cutting herself and injecting ink, a process that resulted in awful looking homemade tattoos. 'Samantha' and 'Bec', both fifteen years old, left the refuge not long after I arrived, to return to 'work' in Kings Cross. They had failed to meet their curfew and were never seen again. Scotty took an instant liking to me and wanted to become my boyfriend. I don't remember his story, but prior to leaving the refuge he told me I was special and "not like us".

He was right: the refuge was not for me, but I could see myself working in one, one day. I seemed to get through to these lost souls in ways others could not, and on my last day there James smiled at me as I bid farewell. The youth workers commented on this for until then they hadn't detected an ounce of emotion in him. They added that I should look into social work as a career choice once I turned eighteen, and maybe return someday for a course placement. I did have a way with people in general; I seemed able to draw out an individual's innocence and humanity and get them talking instead of fighting or checking out altogether. I thanked the youth workers for their advice but informed them my life revolved around art and that I hoped to become a commercial artist or a professional writer. Clutching my old suitcase and tired plastic bag once more, I waved goodbye to the carers and their sad kids as my taxi sped off playing the latest one-hit wonder over the radio – 'I Ran' by A Flock of Seagulls. 'Very apt,' I thought – but where exactly would I be running to now?

At the Minda Children's Court, a fortnight after my apprehension at Cabramatta, the magistrate made a recommendation for a control order to be served at the 'juve' adjacent to the court house. This was the same year Barbara Holborow, the legendary Children's Court Magistrate, 'the children's champion', was first appointed as 'Your Honour' by the Bar. My memory of this occasion does not serve me well but perhaps it was *she* who presided over my case. I very much doubt it, though; Barbara would have made no such recommendation. I had committed a crime, yes, but I was no criminal. Fortunately, my District Officer intervened in my favour and I was placed on a good behaviour bond instead of serving time in detention. Letitia was present as my support person but we didn't have much to say to one other. Letitia, my saviour in life, had already let me down more than once and I trusted her now as much as I trusted her daughter. I was going to make my own way in life and to hell with them all.

The Minda Juvenile Detention Centre was notorious for its 'internal mishaps', especially in the girls' dormitory. I had certainly dodged a massive bullet there. I had tried to continue on with school while at the refuge but it proved impossible. I returned to Cabramatta High in mid-August to say goodbye to all my friends and teachers. I took lots of photographs with a beat-up old camera, and cried my eyes out. Cabramatta High School was my *true* saviour and my sanctuary. I loved her and I'd never forget her. In fact, the years spent there were the happiest in my life.

Maria and I met up again and went on a double date with the delightful Argentinian twins Mario and Luis. We caught the ferry to Manly from Circular Quay and spent a beautiful and rather romantic day together. As we sped through the rips Maria asked me to sing Barbra Streisand's *'Run Wild'. Shyly, I did as asked, and it seemed very lovely and innocent.

I never saw Mario again after that gentle day, though I forget why. Life then took a different turn for me, though not for the better. My District Officer helped me find a job so I could get out of the youth refuge and become independent. I was trained as a 'checkout chick' by a brand new Coles New World outlet inside the refurbished Fairfield Forum, and it was here that I befriended a different brand of individuals.

Carolyn looked like a nice girl. She wanted to move out of home and was looking for a flatmate. I immediately put my hand up and although I had nothing to contribute in the way of furniture or white goods, we moved into a two-bedroom flat in Clifford Avenue, Canley Vale. With her mother's help we raked in enough stuff to make the walls liveable. Up onto my bedroom walls went my James Dean, Marilyn Monroe and David Bowie posters: the three people I worshipped for reasons I could not fathom.

After toying with an assortment of pseudonyms, I shortened my name to *Adel, triple-pierced my ears and wore miniskirts and skimpy clothes to my heart's content – anything to defy the dictators back home. I earned barely enough to cover rent and cigarettes, and, because food was scarce, I lost twenty unwanted kilos. I looked amazing and although hungry I was *free*. Nothing could taste better than this.

Carolyn and I were making odd friends along the way, people we'd meet on city outings or who were mutual friends from work, such as fifteen-year-old Carla. Carla could barely fit her enormous breasts inside her Coles New World uniform, and always managed to look terribly uncomfortable. In the clinical sense Carla was also a hopeless nymphomaniac; she was forever doing someone or *something*.

One day as we walked back to my flat along Cabramatta Road, Carla felt one of her impromptu itches wash over her. She began thumbing traffic until a car stopped for her.

"Feel like some quick fun?" she brazenly asked the stranger.

And with her next breath Carla jumped into the stranger's passenger seat calling out to meet her later on at her house for coffee and full disclosure. Because of the numerous indiscretions she subjected herself to, Carla contracted a veritable smorgasbord of STIs; she was always scratching something. Carla displayed genuine affection for me and wanted me around her frequently, which was great because it ensured I was fed and watered. Although some of my attitudes towards sex were a little draconian, I never judged Carla – what she did with her body was *her* business.

Carla lived with her two sisters and their children. The eldest sister was married to an able seaman in the Australian Navy, a 'pusser' as they liked to call him. One evening I was invited to a party at their house. When I arrived the place was teeming with pussers, some of whom were going in and out of Carla's bedroom like sheep. One of the 'able seamen' grabbed me and placed his navy cap onto my head.

"You're mine for the evening now, beautiful!" he smiled knowingly, high on alcohol.

I yanked the cap off, told him where to shove it, and ran out through the front door. He could pour his 'able' semen into someone else, thank you very much.

On New Year's Eve 1982, Carolyn, our colleague Lisa and I headed out for some fun at The Rocks in Circular Quay. Random strangers kept asking for a kiss and, keen to learn, I obliged them. I was a lousy kisser but we had a great night nonetheless, leaving for home well after the midnight fireworks display, a little drunk and dishevelled. We were young and enjoying life.

As we waited for our train I got talking to a gorgeous looking guy who had missed the ferry back to Manly, thus finding himself with nowhere to crash for the night. This handsome guy's name was Pierre.

"Why not come back to our place?" I suggested coyly. What an amazing confidence booster alcohol can be. Pierre's eyes lit up.

"Hey, that would really help me out, thanks!"

I glanced at Carolyn, who seemed annoyed; Lisa, though, appeared pleased. It had not crossed my mind that Pierre might be a potential hook up for the night, but Lisa was definitely entertaining the idea.

When we got back to Canley Vale, at around two in the morning, Lisa was all over Pierre but he clearly was *not* reciprocating. Astonished as I was by the realisation, he appeared more interested in *me*! Lisa got the message and trotted off to bed, and Carolyn was asleep the moment her head hit the pillow. I began to set Pierre up on our foam lounge, bidding him goodnight, when he suddenly reached out for my hand and asked me for a New Year's kiss. Pierre was stunning looking and the butterflies fluttered in me until I thought I'd been knocked from my emotional axis. I had no idea how one 'made out' so I offered Pierre a quick peck on the lips, then ran to my bedroom before he could pull me back into his arms.

"Not like that! Where's your tongue?" he teased as I shuffled with the knob on my bedroom door. I felt my cheeks reddening.

"I don't kiss any other way, sorry." And I shut myself in.

A few moments later there was a soft rap on my bedroom door. Pierre asked me if we could go for a walk outside, as it was a hot night and he couldn't sleep. I agreed, quickly put back on the clothes I had just discarded and slipped quietly downstairs. I'd really *hoped* for that knock … *thank you Lord.*

During the walk Pierre informed me he was staying at a hotel in Manly on a modelling assignment. There were many other things we spoke about but Pierre, whose parents were French, wanted to know more about me and *my* European heritage. I related my life to him, the less sordid parts of it, and he appeared fascinated with it all, saying I was the most interesting girl he had met in a long time – and why on earth was I living like a squatter.

Pierre had found the 'average girl' annoying and insipid. Most were "empty-headed bimbos with nothing to say and too much on show," according to Pierre.

Pierre thought I was markedly different and wanted to get to know me a whole lot better. I was flattered but frightened. Why would someone like him want anything to do with someone like *me*?

The next morning, I said goodbye to Pierre knowing I'd never see those beautiful blue eyes again. In the background Toto's *'Africa' was playing on MTV. It became my favourite song of that year.

Two weeks later there was a knock on the front door; opening it I found Pierre standing there clutching a bottle of bubbly and sporting a huge smile.

"Hey beautiful, it's my birthday and I was hoping to celebrate it with you!" He announced.

I had a friend's birthday party to go to and had promised to attend. I was in such shock that Pierre had returned to me that I couldn't think of an excuse to cancel my commitment just so I could just fall into the arms of this mythical creature. So I declined Pierre's invitation, hating myself for having done so and, alas, that was the last time I gazed upon his beautiful model's *visage*.

God would surely punish me someday, for my lack of appreciation and inaction.

* * *

Carolyn and I began to seriously butt heads, not because I did anything to cause it, but because she was growing jealous of me. This realisation hit me like a pile of bricks; but what was I doing to make her feel this way? I had no boyfriend, I was always broke, and I had stopped socialising. Yes, I flaunted my new figure – the by-product of starvation – but I didn't capitalise on it. It turned out a neighbour, a young man named Glenn, had caught Carolyn's discerning eye and whenever she stopped to chat with him, Glenn would ask about me.

One afternoon Carla and I bumped into Glenn at some nearby shops; he was in his school uniform. Glenn was built like a footballer and it didn't take long for Carla to begin acting inappropriately with a view to getting him into her pants. But Glenn couldn't care less about Carla's advances, his stare remained fixed on me. Not to be discouraged, Carla invited Glenn back to our flat, but there was something about Glenn that did not sit well with me.

Carla didn't get her way with Glenn. He ignored her and spent every moment of his stay asking me personal questions. I guess I enjoyed the attention but the more I spoke with him, the more that sense of 'something' grew. Glenn was the son of an autocratic police sergeant and there were clearly issues that divided them. Glenn was finishing Year 12 and couldn't wait to break free from his father's clutches so he could venture out on his own, in much the way I had.

Glenn became my needy puppy dog, following me around adoringly wherever I went. Coles New World had reduced my hours to practically nothing so to make ends meet I found a part-time job at a takeaway pizza shop opposite Canley Vale station. My shift finished at midnight and Dave, the shop owner, was making it clear he had other 'duties' he'd like me to perform. Dave was a much older man and not at all attractive; I felt unsafe being there alone with him, especially at closing time, so I engaged Glenn to become my chaperone. What was happening with me all of a sudden? At school I found myself hard up getting the least popular kid to like me and now I had men vying for my attention. It must have been the weight loss ... could it be that men really *are* that shallow? Apparently so.

As the clock struck midnight there was Glenn faithfully waiting on the shop's doorstep to walk me home. I was so grateful to him because Dave *had* tried something in the back room that night and I'd warned him Glenn was now my boyfriend and he did *not* want to upset him.

"What if I really *was* your boyfriend?" Glenn asked me wistfully.

"No, I don't think so Glenn. You're a friend, a very good friend."

Glenn was not happy with my reply. One night when he arrived to pick me up from the shop, he looked markedly different. Reaching the car park inside our block of flats, Glenn stopped me in my tracks, brusquely taking me by the shoulders.

"Just try kissing me once and see how you feel Angelica. Give us a chance for fuck's sake!"

I felt panic welling up. Would Glenn force himself on me? Could I take a risk by rejecting him again? There was noone around and with his strength and stature Glenn could easily drag me off somewhere and seriously injure me. I leaned in and kissed him slightly. Glenn forced a very open mouth and sickeningly wet tongue to my mouth. It was disgusting; I felt as if I was being eaten alive.

I was not raped that night but it had been a distinct possibility. I feigned satisfaction and offered Glenn the usual gratitude before running breathlessly up the stairwell to the safety of my flat and housemate. Closing the door behind me I could hear my heart thumping fiercely, the blood burning my ear lobes. When I felt it safe to do so I told Glenn that under no uncertain terms would there ever be an 'us'. Glenn attempted to stir up jealousy from me by having a fling with Carolyn, but by the time he'd finished with her I was out of Clifford Crescent *and* Carolyn's life.

I was living a Bogan's life. I had no contact with my family and avoided their haunts. Scenes from *Puberty Blues* were becoming reality. I was running around with unemployed teenagers whose main interests were booze, drugs, sex, and shitty parties. Their stomping grounds were not the golden sands of Cronulla beach, though; our 'barrio' was a haven for criminal activity and a fast developing cultural ghetto.

I was embroiled with people who harboured no ambition and even less potential, just like another Glenn, who Carla dubbed 'Mullet'. Mullet had extremely bad skin and worse teeth. He was one of Carla's night time pickups, when nothing better was available. He was considered cool because he had his own place and drove a 'muscle car' panel van fitted with police speakers and 'come fuck me' decor.

Mullet's home was always open for 'business'. In my naivety I did not grasp that this *business* might involve drugs. He invited us over for pizza and a video and upon opening his front door I was hit by a stench to draw the wind from my lungs. Once inside, I noticed that Glenn's house was covered in dog shit, every inch of it, including the steps leading to the upstairs quarters. I didn't want to spend a minute in this cesspool – let alone eat here. I really needed to vomit. Carla did not seem perturbed by any of this; I guessed she had spent plenty of nights here and had become acclimatised. She begged me to stay, reminding me I had no money or means to get back to Cabramatta from Mullet's home in Merrylands.

I don't know how I got through the next few hours. I think I held my breath for most of the movie and cited a sore stomach so I could refuse the pizza. Fearing I might not get out of here this night I asked to make a phone call, but Mullet's phone was in his bedroom upstairs and to reach it I had to dodge the dog turd on every one of those infernal steps. Reaching the putrid room, I noticed the telephone was on the other side of Mullet's bed against the far wall. To reach it, I had to step over more shit, jump on Mullet's filthy bed, and put a greasy receiver up to my ear. Gagging, I dialled the number only to hear the engaged signal. I'd be stuck in that faecal level of hell for whole of the night, unintentionally and unwillingly listening in on Carla's lurid moans downstairs.

Our group visited Kings Cross often. I found myself fascinated and disturbed, in equal measure, by the locals and their minstrels. There were a lot of street kids loitering in and around the place and I wondered what they might do there. I refused to believe that some of the beautiful young girls I saw in Victoria Street and William Street sold their bodies for money, but this is how 'Samantha' and 'Bec' from the youth refuge made their living, and Carla was quick to corroborate their stories. Film romanticism had led me to believe that beautiful girls didn't have to resort to soliciting, that gentlemen lived in abundance and would look after all the damsels in our world. But reality, in Kings Cross, is harsh: girls as young as nine worked as prostitutes in the back rooms of clubs guarded by corrupt cops paid off to maintain a 'business as usual' underworld commodity.

The people I was living with were dealing in heroin, I discovered. They didn't tell me this but, after wondering about the constant stream of visitors, in and out of the joint at all times of the day or night, one lazy afternoon I found out about the trade for myself. Answering a knock at the door, I faced Joe, a guy who was in my year at Cabramatta High. Joe was part of the 'cool' group at school, and we never exchanged as much as a word because I found him so intimidating. Joe seemed as shocked to see me as I was to see him.

"Adalgisa! Oh my God, what the hell are you doing here?" he gasped.

"I live here, why … oh and its Adel now," I replied triumphantly.

Joe looked at me, utterly dismayed, then paused as if thinking what to say next.

"Oh, okay. So, Adel … does an old school friend get a discount?"

"I've no idea what you're on about Joe, and I don't remember you as an *old friend*. Do you know my flatmates?"

And this is how I found out my 'friends' were drug traffickers. It was time to get out of Dodge City and find elsewhere to live. There was also the problem of Maria.

Maria had been visiting me a lot of late; she seemed different, harder. She was smoking a lot more than when we were neighbours, and drinking heavily as well. And when my friends pulled out their bongs Maria was always up for a tote, and when she was high, she was a bitch from hell, as well as unashamedly promiscuous.

A party was held at the flat, and Maria stayed the night. There were a few guys here and the outrageous way Maria flirted with them made me angry and acrimonious. I ordered her to stop acting like a slut and go to bed. Maria wasn't happy with my outburst: *I had no business telling her what to do and I was just a jealous freak because I was still a virgin and didn't know anything about sex.* It then dawned on me how starved for attention Maria was and that it didn't matter where she was or who she was with – Maria had to grab the limelight. Her hypocrisy made me laugh: she was a virgin too!

This kind of thing had happened before. Maria would get stoned or drunk and take over my home and friends, but tonight I'd had enough and I ordered her out of my home. What did *she* know about life? I'd been living away from home for four months now and had learnt the ropes so *earn your badge bitch!* One thing led to another and my infamous wrath got the better of me. I saw Maria gaining brownie points with my friends over me and before I knew it, it was *I* being ordered out of my place by the others.

"Fuck you all, and fuck *YOU* Maria!" I hissed.

I picked up a large radio unit perched nearby and threw it at Maria's smug face, missing her by centimetres. Then off I went, out the front door, turfed out of *my* home by the people whose rent I contributed to. *Fucking drug dealers! Maybe I should go and pay the police a visit on their behalf.*

Carla didn't betray me like the others; she came looking for me and found me crying and finding warmth sitting on an oil slick in the garage space downstairs. I could still hear the party atmosphere banging on upstairs – it was infuriating, especially with Maria's laughter and smug chit-chat piercing through the cacophony of degenerate activity. *Good old slutty sweet Carla*; her heart was as big and her nature as loyal as her voracious sexual appetite and those ridiculous breasts. I learnt then not to ever judge a book by its cover.

* * *

Another Coles New World girl came to my rescue. Valerie and her fiancé Noel rented a large two-bedroom flat in Hughes Street, Cabramatta, together with Valerie's brother Christopher. Christopher was away for work and, until his return, I could use his bedroom rent free. I was touched beyond words by the couple's generous gesture and *so* relieved. Valerie and Noel were clean living lovebirds and I immediately felt a part of their family.

Around this time, I started going out with a South American named Ritchie. Ritchie taught me how to kiss properly and we almost did 'the deed'. Our lips first met one warm summer night on the Tango Train ride at Luna Park. Thankfully, a huge pad and very large underpants, 'Bridget Jones' style, saved my virginity. Ritchie was not impressed and broke up with me soon afterwards.

We have come a long way with women's sanitary items today. Back then, Modess pads were so bulky and horrible they were known as mattresses, and I struggled with them moving around or even falling out. Mother had forced me to go into the water at Bondi wearing one; it became waterlogged and hung down out of my bathers like a large pair of gonads with blood spilling in rivulets down my legs when I got out of the water. Mother really knew how to mortify me at every turn. Whether she did it on purpose or from ignorance, I do not know. At school, blood leaked out from my pad, leaving an enormous patch on my emerald skirt. I was sent to the sick bay for the remainder of the day because yet again, my parents would not come and collect me. Systematic abuse bears many faces and neglect is one of them.

I was not settling down anywhere or on any level; freedom was beginning to lose its lustre. Life was a succession of nomadic moves and poverty was preventing me from experiencing the excitement of youth I imagined I should be having. I was unable to plan for a tangible future and I missed school and my tried and true friends. I had noone to love or who loved me, and Maria, my socalled best friend, was now behaving like both a complete cow and an opportunist.

Since I'd left home five months had passed without bumping into my guardians. Despite my newfound despondency (for completely different reasons) I was pleased not to have to deal with my family. Obviously *they* did not care too much about me being gone or they would have found me by now; I was not *that* transparent or lost.

I wanted more from life. I took advantage of Valerie and Noel's kindness and spent most days at the CES (Commonwealth Employment Service) looking for full-time work. I didn't seem to fit any matches for the type of work I wanted; those positions required a Higher School Certificate or TAFE equivalent. Despair began to sink in, or I began to sink into despair. How was I supposed to support myself *and* go to school?

During one evening at Valerie and Noel's, I completely lost it. I lay down on Christopher's bed screaming like a stuck pig and thrashing about breaking things. It took Noel, Valerie and another person I don't recall to hold me back down on that bed in order to stop me from impaling broken shards of whatever into my wrists. Noel in particular was very attentive and managed to soothe me back into a state of brittle calm. The next morning, I felt deeply ashamed of my behaviour but, although concerned, Noel and Valerie played down the previous night's events and continued to make me feel welcome inside their home. I had found true friends at last. Time to begin pulling my finger out.

I've always felt for our Indigenous, learning at school about their history since Cook's landing. My heart ached for the suffering of black Australians – I knew only too well what persecution and cruelty inspired by cultural difference felt like. On my way back 'home' one evening, I noticed the body of a young person lying in a gutter. On closer inspection I saw that the individual was a young Aboriginal male. I shook the man vigorously asking him if he was okay, the man lifted his head from the ground and cracked a drunken smile at me, his perfect white teeth hiding the foul stench of bourbon and regurgitation.

"Where do you live?" I asked him. "Do you want me to call you a taxi?"

Incoherent, the young man attempted an answer. I then proceeded to help him up onto his feet; I just couldn't bring myself to leave him there alone in that undignified state, Aboriginal people needed our help and I would give this anonymous Koori what help I could.

Hobbling, I managed to prop him up against a telephone booth. I then rang Noel. To my relief Noel didn't say to just *leave him there and come home*, he arrived in his Torana – the second love of his life, after Valerie – and collected *both* of us.

This young man's name was Doug and he slept his boozy stupor off that night on Noel and Valerie's couch. The following day Doug was back to a cognitive state and able to explain himself, offering gratitude and proposing amends. Noel blew Doug off, adding noone had done anything more than to act as a decent human being. From that day Doug started calling me 'Sis' and a beautiful new friendship entered my life.

Doug became a permanent fixture at Noel and Valerie's. He lived with his mother in Canley Vale and was not the hopeless drunk he appeared that night … that night was a 'one off' Doug said, not at all like his usual behaviour.

One evening at Noel's it was suggested the five of us play strip poker. The fourth participant was a very young girl Doug had brought over with him; I was the fifth and very much the 'spare wheel' in the group. Feeling mortified that such an unholy game had been proposed, I briskly retreated to my room, from where the events unfolding throughout the night were clearly audible. Maybe Maria was right: I really didn't know anything about sex. But if sex consisted of activities that resembled orgies, or covert romps in strangers' cars, I wanted nothing at all to do with 'it'. I was a nice girl. I wanted a romantic experience, just like in the movies.

I was not in love with Doug, but I became protective of him and wished he'd act more honourably and be the type of person to want more for himself. Aside from two girls at school, Doug was the only Indigenous person that I had met or had anything to do with. Like so many 'white' Australians I'd had no real contact with our Indigenous brothers and sisters but wanted to learn more about them. They appeared so segregated from the mainstream and I wasn't sure if this situation was caused by wilful or forced behaviour. As Westerners we were inadvertently taught that the 'Aboriginal issue' still loomed over our nation. As an instinctive rescuer, I was compelled do my bit to resolve this, but in reality my ignorance only served to contribute to the overall mood of pious judgement. But who was I to judge Doug as dishonourable or lacking ambition anyhow? Was I faring any better than he?

I had, to some extent, forgiven Maria for the way she treated me that night at the drug house, although she had not shut up about the radio projectile 'almost taking off her head'. I had to ask myself whether Maria possessed any real empathy or reason and whether I was better off without her. I prided myself on my capacity for forgiveness and friendship however, and so I asked Valerie if Maria could come over to her house and visit one afternoon. Doug was there, as usual, chilling on the lounge listening to a Kenny Rogers record he had brought with him.

Maria had lost a little weight and was prettier than ever. The moment Doug set his deep, dark eyes on her, he was clearly smitten. When the song 'Lady' began playing the scene was set. I felt a pang of jealousy but nevertheless took a step aside and made room for two friends who had obviously fallen in love before they knew it. I really needed to cut the bullshit with Doug. He was not my brother, nor was he some social 'experiment'; I had no right to choose his path. I watched Maria's body language weaving a web Doug was only too willing to fall into and prayed she would not introduce him to even more alcohol or to pot smoking.

I did meet Doug's family, eventually, and they welcomed me with open arms. Doug worshipped his mother; she was a big lady with a number of health issues and I understood why Doug was so frightened of losing her. In time I learnt that our Indigenous communities suffer a short life expectancy largely due to diseases like diabetes that became endemic after the radical change of diet that came with Western colonisation. I assured Doug I'd always be there for him and that if his mother *did* die prematurely, he would never be alone. But Doug would never be alone: the family kinships of our Aboriginal brethren include unrelated tribal members who they address as cousins, uncles, or aunties, thus creating an enduring and reliable support network.

One night, at around midnight, I suddenly felt deliciously sexed up. It was obviously a dream so I didn't hold back. The phantom in the dream was doing the nicest things to me and I wasn't about to stop him. Soon I was lying in bed naked feeling like I'd never felt before and it was heavenly. I was not, as it turned out, having a dream. Christopher, Valerie's brother, had returned home without notice and, finding a young girl in his bed, did not hesitate to take full advantage of the situation. By the time I realised what was going on I was too embarrassed and a little unwilling to stop any of it. I was tired of being a useless, frigid, virgin who knew nothing about sex – so what if a complete stranger would be *my first*?

In the event, Christopher did *not* end up 'taking' my virginity that night – though a hell of a lot happened 'in between'. It wasn't like with Trepiedi, but when the crucial moment arrived I did panic, and with a firm "STOP!" I threw Christopher off of me. Christopher 'finished himself off' over my stomach, and *that* was when I felt as disgusted and victimised as I had with Trepiedi.

Straight after Christopher had left for work the next morning I called Valerie into the bedroom and told her what had happened. I'd anticipated some form of belittling reprimand but all Valerie did was laugh and say, "Good on you!"

I then shyly asked her what was it that had come out of her brother's penis. Valerie looked at me incredulously but, after the biology lesson she gave me, I felt even *more* disgusted with myself. I was also worried I might have fallen pregnant. Leisl had once told me of a girl who got pregnant from 'stuff' that was left on a toilet seat. The 'stuff' crawled into her vagina and fertilised her egg. *Oh my God, could this happen to me?*

I decided I had to try and make this terrible situation work for me, so when Christopher returned from work that afternoon I started to feign interest in him. In the light of day, I saw that he was not an unattractive man but, as with Glenn, I felt absolutely nothing for him. If I was indeed pregnant with Christopher's baby, surely this meant we *had* to get together, right? Even marry? *Oh for Christ's sake, what have I done?*

Christopher did not require too much persuasion. He clearly liked me and was happy to begin dating me. In case I wasn't pregnant – not that I disclosed my concern to him – I asked Christopher to accompany me to a doctor to get onto 'the pill'. Christopher obliged and I managed to obtain a script. The doctor recommended we abstain from sex for two weeks in order to give the medication a chance to do its job, and I let out a sigh of relief. I really did *not* want to have sex with Christopher again and hoped two weeks would be enough for my period to come around so I could extricate myself from this self-imposed engagement.

By the end of the two weeks Christopher had lost interest in me – but there was no sign of a period. I bumped into Carolyn in busy John Street and she mocked me mercilessly.

"Well well well Angelica, I heard someone finally took your cherry!"

'How did the news get out?' I thought. 'Carolyn you pimply bitch, you're wrong!'

I was still very *much* a virgin – even if I was a pregnant one. Life was obviously punishing me for leaving home and now my mother's predictions were coming true. I *was* a little whore.

CHAPTER EIGHT

LOVE AND OTHER DRUGS

———

There was no doubt about it: Christopher's sperm had found its way into one of my ovaries and done its work. Over a month had passed without a period. Mentally I prepared myself for the birth of a bastard child such as myself – or worse, a termination. As a Catholic I couldn't possibly choose the latter. My life was well and truly over.

Life was not all gloom and doom however. Following days of tenacious job applications at the CES, I finally found full-time work with a little continental cake shop in Fairfield called La Swiss. I got the job only because I spoke Italian, but with above award wages in my pocket this meant I could move out of Noel and Valerie's and not have to honour any commitment to Christopher – pregnant or otherwise.

When I mentioned my plans about moving into a place of my own to Maria, she jumped at the chance of doing it with me. Maria's relationship with her mother was growing more stifling by the minute and she wanted out. My gut instinct, given her recent behaviour around my friends, was to say 'NO sorry Maria', but then Doug mentioned wanting to branch out on his own too, so I figured if we *all* lived together he'd help me pull Maria into line. Provided the couple had enough work to fund independent living, we could possibly share a nice place and buy some furniture of our own. Doug's best friend Jim also decided to jump on board, and so plans to move were put in motion.

Nine weeks passed and still no period. By this time I started feeling ill in the morning and my tummy had developed a definite swell. I decided it was high time I visit a doctor to ponder some important decision making.

The doctor listened to my story, and then spoke with some bemusement.

"My professional opinion Angelica is that what you're experiencing is a psychosomatic or phantom pregnancy. It's a rare condition, but obviously due to the misguided information you were given, you've talked yourself into *believing* you're pregnant and so your body has behaved in the same way; however, I *will* take a blood sample just to be sure."

The moment that blood test presented a negative result, my period arrived. I was *beyond* relieved. I now realised the strength of my own mind, but what I needed to learn was how to utilise this strength to better serve my future.

Excited, I made my way up the stairs to assess my new home. I had sent Doug and Maria to the real estate agency to take a look at the flat because I was working, but didn't want to miss out on a good catch. When Maria and Doug gave their approval, I signed the sixmonth lease the very next day.

The flat was nothing flash but it was roomy and well laid out. I made my way into the master bedroom only to be told by Doug that this was Maria's room. I felt a kick to the guts before being 'shown' to *my* room which turned out to be the smallest of the three. Jim and Doug were sharing the third. I then realised that once more I'd been had by Maria. This indignity was soon followed by the news the only person working other than me was Jim. Doug had recently lost his job and Maria was a TAFE student on minimal Austudy benefits, so I had to fork out the better part of our bond. Stupidly, not only did I do this, but I also volunteered to pay for the electricity connection and subsequent billings. Clearly (with hindsight at least) there was no way this situation was going to work over the next six months.

Noel and Valerie bid me an unusual goodbye. I left their place early in the morning tiptoeing around so as not to wake them when all of a sudden, their bedroom door was flung open and there they were, grinning profusely and stark naked.

"Take care of yourself," Noel said, sporting a warm smile, though I found it hard to look at his face while his enormous penis dangled unapologetically between his short legs.

"And," Valerie added, "you'd better come to our wedding."

Christopher came to see me at the cake shop one Thursday night. He was nonplussed about the way I had avoided him because he had in fact met someone else. Christopher hoped we could still remain friends but as things turned out this would be the last time I'd see him; Christopher eventually moved to the United States and married a woman a lot older than him. Also,

I did not see Valerie or Noel for a very long time and, for reasons I cannot remember, I did not attend their wedding.

Not long after we moved in together, Doug and Maria announced they were dating, which really came as no surprise. Doug had been besotted with Maria from day one and Maria ... well, Maria was a *sure thing* from the get-go. The consummation of their 'love' was a traumatic event with big tears from Maria and blood covered sheets to bear testament to her irreversible and painful loss of virginity. Doug's determination to claim it for himself had proved too much for her and she was no longer certain he was 'the one'.

Not only did Maria take my room and my adopted brother's heart, she took the very essence of my newfound independence. Jim proved an opportunist layabout who did not care about much either way, so without support from any of them, I soon (again) became the outsider in my own home. By the end of the first month I knew I could not endure the abuse of privilege that my three housemates were forcing on me. Not only was I paying for all our amenities and a greater part of the food, I was now being told Maria could not afford her share of the rent either.

Maria was displaying behaviours symptomatic with some kind of borderline personality disorder. She was so hungry for attention she would satisfy her need for the spotlight any way she could – including suicidal ideation and two misguided 'attempts'.

Maria's 'set-to-playback' complaint was that she had no money to buy food, and that life at the flat was making her feel more miserable than when she lived at home because *I* was constantly nit-picking about living costs and how everyone 'needed to go get a job'. Maria's defence was that she needed to complete her secretarial course before she could even *look for* a job, so why could I not be a little more patient with her? Noone could afford food or bills, it seemed, yet everyone was smoking and drinking. Why was my patience so thin?

Doug and I finally confronted each other one night and it changed our relationship forever. I stormed out of my room around one in the morning, screaming my lungs out at the three of them. They were huddled together around the dollar-guzzling heater, watching MTV and making so much noise I couldn't get a wink of much needed sleep. All I knew for certain was I had to be up for work that day and if I couldn't get some quality sleep I'd be a train wreck. I turned to Maria and hissed, blaming *her* for everyone's selfish and disgraceful behaviours. Defending his beloved girlfriend, Doug shot up like a missile from his spot on the floor. He then kicked my bedroom door clean off its hinges. It was the first and only time I witnessed Doug completely out of control. The next day he attempted an apology, crying and trying to hold me against him, but the damage was done. I forgave Doug for that episode but would never again trust him.

Soon Maria developed a serious case of anorexia nervosa. She stopped eating altogether and lost close to 20 kilos. What had begun as another attention seeking ploy had now taken a hold of her life. Doug was out of his mind with worry, again lashing out at me for restricting food because of the cost.

"You're earning enough money to buy furniture; how can you let her starve like this?" he barked.

I was angry about the accusation, but as a loyal friend who had shared so much with Maria before I left home I pushed my feelings of injustice aside and set out to help her get better. I knew nothing about anorexia nervosa except that my own eating was the polar opposite of that disease, I downed vast amounts of food – especially at work where it was both plentiful and sinfully delicious. Eventually it dawned on me how very sick Maria really was when she came out of her room one afternoon with a bikini hanging off her emaciated frame. Maria examined herself in the mirror, turning this way and that, frowning at the frighteningly fat person staring back at her. I brought home cakes and biscuits from work, roasted chickens and chips from the takeaway shop, ice cream, anything that I thought would restore Maria's interest in food. Nothing worked.

One day Doug and I lost our patience with Maria and forced her onto the sofa. Doug held her down as I stuffed handfuls of food into her mouth. Her screams were terrifying but by the end of the exercise Maria agreed to see a doctor. She weighed an astonishing thirty-two kilos. The doctor gave Maria a week to put on two kilos; failing this he was ordering her into hospital for a psychological evaluation and mandatory treatment under the mental health act. The threat worked and Maria began to eat again. She also abandoned the flat and returned home, leaving us all stranded and Doug heartbroken and angry. A week or so later Doug too returned home and, feeling uncomfortable with just Jim and me there, I released Jim from our lease. With a couple of months left on our contract, yet *another* former Coles New World workmate came to my rescue. Allira had her own difficulties living at home with her mother, and moving in with me was a welcome 'out' for her. Mothers can make or break who you are, or become, it seemed.

One day, when (of course) I least expected it, after six months away from Bishop Crescent and the clutches of my selfish and brutal 'guardians', my mother walked into La Swiss. Seeing me behind the counter was what she least expected, too, and as words fell out of her gaping mouth like passengers from a sinking ship, my intense feelings of hatred and resentment momentarily melted away. Regardless of any temporary feelings of sentimentality, I still knew I would not be returning home; besides, Gilda did not offer any invitation.

I happened to find in Allira what had turned out to be lacking in Maria – genuine altruism and selfless friendship. Allira was interested in *me*, not what I could provide for her. Allira was a feisty Sagittarian who loved to party and was head over heels in love with a monster sized Lebanese man named Rad. Like me, Allira was obsessed with her figure and hated the hold food had on her. Together we searched for new ways to lose weight, and yet we both consumed ridiculous portions of food that often left Allira completely desperate. I on the other hand, had discovered a better solution for this problem: purging.

My boss's eldest son, Fabrizio, had started paying me a lot of attention. There was no doubt he was a nerd and way too shy, and although I was attracted to his face, his skinny body repulsed me. I found Paul, my boss's chief pastry cook, far more desirable – even if he *was* forty-something. Paul laughed off my flirtations, offering me a wide berth, and so I allowed the salivating Fabrizio into the inner sanctum of my tenacious virginhood.

Fabrizio and I got naked just once at my place, when Allira was out at work. Although I was desperate to lose my hated virginity, I could not get past Fabrizio's protruding hip bones and ribcage. His grotty Y-fronts were a complete turn off too, as they clung to his non-existent behind. The way Fabrizio accepted his father's tyranny while his eyes clearly betrayed the stinging pain he felt inside also bothered me too much to want to be his girlfriend. I needed and wanted a *real* man; my personality and joie de vivre demanded it. Why hadn't I cancelled that stupid birthday party and accepted Pierre's invitation?

The lease was finally up, and Allira and I found a new place in Auburn, a 'multicultural' suburb near Granville – Granville being the locality where Australia's worst ever train disaster had occurred only five years before. Rad, Allira's bodybuilder boyfriend, lived nearby and became a regular fixture at our new abode. I'd often hear Allira cry herself to sleep because Rad seemed hell-bent on avoiding true commitment. Rad was a Christian Lebanese, the son of wealthy textile manufactures. Allira was an Australian- Italian checkout chick, the daughter of an alcoholic single mother. Clearly, there was little chance of any future for the two of them together.

Rad's compulsive bodybuilding schedules took up a great deal of his time, so Allira filled in hers with nightclubs, binge drinking, and eating. Allira now declared me her best friend, and insisted I go out with her and party as hard as she did, though the few times I obliged proved disastrous. On New Year's Eve of 1982 I got so drunk I engaged in 'inappropriate behaviour' on the dance floor with a multitude of men, with far worse to come. I learnt that I was *not* a party girl. My inner joy came from drawing, writing and reading, but the more I shied away from her nocturnal invitations, the more Allira resented my predilections. She had to look for a different party friend.

Thankfully, though, Allira enjoyed rollerskating as much as I did and we often coasted down the streets of Auburn and Granville, indulging in dangerous stunts on busy Parramatta Road; we would cling perilously to Rad's bumper which would tow us along in the 'slower' left lane. With the passing of weeks, however, Allira and I grew apart, becoming reluctant housemates rather than best of friends.

One afternoon as I lay on the lounge room floor doing a pencil sketch for my boss, a knock came on our front door. A man in his early twenties announced himself as Patrick, a friend of Allira's. I informed Patrick that Allira was out and he asked if he could wait for her return. I was a little annoyed as I was engrossed in my sketch, but I couldn't really say no to him.

Patrick had elfish looks and I wasn't too sure I found him attractive – not that it mattered, he wasn't here to see me, and I was far too busy to engage in idle chatter or gratuitous flirtation. I did notice however how his jeans fitted snugly around his front and back and how long and perfect his legs were. Patrick's toned and tanned arms poked out from rolled up sleeves, and his broad smile lit up the room. There was definitely *something* about this guy.

I continued with my drawing. The picture was a reproduction of the little township my boss had grown up in, somewhere along the border between Italy and Switzerland.

* * *

I was dressed up with somewhere to go! A night out at Allira's favourite haunt, the Polish Club in inner city Ashfield. Dancing was therapeutic for me and, provided I could leave when I wanted to, I didn't pass up too many invitations to clubs, especially if I was with a group. My boy hunting days were over so going out on the prowl with a girlfriend was no longer my idea of fun.

Allira had invited Patrick and a couple of his friends out to the club. The friends showed up a little later into the night and I wondered whether Patrick was making a beeline for our mutual friend. The tight jeans caught my attention once more and I was taken completely by surprise when suddenly Patrick ditched his friends to spend some one-on-one time with me, asking me onto the floor for a dance. Alas, dancing was *not* Patrick's forte and whatever could have been that night, wasn't. Patrick had smuggled in a bottle of seventy-nine percent proof 'Blackberry Nip' and, before he could say anything, I poured myself a full glass and, clueless, sculled it. It was the last action of that night I remember taking.

The next morning, I found myself in bed naked.

"How did I get here? What happened to me last night?" I asked Allira, who didn't look too flash herself. She seemed to have vomited half her body weight.

"Patrick and his friends drove us home; you'd collapsed on the dance floor and threw up all over yourself. The boys carried you inside and put you to bed. Sorry Angelica, I was too trashed to help them clean you up."

I was mortified. What if I'd been raped or molested? This would be absolutely the last time I allowed myself to become paralytic. I was far too smart for that.

Patrick called at the flat that night and I briskly hid in my bedroom. I could not possibly face him. Allira rapped softly on my door.

"I'm busy Allira!" I replied tersely.

Ignoring me, Allira barged in and sat on my bed smiling devilishly.

"Patrick really likes you!"

"Yeah right, after mopping up vomit and God knows what else? And besides, he saw me naked!" I gasped.

"Maybe that's why he's so keen on you?" Allira quipped. "No c'mon Angelica, he really wants to see you. He's a true gentleman, I've known him for years, and he's here to see how you're feeling."

The following week Patrick asked me out on a date and I said "*Yes!*" The last date I'd had was with one of Rad's bodybuilding mates for a 'blind' dinner and I knew then and there: oversized muscles were not for me.

* * *

Patrick picked me up in his Ford Landau coupe. For once I did not have mixed feelings about going out with a man; I was really excited. There was definitely something irresistible about Patrick, something I couldn't quite put my finger on, but tonight I felt I was about to find out what it might be.

Patrick took me to Stranded, the nightclub in the Strand Arcade on George Street, a renowned gay club tucked away in a city basement. The Stranded was intoxicating: the music, the decor, the people, the lights, the sheer exoticism it exuded – I was hooked. Patrick had introduced me to the inner sanctum of alternative lifestyle and freedom of expression. Homosexuality and transvestism were alien topics to me – forbidden even, in the light of Catholicism. I could almost hear the parochial echoes screeching inside my head, ordering me out of Babylon lest I too become a sinner. But I ignored the voice of monotheistic judgement and went nowhere. I wanted to learn more, see more, hear more, and I wanted to do these things with Patrick.

Patrick's dancing was truly awful but I couldn't have cared less. Ten years my senior, Patrick was a vibrant, outgoing, attentive and altogether endearing man. Yes, I was falling for him, by the nanosecond. Early into the morning the Stranded presented its 'tranny' show featuring three 'shims' dressed in gothic couture à la Jean Paul Gaultier. They were lip syncing perfectly to the Eurythmics' *'Here Comes the Rain Again'. It was pure magic. One of the 'girls' looked so delicate and beautiful I had to query if she really was a *he*. Straight after the show Patrick and I left for a coffee in nearby Pitt Street. By then, I was giddy with desire.

Patrick asked me a multitude of questions, and I answered them all, anticipating – even suggesting – the next one. I found myself drinking in everything this man had on offer and prayed thirstily for an endless night. I was excited, flattered, and sleepless, and then during a gap in the conversation I forgot myself and lunged forward to kiss Patrick's smiling mouth. Patrick stood still for a second or two, searching my face, but then just as suddenly as I had kissed him, he shot to his feet, grabbed my hand, and announced, "C'mon, I'm going to take you to my favourite place in the world!"

In the warm darkness of early morning we took off from the lights of the Sydney CBD, and landed in a moonlit place somewhere in the Eastern Suburbs. As I sat coquettishly in Patrick's comfortable car, I felt my body tingle. I reached out and cupped his taut thigh; Patrick smiled and I knew he was pleased. My heart had filled to the brim and I couldn't wait to discover what this man had in store for me. Shy as I was, I felt like a vixen under Patrick's gaze. Surely these feelings were not a bad thing?

We pulled into The Gap, the notorious cliff in Watsons Bay. I'd never been there before. A soft wind caressed us as we left Patrick's car. The stars were out in their infinite formations, while the ocean waves beat against the enormous rock face below us. I thought about Victorian lovers caught up in their moment of delicious romanticism, at time when sexual abandon was deemed a sin. I gazed into Patrick's sparkling blue eyes and we immersed ourselves into the kiss that my entire life would be based on.

"This is where many people have committed suicide Angelica," Patrick said as our lips parted, after what seemed an eternity.

Suicide? Why are we here then? I found Patrick's statement morbid and odd. In the arms of this man the thought of suicide was the furthest thing from my mind, yet, right now, right this moment, I was so enraptured that, had Patrick jumped, I could easily have gone down with him. I had tasted the power of love for the first time and if love is the deadliest of poisons then yes, I was ready to die.

And so I jumped.

* * *

The poem I wrote in Year 10, that had been deemed 'plagiarised', because a sixteen-year-old girl could not possibly express herself so deeply about adult concepts, fitted in perfectly with what now lay in my heart and soul as I stood helpless and bound, basking in the glow that was Patrick.

'Night and Day' by Adalgisa G – Year 10

Beyond the Alps lie the embroidery,
Of snow and ice, white upon faded turquoise.
Beneath the seas dwell the corals,
Interlacing with the wild greens of seaweed.
Above the world extend the heavens,
Dark yet sprinkled with oscillating radiance.
To beauty awake the shadows,
Roaming incessantly in search of light.
Silence discovers the thrill of sound,

Mellow, reposing, a vibrant cascade of sensations.
The trees from the Chinese mandarin,
To the majestic sequoia sway,
To the maternal rocking of the wind.
Solitary tulips wound the Dutch meadows,
And await the morning dew with outstretched petals.
The rays of morning glory prod
The highest blue peaks in the distant horizon.
King Sun himself spreads the golden mantle,
Gently, over the obscurity of night,
Forming the surging dawn and compelling the dreamers.
A multitude of plumaged migrants invade,
The infinite borders of the sky.
The spent valleys respond to the lingering warmth,
When their multi-coloured mosaics open up,
In order to greet a new day.
The husky voices of nature
Gossip from the depths of a rainforest,
But are soon quietened when King Sun intervenes,
And casts his fluorescence upon them,
Revealing the most minute possessions
Concealed by this intimidating magnitude.
Graceful creatures frolic vivaciously
Over the perspicacity of their audacious rivals.

The vast coats of deep celestial fire approach;
The joyful choirs cease their fluttering chatter,
To continue inexorable whispers.
Sunset extends from horizon to horizon,
Casting its burning glow over the submitting earth.
As dusk awkwardly breaks up the clouds,
And cools the vivid coats into a mystifying blue.
The offended clouds rush to assist their lady,
To ornament her and worship at her feet.
As the darkness intensifies,
She abruptly parts the firmament,
With a dazzling halo of light;

Her full face is at last revealed,
And her cloud maidens stand aside
To allow splendour for their Queen – the Moon.
Her reflection mesmerizes her beseeching lover.
He performs for her, honours her, breaking the spell,
And secretly adores her candour;
While he rages and victimises the elements.
The Sea is lustful, his waves swell violently,
Surging up to kiss that cold, glowing face.
Has she no heart? She immobilises the world,
She defies the king of light,
And yet the Sea loves her deeply.
She holds him in and gazes down, vain and aloof.

'Tis night and day, existence breaks,
Existence exonerates.
Life persists, life dies.
Nature sings, nature cries.
Shadows lurk, shadows flee.
The Sun is coroneted, the Moon bares her shoulders.
Music erupts and music shudders to insignificance.
The trance of love wavers until it is disturbed.
Man is born, man will come again.
And so the angel of Life defeats once more,
The angel of Death.
And these disperse as Night and Day.

CHAPTER NINE

MADNESS AND OTHER DRUGS

———

Mid-1983, and a new singing sensation is on everyone's lips. Nightclubs everywhere played her debut album and the world just couldn't get enough of this punky blonde bombshell called Madonna. I loved the way Madonna dressed: messy chic versus Boy George, versus Stevie Nicks, versus Nancy Spungen. In every sense of the word Madonna was awesome, and the original femme fatale. At last, I'd found someone to model myself on.

Music soothes the savage beast, and for me music is more than that – life giving. Music is where I retreat to change my mood from quasi-mad to pseudo-functional. Gilda tried to limit my enjoyment of music by sequestering me with opera; she failed, and I managed to escape both of them. The Eighties were a time of musical transition and diversity and, to my eyes and ears, the Eighties were the *best* years. Unlike Mother, my tastes were not restricted to one genre, although during this phase of my life dance music and new wave were my recreational manna.

Patrick and I had a second date at the Stranded, following which he asked me back to his flat in Campsie. I held no doubts – tonight was 'the night'.

Patrick's flat was a harrowing experience. The disarray and filth were beyond belief. Patrick acted as if nothing was wrong, nor did he offer an apology for the mess of his home – the least one might do when taking someone there for sex.

There was kissing and touching, more kissing and touching, and finally off came our clothes. Before I knew it my hated virginity had been taken, just like *that*! It was not the fireworks and all-consuming romance that movies and books depict; it was uncomfortable and unceremonious, but at least I was now a 'complete woman'. Wow!

When we'd finished, Patrick hid from me behind a towel, something I found odd in a grown man but also rather sweet. He had an impressive physique and it was obvious he did some form of regular sport. His Malvern Star bicycle was in the corridor, leaning against the grease-marked walls, and I discovered he cycled daily from Campsie to Menai, forty kilometres, to stay in shape and clear his head.

Patrick and I soon became inseparable. I was hooked on him and the copious amount of sex we were having – filthy flat and all. I was spending so much time at his place that Allira acrimoniously 'asked' me to move in there permanently. And so I did … bye bye Allira.

* * *

Patrick was self-employed, coming and going from home as he pleased. In fact, it turned out pretty much *everything* was on Patrick's terms, including me.

Patrick ran his business from home as a CB radio technician. The second bedroom in the flat was dubbed 'the CB room', with the floor covered in solder and electrical components. I soon gave up clearing the room up: the rest of the flat had been enough of a fix it job. For a man who kept his own person meticulously clean, his surroundings were unforgivable. His bathroom looked like Jame Gumb's basement from the 1991 film, *The Silence of the Lambs*.

Patrick refused to pay taxes and everything he earned from the CB business went straight into his pocket. Always loaded with money, Patrick got away with all this by keeping his Western Australian identity active, including car registration and licence. Patrick parked wherever he liked, leaving a note on the dashboard that read 'TRAFFIC' in order to evade a fine. He also used a different first name, one he wanted us all to call him by.

I was discovering that Patrick was a cad, but he appeared to love me and this was all I'd ever wanted in life so I didn't give two hoots about the improprieties. My heart soared whenever I laid eyes on him and my stomach churned at every thought of him. It was agony not to be around Patrick, and being with him was a delicious, dangerous, insatiable, all pervasive *hit*. I was losing control of my emotions and there was nothing I could do – nor *wanted* to do – about it.

The Stranded Nightclub was our favourite place but Patrick decided to take me on a comprehensive tour of Paddington's colourful gay scene along Oxford Street. With his boyish looks, super fit body and dress sense, Patrick could easily be mistaken for a gay man, but gay he was most definitely not. Patrick was a serious non-conformist who embraced freedom and controversy on any level and, as already mentioned, on *his* terms. I lapped up all of this, hungry for more, I who was essentially non-bourgeois either by inheritance or design. The kaleidoscope of man's basest desires would always be a part of my world. Arm in arm with my precious Malay-born Lothario I now revelled in its unveiling, layer by seedy layer.

Patrick also loved nature, and with him I discovered some of the most beautiful parts of New South Wales, places I'd never before heard of. Aside from The Gap, my lover's other favourite place was Stanwell Tops, a secluded beach in the northern suburbs of Wollongong. Here natural sand dune formations that reached three feet in height were documented as geographical marvels. We took advantage of the solitude Stanwell Tops enjoyed in our usual, primal way, the novelty of exhibitionism being something I did not actually enjoy but learnt to tolerate through Patrick.

Getting 'caught in the act' was no fun. The first time it happened we were on a hillside at a place I don't recall. Patrick had assured me there would be noone around for miles, yet, in the throes of passion, I heard a young child's voice above me frantically calling out to his parents. I looked up to see an entire family on top of the hillside staring down on us, faces glaring with horror and disbelief. The more I fumbled for my clothes to cover my nakedness, the further from reach they appeared to crawl.

The second time I was 'busted', Patrick and I had taken a lovely walk upstream in our bathers, somewhere in Nambucca Heads that was also part forest. Finding a solitary spot we entered the water and went for it. Afterwards, I found my bikini bottoms had floated downstream and out of sight. Patrick ordered me to stay where I was as he returned to base to grab a towel and the rest of our clothes. Murphy's Law states that whatever can go wrong will. Noone had come past this part of the woods the entire time we were there, and Patrick had not been gone ten minutes before I heard rustling in the underbrush. Sitting bare bottomed, as low into the water as I could squat, I threw on my invisibility cloak, remaining perfectly still and quiet. Three young men suddenly peered through the trees at me and one called out, "Are you okay in there?"

"Yes, yes, I'm fine thank you," I gulped.

'That's it,' I thought to myself. 'My time has arrived. These guys are going to drag me into the thickness of the forest, have their way with me, cut me into little pieces, and bury me in a shallow grave, just like all those backpackers who go missing every year. If I survive I swear, I am SO not doing outdoor sex again!'

Patrick was essentially a solitary, self-effacing personality, and that was how he liked things. He was the quintessential Scorpio male, secretive and suspicious; if Patrick didn't want you to know something, you would not be finding out. This aspect of his personality alone was enough to send me into spins of panicked jealousy and self-destructive insecurity. I needed to *possess* Patrick's psyche for my sanity to continue on an even keel. Patrick was the one true love of my life and the only person who had ever given me anything tangible or real. The mere thought of losing him was unfathomable, painful beyond words.

Patrick had me figured out practically overnight and set out to test my loyalty at every turn. He would query my wearing make-up to work, and when I'd tell him it made me feel good about myself, he'd argue that maintenance of my self-esteem was *his* job and I need not seek approval from outside sources.

We often fought over money. Patrick was quite the scrooge, despite money never being an issue for him. He made a habit of purchasing things only *he* deemed appropriate or useful, and seldom what *I* liked or wanted. I offered Patrick a proposal: that I would give up work and become his full-time assistant and housekeeper in return for a small personal wage. It was a feeble attempt at control on my part – I wanted to witness Patrick's every move, rather than enhance his or my life in any way. Naturally Patrick rejected my proposal, seeing right through my intentions. I would have to 'pay my way', all of it – rent, food, and bills, all split down the line.

Patrick soon discovered my Achilles heel: other women. He teased me about certain celebrity beauties, and particularly about Edith Bliss, the TV reporter on the children's program *Simon Townsend's Wonder World!* It did not take me long to realise that Edith resembled his previous and only girlfriend, Cheryl, a woman whose orgasms 'brought down the house' and left Patrick's back covered in welts.

"Show me a picture of this *Cheryl* of yours!" I demanded.

Cheryl was nothing special, so he said, but the way he described her in bed was enough to turn me into a paranoid, jealous Medusa, ready to draw blood and decapitate people. I *had* to find this Cheryl and take stock of where exactly I stood in her multi-orgasmic shadow.

Cheryl had left Patrick for no apparent reason, running into the arms of a much older man with a disability. It was obvious that Cheryl's betrayal had hurt Patrick deeply and left him scarred and reticent about future relationships. The overwhelming need to *meet* the climaxing vixen was further fuelled by a deep sense of personal revenge. Patrick mercilessly tested me on everything only because *she* had created these fears. Why did she get to call the shots over my destiny when I would never do the same as her? The muse who had embedded a question mark into Patrick's psyche, a mark that robbed me of his unconditional love, must pay. Her wild orgasms, things I still had not discovered for myself, threatened our relationship. Above all else, this is what Patrick stood for – sex, lust, and unbridled, undeterred reciprocation.

On my way to work on the red rattler, I'd scan Erskineville station as we passed by, hoping to catch a glimpse that matched Cheryl's physiognomy and that femme fatale glow of hers. I even took days off work just to stand on Erskineville station waiting for her. It was madness I know, but this is how childhood abuse and neglect can fuck with a young person's mind. Cheryl never came but then, one day, I did. Eventually I let her ghost evaporate from my mind and our bedroom too. If knowledge is power, experience is a gift far more precious.

My need to control Patrick and the insane jealousy I felt *all* the time did not stop with Cheryl. I once almost jumped over the counter of the Campsie McDonald's because Patrick informed me that the girl who had served him there was 'extra nice' to him. My eyes followed Patrick's wherever we found ourselves. Who was he looking at, in what way, and why? The only times I found some inner peace or relief from hypervigilance, was when we were completely alone, and with the television turned off. The way I was manipulating Patrick was shameful and it stole a portion of my soul I was too proud to own up to. I had shut everyone out of my life because all I needed and wanted in order to sustain me was Patrick; nothing and noone else came close. If this is how addiction feels, then I was one hopeless junkie!

Patrick would return from his 40-kilometre bike rides covered in acrid sweat and with snot sprayed across his face and hair, but it didn't deter me from throwing myself at him. I'd lost all sense of decorum or standards. I'd wait by that damned door the whole time he was gone counting the seconds until his return, my emotions and rationale completely out of control. There was nothing I wouldn't do for Patrick; he could have asked anything of me and I would have at least considered it. Was it *this* type of unhealthy obsession and co-dependency that created the Rosemary Wests and Catherine Birnies of our criminal world?

Fortunately for me there weren't too many people in Patrick's life who shared his interests. Apart from Allira, Patrick had six friends to speak of, and he rarely saw them because they were *truly* weird and mostly preoccupied with their own strange lives. Patrick was also not close to his rather puritanical English family, who lived a safe distance away in Canberra. Most of my friends – whenever I bothered to call on them – had met Patrick and appeared to like him. With his permanent smile, sporty demeanour and lust for life, Patrick was easy to like.

I kept a very close watch on Maria when Patrick was around because, where attractive men were concerned, she was like a moth to light. Maria and Doug were still together but things weren't going well. Maria complained endlessly that Doug didn't do this or that, smoked too much dope, or drank too much whiskey. Doug became fed up and cheated on Maria with a 'meth mouth' single mother called Faith. Eventually the two moved on to new people and different lives, but I still loved Doug, even after Maria created a rift between us that proved impossible to heal.

Patrick gave his six friends labels I recognised before I could remember their real names. There was Fat Sue and her skinny Asian teenage boyfriend, Richard the Mortuary Assistant, Porno Peter, Diamond Bruce, and Young Talent Time Bruce. I met each of them and felt distinctly uneasy in their company. It wasn't jealousy this time, it was something more, something I couldn't explain and especially with Young Talent Time Bruce. I didn't feel any such reservations with Patrick's highbrow family, however. Rachel, his mother, was welcoming and full of smiles. His father Christopher was more the typically English 'stiff upper lip' type, though the siblings were all polite and congenial. Having met his brood, I figured Patrick should probably meet my embarrassing family. It had been almost a year since I last saw them and introducing them to Patrick was our ice breaker, as it turned out.

Mother liked Patrick, or at least she pretended to. Alfonso … well, I couldn't give a rat's ass what he thought. As with me and mine, it was clear there was no love lost between Patrick and his family. All of them were university graduates, while Patrick was the only high school drop-out, carving a living doing something 'of little worth'. His mother was a mathematics teacher and his father an authority on Malaysian rubber. One of his sisters was an accomplished cellist and his younger brother was studying nanotechnology.

Almost a year had passed and I decided it was time for a commitment, so I began to push for a formal engagement. Patrick was not overly interested in these types of 'bullshit ceremonies' and I knew it, but it made me doubly determined to elicit a ring from him nonetheless. The Spirit of Contradiction would be performing her finest work to date.

If I was honest with myself, I admitted how much I resented Patrick's defiant independence and the uncomplicated freedom he appeared to enjoy. I was not 'wired' like Patrick, though: I *needed* to be needed, to be lusted after and owned. I desired Patrick in a way I could never have imagined. In my head I created many crazy stories about perceived infidelity on his part, but this madness was just the emotional projections of a young, abused and oppressed girl onto the one person who seemed to give a shit about her for longer than a month. I was always in Patrick's face, refusing to let up no matter how angry I made him. The angrier he got with me the harder I pushed. I hated his clients calling into the flat at inopportune times, but for me *every day* was inopportune. I hated his bike rides and the business calls into Ashfield. I was monitoring all of his calls, his mail, his every move, every word and intention, what he liked, why he liked it, what he thought, why he thought it … I was insanely jealous about nothing and everything. I did not understand what was happening to me and felt helpless to change it. Slowly but surely, though, it was driving Patrick crazy – and away from me.

I took to interrogating Patrick about the smallest nuances of his behaviour, turning the tiniest of pimples into enormous mountains and if I didn't like his explanation I'd fly into insane rages that would last for hours, until the explanation changed and was more befitting the scenario my damaged mind had created. Sometimes the rages would turn into self-harming episodes or destruction of property – his, of course. One evening I threw a stiletto at his prized Bang and Olufsen stereo system, damaging the turntable. Patrick glared at me with something near hatred.

"What the hell do you think you're doing you stupid woman? Is this how you think you'll convince me to put a ring on your finger? Keep kidding yourself then Angelica because the way you're going it's never going to happen!"

I would have preferred to be crucified than hear those words. Instant remorse set in, but I'd run out of options in how to show it. I ripped my clothes off and threw myself at him, offering the only apology I thought he would not refuse. But I'd gone too far – he didn't care about 'that' right now. He continued fumbling with the turntable, trying to fix the damage I'd caused – not only to the expensive system, but to our relationship. The tether I'd tried to bind my lover with was snapping by the millisecond.

* * *

I won! I received the engagement ring I wanted *and* a small engagement party. Tenacity and sexual manipulation had paid off, or so I believed.

The small festive dinner was held at one of my mother's opera friends' restaurants in Oxford Street. The small group of guests invited were all mine. This should have told me something but I was too obsessed and drunk with triumph to care. I had my ring and Patrick's commitment; what else mattered?

Saying goodbye to my generous Italian employers in Fairfield, I found a job closer to home in Summer Hill. Patrick could drop me off at work and pick me up, which meant I was away from him for only eight hours of the day instead of ten. My new employers, Alastair and Marianne, were a twenty-something couple who owned and ran a little bakery in the inner Sydney suburb. I met a number of celebrities at that little pies and coconut tarts outlet, with the most famous being the Sydney Swans footballer and pin-up boy Warwick Capper, who at that time was moonlighting as a council worker for the Ashfield Municipality.

One foreboding, tear-filled day, I lost my engagement ring on the red rattler. I had a habit of taking it off to play with it. That ring meant everything to me: it represented a fusion between Patrick and me. I was terrified Patrick would use my carelessness as an excuse to call off our engagement; God knows I was already giving him enough other reasons to. On this occasion, though, I was lucky: Patrick saw the depth of my regret and sorrow and assured me he'd replace the ring with a better one. I was once again floating on air but it would be short lived. Somehow, I contracted genital herpes.

When the doctor confirmed the diagnosis and explained to me what HSV2, the herpes simplex virus 2, was, I just could not understand how I'd got it. STIs affected only promiscuous people who engaged in risky behaviours, right? Right. And Patrick had been my *only* sexual partner, and he'd had only one partner before me, and his penis did not have a single sore on it the whole time I knew him. I suffered with numerous bouts of thrush and cystitis due to our overactive sex life so perhaps herpes had something to do with *these*!

The doctor asked me a few more questions, and the embarrassing conclusion was I contracted genital herpes via oral sex. Patrick must have had cold sores on his lips and apparently herpes simplex type 1, the virus that produces cold sores, was transferred to my vulva, transmuting into the simplex 2 variety. Coping with genital herpes became the most physically agonising period of my life since I'd suffered third degree burns as a fourteen-year-old many years before, after I fell asleep under a blazing sun on Bronte Beach. The prospect of painful, recurring sores for the rest of my life was something I would never get used to. There is no way to describe the sheer torture of multiple burning lesions spread across your entire genital and anal area, especially during toilet visits.

I was off work and sex for almost three weeks. Apart from the physical pain, the worst part was the diminished contact with Patrick, but on the flip side I couldn't help but feel angry with him for placing me in such a situation. Making me angrier still was Patrick's suggestion that I may have been unfaithful. Patrick questioned my virginity and integrity, assuming that me not bleeding during our first time meant I'd had sex before. Patrick insisted I could not possibly have contracted anything from him because his penis had never presented with anything unusual and his personal hygiene was immaculate. A pity the doctor had not seen the state of his flat before I moved in. I also wondered if Cheryl could have infected him. After all, herpes can be present in the host with no visible symptoms.

From then on, our relationship was on a downward spiral. Patrick began withdrawing from me emotionally, and the more he did so the more I demanded he marry me. I was now positively demented with fear of losing him. The rages grew fiercer and my physical assaults on him doubled. Patrick never raised his hand to me during these wild episodes; instead, he would just sit on me and keep me there, restrained. I cried and screamed for hours, but Patrick would just sit there frozen, staring at me in disbelief and bitter derision. I knew that with this insanity I was systematically killing my relationship, but I was like a derailed bullet train – there was nowhere else to go and no way to stop.

Thoughts of suicide began to revisit. If I lost Patrick I may as well be dead.

I tried everything I could to make him understand *my* world, *my* reasons. I even left him to visit my cousins in Adelaide for a week, hoping my absence might help Patrick realise how important I was to him, and that if he only gave me what I asked for, he'd never feel the emptiness of my absence again. I was all about *me*: it did not dawn on me that maybe *I* was not for *him*, and why should it? I was everything he could want!

I hadn't even hit South Australian soil when I immediately regretted being a thousand miles from the man I would marry sooner rather than later. I called Patrick every night from my uncle's place in Magill, pining for him, pouring out my heart to him. I must have sounded so pathetic, exactly like the loser I felt inside. Yet I couldn't stop. I didn't know *how* to stop.

I couldn't return to Sydney fast enough. I had sabotaged my well laid plans and I knew what would meet me was not going to be what I had hoped for. I was wrong, though, and delightfully so. Patrick and I were so pleased to see each other we did not make it up the stairs to the flat intact. Yes! He *had* missed me!

Dreams may reveal different stories, however. One night, during the early hours, Patrick woke up suddenly, sitting up in bed fearful and disoriented with sweat pouring off him.

"Oh my God Patrick, what's wrong?"

Patrick turned to me, eyes wild, mouth trembling. "I just dreamt I was married and had a child!"

* * *

I decided I was going to be 'good' and earn back Patrick's trust. I also wanted to begin using my God given talents instead of wasting my life selling sausage rolls and cream buns to two-bit actors and local yuppies.

I answered an advertisement for a jewellery store in Leichhardt whose proprietor was looking for a trainee jewellery designer. I knew I had excellent drawing skills and great imagination. I had actually designed the second engagement ring Patrick had bought me. I walked confidently into the store and froze. Looking around me at the white marble floors and velvet drapery I felt scared to death, very small, and incredibly inferior. The European counter clerk, immaculately dressed and poised, asked if I required assistance. Nervously I stuttered I was here for a job interview with Mr Cipriano. The salesman ushered me to a rococo chair and assured me the proprietor would see me soon – and had I brought in all my designs? I looked blankly into the young man's eyes. *The ad didn't mention designs.*

"That's okay Angelica", the man smiled. "I'm sure Mr Cipriano will recognise talent once he speaks with you. Just take a seat please. I'll let him know you're here."

Once the salesman had disappeared behind a partition I knew I had to get out of there. A second beautifully presented sales assistant standing behind a second counter looked me up and down; I was nicely dressed, yes, but I did not have the class a place like this demanded – even expected. The job was just too good for me. I was a noone, a nothing, a cake shop girl, not a designer of fine Italian jewellery credited by TV programs around the country. Mr Cipriano would but laugh at me the same way Mother had my entire life. I was a *nothing* trying to convince herself she could become a *something*.

Before I could give Mr Cipriano the chance to see me I ran out of the store and into the welcoming, non-judgemental arms of inner Sydney suburbia. I walked away briskly and did not dare turn around in case Mr Cipriano had peered from his door and was attempting to hail my return. I did not allow my normal breathing to return until I found myself aboard a homebound train, safe in my anonymity and the possibility that maybe just *maybe,* one day I would find the courage to do something worthy of the real me.

I returned home from work one afternoon with my old Coles New World colleague and friend Lisa in tow. Lisa had spotted me on the Bankstown train station and came running towards me excitedly, arms extended.

"Angelica! Where have you been hiding?" She searched my face for an answer she could chew on. Lisa was always a bit of a loose cannon and things had only got worse for her since we last saw one other. Among other issues, Lisa had terminated an unwanted pregnancy to an abusive boyfriend, who was still hanging around.

"Here have a smoke," Lisa offered.

"No thanks, I've given up; my fiancé hates it."

Gushing with pride I showed Lisa my engagement ring. She was thrilled for me and gave me a happy squeeze.

"Wait till you meet him," I said drawing out a Cheshire cat smile. "Are you doing anything right now? Want to come over to our place and see Patrick?"

Lisa happily obliged and, super excited, I ran up the stairwell of our dingy block of flats like a little girl on a mission and flung our door wide open with explosive anticipation. What then met my eyes took a millisecond to register but an eternity to process. Except for my things, the flat was completely *empty*!

I was paralysed. What had happened? Why? Where was he? What was this? What had I done? Was this some kind of sick joke?

Lisa was visibly confused, but when the tears catapulted from my eyes and the moans of emotional agony escaped my throat she threw her arms around me and hugged me, trying to make sense of things on my behalf.

I could not speak. I ripped myself away from Lisa's caring arms and ran downstairs to the flat's lock-up garage. My angry fists banging against the metal had no chance of getting it open and my anguished cries were only bringing out nosy neighbours and stares from passing cars. *Oh my God, oh my God, oh my God, where is he, why is he doing this to me?* My brain fought vainly to work out Patrick's whereabouts and reasons. He could be anywhere – even back in Western Australia. How could I stand still not knowing how to find him, how to get him back – and I *had* to get him back!

Lisa went home but I didn't notice her leaving. The phone was still connected. I rang a few numbers I knew by heart, including Porno Peter's and Young Talent Time Bruce's; neither knew where Patrick was and yet neither sounded surprised he had disappeared. I immediately realised one of his friends was hiding him. I called Allira and she genuinely knew nothing – of that I was certain.

It was getting dark and I had nothing to sleep on inside the cold flat which only this morning had been my home. I was inconsolable and did not know where to turn. Incredibly, I thought of Mother and dialled her number. To my ear her voice was barely audible.

"Come *figlia*, come home. I know what you are going through only too well. Let me look after you tonight."

I booked a taxi for Bonnyrigg, leaving a note for Patrick that begged him to call me at Mother's or at work the next morning – that's if I even made it there. In the note I promised Patrick I would change: I would stop begging him to marry me, I'd stop my tantrums and stop making demands. I would be the Angelica he wanted me to be, I'd be anyone, anything he wanted, *but please, come back to me!*

That most terrible of nights I cried myself to sleep in my mother's arms. It was the first and last time we ever connected this way. Mother told me about her numerous love affairs and how most, my father included, had left her with scars too deep for healing.

"Men are pigs," she added.

Early next morning I woke up feeling hollow and dehydrated. To show up for work was out of the question so I rang in sick and hailed another taxi back to Campsie, hoping the previous day's event had indeed been an unsavoury joke designed to teach me a lesson. I re-entered our flat holding my breath. Nothing had changed: it was still horribly empty. I fell to the ground clutching one of Patrick's Tshirts I found hanging on the clothes horse on the balcony. Lying there on the worn carpet of *our* bedroom I cried until there was nothing left. I buried my face into the Tshirt as if that precious body I worshipped was still inside it. If I didn't get Patrick back today it would be my last day on earth; I simply did not wish to live.

Hours passed and no sign of Patrick. All I could do was wait; wait, and hope. More time elapsed and hope began to die. I then contemplated how *I* would die and by what method. Then, from the suffocating silence, a familiar sound. Rushing onto the balcony I caught a glimpse of Patrick's blue Datsun 120Y, the same car he bought for me to learn to drive, and a gift that had angered me because I wanted to learn to drive an automatic.

With bated breath I waited for the most wonderful sound in the universe and my sole salvation – a knock on the door – but it did not come. Grabbing my shoes I ran down the stairwell to greet him and beg his forgiveness. He was sitting in the car on the driveway, contemplating the garage door before him. He looked as dishevelled as I felt. His eyes met mine and then I heard the ignition turn. Patrick reversed out, and turned into Fifth Avenue. The car stalled and with a typhoon at my feet and the determination of Leonidas in my heart I ran as fast as my body would carry me in pursuit of that little Datsun.

"Stop! Stop! Patrick please stop!" I screamed.

I noticed a malicious snarl on Patrick's face as the engine picked up again and gained speed. I ran faster still, all the way down Eighth Avenue until the little Datsun stalled once again and I was able to catch hold of the door handle.

"No matter how fast you go now you're taking me with you!" I cried. "Drag me along until I'm dead, I don't care. I love you and I'm not letting you go."

The snarl morphed into a pitiful gaze, and with me still clutching the handle for dear life Patrick moved to the kerb and turned off the engine. I didn't give him a chance to unlock the door; I jumped in and grabbed his neck, bringing his face into mine, sobbing and grateful for the mercy he was now granting me. Patrick lost the momentary pity and sat stony faced and speechless. Starting the car once again, he turned the corner towards the flat and pulled into our driveway with me still holding on to him so tightly I must have slowed down his heart rate. All his belongings were stored in the lock-up garage. He'd had no intention of leaving his flat, he just wanted me to *think* he was gone, hoping I'd leave and never return. I was mortified, wounded beyond words, and there was nothing I could offer as restitution, except silence.

Just as I'd thought, Patrick had stayed at Young Talent Time Bruce's, the one who'd had me wary from the start. Patrick had had enough of me – my pressures, my outbursts, and my jealous clinginess. I was no longer exciting and fun. I was little more than a millstone around his neck now. But, just as I thought it was all going to end no matter what I said or did, I was granted one last lifeline.

I was never to mention marriage – not even once. I was to stop being so insanely jealous and possessive, and, I was *never* to throw another tantrum, not ever! I was to respect Patrick's space and livelihood and *no* negotiation would be entered into these terms.

I could do this, I knew I could. No, I *would* do this! My future happiness depended on it. So I gave Patrick my ironclad promise.

That night my passion-filled kisses began to thaw out Patrick's Scorpionic heart and once again I felt whole. My life force had returned and my heart sang the sweetest song I'd ever heard. I thanked God for Patrick's return and then begged Him to slowly return *me* back to me. If I was to keep my promise, I needed to rebuild my life from the inside out.

Oh yes yes yes … I could do this. I could.

CHAPTER TEN

BLACKMAIL AND OTHER DRUGS

Early in November of 1984 I booked myself into the last spot left at the Bankstown TAFE in order to complete Years 11 and 12. I finally began to give credence to the importance an education holds in a person's life. I needed my Higher School Certificate to get into university for a Bachelor of Arts degree and to escape the dead ends of menial labour. I also wanted to find a reason to distance myself from Patrick so I could meet the behavioural codes that might just save our flagging relationship.

Patrick and I had come to an agreement: if I acted differently for twelve months he would slip that wedding band on my finger and happiness would be mine. I became successful in creating the outside image Patrick demanded but, inside, the *real* Angelica was still screaming. I managed to drown the screams with food and before too long I realised I'd become hopelessly bulimic.

* * *

I made a firm decision that I would avoid any form of socialisation at TAFE in order to stay focused on my goal: a good enough aggregate for university entrance. I deliberately sat at the back of the class and snarled at anyone who even looked my way. Had I done this in high school instead of chasing gonads I could have been a star pupil. I knew I possessed abundant intelligence, both academic and emotional, to find success in anything I set my mind to. My three planets in Gemini served me with a sharp wit but also with a penchant for distraction that verged on the pathological. Attention seeking to find self-worth was a major issue too. I loved being around people and their idiosyncrasies so that I could manipulate them, purely for entertainment value – mine and theirs.

The resolve to stick to myself lasted a half day. By the end of the day I'd shifted to the front of the class and knew the names of all my classmates. Our course was a mixed bag: there were people from all backgrounds, with a significant number of Greeks. I'd never met Greeks on a personal level before – nor lesbians, and Kathy, who would not or could not take her eyes off me, was a quintessential 'dyke'.

There was also a large quota of Middle Eastern students, some young, some semi-mature. Then there was a Lebanese man from another course who kept making eyes at me. He was certainly very handsome, as was Allira's boyfriend Rad, but I had already taken a leaf from Allira's experience with Rad and decided not to go there. Furthermore, there was an incident involving our ancient history teacher, who was cornered inside the TAFE lift by an Arab student. He brandished a small knife, menacing the frightened teacher, saying he did "not take instructions from a woman". The teacher had related this incident to our class, adding how it appeared the relatively new Middle Eastern community settling in and around the Bankstown area was somewhat intolerant of their Western counterparts, but particularly of women.

I found myself gravitating towards the boys, as always, and particularly to an unassuming young man named Mark. Mark introduced me to Al Stewart, Cat Stevens and the Alan Parsons Project. Mark was another Scorpio, along with Maria, Noel and a few others; it appeared the sign of Scorpio was dominating my life. Another man, Rhys, caught my eye in the geography class; he was the 'looker' of our course. I would sometimes sit directly behind Rhys, admiring his broad shoulders and muscular back. The other girls thought he was pretty hot too, except for two Greek sisters, Stacey and Barbara, who decided he was too much of 'a yobbo' for their liking. Greek girls are very discerning, I discovered. I often had to stop myself and remind 'me' that I was 'off limits' to other men. Those cheeky Gemini planets urged me to flirt but Patrick was still the love of my life; I would die for, and *with*, him.

Living with Patrick while studying was not ideal, for obvious reasons, so I made a decision that surprised even me: I moved out of the flat and back in with my guardians – my mother and the slug. I don't know what possessed me to do this, and it was a decision I ended up regretting. In order to do Years 11 and 12 full time I'd had to give up the job at La Swiss and go on Austudy payments which were next to nothing. The slug didn't care, though, as he got his cut of it for 'rent', so it did make financial sense.

Little had changed at home, though. I was still judged by Alfonso, and my mother was still out of control. Piero was a little older and a little less painful and if Alfonso would only disappear to Sicily or, even better, suffer a coronary, then 'home' might possibly become a place I could deal with.

Since their arrival in Australia, Alfonso and Mother had refused to do any work outside their operatic field. The Australian Opera wanted neither of them so they thumbed their nose at integrity and societal conscience by remaining ostentatiously unemployed. Our generous Australian Government have since supported them, setting them up in subsidised accommodation and sufficient welfare benefits to afford them a reasonable lifestyle. Why then was our household constantly edging along the poverty line? It was painfully obvious that Alfonso was regularly sending money to his Sicilian relatives. The slug was unashamedly robbing all of us, including his own disabled son.

Mother, in her oblivious downstream swimmer Piscean stupor, never bothered to properly investigate any of this, but unless Alfonso was seeing hookers on a weekly basis or doing drugs, what were our household funds being spent on, exactly? We never bought anything new, we ate the most basic meals, sometimes items that were marked right down because they were virtually off. In my mind I was certain that karma would come for my stepfather, and the slug would perish miserably.

I'd been a fool to return to Bonnyrigg, but I was desperate to change my life and I knew my need to control Patrick would have sabotaged all my future plans. But every day, Mother was screaming at Alfonso, Piero was doing gross things, and I was expected to 'do my bit' around the house as if I hadn't left, thus regressing to the life I'd endured as a fifteen-year-old. Seeing Patrick only three days a week was excruciating but it served to keep my promise to him, and of course to keep me focused on my studies.

Before I left Patrick's flat I had bought the sweetest, white as snow Chinchilla Persian kitten. I called her Tessie. Mother, a cat aficionado, was ecstatic, but Alfonso flatly refused to have Tessie inside the house, so I was forced to buy a small tin shed and house my new darling outside in the bitter cold. I built a brick floor for her, courtesy of a demolished building at Rockwood Cemetery, but despite my efforts to keep Tessie warm and comfortable, it did not take long for my little angel to develop a cold and die. Yes indeed, Alfonso would die miserably for his sins.

Maria continued living next door to my guardians and was happy to have me back. After catching Doug with the toothless Faith, he had been unceremoniously dumped and she was now engaged to a Maltese brute called Mark. I took one look at Mark and knew he was going to be trouble. Mother sewed Maria a 'Scarlett O'Hara' style wedding dress and it was breathtaking. 'Someday soon I too will be wearing a dress like this,' I thought.

I had a catch-up with Doug one evening at his mother's in Canley Vale, and he poured his heart out to me about the *real* reason behind the relationship breakdown with Maria. Doug idolised Maria, but he couldn't take another single unrealistic demand or scourge from her. It was the constant barrage of *me me me* that eroded his Virgoan temperance, sending him fleeing into the arms of the first person that had come along.

"But Faith has missing teeth, she looks like a druggie, *how could* he?" Maria had shrieked at me in disgust.

I just wanted to backhand the stupid girl and tell her it wasn't *about* what Faith looked like; it was about *Maria* and *her* attitude towards Doug and life in general. A painful sense of hypocrisy set in as I recognised in Maria's behaviour how *I* was with Patrick. The sense of hypocrisy was soon followed by a sense of dread: would Patrick do the same with me as Doug had done with Maria?

* * *

My relationship with Patrick was not going to survive, I knew. For one thing, in place of love, we'd started using pornographic videos to get aroused. The last straw was when Patrick suggested a threesome with Maria. I believe once a person begins to behave this way, they're falling out of love with you. Still, I tried to suppress my anger and frustration just in case Patrick was simply administering another 'test' of my character, but unfortunately the anger still came out during periodic explosions that were far more damaging to our relationship than the frequent smaller outbursts. I knew the offer of marriage would no longer be on the table, so I began to relax the few relationship ethics I had been struggling to observe. I began stealing from Patrick, and flirted unabashedly at TAFE, namely with Rhys, the good looking 'yobbo'.

I saw a classified in the newspaper that instantly caught my interest. Channel 10 was looking for a new reporter to replace Edith Bliss on *Simon Townsend's Wonder World!* 'Ha!' I thought. 'Imagine if I got the job and replaced Patrick's fantasy girl, then dumped him for Rhys.' The Scorpio moon in my natal chart was devilishly reaching out to extract pain, the sting fully loaded with deadliest poison.

The network received a record number of applications. It had asked for 'interesting and unusual' and I had just the story for them. I composed a side-splitting satire that described Patrick's six weirdo friends and their incestuous relationships with and away from one other. I used a professional photographer to take some portraits of me and off I went to the post office to lodge my application. I was not expecting a reply but before I had time to forget what I'd just attempted I took a call from Channel 10 in Mother's lounge room.

"Hi Angelica?" the voice greeted me. "This is Brendan Ward, producer for *Simon Townsend's Wonder World!* how are you this evening?"

SHIT! What do I do now?

The urbane Mr Ward asked a few questions which I answered in a most parochial Catholic manner. In 1985 I was forming strong political and socio-economic opinions that definitely leaned towards the right (even the 'far right' in some respects). Mr Ward thanked me for my time, adding he'd be in touch with an audition time and date. I was certain I'd blown my chance.

I hadn't blown it, though. I *was* called in for an audition, but just as with 'The Rose', stage fright took a deep hold of me and I decided not to attend. *Meh, who wants to be a part of some pissy children's show anyway?* I mean, how many ways can one make a wild goanna look interesting or a flea circus erudite?

One evening Patrick and I were having some 'adult time' when we were disrupted by a knock on the front door.

"Don't you answer that!" I cautioned him.

"I have to, I'm expecting a client. I warned you about getting in the way of my business didn't I?"

"Cocksucker!" I barked, as Patrick slammed the bedroom door behind him to check out his visitor.

Sitting up in the bed, seething with a wrath that verged on homicidal, I waited ten minutes for the visit to end. Twenty minutes ticked by, twenty-five ... enough waiting ... then I completely lost it. Every obscenity I could summon up left my raucous throat. I kicked the bedroom door, punched the walls, threw things around; I created a complete fracas. I simply didn't care anymore. I was finished meeting Patrick's demands, accommodating *his* lifestyle, playing the good girl without due reward or consideration. We were over and I would not pretend any longer.

The front door closed. Patrick stormed, red faced, into the bedroom and began yelling.

"What the fuck are you trying to do Angelica – ruin me? Whether you like it or not I'm running a business, *THIS* is my livelihood so pull your fucking head in! I've had enough of this shit and I'm *not* taking it anymore, understand?"

He pulled the bed sheet over me in disgust and ordered me to get dressed; he was taking me home.

My needs would never be met by Patrick. He didn't want children, marriage was not important to him, he was tight fisted; I had to cut my losses and get out *now*. First, though, I had to win over the handsome Rhys's elusive affections. After knowing the power of love and intimacy I couldn't sit on the sidelines between partners. I decided to double dip, and the game was on.

Rhys's sheepish grin was hard to read; did he really like me or was he toying with me? Regardless of true intention, I was thoroughly enjoying the thrill of the chase. I am the kind of person who gains more from the process than a final outcome, and this process was fun. I slipped on my Formula 1 helmet and hit the tarmac of desire with turbo charged gusto. *See ya later Patrick, I'm no longer in your lane.*

* * *

Peter, the Greek guy in my TAFE class, had purchased a brand new Ducati 916. I naturally found motorcycles very attractive – accessories that spoke of rebellion and freedom. When Peter suggested I go with him on a day trip into the Southern Highlands, I couldn't say *yes* fast enough.

I had become a brazen little thing. I had tasted cock as an adult and I wanted more. I made every move possible on Peter but he politely declined, which, I suppose, I admired and respected. Peter had designs on another classmate and a few years later they were married. I did have a wonderful day with Peter, though and the motorbike ride was a complete adrenalin high.

The feelers I was putting out were attracting all sorts, some good, some bad, but none as enticing as Rhys. He brought in pictures of his ex-girlfriends, showing each trophy to the boys with unadulterated pride. This, admittedly, was something of a turn off. His predilection for 'Playboy' types was obvious, but not to be outdone, I started wearing provocative clothes to TAFE and boy did that get the desired effect. Rhys was now actively flirting back with me, but then one afternoon he made a remark I resented deeply: he asked me if the jeans I was wearing were a size ten.

"No, a twelve; why?" I asked, feigning puzzlement.

"Hmmmmmmmmmmmm," he muttered. "I hoped you were a ten."

First red light.

Rhys, though, embodied 'Joe Cool'. Invariably late for class, he drove a yellow Holden HX Monaro GTS. His green eyes were fronded by a fringe which looked deliberately straightened. He wore a flanno and impossibly slim fitting jeans with black Puerto Rican style 'cockroach killers'. The sleeves of his shirts were permanently rolled up to show off toned biceps, and he wore leather bands on his wrists, à la Morten Harket of A-ha (a Norwegian band, big in the Eighties).

Rhys was obsessed with large breasts. I often caught him perving on Greek Barbara's massive 'cans', generating automatic self-consciousness about my B cup 'fried eggs'.

Second red light.

As the academic year passed, I found myself, so typically, paying far more attention to Rhys than my studies. In July my aggregate averaged 375 out of 550 and this nosedived rapidly. If I didn't attend to my studies I would not get the marks I needed to get into university.

Our class attended a field excursion with Rhys sitting directly behind me on the bus. I recounted to the person next to me plans I was formulating to leave my fiancé very soon. Rhys's ears pricked up as he heard Patrick's name. Leaning over me he asked, "Does this guy fix CBs by any chance?"

"Yes he does. Do you know him?"

"Have you got a picture of him on you?"

"Yep." I showed Rhys the picture of Patrick I kept in my purse.

Instant recognition flooded Rhys's eyes.

"That's him," he smiled. "I was round his place just a couple of weeks ago to get my set fixed. Were you the hellcat screaming her head off in the next room?"

I felt myself go a bright red. Any designs I had on Rhys were now flushed down the toilet.

"Yes I was," I replied sheepishly. "But I can explain."

"No, no need." Rhys was insistent. "I'm sure you had your reasons. He looks like a bit of a wimp, and besides it's really none of my business."

I'd heard the six degrees of separation theory, but this was way too close for comfort!

* * *

In October 1985 I began a romantic relationship with Rhys. *Happy Birthday Patrick!*

Unabashed as ever I broke the ice with Joe Cool during a geography lesson, where I intentionally sat next to him. I asked him if he believed in sex before marriage.

One lunchtime Rhys and I exchanged our first kiss in full view of our cheering classmates. Our first date was scheduled for the following Saturday – dinner and a movie in the city. I was beside myself with excitement. Come the night I was dressed to kill, pacing up and down my guardians' porch. Alfonso, eternally the antagonist, said I had to wait for Rhys out on the porch, and that he was *not* to set foot inside the house because "this home is not a brothel". Six o'clock, pick-up time, came, but no sign of Rhys.

At 8.30 I was still sitting on that tiny porch, gutted and near tears. I imagined the slug, inside, snickering with triumphant delight as he sat shirtless, disgusting as Jabba the Hutt. Defeated, I retreated to my bedroom to change into my nightie and remove my make-up, when a V8 engine came roaring up Bishop Crescent and came to a halt down the laneway. I peered around the corner and saw Rhys getting out of his Monaro. *What the fuck?* I was certain I didn't have the meeting time wrong.

Rhys offered no apology. He just smiled and said, "Okay let's go!"

Showing up on a first date almost three hours late was of no consequence at all, it seemed.

Third red light.

I could hear my mother and the slug fighting about me inside. It seemed more appropriate for me to go on this rudely executed date than stay at home listening to *their* shit – so off I went. Gradually, after some prompting, Rhys did offer a half-hearted apology for his tardiness, but no explanation.

Rhys consolidated himself with copious compliments about my looks. His unassuming demeanour, alongside those looks, also assisted him in reeling me in. As a kisser he was breathtaking and his expert hands had me in the back of his Monaro much faster than my sense of propriety and self-imposed 'three dates' law were comfortable with. But once more the intoxication of pheromones was taking me on a joy ride I didn't want to stop. In Rhys's hands I was easier than putty, but a cautious nagging in the pit of my stomach advised me to have fun but not commit.

Because of the constant put-downs from Mother growing up and because of the incidents with Trepiedi and Umberto, sex outside of a relationship (namely marriage) was a dirty word for me. Anyone who had sex just 'for fun' was 'a slut', and God knew the *only* way to keep a man was to provide sex on tap and absolute monogamy, right? I was privately envious, though, of girls who 'bed hopped' and had the confidence to showcase their sexuality in 'men's magazines' or in clubs. The young, curious, experimental, and freedom loving woman inside of me desired sexual freedom, but the guilty, Catholic abandoned child, desperately craved the commitment and sanctuary of a long-term relationship. I was fucked if I did and fucked if I didn't – both metaphorically *and* literally, it seemed!

Mother was steadily growing jealous of me again. In retrospect I *was* an attractive young woman, I just didn't *own* my physical beauty back then. I believed men were 'in it' mainly for looks, and since I had always lacked admirers I believed I had been left wanting in the looks department. Still, what true mother competes with her child? This I simply could not understand.

At times I would stare very closely at myself in the bathroom mirror, trying hard to see the *real* me. Was the face the world saw so pathetic I could not hold down a relationship? The woman in the mirror stared back, silent; I could not hear her at all so why would anyone else? I was romantically invisible, worthless, undesirable … Any man wanting to fuck me was in itself a compliment, so who was I kidding, really?

Mother started with her litany of put-downs again and there was no way I'd revert to that way of life. Despite my aesthetic insecurities I had grown somewhat in character – just enough to stop me from taking too many steps backwards. A mother who found her own daughter such a bitter adversary cosmetically was ludicrous, but this was Gilda, forever needing the prima donna's stage.

I kept on seeing Rhys and at a party held on his home turf, Rhys introduced me to his friends and their girlfriends. He requested I wear my zebra dress, the one that had caught his eye at TAFE a few months earlier, an outfit that would impress his mates for sure.

Fourth red light.

At the party it did not take long for Rhys to disappear while I was left with a bunch of bleached blonde, bourbon guzzling chicks who seemed no more than skanky appendages to backyard hooligans. I received the stamp of approval from *Yobboland* (lucky me!) and my prize consisted of a pub meal next Friday night at a nearby haunt called the Grandview Club.

Fifth red light.

Before we left the party a sonorous cheer sounded from the crowd: Rhys had smoked a massive 'party cone' in one hit.

Sixth red light.

* * *

We 'made love' for the first time in Rhys's tiny bedroom at his parents' place. It was as unceremonious as my first time with Patrick. I felt it was only right to let Rhys know about my herpes, but he did not bat an eyelid, even refusing to wear a condom, the silly man. Louise, his benign mother, and his father, William, were both home during 'the deed', which made me feel uncomfortable and unethical. Rhys had placed a cricket bat against his bedroom door as a barricade, assuring me 'they didn't care' about what might be going on in *there*. I began to wonder how many other girls had passed through his Joe Cool 'anti-seduction' routine.

Unlike Patrick, Rhys had no reservations about being seen naked. He pulled off his jocks and stretched back on his bed like Johnny Wadd. Looking around Rhys's room, his choice of posters seemed to confirm my gut instinct: he was *not* going to be a faithful partner. When he opened his wardrobe it was waist high with 'men's magazines'.

Seventh red light.

There were porn videos under his bed. Rhys pulled one out, telling me it was his favourite because *Ginger Lynn, the star, could "take a large cock all the way up her ass."

Eighth red light.

There were a few things amiss with Rhys's family. Louise suffered from acute agoraphobia and spent long periods secluded in her bedroom. Here she would speak to noone and, often, starve herself for days. Her husband and daughter had her committed to a mental health institution on a number of occasions with little improvement to her overall condition.

William was a typical 'all-round Aussie bloke' who lived for sport, mates and beer. Lyndall, Rhys's only sibling, appeared to keep mostly to herself.

She was newly divorced and never really left the family home, unhealthily dependent on her doting father – possibly a cause of the divorce.

The derision Lyndall directed at her mother was blatant and painful to watch and I felt a twinge of sympathy for poor Louise.

Ninth red light.

Maybe an hour or so after the 'dirty deed done real cheap', the phone rang throughout Rhys's house. Louise rapped on Rhys's door and he stepped outside to take the call. Re-entering the room Rhys informed me the call was for me.

"I think it's Patrick, your ex," he announced dourly.

WHAT?

I took the receiver with a trembling hand. Okay, so Patrick had Rhys's number because he fixed his CB radio, but how the hell did he know I was here today?

Patrick cut straight to the chase.

"Tell me you didn't fuck him Angelica!"

I was so taken aback I didn't know what to say, except the truth.

"Why?" he screeched. "Why would you do that! I would've married you, you stupid woman! I just wanted you to wait and not go into it on *your* terms. I love you Angelica – I miss you, I was going to fight to get you back, but not *now*."

My throat tightened and I saw the error of my ways, as well as the irreversibility of my actions. The words that came out next didn't even sound like my own.

"And now, now you *won't* have me back even if I come back?"

Nothing that was happening in that moment made any sense. Hearing Patrick talk to me this way with so much pain, so much feeling, such genuine heartbreak, it just did not make sense. I was desperate to capitalise on a rare moment of vulnerability. I would do anything to somehow reverse what I had just done.

"Let me talk to you face to face Patrick, let me explain things, please. Where can I meet you?"

* * *

The night before I was to meet with Patrick I returned home from Rhys's and found Gilda waiting for me in the kitchen, her foot tapping furiously.

"I found some foul smelling underpants in the wash!" She spat the words.

"Huh?" I hedged. I knew exactly what she was referring to. I could feel it running down my leg as we spoke. Mother's eyes bore into mine like lasers.

"I don't like all this coming and going. This is not a hotel. And you're acting like a prostitute!"

Here we go with the prostitute thing again. I refused to engage in Gilda's bullshit tonight – or *any* night. I brushed her aside and announced I was tired and going to bed, I had a final exam the next day and had missed a history exam already. I knew I was failing my HSC, stuffing around with Rhys, and there was noone to blame for this but myself.

Returning from TAFE the next day, I found my belongings strewn all over the yard. Gilda was screaming like a lunatic and our neighbours were out, enjoying the show.

"Get out of my house you dirty slut! You think you can tell me what I should or should not put up with in my own home? Get your shit and go live with your boyfriend, see how long *he* puts up with your whoring!"

For the first time in our miserable lives together I let her have it – all of it. I was through with her and her insanity. Gathering my 'shit' I hopped over to Maria's house to call Rhys. He wasn't home. My only other option was Allira, who drove over from Concord West and dropped me and my things off at Rhys's house. Homeless again, I had noone to turn to but him.

I didn't know what to say to Rhys's kindly parents, and Louise did not demand an immediate explanation. Louise helped me find room inside her son's bedroom for all my things. I then caught the bus to Bankstown to meet with Patrick, feeling like I was betraying the whole world.

Patrick looked thinner and his joie de vivre seemed to have dulled. We sat down at a safe distance from one another on a grassy area of McLeod Reserve and talked until the afternoon turned to evening. Before we parted, I dared to embrace and kiss him. I needed to explore my feelings in order to make yet another decision but found myself falling in love with Patrick all over again. Truth be told I never fell *out of love* with him. Then again, was it really love I was feeling or a disguised, desperate neediness? At the tender age of twenty I don't think I knew the difference.

A week or so later Allira handed me a package. Recognising the handwriting on the front of it I ripped open the padded envelope with zeal. It's funny what can cause the heart to skip when one sees, smells, or tastes desire. Patrick's handwriting had this effect on me right now. Inside the hallowed envelope I found a record, a single. Playing it on Rhys's stereo I wept bitter tears. The song was *'Separate Lives', by Phil Collins (from the 1985 film *White Knights*). I knew straight away this was Patrick's way of saying goodbye to me, but I wasn't giving up on him. Confused and lost I began sleeping with Rhys *and* with Patrick, trying to make a definite choice. Neither man knew I was deceiving the other. If the Eastern philosophy of cause and effect is true, then karma was going to get brutal with me; I was going against all that was moral, honest, and my authentic self.

In the end I chose Patrick. I took my belongings to Allira's and, like a coward, called Rhys from her place, disguising my voice as Allira's. Rhys did not take any of it well and begged 'Allira' to knock sense back into me; he was genuinely in love with me. It was close to Christmas and Rhys had bought me every present he knew I'd like.

"Tell her not to leave me and that her presents are here waiting for her," he pleaded. 'Allira' had nothing more to say and hung up the receiver with a heavy heart.

Almost immediately I moved back into Patrick's place. I replaced my beloved Tessie with another Persian I called Sweetie, but something had changed there and his home no longer felt like *our* home.

My former employers Alastair and Marianne found a spot for me at their cake shop in Summer Hill and life returned to a semblance of normal, but not for too long. When you begin to seriously piss off the driver, that karma bus gets its revs going and heads straight for you.

CHAPTER ELEVEN

DOGMA AND OTHER DRUGS

———

A ccording to the rites of the Catholic Church, on 17 January 1987 I
became Rhys's wife.

* * *

Patrick had seriously kidded himself. He thought he could handle the fact that
his 'virginal' girlfriend had shared a bed with another man, but he could not.
We argued about it at least every other day.

Instead of ordering me out of his life Patrick decided to set me up. He knew
I had been pilfering money that was left in pockets and in and around the flat.
He caught me out one day, and nothing I said helped my cause. Heartbroken
and defeated, Sweetie and I moved out and into a bedsitter close to work in
Summer Hill. It was Patrick who helped me move here.

By now Maria had dumped her fiancé Mark, citing 'sexual cruelty'. She
had given me her engagement ring in exchange for a $400 loan she needed to
get out of some undisclosed 'trouble'. I kept the ring as collateral until Maria
repaid all the money. I had learnt not to trust her anymore. At the same time,
I did not have a bond for the Summer Hill bedsitter, so I borrowed it from
Patrick and gave him Maria's ring as collateral. Life was becoming a comedy.

In Fairfield I bumped into Mark and was subjected to a lengthy oration
on Maria's character and her lack of morality. He then asked me to visit him

at his house in Seven Hills for a further counselling session. Going completely against my grain, I took the long train ride along the Blacktown line, not realising Mark's only purpose for this meeting was getting Maria's engagement ring back.

When I arrived at Mark's house there were four other guys there and the lounge room was filled with pot fumes. Fear rose into my throat; it may have been unfounded but as I found out later in life, my gut never lies. Suddenly I needed to use the toilet rather urgently, something that would happen often as a result of anxiety. Locked inside the loo, where I could not decipher the mood in the joint, I grew even more fearful. During my time spent on that blasted toilet seat, my eyes were fixed on the doorknob and I half expected it to turn suddenly and one or more of the guys to barge in. My gut instinct was correct and the fact that I was not raped or seriously hurt that day forced me to believe in destiny and intuition. The ambience was saturated with malicious intent. When finally, I managed to step outside of the house, unharmed, I let out the greatest sigh of relief. *What on earth possessed me to come here?* I barely even knew Mark. Me, my promises, and altruistic principles … if ever I'd said *yes, I'll do this for you* to someone, I'd keep my word under any duress. I had learnt to put my own needs way below those of others.

Patrick was coming over regularly for sex, and 'no self-esteem Angelica' indulged him, although I felt cheap about it. Our relationship was over but I simply did not know how to let go of him. I often asked myself, and still do, whether *I* had destroyed what might have been a productive union.

I gave Patrick $300 for Maria's ring, the cost of the bond for the bedsitter. He refused it preferring to keep the ring. Maria had repaid, grudgingly, the $400 she owed me and therefore the ring *had* to be returned to her. It became painfully obvious Patrick was saving the ring for someone else – but who, if he was still screwing me? Then, just like that, Patrick stopped screwing me. We had a massive fight and I ordered him out of my home. I would just have to retrieve that damned ring from his flat myself.

Sometimes when a person needs to accomplish something of importance they do so irrespective of personal limitations, and breaking into Patrick's flat was going to be such an accomplishment. I had to get Maria's ring back. Somehow I managed to pull myself up and through the stairwell's manhole, locating the manhole that led into Patrick's lounge room. I crawled through dust and cobwebs inside the roof space and kicked in the manhole cover in with one foot. Squeezing my frame into the small hole, I jumped down the cupboard chute, subsequently destroying both shelves, and triumphantly found myself inside Patrick's lounge room. Go Angelica!

Heading straight for the strongbox Patrick kept in the 'CB room', I decided to retrieve Maria's ring and keep any cash I found for 'services rendered'. Instead of finding dollars or bling, what I did find in that box caught me completely off guard and changed my life forever.

Inside a big yellow envelope, addressed to me, was a very long letter from Rhys: sixteen pages of heartfelt love, anger, pain, and supplications. It was Rhys who truly loved me! I had made a huge mistake – nine red lights and all.

* * *

Life often imitates art. *Simon Townsend's Wonder World!* sent Edith Bliss's replacement, reporter Hugh Munro, to Alastair and Marianne's cake shop for a story on how cakes are made. Alongside my colleagues and employers, I was featured in the clip, feeling rather bittersweet about my first appearance on national television. I could have been that reporter, had I not felt so goddamned incapable.

Following the discovery of Rhys's letter (that had been concealed by Patrick in a final act of treachery) I set about finding Rhys to beg his forgiveness. I called his mother and, with unconcealed austerity, she related how terribly I had hurt her son.

"He barely ate for a month after you left, Angelica. He lost so much weight."

When I found Rhys, he wasn't exactly running back to me with outstretched arms. He was now working in sales for a large department store at the Westfield shopping centre in Burwood. He spoke to me in a quiet and condescending manner and had no qualms in telling me how several girls at the store had shown an interest in him, and, that he was now 'pretty much over' me. Rhys's pained eyes told a different story however as he muttered, "I tried to kill myself you know. I almost jumped in front of a train. You really hurt me."

A few days later Rhys cautiously asked me out to dinner, but we would not be dining alone; two of his closest mates tagged along just in case my 'true colours' resurfaced. For now, at least, Rhys's trust factor in me was a big fat zero.

Eventually Rhys's reserve melted and he presented me with the eight belated Christmas gifts he had bought for me. Louise and William were somewhat reserved, still, and their 'welcome back Angelica' was definitely unceremonious. I knew I could not fuck with this man's heart a second time, but I still had to ask myself why I was really back here.

Rhys began spending most of his free time at my bedsitter, and the initial tenderness he displayed helped me feel more secure about him. Rhys then compounded my newfound security by speaking the words I had so wanted to hear coming out of Patrick's mouth – *will you marry me*. Ah, those magical words … I realised then it was those words I was in love with, and it could have been *anyone* uttering them.

Allira came into the shop to see me and there was something distinctly different about her. I asked her to be my bridesmaid but she gently declined, which shocked me. Who declines being someone's bridesmaid? I then asked Allira about Patrick and with a well concealed smile she informed me he had met someone and had asked her to marry him. A stabbing, all pervasive thunderbolt of pain tore through my body. The only words I heard myself ask were, "Is she prettier than me?"

Allira shot me a disdainful look and declined to answer.

Allira and Rad had finally called it quits after years of struggles, with tradition and culture the cruel winners. A few weeks after the cake shop visit, Allira called out of the blue to explain why she could not be my bridesmaid: Allira, of course, was the 'someone' Patrick had proposed to. It was the last time I'd hear from or see my friend. I had no other choice but to accept Rhys's offer of marriage.

* * *

Rhys was not the bogan he sometimes portrayed. He was attentive, caring, witty, intelligent, and funny. His comedic 'love letters' left me in stitches and were a far cry from the beseeching tearjerker I'd found in Patrick's strongbox. Nevertheless, his predilection for porn and centrefolds was getting in our way. I was finding girlie magazines stashed all over the place, and on one occasion I completely lost it with him. Rhys knew the porn made me feel insecure and unattractive but he would or could not stop himself. I was now competing with professional busty blondes who treated sex as an art form, not an emotion. My bulimia took a definite turn for the worse.

I found Rhys's photo collection of ex-girlfriends inside his room and demanded he trash them. His most recent 'ex' was a Greek girl named Damaris who was not classically beautiful but possessed an undisputed sexiness of a kind I could not pull off. As with Patrick's Cheryl, I developed an unhealthy obsession with Damaris that began to devour me. The previous girls in Rhys's life had been handpicked for their looks and erotic charm and one of them was even Penthouse magazine's 'Miss July' for 1986. I did not feel equipped to compete with any of them, and besides, my Catholic upbringing frowned on exhibitionism, condemning even a hint of anything which revolved around sexual exploitation of any kind.

Rhys slandered Damaris with every breath he took. I found it surprising he could be so spiteful about someone he had claimed to love. He considered Damaris to be promiscuous and common, adding she had slept with every one of his mates and "some chicks too".

"She was my hand-me-down anyway," he said, dismissing her proudly.

During one of his many fights with Damaris, Rhys had reduced her to tears after calling her every defamatory name imaginable. He then turfed her out of his car onto the street. Recalling Damaris's tears and her beg for forgiveness appeared to give Rhys a kind of morbid rush; I could feel the horrible power trip in his voice and see it in his face. As disgusted as I felt, though, I decided to ignore this latest red light (the tenth!) and focus on the positive: Damaris was one rival I did not need to worry about.

Furthermore, according to Rhys, Damaris began to display significant mental health issues. She was subsequently admitted into the same sanatorium his mother had been in and medicated with anti-psychotic drugs that caused her to pile on weight and develop excessive facial hair. There was no regret or sympathy in Rhys's voice as he recounted Damaris's misery – in fact, he appeared to sanction her situation as some kind of just desserts for being 'such a slut'. There were now more red lights flashing before me than I could count, enough warnings to get the hell out of this relationship; but the promise of marriage loomed over me in the way a promise of heroin looms over a hopeless addict. Meanwhile, this Damaris fascinated me and I just *had* to meet her. As it later transpired, Damaris wanted to meet me, too.

* * *

Aside from addiction to porn, Rhys had a second, perhaps more serious problem: an obsession with his hair. He styled it literally for *hours*, and *this* was the reason he had arrived so late on our first date. His mates would mock him about his 'hair issues' and in my naivety I decided that rather than it being a problem, it was simply a reflection of profound personal pride, and better this 'problem' than the copious drinking, smoking, and gambling that his mates engaged in.

By the end of 1986 we'd moved into our own place in Lakemba, a suburb long popular with Lebanese Australians. Rhys didn't like Sweetie so I sadly 'donated' him to my grandmother who fell in love with him at first sight. Letitia had been living on her own in a Housing Commission granny flat for some time after Alfonso, fed up with her complicit behaviour against him, successfully persuaded her to leave Bishop Crescent.

Rhys and I were soon fighting like beasts and he soon became a lot less sweet. His hair obsession was driving me nuts and actually posed a serious threat to our future. By now bulimia had a fierce hold on me and I rarely kept much down but, because the disease was effectively controlling my weight, I did not view it as a health hazard. I again left Alastair and Marianne's cake shop after an irreconcilable argument with a fellow employee, but soon found a similar position in an upmarket cake shop in the Sydney CBD. The conditions there were far worse, with none of the staff hired as permanents and most of them on overseas working visas.

Not long before my impending nuptials I suffered an outbreak of herpes, and again the pain was excruciating. Now that I was to become a 'respectable' woman, Mother had talked me into reconciling with her and something possessed me into confessing my loathsome virus to her. Gilda was shocked and I'm more than certain it compounded her 'loose woman' opinion of me – not that I cared; after all, who was *she* to judge me given her *own* promiscuous track record and frivolous terminations?

Only weeks before I was to walk down the aisle, Rhys delivered some shattering news. The department store he worked in was prosecuting him for larceny and he had been sacked on the spot for the offence. I had every reason to bail out on the wedding *and* the relationship, yet something continued to keep me exactly where I was. I guess given my own shoplifting past I couldn't exactly point the finger, right?

I didn't ask Mother to make me a wedding dress as she had with Maria; I bought a second-hand one from a 'White Elephant' store in Fairfield and modified it myself to resemble an Elizabethan gown. Mother insisted on an eight-foot-long veil that would trail along the infinite aisle of Sydney's majestic St Mary's Cathedral. Maria insisted on being my matron of honour, and as usual the day became all about her; she even refused to buy her own shoes, which helped me cut costs. We were now on a single wage – mine!

My new parents-in-law seemed genuinely happy for us. I had been welcomed into Louise's arms as a second daughter when I took my time and helped her out of the agonising agoraphobia that had sequestered her. Unfortunately, and as ingrained mental disorder would have it, the agoraphobia was replaced by acute obsessive compulsive disorder. Like Rhys with his hair, Louise spent hours by the stove, heaters, side gates and doors, to ensure they were turned off or locked. Louise also prayed out loud ad nauseam, asking God to keep her children safe – not via a single request mind you, but by listing every possible toxic scenario that might occur. This sad ritual took more hours out of her sad life.

I did not recognise it at the time, but there was an unmistakeable connection between Louise's obsessions and Rhys's hair obsession. There is no doubt Rhys was body dysmorphic, and tragically he would pass this hopeless condition on to one of our children.

* * *

Rhys's larceny charge saw him brush right past a prison sentence. He was given the maximum community service penalty and a good behaviour bond. Outside the court I cried with relief but the moment we were home I raged at him with all the fierce abandon that lived inside me. A friend of Rhys's came over during the tirade and, resenting the impromptu intrusion, I dragged Rhys into the bathroom to warn him that if he did not get rid of the friend *immediately*, I would. Rhys just laughed in my face, so I grabbed his right arm and impaled his wrist onto the jagged piece of broken ceramic that served as a towel rail. Blood began to spurt everywhere and I realised how much injury I had just caused him. Forgetting my wrath, I watched helplessly as Rhys bled like a stuck pig. I then begged for forgiveness.

I think Rhys was as shocked and dumbfounded as I was, for he started laughing as if nothing was wrong. I rushed out to the friend sitting quizzically on our lounge, and asked for his help. The friend assisted Rhys by placing a towel around his wrist to stop the bleeding, then bundled Rhys into his rickety old car and drove him to nearby Canterbury Hospital, the same one where Rhys was born in.

I was crying uncontrollably from shock and remorse, but instead of being angry with me, Rhys began consoling me. I didn't understand his reaction at all; if nothing more, I had expected him to call off the wedding.

Rhys served his three hundred hours with the St Vincent de Paul Society 'op shop' in Bankstown, first as a furniture delivery person, then later as a driver. Rhys's assignment was to begin by the end of February, following his return from our Queensland honeymoon which William had kindly paid for. In the meantime, Rhys received minimal unemployment benefits, so the burden of daily living costs was falling solely upon my shop assistant's wage of $11.50 per hour.

I was demoralised and disappointed. I no longer wanted to go through with the wedding – but how would I tell Rhys? He might try and hurt himself again and Louise would hate me. I didn't want anyone hating me – I *hated* being hated. Other nonsensical reasons that compelled me to forge ahead with this wedding included my mother having hand sewn four bridesmaid dresses for nothing, having to live on my own again, Maria berating me with her *I told you so's*, not getting back our deposit on the church, William (with his ocker mentality) thinking 'typical wog', the cows never producing milk again, and the possibility our world might implode and spores of anatomical aberrations would pollute the cosmos! Any excuse seemed a viable option, except the option of listening to my true feelings which were screaming out *NO Angelica, don't do this!*

And then there was the best excuse of all: if I left Rhys I may never find another person who would wish to marry me.

* * *

The weekend before the wedding was my girls' night out and Rhys's bucks' party. Our mutual friends came up with the ingenious idea of taking us to the same location, Kings Cross. Maria made up some bullshit 'boyfriend' excuse and did not attend, so I became Vanessa's slave for the night, Vanessa being the employee who had caused me to resign from Alastair and Marianne's shop. Vanessa manacled me to a heavy duty frying pan and refused to take it off. Marianne, who I chose as a third bridesmaid, organised us to go see the 'Carlotta's Les Girls' show in Roslyn Street. Painful memories of the Stranded replayed in my mind's eye, piercing my heart. Why did I leave Patrick? I did *not* love Rhys.

Halfway through the night we bumped into Rhys and his mates. Naturally his friends had taken him to a 'strip club' which was in fact a smutty live sex show. Any sense of frivolity that had momentarily taken me out of melancholy introspection and doubt came to an abrupt end. I felt disgusted, hurt, indignant, and angry. Had Rhys fucked one of those sluts on stage? He certainly looked high as a kite. Later in the week, Chris, one of Rhys's groomsmen, gallantly leapt to his defence.

"Rhys did not go anywhere *near* those girls Angelica – I *swear*. Yeah, he was asked up on stage, as the buck, but I took his spot; I mean you saw him; he was drunk as a skunk. He couldn't have fucked his own hand!"

Friday 16 January, the night before the wedding: I paced the floorboards of my former bedroom in Bishop Crescent like a tiger on meth. Maria came over and I begged her to change my mind. She was too wise to even try.

"It's too late now Angelica, you should've cancelled everything before when I told you to."

She was right; I simply could not do this to anyone now although it seemed perfectly okay to do it to *myself*.

I woke up the next morning with renewed resolve. I was marrying a *good* man; he loved me, and I was going to make it work. I rushed to the local hairdresser at Bonnyrigg Plaza only to find all the available hairdressers already working on my bridesmaids' hair. I was the bride, the most important member of the wedding party, and yet it was *me* who had to wait my turn? I darted an angry look at Maria, who as my matron of honour should have vacated her spot immediately but, as I would have expected, Maria did not flinch an inch.

Time was running out. I returned home, pulled my hair into a hurried bun, and Mother threw one of her wigs over it. I then jumped into Marcelo's white Holden with my stepfather sitting next to me, on the longest drive of my useless life. I couldn't translate the myriad of hints to save myself the universe had whispered to me over the past few weeks, and yet I considered myself intelligent and sensitive enough to pick up on others' situations. Today, this emotionally intelligent woman was going to commit the most infernal act of treason imaginable against her own person, to avoid *upsetting* anyone else.

Reaching the front portals of St Mary's Cathedral, I looked up at what awaited me inside. Alfonso held my hand and together we climbed the thirty plus steps towards that consecrated entrance. I stopped for a moment, tasting acid in my mouth, a familiar symptom of nerves and fear. Everything inside of me begged not to take another step.

The first bars of Bach's *Toccata and Fugue in D minor* that poured from the cathedral's imposing pipe organ, an ominous piece handpicked by Rhys, heralded what was to unfold for me, soon enough. I bravely placed one foot before the other and crossed the threshold into the abyss.

Arriving at the altar I could hear my mother's voice belt out Schubert's 'Ave Maria' from above me. Looking up, I saw how Gilda took centre stage even now. Any conscientious mother would counsel her daughter on making a poor choice, but not Gilda – *La Soprano*. This sad occasion was just another platform, another stage for her to shine from. Although, essentially, she was never a mother to me, I did not feel completely disconnected from her that day. Somehow she was giving birth to me anew, delivering me from the dark, insular warmth of a toxic womb into the guardianship of a man I was not ready for and did not understand. Who knew what our future might hold?

I gazed into the eyes of my soon-to-be husband: he looked so handsome in his black tails and artificially straightened hair. Rhys smiled warmly at me and then, in that same moment, sought approval from our guests. Had Rhys *only* looked at *me*, held *my* eyes in his, I may have actually believed the illusion playing out before me.

CHAPTER TWELVE

THE MOST BEAUTIFUL GIRL IN THE WORLD

—————

O n our way to the wedding reception Rhys and I engaged in another vicious fight. He told me I'd had bad breath when he kissed me at the altar and I retorted that at least my dick hadn't been inside some Kings Cross slut.

The reception was held in Louise and William's backyard because we could not afford a 'proper' venue – something for which Rhys was principally responsible. Besides a few trays of homemade lasagne, my guardians offered up an operatic duet and I cringed as Rhys's Neanderthal mates laughed their heads off at them. Gilda and Alfonso ought to have picked their audience more wisely but I wasn't about to offer any apologies on their behalf.

On our wedding night we got stuck into each other again, when my new husband said something was wrong with my vagina. I tried my best 'porn siren' act for him, even posing for lewd pictures, but it was not enough. There was always something else I had done wrong. We fought throughout our honeymoon because everything about it was complete and utter crap. The truth was, *we* were crap.

A person died in the motel room adjacent to ours and I saw the body bag careered off by paramedics. Our room was a dingy $20 a night 'hooker hovel', all we could afford for our four weeks on Queensland's Gold Coast – Rhys's choice not mine. Between screams, profanities, and having to wait around for Rhys's hair to look perfect, Rhys took more lewd photographs of me. Only eight days into our trip I had packed my suitcase and was headed for home ... but then he *promised* to do better by me, and I stayed.

Something was indeed wrong with my vagina. Sex felt unnatural and uncomfortable. A doctor in Queensland diagnosed me with cervical warts; I had no idea what that meant but it sounded serious. The final, universal 'get out of this' nuance was delivered to me when my grandmother informed me our flat in Lakemba had been broken into, frightening her and my thirteen-year-old cousin Valeria out of the joint. They had stayed there minding the place for us. The front door was almost kicked off its hinges and anything of value stolen, including something that couldn't be of any importance to anyone but me: my Vatican City Christening certificate.

* * *

Even though it had been violated, I was happy to be home again. At home I was able to escape my lot from time to time. I went to see my doctor under strong recommendations from the Queensland physician and was told I would require laser surgery to remove the warts. There was a huge cluster of them and they looked horrible. The recovery period from the laser treatment was two weeks, with no intercourse for a further four. Additionally, I had to undergo a pap smear every six months because cervical warts are often associated with cervical cancer. I now belonged to the 'high risk' group and would remain in it for the rest of my life. I called the CBD cake shop to get the two weeks off work, but was eloquently advised that as a casual my position could be filled within hours. So, I packed my underpants with Modess pads and continued working – otherwise we could not afford to pay the rent. Money was so tight we ate our meals at Rhys's and my parents, just to have enough left for bills and petrol. It was a bleak start to our new married life.

Much to my disappointment, we had no choice but to give up marital independence and move back in with Rhys's parents. This may have been a blessing in disguise, as Lakemba was rapidly becoming a kind of Middle Eastern ghetto, full of anti-Western sentiment and a marked rise in crime.

While we were still living at the flat in Colin Street a pair of teenage schoolgirls had gone missing; the remains of one of them was found buried beneath the pavers of a business run by non-secular 'Bedouins'. Returning home from work one evening, I was walking alone from Lakemba train station when I noticed a white Holden Statesman creeping slowly behind me. With my long, bleached blonde hair and tight fitting shop girl's uniform I stood out for all the wrong reasons. Frightened but alert, I cut my journey along Colin Street short by pretending I lived inside another block of flats. If I had to, I would not hesitate to kick in someone's door down to seek refuge; I'd be damned if I too would end up beneath some greasy kebab shop's pavers like that poor girl. Sydneysiders were still in shock over the brutal 1986 murder of Blacktown nurse Anita Cobby, with the trial having just commenced in March of 1987. Then there was the terrible shooting by Richard Maddrell of four teenage girls at Pymble, which took place soon after our wedding.

Not long after the Holden Statesman episode, there was a news report on how New South Wales Police had linked a white Holden Statesman to a number of recent failed kidnap attempts on young women in the Bankstown area.

* * *

Louise, who I now called Mum, and meant it, was diagnosed with advanced breast cancer. The doctors removed her left breast and all the glands under her left armpit. The cancer had gone unnoticed for two years, and it was a miracle Louise's life was saved. Louise was also fortunate to have me living with her, for I decided to take care of her post-surgery when everyone else would not. Between her husband and daughter, Louise was treated with the kind of regard one might observe in a piggery; it was no wonder she suffered from so many emotional and physical ailments.

I was forced to leave the CBD cake shop because the laser surgery had been so invasive. The lack of rest brought on some serious consequences and I could not get out of bed for two weeks post resignation.

Rhys and I were now *both* unemployed, with my new husband still serving his community service hours. Oddly but thankfully, Rhys was made a full-time employee; apparently, he had worked so well the St Vinnies manager could not do without him. Rhys's new job offer was both a miracle and a blessing, but it provided me with another set of problems. Rhys was still a driver and deliveryman, but his offsiders were other court order individuals on community service hours. One of them, a Lebanese offender, paid various lunchtime visits to the local brothels, and even offered my husband a 'freebie' as an act of good will and camaraderie. Additionally, Rhys never missed the chance to confide in me how many of his welfare clients were sexy single mothers, willing to give a little of their 'time' for an extra stick of furniture or a 'noone-will-miss-this-one' whitegoods item.

I could see how life would pan out with Rhys as my husband: a perpetual competition with other women – any woman, provided she had big tits, a small ass and the inclinations of a street whore. To keep my husband's eye on *me* and me only I had to be more beautiful and sexually inviting than all or any of them. I felt constantly jealous, and the increased self-consciousness had me hating both myself and my adversaries. My eating disorder spiked once more because I had to do whatever it took to keep Rhys faithful. I could never be slim or sexy enough for Rhys and he mercilessly picked me apart at every turn. When the first sight of cellulite appeared on my thighs Rhys cautioned me on how disgusting he found the condition.

"You better do something about that Angelica. I don't want you having dimply tree trunks for legs, ugh!"

Despite Rhys's open ogling of other women and 'tongue in cheek' put-downs, I tried to make us work. I still found him attractive and my libido was healthy. Ironically, Rhys's had declined significantly. He now used petty excuses to get out of sex like, 'my parents are asleep in the next room', gratuitously forgetting how he snuck me into his bedroom back in the day, barricading his door with a cricket bat. 'So let's move out then!' I'd protest, but it was clear Rhys had no intention of leaving the maternal nest where Louise still catered for him like he was five years old. She adored her son. I felt more trapped in this home, even with benign in-laws I cared for, than I did in ugly, perilous, Lakemba.

Without love all I had was sex to fill a void in my romantic life. Our fights grew more vicious by the day and eventually, to release some of the pressure, I returned to my old self-harming ways. A rather brutal episode took place in front of poor and already tortured Louise. After a particularly violent confrontation where Rhys had literally ripped a shirt off my back, I grabbed a sliver from a glass I had smashed and began slashing myself from collarbone to belly button *hari kari* style. It was not a deep gash but it was enough to shock Rhys into instant withdrawal. Louise gently tended to my wound as I cried uncontrollably. I couldn't have guessed what she might be thinking now about her devoted daughter-in-law, but perhaps now, via the pain and disappointment of our husbands, there could be an unspoken kinship that she quietly understood and accepted. I felt that Louise and I *had* formed a close bond but then again she also openly worshipped her only son, rarely reprimanding his behaviour or misdemeanours. Much to my detriment as his wife, Louise compensated for an abusive marriage and a hateful daughter by babying Rhys every chance she got. She defended him against William's too obvious bias for Lyndall, and from Lyndall herself, who made no bones about how much she despised her brother. I was now part of a family divided and at odds with itself in ways that were far more draining and sinister than my first impressions even hinted at.

Eight months after moving back in with Rhys's parents I finally put my foot down and insisted we move out, back into a place of our own. I had full-time work again as a consultant with a picture framing shop in Town Hall Arcade, working for two young and cheerful Sikh brothers.

Rhys was not happy about leaving his parents' place and opposed every rental suggestion I came up with. When I found a little flat in fashionable inner city Petersham, however, I would *not* be swayed. I hated the notorious Western Sydney suburbs; I wanted to rub shoulders with people who lived clean and actually cared about their lives and environment. We won the Petersham application and moved in straight away. I hoped the lifestyle change might also give our troubled marriage a new lease on life too – pun intended.

It didn't.

Rhys's narcissistic and voyeuristic reports grew more audacious. He even started visiting a certain hairdresser in her own home for 'private styling', telling me how *gorgeous* she was and the moves she kept making on him. The violence in our relationship grew and grew. This was mainly the emotional abuse from Rhys, to which I began to retaliate physically. Finally, I knew I wanted out. I couldn't live like this any longer. There was no purpose to our union and nothing had improved. Unfortunately for me though the universe *did* find 'a purpose' to stay put. On the recommendation of a doctor, I stopped taking the pill for a while to give my body a break. To avoid falling pregnant we used the 'Catholic method' – climax withdrawal. My period was late and, horrified, I rushed out to obtain a blood test and it returned a positive result. No psychosomatic pregnancy *this* time! *FUCK!!!!!! What do I do now?* As a Catholic, I was strongly opposed to abortion but at the same time I no longer wanted a life with Rhys; but then again could I truly raise a child on my own? Mother had but I'd be damned if I'd put a child of mine through what she had put me, and what was more, a child deserved to have a father in her life.

Rhys returned from work one afternoon, his eyes downcast. He then proceeded to tell me something, asking me to sit down first. Before I obliged him I informed Rhys that I too had something to say to *him*.

"Okay then, you go first," he replied.

"I'm pregnant."

Rhys looked up at me with the shadow of gloom disappeared from his face as if old dusty drapes had suddenly been stripped from misshapen and tired windows.

"Are you serious?" He smiled in disbelief.

"Yes." I handed over the lab results.

"Angelica this is fantastic!" he said, laughing and lifting me off the floor for the first time ever. "This is exactly what we need! When I walked through that door I was going to ask you for a divorce! I just can't take your jealousy and accusations anymore Angelica, but this – *this* will save us. I still love you Angelica and I can't wait to meet our child. I want a football team of kids! This is the best news since Canterbury won the premiership in 1984!"

Rhys's enthusiasm was infectious and although deep inside I knew I was only prolonging our misery, I contemplated the old adage that a baby often brings parents closer together. My little one – whoever he or she was – would be a bicentennial baby, due in early September of 1988.

During the course of our pregnancy Rhys failed to change in any way. I felt trapped. Had he spoken first that afternoon when I found out I was pregnant, could it have silenced me? Would I have aborted my child, or chosen to soldier on as a single mother?

Soon after, on 2 May 1987, Rhys lost one of his groomsmen. It was the one who 'took the bullet' for him on his bucks' night. Chris had been hit by an allegedly 'off duty' drunken police officer as he rode home on his motorcycle one night. The inquest into Chris's death took place inside a closed courtroom and Chris's mother was forced outside and kept in virtual darkness regarding a just outcome. The police officer was found to be innocent and was re-instated. Chris had died in hospital only days after the accident from his horrific injuries. On admission, one of his feet was found to have been severed on impact. He was just twenty-three years old.

* * *

I was sitting in my little framing booth inside Town Hall station one morning flicking through the newspaper, when a familiar story caught my attention. On 2 February 1986, Anita Cobby, a twenty-six-year-old Sydney nurse, was brutally raped and murdered at Prospect, following her abduction by five men as she walked home that night. The senseless tortures Anita endured before her throat was slit sent

Sydneysiders into a spin of horror and precautionary behaviour. For a very long time after that unfathomably vicious attack, women ceased taking unnecessary risks, feeling completely unsafe on our streets. Because of five degenerates, an ambience of melancholy and destruction hung over our fun loving state.

The article was as heart wrenching as the crime that preceded it two years before. The article featured Anita's father – the kindly and much loved Garry Lynch – and had the following title:

'I have forgiven their souls, but not the humans'

Mr Lynch also stated, 'We feel honoured and grateful that we were chosen as Anita's parents.'

The feature spoke about Garry's mission – to educate nurses working at the Sydney Hospital, where Anita was an employee, and to ensure his daughter would never be forgotten.

An address for monetary donations to finance Garry's tribute project – the Anita Cobby Memorial Fund – was also supplied but I decided to send in something a little more personal.

My heart went out to Anita's parents. Losing a child must be the most difficult of all personal experiences. I would soon become a mother myself and Garry's and Grace's pain resonated with me more than ever. To lose a child in such a way, knowing she had suffered unspeakable acts of torture for literally hours on end, must surely slice through a parent's soul.

I had a beautiful eight by ten Sacred Heart print that was given to me for my Confirmation only months before the wedding. Peter, my boss, framed it for me, adding a brass plaque below the Christ that bore a few words of comfort for the Lynches. I sent it, together with a long letter of shared sympathy, to the Memorial Fund's address. I did not expect a reply and not receiving one didn't matter to me; the only thing I hoped for was private recognition that a member of the community cared enough about the Lynches' loss, and how I appreciated what they were going through. I patted my growing tummy protectively. If I was carrying a girl, I prayed, as any new parent would, that nothing like that would ever happen to her.

* * *

A young woman stood in the shop's doorway glaring at me sheepishly while puffing out her chest.

"Do you recognise these boobs?" she said, grinning.

I hadn't the vaguest clue who this strange person was. Town Hall was always teeming with vagrants and weirdos.

"Letter? You wrote to me?" she continued.

I had to look twice at the crazy woman before the penny dropped – *Damaris!*

So, Damaris finally stood before me. And she was not the sex siren who had raunchily exposed her impossible legs and centrefold boobs all over Rhys's car bonnet, as seen in the photographs he'd kept hidden in his underwear drawer.

Yes, I *had* written to Damaris a while ago. I didn't know why, other than the fact that her account of life with Rhys might shed some light for future decisions I might take with him. I liked Damaris straight away. She had a way about her that was fresh and European, despite an obvious mental condition. It did not take long for me to discover why Damaris was unwell. Just like with the kids at the Fairfield refuge, I seemed to inspire troubled souls to disclose to me, and boy did Damaris open up!

Her father had been sexually interfering with Damaris since she was a small child, and as older generation Greeks the family guarded their secret well. In the end Damaris replaced one type of abuse with another by allowing Rhys and his friends to disrespect her in a similar way. No wonder the poor girl had lost her mind. I hated Rhys for the part he played in Damaris's moral destruction, but worse was to come. Damaris was convinced she had carried Rhys's baby, but that *God took her to be with Him*. Instead of the usual bitter jealousy I'd felt towards my 'predecessors', I felt only a deep compassion for this young woman. Everything she cared for and trusted had been rudely taken from her.

I never saw Damaris again after that strange day, although we exchanged more letters over the following month. Her letters were unhinged but real, and unfortunately I could do no more for Damaris as her mental deterioration progressed. I hoped the drugs she was being fed at the sanatorium took some of the emotional pain and memories away and that someday Damaris would find peace. Wherever you are today Damaris, you are not forgotten.

* * *

Working in the Sydney CBD had some perks. Actress Heather Mitchell, playwright David Williamson, film critic and presenter Bill Collins, and Mark Lee of the 1981 *Gallipoli* fame, had all wandered around the Town Hall Arcade at some stage and two of them had been customers in my shop. I was never prone to star struck hysteria, but having these 'iconic' Australian celebrities meander by my shop made the attainment of success seem possible. I still longed for fame and fortune as an artist, and who knows, maybe a 'famous customer' might just help me someday.

With Peter's permission I started a little business on the side as a pencil portrait artist. My only client was a woman who wanted her pet dog immortalised. I did my best, although animals were not my forte, but the lady did not like it and the venture ended.

My next artistic endeavour was a series of short stories for magazines like *Cleo*, *Woman's Day*, and the amateur sex manual *Forum Magazine*. *Forum* complained that my story was too violent and declined it. Today, blockbuster novels like *Fifty Shades of Grey* are a hit, yet the sadomasochistic connotations in *my* story were no more violent or derogative to women than many public opinions on *E.L. James's. Lastly, I tried to help my mother's operatic cause by sending a lengthy 'sob story' to Jana Wendt at *60 Minutes*. Much to my delight I did receive a phone call from the current affairs queen, (also dubbed the *Perfumed Steamroller*) but she did not follow through with a report.

As I continued to learn more about our world and its society, I publicly vented my opinions, posting them to the *Daily Telegraph* and *Daily Mirror* 'Letters to the Editor' section. Almost every entry was printed.

Meanwhile my baby continued to grow inside me. Sitting down all day in a confined space five days a week surrounded by food meant I managed to pile on the kilos in very little time. Almost at full term, I weighed a whopping 100 kilos and had developed toxaemia. The swelling made my feet and hands look humungous, and I was duly admitted into hospital for observation, something I found devastating.

The first night in I rang Rhys and begged him to pull me out of there. I didn't know why I was feeling this way; I'd never been in hospital before and I panicked. Perhaps my fear was that with me gone, Rhys would bring home some floozy he'd delivered a fridge to. I was inconsolable but my cries fell on deaf ears. Rhys just yelled at me not to be so stupid and hung up.

* * *

Garry Lynch responded personally to the letter and gift I had sent to the Anita Cobby Memorial Fund. I was blown away. The family had received hundreds of cards and sympathy letters. Below is Garry's note.

My Dear Angelica,

What a courageous person you are to have written such an honest and caring letter to my wife and I and we marvel that with all the horror of your early life you can still find a deep faith in God and we are proud of you for your perseverance with your love.

Some of us have to be very severely tested in our physical life and none more so than our Beloved Anita, and her sacrifice has placed her with God and beside Jesus!

You have suffered and have been sorely tested and having gone through the fire, you are among the chosen ones whose duty it is, to do all in your power to offer support, either by words or direct action, when you find someone in need of a word of loving support which may lift even the smallest bit of their heavy load from a troubled heart.

We ourselves have been very heavily tested and through our faith in God are now able to be of some help and support to a great many, who need our support and the rewards from our efforts are more priceless than Gold.

We are going away until the end of September and when we return would love to hear from you again. You are very special.

Garry and Grace

Attached to the note was a photograph I was familiar with from the many newspaper articles and current affair programs that filled our senses since Anita's senseless murder. On the back of the photograph Garry wrote: 'ANITA Her light shines forever; To: Angelica for caring; From: Grace and Garry.'

* * *

My baby was now overdue by almost two weeks. I was as round as a balloon and felt terribly uncomfortable to say the least, but the medical staff at the Royal Hospital for Women in Paddington insisted I would be okay for a natural delivery.

Three weeks earlier I said goodbye to Peter, Francis, and Town Hall Framing to have my child, convincing them to take on Maria who was unemployed and despondent. Peter had become a good friend over the twelve months I was his employee, but soon he would be closing down the business to travel to India for an arranged marriage. Maria would only be required to work at the shop for a couple of months.

In the very early hours of 26 September I woke up in pain and it felt different from the Braxton Hicks I had become accustomed to. Rhys called the hospital and staff asked him if my waters had broken; they had not, so they advised him to keep me at home until they had. I flatly refused, demanding to go in immediately, as the pain was unbearable.

Upon arrival into the maternity unit I wasn't even one centimetre dilated. My waters were artificially broken and I was placed on various monitors in a little room somewhere away from the mainstream. Almost twenty-one hours after our arrival I was declared 'ready to give birth'. The debilitating contractions had me crying, swearing and screaming like a banshee. The anaesthetist gave me an epidural but I carried so much fat on my spine it took him several jabs to find a suitable spot. The room was full of people, mostly medical staff and students. I really didn't care if an entire circus entourage was staring at my swollen and hairy vagina; I needed this baby *out*.

Earlier in the day there was some discord between Gilda and Rhys because Mother wanted to be at her grandchild's birth. Rhys stood his ground and I vehemently supported his decision. Mother was not getting centre stage this time.

Around 12.45 in the morning on 27 September 1988, the heart monitor started to beep frantically. All I could make out was the voice of a midwife saying, "The baby is in distress!"

Terror shook my core. What was happening with my baby?

My child had opened its bowels inside of me and chunks of green matter were coming out of my uterus. A tube was placed inside *it* and the baby's mouth so it could suck out the particles of faeces. I was now being pumped with induction drugs and baby must come out *immediately*.

I tried pushing but couldn't feel a thing due to the epidural. I was given an episiotomy from 'here to there' and at 1.30 in the morning a little girl was pulled out with forceps. I could hear the gurgle of her tiny throat as the tubes cleared her airways. I was desperate to know she was alright and completely healthy. Rhys readily assured me she was and that the nurses were just cleaning her up. I would soon meet my little daughter.

Alycia Felicity was finally placed on my chest and I cried happy tears. She weighed a whopping 4.17 kilos and was a long 53.3 centimetres. She was pink, clean, blemish free, and breathtakingly beautiful. I fell in love with her straight away.

I looked up at Rhys whose eyes were filled with wonder for our child. That was the only time I can remember feeling close or loving towards my husband.

"She's beautiful Angelica, thank you," he said as, ever so softly, he kissed my brow.

As the medical staff worked on freeing me from the meaty placenta that follows birth, I held Alycia close to me, absorbing her sweet fragrance and almost inaudible breaths. I was totally enveloped in our creation: at long last my life actually made sense. Alycia's little eyes looked up at me as if to say, *so, you're my mummy?* I squeezed her into me with all the adulation any proud mother feels towards her newborn and suddenly I understood why mums so often say the pain of childbirth is forgotten once you're holding that child in your arms.

During this hallowed moment life had changed eminently for the better. My beautiful, chubby, pink, healthy, sleepy baby was soon everyone's main focus and delight. My room was flooded with visitors, chocolates, gifts, and flowers. I couldn't wait to take my Alycia home and begin playing Mummy to her. It no longer mattered that I did not love her father; Alycia filled me with a joy no man could offer. Oh yes, the pain was *so* worth her, and I certainly made the right decision in not having an abortion.

CHAPTER THIRTEEN

MAGICK

———

Alycia was beautiful and my reason for everything. My pure joy. I could not imagine a prettier, sweeter baby. She stole my heart completely. She was a good baby, too. She slept right through the night from the first day and when awake she was happy to lie in her cot just gazing around her room. I did my best to give Alycia a pretty room, given everything came from St Vincent de Paul's. Even with my beloved first child, I was not afforded a decent start.

I grew so confident in Alycia's predictability that I started attending the hour-long gym session across from our flat, in an attempt to shed some of the disgusting 33 kilos I had put on throughout my pregnancy. In retrospect I realise how serious leaving her alone was, but as a new mum, trusting my baby like that was just one of those silly mistakes new mums sometimes make.

I met up with Garry Lynch in dreaded Blacktown where Anita's family lived. Looking around me, hoping to spot him outside Blacktown railway station, I soon recognised the benign, lined face I'd seen so many times on televison, in the newspapers and in magazines. Garry hugged me briefly, sporting a warm smile. We boarded his car to meet with Grace – or 'Peg' as he affectionately called his wife, at their home in Sullivan Street.

On the way to the Lynches' house, Garry took the fateful route walked by his beautiful daughter when she was set upon by the five human beasts who had so brutally taken her young life. I felt a chill run up my spine and from that day the name Blacktown took on a whole new meaning for me.

Grace Lynch was the typical 'wife next door' type: courteous, unassuming, happy to allow Garry to take the debating platform; a subtle strength.

Grace offered me a cup of tea and some sweets. I don't remember what we spoke of overall, possibly about crime and punishment, and naturally about their precious daughter. What *did* burrow inside my memory, never to be relinquished, however, was Garry's disclosure about the media reports on Anita's dreadful death. Garry explained that what the media had released to the public about her demise was not even the tip of the iceberg of what was actually done to her. To then be told that, following the multiple acts of rape and torture that Anita endured, she had remained conscious until John Travers slit her throat from ear to ear, tarnished me with an inner stain I knew I'd never be able to remove. And as for the two people standing before me? The very ones who brought Anita into the world and raised her? How deeply ingrained was *their* inner stain? My thoughts then turned to Alycia, but fortunately did not linger there too long.

Garry added another chilling detail to the brutal story. In order to make a positive identification of his daughter, Garry had to heavily rely on the appearance of Anita's hair, such was the extent of her injuries.

Looking up at a wall in the family room, I saw the framed Sacred Heart I had sent Garry and Grace. That touched me deeply. I was later shown pictures of Anita as a child, as a teenager, as a nursing graduate, at her wedding; she was such a beautiful woman. *How* could they have done what they did and why? How does God allow such things to happen? God, this omnipotent nonentity who was slowly evaporating from my soul and mind. There were so many inconsistencies concerning the God of my upbringing that I was left completely wanting. There simply needed to be another story, and yet, here were two individuals who still believed in a power that failed to intervene at a most crucial time.

"What can I do, *how* can I help?" I asked Garry, fighting back tears.

I knew I couldn't go about my life like before – not after everything I'd just heard. I had to do *something*. I was a good writer, a good communicator, opinionated and logical, *and* I had spirit. At TAFE, Tom, my modern history teacher, played a game which determined the individual potential of his students. Tom pointed an assured finger at me and, turning to the class, he declared, "Here sits a world leader!"

I certainly did not see myself as one. I was more the organiser type – I hated the limelight. I was a background person and I enjoyed the thrill of the chase far more than the prize. Also, leaders get shot, and although I'd been miserable I was not yet ready to die.

"Angelica, you can support others the way you've supported us," Garry replied. He then told me about a group being trialled in Parramatta called V.O.C.A.L, or the Victims of Crime Assistance League. Maybe the quest to assist others could begin here?

I returned to the Lynches a second time, with Rhys and Alycia in tow. Grace produced SAO biscuits with cheese and tomato this time. Rhys was deeply moved by the Anita Cobby story, too. I had to change Alycia's nappy and Garry offered me Anita's bedroom.

"Oh I couldn't possibly do it in there!" I protested.

But in I went, for Garry had insisted and I couldn't refuse a holy man. Entering Anita's room, I felt like I was about to desecrate a shrine. On the bed Anita once slept in, I very carefully rolled out the nappy change mat. Anita loved to draw and some of the artwork that had been used in the newspaper stories hung above me on her bedroom walls. I lost sight of Alycia for a second as I dug into the nappy bag to retrieve some Wet Ones. While I had my back turned to her, she had grabbed a seashell from a nearby shelf. The delicate shell had been the subject of one of those hallowed drawings. I swiftly grabbed it from Alycia's tiny hand just as it appeared she would toss it to the ground. My heart skipped a beat; these simple items were all that were left to mark a precious, now extinguished life. They were cherished and priceless. Once the sound of my beating heart quietened, I felt something in the room. It was nondescript and fleeting, but whatever it was left an indelible imprint on my soul. Anita aiming to catch her shell perhaps?

Garry told me Anita visited their home often and that her visits gave him and Grace a greater sense of peace and purpose. I did not doubt this for a moment. I knew there *was* life after death.

* * *

Rhys finished up with Vinnies due to back problems resulting from constant handling and lifting of heavy furniture and whitegoods. He now worked as a Night Captain for Woolworths. I was relieved to know he was no longer visiting private homes but still, it did not stop him tormenting me with reports about who was or was not attractive here as well. I had recently lost 27 kilos on a 'carb free' diet which Courtney Love swore by after using it to prepare for her role as a heroin addict in the 1996 film, *The People vs Larry Flint*. Regardless, my stomach was overstretched from the pregnancy and my once taut stomach was never again to rebound.

Once the honeymoon period of a new baby dissipated, Rhys and I were at each other's throats once more and I began to daydream about what might have been had I not ruined things with Patrick. I could not forgive Rhys for the emotional suffering he had put me through – was *still* putting me through. He was autocratic, spoilt, and cruel. He would seize any opportunity to put me down and keep me there. 'If not for Alycia,' I frequently thought, 'I would walk out on this marriage today.'

A moment I would never allow myself to forget had occurred when I first breastfed Alycia at the hospital. My nipples were so sore they had cracked open, with blood pouring out which then mixed with the baby milk inside Alycia's mouth. Breastfeeding had been highly recommended by the nurses to pull the uterus back into shape, but the pain felt exactly like labour contractions. I was in tears and shrieking from the agony each suck incurred, yet I persevered. My daughter was worth it. Instead of attracting Rhys's understanding, praise and support, he looked at me ostentatiously and hissed, "Look at all the other mothers breastfeeding in here Angelica. I don't see any of *them* whining the way *you* are!"

Rhys's hair-based body dysmorphia was now relentless. Every single day he was at it, never for less than two hours and sometimes up to five. His record was an incredible *nine* consecutive hours because he needed to look his best for a work staff party. Rhys also made no effort to mask his ongoing ogling and voyeuristic behaviours. He was vocal about my pregnancy weight gain and how it disgusted him. In his eyes my appearance defined who I was inside and how this reflected on him to a watching world.

Money passed through Rhys's hands like water. He was obsessed with performance cars and during our first two years together he owned four of the infernal petrol guzzlers. We were so poor from mismanaged debt that one week, unable to purchase groceries, I approached a local Salvation Army depot for food stamps.

I remembered how 'Miss July' had told me she'd earned $5000 for two *Penthouse* spreads and a whole lot more for the Black Label edition, so naturally I began toying with the idea of doing something like this myself. My body was far from the 'glamour' ideal but I still had a chance with *Picture Magazine*'s 'Girl Next Door' competition. The only person I told about this was Maria but, of course, instead of seeing it as my desperate attempt at making ends meet, she went into competition with me by seeking out a 'Page Three Girl' stint for *The Mirror*.

Maria's name was coming through Rhys's lips often nowadays. Everything was *Maria does this* and *Maria can do that*. Yes, Maria had the type of body Rhys would kneel for, and yes, Maria worked hard at maintaining it, but Maria was not a healthy girl on the inside – either morally or physically. Anorexia nervosa remained at bay but Maria was a heavy smoker, loved to drink and party, and had begun investigating recreational drugs. She was now engaged to John, an Italian health food shop owner, but Maria did not take a leaf out of John's entrepreneurial book. She was more interested in the shop's takings.

Emotional and material security did not make Maria a better person. I felt alienated from her and the only reason I remained in touch with her was because *she* pursued a friendship with *me* and I didn't know how to discourage her. Confrontation has never been my forte and I still had a long way to go before I would learn how to use diplomatic assertion. Maria was an attention whore: she knew she could lure men at a glance and absolutely relished the challenge. So she did very little to deflect or redirect Rhys's puppy dog eyes and salivating nods.

One day, as we sat around the dining table for lunch at the new home she shared with her fiancé, Maria produced a handful of photographs. Deliberately handing one over to Rhys, she asked, "Rhys, do you think I look fat in this picture? It's probably my worst one."

Rhys's eyes lit up. "Hell no! You look fine!"

"Let *me* see," I asked curiously, reaching out for the picture.

There in glorious technicolour was a perfect size eight Maria seductively showing off her blue micro bikini. *Pffffttttt!!! The bitch did this on purpose!* I itched to reach over to my socalled friend and rip the smug look off her face. Okay, I did not love Rhys, but that didn't mean I'd take this type of disrespect either. I despised homewreckers.

Rhys's view of women was pathologically distorted. For Rhys women were primarily a decoration, an extra on his beloved car, or a glittering prize of sorts. I don't think he appreciated a woman having much of a functional brain, in case she undermined his authority or uncovered the misogynist that dwelt beneath that quiet exterior.

Rhys's open discussions on women often included the following: under no circumstance must a woman divulge that she defecates, urinates, passes wind, or picks her nose; she is not to put on weight, have stretch marks, cellulite, or suffer halitosis or wardrobe malfunctions. I remember Rhys bragging once that he didn't ask a girl he liked out because his mate told him he'd 'heard her fart'.

When I lived in Summer Hill my ensuite echoed dreadfully, so in order to avoid one of Rhys's discourses on why 'women don't shit', I had to go through a painstaking ritual of filling up the bowl with toilet paper and then sitting right on the edge of the toilet's lip so that the poo or pee would slide down the S bend and into the paper, thus muffling any splashing or plopping sounds. If, God forbid, flatulence made its vile and vaporous presence felt as it escaped my 'oversized derrière', I would soon receive a barrage of insults: *butcho lesbian, wharfie, bushpig, masculine, buzzard*, etc. etc.

Only days before Alycia's first birthday, I gave into the nagging impulse and telephoned Patrick. I was surprised he was still at the same place and number, but much to my sadness there was no *Hey Angelica, how are you? Nice to hear from you.*

"Why are you calling? You're a married woman with a child; what the hell are you doing contacting me? Wake up to yourself Angelica, it's over between us!"

I did not call Patrick again but the notion that we could have been good together continued to live inside my head. If only I had left that damned strongbox alone.

I tried so hard to deal with Rhys's blatant 'appreciation' of the female form but found it demeaning and disrespectful towards me as his wife, and as the only person he needed to feast on. Surely this behaviour constituted emotional infidelity?

For Rhys's twenty-fourth birthday bash I hired a stripper. This was to try and 'train' myself into accepting his predilections. It didn't work out too well and I found myself battling the urge, as she unzipped my husband's trousers, to jump up on stage and pull the slut off him. But why did I care anyway? I didn't love Rhys, I don't think I even liked him. I guess I had felt cheated of what was mine for so long I refused to give any more up – even if I no longer found any use for it myself.

My inner torment was manifesting itself in dreams. Before Rhys and Patrick, the ghoul who had chased me in my sleep was Mother; now it was Rhys. I never slept soundly or blankly. My dreams were extensions of the life that I'd become convinced I was cursed with.

* * *

Regardless of personal pain, I gave in to Rhys's relentless demands for a second child. Mea culpa.

Although I worshipped Alycia, morally I was not ready for another child, and if I did have another there'd be no way out of the marriage. I couldn't understand myself at all. I'd left home without life skills or resources and made my way through circumstances of all kinds since; why wasn't I now able to move on from a dysfunctional marriage? Here I was, going toe to toe with Rhys, arguing like a demon and yet I'd always end up giving in to him. Perhaps I was terrified of going it alone, but truth be spoken, I was afraid of hurting the peripheral people in my life more … like my well-meaning parents-in-law, people who were there for me, and were the proudest grandparents anyone could ask for. Louise and William had treated me far better than my own parents ever could. And there was *another* factor: living with the fallout of never having experienced the love of a true father figure, I did not want Alycia to grow up without her natural father. All of these 'reasons' compounded my martyrdom.

In September 1990 I realised I was very much pregnant. I hoped we were having a boy, to keep Rhys happy and to keep me from having to conceive again. Rhys was the last to carry the family name, so having a boy would get him off my back. Louise had several miscarriages which were identified as males and apparently something about her blood group made her unable to carry a son. Rhys was an unexpected fluke. While pregnant with Alycia, I'd been told my and Rhys's blood were incompatible and that Alycia would require a special blood test at birth to determine her ability to generate antibodies efficiently.

In the meantime, for monetary reasons (and a free trip to Adelaide) I applied to go on the TV variety show *Wheel of Fortune*. I loved solving the puzzles at home, and after the *Simon Townsend's Wonder World!* fiasco, I was still itching to somehow get on television. Getting to see my cousins again was a bonus – I so missed them. The last time I'd seen them was during the Grand Prix in November 1987, when I'd travelled there with Rhys. Without the privilege of 'proper' siblings I had adopted my cousins instead. Valeria, especially, was the one I felt closest to. Given some of the cards and letters I'd received from her over the years, I felt she reciprocated my feelings. One fine day I'd return to South Australia and we'd be reunited, for true love knows no boundaries and I'd never enjoyed Sydney like I did Adelaide.

Alastair and Marianne were giving me the odd day's work here and there, which saved our bacon from week to week, but with a two-year-old at home and a second child on the way there was not a lot I could do outside of casual hours. For a while I worked for a shameful $5 an hour inside a tiny kiosk at the Central Railway Station. My employer was a matriarchal Russian fake blonde who expected a lot for the little she paid me. I made up for what was owed by stuffing myself with her delicious piroshkies and chocolate slices. I lasted a month; it was all just too hard, with Rhys working nights and needing his sleep during the day.

I spotted an advertisement that asked for people to do some ironing from home. Snapping up the opportunity, I brought in a tidy sum doing that. I also applied for a 'Mystery Shopper' position, travelling all over Sydney on buses and trains conducting surveys, with Alycia in her pram. In the end my combined efforts conquered both our financial commitments *and* Rhys's penchant for petrol guzzling 'mean machines'.

I wanted my driver's licence badly: it meant not having to struggle with prams and baby bags on public transport, but I still refused to learn to drive a manual – and particularly Rhys's car. Rhys had absolutely *no* consideration for any of my wants and needs – it was always about him. He would not agree to an automatic car for me to learn in and I felt like the most neglected of wives. I continued to wonder about how pampered I might be had I waited for Patrick; he knew how to make and *keep* money.

One afternoon I heard a knock on our front door. There, standing in the foyer with a big happy smile was Doug. I was overjoyed; it felt like forever since we'd last spoken. Maria had managed to divide us, but in the end, even under so much duress, true friendship was never completely lost.

I introduced Alycia to Doug and he was smitten by her bucktoothed cuteness. Doug picked my daughter up and playfully flung her over one shoulder, and my little two-year-old was not the least bit afraid of him. Doug loved kids and wanted some of his own – part and parcel of a tight-knit Indigenous culture. My love for Doug came flooding back as I told him how desperately unhappy and isolated I felt under Rhys's thumb. A sympathetic hug from someone who knew me well momentarily filled the weeping void.

Around the beginning of 1991 I was hanging out clothes in the downstairs courtyard when something caught the corner of my eye. A book or something like it had been placed on the brick fence out the front of my block of flats. Looking around I picked up the book, *Mind to Mind. The book was written by a clairvoyant and spiritual healer named Betty Shine. No one was around trying to claim it so I opened the cover in case its owner had written contact details inside. Scribbled in pen was an appointment time for 4.15 pm, with beneath that the name 'Sally' and a northern suburbs phone number. I dialled the number but the line was disconnected so I decided to keep the book and then put it away for posterity.

* * *

Rhys and I had yet another huge argument. It was his birthday and his parents gave him $400. I thought he might spend it on new things for our second child but instead he intended to blow it on more 'boys' toys'. I was very jealous of the love Rhys's parents lavished on him; I could only dream of such generosity coming from *my* former guardians.

When you don't love someone you resent them having more than you and I certainly resented Rhys in this way, and every other way. The tantrum I vented onto Rhys saw him frenziedly tear up the fifty dollar notes in a fit of rage the like of which I had not seen before. Rhys put a rip into our brand new vinyl lounge when he picked it up and impaled it on the second settee. This sent me into hyperventilation and Rhys was forced to call an ambulance in case I had hurt the baby growing inside me. It was a very dark day in my lacklustre life and all I could think of was how to escape this horrible, frightening marriage.

But the new life due in a few months ensured I'd be remaining inside my emotional hell. Where would I go and what could I do? I had no warm 'family hearth' to fall back into. Slogging it out there with two babies all on my own would be too hard; I'd already had a taste of that, just on my own. I knew I couldn't leave and that I'd become none other than a self-imposed prisoner of misguided, fear-fuelled decisions.

My waters broke on their own this time. It was 1 May 1991. Once again my husband drove me to the Royal Hospital for Women in Paddington, and yet again I was barely dilated. Nineteen hours later the familiar and dreaded contractions began. I begged the nursing staff to get me some pain relief but I was a public patient and the anaesthetist was preoccupied with a long list of private patients. The gas made me ill so I opted for 'white knuckle' pain management, swearing and screaming my head off and almost yanking the bedhead out from behind me. Rhys, as always lacking both initiative and altruism, was more interested in making adjustments to his video camera so he could film the birth.

During the twenty-first hour of labour I was at last granted an epidural. It had not been administered correctly and only the left side of my body had become anaesthetised, leaving the pain to concentrate in my right side. This relentless agony was so distressing that on more than one occasion I thought I might faint. Around 2.30 in the morning I felt the urge to push, and so at long last the process of delivery began.

Because I could not feel my left leg one of the nurses had to keep it propped up for me. The pain in my right leg was unimaginable but at least I did not feel my vulva tearing.

At eleven minutes past three in the morning on 2 May, another beautiful baby girl was born to me. We called her Kristen Danielle. She was smaller than Alycia, 0.69 pounds lighter and 1.2 centimetres shorter. Kristen had a yellow tinge to her, which the midwife said was caused by jaundice. My second daughter was the polar opposite of Alycia, sporting a thick, dark mop of hair and big brown eyes. Unlike my sleepy, happy firstborn, Kristen looked serious and did not cling to my chest the way her sister had. This time around the hospital staff seemed cruel. Only moments after Kristen's birth, they forced me out of bed unassisted to transfer me to another room. Because my left leg was still numb I fell onto the floor and almost ripped open my episiotomy stitches. I was then wheeled into a corridor and left there on my own for almost an hour as hospital staff waited for a vacant bed.

Rhys was nowhere to be seen. He had followed the nurses who were now bathing Kristen and testing her for jaundice. I remember sitting in that poorly lit corridor, still in agony, pondering how life could be so spiteful to a well-meaning person like me. I couldn't take any of what I'd done back. I was trapped, condemned to a loveless life, with my daughters raised by a sad mother, an obsessive compulsive father, and in a home where every move was forced or strained. I was, I realised, no better than Gilda, the one person I had vowed never to become.

Even without the uterine pain of breastfeeding I was more determined to nurse Alycia than I was Kristen. With Alycia the never-ending flow of visits and fuss brought on by friends and family had not fazed me, yet with Kristen the very thought of curious onlookers made me cringe. All I wanted was sleep … lots and lots of mind numbing sleep. I took full advantage of the nursery, allowing staff to look after my baby, feeling resentful and angry whenever Kristen was brought to me for feeds and nappy changes. Could people not see that all I asked for was some alone time, some 'me time', some peace and quiet? Reality was not about 'me time', however. I didn't know it at the time but I was hopelessly in the clutches of postnatal depression.

Once I took Kristen home my mood began to pick up a little. In spite of everything, I got down to the task of mothering two adorable, healthy little girls. As the cost of living rose and I found myself unable to work, we submitted an application for government housing. I really wanted to remain in Sydney's trendy inner city, but for this locality the waiting list was over a year. A three-bedroom townhouse came up in Auburn, a 'multicultural' suburb in Sydney's Inner West. Rhys wanted to wait out the year, saying Auburn was 'full of Lebos', but I wasn't coping with the financial strain and the children's bedroom at the Petersham flat was far too small for two kids. Also, the lesbian living below us was continually holding noisy parties, and her open and sonorous love life was starting to bug me. We accepted the offer and moved out; Kristen was just one month old.

Auburn is a predominantly Turkish, Middle Eastern, and Asian suburb. Having lived here once before with Allira I was familiar with the area and did not feel overly estranged. My social, jovial personality helped me familiarise and integrate with the locals and so I was rarely met with racial derision or ostracising. Only once did I suffer a significant episode, from a pair of Muslim women in black burqas with only slits for vision. It occurred inside the Commonwealth Bank and my colossal response to their unfair and unprovoked slandering was well received by the other customers. What these 'ladies of the garb' had failed to realise was that I had learnt a number of choice Arabic words myself and I knew what they were saying about me. The Lakemba near-kidnapping was just about forgotten by now and I was willing to co-habit with my Bedouin neighbours.

Each month, Rhys's hours at Woolworths were cut back more and more. I started harassing him about finding another job. Australia was on the verge of a major recession and jobs were scarce. Paul Keating, the then Treasurer (and later Prime Minister), famously described it as 'the recession we had to have'. Additionally, he proposed changing our flag, turning Australia into a republic, and during a time when our 'own backyard' was in dire need of welfare assistance, he gave precious funds to multiculturalism and the arts. Keating and his feudal consorts dubbed this audacious madness 'big picture politics'. It may have been around this time that I turned my thoughts to local politics, making some enquiries at my local council.

One evening while we were watching *Australia's Funniest Home Video Show* Rhys suddenly exclaimed that he could stage a situation that could win us a major prize. Out came the detested video camera and I was ordered to play a role not too different from how things were in real life. If I had to name one director who used the same modus operandi as Rhys, it would be Charles Chaplin. He was never satisfied with the first, tenth, or twentieth take, but kept forcing his actors to repeat themselves until he finally deemed the scene perfect. The skit for *Australia's Funniest Home Video Show* only served to compound my hatred of acting – and of Rhys.

In the meantime, I dusted off the book I had found in Petersham, *Mind to Mind*. All this clairvoyant and psychic healing business was extremely interesting, but far removed from everything that had been ingrained in my head concerning Catholicism, God, and the ever after. What I discovered inside the pages of this little book, though, made a hell of a lot more sense to my inner scout. It was also positive and uplifting fodder for the soul: no guilt mongering, no fire and brimstone or eternal damnation. I scoured Auburn library for another Betty Shine book but returned with another written by a famous British medium called Doris Stokes. This was the same medium a furious Don Lane had defended from a sceptical James Randi in the famous *Don Lane Show* episode.

A light switch seemed to flick on inside my head and I was now searching for more bulbs, until I could light up a ballroom. Metaphysics and esoterica were the answers I'd been looking for since I first began to rummage through Mother's 'scary' magazines in Rome. This belief system addressed questions such as, *Why does God forget 'His children' and allows the righteous to suffer?*

If I kept at it, perhaps I'd find an answer to my own suffering as well? I felt renewed, as if I'd just uncovered a gold mine, and it reminded me of a bumper sticker I saw that read 'Magic Happens'.

CHAPTER FOURTEEN

FAUST, WHAT FACE DOST THOU WEAR TODAY?

———

Rhys's idea for *Australia's Funniest Home Video Show* proved very successful, so much so that even a few nightclubs played our clip on their big screen.

In September 1991 our clip appeared on the show, with the producers naming the segment 'Legcam'. The plot for Legcam was simple: it featured me talking into the video camera as if I was sending a message to an overseas relative. Discussing this and that at the Auburn Japanese Gardens with little Alycia on my lap, Rhys suddenly pans and frames his camera lens on a 'yummy mummy' passer-by. Maria strolls in the background wearing high heels and short skirt as she manoeuvres two month old Kristen inside her pram. Discovering the reason, the camera is no longer on me and our daughter, I turn and exclaim at the top of my lungs, "What are you doing you BLOODY PERVERT?"

Jealously enraged I charge at Rhys and knock the camera from his hands … a clear case of life imitating art.

The thirty second set-up did us proud. We won the weekly first prize, a nine night Sitmar cruise for two adults and two children on the TSS *Fairstar*. This wonderful opportunity was only marred by my discovery, when I applied for a passport, that I was not an Australian citizen. Once again I was horrified and disgusted with my guardians; back in 1975 they had obviously applied for Australian citizenship and forgotten all about *me*. Only two months before departure, on 12 December 1991, I took my citizenship oath at The Rocks, overlooking Sydney Harbour. I did not understand how I was allowed to vote all those years – and besides, shouldn't marrying a native and having naturalised children automatically *make* you a citizen?

Our Legcam clip was then chosen for the show's Grand Final, taped on 20 September 1991 in Brisbane. We won the third prize this time – of airfares to and accommodation in Anaheim and Oahu. We were beside ourselves. The only glitch was money for meals and spending money. We had zero savings and were forced to defer the two-week trip for as long as the network allowed us, until we could save up some extra cash. Rhys had lost his job as Night Captain and was now unemployed, in the thick of a national recession we 'had to have'. I was getting a few days here and there with Alastair and Marianne in their new wedding cake showroom, but that wasn't nearly enough to keep us going, let alone save up for a holiday.

A friend of mine told me about market research groups that were being held all over the city and Inner West. I promptly put my name down with an agency and began attending various groups under different aliases. The hardest thing about these groups was remembering which name I had with what agency. Not long after I started, Rhys jumped in on the action and together we made a neat sum. One focus group I attended in Parramatta had to do with a TV pilot for a new hospital drama called *All Saints*. I thought it was a pathetic episode and vocally spoke against it, turning the entire room against it by the end of the research session. Fortunately for actors like Eric Thompson, the other focus groups must have voted *for* the episode because *All Saints* went on to become a great success, and I for one a devoted viewer. My favourite *All Saints* character was Bronwyn Craig, played by Libby Tanner, who later, in 2002 and 2003, received Logies for her performances.

During this time in our lives Rhys went completely stir crazy with creative juices. He figured if only *one* of his many ideas could make it like Legcam had, we could change our living conditions significantly. Rhys's creations completely took over from looking for work, and the family imbalance it caused sent me into a new spin of despair. I *hated* Rhys being home all day; it interfered with the routine and the semblance of peace I enjoyed either on my own or with the girls. Rhys was also forcing me to perform more ridiculous roles for his stupid video clips almost every other week. Here I was, having to fulfil daily domestic and motherly duties while my husband entertained himself with idiotic experiments. My resentment barometer was close to blowing a gasket.

For almost four years Rhys remained hopelessly unemployed. The anger and frustration I felt cemented the deep-seated knowledge that I did not love and would never love my husband – no matter how hard I still tried. I busied myself in any way possible just so as not to pick fights with Rhys. I had already learnt that Rhys's flash temper could reach its peak without warning and that the devastation caused was simply not worth it. Rhys and I were a lethal mix, given my own temper, which could reach homicidal heights just as quickly.

In between our many ventures, care of the Department of Social Security, the Housing Commission, and TV networks, I was posting out up to twenty job applications a week for Rhys, hoping that *someone* might take pity on him and pull my husband out of the house with a job offer. To save for the overseas prize we had won the previous year, I travelled every day to Meadowbank to assist in the set-up of a brand new Franklins 'Supa-Centa'. Without providing a tax file number, three weeks was all I could get away with. The $1000 netted was the only sum we would take with us overseas.

On 21 November 1992 our family of four boarded a Qantas jumbo bound for California. Our excitement was marred somewhat by Maria who demanded we split the prize, given her appearance in the video. If by now I wasn't convinced my former best friend was an inconsiderate and selfish narcissist, this ridiculous and impossible demand had sealed the deal.

"So tell me Maria, do I just stay home and *you* go with Rhys and *my* children, or should I just take your fiancé instead and Rhys can run your shop for two weeks?" I humoured her, hoping to open up some logic, thickly hidden beneath those oversized eyelashes.

I was a classic 'people pleaser' who suffered from Caretaker's Syndrome. Deep inside I wanted to dislocate arms and break necks, but on the outside I smiled sweetly and endured what in fact were a myriad of systematic abuses. My friendship with Maria was now a host/parasite relationship: she was a self-appointed alpha female and I her little lap dog. Exacerbating everything that was vile in our relationship was Rhys, who now unashamedly worshipped the ground Maria walked on. To appease her bullying, Rhys promised she would 'star' in his next video and twothirds of the ensuing prize would go to her – no questions asked.

In February 1993 John married Maria, who was then three months pregnant. I was not matron of honour or even a bridesmaid. Rhys and I received an invitation late in the proceedings and I, congenial and polite as always, decided to attend when what I *should* have done was tell the bitch where to get off, finally ending things with her.

* * *

Disneyland was fantastic and I loved every minute of it. Alycia too enjoyed herself but Kristen, at only eighteen months old, was entirely unmanageable. Rhys and I took turns at the hotel with Kristen because everything about our special adventure frightened her – even Mickey Mouse. The flight too was a disaster. Kristen would not remain in her seat, crying, kicking and screaming. With all reasonable parental controls and resources failing us, Rhys and I were ready to choke our youngest daughter. I resorted to dosing Kristen with Phenergan, placing my sleeping toddler on the floor under the seats in front of us. Finally, some peace. Then an androgynous flight steward saw Kristen's tiny feet inching their way into the aisle, and boy did we receive a well-deserved reprimand from the outraged steward, complete with a lecture on what turbulence might do to a two-year old's body.

Rodeo Drive was a rort, no fancier than Sydney's Queen Victoria Building or Bondi Junction Plaza. Hollywood, and the obligatory celebrity homes tour, paled in comparison with the millionaire homes lining Sydney Harbour, Point Piper, or Palm Beach. Hollywood Boulevard was filthy and unkempt. I was particularly appalled by the presence of a squashed hamburger covering my idol's star. I knelt down to peel off the offending waste from Marilyn Monroe's special tribute. Years later I read Anthony Summers's account of Marilyn's life and felt a little less enamoured with her. As with my newfound love of snakes, I only decided to fall in admiration with Marilyn to spite Mother.

The heavily processed food in America is horrid and I suffered diarrhoea my entire week in Los Angeles. Con artists and beggars smelled us out, trying to solicit money from us pretty much wherever we went. For me, there was nothing endearing about the City of Angels; it was more like the city of hobos and smog. Nevertheless, invaluable memories were created at locations like Magic Mountain where I boarded 'The Viper' – the world's tallest and fastest rollercoaster, and sat next to a Japanese tourist who was so frightened she did not stop screaming and crying until the end of the ride. I also enjoyed Universal Studios where as a movie buff I could not get enough of the original set props for legendary films such as *Psycho*, and *Jaws*' own mechanical shark.

I bought Rhys a replica cavalry handgun from Knott's Berry Farm, and came face to face with a vomit-laden Regan MacNeil and Elvira, Mistress of the Dark, at the Hollywood Wax Museum. All in all, Los Angeles was an experience, one I would not have lived had Rhys not conjured up a legitimate way to ogle Maria's legs and backside. With the thick ring of smog that circled the entire San Fernando Valley, though, I pondered the sheer number of Californians who might die of lung cancer that year alone.

Oahu was a much nicer and more relaxing experience. Its touristic aims were somewhat repetitive and the place is too blatantly commercialised, but visually it was beautiful – with its surrounding oceans, dividing ranges, and the majestic volcanoes, Waianae and Koolau, which formed the island over two million years ago.

We visited the famous Hanauma Bay, immortalised by Deborah Kerr and Burt Lancaster in that legendary kissing scene in *From Here to Eternity*. I watched a much awaited *Bram Stoker's Dracula* at the Waikiki Cinema while Rhys babysat the girls at the hotel, probably consoling himself with the porn channel once our babies went to sleep. Gary Oldman was brilliant in the role of Dracula; I promised myself that someday I would visit my favourite anti-hero's castle in Transylvania. We ate chocolate covered macadamias till we burst, and feasted at *luaus* held over magnificent sunsets, flanked by beautiful indigenous dancing girls and muscular fire-eaters as they wowed the audience with their home grown skills.

There was a boat trip on 'The Barefoot Catamaran Cruise' where Alycia and I took a perilous ride on a floating trampoline. A sunshine-filled day at the *Paradise Park* finished off our 'Aloha' trip beautifully. In Hawaii I did not get sick once: the food was so much fresher and the air cleaner. The only thing I regret *not* doing was to pay Pearl Harbor an honorary visit on our way back to the airport. Rhys preferred to browse the endless shops that sold nonsensical merchandise than pay homage to a significant part of World War II history. Cultural acumen was never high on Rhys's list. I myself am not a fan of war, but I do believe in showing respect to the men and women who bravely fought for their country by visiting the tributes laid out in their honour. One day, I hoped, I would walk on hallowed Anzac ground in Gallipoli, where our country lost 8709 Aussie heroes in the most senseless of ways.

Our momentous trip did nothing to bring Rhys and I closer, although we did not fight anywhere near as much as we did at home. The trip did not draw any sentimentality or romance to us, and I was grateful the children were in our 'marital' room, as for me, avoiding sex had become something of an art form. I was not frigid; self-imposed celibacy was a tool for self-preservation, and an added burden that weighed heavily on an already tortured soul.

* * *

In 1995 the domestic violence practised by Rhys and me rose to fever pitch. Rhys had perfected a method that kept me at the level he wanted. He had begun smashing things around the house, putting holes in walls and doors, and continued to denigrate my character and appearance at every turn.

I am very houseproud and love beautifying my home, so to avoid damage I stopped firing back at him during discussions or arguments, allowing Rhys to have his own way time and time again. I began developing painful mouth ulcers, and suffering long spells of influenza and bronchitis from the stress and mental anguish that emotional suppression can frequently cause. The girls too displayed their own stresses, when childhood asthma and nasty attacks of eczema began presenting in *their* lives. Alycia in particular had such breathing difficulties that she'd cough so hard her tongue curled back into her throat. Even with these physical manifestations I did not enter a contract to leave my unbearable marriage. It did not cross my mind that the beauty of my home did not matter, but it was the very real damage against my children's minds that was the reason to end things with Rhys. In some untapped recess of my ego, I think I was waiting for a 'Good Samaritan', a saviour of some kind, to rescue us – but who?

By this time in my life my bulimia was out of control and to battle the fat I was piling on by the day, I began using amphetamine-based prescription drugs to suppress my appetite. As a result, I was sleeping only a couple of hours a night as my mind clicked over ad infinitum. The mental fatigue I was experiencing was masked by a physical stamina, which only served to exacerbate my aggression levels. Every time Rhys started on me the feeling of invincibility and fearlessness stopped me from backing down like I had before. I prayed for Rhys's death but continued embarking upon endeavours that would keep me from wanting to kill him – or myself. Life was almost as unbearable now as it had been living with Gilda and the slug.

On the weight loss drug Duromine I managed to lose 12 kilos and started feeling almost fabulous again – although a *true* bulimic never does look perfect by any means. By losing weight I was actually doing myself a disservice because Rhys was now lusting after me again. In order to reduce the torturous ritual of unwanted sex, I continued keeping myself busy and out of reach; I even went so far as to steal a medical certificate from my doctor's desk, falsifying a diagnosis of debilitating vaginitis. Silly Rhys fell for it hook, line, and sinker … he fell for a lot of things: irregular periods, stomach cramps, headaches, cystitis, etc etc. I was sick to death of feeling like a porn star. Sex was never about love with Rhys and there was rarely any sentiment in it. Sex with my husband was an hour of cold, mechanical, staged lust that I couldn't wait to end.

Rhys had embarked on various writing projects, one of which was a film script that encapsulated most of *his* erotic fantasies. He had added some spice by trapping his heroines inside a voyeuristic and predictable web of intrigue and suspense. I helped edit and type the long script, but for all my efforts I received an earful of insults because my 'critique' was in sharp contrast with Rhys's staged projections.

Eventually, and much to my relief, the script was finished. Rhys submitted it to the newly formed short film festival program, Flickerfest. Much to our surprise it was picked up and read on stage by a panel of secondary film and TV commercial actors. The Harold Park Hotel in Glebe, a known watering hole for the acting industry, was Flickerfest's rehearsal stage; one of the volunteer actors happened to be Daniel Wyllie of *Spotswood* (1992*)*, *Romper Stomper* (1992), and *Animal Kingdom* (2010) fame. Lyndall and her husband Kevin honoured their relative by sitting through the painful three-hour reading, with Lyndall herself nursing a longing to break into any facet of film or television. Not long after the reading, Lyndall embarked on a television and broadcasting vocal training course.

The script and story were terrible, provoking some well-masked condescension from a few of the actors (namely Daniel Wyllie). There would be no future for Rhys with this venture.

Not to be defeated Rhys's determination to break into film and television saw him send unsolicited sketches to the comedy show *Fast Forward* (which became *Full Frontal* in 1993). Again I offered to assist Rhys with editing, forwarding a few ideas of my own in the interim. The show's producers liked some of what they read and encouraged us to submit material on an ongoing basis. In addition, Rhys sent material to a variety club called The Comedy Store in Petersham. The club showcased a string of renowned stand-up comedians such as Vince Sorrenti and Steady Eddy.

One day Patricia's sister Susan rang our home, asking whether Rhys had sold a couple of his scripts to a radio station. Susan had read some of Rhys's work and recalled a few punchlines that she had then heard on air on a major radio station. Following further investigation Rhys discovered that The Comedy Store borrowed material from the radio station and vice versa. Without copyright protection his material was legally plagiarised, simply by making a couple of 'semantic adjustments'. As much as this incident angered Rhys, it did help him realise that his natural proclivity for comedy was rousing interest. With renewed motivation Rhys set about putting together a script that retold all the funny sketches he accumulated over the years. On this occasion I left everything up to Rhys while embarking on an idea of my own which, oddly enough, had been encouraged, and then facilitated, by my mother.

Meantime, I took a deeper interest in social issues – primarily in the areas surrounding child protection and welfare. I discovered that between 1989 and 1993 an average of twentyseven children under the age of fifteen had been murdered each year in Australia and that twothirds of these were five years old or younger. Keeping my ear close to the ground I heard over the radio about an activist who advertised her resolve to bring back capital punishment for violent crimes – mainly against children. Noting her details, I contacted the activist, 'Patricia', immediately. I couldn't do a lot on my own but with a team of forceful, dedicated warriors, I was more than willing to do *something*. I could almost hear Garry and Grace Lynch inside my head applauding me, and just like that I had found my calling.

As a loving mother, fiercely protective of her children, it nauseated me that evil perpetrators roamed our streets or extracted $80,000 a year from tax payers by being catered for in jail. Two horrific murders began haunting me, those of six-year-old Damien Noyes from Whalan and nine-year-old Ebony Simpson from Bargo. Repetitive nightmares about my own daughters, so ghoulish, so real they destroyed my sleep at night, were turning me into a hypervigilant maniac, obsessed with home security much like Louise and her OCD. I truly *had* to do something!

Patricia was a corpulent German woman, a character straight from a Gestapo postcard. She was larger than life in personality too, an exuberant powerhouse commanding respect – exactly what we needed to lead an important campaign. I immediately jumped on board her petition and hit the streets with fervour, collecting signatures every chance I got. For maximum emotional impact, the petition forms showed pictures of children who had recently been violated and murdered.

- Damien Noyes: age 6. Went missing from a playground in NSW on December 22 1992. His body was found in a car park at Penrith Railway Station.
- Kylie Gill: age 8. Was kidnapped, raped and brutally murdered. Later dumped in the gutter near her home.
- Kylie Maybury: age 6. Tortured, raped and murdered.
- Nicole Hanns: age 5. Was stabbed to death by an intruder in her own home – 1974.

Nicole Hanns's mother Gwen was coincidentally Patricia's best friend.

To get myself 'out there' I invoked my local council's help. The area newspaper, the *Review Pictorial*, published a decent editorial on page two; it was titled simply, 'Call for Capital Punishment' (28 April, 1993).

"I am a very proud and devoted mother, and one who would do anything to protect her children's safety and wellbeing."

This is the proclamation of an Auburn mother of two, fighting for the reintroduction of capital punishment.

"I am not a prude, a puritan, a religious zealot, a conservative leftist, nor a misanthrope," Mrs Angelica — said. "I'm an everyday Australian who loves her children and children in general and who, like the majority in our society, wishes above all else to feel safe and be safe from some of the cold blooded, mindless killers and rapists who roam our streets."

"In just four months we saw four children assaulted and butchered. Unfortunately, once a murder – as horrific and unjust as it may be – is out of the news headlines, people's anger dies down and they forget, continuing with their day-to-day routines. They do not try to foresee the possibility that such crimes may re-occur, and they continue to take their lives for granted without acting on their previous outrage and concern. Patricia and I are not among these people; we foresee that these crimes will re-occur. Thus we take a stand in what we believe and try our hardest to do something tangible about it."

"Our aim is to raise four million signatures before presenting these to Parliament and calling for a referendum. We would like to see capital punishment reintroduced in Australia for extreme cases of murder involving excesses of sexual and/or violent activity; where there is absolutely no doubt that the offender committed the crime."

Before joining the campaign Patricia had collected 80,000 signatures, with the assistance of a couple of friends. When I hit the streets of Sydney – either alone or with my girls in prams – I was a woman possessed. I fostered no compulsion for the eradication of paedophiles, rapists, and child abusers, but it allowed me to sleep at night and took me out of Rhys's self-absorbed life and demands.

I travelled to practically every corner of Sydney, discovering how a majority of people were willing to listen, with most of them signing the petition. I left forms in pubs, clubs, schools, wherever I could. Thirty thousand signatures later, I was satisfied I had done a good and important job; as was Patricia, who was now on the phone with me every other day – much to Rhys's annoyance and eventually mine, too. What I came to realise during this unusual journey was that there is a distinct demographic division in terms of *for* and *against* public opinion. People who live in affluent areas like the Northern or Eastern Suburbs, appeared less sympathetic to such a cause, sometimes even displaying concern for the perpetrator's human rights. But those in the lower socio-economic and working class areas like Sydney's west and south seemed as enthusiastic about punishing the villains as I was. The west and south are, coincidentally, higher crime rate areas … was there a correlation? And could these results suggest a legitimate view of 'if it doesn't affect me, I don't really care'?

One afternoon I lost three-year-old Kristen somewhere on the main street of Auburn for a throat-clenching fifteen minutes. Those terrifying moments in my life were intensified by the campaign's objective, and I realised how deep in horror I had immersed myself.

When I turned around from browsing at a window display my beautiful daughter was not there. She'd gone. I could hear the gut-wrenching screams coming from somewhere within me as I ran frantic and disoriented up and down the street looking everywhere and yet nowhere. *"Kristen! Kristen! KRISTEN!!!"* I called out, circumnavigating Queen Street and returning to the spot where I had initially lost her. There like a desert mirage played in slow motion, was my baby; she'd been held in place by a tall brunette lady who saw the look on my face and knew I had to be the child's mother. Without words, I hugged the woman, blessing her a thousand times for holding on to my child. To this day I've not forgotten the woman's face nor the feeling of immense relief and exhilaration I experienced the second I found my wayward little girl. The 2009 film *The Lovely Bones* captures succinctly what a parent feels when their child goes missing. Almost losing Kristen brought home that kind of anguish and helped strengthen my resolve to bring perpetrators to justice and to their own physical demise.

A focus on responsible parenting also brought to the forefront an active decision to track down my biological father. I never truly stopped thinking about the *Sperm Incognito* and an attempt at locating him was ultimately *my* decision. If my decision then upset members of my family, for me that was an irrelevant and minor detail; after all, what had any of them ever done for me? I owed them nothing. Finding Ettore might answer a few questions about *me* for, aside my strong singing voice and some literary kudos, I was *nothing* like my mother.

Equipped with just a few scraps of information I called the Italian Consulate in Market Street and asked for help. The best they could do for me was supply me with a list of people using my father's surname who might still be residents in Rome. By condensing the list down to three names and sending each a very short enquiry letter, I managed to track down my uncle. I also noticed one of the three names belonged to Adalgisa di Marchi. I had no idea what to expect if anything. My family had related so many negative things about my father, the chances were that I was seeking out a lunatic; yet if he was indeed a lunatic, it was a fact I needed to find out and process for myself.

I wanted nothing from Ettore except an acceptance I was indeed his – this and a photograph of him, so I could see my face as genetically *someone's*. I did not feel I looked much like my glamorous mother. Additionally, I wanted to know if I had siblings. I wasn't about to give up my need for a sister.

Late in January of 1994, I received the correspondence I craved for and anticipated. I could barely contain my excitement as I tore open the envelope bearing that familiar 'French flag' coloured border. Even Rhys was excited for me. Besides the birth of our daughters there weren't too many personal joys we celebrated together, so as I scanned the one-page letter trying to ingest everything in one bite, the following sentences, delivered in almost perfect English, pricked my eyes like needles. Ettore had typed:

Rome, January 14th, 1994

Mrs G,

Here I am! I am Ettore di Marchi.

Of course I have understood that, after twenty-nine years – frankly a 'little' tardy – (in my opinion), you are now in a hurry of knowing who is your father and, above all, IF I am your father! I am sorry to disappoint you: no, Mrs G, I am not your father!

I am a fifty-five years old man. I have been happily married twenty years with an Italian lovely woman I am very fond of and we both have always wished to have a child of our own, but, unfortunately, we couldn't have one.

Therefore, I am sorry to let you know that – for what I am concerned – you have neither brothers, nor sisters.

You wrote to my only uncle who, poor man knows almost nothing of my life either as I am a very reserved person, or owing to sporadic relations always clasped among me, my parents and him.

You also wrote to my mother, but she, poor woman, is now eighty-three and is very ill, suffering with mental disorders and other diseases. Thus she also can't help you, just like my old father who is eighty-six and unfortunately is seriously ill too.

Anyway, thank you for your refined tact and convenient solicitude towards them all I will certainly never forget!

For what concerns the supposed, debatable and troubled event occurred between me and your mother, you must consider that, in case, it happened thirty years ago! My memories of that so far and confused period of my life are necessarily, for biological reasons too, so indefinite and fragmentary.

Nevertheless, if you really wish, after all I have affirmed, to contact me again, PLEASE be far-sighted and discreet next time and write EXCLUSIVELY to the following address:

[Rome Address]

Truly Yours

(Ettore's Signature)

Bitterly, I realised Gilda had lied to me. The name I was christened with was not taken from an opera as she had told me. Ettore's mother, it turned out, was called Adalgisa; I was in fact named after my paternal grandmother, Adalgisa di Marchi. My sense of identity, of my being *me*, of what me looked like, took a 180 degree turn – even in the face of my biological father's outraged, poisoned pen denial.

As a teenager staring into that bathroom mirror in Bishop Crescent I'd hoped to catch a glimpse of my soul, and my authenticity. One time alone, I felt a definite force well up inside of me, and it was terrifying. There was a beast lurking within that, let loose, would plough through everything that lay in its path. Was it the beast of the di Marchis, and on what side of the biological 'blueprint' did I belong? Either side I was truly doomed. Whether life would change for me or not, from this day on the blueprint was certain to taint all that I touched.

CHAPTER FIFTEEN

MOMENTS, SEASONS, ERAS

———

Patricia's friend Gwen and I became very close. She had fought for over a decade to have John David Lewthwaite – her daughter's murderer – kept behind bars longer than his original twenty-year sentence. Despite enormous public outrage Gwen's tireless campaigning saw Lewthwaite serve an additional six years prior to his release in 1999.

In 1974 John Lewthwaite stabbed five-year-old Nicole Hanns seventeen times as she lay sleeping in her bed. The attack was so frenzied the knife snapped. Eighteen-year-old Lewthwaite had broken into the family home with the sole purpose of sexually assaulting Nicole's nine-year-old brother, Anthony. Lewthwaite, already known to police, committed his heinous crime while on parole. This and many other crimes of a similar nature outraged me to such an extent I was unable to control my anger and hatred. I began to seriously doubt mankind could harbour any *real* goodness or empathy. My experience of watching censored and poetic movies had led me to believe that no matter how extreme the violence exerted on others, a mother holding her child would be spared, for the innocence of *that* child. How was it possible then that in today's socalled civilised world, horrors against babies still took place? I certainly had much to learn, including that movies are not accurate depictions of history or of real life.

In Gwen I found a fellow rager, one who shared the same passion for shaking things up, so for now at least I no longer stood alone, carrying overwhelming feelings of hopelessness.

The capital punishment campaign drew the support of two politicians: the independent member for Tamworth, and National Party and member for Parkes, MP Michael Cobb. Although not a supporter of Capital Punishment per se, the Labor member for Smithfield Carl Scully, who in later years rose to prominence as Minister for various portfolios, including police, did however work closely with Gwen and made recommendations John Lewthwaite be kept in gaol for a much longer time than was given to him. With well over two hundred thousand signatures, Patricia and her team took the petition to Parliament, attracting a certain amount of media attention, including a brief story in *Woman's Day* magazine. But, alas, no semblance of a referendum and on 3 July 1993 a highly contentious story appeared in *Truth Magazine* that disclosed just how Patricia had funded her campaign.

Gwen was on the phone at once, frantically attempting to call the alert. As Patricia's left and right hand workers we felt violated, and hoped to somehow resolve the calamity by immediately cutting ourselves loose from our leader. Patricia had started to go sour on Gwen anyway, since the media attention Gwen received regarding her daughter's case had begun to overshadow her own efforts. I felt like a Judas ditching Patricia, but prostitution was not a scandal I wanted to be involved with. Gwen had heard of the victims' support group Garry Lynch mentioned to me and, together with her long suffering husband Peter, we marched in and signed up.

V.O.C.A.L, an acronym for the Victims of Crime Assistance League, was founded in 1989 by a Newcastle mother named Dawn Gilbert whose daughter, nineteen-year-old Tracey, was shot dead at her place of work by a disgruntled stalking ex. Anita Cobby's brutal murder stood out as a beacon of horror among many other horrors, like the one endured by six-year-old John Ashfield of Nowra. Little John's mother, Gunn-Britt Ashfield, and her then boyfriend Austin Allan Hughes, had beaten the little boy over a period of several hours by placing his head under a phone book then bashing it in with a hammer. The bestial act was executed in front of John's four siblings. John sustained a retinal haemorrhage and extensive bruising to his entire body and passed away the next day in hospital. His aunt and grandmother attended the group, relating to us how John had relentlessly been a scapegoat for his mother's immoral and cruel excesses. Being privy to such knowledge, and as direct blood relatives, why didn't his aunt and grandmother remove John from his home? I most certainly would have, no matter the consequences – legal or otherwise.

The shocking case of another tiny victim, two-year-old Daniel Valerio, beaten to death in 1990 by his stepfather, sadly answered the above question. Australian Child Protection Services simply could not, or would not, reach every child, and kidnap offences carry heavy penal sentences; they are often futile attempts, too, given extensive parental rights. In later years the Valerio case served to radically amend some of the guidelines and policies by which our Federal Government served our most vulnerable resource – children at risk – but it was still not enough.

As V.O.C.A.L's only 'non-victim of crime member', I stepped into Long Bay Jail as Gwen's 'primary support network' for a Serious Offenders' Review Board meeting. The delegation was summoned to grant John Lewthwaite a C3 classification which would enable him to apply for day release from Cooma Jail, where he was serving the secondary portion of his sentence. Gwen vehemently opposed the application, standing her ground and protesting the deliberation, demanding it be overturned. Gwen argued that Lewthwaite was neither repentant nor 'cured' of his paedophile urges, given a number of inside reports on his prison behaviour.

Looking around me at the squalid walls and corrugated iron bars, I swore I would never step into a place such as this of my own volition. I felt like I had just walked through Satan's gates. I watched mesmerised as several officers went about their duties, and sighed with relief when not a single inmate came into my line of sight. I asked myself how anyone would even *want* to work with such scum.

* * *

Gilda's coveted first, and only, performance inside the Sydney Opera House took place courtesy of an Armenian composer who'd organised a program of Italian, Spanish, and Armenian lyrical pieces. The concert was held on 13 October 1991. Naturally I was expected to be present at Mother's big 'Aussie launch' and breakthrough, the reason she had abandoned South Australia and forced us all to follow her here. Maria, always unwilling to miss an opportunity of being seen, tagged along with her then fiancé, John.

Mother sang Bellini's 'Casta diva' in Act One, and Torroba's *La Marchenera* in Act Two. As always she was the consummate professional and was well received by the audience. That Gilda was a talented woman was never in dispute; my issue with Mother centred on her inability to quit, and that there were too many casualties of her obsession. Coming to Australia at age forty was also an enduring mistake. If Gilda's career was failing in Italy, it would surely lay dead before hitting Australasian shores. Ten years on from this I read Chrissy Amphlett's 2005 autobiography, *Pleasure and Pain*. Chrissy, frontwoman for Divinyls, was a woman I admired, yet her steely determination and unrelenting ambition very much mirrored Mother's. The distinction I drew between Chrissy and Gilda however was that unlike Mother, Chrissy did not mingle motherhood with her craft. Chrissy died from health complications (multiple sclerosis and cancer) in 2013, still unselfishly childless.

Children need and *deserve* unconditional nurturing, lest they become emotional cripples or abusers themselves. Mother had placed her craft and career well above me or anyone else close to her and boy did we feel it!

The Armenian composer, Edwin, wanted to create a musical of his own. I was enamoured with Rob Guest's performance in *The Phantom of the Opera* and suggested a rendition of the 1953 Vincent Price horror movie, *House of Wax*. Mother told Edwin that Rhys was a scriptwriter and I was a lyricist. Seeing dollar signs around him, Edwin urged us to write a libretto right away. I was no lyricist – only a woman who loved writing – but I was willing to give it a crack.

In the meantime, Rhys had struck a little luck with his collection of comic scripts and sketches. Henri Szeps, of *Mother and Son* fame, heard about Rhys's project and promptly negotiated a TV pilot, endorsing Rhys's script. After a few months waiting for a production commencement date, Rhys's triumph and excitement was suddenly derailed. It appeared Mr Szeps had failed to convince producers and with that, everything went up in smoke. I did feel mildly sad for Rhys; he was a talented comedy writer and I hoped that maybe, just maybe, success would change his outlook and perhaps even save our marriage.

There must have been a spy drone hovering over our Housing Commission townhouse because every idea Rhys formulated seemed to manifest in other people's hands. One of his ideas involved a children's animation story based in a colony of ants. Then in 1998 came *Antz*, featuring the voices of Woody Allen, Sharon Stone, Jennifer Lopez and Sylvester Stallone. Rhys had drawn up the draft plot for his film in 1993, later discarding the idea without discussing it with anyone. When the DreamWorks film came out we were both in shock: the plot was almost identical to Rhys's. How was this possible?

* * *

It was around this time that my eldest cousin Valeria announced her wedding to her long-time fiancé. I was ecstatic when she informed me I was to be her Matron of Honour. It was my first time in a wedding party – something my so-called best friend Maria had denied me when she married John. So in August 1993, with five-year-old Alycia, I took a coach to Adelaide, delighted to be supporting my beloved cousin on such an auspicious day. I was also very excited to meet Valeria's German 'pen pal' Herr Jens Lindemann, who I liked instantly. Jens had travelled for the occasion all the way from his home town, Parchim in northern Germany. Before departing the gorgeous Adelaide Hills, where the wedding was held, I made Jens promise me he'd become my pen pal too. I was to see him again in 2001 when he visited Sydney, and twelve years after that in his German homeland.

Back in Sydney, Rhys, not to be defeated following his close brush with fame, coerced me and three of his friends to attend an audition for 'Red Faces' at the TCN-9 Studios in Willoughby. This was a spoof on talent shows, a regular slot on *Hey Hey It's Saturday* (one of Australia's longest running TV variety shows). On 11 August 1994 the show's floor staff rolled around in stitches when our act, The Phluorescent Bronchial Phlegm Band, pounced in front of the cameras with its ridiculous ensemble, like something out of a Rob Zombie flick. Yet again, though, it was not to be. I don't know what the producers wanted, but the fact that their boom man, with tears in his eyes, dropped the microphone from cackling so much, spoke buckets.

Five years on from my initial application, Grundy Entertainment invited me to audition for *Wheel of Fortune* and on 21 October 1994 I was flown to Adelaide where the show was taped. Unfortunately, I bombed out on the first go when a dubious 'Bankrupt' cleaned me out. That night after the taping wrapped up I called Rhys from a public phone booth outside my hotel to relate the experience. Instead of feeling proud for making it so far, Rhys began berating me about my loss. I tearfully walked back to my hotel room where my cousins Rodolfo and Bianca sat waiting, jubilant to have me in their sights even for just one evening.

A shitty call to Rhys was not an end to what should have been an innocuous experience. When *Wheel of Fortune* went to air, during the first commercial break I received a call from a man who said he was watching the show and wanted me to know how beautiful I was. A little disturbed but not overly concerned, I thanked the strange caller for his compliment and hung up. *He had to have got my number from the White Pages, how bizarre.* But then the same man rang during the next commercial break. This time his words were more concerning.

"I'm sitting here touching myself over your beautiful face, Angelica."

I yelled abuse down the receiver, threatening to have the police put a trace on his number if he dared call me again. The shock and disgust left a scar. It took me a few weeks to stop looking over my shoulder each time I left the house. Thoughts of victims from the V.O.C.A.L group flooded my mind and I realised, albeit minimally, how it might feel to be stalked and possibly murdered.

A second and very peculiar event resulted from my appearance on the show. It involved a retired New South Wales Police sergeant who contacted Channel 9 to have the network pass on his details onto me. 'Mr Dean' heard me plugging my unfinished autobiography and decided I could become his literary ghost writer. Mr Dean then related the most fascinating story.

Stating he was 'not much of a writer', he asked if I was interested in jumping along for the ride. Mr Dean's beef was to do with police corruption – not so much against the public – but among officers and their interpersonal relationships. Although I found it virtually incredible, the bullying and harassment Mr Dean claimed to have suffered at the hands of his colleagues had mostly to do with religious bias. When I agreed to collaborate, Mr Dean backpedalled, claiming the project might endanger my young family. No amount of arguing would change the former sergeant's mind, so the glimmer of opportunity slipped through my fingers again.

Secretly, I had a thing for the police. It had little to do with hot men in uniform, though, and everything to do with what the force stood for: courage, service, and honour. For a man or woman to rise from their safe home each morning and go out with no guarantee they will return home that night, takes a lot of guts and integrity. These men and women put their lives on the line to keep us safe and for this alone they earn my respect and esteem. If only *I* had chosen this path instead of a distorted image of marriage and children. Law enforcement was a career that grew more appealing to me by the day. Three of my former classmates at Cabramatta High School had taken this pathway, with one of them a successful and renowned detective formerly assigned to the Cabramatta beat, as dangerous a mission by now as the once notorious Kings Cross.

New Weekly magazine published a short piece of mine called *To My Biological Father*. The piece included a photograph of me handling a diamond python at the Gosford Reptile Park. It was inaccurately edited but I received $100 for my efforts and felt I was putting something 'out there' as a rebuttal to the nasty letter the *Sperm Incognito* had sent me. Like Ettore I loved snakes, and when Ettore sent me a photograph of him wearing two cheeky pythons around his neck, I couldn't resist sending him one back – the same one *New Weekly* had now published. *Touché!*

At this point I hadn't given up hope that one day my father and I would be reunited, and that he might even learn to love me.

With great trepidation I told Letitia I had managed to find Ettore and get in contact with him. Not in my wildest dreams did I think she would betray my confidence to Gilda and the slug, who I knew would not take the news well. The fallout that came from something so personally important to me was further testament to my guardians' selfishness and narcissism. Then, on top of the insults and recriminations thrown at me, one by one the skeletons began pouring out of the overfilled family closet.

Mother, who had not yelled and carried on at me for a number of years, unleashed the demon once more. Our relationship had no doubt been plastic but it was comfortable; there were times where I even enjoyed discussing metaphysical topics with her and managed to receive a few reasonable answers. Nonetheless, Gilda's take on mysticism failed to draw much respect from me because no matter how I worded things, *her* view held a higher validity than mine. God and the Bible always had to play their part too, and Gilda knew only too well that for me there was no longer a monotheistic deity that reigned supreme over my life. When the Ettore affair was divulged via the poisonous mouth of a woman I had trusted, the old Gilda came flooding back with a vengeance. She was utterly and vociferously disgusted with what she considered my 'betrayal' of her.

I really did not care for the personal realisation that Ettore being a prick had made *Mother* right. Finding my biological father was all about *me* and not the mighty prima donna soprano. Gilda just wouldn't see that a child needs to understand her roots, that a clear sense of identity is necessary for future growth. Gilda may not have been affected by the fact that she had precious little time with *her* father as a child but it was not the same case for me – I was *very much affected!* My entire life was about meeting a man who'd love and care for me: the missing male component to an equation every child has a right to.

Alfonso, naturally, did not skip the chance to join in Mother's acrimony – not that I gave two flying fucks about anything he said or thought, anyway. This was *my* journey, not his. He chose to leave Sicily and his family – and perhaps for good reasons. Yet he continued to carry his Sicilian family economically and this too was *his* choice. I chose to seek my biological father out; I never accepted Alfonso as a surrogate father and could not. Alfonso's lack of insight and subtlety towards me had, from day one, paved the way to rejection.

But now let's get back to that closet.

It was established that Ettore was a misguided 'fling' and I its unwelcome result. My grandmother Letitia, who fundamentally controlled every aspect of Mother's life, urged her daughter to have an abortion, asking Ettore to finance it. Mother refused, hoping that by having me she might entice Ettore into remaining in her life, thus making her a 'respectable woman' in a nation that condemned her current status. Refuting both counts, in a fit of rage Ettore allegedly bashed Mother when she was eight months pregnant, before exiting our lives forever.

I was indeed named after my paternal grandmother, not an opera, but that did not affect Ettore's resolve to flee responsibility. Letitia then claimed Ettore had spotted her wheeling me about in my pram, and he tried to run over us in his car. 'Afraid for my life', Mother temporarily relocated me in Düsseldorf to live with Letitia's brother and his young family for a year. There are photographs and Facebook conversations I have saved that corroborate my 'adoptive' family's involvement, but these have nothing to do with Gilda's rationale for my being there.

Letitia tried repeatedly to convince Mother to have me placed in an orphanage. Mother visited the said institution but reported that the conditions were so austere she could not bring herself to leave me there. For me, the fact that Mother even considered the option gives me enough rope to want to hang her. How *any* mother can seriously contemplate abandoning her child is a feeling so removed from my own chemical make-up that the most 'reasonable' reason just does not sound good enough. Yet my beloved Auntie Gianna did just that, albeit forced to by my Uncle Eduardo, who point-blank refused to raise another man's child. In later years Auntie Gianna began searching for her daughter, who she'd named Gioia, but found no birth records for her. Ironically, Mother had considered adopting Gioia but once again Letitia stood in her way, condemning children as 'career assassins'. Gioia could very well have been that sister I'd always longed for.

Gradually I began to understand why Ettore wrote that meeting Letitia had disturbed him from the moment he laid eyes on her. Letitia's penchant for ditching offspring should have come as no surprise given she abandoned her own firstborn. It then occurred to me Letitia might have a problem with firstborns generally; she despised my cousin Valeria, taking any chance she got to single her out from Rodolfo and Bianca. Later in life, however, Valeria, the cousin I loved with all my heart, my nominated stand-in sister, would do exactly the same thing to me as our grandmother had done to her.

Despite all these family skeletons, the most shocking of revelations, one that hit me like a ballistic missile, came from Mother when she confessed how Letitia – my 'saviour' – had set me up to receive those infernal punishments. Letitia would report my 'terrible deeds' to Mother, Mother would dish out my punishment, and Letitia would rush in like Florence Nightingale, looking all saintly and indignant, to rescue me. It appears, then, that my grandmother may have been suffering from a version of Munchausen syndrome by proxy; yet how did she bring herself to act this way when I idolised her as the 'father' I did not have *and* the mother I should have had? The facts now clearly show that Letitia was in fact the principal protagonist in the endemic dysfunction suffered by *all* the members of our family. It also appears that the warping of her character began when Letitia was a young and impressionable girl living in fashionable Madrid.

As a teen, Letitia enjoyed a brief stint as a singer but her 'aristocratic' family forbade her to continue along this track. To perform on a stage was considered frivolous and demeaning, so when Gilda came of age Letitia vicariously lived out her performing dreams through her condemned daughter. She began grooming Mother by setting her up with 'important dates' that might lead to connections within the opera world. One such connection was an avant garde painter well known around Madrid's artistic circles. There was clear pain in her eyes as Mother divulged how the painter had wanted to do a nude of her. Barely fifteen years old and extremely shy, Mother made her feelings of agony so clear the artist mercifully ended the sitting and sent her home. Gilda explained how a 'privileged' Catholic upbringing, courtesy of her maternal grandmother in Benidorm, had prepared her for a conservative life as dutiful mother and wife – not some brazen 'artist's model' or covert mistress. A convent education, elocution training and virtual internment inside the sparse matriarchal villa had ensured that inappropriateness of any kind would not interfere with impeccable manners and seeking daily improvement.

But Mother's grandmother's vision was not to be. Deeply preoccupied with escorting Gilda around the world in order to turn her into a successful prima donna, Letitia continued to fail as a mother by abandoning her two vulnerable sons, Eduardo and Miguel, who at eighteen years of age, were just starting out in life. With the boys losing their father to politics and womanising, maternal abandonment further compounded their negative views on women, relationships, fatherhood and self-esteem. My uncles became rageaholics and alcoholics and, consequently, abusers in their primary relationships.

Miguel, my favourite uncle, died childless from cancer of the oesophagus in 1988, completely devastating his brother Eduardo. For years to come, Eduardo made his undeniable dislike for me and his sister apparent because we had 'stolen' the mother he adored. It was pointless trying to reason with him because he'd never accept the bitter truth. Letitia could do no wrong in his eyes – Letitia, the woman I looked up to, the teacher I took so many life lessons from, my nurturer and confidante. This woman was in fact none other than our own smiling assassin.

Mother's 'family truths' tirade concluded with the following.

"Up until you unearthed this monster, I had forgotten everything he did to me. The only time I am reminded of him is when I look at *you*. It is *his face* you wear!"

So ... was *this* the reason Mother treated me with so much derision? Was I Ettore's spectre, come back to haunt her? Indeed, it is true I wore his face. Following two other condescending letters from the *Sperm Incognito* I begged for a photograph of him; when I looked at it, I stared at myself. Ettore had my very soul in his eyes, in his nose, inside those goddamned pythons. Now I knew what lay behind that bathroom mirror in Bonnyrigg.

* * *

Maria left John, claiming spousal abuse, and moved out into a rented house with her eight-month old baby daughter. She told me how the last straw had arrived when she caught John masturbating to an underwear catalogue. Once again, I found myself drawn into feeling sorry for Maria and helped her out where I could.

Alastair and Marianne finally launched their new wedding cake showroom for the Sydney elite, and it was spectacular. I was employed as a sales consultant on weekends and Thursday nights, which saved us from financial ruin. Not long after that, Rhys broke out of the unemployment drought that had sequestered him for four long, inflammatory years. Still hell-bent on breaking into film and television, he managed to get a media related job, as a monitor for a company in Redfern who sold television, radio, and newspaper transcripts to commercial vendors and clientele with vested interests. It was I who compiled his application and *I* who sent him back for a second interview when he failed at the first then refused to return.

So, now that Rhys was out of the house again I felt better about life, my only concern being that, working in an office filled with young city beauties, Rhys's body dysmorphia worsened. If I did not get out of bed and push Rhys out the door he'd run late most mornings. Again, the hatred and frustration I felt reached fever pitch. Could my husband not see how he was destroying us? I'd scream at Rhys that what he was doing wasn't normal, that he needed to see a doctor, but my cries fell on deaf ears, as always. I needed out of that marriage. My only relief from it came when the front door closed in the mornings, only to be quashed the moment I'd hear his car pull up in the driveway each afternoon.

Realistically, my marriage was dead and totally unsalvageable. Even though I occupied my life with other ventures and did not stop to reflect on the internal void and misery I was feeling, being around a husband I despised and disrespected felt like being stuck in quicksand with a rope only inches out of reach. To offer myself hope for a meaningful existence, I began to visit clairvoyants and immersed myself in spiritual research. As the road to enlightenment grew clearer, I called upon influential enablers, putting forth ideas for entertainment based on the spiritual facts I was discovering. One of these enablers was the film director Vincent Ward (director of *What Dreams May Come*) and, boldly of me, director extraordinaire Steven Spielberg. I brazenly obtained Steven's contact details from Thomas Keneally's wife, not so long after his *Schindler's List* success. I collected a cache of famous refusals, with the one below from composer Claude-Michel Schönberg (of *Les Miserables* and *Miss Saigon* fame). Mother's friend abandoned the *House of Wax* project so I forwarded the libretto to Mr Schönberg while he was in town with his *Miss Saigon*.

20 June 1995

Dear Mrs _____,

Thank you for your letter of 15 June 1995, and of thinking of me for your project.

I am currently working on a new musical with my partner Alain Boublil which is scheduled for production at the end of 1996 and have no plans until that time to consider any other projects. In addition, both Alain and myself only undertake to write a musical when we have had the original idea. We don't work under commission.

Yours Sincerely

Etc. etc.

In the newsagency I came across an Australian magazine called *Psychic Interactive*. Taking a copy home, I saw that private readings between subscribers were encouraged with the closest 'prediction' chosen for a prize. It was absolutely wonderful to receive all these amazing letters from Australians around the nation that were bizarrely accurate given all they had to go by was a photograph and my time of birth. One man, Phaedrus, really stood out and although I did not nominate him as my profile winner, his numerological assessment drew me in and we became pen friends.

Phaedrus, whose real name is Trevor Pearson, hails from Christies Beach in Adelaide but spent twenty years of his life studying Numerology and Vedic Astrology in India. His esoteric knowledge surpassed anyone else's I'd come into contact with, bar the eclectic author Linda Goodman. We began writing to one another in 2000 and continued until 2009, exchanging dozens of letters (which I've kept). While still in New South Wales I made two trips to Adelaide to meet Phaedrus; he was a devout vegan so we'd catch up inside his favourite organic cafe in the city. Physically, and in terms of lifestyle choices, Phaedrus was the classic hippie. With me knowing next to nothing about Cancerians, Phaedrus became the first crab to touch my heart. Throughout the vile storm that was my marriage, Phaedrus's words comforted and sustained me. He even compiled a numerological table that spans my year of birth till the year 2033, with each year based on my full birth name calculations. The year is then represented by an 'essence number' that determines how the year might unfold for me. The present one, 2016, falls under the '5' essence number, with '5' representing individuality, non-attachment, life lessons learnt through experience, storytelling, surrender and release. Wow! How true was this for me.

Towards the end of 2008 Phaedrus showed signs of dementia, perhaps even Alzheimer's. I did not abandon my dear friend, but around this time life was changing rapidly, and my ability to respond to letters that were now making little sense wavered, and eventually tapered off altogether. By the time I was ready to resume correspondence with Phaedrus he had moved back with his sister and I did not know how to find him. The cafe had not seen him in months either. I will never forget Phaedrus or his knowledge. Phaedrus was a gift I treasure, just as I do his many letters, ones I may publish on his behalf someday.

Also in 2000, I went to see another personal spiritual hero live on stage, author Neale Donald Walsch. I was accompanied by Kelly, a heroin addict who had lost her five-year-old son to brain cancer in 1999; I watched him take his final breath wrapped in his mother's arms. Because Neale had saved me via his *Conversations with God* books, I desperately wanted Kelly to be saved by him too. Alas, heroin is a great seducer, and my beautiful friend missed twothirds of the program scouring Sydney for a dealer. Although happily married to Rhys's best friend and mother to another son, Kelly never recovered from her son's death eventually joining him when she died peacefully in her sleep in 2014 aged fifty-four. For many years I had been Kelly's only real friend.

Alongside spiritual endeavours of 'the third kind', I wanted to establish some kind of future for my girls. My beautiful four-year-old Kristen had been accepted into a well-heeled modelling agency which lent its staff to film and television. Albeit finding herself at the top of their selection list, my stubborn little Taurean rarely jumped through production hoops as directed. Defeated, I pulled her out of what was in actual fact an awful kiddies' meat market. A carbon copy of Letitia I was *not*, nor would ever become.

Jumping back to my the 1990s and my moribund marriage to Rhys, I was growing more detached from him and keeping myself busy and out of the marital bed in any way I could. In 1999, for my thirty-fourth, I jumped out of a plane (with a parachute), but before I reached those heights, in 1994 I decided to organise a Cabramatta High School reunion. My fondest memories still revolved around my high school years and I just had to see these guys again. I poured myself into seven months of solid work, sifting through hours of electoral microfiche while my young daughters slept in their strollers. I managed to locate over twothirds of former students and teachers from the Class of '81.

The Cabramatta High School Reunion took place on 7 April 1995 and was an enormous success. Auspiciously, 181 students and teachers attended the Grand Ballroom of the South Terrace Function Centre in Bankstown. Dressed to the nines and sporting huge sentimental smiles, my former 'Cabra Highs' made the arduous task all the more worthwhile for me. Post reunion I received dozens of thank you letters and cards from ex-students and teachers alike, praising me for reconnecting them with old friends they hadn't seen since the early Eighties. The high school itself sent me a commendation letter and my work was published, complete with inaugural photograph, in the local Liverpool newspaper.

Once again, no pat on my back from Rhys, no recognition from *him* of a job well done. According to him, I had wasted a lot of time and effort for very little return. Even an experienced events manager couldn't have achieved what I had without an assistant. It was yet another reason to leave the marriage, but rather than jump ship and save myself, I committed a further act of treason against my soul. I gave in to Rhys's nagging and prepared my body for the son he so wanted.

Armed with an in-depth text that explained how to choose a baby's sex, I followed the instructions to the letter and on 3 March 1996 at 7.47 am, little Edan Khaellan was born, weighing a massive 4.3 kilos. In sharp contrast with what I'd been told by a midwife, Edan was my longest labour yet at fortyeight hours, though the birth itself was relatively painless and did not require an episiotomy. Our son was a bundle of joy, but also one more reason to remain in a defunct and loveless marriage. Edan's birth was also memorable as the second time Rhys gave me some praise with any credible sincerity. I'd finally produced an heir to the family name – the 'Golden Son' Rhys so desperately needed.

The first time Rhys praised me was when I signed up for a singing competition at the Marrickville RSL in 1996. The contest paid a whopping $10,000 to the winner, which spelt a deposit on our own home. I desperately wanted to get out of Housing Commission accommodation and its perceived mediocrity. I did not want to endure the welfare legacy my guardians seemed so comfortable with.

Eight months pregnant with my baby boy I stepped onto the stage and, stronger than ever before in my life, I belted out Barbra Streisand's *'Evergreen' and Bette Midler's *'Wind Beneath My Wings'. I knew this night would be the last time I'd sing to a live audience so I made the most of it. Judging from the reaction I still possessed a notable instrument. One man approached our table congratulating me in person telling me I had the money in the bag. It was also the first time Rhys had heard me sing and he appeared completely blown away by the experience. Although I still despised my husband, his proud tears warmed him to me somewhat, if only for a fleeting moment. If only he would stop doing all the things that had destroyed our relationship I might still learn to care for him.

That night, a local songstress with poor pitch and no memory for lyrics took home the cash prize. In life it's so rarely what you know but *who* you know. I once asked Mother why she had not achieved fame as an opera singer given her talent and extensive training, and she replied, "Because I would not succumb to the casting couch."

I then asked her if, knowing what she knows now, did she consider the casting couch a viable option; I did not receive a reply.

It took more effort on my part to have Rhys commit to a savings plan. Yet he did so, and in 1998 we finally had enough collateral saved up to build our own home. It was during this time that I revised my autobiography.

Rhys and I purchased a decent sized block of land for $52,000 in St Helens Park, a suburb in the now established city of Campbelltown. The house cost $70,000 to build and it had five bedrooms, an ensuite, walk-in robe, and a huge family room that comfortably accommodated Rhys's new pride and joy – a restored 'pub-sized' slate pool table. The only thing our budget didn't cover was turf for the large front and back yards. There was $700 left over from the building contract, which I decided to use on landscaping. With three young kids running around the last thing I wanted was mud trampled into our brand new carpets. Knowing Rhys would buy another 'toy' with this money, I did not reveal our residual fund to him, quickly ordering turf before I'd lost my nerve. I then told Rhys my parents had given us the turf as a housewarming gift. Naturally Rhys proceeded to thank them behind my back but Alfonso denied making the purchase … So, I copped another major slamming from Rhys. Either the slug was seriously stupid or he just enjoyed making my life a misery.

Tommy and Sebastian, my beloved cats, also came with us to the new house, settling in quickly as cats do. We *all* settled in quickly and for a brief period of time everyone seemed happy with their new lives. Everyone but me. Three great children, a brand new house and a good job for Rhys is all it takes to make for a harmonious life right? I even lost two-thirds of my excess weight, yet Rhys and I seemed to fight more viciously than ever before. The body dysmorphia grew worse, as did the porn addiction. It was never enough for Rhys: the more he got from life, the more preoccupied he became with his hair and with women.

Late in 2000 I organised a twenty-year Cabramatta High School reunion with three other ex-students, one of them a former school heart throb called Leonard. Tall, blond, and confident, Leonard was everything I looked for in a man. In no time at all I was head over heels in lust with him.

Until Leonard, I thought I had completely lost my libido. When Rhys touched me I'd recoil like the trodden Snake that I was, and of course I was already a master in the art of avoiding sexual contact. When Leonard unsuspectingly tiptoed into my life, however, he revived a passion so strong I was immediately transported back to how things had been with my beloved Patrick.

Alas, Leonard was unattainable. He was a happily married man with two young boys and his wife, a fitness instructor, looked like she had been forged from the fires of a gladiatorial arena. My stretch marks and cellulite would never compete. What rendered Leonard more irresistible however was the way he spoke about his Amazonian wife, her name playing adoringly on his lips with every sentence that left his mouth. If only I had been so lucky to be the wife of such a besotted husband, how much genuine gratitude I'd have bestowed on him in return.

One of my personal rules concerns respect and reverence for marital relationships. Leonard was now a catalyst for unrequited love but I honoured his delicate position, and consciously maintained a safe distance from the object of my desires. What the 'Leonard experience' did for me was force me to see clearly the stark reality of life, the fact that I existed within a dead and irreconcilable marriage. Every single day I forced myself to ignore my needs and feelings of indignation in order to uphold the hallowed family unit. I actively chose to live in hell because my children had to have what I did not, but all I really succeeded in doing was to systematically, drop by drop, annihilate portions of my spirit.

Maria, who thoroughly relished Rhys's passive adulation, fuelled my resolve to leave the marriage. Knowing her motivations, I guessed she just wanted a single friend to go man hunting with. She was also badly in need of extra cash now that John had filed for bankruptcy and stopped paying Maria child support, I stupidly convinced Alastair to employ her services in the luxurious new showroom. Instead of offering gratitude Maria set out to sexually manipulate Alastair in order to undermine my status as his primary sales consultant. There was no doubt Alastair was fiercely loyal to Marianne but it was obvious he also appreciated Maria's short skirts and tight curves. Eventually and knowingly, Maria achieved her objective, and another lifelong friendship was compromised by someone I had once called my best friend.

Maria's personal life was out of control, irreverent. She was sleeping with anything that had a pulse and dabbled in unlawful drugs. One of the new pastry cooks Alastair had hired was also heavily into the drug scene and Maria latched onto the twentyone-year-old like a professional hustler. Danny wasn't interested in Maria, though, finding a lot more in common with me – even if I *was* twice his age.

Danny and I grew close. Although troubled, he was an intelligent man with drive, ambition, and a sound work ethic that Alastair appreciated. Danny introduced me to something that grew into a passion: trance music; I just couldn't get enough of it.

There was a downside. Going to multiple raves, the only way to survive endless nights that turned into days was large doses of amphetamines, and Danny began to deteriorate quickly. Along with his addiction, Danny decided to share with me the pain of my marriage. He became my confidante and for someone so young and erratic, Danny was now a great comfort to me, my new best friend.

Danny was so outraged with the way Rhys treated me that he offered to have him seriously hurt. It took every ounce of moral accountability and a responsibility towards my children not to accept his offer. Sadly, but perhaps karmically, a year later and at the tender age of twenty-two, my beautiful confidante was diagnosed with Hodgkin's lymphoma, a kind of blood cancer.

* * *

In 2002, only a few days after our fifteenth wedding anniversary, three major events gave me the strength and courage to finally leave my hopeless marriage.

My son Edan was, at the age of three, diagnosed with autism. I immediately embarked on a campaign that would disprove these findings while 'temporarily' accepting the intervention plans meted out by local government. While I was merely sceptical of Edan's slow intellectual and social development, Rhys was in complete denial. The 'Golden Son', carrier of the prized family name, had to be a perfect specimen – not labelled as a retard!

Rhys submerged himself to the point of hysteria into teaching Edan how to talk correctly, do sums, solve puzzles, and learn from educational worksheets – anything at all that might confound the theorists. I tried to remove myself from the long torturous lessons, listening with clenched teeth to Edan's laments as Rhys pounded our son with attempts at autism antidotes. But one day my maternal ears caught sounds I would *not* ignore.

Rushing into Edan's room I saw my five-year-old son cupping his head; his forehead was red and there was an indentation on the wall above his bed. Edan just wasn't 'getting it' so Rhys had lost his temper and smashed his little head into the wall. I grabbed my son from the bed, kissing and rubbing his head over and over until his little caramel eyes had lost their frightened look. Glaring at my pathetic husband, who stood there ranting in arrogant and remorseless tones, I hissed, "Touch my son again and I'll kill you."

* * *

By this time, I had learnt so much about spirituality and Metaphysics, there seemed to be no books left that could teach me more, other than the ones I came across via an Australian esoteric author, *Dawn Hill.

Dawn had put me onto the Neale Donald Walsch's *Conversations with God* trilogy. These books had given me permission to become the authentic *me*, enabling me to leave the marriage. When the Universe sends you cues such as Leonard, violence against your child, books, and so on, you *need* to pay attention. When Rhys recognised the strength I was gaining from Neale's books, he destroyed the most important one – Volume One – before my eyes. Rhys's own eyes widened with rage as one by one he tore the blessed pages, spitting profanities at me.

The final cue arrived when Alastair reduced my three working days down to one, tightening the screws on our finances. Business had taken a sudden dive and Alastair decided Maria was the 'better consultant' after all. He went as far as to feature her in his new glossy catalogue and I felt certain he did this because he found her sexually appealing, and therefore marketable. Triumphant, Maria made no effort to share her hours with me, or to dispute Alastair's decision. I hated both of them – he more than she because he should have known better.

I swallowed hard but, taking a huge breath, I told Rhys our marriage was over. A different and difficult phase in my tortured life was about to begin, one that carried no more joy than if I'd remained in my present hell. Yet although the burdens would become greater, just as they had when I left my guardians' home back in 1982, I'd at least carry them freely and on my own terms. Everything bears a price and for me, yet again, the price of freedom tasted like the sweetest of victories. Surely other, new burdens could only be less toxic than the ones I'd endured over the past seventeen years?

Soon after the split, Alastair approached me sporting a benign gaze that was veiled by sorrow. Talking into my angry eyes he began pleading his case.

"Angelica, had I kept you on instead of Maria you would never have left your marriage and it was time for you to do this. I forced you out of your comfort zone and I want you to believe I wasn't trying to hurt you."

Whether it was true or not, what Alastair did was a callous act I did not expect and would never forgive. Yet, truth be said, everything happens for a reason, and being pushed out of my comfort zone definitely did help force my hand with Rhys.

CHAPTER SIXTEEN

SOMEHOW I'LL FIND MY WAY HOME

———

The next twelve months had me question whether I'd made the right decision; never in my wildest dreams had I truly believed I'd leave Rhys. Abandoning the familiar is never easy and the moment you stumble, your defeatist ego begins tricking you into submission with memories, of the 'advantages' of before.

It's easy to see, then, why so many battered women do not leave their partners; getting rid of Rhys proved horrific. He *did not want to leave* and had put up the fight of his life.

Repentant supplications came first. These were not easy to dismiss because Rhys's raw vulnerabilities surfaced like never before, and my sense of compassion was sorely tested. But then the wrath arrived, something I understood far better and was emotionally easier for me to handle. Wrath is what I grew up with. The combative adrenalin rush Rhys's wrath extracted from me was in fact a form of bitter release; it felt both morbidly euphoric and completely justified. *Bring it on Rhys; I'm ready for you this time.*

Aside from the strength *Conversations with God* and lusting after Leonard had given me, the beginning of the end arrived courtesy of the family computer that Rhys left behind when I forced him to move back to his parents. I had only ever used a computer for Alastair and Marianne's MYOB showroom program, having no interest whatsoever in computers or the internet. For me technology spelt maths, and maths and I were never friends, mainly because of the bitch who traumatised me with times tables at Umberto Primo school in Italy. Despite vociferous resistance from me, my cheeky daughters went against the grain and introduced me to an online social medium called NineMSN Chat.

"You can talk to people from all over the world, Mum," they chimed in tandem.

Kids absorb and understand a lot more than we give them credit for. Alycia and Kristen knew Dad had made Mum very unhappy, and believing our children were more 'me' than him, I felt they would not judge me for leaving their father. As well as being my progeny, the true family I never had, these girls were also my very best and most honest friends.

On NineMSN Chat I began to connect with a variety of single men in various interest rooms, but mostly in the '30+ Romance' one. In the meantime, the news that Leonard had left his wife knocked me for six. Ironically, Leonard and his family had moved down the street from us with his sons even attending Alycia's and Kristen's school, with his eldest in Alycia's class. Leonard had returned home one afternoon and found his wife in bed with her gym colleague. When he related this episode to me, the deep pain I could see in his eyes was dreadfully disconcerting.

"She was lying naked with him on *our* bed! She didn't even have the decency to turn our wedding photo around."

My heart went out to Leonard. On a different level, I knew what it felt like to be emotionally cheated on, yet I did not waste any time trying to endear myself to him ... I was starving for love. My efforts proved completely fruitless because Leonard was wholly in the grip of post-marital grief, something I did not completely understand given I had moved on so quickly from Patrick to Rhys. Or so I thought.

Not to be defeated, I cast a Wiccan love spell on Leonard. Two of my astrological virtues (which, channelled poorly are potential worst enemies) are my iron will and a certain misguided tenacity. The use of White Magick asks that permission be sought wherever possible. Without asking a recipient for permission, a White Magick spell will fulfil its intention inappropriately and may harm the spell caster. In the Wiccan Rede, witchcraft's code of conduct, spells that are used in order to manipulate, dominate, or control another person, are forbidden. I had been successful with spell casting before, as my knowledge of and belief in Metaphysics grew, yet this one backfired on me in a most unusual way.

Leonard began calling me almost daily. He'd drop in at my home unexpectedly and arranged for me to visit him at his little makeshift flat in Ambarvale. At no stage however did Leonard attempt to initiate anything at all sexual or romantic. Meanwhile, I was dying inside. I wanted him so badly that I began stalking him with my mind; I was consumed by thoughts of him morning, noon and night. Leonard's undeserving wife had caught a whiff of our one-sided dalliance and found the audacity to have a go at me a couple of times, at our children's school – something I chose to ignore but scorned internally. What is it with cheating partners, getting all high and mighty with those swooping in on their discarded?

As I waited for Leonard to get a grip, I started chatting to 'Stephen' on NineMSN chat. Stephen was a MIG welder from Tamworth, a former policeman, and a Scorpio. Needless to say these secondary attributes piqued my interest. From his miniscule profile picture, it was hard to make out what Stephen looked like, but the words he typed to me made the possibility that he might be ugly as fuck irrelevant. When at last we exchanged telephone numbers, his spoken voice drew me closer to him than Leonard had, so I decided to throw caution to the wind and dive into unchartered waters with a smile on my face.

I was now desperate for a true relationship. I wanted to feel the euphoria of skin on skin, of sweet caresses and pillow talk, of compliments, respectful male dominance and charm. I'd get up at six in the morning to chat to Stephen on MSN Messenger, and would stay up all hours of the night with him, often ignoring my children and the essential duties I owed them. I was completely hooked, with physical and mental fatigue a trivial inconvenience.

One morning I was seriously running late for our school run, but finding myself still in conversation with Stephen I chose not to close down the computer and assured him I'd be back in a jiffy and to 'just hang in there'. When I pulled back into the driveway I knew something was terribly wrong when I noticed our front door wide open and the boot of Rhys's Holden Apollo stacked with computer parts that looked a lot like mine. I ran inside, demanding Rhys return the computer immediately; Rhys responded by grabbing me around the throat and pushing me down hard onto our bed. Holding me down, Rhys screamed insults into my face. He then unloaded as much spit and phlegm at me as he could muster, until my face was dripping.

"I want you out of this house you filthy slut! I told you, you and the kids could live here, but *no* other fucking man is to step inside *MY* home while I'm alive, understand?"

I could no longer be quieted by Rhys's violence and I lashed back. This was *my* home too and it was *he* who had destroyed our marriage. If he wanted me out, he could just fucking wait until I was good and ready to go.

That afternoon when the kids returned from school, I called Stephen and arranged to meet with him at a hotel. It was reckless behaviour on my part but I'd had enough of acting 'appropriately' and thinking of others. I was ready to do something for me, and me only.

Rhys returned to the house the next day, computerless, demanding Stephen's phone number. I refused and told him to get the hell out. He ran into my bedroom and ripped through my belongings until he'd found it. I again yelled at Rhys to get out of my home or I was calling the police. Laughing in my face he reminded me it was still *his* home as well and that I'd allowed him to keep the front door keys. Rhys then ventured outside to do something or other inside his car – most probably call Stephen's number. Unwilling or unable to stand another second of bullying in my life, I gathered the children and bundled them into my car.

"I'm going to the cops, I'm sick of you trying to run my life! It's over, do you hear me? It's *over*, there is no coming back to you – *ever*!"

Rhys revved up his car and followed us. The drive to Campbelltown Police Station became a dangerous car chase that only ended when I reached Queen Street and ran into the police station, frantically pleading with the front desk officers to do something about my ex-husband, who was taunting me with calls to my mobile from somewhere around the corner. The police advised me to stay away from home that night; they could not guarantee my safety otherwise. Furthermore, the children should not be witnessing any of what was going on between Rhys and me, and I was advised to ring someone who might accommodate us for the night. I called Debra, my walking friend, who was recently separated herself. Debra flung open her door to us and the police offered us an escort to her place. I then called Stephen and explained what had transpired, adding that in the light of such circumstances, it would be sensible to drop our meeting – *any* meeting. Stephen told me he *had* received a call from Rhys and wasn't afraid of him, and that he still wished to meet me.

As I slept that night on Debra's foldout sofa in the family room, a very scary thing happened. I was suddenly and brutally awoken by an old man's face staring and screaming only inches away from mine. Sitting up, I looked around me cautiously but only the stillness of the night responded. When I discussed the event with Debra the next morning straight after our school drop offs, she told me that her youngest daughter, Brittany, often complained about 'visitors' coming into the house, and that one of them was a cranky old man. Could this mysterious cranky old man be warning me about Rhys perhaps?

Rhys barged into our house again, and this time I didn't care if one of us died in the process of reaching a conclusion. I could not live like this any longer: I now *demanded* absolute freedom and the right to be *me* again, the right to live as *I* wanted to – come what may.

I walked into the kitchen, hot with angry tears, and began smashing everything I could get my hands on. I had been fearful of Rhys long enough and today it was *he* who'd be shown what violence looked like. I was aware that Kristen and Edan were in the house but was too far gone with despair to care. Rhys wasn't taken aback in the least, smirking as he berated me: "Do you *really* want to see who can cause the most damage Angelica – huh?"

Rhys proceeded to punch himself repeatedly on the side of the head until it swelled to double its size. He then called the police and screamed down the phone that he was being assaulted in front of his children by his ex-wife. I could not believe what I was witnessing. My hatred and pure wrath now reached fever pitch – Rhys wasn't going to win this one. Flying back into the kitchen I grabbed a knife, any knife.

"It ends *today* you miserable bastard! It ends *TODAY!*" I cried.

Rhys ran around the house like a lunatic, laughing and goading me; we must have looked like the protagonists in a cheap horror flick. Kristen came out of her hiding place as she saw me waving the knife about and begged me to stop. I was crazed with anger, though and, raising the knife above my head, I yelled at her to go back inside her room.

The police were suddenly on my doorstep, loudly knocking on the front door. Kristen, wild-eyed and frightened, opened the door to let them in. I dropped the knife, kicking it under the bed my ex-husband was still sitting on, grinning at me like a triumphant retard. I had lost all sense of reflection and logic; years of unresolved and unchannelled pain poured out of me like the flood from a busted dam. All I could feel was raw, lurid rage and the overwhelming need to rid my life of Rhys, just as I had done with Alfonso and Mother.

I was certainly *not* a perfect mother but there were certain moral lessons I had instilled in my children and one of these was to always tell the truth. My little Kristen did just that, as she explained to a benign police officer exactly what she'd seen. Then, before all my gawking neighbours, I was carted off in the back of a paddy wagon. Once again *I* was the bad guy, implicated and punished for another's inability to accept reality or abide by *my* rights as a human being.

If that ride to Campbelltown Police Station were a piece of music it would sound like Albinoni's *Adagio in G Minor*. I felt wronged, sad, defeated, spent. I had tried *so fucking hard* at my marriage, one that had clearly been doomed from the outset because of Rhys's and my psychological issues. Was this ride, then, the sum total of eighteen years of impossible work? The books on spirituality I'd read gave various reasons for our union – the children had chosen us for parents, I wronged Rhys in another life, we needed to atone for past karma. I did not care about any of that anymore! What was transpiring right now was wrong! Rhys *was wrong!*

I was placed in a cell next to an agitated man of Arab appearance. The tears fell out of my head like exaggerated emoticons, only to be surpassed by inconsolable sobs. I had been arrested! I was a criminal once more! I *was* the bad guy!

I badly needed to pee. One of the male officers called over a female officer and I was asked to urinate in an open cubicle, under her supervision. Five hours later I was released. I gave the police a taped interview, recounting what really happened. Examining my knuckles and observing my reaction to cross examination, it didn't take the police long to realise I had not assaulted Rhys and that it was *I* who in fact suffered from battered wife syndrome. I had cried throughout the entire process and by the time I'd reached home I was emotionally drained and close to physical collapse. Rhys was asked to go to the police station for questioning the next day, and was subsequently released with a caution. Very little is done, even now, about domestic violence in this country.

For what it was worth, however, Campbelltown Police treated me with utmost dignity and I thanked them both face to face and via my local newspaper. But things did not end there. I soon found myself served with an Apprehended Violence Order (AVO) which I received via the Campbelltown Court. It would be one of many court appearances and calculated systematic harassments. Rhys would not go out quietly.

* * *

I fled my marital home. Fortunately for me it sold quickly at a good price. I needed out of that marriage and its persecution as soon as possible, and ordered my solicitor to dispense with the extra entitlements. I wanted everything divided equally so Rhys would leave me alone but, because I held primary custody of our children, I still walked away with 70 percent of our equity.

Desperate to house my children in adequate surroundings, I moved into a three-year-old house in Oswald Crescent, Rosemeadow, only 1.3 kilometres from the home we'd built in Gunn Place. I didn't want my children living in a hovel or going to a different school, just because their parents couldn't get it together. Children get caught in the crossfire of adult shortcomings, recriminations, and selfishness – I knew this firsthand and had already exposed mine to too much. I'd be damned if I'd add to their stresses any further.

The first night I returned to our new house I knew beyond the shadow of a doubt I had turned off all the lights, but even before re-entering, all were switched on. In the front foyer Alycia said to me and Kristen, "Did you hear that?"

I had heard nothing.

"No," Alycia insisted, "two children's voices were saying *Shhhh here they come!*"

* * *

Paris was a clairvoyant who worked out of a new age shop inside Macarthur Square; I had consulted him before moving out of Gunn Place. Being naturally judgemental, as we all are, I thought he looked like a typical fake, sporting all the obvious embellishments. Yet Paris was probably the most brilliant psychic I'd ever seen, or *would* see henceforth. As well as being a bulimic, I was well on the way to becoming a divination addict as well.

Paris used Western astrology, runes, tarot, numerology and a palm reading to 'work out' my life's pathways. He was spot on about my past and present but when he read my future, it meant little to me.

"There is love around you. You will meet many men. I see you typing on a keyboard. I see your future work in front of a conveyor belt; you are placing items on trays. Later I see you working with children, but they are not normal children. I see you locking them up at night. There is a restless spirit around you. It wants you to listen to her. I see her moving about the house, she is naked; she has dark shoulder length hair and dark angry eyes."

Along with divination, I was addicted to NineMSN Chat. I needed and wanted love again, *real love!* My heart needed years of mending and surely there was a man out there who carried a good needle and thread kit?

A friend of a friend made a remark that compounded my addiction … she said, "Stuff spending a fortune going out every weekend hoping you'll meet a man! All I have to do is get myself a bottle of wine, sit at my computer, and the men come to me!"

She certainly made a valid point, and since I now struggled financially on a single parent pension, child support, and one day a week of paid work at the cake showroom, I felt justified frittering my life away as a faceless flirt in cyberspace.

In juggling expenses, I was constantly 'borrowing from Peter to pay back Paul', but we managed. I fine tuned skills I'd developed from years of managing Rhys's spendthrift and imprudent ways.

My close friends – some of whom I grew up with – appeared to give me a wider berth now that it was no longer me and Rhys coming over for barbecues. The fickleness of throwaway friendships was never more painfully obvious to me than during this critical time in my life. I felt my friends were judging *me* as the one at fault for the break up – after all, I was the loud and vulgar one, the visibly more aggressive and opinionated one. Not worried, I took this incidental isolation as a situation that afforded me more time on social media and, with the exception of relentless and opportunistic calls from Maria, the chat rooms became my social lifeline.

Rhys had the children every second weekend, and during this time I'd meet up with the latest online man that had somehow engaged my sensibilities. Stephen, the former cop who'd appeared so keen, thought better of my situation and bailed out. I didn't begrudge him that: why add unnecessary drama to your life? Besides, Tamworth was a long way from home.

For a short while Rhys lay low, which certainly gave me much needed breathing space and helped me cope with my new sole parent status. A person can easily dismiss how much a spouse actually does with the children or around the house, before they find themselves without them. But, this had been *my* decision and one I was glad for, and what's more I was completely committed to making it work. Soon enough I'd meet someone wonderful who would help me and the fairy tale ending, the one I spent hours dreaming up in Rome and Adelaide as a lonely and wanton little girl, would be mine.

One afternoon I was 'talking' to a man whose chat room handle was 'jjjumpingjackflash'; he did not have a profile picture so I had no idea if I would find him attractive or not, but his conversational style briskly won me over. I was so engrossed in our repartee I forgot to pick up the kids from school. I briskly bade 'Nick' goodbye, writing his handle down so I could find him later on and so I could add him to MSN Messenger. Returning from school I couldn't jump back into cyberspace fast enough. Frantically searching for my new friend on the MSN search engine, but could not find him. I tried another dozen times but only the detested 'no result found' met my eyes. I had obviously misspelt the handle, but surely Nick hadn't deleted his profile? I was devastated. It's not easy finding a guy on cyberspace who wants to do more with you than show you his dick or ask you to 'cyber' (have online sex talk)?

Three days later I was chatting to someone else when the familiar orange conversation alert flashed at the bottom of my computer screen. There he was – jjjumpingjackflash! I could feel a huge smile spread over my face as I typed, 'There you are! I thought I had lost you forever!'

I arranged to meet Nick at the cake showroom following my Saturday shift there. Nick lived nearby in Bexley North and we could grab a round of drinks at the Canterbury-Hurlstone Park RSL, next door to the showroom. This was the place William, Rhys's father, had visited all of his life since its 1927 inception as a mere tin 'men's shed'.

As the appointment time drew closer I found it difficult to concentrate on my shop duties. My eyes darted back and forth to the front door of the showroom expecting a gorgeous man to walk through it. Finally, right on time, a typically 'Hellenic' looking personage peeked through the portals of Alastair and Marianne's showroom. I couldn't be sure it was Nick as I had no reference picture, but the knowing smile gave him away. Despite being a little pudgy and completely bald, Nick was tall and, well, 'reasonable' looking.

"Look at that hair!" he complimented, scanning every feature on my face with undisguised pleasure.

Look at my hair? Surely my hair wasn't an overriding 'best feature'? Oh well, at least it wasn't Rhys's pathological preoccupation with enormous mammaries!

* * *

Nick was a bad dresser, he had red patches on his bald head, no car, and he was the archetypal *wog* I'd so carefully steered clear of. But, I liked him and I agreed to see him again. After our drinks at the RSL I offered to drop him back to his granny flat and even allowed him to kiss me on the cheek. From that day until our first date, there was nonstop texting and online chatting between us. Nick accessed NineMSN Chat from a public computer, and it concerned me that a man of thirtythree had so little collateral. As much as I needed love, I also needed protection and a 'prosperous' life of sorts.

On our first date, I picked Nick up from his granny flat and we had dinner at a Mexican place in Hurstville. This was followed by the ethnically flavoured 'chick flick', *My Big Fat Greek Wedding*. Needless to say, I was not even slightly impressed.

Despite all the evidence pointing to another epic relationship fail, the years of living a sexless, passionless life prompted me to take Nick home that night. After the movie at Brighton-Le-Sands we spent countless hours and a bottle of wine making out by the ocean, so I guess I was pretty fired up. I woke up the next morning next to a snoring gorilla. *SHIT! What have I done!* Nick was possibly the hairiest man I'd ever seen, I found eczema on other parts of his body, he had an upturned penis, and what looked like a pouch on his mons pubis. All these less than fine features left me feeling positively *ugh*! Additionally, his side of the bed was drenched in sweat, leaving no doubt that Nick suffered from severe sleep apnoea.

When Nick left my place I pondered what to do, or even to think. He seemed so nice. I had chosen Rhys for his looks and realised looks mean nothing. It's a person's behaviour that counts. Even though my gut was vociferously saying *NO*, I agreed to keep seeing Nick, and for our second date he invited me to a work party at the hospital where he worked as an operations assistant. I breathed a sigh of relief when I saw him wear a normal shirt and trousers; suddenly Nick looked a whole lot better, and I began feeling hopeful.

* * *

I was sitting in the car park of the hospital he worked in in the shire; Nick was late getting out of theatre and memories of Rhys's tardiness triggered a level of anxiety I wasn't prepared to welcome back into my life. I was also nervous about meeting Nick's friends so soon. I was fresh out of a long married life and my self-esteem had taken a beating, so I was not prepared to be surveyed by people I did not know and who might judge me. It took every ounce of deliberation not to start the engine and drive away. Just as I was about to act on my impulses Nick tapped on the window, still wearing his hospital blues. Nick assured me he would only be five more minutes changing into his civvies and his big warm, happy smile made it impossible for me to leave.

Nick's personal friends and colleagues sat around a big table in a function room attached to the hospital's main building. My date then zealously introduced me.

"This is Angelica, isn't she beautiful?"

I could feel myself warm to a deep shade of crimson; I was never introduced this way by Rhys. Rhys could only ever find fault in my appearance … was I really beautiful?

Those words clouded my gut feelings like thick fog and I immediately pledged my love to my Greek benefactor. At the party Nick's only non-Greek friend was Howard, a heavily tattooed and pierced 'heffer' who worked as an operations assistant as well. The other Hellenics were amiable types who did their best to chat to me, imparting affable pointers concerning my 'boyfriend'. I was glad when it was all over. I had spent the last eighteen years socialising with the same people and now found myself unable to say very much at all. What did I know of modern Greeks anyway?

Stupidly, and only three weeks after meeting Nick online, I asked him to move in with me and the kids. Certainly I was thinking with a whipped-up groin rather than a level head. Jumping from a terrible marriage into an uncharted fling was risky, but it was just so difficult for Nick to see me regularly without a car, and patience and abstinence were never strong points of mine.

The kids did not seem to mind having a new man around. Nick was comical and congenial with us all. In retrospect I believe they were happy to see me smile again, rather than accepting Nick per se. Yet it did not take long for events to jolt my gagged gut into cutting through the fog and screaming out *I TOLD YOU SO!*

I had indeed jumped from the frypan into the fire, and this particular brand of souvlaki was badly overcooked.

CHAPTER SEVENTEEN

REBOUND

———

Rhys was stalking me again. He saw that there was another man in my life and World War Three was declared. Settlement was taken care of before Nick came on the scene, so the only way Rhys could torment me now was via the kids and every government department who offered him the time of day.

The first of these departments was Centrelink, who decided to investigate my single parent status, following Rhys's claim that I was now in a de facto relationship. The Department of Community Services then asked about an incident in which Edan had slipped inside our backyard and hit his mouth on the concrete veranda. As Edan's gum gushed with blood it was Nick, not I, who scooped him into his arms and rushed him to Campbelltown Hospital. I had frozen with shock, much to my maternal shame.

When these attempts failed, the local sheriff, who was coincidentally our former next door neighbour at Gunn Place, served me with Family Court orders relating to custody of Kristen and Edan, who were still minors. Furthermore, an altercation between Nick and Rhys on our front lawn ended with Nick and me receiving AVO charges.

Rhys had arrived to pick up the kids for weekend access, but because Nick decided to go outside and supervise the pick-up, Rhys became violent, threatening Nick both physically and verbally. I grabbed a stick and waved it at Rhys to defend Nick who, realistically, required no assistance from me. The magistrate decided I was a definite threat to Rhys and my criminal 'resume' received a second AVO.

Nick showed up in my life at exactly the right time but, I soon realised, he was the wrong man for me. He was a hopeless substance abuser and the more I nagged him to stop his drug taking the more drug paraphernalia I found concealed in my home. I also learnt that the Greek community in which he was deeply entrenched consisted of drug takers *and* dealers. Not knowing how to handle any of this I did the only thing I *could* do, and started smoking with him.

I had never been drawn to drugs or alcohol, but as the months went by I found less in common with Nick and this meant if *I* didn't walk into Nick's world, there wasn't going to be a 'world' with him for me, at all, and I wasn't ready to let go of him just yet. I simply would *not* be wrong a third time.

Family Court is not for the fainthearted. I hired a solicitor to see me through the first day and I may as well have flushed $2000 down the drain. After agreeing to mediation and getting past round one, I had to return to the courtroom because Rhys objected to us taking the children to Adelaide to visit my cousins. This time I represented myself, and won. When Nick and I walked out of the court house into busy lunch hour Goulburn Street, I saw Rhys approaching with a demeanour that spelt trouble. Before I could take another breath Rhys had gone toe to toe with Nick, who unflinchingly stood his ground once again. What happened next was nauseating, with me feeling more embarrassed and self-conscious than ever before in my misshapen life. Rhys, with unbridled ferocity, berated Nick with profanities and degradations about me – the mother of his children.

"I fucked that slut two thousand times! I've been up her ass a hundred times! She's swallowed my come and polished my knob! I was there before you and those are *my kids* you fucking wog, you bald cunt!"

The business suits and the well-to-do 'lunch ladies' walking by took notice of the spectacle, probably wondering who 'her' was. I tried to make myself as small as possible. I felt no more vindicated by Nick's rebuttals than having a bucket of iced water thrown over me.

"Go put on one of your mother's skirts, you cross dressing poofter; go on, go smoke some pole!" Nick spat back.

The slurs continued, back and forth. I was certain Nick would throw a punch at any moment – it was what Rhys was aiming for, but Nick outsmarted him and kept his hands firmly by his side throughout the ordeal. Rhys walked away laughing, convinced he had mortally wounded Nick's dignity, but it was *mine* he had hit – a perfect bullseye too. Nick didn't give a shit; he copped far worse daily from his Greek matriarch. He was the black sheep of the family, the one that hadn't settled down with a 'nice Greek girl', and *Mitera* couldn't stand it. Also, she could not stand *me*.

One afternoon during a forced visit to his childhood home in St Clair, and as her precious baby son sat on the toilet safely out of earshot from her acid tongue, *Mitera* approached me and snapped, "Why you with my son? You married, you older, you have kids, you no good for Nick."

Shocked but defiant, I managed to get the right words out.

"Thank you for your concern but I think these factors are for Nick to decide on, don't you think?"

* * *

Pretty much from the day he moved into our home, Nick had been lying about everything. Nine out of ten were white lies, but as our issues grew larger, the lies darkened.

Nick was supposed to have saved up $1000 for our trip to Adelaide but didn't, and I almost called it off and had a huge fight with him over it. For an entire hour I abused Nick yet, and almost in tears he insisted, "We are going to Adelaide, I promise you!" And yes we did go – taking long, dangerous turns at the wheel and almost falling asleep with my three babies sitting unsuspectingly in the back.

We stayed at my cousin Valeria's house. She took one look at Nick and decided she didn't like him. Valeria virtually kicked me and Nick out of her house forcing us to 'camp' in her front yard. The kids were welcomed inside and treated completely differently from us, which was fine so long as *they* were happy. Nick and I left the kids with Valeria and spent one night alone at a quaint bed and breakfast in Hahndorf. It was anything but romantic. Nick was high on alcohol and the sex was how I remembered it with my ex-husband: empty and staged.

Our drive back was an even greater disaster. We traversed the worst dust storm imaginable, which left my car and our belongings covered in fine red dust. I was grateful for Nick's presence for it was he who got out and ran alongside the car, keeping us inside our lane and preventing us from colliding onto oncoming traffic. In addition to this, I had a message on my mobile from my doctor advising me to see him as soon as I'd returned to Sydney. My pap smear had presented with some abnormalities and I was graded CIN1 for cervical cancer. The cervical warts that manifested back in 1987 were directly linked to it.

Bringing Nick into my 'earth plane' seemed to attract ailments of all types, physical *and* spiritual. It was time to utilise some of what I'd learnt from the many esoteric manuals I'd fed from over the years.

Turning to my Wiccan spells for help, I asked *Source* to freeze the offending cells. *Source* owed me a favour, for I had helped Letitia's cat when he was dying of cancer. Letitia had been inconsolable; Sweetie was her life and only companion away from Mother. I witnessed the way Sweetie's body had wasted away, his thick Persian coat coming off in clumps. Although I no longer respected Letitia as a person, her tears touched my heart and so I cast the *Pain Freedom Spell* on her behalf. Sweetie made a full recovery that left everyone baffled and, along with Sweetie's cancer, all signs of the CIN1 anomaly disappeared.

Around this time, I witnessed ominous manifestations in my home which brought back memories of the reading Paris had given me a few months earlier. Alycia had seen a young naked girl with dark hair and angry eyes who ran out of our family room and through the glass doors into our garden. With paranormal activity intensifying, we decided to name the spirit 'Sarah'.

I noticed this activity at its peak whenever Nick and I were intimate. I had returned to unnatural promiscuity in order to keep Nick interested and faithful. He spent far too much time on my computer and alarm bells started sounding. One night Edan woke up vomiting. I stripped the bed, cleaned my son up, and set out to remove the vomit covering his bedroom floor. I went to the laundry to retrieve the product I needed for this and it was gone. I checked the kitchen cupboards – nothing. I knew it was where it was supposed to be so I decided 'Sarah' had moved it in the same way she moved everything when it was most needed. Frustrated I called out, "Sarah! Give me the fucking cleanser NOW!"

I then felt myself being psychically led into my bedroom where, lo and behold, there it was, sitting right next to my bed on the bedside table, a spot that had been empty only moments before. I had to wonder if my interest in Metaphysics and practice of Wicca had attracted Sarah to our home. The use of a ouija board was how little Robbie Mannheim became possessed in 1949 and for that reason alone I was most careful with all methods of divination.

Sarah had begun to affect everyone, including visitors. Alycia's friends were reporting, when they stayed overnight, sounds of footsteps, as well as an all pervasive fear, like something or someone was watching them. Lights flickered on and off at different times of the day, doors slammed shut, and one night Kristen ran out screaming from her bedroom because 'someone' had yanked off her bed covers. On another occasion when Nick and I were having sex, I felt the temperature of the bedroom drop suddenly. An icy cold hand touched my face and then Nick jumped out of bed, all colour drained from his face.

"What the fuck was that?" he cried.

I saw nothing but felt a denseness that could only have been Sarah's etheric body. More pronounced however, were the words on repeat in my mind's ear: *get rid of him, get rid of him, get rid of him.*

The next morning Sarah reaffirmed her wish in the most tangible way to date. A beautiful mosaic mirror that my cousin Bianca had created came off the wall before my very eyes and seemed to fling itself against the opposite wall in our corridor. When it landed on the ground breaking into a hundred pieces, I knew we were living inside a genuine poltergeist nightmare. I was now afraid of, and mindful, that this soul had developed sufficient anger to possibly hurt us. I returned to Macarthur Square to consult with Paris.

As much as I was frightened by Sarah, she also validated that I was indeed clairvoyant and clairsentient and that the things that happened to me in Rome as a child were *not* the figments of an overactive or traumatised imagination, but as real as day and night.

Paris painted a bleak picture of not only Sarah, but Nick as well. Sarah had been the victim of a vicious rape and murder and it is unclear whether her body and killer were ever found. Perhaps this was her pained message to us. Something about Nick seemed to anger Sarah more and her fury would intensify when we had sex … I guessed it made perfect sense. Paris assured me Nick was not the one for me – not even close. He carried many personal problems and had somewhat lost his sense of identity. Without advising me to leave, Paris suggested I'd be doing other things that did not involve Nick, adding that once Nick left my home, Sarah would too. I had no intention of kicking Nick out. I loved him and needed him – pot addiction, lies, sleep apnoea, upturned dick and all.

There was a clairvoyant in my neighbourhood who came highly recommended for spiritual cleansing. I'd happened to pick up one of his business cards at a meeting held in the Mount Annan Spiritual Church a few weeks before. I decided that it would be 'Sarah' to leave my home long before I'd ever rid myself of Nick.

* * *

My third day in court proved highly fortuitous. A second hearing was held in my absence because I had collapsed in my driveway from the worst case of cystitis imaginable. In the last hour, Nick, my champion, had accessed his family's solicitor to represent me for a trite $500. It was a monumental mistake, however, for Nick to take Kristen with him. When Rhys saw Kristen with my boyfriend he was furious and demanded an adjournment which, strangely enough, the court granted him. I should have known better than to send Kristen along but foresight has never been my forte.

On this occasion I felt unusually calm and made the unconventional decision to represent myself. After wasting so much on taciturn solicitors how hard could it be? I was an intelligent, eloquent, and logical person and, the magistrate was a *woman.* This glorious woman listened to my submission with obvious intent, slamming Rhys down hard after a monologue of put-downs against me. A final 'sit down Mr So and So', as Rhys argued out of turn at each word that came out of my mouth, and the fight was won. I received full custody of Edan and Kristen, and Rhys was given alternate weekends and part of the school holidays. Nick and I danced out of the building sporting wide grins, but the moment of victory was soured by a torrent of acrimonious words behind our backs. Rhys also spat on me. Nick gave chase to him but the coward managed to get away. Disgusted, I reported Rhys; I couldn't take any more. We made our way to nearby Surry Hills Police Station, certain the court's front foyer cameras had captured the incident. Not so, and charges were not laid.

On another occasion when Nick drove the kids to Campbelltown Police Station for Rhys's access pick-up, my ex-husband followed my car all the way to Rosemeadow shops, forming a block on the exit path to antagonise Nick. It was a childish and dangerous act, with Nick having to mount the median strip to get himself out. Rhys's intimidation tactics aside, there were other terrors occurring at home.

Intellectually I understood that Rhys was hurting, but Rhys would not understand that *he* was the reason for his own pain. All of us are on a learning path, with some receiving harsher lessons than others. My spirituality told me that the sooner we stop repeating the same mistakes, the sooner we are released from the karmic wheel of debt.

Little by little I began to see Paris's reason for steering me away from Nick.

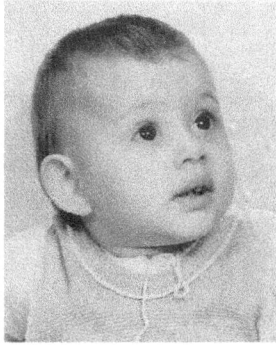

Me at ten months of age.

Me aged one in Düsseldorf, Germany.

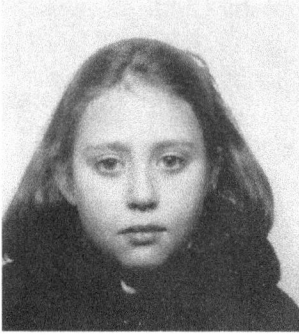

Me aged eight. Passport photo for my trip to Spain.

With the Colusseum behind us in Rome. L-R: Letitia, Auntie Gianna, Gilda, and me.

Me at my first cake shop assistant position, holding up a pencil drawing I made for my boss. This was his hometown in Northern Italy.

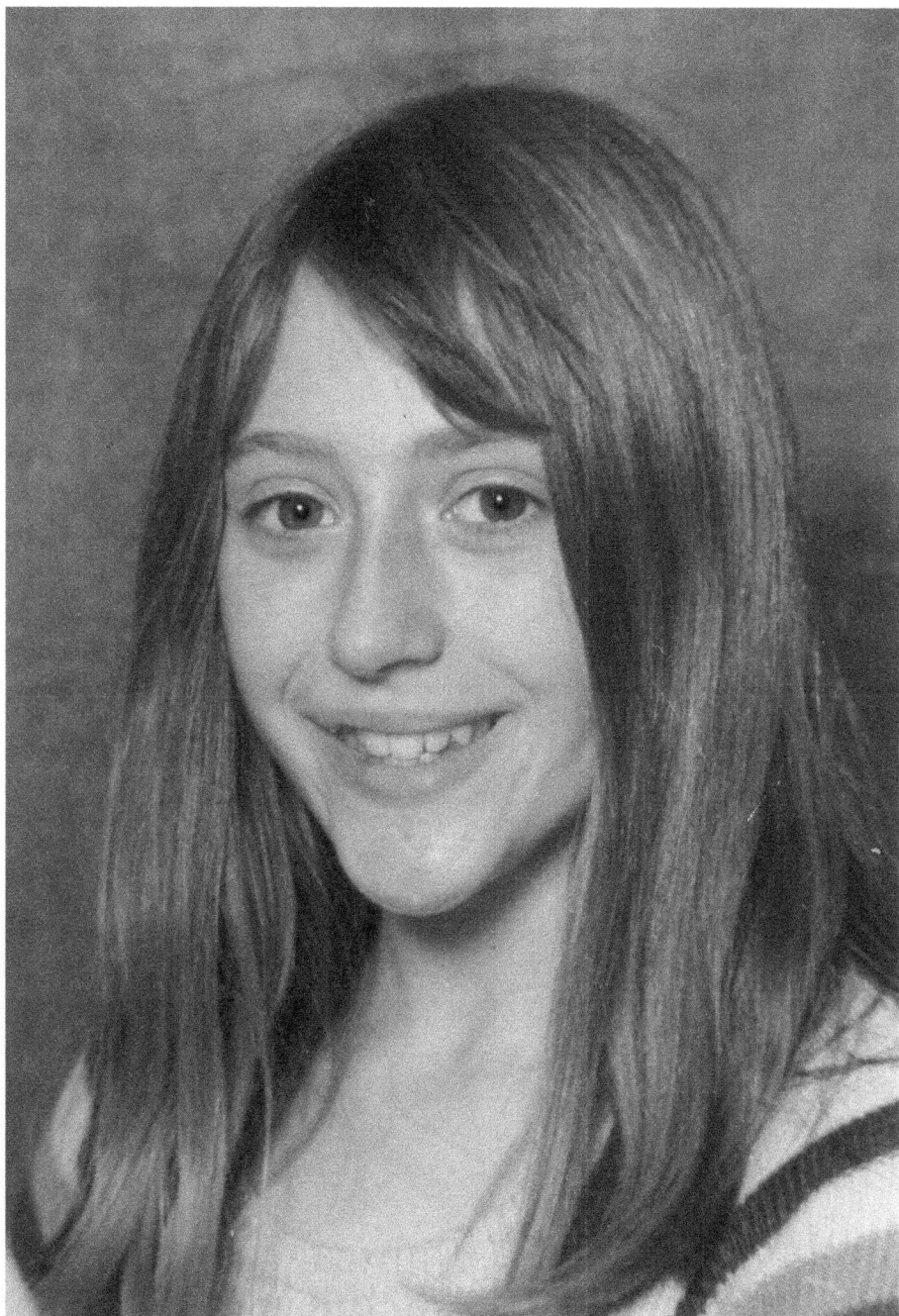

Me aged thirteen whilst frequenting Cabramatta West Primary.
Again out of correct uniform.

The head shot sent to producers for the advertised reporter's position with Simon Townsend's Wonder World, *as Edith Bliss' replacement.*

Red eyed and drunk on Sydney's red rattler on our way to new year's celebrations at circular quay.

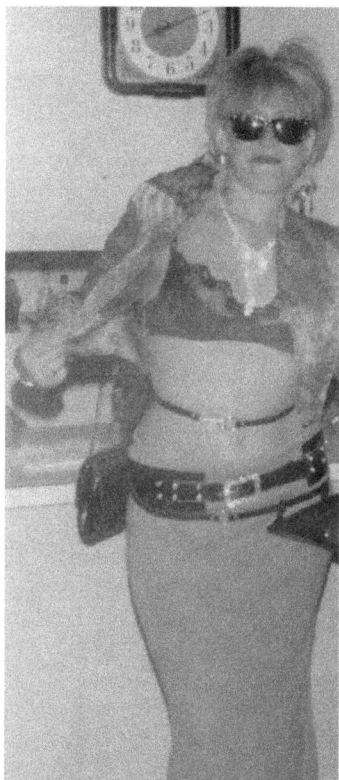

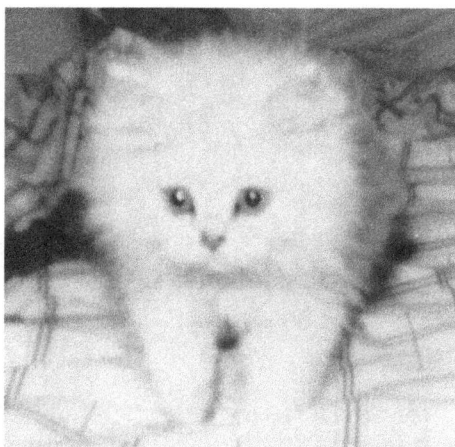

Above: Tessie, the little Persian forced to sleep outside by Alfonso.

Left: Dressed as my idol Madona Ciccone during yet another New Year's Eve.

Below: In order to marry Rhys in the Catholic church I had to be confirmed – reluctantly I might add.

Above: First marriage inside St. Mary's cathedral in Sydney. Dragging that infernal train – my mother's idea

Left: The saddest bride in the world.

I began finding an affinity with animals at a very young age. Here I find myself on the Gold Coast during my honeymoon sporting the cheap bleached blonde hair Rhys wanted so much.

As a snake Chinese zodiac I was always fascinated with these creatures. The fact Gilda hated snakes also helped me want to get to know them better. This is the photo sent to That's Life magazine regarding my biological Father, Ettore.

Left: Janos' crayon portrait of me – Rome, 1972.

Below: Kristen aged one at our housing commission townhouse in Auburn 1992.

Alycia's first birthday in Revesby NSW – 1989.

My chubby Edan looking dapper in his christening outfit – Auburn 1996.

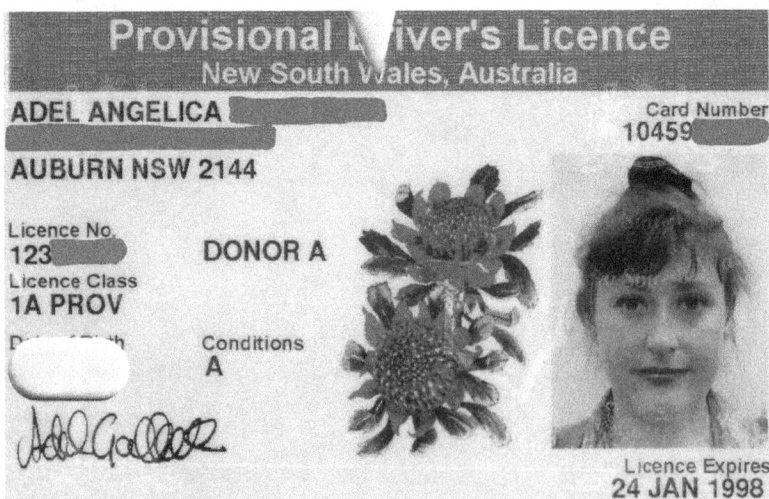

One of the most poignant moments in my life; also my first taste of real freedom. I obtained my licence aged thirty five after five failed attempts due to nerves.

Left: More animal love. Here I am with my little Alycia during one of my many visits to Adelaide at the Cleland Wildlife Park.

Bottom Left: One of the many photos taken of me by Eser during our two years together. Black hair in order to help undo some of Rhys' emotional damage became an absolute must.

Below: Wishing for love during my European trip in 2008. The famous Trevi fountain in Rome.

Left: Another dream come true. Me inside Stonehenge; Amesbury, England – 2008.

Right: Adam and I in our corrections uniform during the early days of our courtship; Springton, South Australia, 2010.

The happiest day of my life; August fourth 2013.
I finally marry my sweetheart Adam Heath Brewer.

Left: Adam and I on honeymoon in 2013 at the "love locks" bridge behind Notre Dame du Paris where we attached our own special love lock keeping the key.

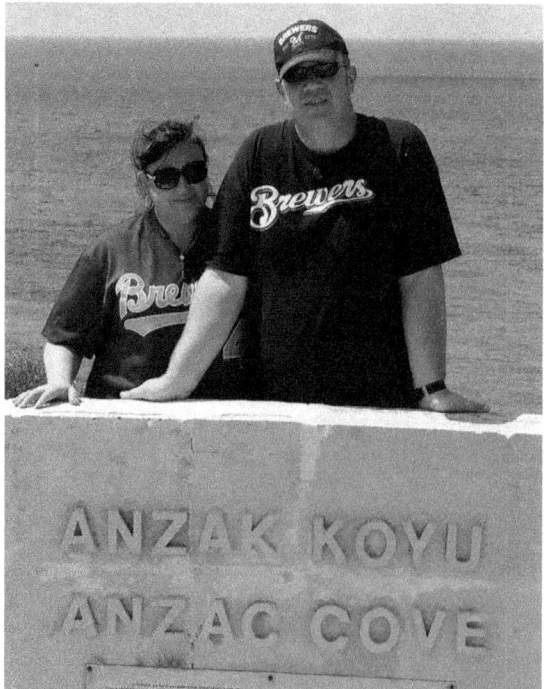

Right: Adam and I at Anzac Cove in Gallipolli, 2013.

On my fiftieth birthday with my beautiful son Edan.

Kristen's twenty-fifth birthday in Angaston with Alycia. My beautiful girls.

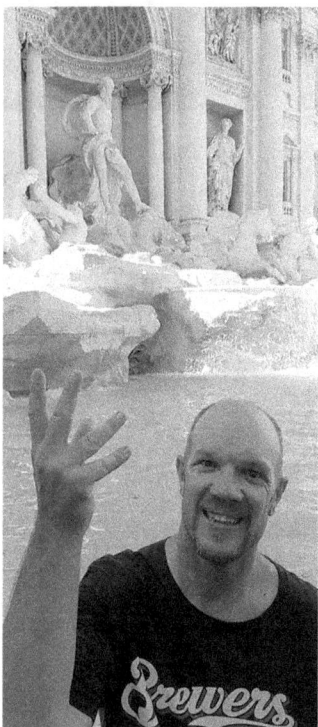

Above: During our 2016 Italy trip for Adam's World Championshop Clay Pigeon Shoot. The blondie hair is back, we've both lost a tonne of weight, and the gorgeous Amalfi Coast is at our back. Happy times.

Top left: Following a PTSD episode back in my birth city, I say 'vaffanculo' to this place. I've found true love and I don't need you anymore Trevi. My job here is done!

Bottom left: And Adam decides to join me... not a fan of the eternal city either.

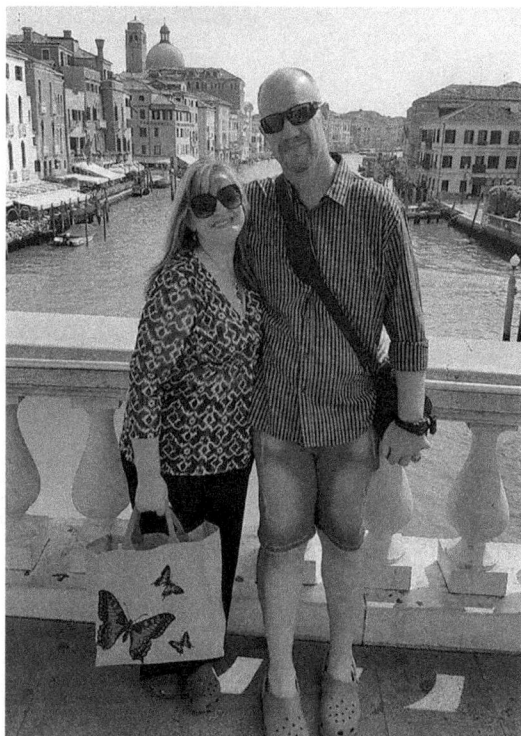

Left: Italy trip, Venice 2016.

Bottom: No longer afraid of the Colosseum. Rome 2016.

At her home in Boras Sweden, Lotta and I during our 2013 honeymoon. Even with minimal contact, a thirty year friendship will survive if the heart is willing.

At Noel's wedding to Danielle. Another friendship that has lasted the test of time. Sadley, Danielle and Noel have since separated.

Gwenn Hanns (RIP) and her husband Peter Hanns with my eldest, Alycia. Circa 1998.

With my earth plane sister, Sharon, on her wedding day in November 2015 as her maiden of honour. True family is rarely blood related.

Me and Rachel Iasiello, beautiful soul, fellow Italian, spiritual daughter.

Alycia's dog Gogo introduced me to the joys of dogs and the purest love only a dog can offer.

And then care of Kristen, along came Conan in 2014.

And they did live happily ever after. Flaxman Valley, part of the distinguished Barossa Valley, South Australia – Wine Country.

When Kristen decided to relocate to England, Frodo became my son instead of my grandson, and naturally, Conan's brother instead of his nephew.

Mango, my longest living furbaby. 24 January 2005 to 13 August 2019.

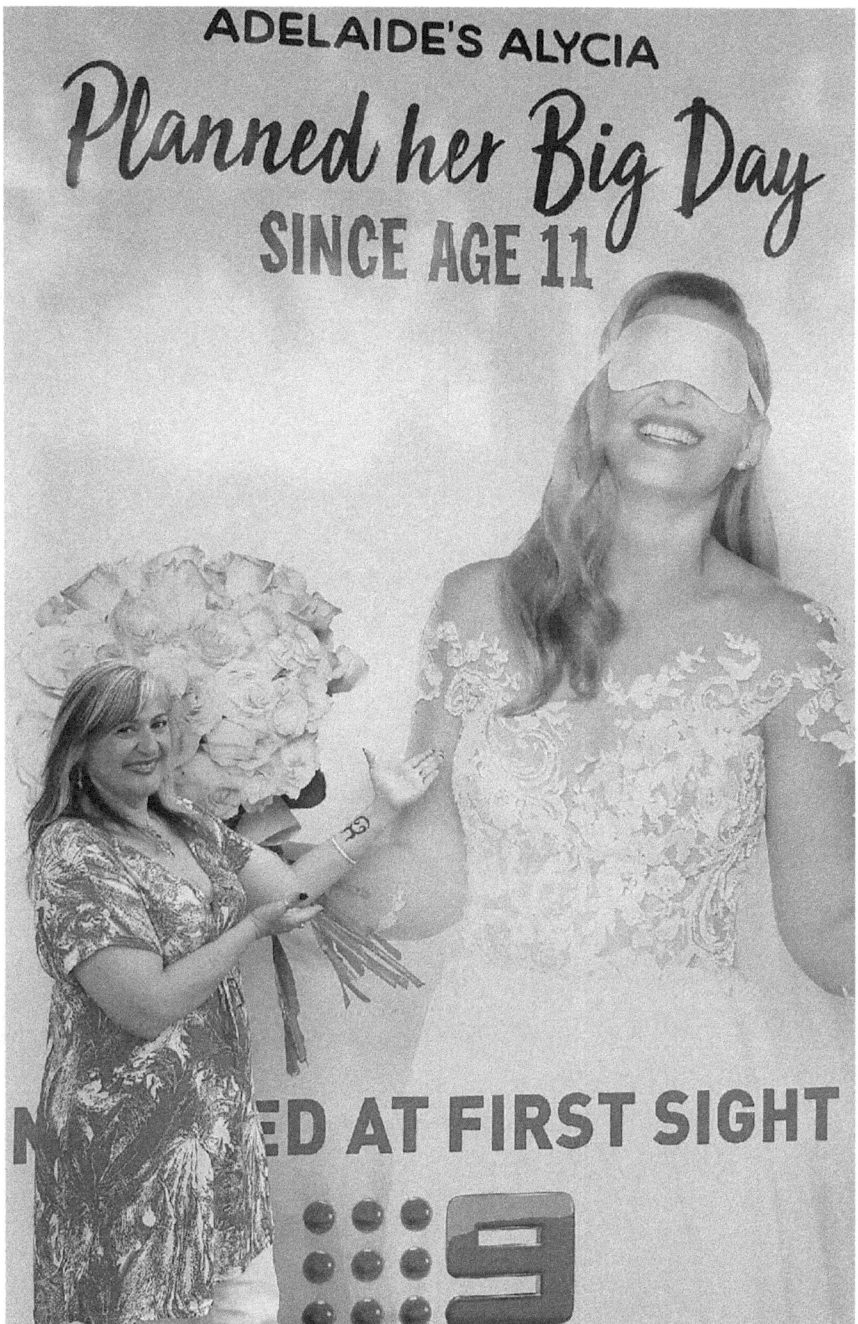

Standing in front of a channel nine billboard of my daughter Alycia in the Adelaide CBD. A very proud mother of a TV and Instagram star! January 2018.

Beautiful Kristen, how I miss you.

He was definitely hiding something from me on the computer – *my* computer, and I had every right to find out what this something was.

I wasn't very computer savvy but by playing around with the PC long enough, I discovered how to retrieve messages and pictures from the hard drive. Nick had subscribed to to an adult "dating" site and was 'chatting' to a variety of older women whose profile pictures left little to the imagination. I also managed to hack into Nick's emails, quite by accident, finding several provocative proposal emails to two separate women. I waited angrily for Nick's return from work as I geared myself for the pounce. All I got back was denials and excuses. I had expected them but I didn't *have to* accept them. I continued to drill Nick until I had him in tears, only then did he confess portions of his crime. The emails, Nick defended, were written to appease a couple of online stalkers who had become obsessed with him.

The heart only listens to what it wants to hear and feel, rarely to the truth. I knew Nick was cheating but I was hooked on him. He had been my knight in shining armour in the fight against Rhys. He thought I was outstandingly beautiful and called me his 'little Spanish meatball', the kids liked him, he spoiled me … surely a few emotional betrayals were worth the payoff …

I begged Nick to stop. He agreed but did not stop, and so I told my gut to shut the fuck up and leave my heart the hell alone.

> *There's a story … a legend, about a bird that sings just once in its life. From the moment it leaves its nest, it searches for a thorn tree … and never rests until it's found one. And then it sings … more sweetly than any other creature on the face of the earth. And singing, it impales itself on the longest, sharpest thorn. But, as it dies, it rises above its own agony, to out-carol the lark and the nightingale. The thorn bird pays its life for just one song, but the whole world stills to listen, and God in his heaven smiles.*
> From *The Thorn Birds* by Colleen McCullough

* * *

Maria started to date Nick's best friend, Con. Con was far more respectable and honourable than Nick. He owned a successful real estate agency, had a nice car, good clothes, and plenty of cash to splash on the ever demanding Maria. In addition, Con had strong connections with the best drug dealers in his area and Maria was now a 'designer drugs' junkie. Before dating Con, Maria spent a year with David, a dubious nightclub owner and sexual health supplements 'rep' who rented a yacht from rich associates, giving Maria a glimpse of the Sydney elite's high life (pun intended). I could not care less about the direction Maria was taking, though; I'd stopped loving her a long time ago.

One night we went to Sydney's biggest and best gay nightclub – ARQ, in upmarket Darlinghurst. It was here where I tried my first 'E' under my former best friend's watchful eye.

I remember very little of that night. I know I was feeling the 'lovey dovey' buzz everyone speaks of, and danced on air through to twilight, hoping to catch one of the intermittent laser lights in my hand. The crux of the experience came when, dazzled by the lasers, I perched on the mezzanine and tried to dive down to catch those pretty lights that bounced off the revelling crowd below me. A family friend, who in fact *was* keeping a genuine eye on me, grabbed me by the belt and set me back on my feet with a sharp reprimand. Back home I continued to find myself inside altered states and, as they say, the sex was mind-blowing … but not so the twenty-four-hour 'comedown' to reality.

The big tattooed brute I'd met eight months previously at Nick's work Christmas party 'added' me on NineMSN. He then asked me for 'a most unusual favour'. Howard begged me to cast a spell to get him off drug trafficking charges. I wondered if he was stealing morphine from the hospital coffers too. Stupidly, I obliged. A month or so later I received an elated email stating he had beaten all charges and whatever I had done worked a treat. As my reward Nick and I were sent a special invitation to an 'elite location'.

The special location was nothing more than an 'outback do' in the backwater suburb of Bringelly, at a place that looked more like a hippie commune than anything 'elite'. The entrance was heavily guarded by bikie-looking men who checked every guest's itinerary and credentials. Nick asked me to wait in the car while he consulted with a doorman who looked like a hero from Norse mythology. The giant summoned Howard to the entrance and, following a string of congenial gesticulations, Nick signalled for me to park in a certain spot inside the strange arena.

Everyone in the place looked like a bikie. I'd never really taken notice of bikies before. The only time I'd heard anything about bikies was whenever Rhys and I drove past the Milperra pub. Rhys's eyes would light up and he'd exclaim, "Look! That's where the Father's Day Massacre took place!"

The men wore vests with 'Rebels Australia' embroidered on them. I wasn't sure who these people were but a poster at the Surry Hills Police Station displayed a long list of outlawed bikie gangs, and the Rebels were definitely on it. There were rows and rows of ornate Harley Davidson motorcycles on display, alongside a few hot rods. The girls hanging off the dishevelled brutes acted and dressed like suburban pole dancers.

The event taking place at the Rebels Clubhouse not far from Rossmore, was titled Porn and Prawn Night, and a measly ten bucks bought you a beautiful platter of fresh prawns, hot chips, and a schooner. Following the meal, Nick and Howard disappeared into some huts lining the driveway. I watched inquisitively as a couple of burly clubhouse members hovered around the huts like sentinels. My eyes then landed on a massive bikie who was easily seven feet tall; he was covered in facial piercings and looked meaner than King Kong on heat. Howard came out of the hut and beckoned me over, introducing me to some heavily tattooed women sitting around a table outside the food pavilion.

"Hey girls, take good care of my friend Angelica while Nick and I go have a catch-up yeah?"

I prayed Nick's 'catch-up' wasn't going to last all day while I was left with these dubious ladies of the night. Oddly enough, the ladies were actually very nice to me, and chatted enthusiastically about their kids and family life. It also appeared they generated enough revenue to afford their children the very best education and home life. I began to wonder what exactly it was they did for a living.

I could hear familiar stripping anthems emanate from the pavilion. Catching a glimpse of the stage, I could see scantily clad women beginning to 'do their thing'. The men sitting around below them had discarded their prawns and were now greedily absorbing every move the women made. One woman at my table turned away from the entertainment and asked me about my situation with Nick. I explained I was Nick's girlfriend. The woman looked knowingly at the others and smiled.

"Well, it won't be long before you become one of us then? Get ready for a hell of an initiation girlie; I hope you're not shy."

'A what?' I thought to myself, but did not dare probe the group for more information. I didn't *want* to imagine what the woman meant. I felt very uncomfortable here and couldn't wait to leave; what was Nick doing in those huts anyway?

* * *

Things with Nick were spiralling out of control fast. I spent more time trying to uncover his lies and catch him cheating on the computer than I did having a 'normal relationship' with him. Nick was high more than he was sober, asleep more than he was awake, and despite all my good intentions to build us into a productive family, his mother continued to drive him nuts about his living here with me. Nick spent all his wages on drugs, Magnum ice creams and the like. I had ballooned to 100 kilos and felt horrible, and the relentless nagging and questioning that was now a staple in my demeanour quickly brought everyone in the house down.

I returned home from work one afternoon and saw an old white car parked in the driveway. Nick sometimes borrowed his mother's car in order to give mine a break. I went inside and found Nick sitting at our outdoor table, tears streaming down his face. When I asked what was wrong Nick walked over and hugged me tightly.

"Angelica I can't do this anymore. I can't live like this with you telling me what to do all the time; I cop enough of that from my mother. I've packed all my stuff; it's in Mum's car. I'm sorry; I'm going to go back to my parents. I love you so much but I need to be me, I'm sick of all your rules!"

I felt the floor falling from under me. My stomach clenched, my heart stopped beating, my throat closed up. The feeling of dread that gripped me was the greatest since finding Patrick's flat emptied out, all those years back. Nick was *not* leaving me, not tonight, not tomorrow, and not *ever*! As bad as he was for me I needed him in my life.

I flung my arms around his neck, screaming, begging and manipulating him into staying. I felt like Rose in the 1997 film *Titanic*'s death scene. Forcing Nick to kiss me, I hoped he'd be reminded of how amazing and sensual it was to be with me. After only moments ticking by, Nick began to feel the ardour he had for me, and clutching seconds of triumph inside my hand, I begged Nick to stay, over and over again. No, tonight Nick would not be leaving me.

* * *

My beautiful Auntie Gianna passed away suddenly and tragically, on 15 March 2003. She had gone into hospital for a simple knee operation, and the next morning, on her way to the toilet, she collapsed and died of a brain aneurysm. She would not have known what hit her, which was the only consolation anyone who loved her received.

I was in shock. Auntie Gianna was the only person in my family who I'd loved deeply and she wasn't even a blood relative! I flew to Adelaide to attend her funeral, entrusting Nick with my three children as well as with Lucky the cat. Everyone was inconsolable but most of all my little cousin Rodolfo, who had worshipped his mother. Watching Uncle Eduardo howl like a child as he bent into his wife's open casket was also particularly painful to watch. Pleadingly, he kissed and touched the plasticised face of a corpse. When his son tried to drag him away Eduardo resentfully lashed out, refusing to let go of his Gianna. This sad spectacle was a lesson in humanity for me because I never believed my uncle could wear so much vulnerability on his sleeve. All my life Uncle Eduardo represented the immovable, stoic patriarch, and to most of us he was no more than an arrogant dictator.

At Auntie Gianna's wake I witnessed more of the unimaginable: a hissing squabble between Bianca and Valeria over Gianna's few personal effects such as photographs and a few pieces of inexpensive jewellery. This made me feel a little nauseous for I'd always believed my elder cousins had more dignity. The catfight was in fact a snapshot of what was to come later on in our lives and the behaviour that would leave me bleeding for a very long time.

Letitia was dressed to the nines and frosted with jewellery, some of which she would proudly boast about, like her gold Longines watch and a huge ruby encrusted ring. I couldn't feel further removed from my tribe if I tried. Letitia had often criticised my Auntie Gianna, calling her a gold digger and opportunist, yet here she was on this precious day looking like Bathsheba before a lusty David.

* * *

When I returned to Rosemeadow the house looked like a typhoon had hit it. The kids told me Nick had been on the computer the whole time I was away – when he was home that is. I yelled my lungs out at him: *how could he let this happen?* Still in emotional pain from the funeral, I had no room for lack of consideration. The stark reality of Nick's actions was not deliberate oversight or neglect, but a way of telling me it was over. But I would not listen. I knew Nick was scouring the net for other women, and under duress he readily admitted some very disturbing facts that should have had me running for the hills.

I plodded along with Nick until early September 2003 when finally, after another awful lie and betrayal, I had to call it quits for my sanity's sake if nothing else. But before this bitter end arrived I decided to enter his special brand of hell one last time.

One ominous lunchtime, I had rung Nick all day long from Alastair and Marianne's. His mobile and our landline just rang out; something sinister was afoot. I rushed home expecting Nick to be gone for good but instead, there he was sleeping soundly – albeit abnormally quietly given his chronic sleep apnoea. I shook Nick vigorously a dozen times screaming into his face and jumping on him, but he barely twitched. I then rummaged through his clothes and around the house for evidence of something that might explain things. Nick had once overdosed, long before I'd met him. It was over a bullying and harassment situation at work, the type of situation I too would come to know, not far into my own future. Con informed me that what had saved his friend's life was Nick's incredibly strong heart. I panicked.

Sitting inside my washing machine were the items I was looking for. In the pocket of a pair of Nick's jeans I pulled out an empty sheet of Xanax, with six tablets also missing from a sheet of Prozac. I immediately called an ambulance and Nick was taken to Campbelltown Hospital, with a paramedic assuring me his life was not in any danger and that he really only needed to sleep off the cocktail. I felt angry and resentful, decided Nick had a lesson to learn and made the opportunity.

That night, when I visited Nick in hospital, he refused to speak to me and called us off for good. Nick claimed I had embarrassed him beyond redemption and placed his job in danger. Smugly I thought to myself, 'What if I called your superior at the hospital, Nick, and told them how you'd attend theatre completely stoned most days?'

Nick thought himself invincible, and I certainly deserved all the pain I received for begging this loser to give me another chance. "It's not like I haven't used hard drugs before," he snapped. Then with a hint of pride Nick told me how he and a nurse he dated at St George Hospital had shared morphine shots she stole from the drugs register. Was I insane enought to believe I could hold down a relationship with a lying drug addict who had outlaw bikie affiliations, as well as being someone who could not keep his dick out of online dating sites? There was no doubt I suffered from battered wife syndrome, but my need to keep Nick, while blocking out all reason and self-respect, was so unlike the core me. Not only was I hurting myself, I was putting my children at risk too. Denial is not just a river in Egypt!

But still we kept going. Together we applied for positions as Youth Officers at the a Juvenile Justice Centre in nearby Airds, after a friend of mine pointed out the advertisement in a local paper. Annie was a former Juvenile Justice Youth Officer and believed my personality suited this role. Not for a moment did I believe Annie but I filled in the application form regardless; the money from casual cake shop work was no longer a viable income for me. At the same time, I applied for a Hospital Assistant's position at nearby Campbelltown Hospital, hoping Nick would act as my referee. Additionally, I attempted to bring another shred of commonality into our lives by getting my nipples pierced, along with Nick. His bikie mates owned a tattoo shop in Liverpool and one of the girls I'd met in at the Clubhouse did the job. I almost fainted just with the first nipple.

The application process for the Youth Officer's position was lengthy and included a two-hour psychological test, which I failed; I was not allowed to reapply for twelve months. Incredibly, Nick passed his psychological test but bombed out at the interview. The irony of this outcome is that the American psychological test was designed to flush out the liars among the candidates, and Nick was the greatest liar I'd ever met.

I organised a night out at The Albion in Parramatta with Annie, Con, Maria and a few others. Nick had 'gone somewhere' in my car and would not answer my calls. I rang Annie and told her I could not pick her up as promised because Nick had the car and was uncontactable. Eventually Nick returned, staggering through the door like a zombie, his pupils mere pin points in the light. I wondered what diabolical concoction he might have ingested this time, and then realised I'd had enough of his shit. Nick had known tonight was important to me, and he really didn't care. He was a hopeless, useless drug addict, nothing more. Nick was so incoherent and absent it seemed a miracle he'd got home without wrapping himself around a tree. Somehow I managed to get Nick back into my car and drove to Annie's as he sheepishly tried to light a cigarette by its butt, almost sparking a fire in the front seat. Annie, seeing how intoxicated Nick was, snapped at me in classic Leo fashion about Nick's ongoing irresponsibility and a lack of respect for me. The car suddenly became very quiet, with Nick still attempting to light his cigarette.

At The Albion, Nick went straight to the pokies, drinking schooner after schooner of beer. His need to be in a constant stupor was astonishing and something I did not comprehend. For all the wrong reasons I loved Nick and continued telling myself I *could* live with all of this – after all, Rhys's emotional addictions and body dysmorphic disorder had been much worse, right?

* * *

I finally found the courage to kick Nick out but before I did so, I needed to honour a booking I'd made with a high school buddy at the Brahma Kumaris retreat in Leura. At this point in my crazy life I needed this getaway; the retreat was the only place in the world I could let go of the endless 'mind chatter'. Brahma Kumaris is a school of meditation based on – but not exclusive to – Hindu teachings. With no available babysitters I implored Nick to stay at my house and look after the children one last time. He owed me one, for fuck's sake!

On the first night of the retreat I rang Nick to check on the kids and everything seemed fine. There was no amiability in his voice but at least his words weren't slurred. The following night everything was different. When I called home just before bedtime Kristen told me Nick had gone to his parents' place and had not returned as promised. I continued to call at half-hour intervals, hoping Nick had had a conscientious revival and come back to the house. Still no Nick or calls to the kids from him. Panicked, I called home every ten minutes, then every five minutes, and so on. My meditation buddy grew impatient, telling me I was worrying unnecessarily. In a selfish way my feelings of panic were not so much for the children's safety – they were good kids and one night alone should not bring about any issues. My panic was about *me* not wanting to accept that Nick would betray me again, that he would shirk basic responsibility by failing to look after children he knew who trusted him and cared for him, just in order to satisfy his own base needs. After everything Nick had done for me in the light of Rhys's brutality, why was his behaviour now so equally vile?

Finally, around one in the morning, I got hold of Nick on his mobile. I barely had any battery power left on my mobile and had forgotten my charger, so my words had to pour out quickly and resolutely.

"Don't do this Angelica, for fuck's sake it's over!" Nick bellowed through static.

"Just tell me where you are! How can you do this? Are you with another woman you *fuck*?"

"Yes I am. I AM! It's over Angelica." Then Nick's phone switched off.

Just as the last power bar was about to fade, Kristen called to tell me that Alycia and her friend Mitchell had gone missing. I further questioned Kristen, asking her what Mitchell was even doing there in the first place. Kristen seemed unable to convey a background story but it was obvious from her voice she felt insecure and frightened. I needed to get home immediately.

I was so concerned for Alycia's safety, all I could think of was getting the police to initiate a search. My friend quickly dismissed my thoughts, encouraging me to proceed with the two-hour trip home instead. We alerted the retreat's on-call staff, packed our belongings and stole away into the night, dreading the anxious drive back to Rosemeadow.

We arrived at three in the morning, relieved to find Alycia and Mitchell safe and sound and pretending to be asleep. Mitchell was Alycia's best friend in high school and, finding a free run of the premises, the pair decided to go on a moonlight exploration of the pipes at the Rosemeadow Oval, across the road from our house. I was out of my mind with anger and frustration and could not string two words together other than the foul curses I'd become so adept at. My friend pushed me aside and gave the children a more composed and eloquent lecture on my behalf.

Nick exited my life soon after I hosted a thirty-fourth birthday bash in his honour. The man had no morality and no accountability. He was instinctive and primal. The last *compos mentis* words he uttered to me were, "I don't know why I've treated you so badly Angelica; you're the only person in my life who really cares for me."

* * *

My firstborn, Alycia, informed me how now and again she'd levitate from her bed, glide off her window sill, and fly in a circle around the rooftops of our Auburn townhouse. Rationality would then set in and back she went inside her bed as if sucked into it by a powerful vacuum. I too had such an experience once, as I lay next to Rhys.

It was late one night and I had been pondering how I might continue with this man. Years of abuse and subjugation then forced my soul from my body. I needed to move away from my dormant tormentor; even one night away from him was better than none. Early the next morning I found myself lying on the lounge downstairs and I *knew* I had not sleepwalked there.

With Nick both my soul *and* my body were forced from him by the lifestyle he led and his rejection of me. But I wasn't going to leave without a fight or adequate vindication. First though, I needed to conduct some serious research.

All I ever wanted in life was to love and be loved. I didn't deserve any of this pain; yet even with the vast stores of esoteric knowledge I gathered and had learnt to recite verbatim, I had not grasped a simple and basic concept – that all I had endured leading up to this moment, I attracted to myself, because of misguided need and want. I held no self-worth and continued to barter myself to the lowest bidder. I chose actively to ignore truth and consequence in exchange for a twominute fairy tale – or rather, a sordid 270day sex saga.

Shame on Nick for tricking me once, but shame on *me* for falling for the 'quick and easy' more than once.

CHAPTER EIGHTEEN

*PAIN BODY

———

Pain arrives in many forms. My year-long fissure tear, the one I had to have because my ex-husband wanted to fulfil a porn fantasy, was a memorable physical pain. A second form involved the illegal purchase of the house I moved my children into only six months after I left Rhys, because it had been placed for sale and I just could not uproot them so soon after the separation. The salesperson who tricked me into taking out the loan (by approving me for a loan for which I was not really eligible) turned out to be a 'client launderer' and I was almost convicted alongside him. Third is spiritual pain, the type that turns a well-meaning, self-sacrificing and devoted lover into a crazed villain, because I could not take any more betrayal.

Alex Forrest, the principal antagonist in the 1987 film *Fatal Attraction*, is a character I have identified with more than once. That Sunday, the day following Nick's final treachery against me, I located my inner Alex and took my revenge.

Nick's phone was turned off the entire morning so the dozen or so abusive messages left on his voicemail fell on deaf ears. An unsuspecting hospital employee picked up the operating theatre's admin phone and faced my music instead.

"I need to speak to Nick P. *immediately* please!"

"I'm sorry, he's in theatre," the man's defensive voice snapped.

"I don't give a fuck, get him *out of theatre!* It's either this or I'll be there in fortyfive minutes and I'll pull the miserable bastard out of theatre myself!"

I then gave the employee at least another four earbashings, including countless threats and personal disclosures about Nick's true character.

Eventually, he too stopped answering the phone. Much later that afternoon I received a furious call from Nick.

"Angelica, let this be your first and final warning – leave me the fuck alone! If you contact me or anyone associated with me again, I'm going to slap you with an AVO. Do you want another one? Really? It's over! I fucked up yes, but you weren't letting go. Now fuck off and go on with your life."

As brutally as he had spoken to me, Nick hung up the receiver and that was the last time I would hear his voice. No, my rap sheet did not need another Apprehended Violence Order but *I* needed answers, closure, and finality, whatever it took to mend a shattered heart.

I succeeded with tracking down Nick's 'nurse' ex-girlfriend, the one he boasted fucking while high on morphine and wearing *her* stockings. The story I received from this woman was worthy of a *Today Tonight* story.

Nick was a serial 'lover'. What he had done to me he'd done to the 'nurse' and countless other women. He was also still married to an American woman he'd met during a whirlwind six-month visit to the United States, in order to obtain residency there. I remembered seeing Nick open, shut, minimise, or hide, various online conversations, and a quick sweep on my PC's hard drive produced the desired evidence. He was begging his wife in the US to finance their divorce, but she flatly refused. Before Nick lined up his next victim, he'd prepare by alienating the last one. Those 'others' all marched away, but not this little black duck. I was a tenacious pit bull – I required *added* brutality.

Nick chose his hosts carefully and systematically. They would be found online, searching for love and often fresh out of a failed marriage or long-term relationship. Aesthetically they were older, larger and less attractive to a certain type of male. They all had children in their care and were reasonably self-sufficient or reliant. It also appeared Nick preferred brunettes. It would then take Nick around six months to move on, from one feathered nest and into another.

Because of my will, we were together nine months, well past Nick's usual 'due by' date. During this period Nick lied about absolutely everything – even the most nonsensical items. He was a hopeless drug addict and an emotional cheater. His entry ticket into our lives consisted of the way he appeared to understand women and their many crutches. Nick was attentive, loving, good with the kids, helpful, rewarding, satisfying in bed, and seemingly adaptable – *at first*. Along with their hearts, Nick also took souvenirs from his lovers – odd bits and pieces that tickled his fancy, much in the way serial killers do. I noticed that Edan's 3D piece of nail art and his transistor radio were missing. Also missing was something else far more important that I had not considered, something Nick doted on daily: Lucky, our cat.

I felt used, and lonelier than ever, but I could only blame myself and no other, not even Nick. I had been desperate. I'd rushed into a classic rebound relationship with someone I barely knew who had charmed his way into my life from behind a computer screen. Expertly, Nick parroted all the things I needed to hear. As with Rhys I *had* seen the signs early on but refused to acknowledge the facts. Misguided optimism and my innate trust in the eventual goodness of mankind helped me gloss over the lies. I swallowed far more than his cock because I *wanted* to, because I *needed* to, my self-esteem demanded it. Everything happens for a reason and the reason for Nick was his support during those soul destroying court hearings, the malicious access visits, and the harassment I received, via departmental inquiry, because of Rhys.

Following the fulfilment of Higher Purpose not everyone is meant to stay. If you force them to they'll push back thrice as hard and your own pain will be tenfold. There is another woman out there who has signed a similar contract with Nick and it's now her turn for learning.

* * *

A broken heart is an excellent dieting tool. For eight weeks' solid all I could do was cry and smoke so the 10 kilos I had put on while with Nick melted away. I had begun to lose a grip not only on my emotions but on my family as well. Alycia now had a boyfriend who she was seeing indiscreetly. In the end I allowed my impressionable sixteen-year-old to 'see him' under my roof, to help preserve as much of her dignity as possible. As one ought to expect from a teen, Alycia grossly disrespected the privilege bestowed on her, and so the fighting and struggling between mother and child was on.

When I started full-time shift work as a Hospital Assistant in Campbelltown Hospital, Kristen became Edan's unrewarded surrogate mother, and as life would have it, Nick was no longer there to share my hospital stories. The job in the hospital's kitchen services department meant I was now able to pay my bogus mortgage without fearing destitution, but it did push my once gregarious Kristen into adopting a sad and hypervigilant personality that no child deserves.

Edan's disability seemed to remain static. With misguided punitive measures such as threats of 'jail' and 'the worm factory', Edan appeared compliant and subservient. I still hadn't given up hope that his Asperger's would one day magically resolve itself, but I was better equipped now to deal with its reality. Disability aside, Edan was a beautiful and sweet little boy who I adored and cherished. I felt his sisters adored him as well, despite their frequent bouts of exasperation with his quirks and absurd routines, like 'Semmen' (his way of saying 'seven', which became a synonym for his Asperger's-driven routines).

Work took up a large part of my life but instead of devoting the remainder of the precious time I had left to my children, I again found myself seated at my computer browsing dating sites. The rush of the contact email was just too difficult to renounce. While some people learn their lessons straight away, I certainly took my time. The spirit of contradiction would never allow surrender to the obvious; someone out there was looking for a genuine soul to live out their life with and I was *it*. My online handle was now the seductive Fire_Dance_With_Me, a take on the Twin Peaks 'Fire Walk with Me' line.

Running around a large hospital for eight hours pushing heavy food trolleys certainly improved my fitness. I lost a further ten kilos and started to look like my old self. A flash of memory took me back to Paris's prediction where he'd seen me placing trays on a conveyor belt, which is exactly what I did during hospital meal allocation. A trained dietician would stand at the head of the first station on the conveyor belt to assess the menu sheets assigned to each patient. The tray would then pass by other food stations – meats, vegetables, liquids, desserts, and so on. The person on each station would rapidly skim over the menu sheet and place the appropriate item on every tray. It was a tricky job but I soon learnt to master it and was considered one of the fastest and most efficient workers on the belt.

On the wards, however, I was certainly not so fast or efficient. I just could not resist engaging with the patients and was often the last one back to the kitchen. Our leading hand, Mary, an acidic Anglo-Italian matriarch who made no bones on how she felt about me, never missed an opportunity to publicly berate me about my tardiness or any service she viewed as substandard. But my colleagues viewed me differently. I was a breath of fresh air, someone who amiably disrupted Mary's tough 'galley' autocracy with comedic banter that left most of them in stitches. I began to forge some truly lovely, lighthearted friendships.

I didn't quite realise how sheltered I was from the collective pain of other people's lives until I frequented this hospital. There was some degree of suffering on every ward, with Maternity possibly the only happy place. An image that still haunts me today is of a young man in isolation who had the most severe case of eczema imaginable. He wore mittens so as not to scratch and his bed was covered in dead skin. There wasn't a patch on his feeble body or his scalp that was not red raw or flaky. I saw the pain in his eyes as I laid his food tray on the table beside him, or could it have been resentment because I was not in a similar position? The smell of exposed flesh was overwhelming.

Then there was a young woman, also in isolation, with an obvious intellectual disability. This girl rocked repeatedly in her bed, only uttering a single word, or perhaps it was just a sound. My heart bled for her and the very next day I brought in an unwanted plush toy from home for her to nurse. I noticed the rocking significantly decrease after she received the toy, and rather than ignore me as she had done previously, a mild acknowledgement came into her eyes whenever I walked into her room.

Triage, a room guarded by security personnel against unruly or violent patients (usually as a result of substance abuse), was a place we were advised to service with caution. On this particular day the tray belonged to a teenage girl who was a renowned self-harmer. I myself did cut a few times and Lydia, from the Fairfield refuge I briefly resided in, was the first girl whose self-harming scars made mine look risible, but none of that prepared me for *this* girl. There wasn't a visible part on her body, bar her face, that was not marked by a racecourse of painful scar tissue. When a new employee, Daisy, joined our kitchen, I caught yet another glimpse of this unusual phenomenon. On the inside of Daisy's forearms were the numerous horizontal lines that spelt *trauma* at fever pitch. Daisy kept her palms down and her arms close to her body, hoping to disguise her cutting, and whenever possible she'd wear longer sleeves. Wanting to understand, I tentatively asked Daisy why she did it. Her mother had died and unable to vocally express her grief, Daisy cut herself to release internalised pain that was sometimes near suicidal in nature. She was eighteen.

I soon recognised a distinct hierarchy within the hospital system. Doctors and surgeons are the undisputed gods who treat nursing staff like slaves. Naturally, with shit steadily flowing downstream, the nurses treat ancillary staff almost as poorly. A few of the nurses took their frustrations and fatigue out on the patients, a practice I found deplorable as well as unethical. I am 100 percent for optimum and humane customer service, as well as of the opinion that if you can't hack it, don't do it! These people, as trying as some of them were, needed our assistance.

Once after I placed my tray on a sweet old lady's table, she weakly clasped my wrist, begging me to call a nurse in to see her.

"Oh dearie, would you please call a nurse for me? I've been pressing the button a long time and noone will come. I'm afraid I might soil my sheets again. I really need a bed pan."

"Of course I can." I smiled compassionately.

The patient buzzers were going off left, right and centre but noone was answering them. The ward's reception desk was unattended and I could see the nurses sitting around, casually drinking coffee in their staff room. I rapped softly on their door.

"Excuse me. The lady in Room Nine desperately needs a bed pan."

I may as well have presented them with an unpinned grenade.

"I'll be there when I'm done," a fat one snapped at me, and off I went, acidly dismissed.

I finished my deliveries and returned to the kitchen. Two hours later I started my tea and coffee round. The sweet old lady in Room Nine looked pained. She had not yet been attended to.

"Could *you* bring me a pan dearie? I just can't hold on anymore."

How could those sows simply ignore her like that? Where was their duty of care? I stormed into the staff room where the fat bitch who had dismissed me continued sitting next to a plate of cream laden scones, chatting away.

"*Excuse meeeee*, but the lady in Room Nine is going to seriously shit herself and if you don't attend to her right now I'll be telling her to go ahead with it and it will be *you* who changes her sheets. Or do you intend leaving her to stew in her own muck?"

The grenade had blown up.

Aside from Mary's tyrannical outbursts and some nursing arrogance, the worst parts of the job were the smells and sputum laden trays. The most nauseating rooms were those of diabetic patients whose limbs were slowly rotting. I soon learnt to place a dab of Vicks VapoRub under my nostrils to avoid holding my breath in when entering those rooms. These patients were not only losing valuable body parts but their dignity as well; the last thing I wanted to do was burden them further with my heaving facial grimaces. In this job I also touched my first corpse.

I entered an old lady's room to offer her tea and biscuits. She appeared peacefully asleep and so I decided to nudge her gently in case she did not wish to miss out on afternoon tea. A nurse rushed into the room a little animated.

"I'm sorry, this patient is deceased and I was about to post a note for staff on her door."

No shock was greater, however, than when I found a high school classmate attached to various tubes in the ICU. Kim wasn't someone I knew well at school, but when you see a person from your Year in such a pitiful condition, you certainly begin to contemplate your own mortality. In high school everything is subjective and the world is waiting to be discovered. Experiences are purely sensory, and the future looks shiny and bright. High school offers you your rightful place in the world and you're either the popular kid, the nerd, or the class clown. School lends you a springboard from where to launch future choices based on the relationships you had with your peers and teachers. I was now coerced to contemplate the dire choices Kim had made. I did not find out exactly what was wrong with Kim, but it looked serious for she could barely string two words together.

I then bumped into another former classmate, this one part of a playground 'Romeo and Juliet' romance that I had believed might stand the test of time. Kate had been struck with a rare autoimmune disease that was slowly paralysing her. She asked me if I'd heard from Robert, her Romeo. I was surprised Kate had lost touch with him, but thinking back it made perfect sense. I had contacted Robert for the 1995 school reunion, but he was not able to attend because multiple sclerosis had rendered him wheelchair bound and, inexplicably, his wife would not allow anyone near him. Robert then politely and apologetically asked me to never call him again. Kate and Robert, the golden couple of Cabramatta High, were indeed a Shakespearian tragedy and their destinies spoke painfully about the fragility and capriciousness of life.

* * *

'Facetious_Wit' 'added' me on a dating site called Find Someone. For maximum exposure I was registered on at least four sites, some indication of the degree of my addiction. Facetious_Wit's real name was Graham, and he did not show me his profile picture for quite some time. As with Nick, I didn't care about that; I was falling in love with Graham's online conversations and, as the handle suggested, his mercurial wit.

Graham pulled out the magic word from his vast bag of emotional tricks. He was looking for *marriage*. Here was a childless, intelligent, funny older man, who lived in the beautiful Northern Beaches, was the general manager of an RSL and was now discussing happily-ever-after with me. My heart skipped many a beat as future prospects played out before me like a fluorescent, holographic dream.

Graham finally sent me his picture, with the inscription 'Be kind'. There was nothing to be kind about, though; he wasn't Gerard Butler but he was not unattractive – not to me anyway. We organised a date at a favourite Italian restaurant of his in Leichhardt, yet somehow our interactions were suddenly marred by a silly online argument and only a few days later Graham decided to phone me rather than reschedule online. His speaking voice was wonderful. I was smitten and could not understand why Graham had begun to push strange buttons on the computer screen. He was becoming downright nasty without the slightest provocation. It would seem the darker Gemini twin had emerged. I had always believed the Gemini duality to be a myth. However, the true nature of Graham's sardonic laughter became evident soon enough: Graham was a manic depressive and an alcoholic, and I had fallen in love with him. I was doing it all over again, just as I had with Rhys and Nick. The stark reality, the cruel lesson of so many precarious relationships, is that love does *not* conquer all.

I met Graham for the first time several months later at Darling Harbour's Cockle Bay, at a place called Nick's, ironically enough. Graham the Gemini was taller and much slimmer than the photograph he'd sent me, but after a few moments in Graham's company it became painfully obvious that life with him would prove difficult. I too had a comedic streak, but mine was slapstick and easy to capture. Graham's wit was acidic and cryptic; I had no idea where to stand in his presence.

The relationship that might have been became instead a long online and phone friendship. The same friend who'd accompanied me to the Brahma Kumaris retreat, that fateful night of Nick's betrayal, decided to jump on board and befriended Graham as well. She accompanied me to his home overlooking Palm Beach. This friend was stuck in an abusive marriage and it appeared to me she was readying herself for an affair. From slices of information fed to me on occasion by Graham, my old high school buddy was more his cup of tea than I ever was, anyway.

* * *

The search for love continued. Instead of going out partying with friends and meeting people the regular way I sat at my computer night after night, ignoring everything and everyone. Cigarette in mouth, clicking away on the latest friendship request, I relished the rush of anticipation that comes from the little unopened envelope icons sent by strangers. Co-dependency is an insidious disease, even when your insight comprehends very well where it comes from.

I found that each time I was on Find Someone, a certain guy kept messaging me, often interrupting serious conversation with other prospective beaus. The way he wrote smacked of 'foreigner' and I soon discovered Eser was a Turk in Australia on a working visa, hoping to obtain permanent citizenship just like Nick had in the US. His photograph wasn't bad but Eser was not what I was looking for, and the fact that he was from an Islamic part of the world bothered me too. I would never stoop to being someone's meal ticket, let alone a Muslim's. Some of what I had come across in Auburn during my years of living there did not resonate with me or my desperate need for emotional freedom. I had defiantly given up *my* religion and I'd be damned if I was now going to walk into anyone else's.

For three months solid, this Turkish man, who somehow managed to live in fashionable Rose Bay, harassed me day and night into meeting him. In the end I became so fed up with the stream of uncouth insults I berated Eser with, just to make him back off, that I deleted him from Find Someone, and that was that.

Early in April of 2004 I was still single and still desperate. Scrolling through more profiles on Find Someone, a picture of a man with dark smouldering looks stopped me in my tracks. There was something slightly familiar about his face. Opening up the profile I recognised the introduction: 'I am a man who enjoys the little things of life, from the strongest to the most delicate. I love the beach, sunsets, food, cooking, and intelligent conversations with distinguished women.' It was Eser! He had changed his handle to 'Sunsetluva' and the picture posted here was ten times better than the one he'd introduced himself to me with. In this photograph he looked like a model for a men's cologne. A strange stirring washed over me. Maria came over and I just had to ask her opinion, given her shrewdness concerning all things male.

"Mmmmm, nice," she affirmed. "So why don't you just go for it and try something different Angelica?"

Holding a long tail firmly between my legs, I re-added Eser to my contact list and apologised for the rudeness I'd displayed a few months earlier. Eser was understandably reserved this time around but accepted my request as well as my apology.

I decided to take Maria's advice and get to know this handsome Ottoman. My cultural prejudices still loomed large in my sensibilities, though, and this meant poor Eser received a different brand of insults.

When Eser sent me a long email about the way I had influenced him musically, I decided I *would* meet with him. I had explained my love of trance to Eser, and that ARQ was the Sydney nightclub that played all the best trance tracks and remixes. Although ARQ is a famous gay haunt (albeit open to all) Eser visited ARQ on his own and realised just how much the music had touched him on a spiritual level. In his email, Eser said he had felt my presence, with memories of me now crystallised in progressive trance music, and soon I discovered there were other things that connected me to Eser. To hell with my prejudices. I, who prided myself an intellectual, was dealing with a highly sensitive and deep thinking equal, not some sleazy, wife hunting 'camel fucker'.

Intrigued anew, I agreed to meet Eser on his own turf after he invited me to dinner at Bondi's popular Ravesi's Restaurant, overlooking that famous Sydney beach.

I pulled in outside Eser's block of flats on Old South Head Road and called him from downstairs on my mobile. A slim man, around 5 feet 9 inches tall and dressed in fashionable black jeans and Tshirt, approached my car from across the road. Eser surprised me with a bouquet of multi-coloured gerberas, which he handed to me through the driver's window as I stared directly at his crutch.

"Are you the beautiful lady I am expecting? If you are, these are for you!"

Eser's accent was thick but far from coarse; his voice was velvety and his smile infectious. Without a second thought, I grabbed the delicate bouquet and threw it onto the back seat, thus allowing Eser the passenger seat. Eser looked a little taken aback by the brusqueness of my actions but quickly recomposed himself, planting a kiss on my cheek. I was more than impressed.

I could feel Eser's gaze on me during the drive from Rose Bay to Ravesi's. I don't think I could have felt more beautiful and perfect than during those moments of strange adulation. Eser was unabashedly drinking me in.

Eser was also the consummate gentleman, opening my door and stepping aside for my descent just like a well-trained footman. Everything about this gorgeous man spelt class, grace, and decorum. I felt terribly rude and shamefully guilty for having put him through such a disrespectful mill of pursuit.

We spent a wonderful night at Ravesi's. Eser appeared besotted with me, holding my hand and observing it as if it were made of the finest china. This night was one of the most romantic experiences of my life; even that kiss I shared with Patrick at The Gap seemed to pale in comparison. Watson's Bay is only a few kilometres from Bondi, of course.

After dinner we strolled along the beach with the moon lighting our happy smiles. Eser explained his deep love for Australia and how it began. He told me about his life in Istanbul and how he dreamed of another within a Western culture. He related his search for true love as opposed to the arranged seven-year marriage he was forced to endure. Personal wishes aside, Eser also loved his homeland deeply and made Turkey sound like a beautiful place to visit. I could smell, touch, and see the kaleidoscopes of colour, culture and aromas like a shimmering oasis before me, and so Turkey became a place I definitely wanted to visit. Gallipoli had always been on my 'bucket list', but following Eser's descriptions the mainland came into full view too, in just one magical evening.

I became intoxicated by Eser even if self-righteous ignorance continued to sabotage the beauty emerging before me. *Eser was too skinny, his arms too hairy, his semantics too absurd* ... but then Maria's words interrupted the stream of my prejudiced consciousness: *Try something different Angelica.*

CHAPTER NINETEEN

GÜNEY GÜNEŞ

———

My dreams were always brutal. I was plagued by continual images of Mother or Rhys trying to hurt me in one form or another. Whenever my 'anxiety dreams' varied, the images involved terrifying ghosts, chases, murder or snakes. One dream in particular felt distinctly prophetic and I was compelled to investigate. A little girl trapped in the foundations of a decrepit home somewhere in a North American state was calling out for help from her grave. Not such an unlikely scenario, really, in a continent where on average 800,000 children are reported missing each year.

In another vivid dream, an entire family appeared before me swathed in flames as they stood from oldest to youngest in front of their burning home, glaring and filled with hatred. My tortured psyche certainly unleashed its venom during REM sleep, with the residual pus of a life poorly lived, of innocence consumed by predatory characters, of maternal fascism and cruelty, playing itself out in the surreal and utterly frightening. Alas, there was no escaping life for me, not while my body insisted on living it.

* * *

Eser and I had many things in common, but after a few dates I once again worked my very best to sabotage a potential relationship. There were trivial 'faults' I used: his flat head, arms that were too hairy, an awful car, embarrassing language malformations like *don't make laugh of me* and *these chips are crab* [crap]. These dreadful faults helped mask the fact that Eser was too endearing, and that I was falling in love with him by the minute.

Eser was an elegant, charming, educated gentleman with old fashioned values and a modern outlook. Back in Turkey Eser had worked as a financial accounts manager inside a multinational company. Here in Australia, his beloved adopted country, he struggled to find anything remotely suited to his expertise, due to the national accreditation regulations. During his first 'pilgrimage' in Australia, Eser survived as an indentured lackey to a kebab shop owner operating on Bondi's well-frequented beachfront strip. On his second sojourn in the land down under, Eser paid for an expensive Eastern Suburbs lifestyle by working the graveyard shift at a customer service consultancy in Frenchs Forest. Eser's trilingual skills, the result of five years in Germany as a youngster, were his entry tickets into the kind of semi-professional role he could relate to. In my job at the Campbelltown Hospital I met many immigrants just like Eser: qualified lawyers, accountants, and teachers, all reduced to menial work because of a discriminatory bureaucracy. Yet Eser decided to smile through it all, just glad to call Australia home for now. A far cry from the derisive, ungrateful attitudes of Gilda and Alfonso. Mother would never let up on how the detested and racist 'Anglo Saxons' had 'cheated' her out of a career, forcing her into Housing Commission living and a few dollars a week for everything else.

My second meeting with Eser took place at McDonald's in Mount Annan, where once again I made the mistake of prematurely introducing my new 'friend' to the children. Eser presented me with a gift I was not expecting, an elegant rose quartz and silver pendant. Rose quartz, the crystal promoting love, was an unusual gift for a second encounter but the handwritten tag that accompanied it saved the day. It read simply: 'I hope you find it.'

For our third meeting I invited Eser to join me and the children at a local Easter Fair. Eser, clearly determined to endear himself to my kids, kept us all entertained. By home time I had made my decision: Eser would be mine. I bestowed on Eser's lips a kiss that he did not expect but appeared to greatly enjoy.

Our fourth meeting took place at ARQ, the nightclub that had inadvertently brought us together. The intoxicating mix of progressive trance, laser lights and the open lovemaking on the mezzanine above drew us in like moths to flame. The dance of copulating serpents and the passionate kissing left no doubt we were heading towards lusty romance. We were completely absorbed in each other and wished for the night to never end. A week later, during a childfree weekend, I allowed Eser to make love to me. As I gazed into Eser's roving eyes, suspended above mine, I was suddenly gripped by doubt. Maybe I was just a 'Green Card' into Australian citizenship. Eser did not appear as attractive to me in that moment and I wanted him to stop, but lacked the courage to voice these feelings. So, I began looking for more faults.

* * *

Through Eser's eyes I began to discover many of the beauties of Sydney's Eastern Suburbs, and through me Eser fell more and more in love with trance music, as well as me. My shredded self-esteem, though, made the latter seem improbable.

One day I bought a car to replace my decrepit Sonata and Eser insisted he'd remove the stereo Nick had bought for me for Christmas and install it in my new Camry. I had left a *Godskitchen* trance CD inside the stereo system. When I met up with Eser after work, he was waiting for me by my car sporting a Cheshire cat grin. Eser then scooped me into his arms and told me he loved me more since listening to the first track on my CD. The music had spoken to his soul, drawing him closer to me on a spiritual level. The track in question was Paul Oakenfold's *'Southern Sun'.

"When I listen to this music I feel like I could fly," he mused.

Thanks to Eser and his view of the world, my life began to transform into a vortex of sensory pleasures. Eser became everything I'd ever dreamt of, for a 'lowly Muslim' I had repeatedly rejected out of ignorance.

Eser seemed to embody style, intelligence, refinement, manners, ethics, altruism, art, music, literature, history, humour, and a love of food and cooking. The kids respected him too, especially Alycia. With this man there were no substance abuse issues to look out for, and from what I could gather no obvious problems involving infidelity, prevarication or covert porn consumption.

Eser thought I was gorgeous exactly as he'd found me, with some of the most beautiful photographs of me captured by his adoring lens. On the kids' access weekends, we spent dizzy days and nights at his Rose Bay flat, watching foreign art-house movies, eating wonderful things he had cooked or discovered inside elegant restaurants, making beautiful love, and laughing our heads off at our own nonsense. Eser was a culinary connoisseur, but no meal captured his imagination more than his native fare. Listening to the methods provincial

Turks used to make their baklava, as well as what it felt like to bite into one, was like hearing music sung from an ancient libretto. Eser's exotic descriptions of Turkey transported me to this wondrous place and I felt ashamed of my prejudice anew.

Walking with Eser past sunsets on Bondi Beach and Tamarama Beach, hand in hand, smiling lovingly into each other's eyes, helped me realise how easy love can be once you allow yourself to let go of insecurities. Watson's Bay, the magical place Patrick took me to for that 'movie kiss' so many years before, became a completely different platform with Eser. Here, entwined in my Turkish delight, I spared no thought for Patrick, the man whose love I had to earn. Eser and I lived for the things we *both* loved, things that were one and the same. Eser showered me with presents, unique surprises and romantic gestures of every kind. Whenever I found myself with Eser, I felt myself enveloped in a blanket of dense, chocolatey velvet I did not ever wish to come out of. This richness of life, and the multileveled iridescent sensations never before experienced with a man, inadvertently brought out the greedy, needy, and imbalanced Angelica, who for so long had silently screamed for want of such spoiling. When this side of me emerged, it was only a short while before I began placing impossible demands on Eser and his gentle kindnesses.

I wanted Eser to see more of me more often, so to placate me Eser pledged two visits a week at Rosemeadow. Rosemeadow is an eighty kilometre trek from Frenchs Forest, and at three in the morning (the end of Eser's shift) a most brutal commitment I should not have insisted on. Weekends consisted of alternating between one at his place (during access visits) and the other at mine with the children.

During the first two months of our dreamy relationship, it was obvious that Eser was as keen to see me as I was him, with the dreary travel across Sydney not appearing to faze him. But as things progressed, some carefully veiled complaints and excuses began to emerge.

I was so determined to *own* this miracle relationship forever that I escalated my behaviour, much as I had with Patrick. I rang Eser incessantly during his shift, demanding lengthy chats. Eventually Eser allocated me a strict time slot after 9.30, which I repeatedly contravened. I'd set my alarm for three in the morning to talk with Eser, showing little or no regard for his need to unwind after a long shift. If Eser was more than ten minutes late arriving at my place, I'd call his mobile demanding a satisfactory explanation. I began talk of marriage, knowing marriage had not gone well for him back home. Failing this, I made him promise to move in with me, knowing only too well how he felt about dreary Rosemeadow, compared with his beloved Eastern Suburbs. Eser was soon trapped between a sword and a hard place. His job, too, left him feeling demeaned and unfulfilled, and I knew just how much professional success meant to Eser. This issue alone required a resolution before he could ever 'settle down' with *anyone* – let alone a desperate, love starved woman like me.

To travel night after night from Frenchs Forest in order to live with me was a ridiculous expectation and I knew it, and for everything I asked I had the answer before asking it. Eventually Eser's mild yet calculated resistance to my demands began to infuriate me. And so, little by little, I systematically tore our relationship apart.

Was I a spoilt child unable to get her own way? I doubt that. I think I was, to put it simply, terrified of finding myself alone and unloved once more.

In my defence, Eser was not quite as completely perfect as I described him. I had begun to see through his deep-set veneer and was aware of a few characteristics that pointed towards 'rational egoism'. Having lived a sheltered life in an essentially non-secular Islamic culture, a life Eser despised as he watched the freedoms of Western countries from afar, Eser was *not* ready to be tied down to some Campbelltown divorcee, especially one burdened with three questionable children. True to his dual star sign, Eser was a perfectionist and high achiever. The Virgo in his chart was ambushed by mild obsessive compulsive disorder and a suspicious and nervous disposition he desperately tried to hide.

"I loved people like Madonna," Eser told me, his eyes lighting up as he recalled music clips he watched on television as a young man in Istanbul. "My room was filled with posters of American idols and I would lie in bed dreaming of the day I would live in a country like theirs."

How neat that Eser had loved Madonna – *my* idol. Then, almost as if linking the two together, Eser disclosed he'd been a virgin up until his marriage to a 'typically Turkish girl'.

"In Turkey, women are not readily available for sex unless they are prostitutes. For a man to 'just have sex' is pretty much impossible, so to get regular sex he has to choose a wife or have one chosen for him. For this reason alone, there are many gays in Turkey."

Jean Sasson, in one of her *Princess* books, said something similar about homosexuality in Saudi Arabia – namely among women – being due to the rigid restrictions placed on both sexes there. Eser and his wife were only ever really friends, but as his need for sex intensified it became evident it had to be *her* or noone at all.

Eser also informed me that he and his family kept their religious beliefs a secret. His family subscribed to the Alevi faith, a non-mainstream version of Islam with Christian overtones and therefore frowned upon by mainstream Muslims. In 1514, forty thousand Alevis were killed by the Ottoman Empire because they were thought to have been radical extremists who had sided with the Persian Empire against them. The prejudice against Alevis had not left modern-day Turkey, and Eser emphasised the importance of religious anonymity back home, as well as in Australia.

As Eser's dissatisfaction with his wife grew, he began ignoring her more and more. With some pride, Eser boasted how he refused to sleep with her for a year, something which only served to destroy her self-esteem. Eventually, after seven long and indifferent years, Eser left his wife. He indulged in prostitutes and a brief affair with a lonely single mother who, he said, "pissed herself during climax". A close friend, Can, decided to visit Australia and convinced Eser to go with him. With only shards of the English language, they obtained substandard jobs in a Turkish kebab outlet along the Bondi beachfront strip where they scraped together enough money for rent and a single car. Can ambushed the vehicle at every turn in order to keep Eser at home while he'd party alone. Unable to tolerate this virtual enslavement, Eser returned to Istanbul broke and disillusioned but nonetheless vowing to revisit the sun-kissed land he'd fallen in love with, a land of beautiful women and simple freedoms.

Eser's mother had died when he was nine months old. His father was a Gemini with a split personality, loving one moment and cruel the next. He soon married Eser's aunt, mainly to get help with the baby. Not long after the wedding, Eser's aunt gave Eser a sister. From the outside the family looked happy and productive, but Eser lived in fear of his father's regular beatings, a fear that had left deep psychological scars. I'd witnessed the way Eser's impenetrable and dignified demeanour had dissolved into babbling sobs when he recounted those beatings to me. That one occasion was enough for me to comprehend the level of emotional repression he held in check.

Eser was pedantically neat in the way he arranged his life. I would amuse myself by reshuffling the perfectly stacked, colour co-ordinated Tshirts and jumpers, and by re-arranging his cologne bottles that were lined from tallest to shortest, thus creating all manner of asymmetrical chaos. What I was in fact doing was fucking with a damaged mind, one that did its utmost to hide its pain – unlike me. In spite of the buried familial hurts, Eser faithfully made annual pilgrimages to Istanbul to visit the people he still referred to as Mum and Dad. As with me, Eser's parents had maintained a deep psychological hold on him.

Because I made myself 'unconventionally available' – my modus operandi for holding on to men – Eser felt comfortable enough to begin sharing me with his predilection for porn. So once again I was back in the 'permissive' hell that had been life with Rhys, Nick and, to a lesser degree, Patrick. Why did men need this outside stimulation when I never denied them my body or most of the 'things' they seemed to like?

Meantime, Maria, who thrived on male admiration, had committed an act of treason, the absolute decider for me to let her go. I had given Maria strict instructions regarding Rhys not finding out I had met someone new. After the Nick experience I simply did not wish to risk more of the same. Maria, now engaged to Nick's best friend Con, had spotted Rhys in a city nightclub. Taking advantage of an opportunity to be admired, she got into my ex-husband's face then casually told him about my new relationship. If not for my own friendship with Con, I'd never have found out.

Just as with all of Maria's exes before him, Con would often pour out his heart to me about her endless petty demands, her indiscretions, her sexual put-downs. I'd had enough of Maria. Twenty-five years in a parasite-host relationship had finally taken its toll. Just before this final act of treachery, I had already decided to remove Maria from my life when she so generously asked me to be Matron of Honour at her wedding, but only on condition that I lost weight first.

"I want my wedding to be perfect," she'd stated.

So, I performed a surgical removal. Maria's email to me was every inch as brutal as her friendship. She accused me of being jealous of her looks and her ability to attract any man she fancied. She was right about that: any man she fancied had her over her lounge for a joy ride, then they'd get off and leave the fun park for good. Once my outrage over the email blew over, I let out a sigh of profound relief. The 'friendship' was finished, hurrah! *To hell with you Maria, you pompous drug-fucked slut!*

Four months after our blissful, perfect romance began, Eser delivered a high-speed bombshell. When I recognise beyond the shadow of a doubt that I'll never achieve my objective, I cloak my sense of loss and defeat with arrogance and futile persistence. I began to drive my deliberations at a higher speed than Eser's.

"So when are you moving in with us, Eser?" I'd mock.

"I'll *never* live with you in Campbelltown Angelica! I hate Rosemeadow and I *don't* want to be married. I've done that already and I don't feel a need to do it again. We are not working out, Angelica; you upset me too much; *you shorten my life!* I also think your kids are very disrespectful and I don't like that. I think we need to split."

If there were words to describe how Eser's words cut through me I would use them, but there just aren't any. As an experience, finding Patrick's flat empty comes close, but as with Nick, the instinct that kicked in following those feelings was to try to stop the worst from happening. I had turned a blind eye to the moral filth that Nick had brought into my life simply because I could not function on my own, or so I thought. But with Eser the situation was completely different. Eser was my perfect match, my true love, a valuable being more precious and more perfect for me than any Patrick. I could not allow him to leave me. He was just sick of my nagging, so I'd stop doing it, I'd stop it right away. He couldn't have meant what he said – how could he? He had put up with all that initial rejection and all of my immature insults, but then enjoyed my affections for almost as long as we'd been together. Eser just needed some space now, that was all. I knew he was fed up with his job and its early morning finish, and his German colleague was bullying him. Eser was just unable to pretend a day longer, and I was making demands he could not fulfil under current circumstances. If I backed off and gave him time to fix his life, everything would be okay between us, I knew.

But then what if Eser *did* mean all he said? Under Eser's stony gaze I started to throw demeaning supplications. Then I dared to ask the question, "Is there hope of us staying together, if I change, Eser, if we do things *your* way?"

I doubt Eser's pulse went above eighty-five when he answered.

"No Angelica, there is *no* hope."

How I managed not to crash my car on the long drive back to Rosemeadow on that fateful day was beyond all belief. My eyes were blinded by tears and my ears could only hear replays of the words he'd uttered, words which rocked my world into total oblivion. In an attempt to soothe myself I pressed play on the CD deck, to hear the trance track that had so enriched our love, 'Southern Sun'. I played the track over and over. It only intensified my pain.

The very next day, sick and pathetic from a long night of blackest suffering, I dialled Eser's number, intent and defiant. I was *not* taking no as an answer. How dare he? It had been *Eser* who had chased *me*, Eser who had *begged* for *me*, Eser who had led me down a garden path more spectacular and lush than any landscape I could have foreseen. No, Eser was not getting off scotfree. There *was* hope for us … there is *always* hope.

CHAPTER TWENTY

I'M SWIMMING IN THE DARK BESIDE YOU

———

Sometime in 2005 Letitia died, aged ninetyfive. To this day I don't know what finally killed her. I can only guess it wasn't the countless cigarettes she smoked over eightyfive years of her life.

I decided not to attend Letitia's funeral – not because it was held in Adelaide, but because as a hater of hypocrisy, and privy to what I now knew about her, there was no way I'd put myself in a position where I might be expected to appear mournful. As a child I had truly loved my grandmother; she had been my hero and saviour and to this day I find myself paraphrasing the pearls of wisdom or domestic solutions she taught me back then. Letitia had been the only family I sincerely looked up to, the one I had any respect for and it was all one big fat insidious lie.

The worst type of self-imposed agony is holding on to something you know will not last. Eser told me there was no hope for us, yet I would not let go.

After sixteen months of hard work at the Campbelltown Hospital, work I actually enjoyed and that helped keep me in shape, I came across a second youth work classified that outlined various positions at the Airds Juvenile Justice Centre in. In the meantime, Eser and I applied for an online test with the Australian Security Intelligence Organisation (ASIO), who were looking for multilingual staff. Much to my surprise I passed the test (Eser did not), but when the department informed me I would be required to work anywhere within Australia or abroad within one day's notice, I instantly realised it was not the kind of responsibility a single mother of three could undertake.

I had grown tired of the smells of the hospital, and the tragedies I would witness most days. I was even more tired of the bitch Mary, who as my leading hand had made it her life purpose to antagonise and bully me at least every other day. There had been fleeting moments where Mary would appear to soften towards me, but the moment I lowered my guard she'd briskly retreat from any semblance of congeniality. I could only put her behaviour down to my exuberant nature, and the popularity I enjoyed among the other girls there. Mary's loyal sidekick, Maude, was the mother of a local murderer who had killed his girlfriend and then dumped her body inside a wheelie bin. Mary and Maude seemed to me a sure case of birds of a feather nesting together.

Once more I embarked in the arduous task of an application process for the position of Senior Youth Worker. Eser was away in Turkey for another long month, trips which seemed to occur around his birthday. These family visits were terrible for me because I was unable to manipulate our complex situation. I was also making myself sick wondering what Eser might be up to over there; I knew about the many 'rub and tugs' he had received as a bachelor.

During those agonising four weeks the moment I got home I'd attend to nothing else but checking my email for communication from Eser. There would be no words from him; I was lucky to receive a single phone call for his entire absence. There really was *no hope*, yet my complete lack of self-worth and obtuse stubbornness somehow managed to stretch four months into two years. All to be with a man who, although essentially good, was hell-bent on pleasing himself first and foremost.

On 2 May 2005 I started a six-week training course for the New South Wales Department for Juvenile Justice as a Trainee Juvenile Justice Officer. I met a lady at the psychological test who covertly informed me how to tweak the test answers in order to give the idiots their desired score. It worked. The test supervisor had explained the test was designed to detect lies, so I found it particularly ironic that two years ago, by being the true me, I had failed, yet by lying – as Nick had – he passed with flying colours.

I saw Eser every second weekend now and we were just going through the motions. Even so, I was still very much in love with him. In a final attempt to salvage the unobtainable, I suggested the kids and I move somewhere nearby, like the backstreets of Bondi. My message was met with a dozen reasons why it was a foolish notion. The greatest mistake I made with men, and kept on making, was my readiness to change my lifestyle choices, values and needs, in order to accommodate theirs. In the end I'd find myself alone anyway, simply because I was not in their lives for *me* first. Additionally, my boundless need for 'love' meant I was continually sacrificing my own children's needs and wants. I was a hostage to 'love', too deluded to have a clue how to break free. What a poor role model I'd become to my two wonderful young girls.

* * *

The Airds Juvenile Justice Centre was an eye opener. No amount of training had me prepared for it. The centre catered for juvenile 'delinquent' boys aged ten to fifteen, with Aboriginal detainees overrepresented. As so often in my life, I took a breath and jumped in.

The public seems to believe kids' crimes are innocuous, and most of the time they *do* fall into the class of petty crimes, but the centre also held boys as young as twelve who were being held on charges of murder, armed robbery and sexual offences. Additionally, a number of the boys housed here were extreme mental health cases who required medical rehabilitation – not a prison system staffed by cowboys. One boy, observed masturbating on camera, concluded his business by licking the ejaculate out of his hand. Another boy violated his own anus with an empty tube until his sphincter bled. I was painfully shocked, too, by the 'recreational banter' I was inadvertently privy to inside the common areas. When a fourteen-year-old detainee, his penis swelling inside his tracksuit pants, 'shared' what he'd like to do to me, I began to question whether I really wanted this job.

Aside from lessons about disclosure – some fabricated, some real – I learnt a lot about nepotism and cronyism in the workplace. Maria's and Alastair's behaviour towards me in the cake showroom had offered me a glimpse of what entitlement looks like. At the centre, an establishment that promised full-time work soon revealed an exclusive boys' club which blatantly raised its Polynesian employees above all others. The rosters were made up well in advance. The three Polynesian recruits in our course group were therefore 'looked after' and the rest of us received around fifteen hours a week. After a month at the centre, I transferred to the older and more notorious boys' centre in St Marys, the Cobham Juvenile Justice Centre. Prior to submitting an indignant resignation, though, I made certain the Centre's general manager received a good piece of my mind regarding in-house corruption.

Cobham is where the *really* bad boys live: recidivist rapists, multiple murderers, vicious armed robbers, gang members, and, unfortunately, still *way* too many Indigenous kids. Shitting bricks is an understatement. Little boys with big mouths I could handle, but many of these teens were the size of *men*. Strong communication skills were my saving grace – that and my own inglorious past, which meant I could relate to them, to some extent. Other useful 'tools' included an innate sense of humour and a mercurial wit, which got me through the first few shifts, until Cobham became familiar territory.

I began to identify the staff as the primary operational problem, in both the Airds centre and Cobham, rather than their charges. It was painfully obvious that each unit and their team worked independently of general protocol or standard operating procedures. The unit co-ordinators were often a law unto themselves, choosing their favourite lackeys for the choice tasks. As a 'newbie' I had little choice but to adapt to each unit co-ordinator or find myself side-lined. Consequently, I welcomed the Unit Support role – it kept me out of the units and as a busy 'floater'. Hours could really drag by inside a 'settled' unit, a little world full of testosterone, ruled by a would-be dictator of a unit co-ordinator.

I was supervising inside the school one afternoon when a boy I had established a rapport with showed me an ink cartridge he had stolen. The item would undoubtedly be used for a makeshift tattoo gun. As we made our way back to the unit I extended my hand to the boy, demanding he pass the cartridge over to me.

"No way Miss!" he retorted. "You're nice, you won't tell anyone!"

"Oh yes I will, if you don't hand it over right now!" I used a stern voice, followed by a cautionary smile.

The smile was not returned. I was sorely challenged; it would have been so easy to just turn a blind eye and keep walking, but I hadn't signed up for corruption or fearmongering.

"You *will* hand it over to me or I'll call for back-up and have it *taken* off you!" My smile was now defunct.

The boy was no longer smirking. Nor were the other boys walking with him, who had cottoned on quickly to what was happening. The boy, muttering profanities under his breath, slapped the cartridge into my open palm. I decided to teach him a lesson about mutual trust, so instead of treating him with a mandatory minor misbehaviour report I pushed the cartridge deep into my pocket for later disposal. Needless to say there was no retribution from the boy and the incident remained anonymous.

Testosterone, puberty and a criminal mind, are terrible burdens to have to endure all at once. I had been posted on video surveillance duties inside the infirmary where a seventeen-year-old youth had been placed inside a 'soft room' for 'protection of self'. It was now my job to observe the youth closely and report any serious act of or attempts at self-harm. I watched hopelessly as he picked at the self-inflicted wounds on his forearms. He had been stripped naked and made to wear a 'suicide gown' that could not be ripped into shreds. Screaming with frustration the youth began hitting his head against the 'soft' walls so ferociously he managed to knock himself out. I called my supervisor over the radio and two male officers arrived and entered the cell. The boy stirred, then lashed out at the officers, and he was swiftly subdued and handcuffed. There was blood on the cell walls from the boy's cuts and I could not help but feel rage towards a system that did not appropriately cater for chronic and severe mental health issues, let alone offer suitable treatment for people below the age of eighteen. At the end of the day this particular young man's issues were deemed to be 'behavioural'.

The rate of suicide or death in custody among young men under the age of twenty-five is phenomenal, and far exceeds that of females in custody. The primary cause for this is so far undetermined, but untreated depression and romantic break-ups seem to be strong contributing factors, and for these reasons alone frequent visits or phone calls from girlfriends were encouraged at Cobham, something I applauded.

Eser had become a casual boyfriend. Stupidly, I had introduced him to my mother who couldn't get enough of his Mediterranean charm. My friends and eldest daughter were also enamoured with Eser's refined attitude, and of course it *had* to be big, crass, coarse *me* who had devoured and denigrated the relationship. Perhaps it was; perhaps I needed to take a step back and take a good look at how I behaved in a relationship. But for Eser and me any positive introspection had arrived too late. We were now so estranged from one another that I returned to the internet to begin the hunt anew. I then stumbled across a faceless profile which turned out to be none other than Eser's romantic back-up plan.

Eser and I split in March 2006 when, after returning from his yearly Turkish pilgrimage, he openly accused me of having given him herpes simplex virus 2. The pain and indignation his finger pointing created inside me was indescribable. In eighteen years of marriage I had not given Rhys a single STI, nor Nick, and definitely not Eser. It was, I knew, Eser's only way of telling me, in no uncertain terms, to fuck off, he'd had enough.

On the flip side, Eser's departure felt like a huge weight had been taken from my shoulders. Emotionally I had swum against the tide for months, meandering this way and that in my desperation to sway Eser's steely determination. Now, in the light of such an uncouth accusation, I had no recourse but to let go. After all, apart from anything else, did I really want to catch whatever the bastard had caught over there?

On more than one occasion, metaphysical research has shown me that when a person refuses to let go of a situation or a person who no longer serves them, the Universe will create ways – often both cruel and precipitate – that *will* force them to let go. A clairvoyant once told me my astrological chart was among the most tenacious and resilient she had come across. She likened me to a pit bull and the way its jaws will lock onto something, with no way of persuading it to release its victim.

Just as I began to enjoy my 'front line' Youth Officer's role, I found myself rostered more and more into Admissions, which pretty much kept me separate from the units and the boys. In Admissions I found myself running into another 'Mary' type, a morbidly overweight woman who acted like she owned the place. I pleaded with rosters to have me posted back inside the units or as Unit Support at the very least, but my requests fell on deaf ears. Three months inside a place that had seemed to promise me a professional future, and it was turning into a nightmare.

In early August 2005 I discovered the Admissions co-ordinator had sequestered Anne and me. Anne, a voluptuous blonde, was one of the women I had trained with at the Airds centre. The co-ordinator, a man in his fifties, was renowned for doing this type of thing for the sole purpose of securing 'eye candy'. I understood how a woman like Anne might fit into his mould, but me? I spoke to the General Manager about the problem but nothing was followed up. Demoralised, it dawned on me I would need to move on once more. Of the ten juvenile justice centres in New South Wales the only other within reasonable travelling distance was the new female detention centre at Lidcombe, the Juniperina Juvenile Justice Centre (formerly known as Minda).

I was totally at ease working with boys now and I saw firsthand how ferocious girls could be when Cobham housed the occasional overflow from other centres. I had no wish to work with females, but what choice did I have? I was already coming dangerously close to giving the fat Admissions 'Mary' a piece of my mind. What I could not have envisaged, however, was that I was about to embark on an experience I would never forget and that would bring a part of my past life to full circle.

'When the student is ready the teacher will appear' – Buddha Siddhartha Gautama.

CHAPTER TWENTY-ONE

A PRICKLY SPIDER FLOWER

———

Whether by accident or design, I grew up brushing shoulders with the highly visible criminal element of Sydney's western and southern suburbs. I also grew up with an iconic TV drama series called *Prisoner*, which spoke to me on certain personal levels. Yet not in a million years would I have dreamt I would one day work inside a prison myself – I simply did not possess the courage or the confidence.

The Juniperina Juvenile Justice Centre hired me almost immediately, placing me on a Section 27, an ongoing threemonth contract renewable by the Unit Manager at the General Manager's discretion. What a relief – no more sitting by the phone waiting for shifts. I would work six days on, three days off, on a rotating roster, earning both recreational and sick leave. Life was looking up. Could the old adage be true, that when one door closes another opens?

Unlike at Airds centre and Cobham I did not have to earn the staff's friendship here. The Youth Officers were appearing in droves wanting to shake my hand. Juniperina was a completely different world: the buildings were brand new and up to date, with an open plan layout without the harsh barriers that stated the obvious, and although a prison, the place screamed out 'rehabilitation'. I was placed in Banksia Unit, on Malulani's team; Malulani was a corpulent Cook Islands matriarch with a stern demeanour that masked a kinder inner disposition. There were a number of Pacific Islanders here too, but they did not dominate the place like in the boys' detention centres. I actually really liked the 'Fobs'; they were always on a high and seemed particularly friendly.

The first shift at Juniperina was markedly different from the ones I'd experienced at the Airds centre or Cobham. This time around the detainees snubbed *me* and it was I who had to put in the time to get to know them in order to gain their trust.

That first evening after dinner, I took a girl to the nurse's clinic from the Boronia High Needs Unit. 'Yeah no problem,' I thought; I had done this type of movement many a time before at Cobham with no issues. As I soon discovered, though, at Juniperina getting the little shit *back into the unit* became the issue. 'Heidi' was only thirteen and had been in and out of 'juve' since the age of ten. We exited the clinic and Heidi fixed me with her big hazel eyes.

"I'm not going back to the unit and what are you going to do about it?" She was mocking me.

Goddamn it! My first shift in this idyllic place and now this?

"Well," I mused, searching my mental bag of tricks for the correct formula, "I could call for back-up over the radio or, we could simply get to know each other better as we walk back?"

Heidi stood still for a moment weighing up her options.

"I don't want to walk," she proclaimed defiantly.

"Oh really? Well what do you want to do – skip?"

Heidi looked at me and smiled. "Yep, that's what I want to do, skip back to Boronia."

"Okay," I said. "I'll probably get spoken to when the supervisors look on the cameras but hey, it's not about me is it?"

I was a star sign fanatic by now. I could give you the star sign of most renowned personalities at a glance. I soon utilised this knowledge on colleagues and even the detainees in order to better manage my relations with them, believing that each and every one of us responds to our basic planetary traits on a negative or positive bent. On this particular occasion I decided Heidi was most probably a Gemini or a Leo, a personality fuelled by defiance and mischief.

"What star sign are you Heidi?" I asked, certain I had the little shit pegged.

"Guess!" Heidi replied smugly.

I picked out every sign except the correct one as we skipped back to the Unit, arm in arm like two silly sisters. Just before we entered the unit I asked her, "Well, what is it then?"

Heidi used her fingers to mimic a set of pincers.

"Nahhh no way, Cancer? You? Cancerians aren't pains in the ass. They're easy to get on with."

But as a matter of fact, young Cancerian girls are extremely troublesome. They only settle down somewhat later in life.

* * *

The more I got to know the girls, the more Juniperina became the perfect working environment for me. Sure, behaviourally these girls were ten times worse than their male counterparts, but I found it easy to understand them; I might even say they were therapeutic, given my own background. Being with these hopeless souls was like looking into a full-length mirror of my own past.

Winning the trust and affection of the girls however came at a price. One unit co-ordinator 'advised' me I wasn't writing enough minor misbehaviour reports, which meant I was not doing my job properly. This person, a troubled woman herself, chose to overlook the fact that I possessed sufficient communication and negotiation skills to make minor misbehaviour reports irrelevant. Because I 'dared' to repeat this to her, this co-ordinator made it her personal mission to trip me up whenever the opportunity presented itself, particularly in front of others. I can deal with constructive criticism in private; publicly however … well, try to shame me and you'll get a mouthful back, which is exactly how I dealt with the said person.

Another unit co-ordinator, renowned for being a 'dragon lady' and who noone wanted on their team, felt it was her job to systematically correct everything I did in front of the detainees, cordially reminding me that the 'residents' were not my friends. Both of these ladies eventually recognised my talent with the girls and became both allies and confidantes – although the former co-ordinator was dismissed for 'professional misconduct'. Ha!

In spite of the glimpses I'd caught at the Fairfield youth refuge, the girls I came across at Juniperina weren't anything like I'd imagined. Their stories seemed to have been obscenely exhumed from the screenplays of horror films, the kind that would rip out my heart rather than offer cheap thrills. I now believe nothing is mere coincidence, so perhaps I had come to this place to learn that in comparison, my own past had not been so terrible. Irrespective of the horrors, every day at Juniperina proved an adventure and because I often got through to the toughest kid where others failed, Juniperina also gave me strong feelings of self-worth and achievement. I had spent a lifetime picking up other people's emotional pieces and nothing had ever been returned to me as it was by these lost souls who concealed their pure hearts behind Medusa faces. Who would have guessed that the very soil I'd stood on in 1982 as a delinquent teen facing court would one day be the place I worked in, helping girls who seemed so similar to that younger me?

At Juniperina I received a lot of specific training refreshers, but none as frequent as the Alcohol and Other Drugs courses. These kids were consumed by drugs. Cell searches always turned up some form of substance with the most common being crushed Panadol, which the girls snorted. The worst drug deviation I witnessed was a girl on methadone who regurgitated her dose directly into another detainee's mouth. I decided then and there that drug taking and dealing was possibly the vilest form of abuse, bar child molestation. Later in life I had to catch myself from judgement, when I acknowledged I was both a food and relationship addict. Addiction is addiction regardless of what you indulge in.

At the end of my first Section 27 I was immediately renewed and my 'talents' saw me transferred from the cushy, privileged unit of Banksia, to the Boronia High Needs Unit – one which had burnt out many a Youth Officer before me, and since. Whereas Banksia had every luxury an incarcerated girl could ask for, Boronia was rudimentary and austere. Boronia was an induction unit and the only 'travel pass' into Banksia was consistent good behaviour, the attendance of behaviour modification programs and an adherence to all the institutional rules.

My radio call sign thus became 'Boronia Angelica'. It was inside this 'terrible' high needs unit that I spent the next three years of my working life.

* * *

Unfortunately, mainstream society knows little about these, their less than productive peers, some of them as young as ten. Please, allow me to enlighten you.

Among the long-term detainees I was privileged to meet at Juniperina was Lenny. Lenny came into custody on charges of attempted murder and aggravated assault, and spent four years there. By falsifying her ID she also managed a brief stint at the Mulawa Women's Correctional Centre in Silverwater.

Externally, Lenny was a force to be reckoned with: tough, assertive and silver tongued. Her reputation, both inside and outside Juniperina, preceded her; noone dared to fuck with the Vietnamese spitfire. Lenny was embroiled in a high profile Vietnamese gang who called Cabramatta home … Cabramatta, my old stomping ground, was now a suburb with just over 50 percent of its population of Asian descent. Lenny was the girlfriend of a respected gang member and the head of its female division. High on the drug 'ice', the same potential killer Maria had dabbled with, Lenny stabbed a rival groupie on the back of her neck, and a second girl in her eye. In her drug-fuelled paranoia, Lenny was convinced the girls were making a pass at her man. Both victims survived and Lenny did her time just shy of her twenty-first birthday.

Somehow, but never entirely, I managed to pierce through Lenny's steely exterior. I discovered a young woman who in her own unique way possessed a logical set of moral codes and also, rare for her young age, twenty/twenty vision. Lenny's downfall was men and the pursuit of romantic love. Her feisty personality was attracted to and attracted the quintessential 'bad boy'; anyone less would have bored her. But as with all host/parasite relationships, Lenny paid a high price for each rollercoaster ride she embarked on, and the path to criminality was paved. Lenny was raped, bashed, extorted, and left heavily pregnant. Her dubious family raised Leah, the daughter Lenny gave birth to not long before committing her heinous deed, and Lenny never truly got to know or grow close to her.

One day while I was on loan to Banksia Unit, which for me was a rare treat away from the crazies, I stumbled onto a bitter argument between Lenny and one of the oversized Pacific Islander Youth Officers who everyone affectionately knew as Uncle Bob. Bob, towering over Lenny, was spitting useless directives from a toothless mouth. I could see that Lenny, all five feet of her, was growing more and more agitated and that the issue could have been resolved differently and borne a healthier outcome. Not everyone is born to be a successful youth worker and there are a few individuals who ought to know when to get out of that fragile environment, lest they become a liability to themselves and those they work with – and for.

During our training we were told never to undermine another Youth Officer in front of the detainees. Although I understand the rationale behind this, I saw it differently. For me, safety of self and others comes before ego and if this means I am able to defuse a potentially dangerous situation more successfully than my colleague, I will not allow protocol to get in the way. I knew how volatile Lenny was and Uncle Bob, who had worked there for ten years, knew that too. The situation at hand had nothing to do with a refusal of directives and everything to do with wounded pride, so I stepped in and *demanded* Bob go drink the coffee I had 'made for him' in the staff room.

At Cobham and the Airds centre, I had got to know a people who were previously foreign to me, Pacific Islanders. I found that when sober, Polynesians were a joy to be around, but pour a little kava into the mix and these colossuses of humankind could become unmanageable and downright frightening. Ego too stands before these proud people and both Uncle Bob and Malulani were, among others, forces to be reckoned with when displeased. But this was not the time for self-righteousness.

My rapport with Lenny lasted the three years I worked with her. She called me her 'Angel', and decided I deserved the same love I had given her; and so, because she understood I needed more love in my life, Lenny tried to set me up with another youth worker at the centre, a Gemini. (I will come back to this later.)

Another long-term detainee, held at Juniperina under the mental health act, was 'Kristy'. Kristy's story is far more macabre than Lenny's and involves demonic possession.

Fifteen-year-old Kristy became embroiled in the most terrifying case of religious brainwashing I'd heard of in this country. Her father and brother convinced Kristy her mother had been possessed by the devil and that if she did not help free it, her mother's soul would be lost to Satan forever. A neighbour testified at Kristy's trial that she had seen Kristy hold down her mother's legs while Kristy's father and brother inserted surgical needle holders up her nose and into her brain to free her of the 'malign demon'. It was also reported that Kristy's mother had attempted to flee her attackers but was dragged back several times by her family, ending in her death. Over the six years she spent incarcerated, Kristy vehemently denied any involvement in the murder of her mother. Her unrelenting denial prompted the New South Wales Department for Juvenile Justice to have Kristy charged under the mental health act, with ongoing reviews and assessments bearing no discharge dates until the board was satisfied with Kristy's restored sanity.

During these six long years Kristy was a model prisoner: polite, studious, obedient, graceful and congenial. I remember taking her to TAFE college and university so she could finish her Higher School Certificate and another course I no longer recall. Kristy would often thank me for every courtesy extended to her, which was not surprising given the way most of the Youth Officers treated Kristy, let alone the other detainees. Whether or not Kristy *was* mentally unstable and if indeed she took part in her mother's demise, I'll never know. My gut instinct was that the twenty-one-year-old woman sitting with me in the work vehicle was, guilty or otherwise, no threat to me whatsoever, and this was all I could go by. Kristy's hopeless situation further compounded my deep dislike for religious practices of any kind.

By the time Kristy was reaching the end of her university course the mental health board was still holding off on making a decision, and Kristy had had enough. With the support of a Christian 'billeting family' who befriended her, Kristy appealed to the media and pleaded with the state government to let her out. A *60 Minutes* story on Kristy was followed by her release from detention not long after. My greatest fear for Kristy was not that she might be insane, but whether religion might again compromise an obvious vulnerability.

The mosaic of teenage personalities incarcerated there was vast and furious. There was 'Donna', a fourteen-year-old girl with bumps in all the right places, who brought a Wollongong brothel to prosecution and subsequent closure when a 'conscientious' client reported the underage employee.

One afternoon shift as I supervised the Boronia courtyard, Donna and 'Kelly', a self-professed lesbian, decided to get it on while 'Sarah', the youngest convicted female murderer in the state at that time, did her best to divert my attention. Sarah had stabbed her boyfriend twentyseven times while her new boyfriend assisted by holding the victim down.

"Play ball with me Angelica!" Sarah commanded in her usual straightforward monotone that seemed completely devoid of emotional colour. Later on, it was established that Sarah might be an undiagnosed case of Asperger's syndrome.

"Yeah okay, but I have to keep my eye on those two."

"No they're okay, don't worry about them!" Sarah assured me.

I needed to worry about them, though, because once I turned my back on the duo – and then briskly turned back around – there was Donna lying spreadeagled on the grass, below unit visibility, with Kelly working her fingers on her like a demon. What to do? As with the ink cartridge incident at Cobham, I chose, in the moment, to do nothing, and continued to play ball with Sentinel Sarah.

Short of coming across as unscrupulous, I would utilise this 'freebie' for posterity. It was no secret that all the girls 'got into' one other every chance they got. The truly unscrupulous ones were those who took advantage of the tragedies that were these children. One of these was a certain Youth Officer, 'Monty'.

Monty got into the job because 'Mother' worked at the DJJ's Head Office. Monty was a young shmuck who acted like his shit didn't stink, and Donna fell for him hook line and sinker; she thought she'd fallen in love. Fortunately, despite Monty's best efforts to camouflage his actions, the centre's cameras caught Monty disappearing into Donna's cell while on night shift, a single post position. Mother's position at Head Office could not get the pseudo-rapist off, and he was eventually added to the NSW Sex Offenders Register. Hopefully, Monty will never again take advantage of vulnerable children.

'Cheryl' was a chubby, smelly, freckled, Cabbage Patch Doll redhead, who relentlessly self-harmed for attention – any type of attention. Cheryl was also a pathological liar who made up the most extraordinary stories to gain sympathy. When head banging, cutting, pulling out medical stitches, smearing her own blood all over her cell, peeing on the floor or masturbating on the cell's camera did not receive the desired effect, she'd up the ante by 'bronzing up' – pretending to be eating her own excrement. Not a pretty sight.

Cheryl was eventually placed on a behaviour management plan, with officers monitoring her every ten minutes during 'moderate' self-harming episodes in order to reduce triggers that might be sparking the behaviours. It was observed that Cheryl would not self-harm up until ten minutes before the check. As officers began their checks, however, Cheryl would move into position against the wall and begin the series of controlled head bangs which might leave a graze but were never serious enough to require medical attention. The officer would then walk past the cell and go back into the office, leaving a trail of acrimonious screams and profanities. Defeated, Cheryl would sit back down on her cot, doing nothing or something for a while. Eventually the poor disturbed kid noone liked simply gave up performing altogether.

'Sammy' had destroyed her frontal lobe through 'chroming' (inhaling fumes from paint). She repeatedly told us there were people in her cell. She would stare at you without actually seeing you until something broke through the unsettling trance. Sammy would try to recuperate a lost sense of *something* by gorging herself on any food she was able to steal from the unit; she would also masturbate for long periods of time. On one occasion when Sammy broke into the unit kitchen to grab a loaf of bread, stuffing it into her soiled track pants, I attempted to remove it from her but she lunged at me with such ferocity I was forced to take a step back and press my duress alarm for assistance. Sammy was then restrained by several officers and thrown into the holding room.

Eventually, Sammy had to be let out on day release due to time served but she absconded and was dragged back to Juniperina on further charges. If there was anyone who should have been detained under the mental health act it was Sammy, together with two other girls who, like Sammy, met with tragic ends. After her eventual release, Sammy was found dead in a dirty side street, still clutching a paper bag to her face.

'Tracey' was an intellectually disabled girl who from the age of ten was a virtual fixture at juve. Like Sammy, Tracey did not belong in custody. I met Tracey for the first time when she was sixteen and she was the only child to deliberately assault me, by throwing a tennis ball at my eye, for no reason at all. Tracey lived for a budgie called Gloria and the eighteenth birthday party she was planning from the inside which might see her freed from a lifetime of rules and regulations she simply had no ability to comply with. Tracey had severe oppositional defiant disorder (ODD) stemming from an intellectual disability. Like Cheryl, she often 'bronzed up', but for something to do rather than to gain attention. Unlike Cheryl however, Tracey actually *ate* her faeces and drank her urine. Upon release she did not receive the help she so desperately needed in the community. Tracey went on to commit additional minor offences and was sent to the Mulawa Correctional Centre where her intellectual disability was mistaken for bravado. Following a number of assaults on staff and prisoners which were harmfully punished, we were told Tracey was found hanging in her cell.

'Paigh' was possibly the worst case of self-destruction I came across at Juniperina. Sexually abused and systematically tortured from the age of eight by the family's church pastor, this beautiful girl with big sugar curls and chocolate brown eyes developed a classic case of Stockholm syndrome. Paigh fell in love with her paedophile tormentor and became pregnant by him. Although she lost the baby, Paigh gave the boy a name and never quite recovered from this episode of her life.

The abuse of Paigh went undetected and unreported for several years. When Paigh lost her son she was suddenly aware that this man was not a cherished lover but a sadistic villain. She finally escaped his clutches by stabbing him and leaving him for dead. Paigh did not discover whether her tormentor lived or died yet if he lived, he did not file charges against her; how could the putrid grub do that without indicting himself?

Paigh attempted to drown her emotional pain by self-medicating with heroin. When heroin was unavailable she would get her hands on anything else that might work, in any way possible. Her growing habit led Paigh into underage prostitution and hard crime. Drug and stress induced psychotic episodes forced her into the mental health wing of, ironically, the hospital I worked in before I came to Juniperina. Staring at the deep scar on the inside of her forearm, Paigh revealed that while in hospital she had wanted to see what her ulna looked like, and had cut into her arm until it became fully exposed.

To finance her escalating drug habit, Paigh began working out of a renowned Kings Cross strip club that covertly serviced regular paedophile clients, under the protection of corrupt police officers. More often than not, Paigh and the other girls were raped and left unpaid. Paigh's final control order at Juniperina took place because she had threatened someone with a blood-filled syringe, yet despite her lifestyle Paigh did not carry any life-threatening viruses.

Inside Boronia Unit, Paigh posed the biggest threat to the nursing staff. She incessantly demanded medication, *any* medication – the more potent the better. Paigh was eligible for the methadone and Suboxone programs and watching her zone in and out daily was heartbreaking; beneath the muck lay an incredibly talented, funny and intelligent young woman, one I quickly fell in love with. The day arrived when I would witness just how mentally tortured and ill Paigh was. She had once again found herself in confinement and was begging staff to unlock the cell door so she could get away from the 'terrifying ghosts' that were trying to hurt her. The fear I saw in Paigh's eyes was real and I believe to this day that it was not just drug induced psychosis beseeching staff through that narrow viewing panel. Low lying entities (such as poltergeists) are morbidly attracted to pain and desperation, especially among young people. Forced by professional conduct, I had no other choice but to turn my back on Paigh's frightened, tear-stained face and her anguished screams for mercy. That night I no longer felt like a Youth Officer and more like the jailer I actually was. Paigh was one of three girls I could not believe would make it past their twentieth birthday.

'Jessie' was another extreme case and possibly the most physically beautiful girl I had seen come through Juniperina.

Unlike Paigh, Jessie solicited openly in and around the Kings Cross district, not only to feed her chronic heroin and ice habits, but because she genuinely enjoyed the dangerous 'bad girl' lifestyle prostitution offered. Additionally, her boyfriend and pimp made certain Jessie was kept 'working' in order to finance his *and* his mother's drug habits. Jessie, unlike most of the other girls, was in no way endearing; she had a nasty streak that could find you dead or injured in a heartbeat if you, for whatever reason, became her enemy. Jessie was daring and astute even within the unit, trafficking, embezzling, and threatening the staff with tales of 'Underbelly-style' executions.

I became Jessie's target when the Unit Manager directed me to let Jessie know she would no longer be receiving mail from her boyfriend. Jessie became so enraged staff had to place her in cell confinement where she was denied cutlery items at dinner time. 'Grace', also in indefinite isolation on the opposite wing of the unit, sat alone outside Jessie's cell eating her meal with cutlery she had only just earned back. Jessie, of course, convinced Grace to slip a knife under her cell door, and so now this angelic looking she-devil was dangerously armed. I almost opened Jessie's door to retrieve her empty plastic plates when I saw her conceal something behind her back. Unsuccessful, Jessie hissed at me through the viewing panel.

"Just you wait Angelica you fucking fat cunt, when I get out I'll get my contacts in Kings Cross to track you and your children down and I'll tell them to tie you up and force you to watch while they cut your fucking kids up!"

I could see in Jessie's eyes she had meant what she said. I also noticed the diminutive Grace snickering next to me and realised her knife was missing. *Here goes another written report.* In Juvenile Justice report writing doesn't stop with a one-page recount; there are alerts to be written up on the data system, checks to be performed and recorded, and punishment recommendations made, which come under a different set of paperwork requirements. The Child Protection Act is 99 percent favourable to the child and if anyone thinks being a Juvenile Justice Officer is a walk in the park, please think again. The number of cases of false allegations directed against JJOs is incredible, so if you're the type of personality kids in custody do not like chances are you'll find yourself out of a job and placed on a Category Two indictment faster than you can say *But I didn't do that!* The average 'burn out' time for a JJO is two years.

Whenever a new kid verbally abused me I chose to ignore their petty slurs and feeble attempts at institutional assertion. The girls were only letting off steam at perceived authority, but once settled in they soon acknowledge what exceptional people most Youth Officers are. The Aboriginal girls called me a 'white cunt' and the white girls a 'dog' but by the end of a week I would be 'Angelica, the best youth worker here'. I genuinely liked my charges and they could see and feel it. Jessie however touched a nerve no other kid had. She had dared to involve *my children* and I lost my cool and made unprofessional counter threats while Jessie laughed diabolically in my face as she tried to goad me into opening her door.

To date, the only detention centre staff member to have been murdered within the New South Wales Juvenile Justice system was by the hand of a girl like Jessie.

Each time the police dropped Jessie off to us, she was so high on drugs she had little concept of anything, let alone her surroundings. She would sleep for hours, cry out for drugs, or go into a frightening trance as she picked behind her ears until the hair follicles had been all but removed. Jessie's primary concerns were all about staying in contact with her pimp boyfriend and the whereabouts of her 'working clothes'. She would try to recreate the feel of drugs running in her veins by re-enacting a heroin shot in front of the other detainees.

"I love the feel of the cold needle going in," Jessie would murmur as she closed her eyes in a pseudo-euphoric flight of fancy.

Before I left Juniperina in 2008 I asked if anyone had seen Jessie; the girls kept tabs on one another on the outside and Jessie hadn't been inside for some time. Noone had seen or heard of her. In my mind's eye I could see Jessie's lifeless face and body stuffed inside a car boot somewhere. Her clientele were the type of persons who would do such a thing. During one of her famous rages Jessie had humoured me by asking how much I made per week 'locking up little girls'. Her reply to mine was, "I make three thousand dollars a week Angelica, so who's the real loser here, huh?"

'Keely' and her cousin 'Kasey', both fourteen-year-old Aboriginal girls, received an eightmonth control order for brutally assaulting a couple in a park for their cash. Keely took to me straight away. She was tiny and sported the big beautiful flashy smile our Indigenous girls are pictorially famous for. As our friendship grew, so did Keely's trust in me.

As a mandatory reporter I was bound to document all client disclosures which were then handed to the Department of Community Services (DoCS). Throughout my 'juve' lifetime I kept just two client disclosures to myself and the first came from Keely. Keely told me her twentytwo-year-old boyfriend had got her pregnant when she was only ten years old and that she subsequently gave birth to a healthy baby boy. Keely's mother took the baby, registered the birth under her name and raised the boy as her own, so he would not be removed by the child protection department. Keely made me promise not to tell anyone and indeed I did not. Assessing the situation, something that was in fact an integral part of my 'juve' training, I could not find a single reason *to* tell anyone. Yes, statutory rape had occurred and it would occur again, given the culture of the forgotten communities many of our Indigenous kids come from, kids just like Keely. Noone even knows where Walgett or Wilcannia are, myself included, so noone is privy to the way these communities function. How much prime media air time is given to childhood abuse, compared with celebrity tripe or international politics? At least this little boy was still with family *and* he had an identity.

No matter how many 'Sorry Days' or reconciliation events our government endorses, it can never restore trust in us, the invaders. The Aboriginal community is still angry, and insofar as we wish we could wipe out the past, it's a past that's still recurring on so many levels. I in no way condone the reprehensible behaviour people like Keely and Kasey have indulged in but in order to begin fixing an external problem, one must first enter its core and work from the inside out. The *Hubbard 'engrams' of Aboriginality and genocide cannot be removed or rewarded with a public holiday here or an 'in memoriam' copper plaque there; first and foremost, we need to fully comprehend how white men impacted on Indigenous life, changing it from 'black' to 'white' without reprieve.

The worst case of self-harm I have seen (outside of internet imagery and Campbelltown Hospital) belongs to 'Tanya Rose'. Like Paigh, Tanya Rose suffered from Stockholm syndrome. She was sexually involved with her father and this was eating away at her soul.

Tanya Rose was a classic cutter: there wasn't a fraction of skin on her inner and outer forearms that she had not sliced through. Her internal pain and external madness led her to swallow razor blades and batteries, stick staples into her eyeballs, break her own arm by having one of the detainees jump on it, burn holes into her flesh with lit cigarettes, and perform systematic genital mutilation that was picked up by a psychiatric nurse. Tanya Rose almost succeeded in taking her own life when she soaked the cast on her mending arm in toilet water, wrapped it around her throat, and waited for it to dry, thus constricting airflow. One of my fellow trainees from Reiby found her the following morning, blue and unconscious and within an inch of her life. Tanya Rose was transferred to the mental health wing of the Children's Hospital at Westmead where I sat in with her over a couple of shifts. It was not a nice place to be in and even Tanya Rose felt uncomfortable there.

Tanya Rose set fire to her cell during a night shift when there was only one staff member on duty inside the unit. No matter what the crisis, to open a detainee's door on your own is a sackable offence, and so the traumatised Youth Officer, once a personal friend of mine, had to wait long, excruciating minutes for the alerted Admissions Officer to lock up his own section and make his way through the air locks and into the unit. A situation like this becomes a matter of life or death for the detainee; in the three years I was at Juniperina, two detainees had perilously set fire to their cell.

'Grace', who I've already mentioned, was the detainee who spent the most time in solitary confinement and on a behaviour management plan, for assaults on staff and detainees alike. She came into Juniperina aged fourteen on a threemonth control order and remained with us a total of eighteen months as her daily custodial charges built up.

Grace had been diagnosed with bipolar disorder and ODD. She was a very intelligent girl but deep, pent-up anger had sabotaged any good intentions and clarity Grace may ever have possessed inside or outside the centre. When I became a master of Shithead (the card game), mainly thanks to hours of oneonone supervision with Grace in 'segro' (segregation, i.e. solitary confinement), I came to know the diminutive firecracker, ready to go nuts on the next unsuspecting victim at any moment, very well indeed. I shared a birthday with Grace so when I'd watch her being handcuffed and dragged off screaming and kicking by numerous Youth Officers, I'd call out behind her, "You're an embarrassment to our birth date Grace!"

Yet in Grace I saw clearly the same resentment, pain and wrath that I carried inside. I had the same type of negligent mother as Grace and shared the same feelings of misplacement, but until Grace and I are ready to charge, a dozen picador's lances won't faze the furious *Toro*. We just continue gouging, not only others but ourselves too.

Grace was the only person I knew to have actually been Tasered by police, though she was barely five feet tall and weighed next to nothing. Following her eighteen-month stint at Juniperina, Grace returned to us and found herself in and out of jail until her eighteenth birthday, when she met a much older man who appeared to preoccupy her for a while.

Just before Grace left Juniperina for good she toyed with lesbianism and started cutting. Grace also disclosed what I already suspected: that she had been sexually abused by one of her mother's many boyfriends, as well as by other family members. The disclosure was made matter of factly during a game of Shithead. This was something the girls had a habit of doing, blurting out horrible facts about their lives when you least expected them, and then looking taken aback by the shock on your face, as if it was 'no big deal'. *No effect* they'd chime, but for me it was *always* a big deal; I never became acclimatised to or desensitised by stories of child abuse, they sickened and horrified me each and every time. I knew evil lurked in the world, and more so inside people's homes than on dark streets, as the movies would like you to imagine. Evil never became my 'norm', however, and I still could not comprehend how a person could defile his own child, or any child.

There was one little girl who came in overnight who played the 'my story is grosser than yours' card with the other girls, declaring her mother would hold her down as her stepfather repeatedly raped her. She also claimed her mother whipped her.

"Okay that's enough!" I'd tell the new detainee, who seemed to show no emotion as she recounted her story.

Sometimes the girls would fabricate or repeat other children's stories for the sake of sensationalism or bravado and although it was our job to know the difference, we were required to shut this kind of talk down inside common areas. Before I could say another word of reprimand, the new detainee had her sloppy joe up and over her head, exclaiming, "Well look then if you don't believe me!"

To my horror I saw unmistakable lash marks etched angrily across the little girl's back. I tried to fight back tears but lost my resolve and walked as quickly as possible out of the lounge area and into the unit office. I had to purge the outrage seething inside me before I was stable enough to proceed with a mandatory reporting incident advice.

The Davy sisters were four Indigenous girls belonging to a family of twelve children who called Juniperina home. The only child not to have known prison was a brother who identified himself as gay. 'May' and 'Kerry' 'Davy' were also prolific heroin users and, like Paigh, were on the centre's reluctant methadone program. Along with three other Indigenous characters, 'Zelda', 'Regina' and 'Paulette', the Davy sisters could bring the centre to its knees with their sudden and irrational flash temper tantrums. My fondest memory of May, who straight out of Juniperina served four years at Mulawa for armed robbery, was cradling her head on my lap as I plucked her big bushy eyebrows into impossibly fine lines.

Although 80 percent of the girls suffered terrible abuses and were almost always attached to an abusive boyfriend, the sheer degree of tolerance and loyalty the Aboriginal girls displayed towards their abusers astounded me. Whether this is a cultural aberration or not, these beautiful children blamed themselves for the treatment they received from their partners and were more than eager to return to them in order to 'offer amends'.

Mary was such a girl. She had been thrown into a bonfire, first by her boyfriend and then by her 'cousins' for a repeat offence against him. As a result, Mary sustained first degree burns to 30 percent of her body; her attacker did this because Mary had forgotten to make him dinner. My heart went out to Mary as I quietly cursed her abuser, but then felt sick to my stomach when Mary retorted, "Don't you put this on him Angelica; I was the dumb cunt who forgot to feed him. This is my job and I failed him so I deserve what I got."

Zelda's story was similar. She had copped a beating when five months pregnant for not bringing her boyfriend a beer when asked to. Besides their endemic bullying, the Aboriginal boys – or rather the *men* in question – were also complacently unfaithful. Here too the girls were expected to endure this insult without too much fuss. As far as Zelda and I went, the only time I faced an allegation of excessive use of force was when Zelda forced our hand on the way back to the unit from the pool area. Her behaviour led to a decision for immediate confinement. Zelda was seven months pregnant at the time and her temper was vile and infamous – she would turn on you faster than Grace, with a bite that was far more ferocious. Spitting was another form of assault Zelda was renowned for and with many of our clients carrying hepatitis C or B, spitting was something no Youth Officer tolerated.

There were three of us involved in the process of 'dragging' Zelda and the subsequent holding room confinement. Zelda fought like a demon, taking a chunk out of the Boronia Unit Co-ordinator's thigh and almost catching my calf with the same massive jaw. She then threw herself onto her pregnant belly and began screeching that we had hurt her baby. Zelda filed three separate misconduct claims against the Department, naming me, the unit co-ordinator and a third Youth Officer as her antagonists. The unit co-ordinator had blood tests done and I was formally interviewed by a Human Resources and Employment Law Services investigator with my team's unit co-ordinator, Claire, present as my nominated support person. Fortunately for me, the CCTV camera that was fixed above the holding room door captured clearly what had transpired between us and the detainee, and all charges of professional misconduct were dropped.

As I stated earlier, it was extremely common for allegations to be made by detainees against staff, but particularly so when a kid took a dislike to any one Youth Officer, often for the most insignificant of reasons. The way the Department is set up, the clients have all the rights and the staff are required to prove their innocence. Many a good Youth Officer has lost their job in this way. One of Grace's tantrums led to the investigation and subsequent sacking of an entire team, of whom three officers had given the Department long service and were considered by all as conscientious, empathetic and highly capable officers. As much as I loved this job and supported these children, I was vocal about systemic failings and pandering. 'Juve' was but a revolving door that many young people, abused or otherwise, called home. In such a facility as Juniperina or Reiby real rehabilitation is virtually non-existent, and programs for the prevention of re-offending irrelevant. Important boundaries are often blurred by politics and in-house preferential treatment. The kids are well looked after, yes, but systemic consistency is often ignored or usurped.

'Celine' was the only detainee I knew who was held under twenty-four hours watch in an obscure mental health facility for acute psychosis and violent behaviour. Prior to her complete decline, Celine was yet another intelligent little girl who had jumped onto the merrygoround of detention at the age of ten. A child like Celine costs the tax payer around a million dollars a year, and all forms of intervention would only see Celine plunge deeper into mental illness.

Celine's mood swings rivalled those of Tanya Rose or Grace. She could go from being a nice little girl who'd play Scrabble with you and crack smartass jokes one moment, to an individual affected by a dangerously heightened state of hysteria the next. My saddest memory of Celine involved an attempted hanging. I checked on her one morning as she was taking a shower in her cell but could not hear the usual sounds. I suspected Celine was up to her self-harming tricks, some of which were put on for attention, like Cheryl. I called for Claire over the radio and together we entered Celine's cell to find her naked body curled up under the water. Claire lifted Celine's head from her foetal position and found a ligature tightly woven around her throat. When Claire removed the ligature with a '911' rescue tool, Celine burst into tears simultaneously gasping for air. She then clung onto Claire like a broken sparrow, her big brown eyes filled with despair and deep, dark unresolved pain.

There were some days and nights when it was difficult saying goodbye to these children, knowing they would sleep alone and unloved in their prison cots behind fireproof doors that could only be unlocked by a bureaucracy that knew nothing about the far reaching tendrils of parental neglect. I had to remind myself I had a job to do and that I was doing it well, and that these girls were the better off for people like me. At Juniperina all detainees are maintained in single cell status to prevent assisted self-harming, drug taking, and sexual activity. Once the TVs are turned off it must be a very long night, locked inside a small concrete block all on your own.

'Amber' was a long-term detainee who like Lenny was well respected by the other detainees. A girl who committed awful acts of assault on the public but who, like Lenny, displayed a cache of logical operational morality noone truly expected. Amber and I were chosen by a Department for Juvenile Justice commissioned advertising agency as promotional material for their new and glossy 'Welcome to Juniperina' how-to guide and video. It was impossible to keep a straight face before the camera due to Amber's knowing smirks, inappropriate questions and wisecracks – all muted out in the final cut of course. I was filmed giving Amber a pat down and as I bent over to her ankles, my handcuffs fell out from my 'juve' belt. Amber said something in 'Alibi', a secret language used by the detainees to evade staff, and I just lost it. This portion of the film was not used and another staff member took my place.

'Korina' had, during a drunken fight, attacked a pub patron's throat with a jagged bottle. This slightly built beauty, who mostly kept to herself in custody, gave away little of her propensity for violence throughout the one-year control order she served at Juniperina. Korina was a 'one timer' who went on to become a law abiding citizen and, in my opinion, an exemplary mother to two children. On the day I left that place Korina and I embraced inside her cell, and it was hard for me to walk out of there as her tear-filled eyes begged me to stay. More love was sown inside this arena of sadness than I encountered anywhere else during my working life.

But not all the detainees were lovable – at least not for a while. There were the notorious fourteen-year-old Samoan cousins who created a media furore by murdering a Sydney taxi driver. The cousins received a ridiculous and much disputed threeyear control order for their callous crime. Because of their physical stature and notoriety, the cousins were well received among the girls and soon took it in turns to run the units with, sad to say, the covert support of the Unit Manager and his despised protégée, herself a Pacific Islander. Along with the cousins, there was a high profile university student from a wealthy

Chinese Northern Suburbs family who had assisted her boyfriend with the kidnap, rape, and holding of *her friend* over a period of three days. This detainee became the unit diva, continually demanding this and that and the other during her one-year control order, and brazenly ingratiating herself to those who counted (on both sides of the fence). Unlike the Samoan cousins, there was nothing cute about this individual's complete lack of remorse and wherever operationally possible her requests were denied by the Youth Officers. Lastly, I recall an Anglo girl turned Muslim who boastfully confessed that a well-known Sydney mosque held an arsenal of weapons in its foundations. In light of the numerous acts of 'Jihadi terrorism' that transpired in and around the Sydney suburbs from 2014, this type of information is certainly damning, but one I can no longer report given its source and the time lapse. Sadly, many of the girls would indeed turn to obscure 'supporters' in search of unity, belonging and love, and most of them would only serve to continue a cycle of abuse suffered from an early age under the guise of 'fostering', when really it is none other than insidious grooming.

On the lighter side, 'Melanie' was the first transgender teenager to have come into a female juvenile justice centre. There was very little about Melanie that was 'girly', though, and whenever it took 'her' fancy, Melanie would show the girls 'she' was very much a *he*. Melanie was a strip search nightmare, with female officers checking *her* upper body, and male officers checking *his* lower.

Severe sexual, psychological and physical abuse was often the precursors for children entering into repetitive custody. Their sense of identity was distorted; they lacked focus or direction, and were almost always numb to ambition or aspiration for their future. Hurting themselves or others appeared to be their only existential purpose, their familiar friend. Sometimes these children would get out on bail or a suspended sentence only to commit an offence that very night in order to return to their safe haven, a place they called home. As I saw it neither the Department nor the judicial system did much to keep young people out of the prison system, with most of them graduating to 'the *big* house'.

* * *

Given these terrible circumstances, you might well ask why *did* I love working at Juniperina so much? I loved it because I saw tangible results, because amid all the pain and horror, there were a hell of a lot of fun times too, and because helping these girls was a cathartic experience that offered me perspective, initiative, and hope. At Juniperina I was able to reach and teach the girls, and in return I received from them the greatest of moral gifts, gifts they could not or would not give many others – their trust.

Some of these girls called me 'Mum' and said how fortunate my children were to have me. Others said they loved me and how they wished I was their mother. Indeed, I loved them too and to this day have forgotten very few of them. Yet it is still most important to remember these kids are no angels and should be handled with caution. It takes a lot of fortitude and skill to catch and tame a venom-spitting cobra.

The hour-long drive home was often fraught with frustration at a system that didn't work and which I and others like me could not change. I was periodically filled with tears and anger about perpetrators that weren't caught or punished for hurting children, mostly their own; but I would then wash away the helplessness in the shower, venturing in the next day full of renewed resolve and enthusiasm for my charges. It was *my* job to pick up their pieces and to instil in their minds a firm belief that better choices would bring about better experiences.

As far as my future at Juniperina was concerned, it was management who became my beast for they despised people like me; I was dangerous territory and perhaps the type of person who threatened their jobs. By refusing to acknowledge that the detainees were not my friends, that failure to write a dozen minor misbehaviours meant I wasn't doing my job properly, that keeping the unit happy and settled smacked of bribery, and that being liked by my colleagues and clients alike was not conducive to 'good youth work', I had sealed my fate in terms of higher duties.

On my resignation reference my referee wrote:

Angelica demonstrates a gift for negotiation and conflict resolution rarely seen in other Youth Officers that I have worked with. Our clients, females ranging in ages from ten to twenty-two, are very difficult individuals to manage, but Angelica appears to be able to settle the most troublesome and damaged with formidable ease. As her occasional supervisor, I have always felt secure and confident having Angelica on my team, knowing that the shift will be a smooth one because of Angelica's approachable nature, sense of humour, and compassion with our clients.

To this day I credit 'juve' as the only work I fell completely in love with, warts and all.

CHAPTER TWENTY-TWO

YOU RUINED ME

———

As I mentioned in the previous chapter, Lenny had made it her personal quest to hook me up with another youth worker. This was Jason the Gemini. After my online experience with Gemini Graham, I wasn't sure I was too keen to try another. The *Urban Dictionary* defines Geminis as: 'The sign that runs from May 21st to June 20th. Although nice and likeable people they possess traits/behaviours commonly associated with bipolar disorder.'

With three planets in Gemini, including Venus and Jupiter, in my natal chart, I knew a little about the Twins' characteristics, but I had also asked the Universe to send me someone *exactly* like myself and the Universe always delivers – often sooner rather than later.

But let me jump forward to whet your appetite a little. There were two major reasons that forced me to abandon New South Wales in 2008: Jason, and the Juniperina management team.

* * *

Jason was a worry from day one. Lenny had sold him to me as the archetypal martyr, a casualty of life. Of course, as the rescuer of lost souls I was a perfect buyer. I really couldn't blame Lenny for the subsequent pain Jason inflicted on me over the next two years; Jason was a master manipulator who made certain people felt nothing but compassion for him, and I so wanted not to fail this time.

I had, once again, returned to online dating. My emotional maturity was still far from developed, as were my self-worth and self-love, the essential ingredients I taught the 'juve' girls but could not adopt myself. Among my online contacts was 'John', a Republican Liberal backbencher with a penchant for 'threesomes'. Today, 'John' is very much a frontbencher, someone constantly in the political limelight. I can't help chuckle to myself each time I see his face on television, knowing all that he disclosed to me in the relative safety of cyberspace. I was never a potential dating candidate for John, nor did I want to be. I was more a useful urban confidante. Despite my aversion to group sex acts, I found 'John' interesting conversation fodder and we even had a chat on the phone once. No mistaking that nasal South Australian voice of his.

Jason, an acting unit co-ordinator at Juniperina, had been separated for five years from a woman he painted as a monster but with whom he was still undeniably in love. At the age of twenty-five Jason was diagnosed with ulcerated colitis and had the large bowel removed, leaving Jason in an induced coma for three days and a scar that ran the length of his body. During early convalescence from this procedure, Jason's wife went into labour and their daughter was born three months premature and weighing only 650 grams, the smallest baby to have survived in New South Wales at that time. Sally developed severe cerebral palsy and lived out her life wheelchair bound and completely dependent on her parents.

The first time I met Jason was during breakfast routine in the Banksia Unit. Jason was Unit Support and took his seat across from me. Nikki, a bouncy Aboriginal girl who laughed a lot then blurted out, "Jason's single Angelica, so now that you're single too, you two should hook up!"

We were both extremely embarrassed, yet from under his cap I did catch a twinkle in Jason's eyes as he surveyed my reaction to the outburst. I then found myself wondering whether Lenny had set up the devil-may-care Nikki as well.

My first date with Jason was at a Thai restaurant in Wollongong, where at least half of Jason's family lived. We held hands but did not kiss. As with Eser, I wasn't too sure about him; I had a thing for tall guys, and Jason was barely two inches taller than me. Although three years my junior, Jason, possibly due to his medical history, looked a great deal older and suffered mild scoliosis which caused him to stoop. I quietly told myself to stop the Shallow Hal bullshit; looks are not a barometer for happiness, as I had found out with Rhys.

When Jason came over my place one evening with his beloved Staffy bitch, Matilda, we ventured for a walk around the Rosemeadow bushland. Jason was an experienced hiker and had discovered natural spots in and around the Campbelltown area I had no idea existed. It was a beautiful night and I soon found myself in the mood for love, until Jason did the thing that turned me off him. Needing to blow out his nose, he blocked one nostril with a finger and disposed the contents of the other nostril onto the grass.

Red light.

A hot tub at Jason's place was a perfectly orchestrated manoeuvre which saw me give in to his advances. I was a sucker for tactile stimulation and Jason certainly knew how to win a woman's heart in the bedroom. Once again confusing sex and need with love, I pledged myself to Jason the Gemini.

A Juniperina colleague leaving the centre invited us to a Kings Cross pub crawl, which became Jason's and my second date. I considered seeing Jason at work the mandatory 'mini dates' one should have before committing to someone, but that was certainly not enough of an excuse to jump into another relationship. On this 'date' Jason was ostensibly by my side the entire night; perhaps he was guarding me from the other male officers who were already plastered. But, twothirds of the night in, it was actually Jason who lost control of his drinking. Being our driver I ordered Jason into my car; he could not even walk in a straight line and staggered backwards, bumping into walls and passers-by. I despise drunkenness, with each serve of substance abuse received from Nick blazing before my eyes like fireballs. During the drive back to Rosemeadow with two other Youth Officers in the back seat, it was impossible for me to mask the depth of anger and disappointment I was feeling. I began to berate Jason so soundly there was no way we'd be taking things further and at that moment I certainly did not want to.

When we reached Rosemeadow Jason was still out of it and asked to go home. Jason lived up the road from me and for reasons I now find incomprehensible and obnoxious, I refused to let him go.

"The night might be over for you but it isn't for me, you drunken mutt," I hissed.

I then unashamedly proceeded to take sexual advantage of Jason, unleashing all the pent-up anger and disdain I now felt towards men in general. I believe this behaviour is known as 'angry sex'.

Another red light.

Things went downhill from then. I knew I should be getting out of the relationship but I was mildly addicted to Jason's unpredictability, his wit and his consummate lovemaking. And there was another minor detail: I worked with the bastard!

One evening I rang Jason as I wanted company. He answered a second call sounding totally weird and then hung up on me abruptly. More curious than genuinely worried, I called him back over and over: no answer. On the umpteenth call, Jason picked up but did not speak. I yelled down the receiver for him to talk to me but still nothing. I was now genuinely worried and climbed into my car to drive the short distance to his house, to find noone at home. I waited around for a while and finally I could see a silhouetted figure approaching from out of the shadows, accompanied by a dog. I recognised Matilda and sighed with relief. Once again, though, Jason was completely inebriated.

"You're drunk!" I told him. "Are you an alcoholic? I don't want to be with an alcoholic! I want absolutely nothing to do with one."

Jason ordered me to leave him be, babbling that I didn't know what I was talking about and that he wasn't in any mood to explain anything to me. He then broke down into sobs and I felt I could not leave him that way; something very difficult to handle was eating at him, I could sense it.

I cradled Jason in my arms and slowly he began to explain how his only child, Sally, had not wished to see him that weekend, his access time with her, and how she'd said she would 'notify' him when it was 'suitable' for him to see her. Jason further explained that this kind of thing happened often, wholly placing blame on his ex-wife for Sally's behaviour. I continued to cradle Jason and remained with him, kissing his brow softly until the tears subsided. Another red light, of course, but the humanitarian inside of me chose to see it as a soft glow. A man who loves a child so deeply must surely have the ability to love his woman just as much?

* * *

Jason turned out to be the moodiest person I'd ever met. Just like Gemini Graham, he could be wonderful one moment and beastly the next, the classic split personality the zodiac speaks of. The cracks were deep and winding and even zig zagged in their boldness. Tardiness, stinginess, broken promises, ridicule, unprovoked anger, a god complex, frequent lack of consideration, complete emotional shut down, professional criticism of my work ethics, accusations, and, when I'd had enough and tried to lash out, even physical and verbal violence could be the serve of the week or day from Jason. On the flip side, the 'good twin' lavished the kind of love and attention I had only really experienced with Eser during our early days. Jason even mentioned the much sought after word to me, *marriage* – the magic solution for a life of perennial yearning.

Jason too could be funny, witty, and endearing. He liked my kids and they liked him. He was a handyman and a hard worker, possibly too hard; he barely took time off and did a ridiculous amount of overtime which usually left me high and dry and on my own. He habitually cancelled organised plans at the last minute in order to accept overtime, and, whenever I'd reprimand him for it, I would endure the following sermon:

"*Never ever* begrudge me my work ethic Angelica. I have a mortgage, a disabled child, and an ex-wife to support and you will *not* dictate to me when I can work!"

No matter how hard I tried – and boy did I try – I could not win with Jason, so I turned my anger and frustrations towards Melanie, the hated ex-wife. Sally, too, happened to be a bitch of a kid, forever competing with me for Jason's attention. Sally made it perfectly clear noone but her mother deserved her father's love, even though it was Jason who had abandoned the marriage. I soon began to demonise and blame Melanie for what Jason had become, and Sally for keeping him there. In the bitter end, though, I realised neither party was responsible for Jason's character.

Several times I attempted to leave Jason. The rollercoaster was too steep and loopy and I seriously wanted off, but Jason managed to talk me out of doing so each and every time. I then began putting pressure on him to divorce Melanie but it only aggravated things because, being a scrooge, Jason wanted to avoid further financial repercussions. He was also terrified of losing Sally, the twisted child who tormented him with every turn of the screw. Bogan Melanie was certainly the type of woman to use Sally as a financial pawn, too.

The rollercoaster was now unbearable to sit in and I began to develop frightening panic attacks. Going to work was no longer a carefree experience for me, with the day's focus subtly shifting from helping the girls to coping with Jason and his cruel 'mind fucks'. Feelings of emotional insecurity and instability created unfounded jealousies within me which Jason noticed and preyed on. The girls, too, picked up on my changed demeanour, knowing only too well who was responsible for it. Suddenly the tables were turned, with the girls taking on roles as counsellors and confidantes on my behalf, and this irked Jason to no end.

"You're too good for him Angelica," the girls would say. "Get rid of him. You're so pretty and he's an ugly short-assed toad, you can do *so* much better. We hate Jason for making you sad; everyone thinks he's a cockhead!"

Jason acted with the girls as he did with me: he was inconsistent, confusing, and completely exasperating. Some of the mortally wounding fights we engaged in were in fact over the detainees; he knew how I loved and protected them and that I openly resented Sally.

"Why would you confide in those dirty little bitches about us?" Jason spat with a level of indignation that diabolically contorted his face. He'd then add, "Why do you care about those diseased criminals but find it okay to criticise my beautiful, defenceless and innocent daughter?"

My rationale regarding Sally was that yes, the cerebral palsy had seriously affected her body but Sally's mind was as intact and crafty as anyone's. She was fifteen years old, extremely manipulative and calculating, and, as guilty as I did feel about her disability, I simply could not bring myself to like her.

Sally was none other than her mother's mouthpiece but Jason refused to accept this; he was blinded by paternal love and the fact he'd almost lost her at birth. No matter the way Sally antagonised me, Jason would side with her. As payback, then, I began pelting Jason with lurid and hurtful obscenities about his precious daughter, later, behind closed doors, acknowledging and castigating my dreadful behaviour. By continuing with this man I was reducing myself to a lower form of personal conduct and acrimonious revenge than I'd never stooped to before. Still, I couldn't bring myself to leave him; I simply did not know how.

Around this time, I applied for a couple of 'acting up' positions at Juniperina. I was an exemplary youth worker, I had completed my Certificate IV in Youth Work, the clients respected me, the staff liked me, I was quite capable of running a unit on my own, and yet each application for higher duties was overlooked. Some managerial brown tongue or newcomer from another centre was always appointed in my place. Eventually the frustration and disillusion became so overwhelming I ended up telling the management team what I thought of them, resigning my Section 27 and leaving my beloved Juniperina. Also, without Juniperina there was no reason to remain with Jason.

Together with an equally disenchanted colleague I found work as a caseworker in a DoCS approved support home at Quakers Hill. The home aided young, homeless mothers and their babies. I barely lasted two months before returning – tail wedged firmly between my legs – to Juniperina as a rostered casual. Jason's bogus offer of marriage and a permanent contract at work were dangling carrots I would never reach. I did not have what it takes to achieve long-term goals (i.e. patience and pragmatism) but I did take another Section 27 and continued, hopelessly, with Jason.

The clients at Quakers Hill liked me. Gaining young people's trust and at times even their affection was effortless for me, but I sorely missed my 'Juni girls'. Community youth work was not nearly as rewarding as custodial work and most of the young girls at the home were uninterested in their babies, something that weighed heavily on me. We were more like babysitters than caseworkers, which was infuriating. The system crippled these people emotionally, then 'enabled' them with rewards for good behaviour. The system thus trained them (like dogs) to behave for 'treats', rather than offering real solutions.

I became so preoccupied with Jason's perceived infidelities that I found myself on guard here, too. Prolonged hypervigilance and obsession were creating mental health issues I had never experienced before. For the first time in my life I sought the help of psychotherapy, and even tried hypnosis to rid myself of Jason's bizarre hold on me. Nothing worked. It appeared I was addicted to, and feeding off, the drama we *both* created.

One afternoon as I drove to Quakers Hill I had a panic attack of epic proportions. I swerved in front of an oncoming truck and missed it by metres as I swerved back into my own lane. When I arrived to work I was in shock and felt I was having a nervous breakdown. Jason was killing me. I had never felt so low, so lost and so completely hopeless and disarmed. That Christmas Jason, sensing I was making a concerted effort to leave him, threw me a bone. I was making plans to sell my house and buy a cute little cottage in the Blue Mountains, organising a transfer back to the Cobham Juvenile Justice Centre for work.

"Don't buy this house Angelica; move in with *me*! We'll go to Tassie for New Year's and pledge to make things work. I love you so very much Angelica, you're really precious to me and I'm so lucky to have you. Let me love you Angelica. I don't know what's wrong with me but I do know I'm going to fix it."

I didn't know what was wrong with Jason either, or how he could possibly 'fix it'. He always blamed something or someone for his extreme behaviours: an abusive father, a selfish mother, an evil ex-wife, a demented halfsister and brother, Sally's disability, the surgery, and, apparently, my demanding and negative attitude.

Stupidly, I canned the cottage and transfer to Cobham idea, moving myself, Edan and Kristen in with Jason. The fighting continued, and after a particularly vicious battle that required police intervention, I decided to call on Melanie for clues to her ex-husband's mind.

"Tell me about Jason," I pleaded. "He claims *you* were the one who hurt the marriage, but I need to hear *your* version of things."

Understandably, Melanie was hesitant to say much at first, appearing rather stunned to be hearing from 'the enemy', but she quickly took the opportunity to relieve herself. The words came pouring out of her mouth and sounded all too familiar.

"I truly believe Jason is bipolar Angelica, but of course he'll never admit it!"

There was a whole lot more, of course, but I needed to remain mindful that within any marriage, each party has his or her own version of events that only the other party can verify or deny.

* * *

The trip to Tasmania, Jason's peace offering, was excruciating. Here he unleashed his most selfish, villainous, and manipulative persona. Psychological crucifixion and emotional blackmail were the order of the day and all I could do was hold my breath and hope the next day might bring us some form of reprieve.

At the Port Arthur former penal colony Jason had made me so upset I wanted to hang him from the gallows that had ended many convicts' lives. I began pondering whether the essence of Martin Bryant's 1996 'massacre' (he shot dead thirtyfive people and wounded twentythree more) there had somehow penetrated Jason's soul, given the level of sadism he seemed to inflict on me. I had so tortured myself, hoping for the miracle of an easy, nurturing love. Why was I willing to put in the hard work needed for a relationship to work when all men seemed to want to do was hurt me and let me down? I was now convinced I was unlovable and undeserving of not only love, but respect too.

Just before New Year's Eve 2007 we spent two days on Friendly Beaches Reserve, a primitive beach in Tasmania's north-east coast. On one of these two nights I took myself away from the emotional noise that was life with Jason and wrote down some thoughts.

December 30 2007

Day four of a much anticipated trip to Tasmania; the consolation prize for cancelling a much hoped for trip to Italy and Germany as well as my little cottage in the Blue Mountains.

Another nasty fight, one I hoped to avoid in an idyllic place as this. The gaps between our fights are widening, but each incident nevertheless leaves me less hopeful of a future together. I have given up a little piece of paradise in the Blue Mountains which was at purchasing stage, because Jason's proposition made a lot of sense and was actually what I hoped for. Some people think having a child together will fix their problems; I thought living together might fix ours.

Yet sitting here now on Friendly Beach in the soft arms of peaceful solitude, I am seriously analysing if I can cope with Jason and his ways long term. There is so much goodness in this man and since Rhys, he has been the only man to show me I am worth keeping and not just good for a short-term adventure; but at what price? A private, fussy, exacting, quasi-alpha male who has learnt to live on his own for the past four years, how will he cope with me and my children who are not in any way regimented or conventional? I'm surprised he even allowed us into his meticulous fortress.

They say Geminis have dual identities. Jason is most definitely such a Gemini; he is not someone I can put up with for the rest of my life. It takes nothing to set him off and a lot to bring him back to the funny, loving person I cherish.

There is so much underlying damage, such guilt and pain within this man, and it all pours out when we fight. "Fuck you! Get stuffed! I will not put up with this! You are not living in my house! I am not the man for you!" he screams at me, his eyes narrowing into venomous, hateful slits. It never ceases to amaze me how Jason's verbal transformation also creates a significant physical one – and just like that. I can't help feeling when he has one of his anxiety attacks its Melanie he sees standing before him instead of me. He is not the sweet, peaceful, smiling "Admissions boy" I fell in love with at work last year. But wait; have I really fallen in love with him? And what does love really feel like? Love is not what we see in movies, that's lust; I have certainly extinguished lust with Jason.

2007, forty-one years old and on another pursuit of what love "might feel like". The notion of love engulfs me, it is all I've ever wanted, what I think about night and day, and all I think I need to feel complete. I have so much natural talent and vocational opportunities that have been thrown at me throughout my life, and I have utilised none of them in the relentless pursuit of what has to be a mythical lasso. Romantic love, ha! Merely the overture of madness.

Am I in love with Jason? I don't know, but what I am beginning to realise is that being on my own, being my own person, and doing things for me alone completely outside of a romantic relationship, are increasing in importance. Wow, amazing! I never thought I'd be writing this down let alone feeling or believing it.

There's another thing I'm realising; I have been dishonoured and disrespected all my life, and as courageous and resilient as I am even today, I'm a shattered mirror; I simply can't do it anymore – and I won't. Mirrors cannot be glued back together and so I must discard the shards and buy myself anew.

Forty-one years old and at long last emotionally freed from the Lady of Shalott's purgatory? Shit, where to from here?

CHAPTER TWENTY-THREE

SEVENTY THOUSAND CAMELS

———

After my separation from Rhys I conversed with Mother sparingly. Being in a familial/marital relationship was the glue that held together the 'we're okay with each other' facade I shared with Gilda. Rhys and the children was the screen I'd hide behind in order to smile convincingly at Christmas, birthdays and Easter. There never were 'stay over at Pop and Nanna's' nights, or trips to Circular Quay as a cohesive extended family, or even genuine cherished cuddles between Grandma and her grandchildren. We were fortunate if she even remembered their birthdays without prompting. Gilda cooked too much, spent most of the day in the kitchen washing up, constantly screamed at Piero and Alfonso about something or other, and would then begin her predictable 'oratorio' on how much Piero had improved. An account of her latest stage performance or literary publication would then conclude a day of tedious narcissism. All I wanted to do on such routine visits was run – run from the millstone and bullshit that was life in New South Wales and a spectacularly bleak past. But then, what about *my* children? Had I not dragged them around to suit my personal needs enough? How could I criticise Gilda when I was messing them around as well?

And mess them around I continued to do. I lasted two months in Jason's home; even Kristen, who rarely voiced her opinion, was now shouting at me:

"How can you live here? He wants everything *his way!*"

Jason was now going through a secondary settlement with Melanie, which did nothing to improve what was left of our relationship. It would appear Jason enjoyed pushing my buttons – it was like daily exercise for him. I could not understand why he behaved this way but it was becoming more and more obvious that mental illness played a part. I felt like a fish on a hook: baited, caught, landed, and then released, with the process repeated a dozen times.

I found a neat three-bedroom duplex in St Helens Park, still too close to Jason's but distant enough from the infernal lifestyle we shared. Completely disillusioned by where my life was heading, I threw caution to the wind, shouted *Fuck it!* and bought myself a brand new sports car and a trip to Europe. *Take that Juniperina management – and Jason, you sadistic angler!*

* * *

Searching for Truth and 'The Meaning of Life' took me down many spiritual paths. One of them was that Brahma Kumaris retreat in Leura, where I learnt to meditate for the first and only time in my life. I went to this beautiful, peaceful place nestled in the bosom of the Blue Mountains many times, on each occasion accompanied by someone new, including my eldest child Alycia. The first time had been when Nick betrayed me, leaving the children alone in Rosemeadow to chase another of his unsuspecting victims.

A silver haired lady who witnessed the sanguinity of my soul during a 'Women's Workshop', stepped out of *my* blue and handed me a brochure.

"I think you could use this," she said, squeezing my hand knowingly, then disappearing nonchalantly back into the group.

Via this mystery lady whose name I later learnt, I discovered Orion Women, a zany female duo dedicated to the emotional and spiritual self-development of other women. As with Rhys and the discovery of Neale Donald Walsch's life changing books, Orion Women's metaphysical based courses helped me distance myself from my deep-rooted problems, to then regroup and renegotiate life.

I met up with Eser once more when I attended an Orion Women weekend course (called 'Seven Paths') held in Willoughby. I needed somewhere to stay and took a chance in calling him. It all now seemed so plastic with Eser. Our conversation was densely punctuated and our physical interactions uncomfortably guarded. Granted, I looked like shit that night and was still in love with another man, but Eser had clearly moved on as well.

I then spent a small fortune and took part in a second course held at a quiet villa on the North Coast. 'Chrysalis' proved a surreal experience, with results I would never have expected; participation in their exercises left me and the others completely unmasked and visibly vulnerable. The hardest exercise – one I did not complete – was when I was asked to use another participant as a stand-in for Mother. The purpose of this was the unleashing and surrender of all pent-up resentment.

"Tell her everything you've ever wanted to say all these years. Let her see your pain, make her hold it, get it all out Angelica!"

The participant certainly played her role well, goading me to come at her at full force. I could not, but boy did I try. Being pushed so hard, indeed in the same way Gilda had always pushed me, brought out little more than resentment towards my facilitators, especially after they accused me of not truly wishing to heal myself. Surely there were less violent ways to heal? I'd had enough mistreatment.

When I returned to St Helens Park I felt no desire to see Jason, and so in the same way that Rhys ripped up Neale's books, Jason flung strips of gifts given to him by me at my doorstep. Standing wholly within my power I suddenly felt strong and invincible against him. At last it was Jason hurting and not me. Mr Gemini, how exactly did it feel being baited, caught, landed, and rejected?

I'd had enough. Before I could change my cautious Taurean mind I handed over $11,000 to Orion Women and booked myself on their next 'Sacred Feminine Tour of Europe'. I was one of eight travellers, including our hostesses. With me the youngest, and most of us acquainted from various courses, there was camaraderie of sorts between us. The only part of the trip I regretted was departing on Kristen's seventeenth birthday. Insofar as leaving Sydney, though … Sydney could kiss my ass.

The first stop on the tour was Singapore. We remained here overnight, catching a connecting flight to Rome the next morning; it would be my first time back 'home' in thirty-one years and I felt a strange sense of excitement, marred by a nagging foreboding.

In Singapore we stayed at the Hotel Furama, visited the Mustafa Centre in Serangoon Road, and took a walk through Little India, and then had a lunch where I tasted my very first naan bread and a yoghurt based drink called mango lassi. We visited a Hindu temple and then had high tea in the Raffles Hotel; we decided against Singapore Slings at the famously peanut littered Long Bar.

Never a fan of humidity, I was glad to be out of Singapore that evening. I thought the Fiumicino Airport in Rome would feel like familiar territory as we sheepishly landed at 7.45 in the morning. Filled with anticipation and wondering whether my childhood memories would come around the corner to jump out at me, I shared these feelings with my fellow travellers who seemed more than prepared to share this excitement with me.

Orion Women wanted each of us to have a different roommate during the tour in order to bond with different people on a spiritual level. One lady noone really wanted to share with, for a number of reasons, was Bernice. Me being the 'nice' one meant Bernice was automatically allocated to me. Bernice was a sixty-something British expatriate who had undergone knee surgery only weeks before departure and who should *not* have been travelling. Bernice also used a noisy breathing mask at night.

Our hotel was located barely five minutes' walk from St Peter's Square, where I had been baptised. A national religious festival prevented us from getting within 10 metres of the square and the need to retrace my childhood steps suddenly felt overwhelming. Everything seemed familiar, yet unfamiliar … it felt like being inside a maze I had attempted once, a long time ago.

During our first day a cab drove us through the heart of Rome and we explored the patrician palazzos, cobble stone *viali* and ancient ruins that help make this city so famous. We had dinner along Via Cavour where I was disappointed to discover how brazenly tourists were exploited; we were not treated at all like the locals.

"Watch this," I told the girls smugly, and off I went on a colossal accusatory rant in my diluted Italian. "What's with charging five euros for a half glass of wine, and twenty more for literally *five* gnocchis?" I proclaimed.

I did not entirely comprehend Rome's role insofar as spirituality went, but it soon became obvious our facilitators had designed the tour to tie in with *The Da Vinci Code*, so that on Day 2 we congregated inside the Piazza del Popolo to see the Basilica of Santa Maria del Popolo as depicted in that bestseller. From there we walked to the Piazza di Spagna where I could not resist buying an authentic gelato. I was very conscious of my weight, tipping the scales at one hundred kilos plus, but who gets to travel to Italy every day? The extra kilos compounded problems I'd been having with my feet for some time, however, and they were killing me.

Next stop, the infamous Colosseum, setting for many a childhood nightmare due to Mother and my 'lion phobia'. Obviously, as a rational adult I was no longer afraid to enter the arena; in fact, I was in awe of this place and noone could wipe the smile off my face. I was *inside* the ancient circus of pain, with not a single lion in sight. According to reliable statistics, approximately seven hundred thousand people lost their lives in the Colosseum, along with thousands of imported exotic animals used for extravagant re-enactments, martyrdom and gladiatorial entertainment. One of my uncles on Letitia's side of the family had retraced our genealogical steps to ancient Rome, validating to some extent my paternal half. Via heritage alone, I suppose I *did* feel Roman in terms of bravado, perseverance, a pioneering spirit and industriousness. As was the ancient Roman way, I guess my heritage might also include how my wrath unleashed could lend itself to acts of cruelty. In my core, however, I did not possess the bloodlust or lack of compassion of my socalled ancestors; a combative spirit, yes, but exercised on platforms for human righteousness alone. My wrath needed assistance however. I was a brakeless train that could go from zero to 1000 in a millisecond, once seriously provoked.

At the Trevi Fountain I threw in my three coins and wished for love. I should have wished for a healthier, more peaceful me, but this was not the place for it. Onward to the Pantheon with dinner at Piazza Navona, another childhood favourite; I recalled those beloved Christmas stalls, and the scent of roasting chestnuts. We walked off our meal by visiting the Via della Conciliazione, passing an illuminated Castel Sant'Angelo, my old rollerskating haunt. St Peter's Square at night is something else and I realised for the first time how privileged I was to have been living so close to an international treasure. It's unfathomable to think how someone's life can alter so dramatically just by changing geographical location. I had found that people would gasp aloud when I told them I was a born and bred Roman, as if by living in Cabramatta or Rosemeadow I had somehow destroyed any chance for success that would surely have been mine back 'home'. Perhaps I had.

Day 5 was filled with a visit to the Vatican Museum, a place I had not known as a child. Additionally, I was unaware that beneath the Basilica there was an underground city which held the tomb of Saint Peter. The hidden city was an incredible tour and I was grateful to our facilitators for organising it. Inside the Basilica I experienced familiar flashes: a pundit Letitia telling me important facts when all I wanted to do was run amuck and explore. Michelangelo's *Pietà*, which now sat behind electronically monitored bars due to an act of vandalism perpetrated in 1972, was undressed of offerings; and then there were all those holy water wells which had caused me to hate churches due to *that* unsanctioned exorcism because fear had made me pee my bed.

I was no longer a religious person but I realised religious belief is not necessary to appreciate places like the Sistine Chapel or Notre-Dame de Paris. Art has no creed but for art itself.

For the rest of Day Five we enjoyed free time, as next day we'd be catching a train to Florence. Naturally I was itching to retrace my steps to Via Pietro Cavallini 21 and here was my opportunity. Annette wanted to come with me but this was a pilgrimage I wanted to make alone; I might have no control over any feelings that could surface.

I circled around the place a few times, certain I'd remember my way, but nothing looked really familiar. I then realised the pictures flooding my mind were from the perspective of a child. The 'big road' circumnavigating Piazza Cavour where I once played with my friends, and was afraid to cross, was now not so big. The cinema that had captured my imagination with its posters and screen shots was still operational. *Indiana Jones and the Kingdom of the Crystal Skull* was playing, and so, just like that, I knew exactly where I was.

I found the building where I'd once lived, and, gazing up the six storeys, I felt eight years old once more. Just inside the foyer to the right were the doorman's quarters, rooms used by a paedophile who'd probably accosted a dozen children like me. To my left lay the stairwell leading up to our apartment on the sixth floor. I entered the tiny elevator which felt so much bigger then, the same elevator where my mother kissed my mouth and Umberto pressed his penis against me. Arriving at my destination I took a photograph of a random door, not remembering exactly which one had been mine. There was a myriad of colourful scenarios from my Roman life, but now I was only concerned with one entrance door.

"Cicci! Puttana!" I heard Gilda's voice yell from inside. Playing dress ups as all little girls do, I'd tried on a pair of Mother's shoes, broken them and fearfully put them back. Naturally she found them and I copped a hiding, fleeing for my life through this very door, followed by the ill-fated shoe she hurled behind me. Ah yes, this door had represented much for me.

Next stop was my primary school, Umberto Primo.

I needed to ask for directions – nostalgia failed me once more. It dawned on me I was no longer Italian for I found it difficult to identify with those assisting me. I became painfully aware of my South-western Sydney accent and of how unhinged my language skills were. At that moment my former compatriots were as foreign to me as a Norwegian or South African; I guessed this is what happens when one buys into the illusion of 'origin' or 'race', a belief my mother clung to.

Reaching the school at long last, I found the gate locked and had to press an intercom for service. The voice coming out the other end sounded professional but flat. I explained I was a former student on a visit from Australia.

"*Un minuto perfavore*," the monotone replied. A click on the gate and a gentleman in his late fifties greeted me with a broad smile. Incredibly the *portiere* at the school was the same one as when I was a student there. Twenty-seven years old at the time, he still remembered my favourite teacher and her daughter Ileana, who had been my best friend.

The *portiere* treated me to a tour of the grounds which, again, appeared far smaller than I remembered them. I could not locate the stairwell I'd pushed Alessandra down, but I didn't have sufficient time to look around thoroughly. Due to their confidentiality policy I was not permitted inside the active classrooms but I did manage to catch glimpses of the corridors in which I had stirred up other students during recess, paying the price of detention numerous times. I asked someone to take a photograph of the *portiere* and me before saying goodbye, and then thanked him dearly for his generosity, enthusiasm, and kindness. I could not believe my luck: another milestone of personal history ticked off.

At this point in the journey I wasn't quite sure whether I still loved or hated this place, the city of my birth. The populace appeared different from how I remembered them; I resented being ripped off by merchants or taken for a foreigner, and the food was not served in the huge portions or with the same love I had grown accustomed to as a child. Besides its art, Italy is all about the food and a warm welcome; so no, Rome no longer felt like home to me and I was indeed a foreigner here. Arrivederci Roma ... or maybe not?

On 7 May we arrived in Florence. Things felt very different here – genuine and more natural as well as beautiful. We checked into the Hotel Pendini in Via Strozzi, and this time I shared a room with Jacqui, an elegant Jewish lady I dubbed 'The Queen'. This time it was *I* who disturbed my roommate with my snoring and Jacqui, as a true Aries, made sure I knew about that.

I loved *Firenze*: the art, the culture and the sheer beauty of this small city were captivating. The Renaissance and Medieval periods have always been my favourite. As a child I had been enamoured with films that depicted those eras, and nothing had changed.

The Uffizzi Gallery was spectacular and I did a major backflip when the real Botticelli *Birth of Venus* caught my eye. In the Galleria Academia I met Michelangelo's colossal sculpture *David,* smiling inwardly for its lack of proportion where it most counted. There were tribute sculptures of historic Italians lining the facades of the Uffizi building and it was here I found Niccolò Machiavelli, the origin of the nickname a dear Cabramatta High classmate, Petar, had bestowed on me a few years after we left school – 'Machiavellian Madonna'.

By now my feet were mortally wounded. One of the facilitators advised me to buy a pair of Crocs. I found purple ones for a hefty sixty-seven euros, but to date they were the best investment on my tortured feet. On our last night in Florence, where a Decameronesque stage was once partly the setting for Shakespeare's *All's Well That Ends Well,* I caught angelic sounds echoing from a public area close to our hotel. As I approached the eaves of an old building situated directly in front of the Piazza della Signoria the origin of those sounds came into view. A young soprano of Eastern Bloc appearance was busking with two male accompanists, her crystalline voice filling the air with more beauty this city already possessed. I decided I needed to see more of this amazing country, the one I was born to but which was rejected by me because of the bitter resentments I harboured against a woman of a different disposition. I vowed to return someday – but *not* with a bunch of strange women.

There was no returning to my old life now. My future deserved more of *this* and far less of what I'd experienced. I would give Jason his marching orders the moment I stepped back on *Terra Australis.*

Next stop was Paris, the city of love – yet where was mine? 'Gay Paree' was a dream come true and I was too excited to sleep a wink that night. In Paris, at least Jacqui would not find a thing to scold me about as I would be sharing with my fellow Taurean Annette, and we Taureans are renowned for our patient natures.

* * *

Due to my obsession with Nordic countries as a young girl, I had never felt a desire to visit France or any other Mediterranean nation. But then, just like that, I got the urge and boy was I impressed. The Palace of Versailles was highest on my list. This place had captured my imagination during history lessons at Cabramatta High with a teacher called Mr Okell. The way he'd described the Hall of Mirrors left me wanting more. With its over the top fashions and furnishings, decadent lifestyles, and bitter wars, the sixteenth century wasn't my favourite era, yet a place whose exuberance had driven a nation into a bloody revolution certainly required my inspection.

We arrived at Charles de Gaulle airport at lunchtime and caught a shuttle to our hotel in Rue de Turbigo, Paris. Dinner was at Café Sully where I became adventurous and ordered *andouillettes*, a kind of sausage that sounded like French haggis; they were surprisingly delicious, albeit strong in flavour. It went without saying that dessert had to be crème brûlée.

We travelled everywhere by Metro, which beat haggling with arrogant Roman taxi drivers and was a lot more fun. I loved Paris – it was so sparse and sophisticated, all that people say it is. I spent too short a time at the Louvre where my artistic gaze travelled from one visual feast to the next: The *Winged Victory of Samothrace*, the massive Napoleon canvasses, paintings I knew and loved by Monet, Van Gogh, Vermeer, Corot, Raphael, Rembrandt, Titian, Velazquez, Waterhouse, Whistler, and hundreds more. Then there was the much talked about pièce de résistance, Leonardo da Vinci's *Mona Lisa* or *La Gioconda* as it is actually named, which hung on a wall all to herself. Not *such* a pièce de résistance, I thought to myself. She measured a measly 77 by 53 centimetres and was not anywhere near as captivating as other masterpieces, like Poussin's *The Rape of the Sabine Women,* or Rigaud's *Louis XIV*. Like anything or anyone else who receives persistent public attention, the *Mona Lisa* annoyed me rather than 'wowing' me; nevertheless, it was a case of fait accompli. The famous glass pyramid in the Cour Napoléon courtyard was also familiar from the Dan Brown book and I was smitten by it. Who needs male attention when one can indulge in visual superlatives like these. Jason was now barely on my mind.

After the Louvre, we strolled past the Arc du Carousel into the elegant and expansive Jardins des Tuileries where we enjoyed a lovely lunch under the Parisian sun. We continued on to the Place de la Concorde where Marie Antoinette and hundreds of nobility were guillotined during the Revolution of 1792. Back on the Metro to the Arc de Triomphe and along the luxurious Champs Elysees – home to Louis Vuitton and other luxury international retailers, I observed a myriad of people and styles that seemed oddly inferior to the elegance sported by modern-day Romans.

On to the Pont Alexandre III, one of Paris's most stunning bridges, where we enjoyed spectacular views of the Seine and Les Invalides. Paris, the city that had failed to take my fancy, had succeeded in taking my breath away. Lesson learnt.

On the next day, our tenth, another free day, Jacqui, Annette, and I went off to the magical yet infamous Palace of Versailles, fulfilling a schoolgirl's dream. The place is indescribable and helped me understand why it set the stage for so much bloodshed and civil unrest. The Hall of Mirrors was just as Mr Okell had described it, sumptuous and obnoxious, and the gardens – oh, the gardens – what words can I find to describe them?

Each room was flooded with baroque music, my favourite era in the classical genre. Although the grounds were teeming with tourists, for a brief moment I stood alone, immersed in the luxury and permissiveness that could never be repeated, and should never be reproduced anywhere else in the world. My former close friend and classmate, a French national, told me the palace had been neglected and fallen in disrepair. As a tourist I could not see any of this but I could imagine how the upkeep of such grounds could be a costly matter for the French government. I was very disappointed that the incredible bronze fountains along the manmade aqueducts were not in operation. There was a night time tour available that afforded visitors a spectacular lights and fountains demonstration, but our trip was too short to spend another day there. Perhaps another time, or in another life.

This same night the girls decided to dress up for a Ritz Hotel visit, complete with introductory cocktail, but I was so exhausted I stayed in the room I was sharing with Annette and watched reruns of *Rock My World*. When the girls told me I'd missed out on gold plated taps and toilet seats I wished I'd been less of a drag.

On our last day in Paris we rose to the second floor of the uber famous Eiffel Tower, where the panoramic views of the city were nothing short of spectacular. Alighting into the Hotel de Ville we walked to the Cathédrale de Notre-Dame de Paris where once more I fell into taciturn awe. This place, a pioneer of gothic cathedral design around Europe, took me back in time to Edan who was once so obsessed with NotreDame Cathedral he reproduced it almost to scale on his Etch a Sketch. Edan, a fan of Disney movies, came across the cathedral in *The Hunchback of Notre Dame*. Edan had also been obsessed with the Eiffel Tower, paying artistic homage to that too.

Just behind the famous cathedral stood the Pont de l'Archevêché, also known as the 'love locks' bridge where the heartfelt homages brought a tear to my eye. Thousands of padlocks, most bearing the names of the lovers who had placed them there, sat bunched together as testimony of promises made.

I bid Paris *adieu* hoping to return someday, perhaps alone but ideally with a loved one in tow. Rushing to Orly airport late in the afternoon, we boarded a light aircraft bound for Lourdes, the citadel made famous by Bernadette Soubirous (later Saint Bernadette) and situated in the Pyrenees, a stone's throw from the Spanish border.

During the Catholic period of her life, Gilda had bought me a copy of Franz Werfel's 1941 novel, *The Song of Bernadette,* and I'd found it an interesting account of theological delusion. I was actually rather opposed to the Lourdes visit because I felt certain I could not deal with the kind of blind adulation I was now fighting with every atom of my body. Metaphysics had by now offered me all of the answers I required and the concept of blind religious reverence sickened me. Yet this time around what sickened me even more was Bernice who I found increasingly intolerable. Walking had taken a serious toll on Bernice's knee and she found herself needing a wheelchair to get around. Our group conveniently scattered to different parts of the city and naturally I was the one left behind to do all the disability support. Following my experiences with Piero and Sally, I knew for sure I was *not* 'special needs support worker' material.

It was one day before my forty-second birthday. Lourdes had actually helped me feel far better than I expected. In this unusual place only one thing broke the spell: the countless shops selling crass replicas of Mary in the grotto and other religious paraphernalia. The sea of wheelchairs that flowed steadily along the processional trail to the Sanctuary of Our Lady of Lourdes was eerily beautiful. Benign volunteers, primarily clergy, pushed the chairs with kind smiles that never seemed to waver. I then realised Lourdes was far more than a religious place of pilgrimage; it was an apotheosis for unconditional faith and trust in something far higher than us all, irrespective of devotional denomination. Never in a million years did I expect to take part in a candlelight procession where I walked side by side with nuns and priests of different nationalities … people I'd despised. In Lourdes I was divested of judgement and I found myself relishing an environment I can only describe as one of pure love and unity. Here in a sequestered little market town brought to life by a little girl immersed in veneration, stood hundreds of people from all over the globe chanting *Ave Maria* in angelic unison. I cried, and my heart opened.

Notwithstanding feelings of 'revelation', earlier that day and following much resistance, I was persuaded by our facilitators to bathe in the 'miraculous' waters just outside the stunning Upper Basilica. My hostesses assured me I would not regret the experience and indeed I did not. I sat in line with many others along rows of pews and the only way I can describe how this felt, was like I imagined the European Jews felt while in line for the gas chambers … pure and utter dread, so strong was my aversion for the religious, despite that candlelight epiphany. When my turn arrived, I was directed to a cubicle where a beaming nun greeted me. The curtain to the cubicle was parted and out came Sue from our group, her face looking like she had just walked out of Mount Sinai clutching God's own tablets. I was more nervous now than terrified; might these people somehow 'drug me' into returning to Catholicism?

I was asked to disrobe down to my panties as the nun held a crisp white towel before me. I was then handed a thin linen robe and directed to a large marble tub where I entered the waters. I was expecting the water to feel cold but waded into something completely different, different in a way that's hard to describe. The bathing was brief but totally absorbing. The nun asked me to kiss a little statue of the Virgin sitting at the helm of the tub – if I wished to – and I did so, without hesitation or compunction. When I came out of the waters I realised I didn't need the towel to dry myself; every inch of me was completely dry. Was this the miracle our facilitators spoke of before we left Sydney?

After dumping Bernice by the river and filling up all the little production line bottles on sale with the 'holy water' of Lourdes, I took a meditative walk and offered gratitude to the Universe for giving me such an amazing experience. I also asked *It* for Divine guidance. Below is an excerpt from words I felt compelled to write inside a little address book I was carrying in my purse. These words came to life as I bathed my tired feet from the tranquil bank of the Gave de Pau river.

This morning I bathed in the blessed waters assisted by volunteers who can only be described as "saintly". I was terrified as I waited in line; I felt as if I was about to enter the gas chambers of Auschwitz. Annette, my travel companion, herself Jewish, suggested I may have suffered the Holocaust in a past life … who knows?

Once I bathed semi-naked and vulnerable, I saw what I needed to see and felt some of the pain come out. There is a ball of darkness that dwells inside my heart, but who is not the real me. The real me is kind and compassionate. I ask forgiveness for myself and for those who hurt me, and in turn for forgiveness from those I have hurt too. I don't care about my feet right now, they will heal as I heal.

I know my future is bright now. It said so in my fortune card in Singapore, and the little parrot is never wrong. This isn't a trip, it's a journey, an exfoliation of my soul, trapped for so long inside a fortress of my own making. Bernice gave me a present today which I think I will treasure, a silver fleur-de-lis pendant. I'm not sure of its meaning but I bet it ties in perfectly with what is happening now, for all is connected to the Divine web of life.

I wrote to Alycia about my day today. I have a soul vibration with her. AICYLA. I just had the urge to write her name backwards, I don't know why. I must investigate it. All is as it should be. I am safe and happy and abundant. Love will no longer elude me. I am now free to LOVE!

From what I could gather, the fleur-de-lis is a symbol used widely in monarchic heraldry, and also by scouting organisations, and, it is mentioned in Dan Brown's famous book. I guess I attribute Bernice's gesture to an acknowledgement of leadership. It wouldn't have been the first time I was proclaimed "leader".

* * *

The next morning, on my birthday, we departed magical Lourdes and returned to Paris to catch a train to London from the Gare du Nord. The Eurostar traversed the Channel Tunnel that connects the United Kingdom with its old arch enemy France. What a unique experience, and on my birthday!

We arrived in London in the evening and travelled to our hotel, the Luna Simone on Belgrave Road via London's famous 'hackney cab' service. After haphazardly dumping our luggage, we walked back to the Prince of Wales pub for dinner and a birthday toast to yours truly. I had been in three different cities in one day – what a way to celebrate my forty-second! The patrons at the Prince of Wales were lovely and by far the warmest 'natives' I had met so far on this trip. Landing on English soil was like coming home for me; the UK compounded the feelings I've always had about not being a true 'Latina'.

The next morning, we visited Westminster Abbey, another cultural treat. The two hours at our disposal weren't nearly enough to absorb the rich history to be found inside this treasure trove. I felt tingles up and down my spine as I hovered above the gravestones of great men and women like Robert Browning, Geoffrey Chaucer, Charles Darwin, Charles Dickens, Elizabeth I of England, Mary Stuart, Rudyard Kipling, Isaac Newton, Laurence Olivier, Lewis Carroll and Alfred Lord Tennyson, just to name a handful. In 1971 Mother had taken me to see Vanessa Redgrave in *Mary, Queen of Scots* and I was deeply struck by this tragic monarch's fate, so it was a humbling experience to be standing by her tomb on this day.

After lunch we spent the rest of the day walking the streets of London, absorbing the sights. We passed 10 Downing Street, the Royal Horse Guards, Whitehall, Big Ben, King's College, the Houses of Parliament, Leicester Square, Trafalgar Square and Buckingham Palace. We didn't pass *GO* or collect $200 but were sadly disappointed to discover that all of the Palace's Guardsmen had gone off to war and were replaced by 'Bobbys'. I brazenly chatted up one Bobby from behind the ornate gates. English men are just *so* sexy.

The Changing of the Guard was another experience to treasure. A disrespectful 'clown' had got in the way of the parade and was vociferously reprimanded in front of the gawking crowd, something that gave me enormous pleasure. I am a person of pious deference where national tradition is concerned.

My feet seemed to have completely healed. I wanted to believe the waters of Lourdes had spun their magic but it was more likely the Crocs had fulfilled their purpose. Inside my luggage I stowed three precious little bottles of 'miracle water', one of which I reserved for Sally lest a cure save my relationship with Jason, and a second vial for my brother Piero. The third was mine; who knew, maybe one day I'd need it. My regenerated feet enabled me to fully enjoy London and on the following day, our free day, I chose to visit Madame Tussauds wax museum and the London Zoo, along with Sue, who desperately needed rescuing from a fellow traveller she was forced to share rooms with every night.

As we were getting ready to leave the zoo, which in comparison to Sydney's Taronga Zoo was relatively unimpressive, I received a text message that threw me for a sixer. Kyera, a fairly new employee at Juniperina who not too many liked, sent me a message which read as if it were meant for Jason. The message 'informed' Jason that Kyera had had her second child and that she would love to catch up with him for a drink sometime. Juniperina staff had already given me a heads up on Kyera's suspected affairs with a number of married staff – albeit married herself. In addition to these gross moral indiscretions, Kyera's methodology when dealing with detainees could only be described as downright dangerous.

Kyera had thrown herself, and her gigantic mammaries, upon me less than two weeks after her arrival at Juniperina, languorously declaring how she 'loved' me. I am a very friendly 'hands-on' type of person, but Kyera's uninvited and premature gestures deeply unnerved me, and so the leftfield text I received at London Zoo sent me into a furious spin. Was Kyera trying to hit on Jason? During a forced teteatete with this predatory creature I had confided how much I did love Jason. I now wondered whether my disclosure had become fodder for a nasty femme fatale, one hell-bent on destroying relationships. Sending such texts was not a new modus operandi for me; I had done the same as Kyera to Eser in order to make him jealous. Perhaps karma had now come to bite me on the backside.

I forwarded the text on to Jason almost immediately. His reply smacked of feigned ignorance and my Higher Self knew something was amiss.

On 17 May, Day 16 of our European tour, we hired two cars at Heathrow Airport and began our journey into the South West of England. I held my breath as another childhood dream was about to be realised: Stonehenge!

Our first stop was Glastonbury, home of the Tor and the Festival of Contemporary Performing Arts although I can tell you there is *a lot* more going on here than the abovementioned. Glastonbury is also a melting pot and meeting point for multinational witches and warlocks (and, sadly, for drug users). Something about this peculiar place had me feeling a little stoned *and* a little freaked out. Nevertheless, I thoroughly enjoyed myself and our quaint bed and breakfast was to die for. The worst part of this tript was having to share with Bernice again, and her breathing mask.

A visit to Chalice Well was a delight and highlight. The central well had been kept in continuous use for 2000 years and never failed its patrons. Iron oxide deposits give the water a reddish tinge and it is believed to possess healing qualities much like that at Lourdes – only without the holy apparitions. Bernice and I took off our shoes and waded through a pool that purified our tired feet. Among other treasures the ruins of Glastonbury Abbey boasted the alleged graves of King Arthur and his Queen, Guinevere. As a young teen I was fascinated by tales of King Arthur and the Knights of the Round Table; I'd even hoped that one day I would meet Sir Lancelot and share nights of unbridled passion in his arms.

It was at Chalice Well that I purchased my second bejewelled pentagram, a symbol of divine protection from evil. In the town of Glastonbury, I bought the silver version of the 'Ring to Rule Them All' for Kristen, who I had left behind on her birthday. With esoteric outlets lining a cobbled path along the High Street displaying shopfront names like The Celtic Thread, Stone Age – Prehistoric Pleasures at Modern Prices, The Goddess and Green Man, and The

Psychic Piglet, one does not easily mistake what the place is predominantly about. Add to these The Magick Box and Hemp in Avalon, and there's not much space for doubt.

On the way to Bath, where we immersed ourselves in a hot rooftop spring and then released a few toxins in the saunas below, we negotiated a stop in Padworth a tiny village which was Bernice's birthplace. It was actually Bernice's birthday and, regardless of my exasperation with the woman, I was happy for her. Bernice pointed out her old school and a little medieval church in which she worshipped as a child. Jacqui and I were the only ones daring enough to climb the really steep steeple ladder leading up to the tiny choir and organ alcove where I was offered a deeper understanding of just how overweight I'd become. A second brief stop found us inside the enchanting hamlet of Lacock, a place made famous as the main location for the 1995 TV production of *Pride and Prejudice*, not to mention instalments of *Harry Potter* and *Downton Abbey*.

The city of Bath was very beautiful, with its Romanesque influenced buildings and the surrounding Somerset hills. That evening we participated in 'Bizarre Bath', a 'comedy walk' which proved unique, entertaining, and offered us front row seats to this wonderful citadel. I began to seriously entertain the idea of moving to the UK, with my facilitators appearing favourable to the notion. Sydney held nothing for me anymore and I owed *it* even less. My children and a handful of friends, who had their own lives to contend with, were the only obstacles standing in the way of a new beginning, and I so wanted to start over.

On Day 19 we went crop circle hunting in Wiltshire, stopping at the Silent Circle Cafe, an establishment run by an individual who claimed to be the world's foremost authority on crop circle formations. The facilitators swore he was a real life 'alien'. Staring at the proprietor from a covert vantage point, I could see what the girls meant. Perhaps he was feeling unwell, but the man had a greenish tinge on a rather triangular face and his almond shaped eyes were wide, dark, and catlike.

As we were driving out of the premises and towards the Avebury stone circles, our driver suddenly stopped the car.

"I think I see a circle!"

We all jumped out but in my opinion whatever we saw in the field 600 metres or so away sorely lacked the makings of a crop circle.

The rest of the day was filled with more prehistoric wonders including Silbury Hill (an artificial chalk mound), West Kennet Long Barrow (a

Neolithic tomb), and the surreal White Horses. I was as in love with the South West of England as I was with Paris. Every person in the world (or in an ideal world) should have the means to travel and see these places. Even though I knew I would be returning to a purgatory of my own making, I felt lighter for being privy to such ancient stories. I thought of the Akashic Records and a book I'd read that had described them. Maybe one day, once my soul was divested of its dense 'life' overcoat, I'd see firsthand how my many ancestors had truly lived.

That evening our facilitators had a special surprise for us: an after-hours tour of Stonehenge, devoid of crowds and almost exclusively ours. I was beside myself with anticipation. I had first encountered the place when I was eight or ten and had leafed thirstily through my mother's esoteric magazines, and thirty-odd years later there she was: the ancient Druids' temple, thought by some to have been built by extra-terrestrials, was now almost at my fingertips.

When we arrived I was drawn immediately to the mythical boulders and felt mystically transported from the group. I felt certain I had visited here many centuries before and that my soul essence was as Druid as my birth name. Later in the evening our group held a Druid flower ceremony, but I felt nothing special happen. The feelings of déjà vu were only significant on my own. In the twilight of dusk, I managed to capture some stunning photographs and, for the rarest of moments in life, I felt at one with my Universe.

Waving a sad goodbye to the region of Amesbury, on Day Twenty our group drove back to Heathrow to drop off the cars and head back into London for the next day's Chelsea Flower Show. Another legendary experience was thrown in on our free night in the West End. As an Andrew Lloyd Webber aficionado I had my misgivings about the production of *Wicked*, but artistic anxiety quickly subsided only minutes into the performance. *Wicked* proved a brilliant twist on the old *Wizard of Oz* story.

The Chelsea Flower Show is a haven for lovers of horticulture and we were also blessed to witness our very own Jamie Durie earn a gold medal for his outdoor ensemble. The moment I saw a chance I muscled in on the miniature powerhouse, forcing him into a group photograph.

Day Twenty-two, and 22 May – goodbye precious England and hello Morocco.

* * *

Exiting a relatively state-of-the-art Marrakesh Airport into a dusty red desert environment was only the first shock on this, the last leg of our trip. Morocco was an optional extra on the Sacred Feminine Tour itinerary. I hadn't been keen to go but decided I needed an education. Annette and Jacqui both opted out and returned to their beautiful homes in Sydney's Eastern Suburbs.

The second shock came when the rickety cab commissioned by our hostesses failed to drop us off at our 'hotel'. Our facilitator explained that we needed to walk the rest of the way to our destination because the streets were too narrow for a car to drive down. Lugging our bags, we made our way into dusty laneways filled with children's eyes and suspicious hijabs until our guides stopped in front of a nondescript wooden portal fixed to a rendered, rudimentary building.

This is our exotic hotel? I was mortified, but then the landlady opened the door and we found ourselves inside a chapter of *Arabian Nights*, complete with mosaic floors and a courtyard fountain. I again shared with Bernice because at this point noone wanted much to do with her self-imposed aches and pains. I wasn't impressed and wanted to scream *no, not me again – not fair!* But how does one openly wound another human being's pride? I thought of the fleurdelis Bernice had given me and soldiered on.

Marrakesh was a 'third world' city, basic and very dirty. I was reluctant to eat any of the food served by grotty waiters whose nails were blackened and smiles bronzed from years of tobacco use. Mangy cats lined the dusty streets and the only feature distracting me from a constant wiping off of filth was the *adhan*, the enigmatic call to prayer that was broadcast from rooftop loudspeakers five times a day. *God is great. I bear witness that there is no God except the One God* the chant proclaimed.

As in Lourdes, the despised religious connotations were superseded by the feelings they invoked. Not a lover of Islam and aware of the fierce fundamentalists destroying any fidelity in the religion, I was wary of the people around me, although around this time the tumult declared by El Qaida and ISIL was not yet upon us, so hypervigilance was not an issue.

To visit a third world country is more about education and enlightenment than 'vacation' value. In Marrakesh I learnt that we Westerners are extremely fortunate, even at the (for us) worst of times. The artisans and labourers here worked with medieval tools under dreadful conditions, with poverty obvious, badgering tourists a necessity, and religious observation the absolute ruler, over and above the keeping up of appearances.

Being in an Islamic country, our facilitators advised us to dress modestly once we left the secular safety of Marrakesh Menara Airport. Proof of the danger of the 'tank top' arrived while sitting at a cafe when men in white *djellabas* suddenly poured from all directions into Djemaa El-fna, the main square and marketplace. Their frenzied ululations were directed at someone inside the square; I could not see who had attracted such a fracas, so I asked my waiter.

"There is a woman showing her breasts," he declared in an accusatory tone.

"What are the men saying?" I asked him.

"They are saying, 'you are a prostitute, you have AIDS.'"

One of my fellow travellers, who had seen what preceded the swarm, explained that a girl of Scandinavian appearance and wearing a tank top had been inexplicably set upon. The men packed around the frightened girl, screaming and gesticulating at her as she attempted to deflect her tormentors, using a handbag like some medieval knight with a morning star. I was deeply disgusted. I had seen and heard stories about how people in the Arab world disrespected and despised Western women and the present insurgence seemed to prove this.

In the *souks* we were mercilessly and relentlessly accosted by vendors soliciting us for purchases. Saying, over and over, *la shokran* (no thank you, ارلكش ال) grew very tiresome. Funny how, when it suited them, we were no longer filthy whores. Our bodies were vile but our money was manna from Heaven? I so hated hypocrisy.

At night Djemaa El-fna turned into pages from *Scheherazade*. The only thing to mar the Bedouin ambience was the countless 'free feels' and lurid anecdotes spoken in French or Arabic, all words I knew well, given my time living in Auburn. Hail my profound love of idioms.

Base behaviour aside, the goodies for sale in the square and *souks* where mind-blowing: human teeth, live chameleons, snails by the tub load, frogs, monkey paws, giant grasshoppers … Then there are the tourist attractions like 'free range' snakes and their accompanying charmers. I *almost* trod on a rogue cobra – defanged of course.

The local butcher hung out his cuts of meat, offal and decapitations, in fine Dickensian style. Flies and unwashed customers covered everything and I could barely swallow my *tagine* that evening. The colours, the atmosphere, the dust, all the oxymorons that are Morocco, had somehow permeated my senses, helping me view culture for culture's sake. We Westerners take so much for granted.

In the *souks* where pedlars hunt you down halfway along the overcrowded corridors to procure a sale, one bronze-toothed male came at me head on to let me know how beautiful I was. He was seeking to buy rather than sell.

"You have very beautiful thighs. I am a rich man and I want you to be my wife, and I will pay seventy thousand camels for you!"

'Seventy thousand camels,' I thought and then wondered how they translated into *dirham* currency. Would Nick have paid seventy thousand camels for my hand in marriage? Or Eser, or Jason? Was seventy thousand camels the going rate in Morocco for a fat, middle-aged divorcee, or was I a rare and valuable commodity? I began to ponder the reasons I had not exacted a higher value from my lovers, then realised this was because I hadn't attached one *to myself*. In the desperate search for love and stability I had willingly offered myself to the lowest bidder each and every time.

In Glastonbury Jacqui had bought me a well loved copy of *Louise L. Hay's You Can Heal Your Life*. She had assured me the book would help me. In my spiritual travels it was suggested time and time again that to entice the Universe into giving you what you want, you need to be specific in the way you ask for it. Grasping the prize of seventy thousand camels firmly in my mind's fist, I broke away from the group, returned to the hotel, and began leafing through that pre-loved text.

I *deserved* to be loved. I was *worthy* of love and I was going to *get it*. If the law of attraction is truly real, I was now taking it for a test drive. I turned to the back of the book where Louise had provided several blank 'notes' pages, and started describing in infinitesimal detail the kind of man I wanted to manifest into my life.

I was determined as all hell to fetch my seventy thousand camels, but definitely not here in dusty, sleazy Marrakesh.

* * *

During our last day in Marrakesh four of us attended the local *hammam*, and I was more than eager to have the dust and stench of the city scrubbed off by subservient provincial girls.

My facilitators led the way, with Sue and me in tow. Earlier in the day Sue and I had had some adventures trying to cross the crazy roads, expertly sidestepping the locals and avoiding pedlars. The *hammam* was a pleasant way of ending a fandangle of a day, and an inspirational tour to boot. I was now itching to get back to civilisation, my kids, my home and my cat. Travel is important and amazing but it is also exhausting.

The deep full body scrub meant we needed to strip off completely, but I'd have none of that and held on firmly to my undies. The sight of women running around naked, my companions included, felt most uncomfortable. Intrinsically shy and self-conscious, I have never been one to undress in communal change rooms and the unhappy incident with the Bulgarian singer in Rome was a memory still easily triggered.

After the scrub came a full body massage. Each of us was led into a darkened cubicle where the masseuse began wrestling with my undies and succeeded in removing them. Vulgar images of female rape flooded my mind, along with the idea that these cubicles might be set up as peep shows for the same menfolk who so vociferously despised us? I wasn't feeling relaxed at all, and the way the masseuse was skimming my vagina every time she reached my upper thighs made me feel even less settled. My mood improved once we moved to the French pedicure, and I had all my clothes back on.

Saying goodbye to Marrakesh (we bypassed Casablanca, in spite of Humphrey Bogart), was easy. I was the only one in the group who had disliked the experience but this did not faze me in the least. I am what I am and I like what I like. If the others deemed me uneducated or biased, well that was their stuff to deal with, not mine.

We returned to Singapore for another overnight stop. On the next day, home was only nine hours away; I was more than ready to return to it.

One of the facilitators laughed wholeheartedly at me when I mentioned the 70,000 camels.

"Oh is that *all* Angelica? My bloke offered me a *hundred thousand* camels and a Ferrari!"

The Sacred Feminine Tour had been quite an adventure and holistically life changing. I had barely missed Jason – in fact – I felt indifferent towards the cheating bastard. My gut was telling me he and Kyera were up to something and I was determined to discover what and when.

I now had my lengthy list, written in the back of Louise L. Hay's beautiful book, to comfort me. My reliable gut – the same one I had always ignored, told me that *this* time the Universe would deliver.

I recalled Bruce Willis's catchphrase in the *Die Hard* films: *Yippee-ki-yay!* And bring *him* forth.

CHAPTER TWENTY-FOUR

THE HILLS

———

E urope was now my muse. Its beauty had re-awakened my artistic senses, forcing me to face the banality and trauma that was and had been life in Sydney. I just couldn't do this type of 'normal' anymore.

Whether or not I was in fact running away from endemic problems at this time did not concern me; I simply needed a complete change from everything. I then deliberated on the vow made back in 1977, that someday I'd return to Adelaide. That 'someday' was *now*.

My first move was to contact the Magill Youth Training Centre in Woodforde, South Australia. The plan was to cross over from the New South Wales Department for Juvenile Justice into one of the two Families SA youth detention centres in Adelaide. For back-up I also registered an expression of interest with the South Australian Department for Corrective Services. I had no intention of becoming a Correctional Officer because the adult system scared the pants off me, but if I couldn't get into 'juve' for whatever reason, I was certainly not returning to retail. I recalled a New South Wales Correctional Officer saying to me that Corrections was the best kept secret in the workforce, and indeed, several Youth Officers at Juniperina had already made the transition into adult Corrections. It was around this time, too, that everyone was talking about a new 'social networking' website called Facebook, which I decided to join.

By the end of June 2008 I had a five-bedroom home in Springton under contract and a removal truck that cost me a hefty $3000. As far as the children were concerned, Kristen had gratuitously bailed out of Year 12 during my European trip, and I believed Edan was young enough to adapt to new surroundings in spite of his Asperger's. Alycia on the other hand was old enough to stay behind if she so desired, and she had already been a year or so in the workforce. Despite my personal needs and unlike my mother, I would never dictate my children's destinies. I recognised how traumatising it would be for them to leave their father and friends behind, but it was also a 'nobrainer' that I was the preferred parent. And besides, friends can be found anywhere in the world, right?

This time Rhys did not try and use the children as pawns to stop me. He had married a Chinese lady eleven years his junior and was thus heavily preoccupied. I had been certain that the day Rhys became romantically involved again he would lay off me, and he did.

Valeria checked out the Springton house for me and confirmed that the house was solid and, with a little tender love and care, held promise. Her only concern was the kids' futures as there was no public transport from Springton to anywhere. Springton is a small rural town at the base of the Barossa Valley. Despite these minor inconveniences I decided everything would be okay. My mind was made up: there was not a thing that could deter me from leaving New South Wales.

Gilda cried as she farewelled me, but the tears failed to spill from my eyes. As far as I was concerned this chapter of my sad life was over. I pretended to feel sad for *her* sake, not mine; something told me she'd get over things quickly. With their heartfelt tributes, however, my childhood school friends broke my heart. I asked Leisl to look after a friend whose fragile emotional states I had nursed and fostered over a number of years. I did feel somewhat guilty for leaving, but I knew it just needed to be done; my Higher Self was nudging me all the way.

Jason didn't seem too concerned by my departure. He threw in an occasional *you're abandoning me Angelica* for good measure and continued as usual, even cancelling a final birthday dinner I had organised for his fortieth. Naturally, overtime at Juniperina was the 'reason' for this final, rude snub; true love does not behave in such a way and here lay the answer. Too much damage had been done to this relationship, and though I felt I still loved Jason, the greater reason for my relocation was to get away from *him*. He wouldn't have let me go otherwise and I could no longer be a tortured fish on Jason's hook.

Before my departure Jason gave me the letter below, typed. It offered practically nothing that might even remotely change my mind.

Dearest Angelica,   01/07/2008

I have read your letter and I am pleased you have had time to calm yourself down. Angelica you are a funny lady and I know that you are a beautiful, wonderful, lovely woman. You have never spoken to me with holds barred and I say that with a smile. If I think back over time I have known you, and the very incredible words you have spoken to me, at me, with me, and about me, which have at times amazed, shocked, amused, bewildered, made me cry, and laugh. I could write a book about a woman who on one hand is very wise and all-knowing and on the other hand, immature and lacks confidence and empathy about those, and those around them. I could write many things to describe the amazing Angelica I grew to love in both a positive and a negative way. But Angelica, I have found that you do not understand or accept what you perceive as anything critical or negative about you, even when the negative may be true, or the criticism may help you to understand something. And please understand, I write this now with no intention of hurting you, or, as you often say, to put you down. That my Angelica has never been my intention nor my aim. I am very sorry if I have come across to you this way, or if indeed I have put you down in any way.

I think I understand why you are like this! And I think it stems from your insatiable desire and need to be loved, liked, accepted, and thought of highly. You lack self-esteem, and the ability to know, that you are an *amazing, beautiful woman.* This possibly could have begun from your childhood experiences and lack of praise and love during the most crucial times in your life, resulting in you often giving yourself praise and self-gratification. Angelica you have often not understood me. I don't think wanting and needing these things is bad or wrong. I myself crave these needs, wants, and emotions as well. Maybe when I come across as self-secure, or say I don't need anyone, or care about what people say, it is at that time that I do need people, and crave love, and a sense of belonging. I sometimes try to protect myself from the hurt and pain of knowing people do not like me, or understand me and my ways. I am a good person and I want to be a good man, and to be loved just as you do. I just express myself differently to others, and yes, this is as a result of my life experiences, character, and self-esteem, or in many a case, lack of.

Angelica I know that I have made many mistakes with you during our time together and I know I have not done or been the person you crave. I do not want to, or make any more excuses for my behaviours. We have been there and done that. It is a shame you do not understand DEPRESSION, as I am sure your own daughter Kristen suffers on occasion as I do with this shitty impairment. The kids you work with, according to reports, are the group who suffer most from depression, and this is the area you will continue to work in when you move to Adelaide. I myself struggle with depression and fully understand its effects, and how to cope with them, and explain its grip on me. I know I have made all sorts of excuses about my downfalls and at times, difficult behaviour. Angelica I never meant to hurt you, and I never meant or dreamed of living my life the way I have or do. I do not have a mental illness that cannot be cured, and I can't blame depression for all my faults. I know this, and I am sorry if I have. Maybe it is my own lack of understanding or a defect in character that allows me to do this; I am not sure. I am not going to make any more excuses or blame anyone. I am not going to blame you Angelica or rubbish you in any way.

Yes, I do owe you and yes I do acknowledge this. Yes, I have made many mistakes with you, and no I'm not happy with myself. I have never tried to be better than anyone, and I have only wanted the best for you and those I love. I know we are finished, and that in four weeks you are gone. I did mean all that I said to you about loving you and wanting to be with you, but you are correct, we are very different people. I never tried to con you or deceive you in any way. I do love you, and I wish you only happiness and the love you deserve.

Angelica I am not jealous of you and never will be. I am sad that I could not be the one for you, and I will suffer loneliness as a result. I know that in your heart you meant well for me and tried to do the best for me and us. I know I let you down. Angelica I will never forget you, and I will always love you because no matter what, you did no wrong; you loved me in a time when noone else does. You saw the good in me when noone else can, and it is for this that I love and adore you, and it is for this I am so sorry I let us down. You are a good woman and I know you meant well for me and all that you have known through me. I am a better man because you loved me, this is why I tried so hard to hang onto you, not to hurt you or deceive you.

Maybe I am a weak person, and yes, maybe my Karma will punish me. Time will tell. I do wish you the very best, and thank you for putting up with me when noone else will. No matter the reasons for doing so, you shared your life with me. Thank you Angelica.

[No signature added]

Saying goodbye to everyone I cared about *was* distressing, especially the Juniperina girls, who I had totally fallen in love with. I *worshipped* my job and had things gone well for me there I quite possibly would never have left New South Wales.

On 3 August 2008 I gave, over the radio, final thanks to all the staff who over the past three years had supported me in one way or another. I could not finish my words as I choked on tears of pure heartbreak. One of the Samoan cousins had thrown herself on the floor and, grabbing my leg, begged me to stay. I'm sure she was simply being playful but it made my heart melt and I promised I'd write to her. I then ran out of Banksia Unit where this incredible journey had begun, and into the air lock, not daring to look behind me in case I changed my mind. I had never felt so loved in life as I did inside this place of denial and pain, and by 'those dirty little criminals' as Jason referred to them during so many arguments about our job.

I departed Sydney on 4 August. The removal truck had pulled out of Sydney the day before so I slept at Jason's that final night; this was yet another mistake, hopefully my last. 'Pity sex' feels horrible and to make up for feeling horrible we each began blaming the other for our failed relationship, until, around midnight, emotional exhaustion lulled us into sleep.

I had asked the Universe for someone 'exactly like me' and boy did I get ME. Like Jason I'm an up and down person, sweet and sour, demanding and sometimes selfish. So as the old adage goes, *be careful what you ask for, because you might just get it.*

Kristen had flown out with our cat, Mango, the day before and Alycia had left a week earlier to check things out and decide whether to join us the following year. At seven in the morning, Edan and I waved goodbye to Rosemeadow and set off for the two-day drive to South Australia. Jason didn't seem bothered about waking up to bid us a final goodbye, but was there really a need for one?

Something that had fallen into place incredibly quickly and smoothly turned sour when, only two weeks prior to our departure, I discovered I had failed the mandatory 'psych test' required for entry into the Magill Youth Training Centre. I was now leaving for another state with a nice fat mortgage and no job. Up to a certain point in the journey I allowed myself to panic, asking the Universe if I had made the right decision. Yet once I left the Hay Plain, after an overnight stay there with Edan, I decided *to hell with security – let the games begin.*

In memoriam

Years after I left Juniperina I was able, with the aid of Facebook, to determine what had become of many of the beloved detainees. Those still with us are now in their mid-twenties; below are snapshots of their current lives, at the time of writing this chapter.

Heidi, the first girl I met on shift, who had unsuccessfully challenged me:

Heidi was one of the highly troublesome ones at Juniperina, one on a list of detainees who rarely left the high needs unit. Continually in and out of the place, Heidi told everyone she was a virgin and yet was once segregated for almost two days because she refused to hand over a huge stash of drugs, including two syringes, that were concealed inside her vagina. According to the 1982 NSW Child Protection Act, segregation can be imposed only for a certain number of hours and this time period must be in accordance with the child's age; to impose those two days on Heidi, Juniperina had to obtain special permission from the Minister. Eventually Heidi became too old for 'juve', 'growing up' among gang members primarily of Arab origin in and around the Bankstown district. Heidi (who is on Facebook) is currently living in the Gold Coast area, and appears sober. She is in a relationship with a Pacific Islander gentleman and has given birth to a beautiful and healthy baby girl. Heidi contacted me recently but I have since deactivated my Facebook account.

Kristy, the girl accused of taking part in the murder of her mother and detained under the mental health act:

Kristy and I remained in contact for a short while via Facebook. Kristy deleted her account, informing me that former detainees and youth workers had been bullying her online. She is now back on social media, looking wonderful and happy, but we are not in contact. When released from Juniperina shortly after the *60 Minutes* interview, Kristy went to live with her adopted Christian family in the Blue Mountains, continuing a pious and studious life.

Lenny, the Vietnamese spitfire:

Lenny lives in Canley Vale with her Laotian partner of seven years and their two daughters. Lenny is no longer involved in drugs but maintains strong ties with the Cabramatta Vietnamese community. Her first daughter, unable to gel with an estranged mother and a new father, now lives with Lenny's family in Queensland but maintains regular telephone contact with her mother and half-sisters. In 2012 during a Sydney visit, I caught up with Lenny and five other former detainees and it was a beautiful experience, filled with tears and laughter. By Lenny's request, we are no longer in contact. Perhaps like me Lenny needs to let go of an awful past once and for all. I miss her dearly.

Donna, the teenage prostitute whose 'employers' were shut down and brought to justice on child exploitation charges:

Donna and I kept in contact via phone and Facebook until her death. Donna gave birth to a beautiful baby girl who was removed by DoCS and given to the maternal family due to Donna's serious methamphetamine and heroin use. When Danielle's beloved grandmother died, it was too much for her and Danielle took her own life. I never found out how and it really doesn't matter: she's gone. I could not attend Danielle's funeral in 2011, but I did send flowers.

RIP my beautiful and fragile Piscean girl.

Sarah, at the time the youngest murderess in New South Wales:

I met with Sarah during my 2012 visit to Sydney, alongside Lenny and a few others. She has not changed and there is no doubt in my mind she is on the autism spectrum. Sarah holds down a good job and lives in an affluent part of Sydney. We are not in contact.

Kelly, lesbian extraordinaire:

Kelly and I remained in contact on Facebook for quite a while and saw each other during the 2012 Sydney trip. Kelly is actively involved in an inner city lesbian/feminist movement and was engaged to a Korean girl. Kelly and I had a falling out over political, perceived 'racist' views posted on Facebook by me.

Cheryl, the 'great pretender' dubbed 'Big Red' by staff:

I did not hear anything about Cheryl post Juniperina until recently when I viewed her profile on another ex-juve's friends list. Cheryl is alive and well, seems to have lost a bit of weight, is covered in facial piercings and poorly applied make-up, sports a rather dodgy looking boyfriend and works at McDonald's.

Paigh, the hopeless heroin addict, in and out of mental institutions:

Paigh was my hero. If there is *anyone* on this earth who's made a complete 180-degree turnaround in life, this person is Paigh. When she turned twenty-one, something inside Paigh went 'click'. Paigh had finally grown tired of waking up on the street day after day in a drug induced stupor, sometimes to find a stranger raping her. She then took every possible step to personal healing. By the age of twenty-four, Paigh was awarded a degree, Master of Social Science, and was working with children like her former self *and* their families. A year later she was sufficiently qualified to challenge the bastards who had brought me down professionally at Juniperina for their positions. Ironically the same general manager, who had undermined me, refused Paigh re-entry into Juniperina as an advocate. Paigh invested her victim's compensation payout to see the world and come face to face with the many disadvantaged children who live in it. She worked in South African orphanages and taught all over South America. Paigh's beautifully succinct and inspiring photography is a certain coffee table book winner, as is her own personal story, a project Paigh may visit in the future. Paigh and I had been close friends; she has visited me in Adelaide three times, even attending two very special events I shall mention later. Whenever I need a strong example of immeasurable inner strength, I think of Paigh. Paigh has chosen a path I cannot walk with her but I wish her no ill and hope that, unlike I once was, she is honoured by this person.

Jessie, the 'proud' prostitute and heroin user who had threatened me and my children:

Whereas I knew Paigh was okay and recovering, I heard no more of Jessie – she had virtually disappeared. I held no doubt Jessie lay somewhere rotting. I didn't particularly like Jessie but she fascinated me just as she did Jason. While she was in custody he was continually going out of his way to help her and, given her nasty streak, I could not understand this at all, though her physical beauty may have very well been a factor. I took to Facebook to find Jessie, and eventually I did come across the most awful profile picture of her. Her account was barely active, suggesting she might still be 'working' and using. I then stumbled upon a second account that clearly showcased a serious lesbian relationship with a girl of Pacific Islander appearance. Two years on, I noticed her name on a former detainee's friends list and decided to make contact. Our Facebook exchange, dated 10 November 2014, included the following:

Me: Hi Jessie this is Angelica a youth worker who knew you at Juniperina. I have been searching for you for ages. So happy to see you are here. Do you remember me? How are you? Where have you been?

Jessie: How r u???? Yes, I remember u. I'm good I have a 5-month old daughter and I'm married. I have been off drugs n out of jail for a bit over a year now I finally have my life on track it was really hard after living that life n being addicted for so many years but it was worth all the pain. My daughter is my life. R u still working a Juniperina? Xxx

Me: Heyyyyyy!!! You know I never forgot you Jessie. You were in my thoughts for a very long time because I thought you might be one of the ones we'd lose for sure. Your life was so risky and scary. I now live in Adelaide, I moved there in 2008.

Jessie: Yea I think everybody thought that even myself and I did come close, I was in Kings Cross up until I went to jail last time. I got out 6 June last year then I decided to get off methadone n stay away from drugs n the Cross. I had good support n I finally done it. My daughter's name is (omitted) n my husband's name is Hassan he is from Libya. I was over there for 9 months once I finished on the methadone. Wow what's it like in Adelaide? I used to always wonder how all the girls n staffs at Juniperina were.

Like many people I met in jail, Jessie converted to a fundamentalist form of Islam. Her Facebook page appeared 'radicalised' and completely lacking the identity that once defined her. She had swapped her precious 'working clothes' for a burqa which only served to confirm that Jessie had *not* changed, she had merely swapped one form of addiction for another. Regardless, I was glad Jessie was safe and off the drugs; I just hoped her Libyan husband would be good and merciful to her and their child. The last I heard of Jessie was that she had permanently relocated to Egypt.

Tanya Rose, the worst self-harmer I had met:

I spoke to Tanya Rose very briefly on Facebook. It appeared painfully obvious she continued struggling with life. Anecdotes from former fellow detainee's place Tanya Rose with a daughter while running around with outlaw bikie gang members. The daughter was removed by DoCS due to serious ongoing substance abuse and unsavoury associations. I still do not envisage Tanya Rose's life being a long one because her mental health issues are far too entrenched. Tanya Rose has a large number of Facebook profiles, with one showing activity dated December 2015, in which she states: 'Chasing rock grrrr'. A respondent of Tanya Rose's replied: 'As if you'd write this on your post. Ice is putrid and wrecks lives.'

Grace, the detainee charged with the highest number of assaults on staff and detainees:

For a long time, I chose to maintain in regular contact with Grace. I had seen so much of me in her, acknowledging that behind the oppositional defiant disorder dwelt a good girl wanting to give life a proper go. Eventually, however, Grace succeeded in consuming every ounce of good will, compassion, and sisterhood I attempted to bestow on her. Albeit guiltily, I let Grace go, a little bluntly too. There is a possibility Grace suffers bipolar disorder and the marijuana addiction she shares with a deadbeat boyfriend on a disability pension will certainly not help her condition. When Grace is on a good run, she's endearing, problem solving, and quite intelligent. On a downturn, she is stubborn, vicious, demanding, nonsensical, and downright infuriating: me all over. Grace is currently residing in Goulburn.

May, the Koori girl belonging to a family of twelve, with only *a* brother to never have been incarcerated:

May was another hopeless heroin addict and there were a number of rumours of her whereabouts. The most upsetting of them spoke of her demise but, mercifully, May did not die. May had finished serving two years in adult prison for armed robbery. Following her release, I stumbled onto her Facebook profile and found that, just like Paigh, May was a changed person – happier, healthier, and living a full life back with her son. In December 2015 May gave birth to a bouncy baby girl and I sent her a 'Welcome into the World' gift. May does indeed look wonderfully healthy and has embarked on a hairdressing traineeship. She is in a safe relationship with a mystery man and is an active spokesperson for Aboriginal Civil Rights.

The Samoan Cousins, the fourteen year olds charged with a taxi driver's murder:

The slightly older cousin had steadily defied getting into more trouble following her release from Juniperina three years later. 'P' went on to lead a normal life, supported by her tight-knit Christian family. She has had two daughters with a long-term partner. As promised, we wrote to each other and then continued our contact via Facebook. When I re-entered the child protection arena in South Australia, however, I was forced to delete 'P' due to the seriousness of the crime she was involved in. 'P' was offended by this and our subsequent online conversations became sporadic at best. On the flip side, 'L', the younger cousin, waltzed in and out of adult prison, bound for rock bottom. 'L's moral salvation was her pregnancy and she too gave birth to a girl, returning to her Pacific Islander church group for support. It is unclear whether the father of her child remains in the picture but what *is* clear is that 'L' has become a conscientious and doting mother. 'L' and I were friends on Facebook until she permanently deactivated her profile.

Zelda, the only detainee to have given the Department a reason to carry out an investigation for misconduct on myself and two other Youth Officers:

Precariously, in 2011 I did indeed join the Magill Training Centre as an employee; but more on this later. Here I met an Aboriginal girl named Naomi; she was fiery, stealthy, and sorely reminded me of Zelda. I happened to mention Zelda's name one day and Naomi looked at me in disbelief.

"Oh my God Angelica, that's my sister!" she said, her jaw propped on her chest.

Despite having different fathers and different surnames, Naomi was indeed Zelda's sister. I found various pictures of the duo on both girls' Facebook pages. What is the chance of my working with two sisters in Juvenile Detention in separate states? Even more bizarre was the fact that a friend I made here worked with Zelda in a separate institutional facility. She described the fiery Koori just as I knew her, and the obvious question was then asked:

"This client you're describing, is her name Zelda by any chance?" And indeed it was.

Zelda spent her time in and out of detention in both South Australia and New South Wales. Her fiery temper and drug use had indelibly created her reality, and there was no changing her. She too gave birth to a daughter who was also removed by DoCS. It was discovered the baby was not being fed properly and was left to lie in her own faeces during Zelda's frequent drug and alcohol binges. Today Zelda is still on Facebook and posts many photographs of herself with a child who appears to be a second daughter. Naomi too continues to pop up in these photographs. Zelda lives in Broken Hill and looks relatively healthy and happy. Despite a number of friend requests sent to me, I chose to keep Zelda out of my life. Zelda is just far too much pepper for my soup, I'm afraid.

Keely, the spirited Koori girl who at the age of ten had given birth to a baby boy and kept his identity a secret:

I had all the time in the world for Keely; she was funny, intelligent, and clever beyond her years, *and* she loved me as much as I cared for her. I remained in contact with Keely throughout her short life. When, via a former detainee, I discovered Keely had killed herself, I was dumbstruck and incredulous. Among the girls I thought might commit suicide, and who did so, not for a single moment did I include Keely. Despite a heavy addiction to alcohol and *yundi* (cannabis) Keely was still as free spirited and filled with enthusiasm as I had always known her to be. Prior to her untimely death, she had become the legitimate mother to a second son and was pregnant with her third at the time of the apparent suicide. One of Keely's cousins had found her hanging inside Keely's home. To this day I believe the suicide to have been an alcohol fuelled accidental death on her part, one triggered by a silly fight she'd had the same night with her current fiancé.

RIP beautiful, precious Keely.

Amber, the tough top dog:

Amber had struggled with drugs long after she left Juniperina. She was fortunate to possess great inner strength and a sound support network of family and friends, and she finally kicked heroin to the kerb early in 2014. Today Amber's life is filled with friendship, laughter, and good health. She was in a happy relationship with a man, after years of perceived homosexuality, but the couple recently parted amicably. Amber's beautiful Facebook pictures and posts speak for themselves. I continue to remain in contact with Amber via Facebook Messenger and recently found out via text that Amber is pregnant and has chosen to make the journey of motherhood alone.

Aside from Paigh, the only tangible relationship I maintain with these precious souls is with Korina, the proud and doting mother of two beautiful children. Korina's temper had got her a serious control order inside Juniperina but, like Keely, she was self-effacing, accountable, and amiable. Korina lives in Albury and I would easily nominate her for a Mother of the Year award, given her maternal conduct in the face of continuing personal trials.

Via a former long-term Youth Officer, I recently discovered that the Juniperina Juvenile Justice Centre is no more. The New South Wales Department for Corrections has purchased the site to house an overflow of serious adult female offenders. The current female child detainees will be imprisoned in a new wing built at Reiby, the centre I trained in. Some of the older staff members I had worked with have transferred there while others found different careers. My informant, for example, now works in the disabilities field.

Life certainly came full circle for me, at the Juniperina Juvenile Justice Centre.

* * *

The drive from Sydney to Adelaide was inconsequential, with Edan's behaviour stellar provided I kept feeding him. In Hay, where we stopped overnight, we ordered so much food I vomited yet Edan, always reed thin, ate his entire share without blinking.

Following a minor hiccup where we found ourselves on the other side of the Murray River overlooking picturesque Mannum, a place not en route to Springton – or so I thought – enquiries directed us on our way via the spectacular rock formations just outside Palmer. Tiny Tungkillo and pretty Mount Pleasant came next and then at long last we were only 7 kilometres from the historic settlement of Springton, our new home. Turning into Ferdinand Street I saw my beautiful big house for the first time. I gasped out loud, "This is MY house!"

Springton is a gorgeous rural hamlet on the outskirts of the Southern Barossa Valley with a population of around 350. It's surrounded by rolling hills, livestock, a quaint little pub, and homely rustic cottages; I was in Paradise and I absolutely loved my house. It was a two storey, five-bedroom colonial dwelling with an orchard and three water tanks. Valeria, her husband and Alycia had painted some feature walls and arranged carpeting upstairs prior to my arrival, which was wonderful of them. The downstairs was tiled in slate and my bedroom had its own en suite and walkin robe. There was no doubt I needed to find a job in order to keep this dream alive but even in light of the circumstances, thus far the move to Adelaide was definitely a good choice.

I began to apply for every job I could think of, including the local abattoir. As a confirmed animal lover I was relieved when told I was unsuccessful due to being flat footed, something I had not been aware of, but given how painful my European trip had been it made a whole lot of sense.

Following four agonising weeks of vocational uncertainty, I found a casual carer's position with a renowned Youth Services organisation I was familiar with due to external 'stakeholder liaisons' at Juniperina. My client, who required accommodation support in Mount Barker, was Valerie, an eighteen-year-old girl with pronounced mental health issues. She had been placed in state care following her father's sentencing for the murder of her mother. On more than one occasion Valerie had me read the letters he sent her from jail.

"He's in Mupulawangk Prison," Valerie informed me matter of factly. She then showed me her father's photograph in his prison greens as he stood in front of what looked like a poorly reproduced tropical mural.

Valerie was everything I'd bargained for and more. She'd lull herself to sleep clutching at her mother's greying wedding dress, humming eerie tunes to herself. Her outbursts were unprecedented and frightening, and somehow she managed to exonerate her father's guilt, convinced by well calculated words on his part. Valerie's father clearly shirked responsibility for his wife's murder by blaming her parents and creating a scenario of misguided self-preservation, which no doubt camouflaged a cruel and cold blooded murderer.

I knew I would not thrive in this job, and after a month or so I landed a full-time position with a job network agency, also in Mount Barker. Here I was trained as an area development consultant for their Murray Bridge portfolio. All my life I wanted my existence to feel meaningful outside of motherhood, and this job seemed to promise a little meaning away from my beloved Juniperina. I couldn't wait to ring Valeria with the good news. Since I did not know *anyone* in Adelaide, she was not only my dear adopted 'sister' but my only friend too. We celebrated over coffee and pastries at the famous Lobethal Bakery.

Something between Valeria and me felt amiss, though. I was under the distinct impression I had to gain her approval on all things. There was no doubt she was an autocratic and controlling personality, another resolute Sagittarian female in a long line of archers hell-bent on making my life challenging. There had been an occasion during a past Adelaide visit where Edan, only two or three years old at the time, would not detach from me, screaming the house down because he was made to sit alone in the back seat of Valeria's car. Edan had not been diagnosed with Asperger's syndrome at the time and Valeria would not allow me to give in to him. At one point his desperate cries had me so distraught I ordered Valeria to stop the car, indignantly grabbed my son and defiantly plonked him next to me. He ceased to cry immediately. Valeria made some acid remark about me being an easy target and I felt maternal anger rise into my throat. Valeria had sworn off having children, claiming she and her husband were 'too selfish' to raise any. In my mind I felt compelled to whisper, 'What right do you then have telling me how to raise mine?'

South Australia and Adelaideans appeared somewhat removed from Sydney and *her* people, in terms of open congeniality and exuberance. Often I felt like I was not even living in the same country. Granted, Adelaideans spoke better English and I was perpetually asked if I came from another state. Personally I detest my distinct Italo/Spanish South-western Sydney accent and my frequent use of colloquialism. Any intelligence I possess seems to go down toilet the moment I open my mouth, but this is me, my background and my authentic character. And what the hell is a Stobie pole anyway?

Speed limits in South Australia are ridiculous and the drivers selfish and out of control, yet compared to Sydney, traffic is sparse, except for peak hour bottlenecks on a couple of arterial roads, and the pathways are virtually uncluttered. In my opinion South Australians are spoilt: they whine about having to travel more than twenty minutes to get anywhere. In Adelaide you can drive for an hour and clock up 65 kilometres, whereas in Sydney, with its soul destroying traffic jams, the same hour will net you around 25 kilometres travelled. South Australia is also merciless in racking up revenue through speeding and parking fines. I was clicked *twice* in one week for doing 60 km/h in a 50 zone, and then a year later I was clicked a couple more times. Yes, my fault but come on! Radar and fixed cameras are often positioned in the most contentious of places, and state government knows it.

To my horror I received a thousand dollar fine, as well as court orders to appear at the Tanunda Magistrates Court. I lost a whopping eight points from my licence and with it a hell of a lot of driver's confidence. In 2000 it had taken me so long to gain my licence that I had to deceive Rhys each time I failed my driving test as I funnelled the necessary funds to keep on going. My licence to drive meant everything to me and following many attempts I finally obtained it, counting the achievement as one of the five most momentous occurrences in my life. The fines had built up because they had been sent to New South Wales, prior to me transferring my registration to South Australian plates. Following this sour event, I began to see negatives about moving to Adelaide. Metaphysics had taught me to watch out for 'signs' in situations and whether they are good or bad for you, so naturally I began to assume that in moving to South Australia I had committed another monumental fuck up.

The job network agency that had promised so much delivered very little. I was seriously bullied by the project manager, a rotund bitch half my age whose job was to train me – not mortify me. Outside of dealing with young people at risk I really had no idea what I was doing here. I had built up a significant client base in Murray Bridge and made positive contacts with all the community stakeholders there. South Australian community credos, legislation and bureaucracy were all foreign to me and yet I sat in boardrooms filled with provincial highbrow 'suits', feigning knowledge and making things up as I went along. A growth in infrastructure was gladly anticipated in Murray Bridge – there were plans for the building of a new prison complex that would render Northfield's Yatala Labour Prison and the adjacent Adelaide Women's Prison obsolete. To encourage the stakeholders towards recruiting young long-term 'unemployables', I used the prison proposal as my primary marketing tool. When the prison project was suddenly shelved in favour of a new hospital, so was my position with the agency. The timing was good, as I'd had enough of my manager and gave my CEO a no-holds-barred ultimatum – me or *her*. Only two years after I left the company the rotund bitch also moved on, but such is life.

Soon after I walked away from the Mount Barker organisation my Certificate IV in Youth Work landed me another casual position. With no gaps between pay cheques I began to feel lucky, and the bad omens about Adelaide began to disperse. The SA Corrections personnel I had liaised with in Sydney kept in regular touch regarding future training schools, too. I really had nothing to fear but fear itself, something I still battled with despite the hundreds of metaphysical books that had taught me otherwise. Juvenile Justice still called my name, but for some reason, I was, at least momentarily, unwilling to reapply. I guess my pride was whispering that someone as qualified as I was should not need to jump through all the fiery, red-taped bureaucratic hoops, so fuck you Magill Training Centre, *and* Families SA!

In the meantime, it appeared I had some weird karmic debt due to the suburb of Murray Bridge. My second job there arrived in the form of a placement with four Aboriginal children, the youngest of twelve.

My first shift with the 'Harris children' was disconcerting to say the least. I pulled up by the old weatherboard residence at six in the morning, as instructed, only to return to my car after several doorknocks failed to rouse a response. This placement was a two carer one, with one of the carers working as an 'active' throughout the night. Half an hour later a young woman answered the door rubbing sleep from her eyes, and I was given a half-hearted handover as the children continued resting. Danny, the youngest, had been sick all night, and was introduced to me just minutes before the 'carer' made a speedy exit from the placement. Because my new offsider was unavailable, the agency asked me to do the best I could alone until a substitute worker was found. One look at four-year-old Danny and I knew things weren't right. His lips were cracked and his breathing shallow. While waiting for the other children to rise I tried to cheer Danny up with a favourite story. I was less than impressed.

One by one eight-year-old Steven, seven-year-old Isaac, and a three-year-old cutie named Elisabeth, came out of their rooms. Beautiful children all of them but, as I soon learnt, thorough little beasts, a direct result of serious abuse and neglect. In child protection, residential carers are not allowed to restrain their charges at any time. The standard operating procedure in the event of affray, assault, or a threat of assault on staff, involves placing a call to police and/or barricading oneself inside the carer's room. There was no doubt in my mind that as young as they were, these children *could* kill or seriously injure an adult, or each other. I therefore relied heavily on my solid juvenile justice training and my maternal instincts, skills that served me well during many a precarious shift.

Finally, my offsider arrived and I felt instant relief. The agency had placed me in an uncertain position by leaving me here alone; in youth work allegations of misconduct are rife, with employees rarely coming out on top. The youth worker, a Russian woman, took one look at Danny and scooped him into her arms.

"He looks like hell. I'm going to take him to Murray Bridge hospital."

It was a good thing she did; Danny's appendix had almost ruptured and the doctors who intervened stated he was within an inch of his life. The night shift staff were placed under investigation, and almost two years after the fact I was summoned by the Department's bureau for prosecutions to offer evidence as 'the witness'.

Unfortunately for my psyche, if not my hip pocket, I was given ongoing shifts with the Harris children. Three shifts, two of these twenty-four-hour ones, paid only slightly more than a week's wages anywhere else. I worked alongside a slightly older lady named Jan and my first shift fell on her birthday.

The children and I prepared Jan a cake and from that day we became and remained good friends.

Steven, Isaac, Danny, and Elisabeth were the youngest of twelve children, with all twelve of them 'wards of the state'. Due to ongoing conflict the children were divided into four placements that were managed by different agencies. Their 'parents', one mother and a number of fathers, were serious alcoholics. Steven, the most Caucasian of the twelve, had piercing green eyes and tousled, sun-kissed hair; he was also the most villainous and I must have taken years off my life trying to handle him, subsequently deciding I'd take the worst Juniperina detainee over Steven. At least in detention there are punitive tools available to successfully subdue offending behaviours.

Personal challenges aside, the abuse and neglect these children had suffered was devastating, and the reason a carer needed to remain active throughout the night. The children constantly interfered with one other and, incredibly, the worst offender was little Elisabeth. It took several attempts to teach Elisabeth appropriate behaviour, especially at bath time when she would 'offer' herself. Never in my wildest dreams did I imagine I'd witness such a sad thing in one so young.

During Christmas of 2008 Jan and I were horrified to discover that the children's parents had received a 'parenting supplement' cheque of $1000 per child, a total of $12,000, irrespective of the fact that all twelve children were under the 'Guardianship of the Minister'. This was a shit-covered slap in the face to all honest South Australian tax payers and genuine people in need. Furthermore, the children's Christmas access visit was cancelled, with each child receiving a crappy two-dollar shop gift delivered to them by their social worker *two weeks* after Christmas. Apparently Mummy and Daddy 'could not get there' because they had got so drunk, then both collapsed on the floor after each one bashing the other up. I'd like to add here that my personal critique of this situation has nothing to do with Aboriginality and everything to do with substance abuse. I have had plenty of 'white' charges who mistreated their children in the same – or worse – vein.

Three months on, with Jan and me shedding blood, sweat, and all our stores of patience, we had made significant progress with the Harris children. Even the ever defiant Steven had vocalised that he liked us. Danny, the tiny four-year-old with the wide velvety eyes and biggest smile you'd ever see, would peer insolently beneath huge eyelashes, have me chase him into a room, and then 'resignedly' allow me to give him a brisk hug. Giggling to myself I remembered how the little terror who had almost died due to misconduct once called me a 'fat cunt' because I enforced a directive on him. Coincidentally 'cunt' is a word used frequently among some of our Indigenous and I'm certain it was a favourite with 'Mum' and 'Dad' too. Isaac who was perpetually in combat mode, defending himself from his older and far superior brother, had mellowed so much we were able to have him focus on other things like find-a-word and colouring-in books. But it was little Elisabeth who completely captured my heart. She would run to the door as I pulled into the driveway and excitedly call out *"BELICA!"* as she had difficulty pronouncing Angelica. With her bouncing blonde curls and 'Little Miss' attitude, Elisabeth promised to be a force to be reckoned with, provided life allowed her of course.

In their infinite bureaucratic wisdom Families SA decided Steven and Isaac were now in a position to return to their parents, who had recently relocated to Western Australia. Jan and I fiercely opposed their decision but who were *we* aside from paid babysitters? An impersonal system is only ever really preoccupied with budgets and policies, and children like the Harrises were falling through systemic cracks by the handful.

On the other hand, Danny and Elisabeth were earmarked for foster care and it only took a matter of weeks for them to leave us. I was pronouncedly sad, but what could I do except continue to enjoy what time I had left with them? As the 'Powers That Be' would have it, these precious few days were then handed to another carer, with Jan assigned new charges and me thrown from pillar to post through various placements. One of these sporadic placements was with three little girls whose names all started with the letter E. Those girls were the worst case of neglect I could ever have imagined or have been privy to since. This is one heartbreaking case that will never be erased from my memory.

The three angels, aged eighteen months, five years and seven years, lived their tiny lives inside a caravan with their prostitute mother, permanently shut away from the outside world. The 'mother' worked all night and slept all day, devoured by drugs. The younger girls had *literally* not seen the outside world and were fed scraps thrown to them by their estranged older brother via an open window. The 'E girls' had little or no language aside from what they had picked up from a TV set played to them through the day. Their little legs were deformed from a lack of mobility. The middle child was autistic and the eldest displayed strong sexualised behaviour, possibly due to interference by her mother's clients. Unable to comprehend the world around them, the three girls were fearless and wild and required careful and constant vigilance.

I was instructed to take the youngest 'E' child to the Lyell McEwin Hospital for an autism spectrum assessment. Having a child with Asperger's I did not notice the familiar tell-tale signs in her behaviour; nonetheless, the clinical psychologist took the child through a series of behavioural tests as I watched anxiously from a corner of the room. Suddenly the little girl had had enough and, reaching for her bottle, she lay down on the floor and began patting her own bottom repeatedly. The psychologist then remarked, "Poor little thing, she's self-comforting. Noone must have ever done this for her."

I ran out of the room in angry tears of disgust. What type of monsters allowed such bad things to happen to their *own* children? I wanted to *hurt* these monsters and hurt them *bad.* Children were my kryptonite and it later occurred to me that I gravitated towards this kind of work to atone my own inner torment, but then again I might just be some kind of misguided masochist, too. Perhaps it was a case of the Universe *wanting* me doing this work but before I could understand my duties I had to experience the pain myself. My past was my classroom.

Before leaving this agency for another, the final clients entrusted to my care were a brother and sister whose father had been imprisoned for large scale methamphetamine production, and once more Mupulawangk Prison was a minor protagonist in my story.

These two innocent teens were victims of drug addiction and cultural pride. They were good Italian kids condemned by their aunts and uncles to state care because they had embarrassed '*la famiglia*'. The sixteen-year-old girl struggled with the lack of normality imposed on her but nonetheless continued with her schooling. Tina suffered from severe alopecia, hiding her pain beneath an all too obvious wig. It was a nauseating and abhorrent situation that further compounded 'cultural' criminality and neglect for me. Fuck family pride. These were dependent *children* for fuck's sake!

* * *

Adelaide, the Barossa and the Adelaide Hills districts were absolutely breathtaking and rather reminded me of Europe. Each time I ventured into these localities I had to pinch myself in order to remind me I wasn't dreaming, and that I really *was* an Adelaidean too. For me my life in Springton felt the way it must have for Edmond Dantès when he eventually escaped from the

Chateau d'If. I cursed my old Western Sydney life to hell, giving thanks to whatever forces had led me back to South Australia.

To ratify myself, I uploaded as many scenic photographs on Facebook as possible to showcase to my Sydney friends how well I was doing. I loved my house, Edan had settled in easily and Alycia returned to stay: life was good. But just as I became comfortable the isolation of Springton took a negative toll on Kristen.

A terrible fight ensued over her lack of motivation in finding work or obtaining a driver's licence. Taureans do everything in their own time and pace, responding poorly to pressure and I should have taken this into account before going for Kristen's jugular.

Rhys was visiting Adelaide around this time, together with his wife. Stupidly, I invited them to stay at my house, thinking that being 'nice' was like money in the bank for future transactions regarding the kids. Valeria tried to help Kristen by enlisting her in a youth unemployment program called Greencorps, but Kristen hated every minute of it and resented me for forcing her to attend each morning. Towards the end of Rhys's visit his wife, for work reasons, returned to Sydney a couple of days early, leaving Rhys behind, and thus Kristen took her cue to create dissent among the ranks.

I had vociferously ordered Kristen out of bed after she vehemently refused to attend Greencorps *ever again*. She blamed her allergy on pollen but I wasn't buying it. Kristen ignored me and, enraged, I dragged her out of her bed by her hair. Naturally *Father* came to the rescue, with Rhys gratuitously involving himself in the scuffle. Barking at my heels, he followed me around the house until I tried to shut him out by entering my bedroom. He pushed past me and I completely lost it and punched him in the mouth before barricading myself inside. I hollered for the two of them to get out of my house and return to Sydney, and I came home from work that afternoon to find they had done just that. I was heartbroken, with remorse and emotional pain consuming me. Alycia was my soul but Kristen was my heart and, of course, Rhys had again succeeded in controlling an outcome where I would come out the undisputed victim.

I returned to online dating, hoping a tree change might also bring me romantic fortune. I met a couple of men who didn't even come close to cutting the mustard and because of this I succumbed to the endless stream of text messages Jason had been sending me since Christmas 2008, when he called and wished me a blessed holiday season.

I could not understand why Jason held on – we were toxic together. Also, rumours of a liaison between Kyera and Jason continued pouring into Facebook via my Juniperina excolleagues. My gut believed them, and my heart had no intention of returning to that excruciating degree of pain. But, as the quality of men proved even worse here than their Sydney counterparts, I wearily began to entertain the insane. Had I already forgotten the feelings of independence I acquired that Tasmanian night on Friendly Beach? As a romantic idealist Jay Gatsby had nothing on me, and possibly I too would perish for my folly.

Partly horrified, partly delighted, and just before my forty-fourth birthday, I found a beseeching Jason on my doorstep. Alycia was away in Warrnambool on a working assignment with a mobile photographic company and, freed from family bias, I decided to see what Jason had on offer aside from the obvious. But not even four days into his impromptu visit, and Jason and I were fighting like scalded banshees.

On the fifth evening of this visit from hell I retired early, leaving Jason downstairs to watch television. A couple of intense 'release' nights only found us back where things had been left at Rosemeadow. An SMS alert on Jason's phone surprised me from some bitter thoughts and I found myself compelled to read the message. The name on the screen sent chills down my spine, *Kyera*!

Hi Jason, I hope you're enjoying your holiday in Tasmania, you deserve it. Let me know when you're back so I can come and get the rest of my things from your place. Love, Kyera.

Clutching the offensive device, I leapt out of bed and ran down the stairs to face Jason with the evidence I'd tried to deny myself all these months.

"You've fucked her haven't you? Tell me to my face, you fucked her you filthy bastard. *No more lies Jason, no more!*"

Persistent, sanctimonious denial was all that came out of Jason's pathetic mouth. Why, oh why had I believed him? What a fucking shit of a fool I was, and right now I hated myself more than ever. I had *relocated* to another *state* to escape this man's treachery.

"I was letting her and her boys stay at my place after her husband kicked Kyera out. She had nowhere else to go; have a heart Angelica, what type of bastard leaves a woman, a colleague, with two innocent children out on the street? She was only at my place for a couple of weeks for fuck's sake, get over yourself Angelica; I didn't come over here to cop this shit!"

"Pack your stuff and get out!" I ordered Jason, trying not to look into his eyes for fear I might fall under his mendacious spell once more.

I could taste bile in my mouth. I hated being tricked like this and my body's reaction was a stark reminder. Completely gutted and full of contempt, at that moment I wanted to rip out my vagina, knowing it had been tainted with that home wrecker's DNA. I felt sick, foolish and ridiculous. Also in that same moment, it seemed I had taken a hundred million steps backwards in life – the life I thought I had finally left behind.

"GET OUT!! GET THE FUCK OUT!!" I yelled at him. *Tasmania my ass you low life piece of shit.*

Close to midnight Jason finally walked out of my house, trekking an unlit road with no means of transport and with the bitterness of a Barossa winter at his back. I could not comprehend how he'd prefer to face these hazards than tell me the truth. I *needed* to hear it! I am able to be released by truth; I *can* be reasonable in the face of a sincere confession. This stubborn and pious *denial* is what rips me to shreds inside, and so, gripped by rage, barefoot and in my thin nightie, I chased him, my nemesis, into the darkness.

"Just tell me you fucked her! Be honest for once in your small shitty life Jason. Set me *free* you fuck!"

"Go to hell Angelica. I shouldn't have come; you're still the same goddamn lunatic. You can take the girl out of Rosemeadow but you can't take Rosemeadow out of the girl. What was I thinking? Go back inside, we're done."

Jason had an unregistered gun at his home and he once pointed it at my head, deadly intent on his tortured face. I'd often behave similarly when unable to cope with my own feelings a moment longer. One night Jason handed me a knife and begged me to plunge it into his chest. It would have been so easy for us both to die but it wasn't our time; we were both cowards and our children needed us. Tonight, however, I could no longer handle denial or mind games. I ran back to the house, grabbed my car keys, and jumped into my new Mitsubishi. The section of road leading from Springton into Mount Pleasant was pitch black, but the portion of the brain that retains pain memory could make out Jason's silhouette clearly enough for me to head straight for it. Firmly I pressed my foot onto the accelerator and made a snap decision; things would indeed end *tonight.*

Alas, this is what the face of a fatherless childhood looks like.

CHAPTER TWENTY-FIVE

SOFT REED PLACE

———

The call that released me from casual crisis accommodation employment finally arrived. I had been accepted by the South Australian Department for Correctional Services (DCS) for a twelve-week course as a Trainee Correctional Officer (TCO), starting on 29 June, 2009. I didn't know how to feel … was I happy or terrified?

Sure, I had plenty of custodial and community services experience, but this time I wouldn't be dealing with unruly children but hard-core adult repeat offenders.

I did not run Jason over on that cold autumn night, and that's just as well or I'd be the one sitting on the other side of the vocational fence. Yes, I did accelerate my beautiful new Mitsubishi 380 straight at the slimy bastard, but Jason beat me to the punch by jumping out of harm's way like the twisted but agile dwarf that he was. Karma is a cruel mistress though; in order to at least frighten the bejesus out of him I swerved sharply, turned the car around, then drove into a ditch, totalling my front end.

"Oh Angelica," Jason sighed, looking at the wreck that was now my car. "You stupid stupid, crazy, woman. Okay, okay … I did fuck her! Is it worth you knowing? Is it worth *this*?"

Yes it was! Because of the way I'm wired and the endless stream of lies I've had imposed on me during my lifetime, I need TRUTH! I refuse to send myself mad with doubt and second guessing, especially when my gut is telling me otherwise. But in spite of his confession, which I accepted, the only way to rid myself of Jason right that moment was to return him to Adelaide Airport the next morning. Jason tied my front fender with some rope, promising me to send me money for repairs, but I wasn't holding my breath; the man was a scrooge at the best of times.

For the entirety of that night and all the way into the airport the next day, I verbally abused Jason, then, on arrival, barely gave him the chance to jump out from the back seat. Disgusted, angry and hurt, I pulled briskly away from the kerb, wound down my window and yelled out a final and triumphant "FUCK YOU!" But Jason had in fact lost nothing at all and victory was *not* mine. Just like Jay Gatsby, it was *I* who had been sorely fucked.

A month or so after the Jason debacle my cousin suggested I undertake an anger management course. I contacted Relationships Australia and put my name down for a six-week program held in the Adelaide CBD. Of the twenty participants, only four of us women, I scored second highest for destructive and reactive behaviour. Clearly, I had a lot of work to do.

* * *

As I've said, it was never my intention to work in the adult prison system. I chose to go ahead with the position of Trainee Correctional Officer simply because I would not allow a foreign based 'psyche test' determine my eligibility for a job I knew like the back of my hand. Custodial work was what I was particularly good at.

Just prior to the decision that led to the abandonment of my Sydney life, I had tried venturing into the New South Wales adult prison system but failed the numerical component of their eligibility testing. When I appealed against the Department's deliberation they insisted the requirement for an all-round score was non-negotiable and that I could try re-applying in three months' time. How in hell did maths have anything to do with prison work, aside from an inmate head count? On a metaphysical scale at least, it appeared I was *meant to* come to South Australia because nothing in New South Wales was working out for me.

In complete contrast, the numerical component for the South Australian testing process was a piece of piss and the panel interview, held on 4 June 2009, was rather informal and a lot of fun; definitely a far cry from what I expected. I was measured up for uniforms and had to lose 4 kilos in order to avoid wearing the men's issue trousers. Fortunately, my weight of 100 kilos did not impact on the medical examination, which I'm certain I only passed by the skin of my teeth.

The first day of the course, held at Yatala Labour Prison (YLP), involved a bus tour of all metropolitan prisons. Personally I wanted to work here at the YLP, Adelaide's maximum security prison, and although I had loved Juniperina I had no desire to work with adult women and especially not those convicted of filicide.

I was the first to arrive and then one by one our course mates poured in. The first off the rank was a tall gentleman with greying hair who looked like a biker and was just that; he introduced himself as Colin. 'Mmmmm, not bad,' I thought to myself. Not that I was entertaining the thought of dating a potential colleague … I'd definitely learnt my lesson there.

Next was a guy I immediately dubbed our 'pretty boy': confident, young, built, and attractive; Matt was his name. A beautiful greeneyed goddess sporting a Piscean insignia on the back of her neck pulled in next: Ashley. She was followed by a handsome couple called Jason and Monica who I recognised them from the psychological test. A wide-eyed brunette I had seen at the medical strolled in, head hung low, big brown eyes studying everyone around her; this was Melissa. Jennifer was a middle-aged woman with a happy disposition and of Indigenous appearance; she stood next to and greeted everyone warmly. A tall, rotund man in his mid-twenties with deep-set eyes as striking as Ashley's stood by, quietly surveying the crowd: Darren. Green eyes kept on coming in the form of yet another beaming smile: Amelia. Including myself there were twenty-eight new recruits, and we were now known as Course 159.

We climbed on board the bus and, not wanting to say much, I took the back seat. Just as I had attempted to do at Bankstown TAFE so many years ago, I decided to put my head down, learn my job, do it to the best of my ability and come home safely. Socialising had got me into too much trouble in the past and I needed to truly succeed this time around. Frank, one of the new recruits and outwardly as Italian as Italian gets, immediately started chatting me up. On my left side was Esmeralda, an Indigenous New Zealander who joyfully introduced herself and then chewed my ear off throughout the trip. I should have guessed that these last two larger than life characters were Geminis: the communication sign. By now, and only because of Graham and Jason, this was a sign I wanted little to do with.

Our first stop was Mupulawangk Prison, an already too familiar name. I was so busy being entertained by Frank and Esmeralda I didn't notice the hour that had passed between Northfield and Murray Bridge. As we alighted from the bus two acidic female officers introduced themselves as our tour guides.

One was the image of *Prisoner*'s 'Vinegar Tits' character. Blinking myself back to around 1980 when the TV show had absorbed my interest like no other, I wondered who'd have believed me had I told them that one day I'd be inside a real prison, as a staff member? Certainly not me!

The course lasted six weeks with an additional six weeks of 'buddy shifts' at the jail designated to each recruit, or TCO, as we were referred to by our superiors. Everyone who graduated was awarded a Certificate III in Correctional Practices and a twelve-month probationary contract as an OPS1.

Each morning at precisely 7 o'clock, we presented ourselves inside the YLP training room for roll call, uniform parade, and a marching exercise. Our course instructor was a tubby Austrian man who fancied himself the archetypal drill sergeant. Unfortunately, my two left feet attracted his attention more often than not ... and then there were my unpolished boots, to boot.

Overall our training was loads of fun, though, restraint techniques and self-defence classes included. As a class we all got on well, but as predicted by our instructors by the end of the six weeks definite groups had formed, and some people turned out to be not *quite* so nice.

"This is what will happen with your colleagues inside your prison," our instructor explained stoically. "You will find yourselves more at odds with *them* than with the prisoners. Conflict of interest will become your most problematic concern, so remember what side you are actually on."

As with high school, I belonged to *no* group, mixing with everyone equally. Two women in Course 159 appeared drawn to me, begging for my attention: their names were Melissa, who I have already introduced, and 'Denise'. The class lost two members early in the piece, an Indigenous man who the drill sergeant insulted one too many times, and Michael, a former military man, due to a broken finger which prevented him from completing his tactical restraints module.

When it came to naming our posting preferences I filled in the three spaces with the following: Yatala E Division, Yatala F Division, and Yatala B Division. The drill sergeant looked at me sourly and ordered me to redo the form.

"You have to choose *three* different prisons!" he bellowed.

But I did not wish to go anywhere else and especially not to the Adelaide Women's Prison where I was certain I'd be earmarked given my working experience at Juniperina's Boronia High Needs Unit. The Adelaide Remand Centre was too far to travel to each day so I really had little choice but to write down Yatala, Mupulawangk, and yes, the dreaded Adelaide Women's Prison. If

DCS sent me to option three, however, I had already decided to resign on the spot. I held so much personal bitterness towards the 'mothers' who had abused, or permitted the abuse of, my beloved Juniperina girls, and had absolutely no time or professional inclination towards them as adults in custody. And of course there was my mother's abuse of me to take into consideration.

On posting allocation day I was not even considered for Yatala; the ratio of female to male officers there had apparently been satisfied. There was no doubt in my mind once I realised I was going to Mupulawangk Prison, that the town of Murray Bridge had something to do with my destiny. It was the third job I'd held here since moving to South Australia only fifteen months ago. Working at Mupulawangk Prison meant I'd be coming face to face with Valerie's murderous father and perhaps even the drug dealing father of the Italian siblings I had known in child protection. Wow, such are the parallels, synchronicity, and idiosyncrasies of life, hey?

Our class captain, Anton, the taciturn Colin, handsome Matt, Denise, and a pain in the ass know-it-all whose nasal voice grated on everyone's ear canals, were posted to Mupulawangk with me. Melissa, alongside Ashley, Amelia, Jason, Monica, Esmeralda and 'Travis', were sent to the Adelaide Women's Prison. Denise and I instantly became good friends and carpooled wherever our buddy shifts allowed, debriefing and gossiping to our hearts' content. Some of the officers at Mupulawangk were friendly and forthcoming while others were openly rude and condescending. I saw some similarities with the way Sydney's Reiby and Cobham centres were run and in the way new recruits were greeted. At the end of the day we had been clearly warned: 'When you get to your prison often you'll encounter more problems with your staff than with the prisoners.' There is no doubt in my mind that certain occupations attract certain breeds for certain reasons.

One Saturday in July I met with a gentleman I found online via Facebook's Zoosk dating 'app'. His eloquent conversations had drawn me in and although he looked a lot like Robin Williams (the late actor), I was attracted to the deep blue eyes gazing back at me from his profile picture. I had whined profusely to my classmates how Adelaide had no eligible bachelors and Monica had quickly intervened with, "Just you wait Angelica. I bet you meet someone at the prison you get sent to."

No way! No *fricking way* was I getting involved with *anyone* from work again, not after the black agonies Jason had put me through. I had every intention of making Corrections my lifelong career now – in fact, I was looking forward to the work instead of fearing it. Nothing and nobody was going to sabotage this opportunity … I hadn't give up Juniperina to fail here and not over a bit of cock. The Robin Williams doppelganger would have to suffice.

I had been on my own for eighteen months since my arrival in the land of the free settler and as much as I felt emotionally free, sexually I was hungry as hell. 'Mark' was not the way he sounded behind a computer screen. Physically he was palatable but there was something amiss with his speech and I wasn't all too keen about his heavy smoking.

We met at the Lord Lyndoch in the heart of the Barossa Valley and then, stupidly, I agreed to follow Mark into his 'love nest' hidden among the vineyards, a place he rented from his winemaker employer. You would think that as a budding law enforcer living in Australia's serial killer capital I'd have had more sense than to place myself in such a potentially dangerous situation.

Mark and I kissed that night but it left me less convinced than before. Another date and two glasses of absinthe later and the drought was broken. That thing amiss with Mark's speech was his teeth: he literally had none. Alongside this important deficit was the size of his penis. Unwilling to completely destroy the man, I politely asked him if he'd consider dentures in the near future but my insolence was only met with the classic rebuttal, *I've received no complaints before, why should it matter to you?* It clearly was not going to work between us … not without teeth. I like teeth.

There was an additional problem with Mark – he had taken a shine to one of my school friends, the one who accompanied me to that first fateful Brahma Kumaris weekend retreat (when Nick had failed to look after my children). Mark had 'added' her on Facebook and I demanded she delete him, but by then Mark had already spun a web around her, as he had with me. Incredibly, because of Mark, someone I'd known and loved and cared for since Year 9 fell out of friendship with me almost overnight. I later found out Mark was a registered sex offender. Stupid me and stupid former school friend, who chose a man she'd never met over a friend who had once helped her through the worst times in her life.

The first few days at the medium security programs prison were unquestionably daunting. With a capacity for 300+ male prisoners, 250+ of them allowed free association inside campus style grounds, Mupulawangk Prison seemed a likely death trap. On any shift there were no more than around X number of officers, including upper management, a ratio of approximately 1:11. New officers were a curiosity to existing staff, but also for the inmates. There was no doubt we would be scrutinised by men who were locked up for days on end, and later singled out for our weaknesses and our strengths. And there was no doubt this introductory period would be my hour of reckoning.

Denise's mother had long been at Mupulawangk so the officers made *her* feel welcome and at home. Denise claimed she did not want to hang off her mother's fame and yet at the first opportunity she would tell anyone who she was. I began to see a marked change in Denise right from the get-go, with her gossiping losing its playful congeniality and taking on a far more malicious twist. I, in my usual happy and well-meaning way, continued to extend my hand to future colleagues as I moved from unit to unit and from shift to shift. Overall, Mupulawangk was an attractive prison, with its shady trees and bushes, and soon I ceased feeling threatened by 'what could be' and got on with what *was*. Mupulawangk Prison was run on calculated trust, a palatable and feasible regime with plenty of black humour – something I was adept at, and crass familiarity. Operationally it was an exemplary institution. I knew that eventually, I would do well here.

By the end of the six-week 'buddy shifts' my confidence was marred by an incident involving the drill sergeant, Denise and me. As friendly and forthcoming as I wished to appear, I certainly did not appreciate being forced to come to the attention of my line manager and *not* this early in the piece. In retrospect the incident served to demonstrate there was something grossly amiss with Denise, but because I was yet to learn how not to give people second or third chances I dismissed my gut instinct and begged for Denise's credibility so our friendship could continue unabated.

By the end of the affair, the drill sergeant was banned from re-entering the prison and Denise held a definite upper hand in our relationship. I had no other established friendships in Adelaide so ultimately Denise's effervescent and generous congeniality managed to sell itself to me regardless of the obvious cracks appearing.

On 17 September 2009 I and the twentyfive other 159ers graduated, each of us placing the coveted OPS1 epaulettes onto the graduate next to us. The person next to me happened to be Denise and although my gut continued to say *beware*, I felt an undeniable sisterhood towards her during this triumphant moment. Graduating in Correctional Services was the proudest day of my life. As I marched one last time into a decorated mess full of dignitaries, I felt a hundred feet tall. I vowed to honour the uniform and all it represented. My entire life I had longed to be someone who could somehow impact on society, and on this day I believed I had arrived at that position.

When the time for the receipt of my graduation certificate arrived and I heard my name called out, I was walking on air. I did not even look for Valeria, her husband and my beautiful Alycia, who had all come along as my 'support network'; I was too dazed by immeasurable pride. A peculiar looking man who looked about seven feet tall handed me the coveted piece of parchment as we grinned together for an official snapshot. He was some Labor politician, an upper house member named *Bernard Finnigan, who looked like a rather dubious individual.

* * *

Despite my original plan, slowly but surely I began to make other friends at Mupulawangk, though Denise and I were a favourite pairing in everyone's books, with officers never greeting one without acknowledging the other. Matt was doing well too, with his sweet but macho nature. Fiona, the nasal know-it-all, had too much ambition for someone so new, and Colin was still being scrutinised, but nowhere near as viciously as poor Anton, who, with his openly unorthodox conduct, wasn't doing himself any favours. Me, well I just learnt my job and delivered a service. I wanted to be fair and equitable towards the prisoners, but when you work side by side with people hell-bent on bullying it's difficult to always follow through your good intentions. I was disturbed to notice that one of the staff giving Fiona, Colin and Anton a hard time, cloak and dagger style, was Denise herself. Still, I bided my time with her, hoping it was all just 'new recruit bravado'.

An attractive fifty-something officer began to pay me some attention. During our first shift together I guessed 'Ted' to be a Gemini ... *ouch!* Monica's words about finding love in prison resounded in my ears; I briskly reminded myself of the vow I'd taken, and of how Jason had impacted my work at Juniperina. Following my one night with Mark, my views on sex had significantly altered. Glibly I surmised that a few steamy nights with a colleague did not mean I was making an emotional commitment, so I metaphorically opened my door for Ted to drop by. From the stories I was picking up around the place, Mupulawangk seemed like some sort of harem anyway, so who would judge me?

Ted and I did not even make it to first base. The moment I agreed to begin something, he pulled back completely, citing a great difference in age between us. *Wasn't that my decision to make?*

On Facebook Messenger Ted typed the following: 'I've had a couple of relationships at work already Angelica; they didn't turn out too well.'

'So why go there with me in the first place?' I thought to myself, perplexed.

Much later on I befriended Lynda, one of the officers with whom Ted had had a relationship. By the time Lynda finished a sermon on Ted, laced with confounded bitterness, I realised I had dodged a major bullet in Ted … goddamn Geminis.

Forgetting men for a moment, I returned to the task at hand. I was enjoying my job, despite the periods of monotony and static banality. A rotation of positions and duties kept the job interesting, and the bizarre stories that poured out of exaggerating officers' mouths certainly made for a laugh or two.

The prisoners did not scare me. Sure, there were some serious cases at Mupulawangk and a few definite nutcases, but I had confidence in a system that protected its staff. By securing the person and discarding his crime, I managed to deal with a human being before the maniacal alter ego had a chance of taking over.

Inside the units, two officers per complement of sixty-eight to seventy prisoners was the order of the day. The two of us were in command of unlock, count, all prisoner queries and requests, cell changes, lockdown, 'Intel', and the general running of the unit. Non-unit positions included dynamic patrols, control room operation, industries security, court and inter-institutional escorts, and Admissions and health. Almost every shift is done as a duo and the rosters determine who your partner will be on the day or for an entire run of seven to eight days. It was possible to 'swap out' of a designated position if you found an officer willing to do this with you. Once I'd got past my first unit count, my first 'pat down', cell search, and a few radio calls, I felt confident enough to get to know my 'clients'. When you look for and find their humanity, the prisoners are not so scary anymore.

Adult men are much easier to manage than adult or teenage females. I did a four-day stint at the Adelaide Women's Prison in order to pass the strip search and urinalysis competencies, and in that brief period I saw significant differences between the two both operationally and interpersonally. Following these four days Denise and I were glad to be back at Mupulawangk, resuming our duties with renewed energy and enthusiasm for the place.

My abhorrence for child abuse and infanticide was heightened when the officers at the Adelaide Women's Prison took great delight in telling me a woman I just strip searched, had *bitten* her eighteen-month old baby to death. If the officers were merely trying to test me in the way of personal gumption, they could just shove it. My time in child protection had taught me enough about how to cope with horror, yet this vile image remained branded inside my head, so thank you very much and *go fuck yourself AWP!*

It was good to know that generally speaking Mupulawangk did not accommodate paedophiles or child killers, although it came to my attention that one of our longterm prisoners had murdered his girlfriend's two children and was re-imprisoned here for a different crime. Needless to say, I refused to give this person my time of day outside of the necessary on-the-job duties.

Protectees are kept in maximum security, or specialist prisons like Port Augusta and Port Lincoln. In New South Wales for example, Cooma is renowned as the 'rock spider' prison. Even though I swore I would uphold 'duty of care', personally I much preferred the American system of mainstream association for all inmates. For me 'protection' was a copout and the American system a truer meaning of the term 'natural justice'. As innately humane and inclined towards restorative justice as I am, I remain a staunch advocate of capital punishment for certain types of crime.

On one rather ho-hum lunchtime I was sitting in the mess going through my WAG (Workplace Assessment Guide, a competency booklet that needed to be signed off by senior staff as I acquired various on-the-job skills) when in walked 'Brew'. This massive unit of a man slumped himself on the couch across from me looking positively dismal.

"Awwww, what's wrong Brew?" I asked him.

Brew shrugged his shoulders sheepishly.

"Nothing."

He then changed his mind and added, "Don't you hate it when your texts go unanswered?"

I nodded knowingly. "Let me guess – a girl?"

Brew nodded.

"Maybe she's actually trying to *tell you* something?"

Brew acknowledged the inference without looking up from his phone and I was certain he'd burst out crying any moment. Poor bastard; women can be so heartless sometimes.

I only knew this guy as 'Brew'; it was what everyone called him. Brew was by far the most imposing officer at Mupulawangk, weighing at least 140 kilos and standing well over six feet in height. I had only met Brew a couple of times and thought nothing of him. To me he was just another officer. Following the Ted fiasco, I was even more determined not to date a colleague and besides, Brew was taken and quite uninterested. The only inappropriate thought that had crossed my mind about Brew was whether this giant of a man was 'in proportion' all over.

Two weeks after the unreturned texts conversation I found a friend request on my Facebook page; it was from Brew, or rather Adam Brewer as his name happened to read. 'Interesting,' I thought. The girl must have dumped him after all. I wondered whether Brewer was a German name … my fetish for all things German lingered and with his fair Teutonic 'box head' features, Brew could certainly pass for a kraut; the Adelaide Hills are, or were, virtually a Prussian colony after all.

It seemed Brew was online just about every time I went onto Facebook, and I got this funny feeling he might be waiting for me. Surely not … I was at least ten years his senior, but then again DCS was the kind of incestuous place where looks, age, or marital status did not stand in the way of 'a good time'. Brew and I saw each other at work but were rarely in each other's area, so I got to know Adam from the comfortable confines of a computer screen, something I had become highly adept at.

Adam was shy but strong. I correctly guessed him to be a Cancerian and felt relieved because Cancer is good with Taurus. So despite my best efforts it did not take long to forget my vow regarding relationships with someone from work. Adam was saying all the right things and was devoid of the machismo and arrogance that flourish among Correctional Officers. As our Facebook conversations grew longer and longer, I started to feel a guarded excitement at the prospect of seeing the little green 'online' dot light up by Adam's name.

One lazy Sunday afternoon in Sturt Unit Adam and I stowed away inside the Case Management Co-ordinator's office to play Shithead, the silly card game that had so often helped me keep the Juniperina girls out of trouble. Angela, one of the nicer female officers at Mupulawangk, pulled us out of the office with a big grin on her English Rose features.

"I think there's going to be a riot happening out here soon you two? Time to get back to work?"

Later that evening I found a Facebook message from Angela asking me whether there was 'something going on' between Adam and me. I wasn't quite sure myself … was there? Adam had noticed my manicured acrylic nails and paid me a compliment; did that count as 'something'?

I confided in Denise about the possibility of a budding romance between Adam and me, and her reaction left me positively cold – even offended.

"Ewwwww, Brew? He reminds me of an elephant!"

Denise's outburst actually helped me make a decision regarding my growing feelings for Adam. I was still, as Gilda had dubbed me, 'the Spirit of Contradiction' and I'd continue contravening public consensus. Adam was no elephant – he was majestic. To me he was attractive and I was certainly smitten by his height, one of the attributes I had noted in the Louise L. Hay book in Marrakesh.

As a one finger typist I was going to ring Adam and save my beautiful acrylic nail further angst. The phone call lasted two hours. Now certain there were grounds for something more, we settled on a date: 4 December 2009. A part of me looked forward to it but the saboteur yelled out: *Halt! He's ten years your junior and has mentioned wanting children someday.* Regardless, I met Adam in the car park of Auchendarroch House pub in Mount Barker at ten in the morning. Mount Barker was Adam's hometown and as the many synchronicities in my life would have it, Adam had once worked out of the Repco centre opposite the job network offices I spent part of three miserable months in when I first came to South Australia.

Our date lasted fourteen hours and was entirely lovely. Adam was certainly an officer and a gentleman and made quite an impression. As I was a newcomer to South Australia, Adam wanted to know what part of his beautiful state I was still unfamiliar with. I replied, "The South!"

In his Toyota Land Cruiser Adam drove me 200 kilometres across every corner of this beautiful part of my new world, from Victor Harbor, Cape Jervis, Yankalilla and Meadows, to McLaren Vale and Willunga. Adam surprised me with champagne in glass goblets as we sat on a grassy incline overlooking the sea off Cape Jervis. I brought Paninis.

By one in the morning, despite many obvious cues from me, Adam remained the consummate gentleman and had made no sexual advances towards me. Finally, I grabbed him and planted a big one on his lips. I had a good excuse to, too – I had been bursting for a pee and Adam frantically drove me to the only toilet block he knew would still be open at that time. I had to show my gratitude *somehow*.

Monica's prediction looked like it might be coming true after all.

On our date we saw a horse run towards us on Kangarilla Road at McLaren Flat. Adam stopped the Land Cruiser and tried to corral the frightened animal back into its paddock as I alerted oncoming traffic. A second horse neighed towards the runaway one, thus leading Adam into the correct paddock. My heart melted at the sense of fostering between the two animals and Adam's considerate gesture.

I sensed what had just happened held some kind of meaning that related to Adam and me. I discovered the horse symbolises survival, drive, sexuality, love, the need to offer service, personal change and all that has a power to move us. These were indeed the attributes that were unfolding before me now. It seemed now that the runaway horse was assuring me I was on the right track.

* * *

Almost a year on, Adam and I were living together and travelling to work daily from Springton. Fortunately, we were in the same work group and doing similar shifts. Despite my best attempts at sabotaging our relationship, Adam did not let up on us once. My inner demons would not allow me to believe this man could be the one to truly love me, the man I had described in the Notes in Louise L. Hay's hallowed book ... my *Seventy Thousand Camels*.

It took Adam three months to tell me he loved me. For me those three words were merely a confirmation of Adam's actions; and actions really *do* speak louder than words. There wasn't a single thing Adam would not do for me. Adam pre-empted my very thoughts, presenting me with my wishes before I could even open my mouth. For reasons that surprised *and* worried me, Adam considered me the true love of his life and treated me as such. I had grown so accustomed to arguments, rejection and deceit that Adam's pure, uncomplicated, undemanding type of love frightened me. I knew I would eventually wear thin on this beautiful young man; there was no withstanding the damaged beast that would surely be unleashed, probably sooner rather than later. My profound fear was telling me to end it but I decided to continue playing the waiting game; the prospect of loneliness is far worse than that of impending failure.

Dig deep enough and you'll find the mud beneath the lotuses. Mupulawangk was a haven for treachery. It was inciting, polygamous, and divided into factions. What was worse, these conditions had nothing to do with our 'charges'. I did not join Corrections to be a cowboy. When I joined VOCAL, the victims of crime support group in Sydney, I saw firsthand how victims and their families suffered and so I wanted the perpetrators contained in an environment where at best they would be rehabilitated, and at worst kept from hurting anyone else. Many of the people who joined Corrections, however, did so, in my opinion, mainly to bully others, both 'them' *and* us, the more conscientious officers. These cowboys were the same kind as the high school playground kids who gave the 'nerds' a hard time, and the type of cop who hands out fines because he can. I could count on my fingers the men and women at Mupulawangk who I would share confidences with on the outside.

Altogether I felt more and more alienated from all of my colleagues, but never to the point where it would be obvious that Denise had become my mortal foe; while the others were just protecting themselves, she had made the feud personal. I had given serious thought to leaving Corrections mainly because the monotony was getting to me. Seven consecutive days were far too many to sit around drinking coffee, listening to tired jokes and morbid gossip. I viewed the slander of other officers as Mupulawangk's undoing, with one of the worst offenders my new soul sister Denise. It is with a deep shame that I confess female officers to be the biggest bullies in adult prisons. In their attempt to compete with 'the boys' they lose the very ingredient that is most useful in a volatile and dangerous environment such as this: gentle and understanding – attributes I utilised as much as required, and for which I was respected by all who counted.

I was beginning to find more in common with the prisoners than with my fellow officers. I spent more time doing random wing patrols sharing a yarn with the 'crims', just to escape the interminable bullshit of that claustrophobic office. When you work in such an environment the last place you imagine you'll find solace and sanctuary is with the 'enemy'. But the prisoners at least were *honest* in their dishonesty.

* * *

There are many stories I could recount about my Mupulawangk Prison experience, but this would be a book of its own and I'm bound by confidentiality, among other things. The characters I met in this prison who stood out the most were the ones who managed to touch my heart. If one looks for it, one finds goodness in every arena. Some people make mistakes they pay for for the rest of their lives; others simply don't know how to *be* a different person as they had noone to teach them.

If I was given a dollar for each time a member of the public asked me whether I was afraid of the prisoners, I'd be rich. My reply to each would go something like this:

'They are not the ones to fear. These people have rarely rubbed shoulders with respect, congeniality, or love. Offer them the first two human rights with an open face, treat them equitably, and most times you'll get it back – even during *crucial* times.'

I remember doing my first count as I apprehensively stepped into and down the east wing of Angas Unit. Thirty-five hardened prisoners lined up along both sides of the long, poorly lit corridor, and my cue to proceed came over the Control Room's PA system: "The time is twelve thirty-five, all prisoners stand by your open cell doors until the count has been called correct."

I could feel my legs shaking but I knew only too well that to project fear would be my undoing. To gain respect in such a place you need to *own* your shit. These men had all day, every day, to scrutinise the officers so they could gain some advantage – no matter how small.

I looked into my partner's eyes before proceeding; I knew he would be watching intently by the wing doors for signs of adverse behaviour and that he would also stick to standard operating procedures and lock me inside the wing if, God forbid, I were to be taken hostage by the prisoners. In a Code Brown situation one captured officer is better than *two*. The back-up response time is around ten seconds, but ten seconds is all it takes the hands of rabid rage to inflict a lot of damage to tissue and bone.

One year on and 'the count' became something I actually *enjoyed* ... yep, you can call me crazy. The criminals had got to know me and I now took my time tallying the numerous faces staring back at me. There was always some banter going on among them.

"Three ... twenty-six ... one thousand ..." one or two prisoners would chime in, hoping to trip me up. I'd briskly remind them that to interfere with the count was a breach punishable via regime regression or a fine. I'd then return to the entrance doors and start afresh. The prisoners, itching to get away from their post, would then give the perpetrator(s) a less than friendly scolding themselves.

Compliance came easily to me because, unlike many officers, I made a point of separating the individual from the crime, leaving only the personality.

I also used astrology and had memorised most prisoners' star signs. I found the possession of a sense of humour, carefully assessed compassion, and the delving out of mutual respect, could turn the most hardened criminals into the kind of lions who refused to devour Daniel; they'd neither hurt nor fear you, for even among the unjust dwell moral codes.

The 'lifers' were by far the easiest prisoners. After spending twenty or so years behind electric fences what choice did they have? Often these were men who had committed what is termed a 'crime of passion' and who would more than likely never do so again, even if released early. But it only takes a 'once off' to rob someone of their life. I myself knew how overwhelming emotion will sometimes extract a huge price. Jason had very nearly placed me in the same situation as the lifers I speak of.

The old Italian guy, who'd shot dead his wife and mother-in-law in front of his children as they grieved by his father-in-law's grave, was hell-bent on having me a sample of the basil he grew inside the Ross Unit garden.

"Angelica!" He'd call out my name with an Italian inflection. "*Come stai?*"

I had told 'Pippo' countless times that I would not talk Italian with him because it was inappropriate to do so, but Pippo could not help himself. When noone was about, I'd covertly indulge him, briskly stowing his precious basil into my big vinyl jacket.

My undoing came when I presented Pippo with a small sample of the pesto his beautiful basil had afforded me. The silver haired man with three more years left on his life sentence wanted to thank me personally for bridging the gap between officer and 'crim', but in prison – and justly so – there are eyes watching and ears listening everywhere. I was promptly paid a visit by a supervisor who sternly debriefed me on the conflict of interest policy and the consequences that might arise when prisoner/officer lines become blurred.

The next time I saw my potential friend he presented me with yet another bunch of basil. I looked at Pippo benignly and explained how our occasional teteatetes needed to stop. He looked at me sadly but understood.

"I did a terrible thing Angelica," he said, and I knew he was not referring to the basil, or to my reprimand.

"It's in the past Pippo," I assured him. "We all make mistakes we can't revisit, because it helps noone to do so."

This old man had survived a massive heart attack only months before. He was revived by an officer who is a current friend. The last time I saw Pippo he called out to me from the back of a G4S transport van. His handcuffed hands beckoned for me to go to him but the area was teeming with officers and rank supervisors, so I had no choice but to smile back and keep on walking.

"I'm going to Mount Gambier Angelica!" Pippo called behind me. I turned around once more, nodding acknowledgement. That was the last time I saw Pippo.

Without Pippo the veggie garden soon disappeared from Ross Unit. The officers inadvertently benefitted from Pippo because whenever he found makeshift weapons in his garden he'd hand them over to staff. Whenever he mowed the lawns and came across a drug-filled tennis ball, he'd cheekily throw it back over the fence. Wherever you are Pippo, please know this: we are forgiven by *Source* only once we have learnt to forgive ourselves.

Another lifer was Prisoner *132642. He had stumbled upon his 'ex' and her lover in bed together, forgetting she was an ex for a reason. Both parties paid the ultimate price of blind jealousy.

I found an opportunity to talk with 'John' when he found himself placed in separation for 'safety of self' after copping a serious bashing from a group of cowardly prisoners who wanted his 'Ox' stash. As the only permitted drug (up to March 2016) Ox tobacco is like gold in prison.

"I was brought up by loving parents on a farm," John explained. "I can't use the 'I was abused as a child' story so many other crims do. I never fitted the mould of *murderer*."

I assessed John's pronounced black eye and the cuts on his face as he spoke to me, and wondered how old he was. The many silver threads in his thick beard and the craggy, spent face suggested he might have been in his sixties.

"I'm fiftyfive," he told me.

Great suffering and hopeless regret are ageing emotions, no doubt.

"You should write a book John; let people out there know you're not an evil man. Teach others about the fatal consequences of unbridled jealousy; make a life behind bars count!"

John looked at me with interest. "It's funny you say that; I do love writing and I have entertained the thought of an autobiography."

John was transferred to another prison. He had not seen his assailants; they jumped him when he was asleep and so he was unable to bring any of them to justice. Yet by being forced to leave the only place he'd called home for so long, it was John who was punished. Many would call this 'natural justice'; others will say *Karma finally caught up with the mongrel*; but someone like Gandhi would repeat, *An eye for an eye makes the whole world blind*. Attempting to run over Jason, who had lied and cheated without remorse, was for me a form of natural justice, but was the price, life in prison, worth it? And what of the karmic debt accumulated to someone so insignificant in the grand scheme of things?

Many of the men I met inside Mupulawangk were *not* honourable people. Violence begets violence and prison is a place of survival, not rehabilitation.

There is a pecking order in prison, mostly headed by the outlaw bikies, the same people responsible for lucrative drug trafficking on the inside. Today's society is being crippled by a drug epidemic and trafficking is now a principal reason our prisons are overflowing. Then there are the career criminals who graduate from juvenile justice centres and create the 'revolving door' recidivist effect that has officers gasping *not you again!* during admission interviews. They are the 'poor me' assholes who always seem to have been 'framed' by the cops, who scream down the phone at their girlfriends and mothers because they haven't put enough funds into their accounts for a 'buy up'. The ones who blame their 'cellie' when a makeshift bong is found under their mattress, or ingredients for a 'brew' sit in their cell rotting away.

The most frightening crims are the ones noone sees much of except at unlock in the morning; the thin, ghoulish ones who tower over you but say nothing. I got one of these crim's name wrong over the PA system once. When he poked his deformed head into the office, boring into me with spectral eyes, the officers swiftly reminded me how this man had horribly murdered his mother, breaking her back and cutting off her head. The six foot six zombie glared at the pentagram around my neck and said, "My name is -------! Not the way you pronounced it and *you, you* are a witch!"

The hole above his pineal gland seemed more pronounced now as it throbbed with parochial accusation, and I had to wonder if he he'd been lobotomised for his heinous deed.

"No I'm not -------, this is a protection symbol," I tried to explain to the zombie.

"I *know* what it is and you're still a witch." His body inched away from the office door like a wraith inside a fog and I never wore my pentagram to work again.

Only once did I respond to a serious bashing. A man got his head smashed against a metal railing by his partner's son. According to the perpetrator, the victim had assaulted his mother on the outside. There was copious blood and I was glad I did not freeze. I did however forget that someone with a head injury is not to be laid down and began to place the man in the recovery position. Fortunately, the medics were quick to attend the scene and I was admonished and sent to the nearest computer for a comprehensive report.

In my absence there were many other similar incidents. Jail is not designed to be a happy place, no matter how often our government reviews prisoner rights and privileges. The same issues that land a person inside *occur* inside. Prisoners will fashion 'shivs' from practically anything; they have loads of inventive time on their hands. They even create remote controls out of string and toothbrushes in order to change TV channels from their bunk. Drugs will enter prison, as do mobile phones, with calls sold for around a hundred dollars each. Desperation creates opportunity, with the depraved and immoral profiteering just as they had out on the streets.

One man wore an eyeball on his cheek when his head was caved in by a piece of gym equipment that had been prised loose. Another had his throat slashed. Colin was the officer who called a Code Black on that one. When retribution is called for, there is always someone to deliver it.

Not long after I started at Mupulawangk, a well-known 'crazy' died of natural causes. He had murdered his wife and created prison lore by presenting one of his detached testicles at unlock. These were the stories told to us during the course, possibly to filter out the scaredy cats. When I met the crazy in question, he seemed pretty much harmless and not so scary. The worst thing he ever did to me was to say, "Leave your perfume and nail varnish behind love," following a random cell search or 'ramp', as it is called. When he died, Denise decided *she* had been the first on the scene but it was not as she wanted it to sound. My soul sister was an attention seeking fraud and I wasn't going to accept her look-at-me behaviour for much longer.

Only two prisoners ever gave me the runs. The first was a notorious killer and rapist. He was completely creepy, in Ed Gein fashion. The second was just disgusting and slimy. Both made a pass at me and both got written up for it. As an officer, if you let something slide you will pay for it at some point. Understandably, men in prison will make remarks about female officers, not necessarily to their face, but within earshot. Whether the officer then wishes to do something about it is up to her, but it is highly recommended she pull the prisoner up on even the smallest indiscretion, lest the behaviour continues.

Take the 'willy patrol', for example. During First and Second Watch, prisoners in their cells are checked every two hours. Working in pairs, one officer will take a wing and his partner the other, and this will be their routine for the entire shift. Some prisoners will show off, knowing a female officer is doing the rounds; I suppose it's one way they get their rocks off. The way we'd trip them up, and have a bit of fun ourselves, was to swap wings with our male counterpart so that on the next check they'd be presenting their crown jewels to a male officer who would either write them up or offer them a serious serving.

'Mick' was not in jail for murder, he was more likely a drug trafficker … I didn't really know. I often chose not to read a prisoner's file unless it was mandatory, in order to work with as little bias as possible. Mick was another old bloke who sported a grotesquely deformed stomach due to a humungous hernia. Mick was definitely not one to collect supporters: he was litigious, loud, arrogant, and rude. At only fortyeight years of age, grey covered most of his barbaric red mane and beard and he looked like a proverbial 'geezer'.

As I conducted a routine patrol down the Light Unit west wing, I could hear Mick's booming voice emanating from several cells down. The words 'cunt' and 'fuck' spilled out of his big toothless mouth like rice from a torn sack.

"Hillier! What's with all the yelling and swearing?" I'd reprimand Mick, while trying to withhold a chuckle.

"Sorry Miss, it's just those cunts at the parole board are doing my fucking head in again!"

"What did I just say about swearing Hillier?" I bellowed, trying to refrain from laughing at his preposterous act of innocence.

It was inappropriate to call a prisoner by his first name and likewise for them to refer to me as anything but Miss, Boss, or Officer Such and Such. I think our name badges were a tease and should have omitted our first names.

"Oh sorry Miss, I know I shouldn't talk like that in front of a lady, but why do you screws always have to make surprise appearances?" Mick mused.

I couldn't help smiling outwardly as I proceeded to set Mick straight – if this was at all possible.

"Us *officers* Hillier, are *paid* to make surprise appearances, yeah?" And off I went back to the unit office, giggling to myself, with Mick's quarrelsome, booming voice echoing behind me.

This was just one of many times I intercepted a Mick tirade, but usually it only took a disapproving nod to quieten him down at least until staff were out of sight. Unfortunately, not everyone who works inside a prison understands or accepts the various personality types that are encountered here. I always went that extra mile with people, but then again I was new to the job. Custodial employment has a high turnover rate and as I said earlier, the average burnout period is two years. The problem with our officer to prisoner ratio is that you cannot tailor a response for every individual. A unit has two officers to seventy prisoners and so uniformity needs to be upheld or the shift goes to shit very quickly. We are running a serious institution after all, not a play group.

One morning when I arrived on shift I was directed to take Mick his breakfast in an isolation cell.

"What the hell has he done?" I asked, expecting the worst.

"He chewed off the nurse's ear refusing his meds," my partner replied.

"Let me guess," I replied. "Nurse *So and So*, right?"

Everyone in the prison was thoroughly familiar with Mick's mannerisms and reactions. Even though everyone thought he was a grumpy old prick, we knew he was harmless and, in a bizarre way, even endearing. But Nurse 'So and So' was not so tolerant and she put Mick on paper, citing gross threatening behaviour and fear for her own life. This meant Mick was to be tipped back into a maximum security prison for violence against a staff member. Nurse 'So and So' knew this would happen and took full advantage of the situation at hand. There are staff inside prison who do not belong there, who are only there to dish out punishment, never rehabilitation, and who make life for good staff all the harder and more dangerous.

I could barely see Mick's iconic face through the viewing panel of his cell. I lowered the trap to pass him his breakfast and we talked briefly about regret and lack of self-control … I knew a little about that.

"Miss, could I ask you a favour?" he said pleadingly, the big voice almost extinguished.

"Sure, if it's something I can do."

Mick pushed a crumpled letter through the trap.

"I've written to my mum explaining what I did. I don't want to disappoint her even more by sending her a letter full of spelling mistakes. Would you kindly fix them for me? I'm such a stupid man; I refused the medication because I wanted to be drug free for Mum when I got out. I should've kept my big mouth shut for once and just ditched them in my cell."

"Sure, I can do that," I answered sympathetically, but when I looked up into Mick's face I could see tears welling up in his eyes. I could feel my own eyes stinging and, catching the letter, I clasped Mick's hand for a fleeting moment and gave it a reassuring squeeze.

"Do you really want a screw reading your private stuff Mick?" Calling him Mick and not Hillier seemed appropriate right this moment. I looked down feeling my face and saw the tell-tale wet spots on my vinyl jacket.

"Miss, I used to hate the screws until I met you. You never judge me, you never tell me to get stuffed or write me up. You walk down that corridor and light up the place, always smiling at us – at me! I've never looked at you like a screw but as the kindest lady I've known besides my own mother."

This time what I felt was a huge lump in my throat that seemed to be slicing through my vocal cords. It was time to say goodbye and leave.

That morning I questioned whether this was a job I could do for the rest of my life. There was so much pain in the world, so how long could I last absorbing it before the pain would begin to change me? A few hours later I returned to Mick's cell with a corrected version of his precious letter. He was not inside it. I frantically rang Admits and Health and asked if he had been placed inside the management cells awaiting a transfer to Yatala, but I was too late, Mick had gone. I inserted the letter into an internal mail envelope, hoping the system would be kind to Prisoner *42587, and that his heartfelt words might eventually find their way into Mrs Hillier's hands.

A few months after I resigned from the Department I learnt that Mick's mother had died. He was due for release on parole only days after her death. The best the Department could do for Mick was to authorise his release a couple of hours earlier in order for him to attend his mother's funeral on time. Perhaps the letter had found its way into Mrs Hillier's hands and she was able to leave this world knowing her son loved her and did not mean to disappoint her. I choked back more tears. I could only hope.

* * *

"Have you ever tried Maybury's coffee éclairs Angelica?" a colleague asked.

"No, why? Is he a pastry cook?"

"Not by trade," the officer continued. "He learned how to cook in *here*. You should try his choc slices too, they're pretty good!"

Thinking about delicious sweets, I revisited the many years spent working in cake shops as a young woman and how 20 kilos so quickly found my medium frame. My mouth began to water and so I decided to seek out Maybury and see what all the fuss was about.

'Maybury' was an elusive prisoner. If you didn't know his crime or that he was on the State Premier's personal 'never to be released' hit list, you wouldn't have known he was around. Looking through Maybury's file, I found the original picture taken of him in 1982; he hadn't changed much, bar all the grey threads running through his well-hidden hair. As is the norm for me and my inquiring mind, I became intrigued by Maybury and simply *had* to try his éclairs.

A few months went by and I was lucky if I'd come across Prisoner *31648 a handful of times. Then one day on Swing Shift inside Ross Unit, Maybury walked in carrying a plastic plate covered with alfoil. Looking down at me from under his permanent cap, he asked, "Can you give these to the day officer please; I think her name is Denise?"

"Oh yes, not a problem," I replied, taking Maybury's goodies. "Say, these aren't your famous coffee éclairs are they?" I added.

Maybury's rigid face crinkled slightly in amusement.

"No, they're my famous choc slices. I don't make the coffee éclairs much these days."

"Damn!" I exclaimed in jest, and with this Maybury lifted two slices from beneath the alfoil and handed them to me. Here I was, a policy abiding officer, soliciting sweets from a crim. 'Better in my gut than in Denise's,' I thought.

A few months later I was doing a routine patrol of the prison's kitchen and bakery. Satisfied everything was in order, I spent a few moments in the office chatting to the kitchen staff alongside my partner. Suddenly a rap on the window behind me found Maybury beckoning for me to come outside into the foyer. Maybury then led me to the cool room where he retrieved a large tray of something covered with greaseproof paper. Lifting one corner he showed me the treasure trove that lay beneath.

"Coffee éclairs!" I exclaimed. "You remembered!"

Maybury smiled sheepishly. I then realised why his physiognomy had barely altered after almost three decades of incarceration, Maybury never smiled … his face simply lacked expression lines.

"Be sure to share them with your partner," he recommended, handing me a plateful of the famous sweets. "I wouldn't want to be the reason you get fat!"

I looked at Maybury knowingly. "What do you mean? I *am* fat!"

One afternoon as I waited for 'count correct' by the Ross Unit gates, I made some remark about the living conditions of prisoners here in the enhanced regime accommodation that is Ross Unit. Maybury had been standing quietly nearby, and he boldly interrupted my conversation with a kind of indignation I had not found inside the cool room that other day.

"Yes we are indeed so privileged living here. I don't *live* here. This is where I *exist!*"

Flashes of the faceless post office clerk Maybury had gunned down during a bungled robbery twentynine years before suddenly appeared in my mind's eye. This was perhaps the face and tone *she* had seen only minutes before she died. I quickly reminded myself that although Maybury had repaid his dues to society and that he should not be punished past his sentence, his victim would never receive restitution of any kind.

Knowing someday I would write this book, I asked Maybury to pen down what the word freedom meant to him. Surprisingly, he did so:

To the average inmate, with a family, the idea of freedom is being able to be with the wife and kids, and not see them leave at the end of a visit and not be able to go with them, to be able to spoil them, go where they go and stay with them, and not be locked up and told what to do. This only applies to those who are not afraid to show their feelings and be ridiculed by the tough guys.

Freedom to others is the front gate and the shot or booze in the carpark, the first sexual encounter, and being with their mates.

Freedom to me is the right to choose. To choose to go somewhere, to be with someone, to buy what I want, and to do all these things when I want to. Freedom is to be the authority, not to be authorised.

At different stages of incarceration, all three meanings apply to any one person.

I entered a favourite carwash in Gawler and asked the perennially congenial owner to put extra degreaser spray on my front end.

"Have you been a good girl?" he asked with his usual grin.

"What if I told you I was *such* a good girl, I help keep criminals behind bars?"

Suddenly the owner's benign expression changed to a look of utter distaste.

"Yes well, we won't talk about that. One of those bastards gunned down my cousin at her work many years ago. I hope he's rotting in jail!"

The carwash owner's cousin was Maybury's victim and yes, dear man, Maybury *was* rotting away, day by day, hour by hour, without a promise for release.

It's important to take note of how pain affects everyone, from the perpetrator to the victim and to both parties' families and friends. For a Correctional Officer taking note is a necessary tool to avoid getting close to prisoners therefore blurring ethical lines of demarcation. Maybury had indeed paid his dues and would one day be free. His victim's family's suffering may fade with time, too, but there will always be reminders simply because they will never again see their loved one.

And it's not just a loss of life that creates deep impact, it's also that nagging thought sitting at the base of your spine each time you pass a post office, one that whispers *it could have been me.* This is exactly how I felt the day I met Garry Lynch in Blacktown many years back. Any girl walking Anita's path that fateful February evening could have endured what Anita went through. Crime is never exclusive.

In September of 2011 'Officer Caldwell' played a primary role in my premature resignation from my position with the Department. I hoped any future choc slices Maybury cooked for the bitch – my socalled soul sister – would be forged from copious amounts of 'prison butter'.

Denise's infamy against my character, all to join an elitist mob mentality group which makes the adult prison system reprehensible to me now, produced the desired results for her. My inability to make sense of prison and its charges saw me return to what I knew and understood best, Youth Justice. Youth workers are by far and wide a better breed of people than at least half of Correctional Officers, with its female staff the worst offenders, I'm sorry to say.

The way Denise and the nasal cow who joined ranks with her systematically eroded my career and reputation at Mupulawangk, is something that took me to the brink of suicide and madness more than once.

Prison work taught me the wisdom of the Native American proverb: 'Do not judge a man until you yourself have walked a mile in his sandals.'

I dedicate this chapter to Pippo, Maybury, Domenic, John, Mick and Joshua. Joshua is a young man who has been permanently branded by his criminal record, despite a committed willingness to break free from the dark shadow it continues to cast upon him.

A meme I saw on Facebook once looked something like this: 'Don't remind someone of their past when they are trying to create a better future.'

Bad people are everywhere ... some are found in prison, some live within our family unit, and some are our employers and friends. At Mupulawangk Prison I met some good people who made a bad decision or two. The word Mupulawangk comes from the Aboriginal *mupulawangk* or 'soft reed place'.

I would also like to dedicate this chapter to all victims of crime who cannot write an autobiography because their lives were extinguished by bad people, or, by *good* people out of control. Lest We Forget.

* * *

I made some heated comment on a Facebook thread I don't even recall now, and a nondescript character called Joshua began chewing me up for it. Being me, I had to clear the air and little by little Joshua opened up to me, informing me he was a former prisoner at three of the five metropolitan prisons in SA. He was also a victim of his past, unable to gain employment, which exacerbated his low self-esteem, anger issues and binge drinking. His 'victim' mentality, with the frustration and hopelessness it carries, will most probably see him back in prison. There are no *real* rehabilitation services in this country for ex-prisoners seeking redemption.

One thing led to another and Joshua created a bogus email account so he could converse with me outside of the Big Brother forum that is Facebook. During our exchanges, Joshua opened up about the story he was writing on prison life. He allowed me to read a chapter, which took me back to Mupulawangk and the many stories I'd heard there. Joshua cautioned me that if I plagiarised any of it for *my* book, his publisher would know and I'd be held accountable. The way Joshua describes his experience in one of the two maximum security metro prisons, needs to be heard, so I have not plagiarised Joshua's chapter, I have completely remodelled it for you my reader so that you can discover prison life from the viewpoint of one who can relate such a story far better than I. I now give you Joshua:

I'm back in the prison unit after a month out. This time I know a couple of people, from my last time in here, and first time in adult prison. 'Lizard' thank God, is here too; he'll look out for me. It's good to have a mate who's older and on murder charges, when you've just turned eighteen a few months ago and find yourself in gaol.

Lizard asked me to go and invade a certain rehab place, and bash a guy that is informing on him in his murder case. I agreed to, but I didn't do it. Putting someone on the promise and not following through, will get *you* bashed really quick in gaol. I thought little of it then, and soon I found myself "on the dog" and threatened by a laundry worker.

I am not that strong in comparison to a lot of the guys locked up in here, and even though I'm tall and athletic, I'm skinny and not really hardened up.

I try and get by being polite, and only stuck up for myself once when a huge guy about my age stepped straight in front of me in the meal queue. I didn't want conflict but I had to assert myself too or I'd forever be someone's bitch. This one guy who trained a lot, had ridiculously big muscles and seemed to know everyone, and he was well respected for his young age of 23. He sure liked to mess with me a bit. There wasn't much that I could do. According to him, he was a trained boxer, the most muscular guy in the unit, and was in for armed robbery. After this stint, he became a full patch member of one of the Hell's Angels Adelaide chapters, and was even the person who produced a hand gun at North Park shopping centre and chased *Vinnie Foccarelli with it, assaulted a security guard, and committed an armed robbery when his attempt to shoot Foccarelli failed. This big bloke was actually rich and from an influential background.

I had a new cell mate move in with me who was about thirty. He had a brother who was respected in prison. He had an argument with this rich kid gone bad, who I'll simply name Kronos for the sake of this story. The argument was over milk. In the morning scramble to get from your position outside of your cell, to the table tennis table, and to the good breakfast foods first, my cell mate cut in front of Kronos. My cellie was the dominant one in the confrontation and Kronos backed right down. My cellie told me Kronos shut up because he knew he would smash him. As a further insult, my cellie stole Kronos's milk. 'Peter thieving' (stealing from other inmates in gaol) is hated by all inmates and collectively dealt with to stamp out the practice. My cellie decided to just rub off the number corresponding to Kronos's cell marked with a whiteboard marker, and put ours on it instead. The problem was, cells with two cell mates have their milk marked differently to distinguish whose they are, 7 and 7a for example. My cellie just put a 7 on Kronos's milk, which was my number.

That cellie moved into another cell and stopped drinking the stolen milk, leaving my individual number on it. So, there was this one extra milk sitting in the fridge, I was the only one who had two firstly and then there was that milk with my number on it left sitting in the fridge as I didn't want to be any part of drinking it, for I knew the prisoners would collectively assault me as punishment for peter thieving. So Kronos, who was now in the gym giving me some shit as usual, asks me if I stole his milk. I say, "I think you know I wouldn't do that," which I assume he would because I'm clearly intimidated by him. He responds with an annoyed voice, "I don't know ya from a bar of soap." I didn't get the compassion and understanding I was hoping for. Shortly after that he says, "What did you say about my mother?" I respond, "Don't get me started on her!" In my attempt to stick up for myself, I've publically shamed him by not showing fear and insulting his mother to boot. Reputation and willingness to be violent over any minor affront is everything in gaol and Kronos has just lost an argument with my cellie before the whole unit at breakfast, and had his milk stolen. He wants his reputation points back.

While the *screws are letting the inmates into the gym area to use the weights, we line up outside of the weights room door waiting for the basketball court to get unlocked. The screws are outside in the court yard counting the numbers of prisoners that come down the stairs. While they're outside Kronos shapes up in a boxing stance right in front of me and says, "Do you think you're better than me?" I look next to me at Daz, the older guy who is training me in the gym, someone who is actually looking out for me a bit, and unfortunately, he doesn't involve himself, so I respond, "No." I've backed down from a fight, I've shown weakness and even though this guy is five years older and I'm only of adult age by a few months, it's my problem to be dealt with on my own in a one-on-one fight. Now I'm scared.

My older mate Daz, who was training me, was trying to get me to come outside of the unit to the yard, and to the gym, to keep me training, but I was quite afraid of being attacked by Kronos. He even checked how many push ups I was doing each night, trying to keep me from drowning in the sea of unforgiving pressure, intimidation, and potential imminent violence. I am not coping with it though, or with venturing outside of the unit anymore. Daz, who is training me, has an argument with a Sudanese guy and got moved to another unit.

After Daz was moved, Kronos and another inmate, both of whom are on the SA firearms prohibition list, stood metres from my cell door all day every day. I was now alone in my cell and extremely fearful that I was going to be severely assaulted for being the person to have stolen the milk. At meal times when I usually sat at a table with others, everyone moved to other tables so that I ate alone. I had been ostracised, and I was scared for my safety. Fearful that the two males standing by my door, one of which was Kronos, would come into my cell at any time and hurt me beyond words, I began to think of asking to be taken into protective custody. Being taken into protective custody is also looked down on by other prisoners. You are forever labelled a *chicken* and a *dog*.

I was not savvy enough about the prison system's machinations to know I could just break almost any minor rule and I would be taken to the punishment unit where, after my punishment time was finished, and I'd be placed in a different unit from Kronos and therefore free from that dynamic. I saw no other way out. I eventually asked the screws to be moved to protective custody and they told me I had to tell them the name of the person responsible in order to have this occur. I knew this would make me a dog, and that by doing so Id be putting my life on the line. Prisoners are mostly in custody because someone told on them, so in a prison or criminal community, telling on someone for anything was practically a death sentence. Whilst I was still in the office I heard the officers call Kronos over, and tell him what had happened. My heart sank.

Once I was taken to the solitary confinement and informed about what happened to someone in another cell labelled a dog. I was told, "The only safe place for a dog is in a box." Coincidentally Daz was in the cell next to me as this was happening.

There was another lad about my age who had been moved from a unit due to people attempting to stand over him for biscuits and for reporting to the screws. You can do almost anything you want in gaol as long as it's not dobbing. The inmate rules are enforced far more closely and forcefully than those of the screws and administration. Over the next week or so, I and that lad were being moved in and out of that unit, and another longer term punishment unit, where we were being placed with the inmates who had broken the rules of the prison, or gotten into fights and needed punishment; pretty much the worst place to put two eighteen year olds who were seeking segregation and protective custody. During the day, half of the unit was open at a time, and mainstream inmates could walk into our cells. This was fearfully paralysing knowing that if they found out, they would, or at least try and get us.

We were also being moved between the two units, something that didn't happen with anyone else, so it undermined our fake stories about getting punished for breaking the rules. This placed us at great risk. I still remember people coming into our cell and asking us what we were there for, with us having to plead our cases. I remember on one occasion going to get a coffee, walking out into the unit trying not to look at the other inmates who were mainstream, and every one of these actively seeking out and investigating inmates' stories, looking for inconsistencies. They knew exactly how prison procedures worked, and were inclined to find fault so as to weed out undesirables.

One day during our zig-zagging between the short and long-term punishment units, and while in solitary, the screws rushed out of the unit with the sound of drilling, or street work going on close to where we were. I was in such a fragile mental state from the fear and stress of the situation, I really believed there was a riot and that inmates were trying to drill or cut their way into the punishment unit to get to us. I was panic stricken, and almost not functioning due to the constant fear of reprisals for breaking the inmate code.

One night in the long-term punishment unit, myself and the other eighteen-year-old seeking protection, heard thunderous banging on the perspex windows, and the eruption of barking from multiple levels of the prison. It was like a drum roll, the windows make quite a loud sound when struck hard, and the barking so clearly directed at dogs. Our entire unit was doing it but I could hear it coming from the floor below us too. Knowing I'd be accessible to them in the morning was terrifying. I smoked a fifty-gram pouch of White Ox tobacco in under a week, more than double what I normally would due to the stress. During our constant movements between the punishment units I decided I wanted to die. The only method I had in this cell alone was drinking the floor cleaner. I put some in a cup when I was given the cleaning supplies to clean my cell. I drank it thinking it would kill me. I didn't even get sick, but I remember when I spat due to the foul taste, my spit when left on the floor brightened the floor in that spot due to the concentrated product. At some point I also seriously considered putting a lit cigarette in my eye blinding myself as penance for breaking the code, I was that scared. Thank God I didn't do that, as they'd probably bash me anyway.

Having heard about Yatala's protective custody from inmates in the mainstream prison population, I heard many sensational and alarming stories about it. None had been there, so I guess they believed that it was a very nasty place. I was to find out later some of what they said about paedophiles raping people actually did occur from inmates who'd been in protective custody. At the time I was told that child killer and paedophile *Bevan Von Einem, was the head chef in Yatala's protective custody. I was told that he paid people to bring young males to his cell for sex. At the time I believed this, as the other inmates who had more experience in the system seemed to be sure of it.

I was in a lose/lose situation, and decided to take the option of returning to mainstream in the remand centre instead of going to Yatala. I was asked each day by a unit manager what we were doing or had decided to do with regard to our situations, and remember being told, "Good," when I responded that

I wanted to go to Yatala. I'm not sure now why, but it may have been because then I'd be Yatala's problem. When I told the unit manager I wanted to try mainstream again, I was moved to Unit Three. My cell mate there and everyone else seemed to have figured out what had happened to me. Word gets around quick in the prison system, by prisoners from different units communicating at court, the doctor, infirmary, internal mail, and even the linear vertical toilet sewage systems. When the toilet is emptied of water by pushing the toilet brush into the water quickly, this creates an empty pipe which you can talk through between floors of the prison and of course different units. My cellie was on the methadone program and diverted it to sell to other inmates, so in this predicament with no end in sight, I was trying to procure methadone and borrow a syringe the inmates had, to attempt suicide. My first attempt at this failed. I was aware the prisoners were still trying to get me by pressuring my cell mate to bash me in the cell. My cellie spoke about how not to leave marks on his hands and I heard him say, "Why should I have to do it?" I was then moved once more. I think the inmates, or my cellie, personally requested I be taken out of the unit.

I was sent to Unit One when it first re-opened, which was the induction unit, and only new inmates were there, usually for their first week or two. I got the job as the laundry worker and my Sudanese friend was moved there too, probably due to his issues with other inmates. I was happy here. The older inmates knew that if you'd been in Unit One for more than two weeks you were a dog, and so I was ostracised again by some for this, again eating alone after I'd been there only a little while. When I attended court there were people from Unit Four who asked me about what happened and I was given sympathy by some, but I was also made fun of all day and bitch slapped by one of the younger Aboriginal inmates at the direction of an older inmate. I was forced to be in the court van and in the court cells with mainstream prisoners. But that day I got bail as long as I could get two guarantors to assure I'd be at court by risking $3000 each. After getting many phone calls provided free by the unit manager who had got me into Unit One, I convinced two mates to come into the prison and sign the bail papers to get me out. Luckily the guarantors were unspecified, and I didn't have to attend court again to be released.

I was free! I was safe now. I could hide away from my enemies instead of being forcibly available to them. I was in for two months that time; I think it took about five weeks to get out after I first asked for protection. Five crazy scary weeks. I had no home, nowhere to stay, but I didn't care, I was a lot safer than I was in there. It was on New Year's Eve that I was released, which I spent with one of the guarantors I knew who was a high school friend. We attended a house party with his younger brother and his group of friends. Unfortunately, that resulted in my costing them both the bail money because I forgot to attend court as a result of sleeping rough and going in and out of hostels and detox centres. I lost a large group of good mates and good people from my life, and now they wanted to get me for it.

When I was still at the remand centre, I'll never forget how on Christmas Day the Salvation Army brass band cut through the stress for their ten minutes or so. The usually quiet, or angrily loud unit was filled with Christmas music, and it made me feel joy and happiness for that brief time. Even with all of this going on. I liked the biscuits the Salvos gave me; someone cared and was kind to me in this very harsh period of my life.

People wonder why I have anger issues and can become inconsolably angry, and in the past, also potentially very violent over minor perceived disrespect, or injustice. I certainly am not one of those people wondering. I know why.

Joshua asked me to co-operate with him in order to uncover officer corruption against prisoners. I candidly explained that during my two years at Mupulawangk, I saw no such behaviours. Below is Joshua's referring email.

Subject: RE: Let's get 'em!

Give some detailed descriptions of times when you saw any kicks, punches in the ribs or head, maybe a couple DETAILED instances from your officer mates if they're willing, and when I am able to refer you without fucking myself over by revealing who I am I will help you get published :)

When I explained to Joshua that I truly had nothing, he wrote:

Subject: RE: Let's get 'em!
Date: Sat, 23 May 2015 06:51:09

We almost bridged the gap for a second … the invisible barriers that keep crims down and those who didn't get caught up.

And then our exchanges ceased, just like that.

My daughter briefly dated a friend of mine who did time in a maximum security prison as a Correctional Officer. This friend, who is now a police officer, told my daughter that if a crim was non-compliant many a time he would be taken away from camera view and given a few 'once overs'.

As much as I despise crime, and particularly violent crime, I do not condone officers taking the law into their own hands. Again I refer to the American prison system and a truer version of natural justice in which prisoners themselves dish out punishments.

Postscript

One day during visits at Mupulawangk I looked up as a new visitor approached the officer's podium asking for the table number her prisoner would be sitting at. Behind her stood two very familiar faces ... the Italian brother and sister I had looked after in crisis accommodation!

Shocked, I couldn't even feign a smile, and the look I received from them spoke a million words. Whereas before I'd been their carer, today I was the person keeping them from their father.

CHAPTER TWENTY-SIX

EARTH ANGEL

———

Hot Chocolate once sang, 'It Started With a Kiss'. This is how our romance began also.

I've always loved this song. One day, when Adam and I marry, I'll be using this song – *our* song – for the bridal waltz.

* * *

Adam can only be described as my emotional saviour. I hold the most wonderful man in the palm of my hand. Nothing is too difficult, too much, or impossible for Adam, if it means I'm going to be okay. I am always number one in his eyes and nothing nor anyone comes close in the way of replacing *me*. Every single day of Adam's life is devoted to me, no matter where he is, or what he's doing. Adam will call, text, or email daily just to see how I'm going. Every day I feel cocooned, loved, nurtured, and protected; the man I had asked for in Morocco has been delivered to me at last and, looking back on that list I compiled, Adam ticks almost every box. Louise L. Hay would be proud.

Monica was right … I *did* find love in prison. Another 159er was right, too. During a time of deep regret and overwhelming pain over the Denise 'Judas kiss', Colin had said, "The only reason you joined Corrections and found yourself at Mupulawangk Prison, Angelica, was to meet Adam".

The Universe sends you where you need to go and no amount of kicking and screaming on the way there will alter your route.

After I met Adam it took me three years to grow accustomed to feeling loved, and also to the feeling I was actually *worthy* of love. Abuse and despair were not my legacy after all, yet for the length of these three years, I tested Adam to such an extent I decided he was obviously either dumb or desperate to remain by my side, and so to hell with it, I was just going to keep him.

It turned out Adam was just a simple man with simple desires, someone who wished for real love as much as I did. Yet his simplicity was an external domain; inside, Adam's passions ran deep. He too is a man affected by sadness, having lost his younger brother Daniel to an aneurysm when he was only seventeen. Adam struggled with the fact that the last time he saw Daniel they were fighting over a stolen CD.

"We always fought. He was always into my shit," Adam recalled regretfully, a tear running down his cheek.

Adam, despite his stature and stoic expression, is a soft man filled with good will. He doesn't say a lot unless it is out of interest or rebuttal, and yet he yields gigantic pearls of wisdom that often surprise him *and* me. Adam Brewer is pure Metaphysics personified and manifested.

Adam is my Earth Angel and my twin flame, my good karma repaid, and my Divine protector. When at last I allowed Adam's unadulterated love to wash over me, another form of destructive emotion took a hold of my psyche: the fear I might now lose him to someone else.

* * *

The story of how Denise and Fiona, my trusted 159 colleagues and confidantes, destroyed my career as a Correctional Officer, prompting my subsequent resignation from the Department, is described below in a submission made to the then DCS Chief Executive, just as it was first emailed to my then General Manager at Mupulawangk Prison. When the Universe wants you elsewhere it will create situations or herald certain people who will give you that 'extra' push forward. What happened to me at Mupulawangk was not so much a push as a violent shove that left me weaker than I'd ever felt before, simply because I did not see it coming, and because I was not yet ready to go on *my* terms.

Dear Sir,

From the DCS training school where I first met "Mrs Denise Caldwell" and "Ms Fiona Benedetti", I established what I would deem a very strong personal friendship with both subjects. My friendship with Mrs Caldwell was the closest and most intimate. I and Mrs Caldwell shared a great deal of private information about our lives and feelings.

After arriving to Mupulawangk Mrs Caldwell began to display behaviours and opinions which slowly but surely alienated me from continuing a personal friendship with her. Either on the 4th or 5th of July following a tense shift with Mrs Caldwell in the Control Room, I decided I no longer wanted a personal friendship with her and sent Mrs Caldwell a carefully written personal email from my home computer to her personal Hotmail account. In it I explained the decision for this at all times reassuring Mrs Caldwell I meant her no harm, and hoped this situation would not interfere with our working relationship. Mrs Caldwell replied she was sorry this had occurred and that if at any time I wanted to talk about the issues she would still "be there" for me. I replied by thanking her for her consideration.

From that day, Mrs Caldwell's attitude towards me at work became one of total evasion and throughout necessary work based contact, of direct antagonism. I found her behaviour to be in sharp contrast with what Mrs Caldwell had written to me as her reply on Hotmail. At this point I was unaware that Ms Benedetti had decided to instil the same type of evasion upon me, even though at no stage did I have a quarrel or issue with Ms Benedetti. It would appear Ms Benedetti had made a decision to support Mrs Caldwell in any grievance harboured by Mrs Caldwell against me.

During a very difficult work related phone call by me to Mrs Caldwell, I felt that Mrs Caldwell was being deliberately uncordial and so I took it upon myself to remind her I wanted us to interact well at work, quoting: "If you are nice to me, I'll be nice to you, thank you". I then hung up the Sturt Unit phone. Mrs Caldwell found my statement "threatening" and reported me to the Operations Manager, Mr Garfield.

I was approached that same afternoon by Mr Garfield who asked if I'd agree to mediation as the respondent to Mrs Caldwell's complaint against me. Only prior to Management approaching me, I had sent an email via my DCS account to Mrs Caldwell asking her for mediation if indeed we were unable to resolve our issues between the two of us. Mrs Caldwell did not respond to that email and claimed at the subsequent mediation meeting that occurred on the 20th July 2011, she had not read said email. I forwarded the email onto Mr Garfield to prove that I had approached Mrs Caldwell with a resolution prior to her having approached Mr Garfield for one herself.

During mediation I expressed great disappointment in having to bring an issue such as this into the Managerial spotlight. Mrs Caldwell's "official complaint" was, I had spoken about our troubles to fellow staff members both at work, via private email, and on Facebook. These claims were apparently corroborated to Mrs Caldwell by the "alleged" staff members implied, two which she named on this day. The preferred outcome for this mediation was that neither I or Mrs Caldwell speak of our personal issues to staff henceforth. I decidedly maintained the pledge with my partner Adam Brewer, also a staff member, the only exception for reasons that are natural to a romantic relationship.

Over the forthcoming months staff members who were friendly with me began to inform me Mrs Caldwell was not adhering to the mediation agreement. I continued to receive evasive and antagonistic behaviour from Mrs Caldwell and Ms Benedetti. Other staff members who were sympathetic to Mrs Caldwell, began to avoid me as well. The strain of being the obvious target of a smear campaign designed and actioned by Mrs Caldwell and Ms Benedetti, took an inevitable toll on my self-esteem and confidence at work. I then accessed the Employment Assistant Program hoping to gain some emotional self-management tips from the psychologist assigned to me, "Ms Anne Beckett".

The EAP advice was substantial but not enough for me to feel my original self at work. On the 25th of August 2011 I felt particularly morally low and approached the Operations Manager Mr Garfield, inside his office. Mr Garfield advised me "to take control of my feelings". That afternoon after another chain of adverse events, I suffered an emotional breakdown and was sent home by Officer in Charge, Mr Price.

Since that afternoon I have considerably regressed emotionally and contemplate resigning from DCS to avoid further confrontation with Mrs Caldwell and Ms Benedetti as well as from the staff members who seem to be buying into the accusatory propaganda fabricated against me. Cognition and Ms Anne Beckett are aware of these feelings and deliberations. I spoke to my line Manager Mr Collins, during an off duty walk at lunch time regarding my feelings and the possibility of going point five at Mupulawangk. I felt this would help me cope in two ways: I'd have more contact with my son who has Asperger's syndrome and is displaying erratic behaviours in recent times, and less exposure to Mrs Caldwell and Ms Benedetti. As a result, Mr Collins made a submission to yourself as you are surely aware.

On Monday 19th of September I spoke with you about my wish to be employed on a part time basis and about my feelings regarding Mrs Caldwell and Ms Benedetti. Your reply was that you were aware of the latter issues as Mr Garfield had already spoken to you about them. You also informed me you would put forth a recommendation for me to go point five at Mupulawangk. Later that day I attended "Bullying and Harassment" training which I felt ironic given my current circumstances. I paid very careful attention to this training, asking many questions, retaining all of the information given, and read my copy of the SOP 60 legislature.

That afternoon I decided to follow stage one of SOP 60 titled: PERSONAL RESPONSIBILITY TO WORK COLLABORATIVELY AND RESPECTFULLY WITH OTHERS (please refer to document) to attempt solving the problems I was experiencing with Mrs Caldwell and Ms Benedetti directly with them, and prior to resorting to stage 2 of the SOP, MANAGERIAL INTERVENTION. I did this in good faith as I did not want my problems coming under the radar of management once more. I felt that because Mrs Caldwell and Ms Benedetti would make it difficult – even impossible to talk to them face to face, I could approach them by sending an email from work (attached). I waited two days for a response but did not receive one. Furthermore, on the afternoon of 19th September, the body language portrayed towards me by Mrs Caldwell and Ms Benedetti, strongly suggested my email was poorly received. I did not write the emails as threats to Mrs Caldwell or Ms Benedetti, but as an "option" they could take on board and respond to.

On the 20th of September still suffering low morale from my issues with said parties, I took a sick day to ponder what to do with my situation at work on all fronts. I decided I was not given a proper opportunity to relate to Mrs Caldwell how the disintegration of our personal friendship had affected me and proceeded to write her a lengthy personal email sent from my private Hotmail account to Mrs Caldwell's private Hotmail account. In this email I again put forward an opportunity for her and Ms Benedetti to resolve our issues at a personal level.

Prior to commencement of duties on the morning of the 21st, I asked Ms Benedetti if she had read the email dated the 19th September. Ms Benedetti ignored me and proceeded inside her office within the Visits Centre. I then decided to send Ms Benedetti the final email (enclosed) from my DCS account, explaining the corporate ramifications of a Managerial Intervention as per SOP 60.

At 09.25 that morning Mr Garfield and OPS3 Mr Hulme, approached me inside Angas Unit. After closing the door of the Unit Office, both informed me I would be "escorted" to Admits and Health for a discussion about the inappropriate use of workplace email. I was asked to bring a support person given the nature of the matter. Ms Tanya Collins, my Angas Unit offsider on this day, volunteered, and I accepted her support. I was then escorted by Mr Garfield and Mr Hulme to Admits and Health. I noticed that two additional OPS3 Officers stood outside Angas Unit. This unnecessary hypervigilance caused me to feel extreme humiliation as I was marched out past clients and fellow officers alike. I wish to ascertain without a single misgiving that at no given moment was I a threat to the good running order of the institution.

Arriving inside Admits and Health, I was briefed by Mr Garfield in relation to the workplace emails, including the one sent to Mrs Caldwell over my private home computer. Mr Garfield used a spirited and accusatory tone with me, telling me what I had "done" constituted with the Bullying and Harassment guidelines set by the Department. Mr Garfield then stated I was being relieved of my duties effective immediately pending an investigation. Furthermore, he informed me he was concerned with my mental status and could therefore not allow me to continue my shift out of concern for the good running order of the institution.

I tried to argue my case with Mr Garfield stating I was merely responding to Bullying and Harassment from Mrs Caldwell and Ms Benedetti and not the reverse, but Mr Garfield became more animated stating that what he read in my emails proved it was I who was threatening and harassing Mrs Caldwell and Ms Benedetti with the parties suffering "great distress" as a result of my actions. Mr Garfield then demanded I hand over my keys and radio and that Mr Hulme would escort me to Angas Unit to collect my belongings. I was further directed to wait inside the Gatehouse until my partner Adam Brewer was relieved of his duties in order to transport me home given we had travelled into work together, and I had no other means of transport back.

I now feel it is my right to file an official complaint of Harassment and Bullying according to SOP 60 against Mrs Caldwell, Ms Benedetti, and another against Mr Garfield, given the unfair and biased treatment dispensed by him in this case as well as for the personal humiliation this incident has caused me.

Regards,

Angelica T.

* * *

I resigned from the Department on 27 September 2011. It was Alycia's birthday, and it was possibly one of the biggest mistakes of my life. The career I'd set upon was not to be, and the pride I felt in my heart mere illusion. Mr Garfield, a man I trusted, the manager who'd once told me he hoped I would not leave Corrections because I was a good officer, took my confidence and wiped his greasy, pill popping backside with it.

All was not yet lost. On the upside, it was not hard getting into the Magill Training Centre this time around. I wrote the centre a simple email from Mupulawangk weeks before my resignation and in October I began doing shifts as a Casual Youth Support Worker. With my Sydney experience and a Certificate IV in Youth Work (Juvenile Justice) as well as Corrections exposure, I was more than qualified and employees at the Centre were leaving in droves. It was an optimum time for me to come on board.

The institution was old and run-down but operationally it seemed similar to the Sydney 'juves' I had worked in. The kids too were not so different, maybe less violent – at first that is. From the outset, the youth workers seemed lovely, just as they had been at Juniperina.

I finally achieved what I'd set out to do in New South Wales three years before, and although hired as a Casual I received more than enough shifts at the Centre. Nevertheless, the hatred and resentment I harboured for Denise, Fiona, Mr Garfield, and the spineless mob who'd supported them or hitherto kept silent about their behaviour, began to consume me at my deepest core level. Add to the mix the fact that Valeria had ostracised me emotionally some months before over some innocuous email repartee, and my soul was quickly heading for hell, even with Adam's undivided support.

The problem with emails is a lack of personalised nuance and yet, being a good writer, I thought I had injected enough of that. Where my cousin Valeria was concerned, I think the email reaction was a crutch. There were distinct feelings she would not disclose to me and I had to wonder whether they had anything to do with that Christmas Day incident when Valeria was just an infant. Because I truly loved my cousin, because she was the sister I never had, and because she is a blood relative, her ostracising felt exceptionally brutal.

Insofar as 'Mupulawangk' and 'Murray Bridge' went, these names became synonymous with everything I detested about society and it hurt like hell that my Adam was still a part of the place. I began to unfairly crucify Adam for not leaving Mupulawangk alongside me.

"Why can't you just transfer to Yatala? A big man like you would be welcomed there. How can you work side by side with people who've destroyed me?"

At times my aggression levels and pungent demands were so intense, I pushed Adam to tears. This self-centred cruelty and injustice was manifesting because *I* was unable to move on. These issues were *my* stuff not Adam's, but feeling manically impotent, I was completely blind to Adam's personal needs, even blaming *him* for my current state of mind.

Working at the Magill Training Centre alleviated some of the increased anxiety that sprang from the lack of closure with Corrections. Post resignation I continued to pursue the bullying and harassment claim against Denise and Fiona, but was bluntly shunned by the Department. Because I was no longer employed by them my claim was now considered null and void. Denise was free to laugh behind my back and claim absolute victory. Not a day went by where I did not escape into murderous fantasy scenarios involving my most bitter of enemies. The hatred I felt for Denise was so intense I didn't know how I'd react if ever I saw her or one of her cronies on the street. I needed help.

As with any job and regardless of qualifications or experience, I still had to prove myself on the floor before gaining the trust of new colleagues. There were one or two women in the girls' unit, Unit Five, who decided to give me a hard time, but I had made a decision to do something I've never been able to achieve before: I ignored them. Additionally, I did not disclose too much about myself or act as friendly as is usual for my personality type. This time around, to achieve a different result I had to *be* different; I could not bear another Juniperina and Mupulawangk stand-over situation.

At the training centre I learnt to play Rummikub with a seventeen-year-old boy who had me wondering how such a lovely, intelligent, funny young man found himself in custody. I asked noone but found out via our omniscient media: Travis had sliced open the throat of an eighty-seven-year-old woman with a blunt knife, as part of an 'esoteric' ritual. I was in deep shock and could not manage my feelings, something that has rarely happened to me throughout my community services career. I really liked Travis and felt we had a marked connection, but then this is what sociopaths are good at, creating an illusion.

Then there was the eighteen-year-old girl whose four-month old baby daughter was found dead in her flat. For an entire week the tiny fractured and bruised body lay in hiding. Something told me the petite waif wasn't entirely responsible for her baby's murder, yet her story was far more complicated than it seemed at first glance. By the time I left Magill in March 2012, 'Sasha' was awaiting sentencing. Before my departure she had put a slip into the 'resident suggestion box' informing management I was one of the best youth workers in the place. Whether Sasha was guilty of direct abuse or not, she was definitely guilty of neglect and failing to report her daughter's death, but then she had a perfectly credible excuse for it – battered wife syndrome. Less credible was the subsequent series of coincidences, ones even more bizarre than having met Zelda's sister in South Australia. During a rather intimate conversation, Sasha gave me the name of her daughter's father.

Nonchalantly I replied, "I used to know someone by that surname in high school."

"What high school did you go to Angelica?" Sasha asked.

"Cabramatta High School in Sydney; one of the girls in my year had the same surname."

Sasha's eyes lit up wide. "Was her name Leah?"

"Yes it was. Don't tell me, your boyfriend is her son?"

And indeed he was. *Fuck me!* What are the chances?

As in New South Wales, Indigenous children in this detention centre were over represented. Inside the gym old murals bore the names of 'kids' I had met at Mupulawangk. Crime and neglect is generational and the recidivist rate for 'juve' and prison inmates stands at around 85 percent. Rehabilitation post incarceration is virtually non-existent. Centrelink gives released prisoners a 'starter pack' and off they go, back to the same people they committed offences with, only now the former inmates are a little more 'crime savvy'.

Despite some truly awful crimes and the knowledge that most *would* re-offend, I felt great affection for these wayward children. 'Juve' work continued to be my first and only love, a job I was a natural at. I did not want a manager's position, I did not even want to be a unit co-ordinator anymore, I was happy just being here lending a much needed hand. Unlike their adult peers, juvenile offenders are still malleable, under the guidance of good staff. With kids you are not afforded the luxury of coffees and office gossip ad nauseam. On shift you are always on the lookout for pending disaster, but at the end of that day a simple thank you or the promise of good behaviour makes all the hard work worthwhile.

Whether my maternal streak shone through or the kids were merely amused by me, the moment I'd appear through the unit doors they'd drop whatever they were doing and run up to me, sometimes knocking me to the ground with their enthusiasm. I certainly enjoyed every minute of the fuss and genuine love bestowed on me, but also believed that I made some tangible difference in the children's lives. At the end of the day if only *one* child believed the world wasn't against him because *one* person had treated him differently, it was a good day's work.

* * *

Alas, it was not to be. My return to juve was short lived. The Universe had other plans for me:

DEPARTMENT FOR XXXX TRIBUNAL SUBMISSION
To Whom This May Concern,

Dear Sir/Madam,

My name is Angelica T. I am presenting a written external review submission and I thank you for hearing my case.

In September 2011 I made contact with the Magill Training Centre re. possible employment opportunities as a Youth Worker. On the 23rd of September 2011, I emailed a resume of my experience to the Manager, Marcus Strathfield. Mr Strathfield responded on the 26/09/2011 informing me that he and the Training Officer Mr Garry Bruce were exploring the minimum standards required for me to commence work as a casual or full-time employee within the centre. Following this, I was granted an interview with Mr Bruce. Directly post interview I was placed on a three-week on-the-job training roster at the Magill Training Centre in Woodforde. I received supplementary training by Mr Bruce as well as other location specific training such as Mandatory Reporting, First Aid, Restraint and Conflict Resolution practices. The additional training coupled with my own experience, was then considered sufficient to be granted a contract as a Youth Support Worker at the Magill Training Centre. The decision to take me on board also assisted the centre which was experiencing significant staff shortages. My contract was due to expire on 3/12/2011, but was later extended to 23/03/12 by the then General Manager.

At no stage during my employment at the Magill TC did I receive any negative feedback from Management regarding my performance. On the contrary, the feedback I received was complimentary and supportive. Towards the end of my extended contract, I was informed by Mr Strathfield and his Business Manager that in order for me to maintain ongoing employment I was required to apply for the next intake of new employees. I found this rather strange as I was initially given the impression I had satisfied the standards referred to in Mr Strathfield's email of 26/09/2011. Querying this, Mr Strathfield and his business partner both assured me that the application process was merely "a formality" to satisfy bureaucratic obligations. Accordingly, I submitted my application and was subsequently interviewed by Mr Strathfield, the Operations Supervisor for the Cavan Training Centre, Ms. Diana Jindabyne, a Unit Manager at the Magill Training Centre, and a Senior Psychologist who was coincidentally one of my lecturers during the 2009 Correctional training course at a maximum security prison name provided).

When much to my disbelief I received an official email stating my interview had placed me in the "unsuccessful" quota, I immediately called Mr Strathfield on his work mobile and was informed my application had indeed been declared unsuccessful on the grounds my interview answers placed too much emphasis on security and as such, did not fit with the new training centre's philosophies and business model. Mr Strathfield further added that he envisaged this news might upset me and that he was willing to meet with me face to face to discuss the matter in more detail.

On the 23rd of March 2012 I lodged a request for an Internal Review into the Department's decision. On the 22nd of May 2012 I received an email from HR Consultant Tamara Merchant stating the said Review supported the Department's original decision. The rationale supporting it stated the twenty-one other successful applicants had demonstrated greater suitability to the position than I. It is my contention that this department has treated me unfairly and unjustly for the following reasons:

Prior to working with DXXX I had four years Juvenile Justice training and experience as a Senior Youth Worker in New South Wales, working in three Juvenile Justice Centres. The third Centre where I settled, was the Juniperina Juvenile Justice Centre in Lidcombe, a forty-five bed facility for female offenders aged ten to twenty-one. Here I was placed in the Boronia High Needs Unit on a Section 27, a threemonth ongoing contract which was consistently renewed given my outstanding level of work with detainees. I spent three years full-time within this unit. During this period, I was seconded over two months into a support home for homeless teenage mothers and their children under the jurisdiction of the NSW Department of Community Services, as a Caseworker. When I relocated to South Australia for family reasons, I worked for XXX Baptist SA, and Life Without Barriers as a Youth Worker with children Under the Guardianship of the Minister until I was accepted into the SA Department for Correctional Services where I graduated as a Correctional Officer and spent two years at Mupulawangk Prison, a 327 bed, medium security gaol for adult male offenders. I am currently working part-time with disabled youth and adults in the Barossa Valley, having been accepted into this specialised position purely on other community service qualifications merit. A great proportion of my clients here have been seriously abused and come under the category of Persons at Risk.

I hold a Certificate IV in Youth Work (Juvenile Justice) among other child protection related qualifications, all of which are enclosed. This experience was recognised at the original interview held at the Magill TC to such an extent, I was given immediate employment bypassing a six-week training course compulsory for new staff. My general manager was so impressed with my work he in fact extended the original three-month "probationary" contract. At no stage during my employment at the Magill TC did any managerial personnel question my overall performance; the only feedback received, inclusive of floor staff's, was consistently of a positive nature. I maintained a good rapport with all unit residents, but particularly within the girls' unit given my time at the Juniperina JJC in New South Wales. I was called in for work almost daily and often placed on a roster to secure shifts in advance. Over six months I worked a total of seventy-six shifts which included numerous off site escorts and hospital watches.

I find it difficult to comprehend Ms. Tamara Merchant's declaration that twenty-one new applicants, most devoid of previous experience in Juvenile Justice Practices, were able to demonstrate superior skills than I. Furthermore, it has been brought to my attention that six of these "superior" candidates dropped out of the job very early in the piece. Why then was I not "bumped up" into one of their positions as Number "twenty-two" on this socalled "merit list"? I am also aware that the Adelaide Youth Training Centre is continually re-hiring. Does this not suggest that the "preferred" candidates where in fact not able to cope with what is a highly demanding job, one I was very happy in and capable of?

During my sixmonth stint at the Magill TC my abilities and expertise were adequately demonstrated "on the job", not just verbally as one does in an interview. I also find it unacceptable that the interviewing panel did not bother to contact any of my referees, one of them my former Boronia Unit Co-ordinator who is now an Australian Federal Police Officer.

I find Mr Strathfield's statement, "my interview answers focused too much on security", confounding. Only weeks earlier, a mass escape of residents occurred from the Cavan Training Centre. An ensuing investigation strongly criticised the Department's lack of commitment to security and recommended a range of security upgrades and training for both centres. For the Manager of a Training Centre to criticise a staff member for being "overly security conscious" is beyond belief and smacks of "covert bureaucratic agenda". I would like to point out that two of the interviewing panellists, Ms. Jindabyne and the Senior Psychologist, are both former DCS staff, so how can I therefore be seen as "too security minded" when half my interview panel are themselves former Corrections staff – the antithesis of non-security? Is this not hypocritical and a basic conflict of interest?

The primary scenario question posed during the interview was one that required a security based answer, one I answered according to Departmental procedure. I also added the "desired" interpersonal solution to this scenario, but it would seem this component has been omitted from the panel's final decision. I am also of the opinion the internal review was biased and flawed. At no stage during the process was I interviewed or given the opportunity to present any more information than was on my original request for an internal review form. Consequently, I was not given the opportunity to comment on all the information given to the review Officer. In addition, DXXX took significantly longer than the stipulated twenty-one days to make a review decision. From the day I submitted the application for Internal Review on the 23rd of March 2012, to the Grievance Review hearing date of the 24th of October 2012, this process has taken the Department seven months to acknowledge and action.

I wish to conclude my submission on the conviction that I have not been given a justifiable reason as to why I was found unsuccessful for a permanent OPS2 position at the then Magill Training Centre, which is why I have asked for a further review on the matter. If I am successful at the 24th of October hearing, I am asking to be assigned to the next advertised OPS2 position in order to resume work as a qualified Youth Support Worker, bypassing the compulsory six-week training course given the stated qualifications and extensive "on the job" experience I possess. I am however happy to be updated/trained in any new policies and procedures that have been issued since the end of my contract dated the 23rd of March 2012. Should this occur, I will not take further action against the Department.

Thank you and Sincerely,

ANGELICA T.

Under the initiative of one of Magill Training Centre's senior staff, Chris Devries, a surprise supporter given I barely spoke to him for the six months I was at the centre, almost all the staff signed a petition demanding my immediate re-instatement. The Public Service Association jumped on board at Chris's request, and for seven long months I believed I was going to win. Then, just before 24 October, the tribunal hearing date, and after numerous PSA representative swaps, I was told by the last assigned representative he would only be present at the hearing as a support person, not a speaker. Once again I was left in visceral shock.

In Adam's arms I cried the entire night and decided to withdraw my submission altogether. With an already tortured state of mind why would I front up to what was essentially a court room, and stand there completely alone with most bureaucratic odds stacked against me? I was only setting myself up for more pain and I'd had enough of that. There was no doubt in my mind now I was born cursed, that everything I'd touch would turned to sand – filthy, murky, corrupt sand. My beautiful, lateral minded, realist boyfriend, agreed my lack of 'luck' was, at best, confounding. On that day I also vowed never to trust or join another union.

I had no vocational choices than to return to crisis accommodation, a job I hated, and this was because with every other job I applied for I failed to get a response. A casual position with Australian Customs had given me the opportunity to train with them, but Adelaide Airport was over an hour from Springton with morning shifts starting at 4 o'clock. It would not prove a sustainable position.

I began to convince myself that having Corrections on my resume was the reason for my alienation from the non-community services workforce. Corrections is the lowest rung of law enforcement, with Correctional Officers perceived as major assholes – and many are indeed that; I sincerely don't know how the better half survive in such a toxic environment ... I guess it's a case of survival of the bravest.

My mind was growing more damaged by the day. The blows Valeria, Denise, Fiona, and now DXXX had dealt me, were becoming enmeshed with my ability to cope on a daily basis. As far as my psyche was concerned, Denise was responsible, via osmosis, for this latest mishap as well. Anything that went south for me now was *her* fault. I needed someone to blame and she had started the ball rolling back in July 2011. I lay awake for nights on end watching how in my mind's eye Denise lay dying slowly and in agony by my own hand. I became wholly obsessed with revenge and retribution and started to notice that certain friends, both electronic and real, were now giving me a wider berth.

My Facebook posts were increasingly more aggressive and acrimonious, and people were blocking or deleting me left, right, and centre. Eventually my cousin Bianca followed her sister into the cold war against me and this meant I was seeing less of Rodolfo and his fiancée as a result. I was having trouble doing simple things like taking a shower, I cried at the drop of a hat, my bulimic habits resurfaced and I piled on more weight. My libido disappeared, and every day I entertained ways of ending my life. Yet throughout this personal mayhem, one person remained constant and firmly by me – Adam – always Adam. As is the Biblical meaning of his name, Adam was my 'first man', my first and my *only*.

After reading (on the internet) reports of situations similar to what was happening to me, I self-diagnosed with post-traumatic stress and anxiety disorders. It didn't make sense; I'd always been so strong and elastic and now that I did not need to look for love anymore, why *wasn't* I coping?

I became overly sanctimonious, telling anyone who'd listen for a moment or two how throughout my life I tried so hard to make things work, to honour others, to love, to be co-operative, and to give of me as much as I could, yet nothing worked out and noone was really listening, bar Adam. Despair was promptly replaced by deepest hatred, not just for Denise, but everything and everyone. Coming to South Australia and leaving everything I knew, all of my childhood friends and my beloved job, had been a huge mistake. Originally I came over to be with my cousins and now look what they were doing to me? I even began hating my spiritual beliefs because they told me I had 'chosen' all of this. Okay, say I had, how do I now 'unchoose' it? I mean, what the fuck did the Universe want of me?

* * *

It was May 2012, and Kristen was turning twenty-one, so we drove to Sydney for this important occasion. Because of my decision to come to South Australia I'd missed countless birthdays, and I refused to miss my little yellow baby's big milestone.

On 4 May Adam, Alycia and I took the train to Town Hall for a window shopping spree. I have always enjoyed the Sydney CBD; had I been a wealthy person who could afford a life on the 'right side' of Sydney, I probably would not have moved interstate.

Alycia and Adam snuck into a jewellery shop situated on the top floor of the majestic Queen Victoria Building, making a dismal attempt at diverting my attention to another part of the high class shopping hub. Moi Moi Fine Jewellery, as the shop was called, was where I'd seen a gorgeous ring I had dubbed 'my engagement ring' just in case one day Adam wanted to get hitched to a mad woman. Could it be at all possible Adam was buying my engagement ring right now? Why did this angelic man want to be tied to a woman who was falling deeper into the rabbit hole by the millisecond? Maybe he was buying a friendship ring, to keep me feeling secure.

Exiting the Queen Victoria Building we trailed towards Hyde Park, as Alycia wished to take some photographs there. Alycia was establishing herself as a savvy and talented photographer, and twentyfive years previously Hyde Park had been the backdrop for my marriage to her father.

"You two go over there!" Alycia waved. "I want some shots of this and that."

I know my daughter and I know when she's up to something.

Then, almost as quickly as a gust of wind sneaks through an opened window, I watched my beautiful angel drop on bended knee, holding up a little black box in his hand, which he pointed at me. Oh My God it was really *happening*.

"Adel Angelica T.," Adam muttered, choking back tears, "will you marry me?"

My tears were captured by Alycia's all-knowing camera lens as I accepted onto a trembling finger the huge triangular moissanite diamond I had hinted at. I looked into my angel's eyes and screamed out the most tremendous "*YES!*"

The sun over a thousand deserts began to set as SEVENTY THOUSAND CAMELS rode, gilded and perfumed, into my tired old life. *Good things come to those who wait* they say and I sure waited long and hard, although the beauty and emotion carried by this moment, would remain etched in my mind forever, no matter what terrors still lay ahead for me. In this moment, I was absorbed by a shimmering matrix that exonerated time and space for their crimes against me.

I was ready to become a bride again ... no, not again ... for the *first* time.

CHAPTER TWENTY-SEVEN

HORIZONS FORGED FROM AGONY

———

O n 8 May 2012, four days after Adam asked me to marry him, we found Adam's father, Alan, dead inside his Mount Barker unit.

Alan had been lying flat on his face for eight hours after a final, massive heart attack; he was only sixty-one years old. He suffered his first major attack aged fifty and was fitted with a pacemaker which appeared to have operational issues.

Adam and I became suspicious and called his cardiologist after numerous calls to Alan's mobile which he did not answer, something uncharacteristic of Alan. The cardiologist then informed us Alan had also missed a critical appointment on this day.

Upon entering Alan's unit at around 8.30 in the evening, Adam spotted Alan's body in the spare room. I pushed my fiancé out of the way to shield his senses from witnessing more. I had dealt with death a couple of times and could handle things on my own. I felt devastated for Adam but a part of me was angry with *Alan*. I was certain he hadn't approved of my relationship with his eldest son, just like many of Adam's friends, and decided his cardio myopathy was a spiritual act of protest.

A few days after his passing, I distinctly felt Alan inside our home and became somewhat unsettled by this. I had assisted the funeral duo sent to collect Alan's body because, like his son, Alan was a giant of a man who could not be loaded onto the stretcher unaided, and there was no way I was going to allow Adam to see his father in the condition he died in. Eventually the heavy feeling of Alan's presence lifted and I put it down to him having found his way into the heavenly spheres. But perhaps it wasn't Alan's transition into Heaven that cleared the air in our home; perhaps it was Alan's realisation that it *was* okay for me to become Adam's new life companion – or perhaps his younger son Daniel had helped Alan understand a few things he may have ignored during life. Either way I was glad he was elsewhere and in peace.

For three more months I worked in crisis accommodation for a relatively new company providing nursing and community care. My permanent charges were a family of four children whose mother had mental health issues. At long last, systematic abuse was not an issue. Eventually the two elder girls, one of them a shithead of a kid, were returned to their mother and for three blissful weeks I looked after the younger two: Liam, who had just turned twelve months old, and two-year-old Bethany. Liam stole my heart completely, just as Elizabeth had three years ago in Murray Bridge. I wanted to foster Liam so badly but his exit into a 'good' family had already been planned, and what was more, I wouldn't have had the heart to separate him from Bethany ... *the system* took care of that.

I still think of Liam, my little fellow Taurean, and wonder how he is faring. He was only days from taking his first steps when on my last shift with him I bid him goodbye. Liam was always smiling; he'd crawl sideways like a crab after you at lightning speed, but on this particularly sad afternoon he was sick with the flu and my tearful cuddles were not met with the habitual big chuckles. I had to wonder if the sickness sobs were Liam's unspoken way of saying goodbye.

I applied for a job at Nuriootpa, in the heart of the Barossa Valley, a place I loved. I couldn't believe I was actually doing this because the position was all about working with disabled adults, something I had resisted my entire life due to the personal prejudices instilled in me by Piero, Sally and, to a much lesser degree, even by my own son. At this point in my life vocational opportunities were running out due to the blatant 'blacklisting' of me by DCS and DXXX.

Adelaide had been unkind to me workwise and I could not understand it. What was the Universe trying to tell me now? If I had to go to Mupulawangk to meet the love of my life, why was I now being directed into an industry I thought I would abhor? I mourned the death of my career in Youth Justice; I would never again find a job that fulfilled me in the same way and I could kiss any career notions goodbye too; at forty-seven years old how would I begin again, doing what, and who'd take me?

At the same time, I was still struggling with my mind; this struggle was no longer a mere hypothesis but a very real concern. I was reaching lows I did not know existed. The years of pain had burrowed into my core, morphing it into organic mental illness. Adam was now enduring even more but continued to carry the load evenly and at times almost joyfully. I could not for the life of me understand why or how he did this. Where did all this love come from and why did I not meet Adam sooner? Had I, I may not have reached complete madness, and boy was I feeling it creep into my being now. I realised I had to begin fixing myself, if not for me then for Adam.

My friend Angela, the same one who saw us play Shithead inside the Case Management Co-ordinator's office at Mupulawangk back in November 2009, referred me to her hormone specialist. Adam located a psychologist who specialised in post-traumatic stress disorder and acceptance and commitment therapy. With our wedding date set for 4 August 2013, I needed to get into tiptop condition for my new title of Mrs Angelica Brewer. As far as I was concerned – and despite appearances – the marriage was not about Adam earning me but about me *deserving* Adam.

I got the job at Barossa Enterprises, working in respite care with four sets of intellectually and physically disabled clients. The position was as an 'on-call' casual but my team leader managed to keep my head above water with as many shifts as she could provide. A couple of the clients confirmed my personal prejudices but the others were gentle, fun souls who were grateful for any attention and care they received. I soon discovered that most people with a disability expect very little yet give out a lot. At the end of the day I was forced to accept that the Universe gives you what you need – not what you want – yet I still did not understand how I found myself here.

At home, however, dealing with a disability was becoming a serious problem however. Not too long after Adam and I announced our engagement we noticed a distinct change in Edan's behaviour. Edan developed repetitive and obsessive compulsive traits that were far more insidious in nature than the annoying routines he'd displayed as a younger boy in New South Wales. It appeared that the moment Edan realised Adam was not just another passing ship like Nick, Eser, or Jason, something short-circuited inside his mind. The relentless Tourette's-like noises and tics became intolerable, and then out of the blue Edan declared he wanted to live in Sydney with his father. Again I found myself in complete shock. Never in my wildest dreams did I expect Edan to leave me. I begged Edan to reconsider. He was well set up here in South Australia: he had a fantastic school life with a best friend in 'Special Ed' and a teacher who doted on him; also, he held down a little job on Saturdays at the Springton General Store and enjoyed a rather cushy life with me and Adam within the kind of environment he had always longed for.

A clairvoyant I'd seen had assured me I would be sending Edan to Sydney in spite of my determination not to. She added that Kristen would not be moving back to Adelaide in spite of her promise to, that I was marrying 'an awesome man' but had to get a grip on my emotions or I'd never truly know happiness with him. *If* I accepted the plan the Universe had in mind for me I'd be okay … everyone else around me was intrinsically okay, only *I* continued to live in the past and suffered for doing so.

Three birthdays ago Kristen had bought me *Eckhart Tolle's *The Power of Now* but I did not touch it. Timing and destiny yield perfect moments however, and the book finally found its way into my hands. The chapter that drew me in the most was about something called the 'pain-body', and boy did it apply to me!

* * *

Adam, forever my servant, asked for a transfer to the Adelaide Remand Centre in order to somewhat alleviate the Mupulawangk pain-body. He began work there in November 2012 and consequently I immediately felt a whole lot better. I hoped I had not created unnecessary drama for my beautiful man by forcing him into a position he may not have desired. As it turned out though, Adam was welcomed aboard and, characteristic of my gentle giant, he fell into his new position happily and easily.

Now that my precious children had chosen lives elsewhere, I decided my five-bedroom house in Springton was too large. I desperately wanted to commemorate married life by living in a home that was significantly both mine *and* Adam's. Yes, it was still all about me, much as with my mother had always been all about her. I maintained my victim status twenty-two out of the twenty-four hours in a day, validating the reading I'd received from the Dulwich clairvoyant. My lessons were not yet learnt.

On 11 November, Remembrance Day, I put my beautiful house up for sale and two days before Christmas Day my precious son boarded a plane to Sydney. Everything I knew so well and loved was coming to an end. The pain caused to me by Edan's decision was beyond words. I cried helplessly leading up to the day, yet everyone who cared for me told me it was for the better, that this was my and Adam's time and that I'd done my bit for Edan. It was Rhys's turn to raise his difficult child. Edan's adverse behaviour had escalated to the point where he was no longer communicating with any of us. Perhaps those who *did* care were right.

Just before he walked out of my front door, Edan looked directly into my eyes and stated in his normal voice – one I rarely heard since he'd started masking it with a deep Mr Bean type gruffness – "I'll be back for the holidays Mum. You will be alright and I love you."

Edan rarely told me he loved me without prompting. The next day, with eyes swollen to the size of golf balls, I experienced an epiphany I decided to share with all my Facebook friends:

Ok so I woke up this morning feeling much better. I rang Kristen and spoke to Edan and he is being as silly as ever. Still can't bring myself to go into his room, but that time will come soon enough. IT'S ME TIME! Maybe that's what the Universe is trying to tell me? Or maybe another phase of my life is about to begin which does not accommodate Edan. I don't know. Let's see.

The next nine months were going to be tough, I could feel this in my waters. Forty kilos of accumulated anger to shift before the big day, the sale of my house once the right buyer came along, last minute wedding preparations, psyche and hormone specialist appointments, and holiday visits from my darling children! I also needed to begin work on the Asperger's book Edan and I had in the pipeline, while still attempting to complete this one. Add to the mix work within the many boundaries of my new profession and learning how to separate from my pain-body a step at a time, and 2013 promised to be *huge*. Did I truly have time for more tears?

I was determined to shine as brightly as I could, to muster my inner light, certain I'd never need anyone's approval except my own. I would stand firmly within my Power and claim all of Paradise. I was never in the 'popular' group anyhow; the only reason people knew who I was is because I stood out for reasons I did not recognise. Alas, during my life, I had cast pearls before swine and it was high time I ceased being a people pleaser and learnt to please myself first.

But second to *I* would come the one person who *truly* loved me unconditionally, my beautiful husband to be, and, if indeed there was anything left following 'us', everyone else in order of merit.

Namasthae.

* * *

Course 159 had, it seemed, been cursed.

Alongside me, almost half of my fellow Correctional Officer Trainees' lives were turned upside down, either by their own hand or by outside forces. Of these Matt was the worst affected, on various levels.

During a Code Yellow response Matt had turned, pounced out of his seat, and suffered a prolapsed disc of the lower back which almost paralysed him and rendered him unable to continue working. His WorkCover claim was later cancelled and his name returned to the roster to resume normal duties regardless of the fact that Matt could not drive his car because sitting for more than fifteen minutes at a time was unbearable. Matt soon became seriously depressed and dependent on painkillers.

An MRI disclosed the extent of Matt's injury, with Matt demanding restitution from the Department which of course was declined when it claimed that Matt had falsified documents during enrolment. The Department implied Matt's injury was pre-existent, regardless of MRI results which unequivocally showed it was not. Here stood a young, fit, enthusiastic and capable man, someone who had given so much to the Department during a brief period of service, now being called an outright liar in the midst of a medical crisis with no end in sight.

Outraged and terribly sad for 'Welshy', as he was affectionately called because of his accent and background, I put together a fundraiser that asked our fellow officers to dig deep financially. Matt's young family was devastated by the incident. His beautiful wife worked only two days a week and their second child had health issues of his own. Welshy was a popular guy by anyone's standard and together with a contribution from the Welfare Fund, Adam and I presented Matt with sufficient cash to keep him going for a few more weeks. Two years after that fateful Code Yellow response injury, Matt and the Department settled out of court but the scars the incident had left behind were not compensable. Today Welshy has defied all odds by becoming an armed security guard, a story that even made the evening TV news, and together with his wife has joined the world of competitive boxing.

Ashley, Frank, Jason and Monica, Amelia, Esmeralda and Darren, all suffered break-ups of long-term relationships. Darren's in particular was uniquely brutal and shocking.

Jeremiah was sacked for asking John Bunting, notorious as the ringleader of the Snowtown murders, for his autograph. Jennifer has since passed away, for undisclosed reasons; she was only fifty-six years old. Melissa lost her mother to cancer, her stepbrother committed suicide, her ex-husband attempted to take her children from her, and every man she dated was only interested in one thing. Jason was forced out of the job by Monica, the mother of his children, on the pretext the kids needed a parent at home and that Monica was the better officer. The truth behind Monica's reasoning, however, was far less honourable. Monica had begun a salacious affair with a married fellow officer, which turned the Adelaide Women's Prison upside down. Jason is currently single and a Youth Officer working at the Adelaide Training Centre, on my recommendation. The detention centre was formerly known as the Cavan Training Centre and it is where the Magill Training Centre transferred to when Woodforde closed down, not long after my unfair dismissal and failed tribunal hearing.

Esmeralda, the Kiwi Gemini who chewed my ear off on that first look into prison life, took an astounding two years to complete her Workplace Assessment Guide and was eventually stood down for incompetence. She is now a local bus driver. Anton, the more distinctive member of our course and our class captain, had been called to Head Office for brazenly inviting Prime Minister Kevin Rudd to our graduation. He was finally stood down for 'lack of commitment to the roster' and I am certain Denise had a lot to do with this too, just as she had with Colin and me. Denise, the most poisonous bitch I've ever known (which is saying something), managed to completely turn the prison against us. I never did discover any reasons why Denise turned out to be such a cunt, but years later one of the other Mupulawangk ladies I've remained friends with, Ruth, informed me that Denise's mother, the well-respected officer at Mupulawangk, warned staff prior to her retirement to *watch their backs* because her daughter was *pure evil*. This was almost good enough for me.

Today more than half of my fellow 159 course mates are no longer in the job. Like Adam, Colin (one reason *I* am no longer in the job) transferred to the Adelaide Remand Centre. Colin broke my heart, adding to a long list of confidantes who destroyed my trust in the human race, when he stopped calling and seeing me without offering a reason. Along with many other virtues, it appears loyalty has lost all meaning nowadays.

Darren joined South Australia Police, came first in his course, then married a beautiful teacher from the Barossa. He announced the birth of his first child in January 2016; a classic example of a phoenix rising from the ashes. He now has a second daughter.

The YLP training room is a museum of course plaques, sporting photographs and the names of course participants. Ours is ten times the size of the others (courtesy of the author). It hangs as a prototype for future lecturers in terms of 'what is not acceptable as alma mater material'. In a bizarre way I get a last laugh there!

Unfortunately, and unfairly the two people who created so much mayhem remain at Mupulawangk, all comfortable, happy, and catered for by a group of slimy and spineless 'officers' who in my opinion make the prisoners look like choirboys. Fiona has since married an Indigenous fellow officer. She fell out with Denise much as she had first begun, and according to the three friends I still have there, refers to Denise as a 'fucking moll'. So much for loyalty among who I consider to be the *real* criminals.

In the bitter end I was none other than a disposable key turner. My immense pride in a job that receives little recognition, either politically or within the community, is far better placed in my current work in which I better serve the needs of innocent people. Between a rising prisoner population crisis, substandard funding, and the persistent recruitment of incompetent *screws*, the Department is in way over its own head. Much as I need to thank it (as it continues to keep my beloved husband in a reliable job) I certainly don't have to respect it.

The fallout from this job almost killed me.

CHAPTER TWENTY-EIGHT

THE BUCKET LIST

——————

I have never held a doubt about what happens to us when we die, and I believe I have been clairsentient since I was a small child. I believe entirely in a world of Spirit that sometimes crosses over into the world of the living, simply because neither population are deceased, nor will ever be. As I've often heard, we are souls having a human experience time and time and time again. Yet nothing I've learnt or experienced personally prepared me for the ultimate proof of life after death.

To make things fair and equitable between us and while he lived in my Springton home, Adam paid me a token rent that I'd place in a purple box inside a drawer in our family room. One afternoon I opened the box to retrieve the $100 I *knew* were in there, and instead found $1000 in crisp fifty dollar notes. I immediately surmised Adam had put the money in as a bona fide bonus. So, feeling slightly annoyed rather than grateful, I ran upstairs to our bedroom to take a swipe at him.

"It wasn't me!" he defended himself. "Have you asked Alycia?"

No, Alycia had not placed $1000 inside my purple box and I wasn't the least bit surprised, for Alycia is frugal at best and seems to be always paying something off. Kristen was still living in Sydney and no other person had been to our home over the past month, least of all a kind benefactor.

Alan! I gasped inside my head. Somehow it was Alan who was responsible.

To secure Lyndoch Hill in the Barossa Valley for our wedding, Adam and I needed a deposit of $1000. Alan's life insurance payout was tied up in bureaucratic red tape and we had next to no savings of our own. As I explained earlier, the change in etheric atmosphere suggested Alan was now at peace and aware that his son's decision to marry me was what made him happy. It was Alan who placed the money in the box as a matrimonial blessing for us.

The theory of teleportation through time and space is a concept better suited to Fox Mulder than your average sentient being, but having witnessed psychokinesis at Oswald Crescent and trusting that all is energy whether seemingly inanimate or not, I had every reason to believe Alan had sent $1000 through the ether. Fortunately, Adam was not difficult to convince, bittersweet tears of gratitude streaming down his sweet, loving cheeks. In addition to being the kindest man in the world, my future husband was also blessed with an open mind.

* * *

The morning of 4 August 2013 was a chilly one and I prayed the rain would stay away. It did.

I slipped into my beautiful silver, white and purple bridal gown, lamenting a failure to lose weight for the most wonderful day in an awful forty-eight years of life. 'I would certainly ruin all our photos,' I thought to myself.

There was a knock on my door ... my photographer! Filiz, the beautiful make-up artist who'd attempt to make an older woman look amazing, was still working on the bridesmaids. A bride is supposed to sit there and soak in all the tizz and fuss, but all I wanted to do was get to the Lyndoch Hill Chateau and marry my sweetheart.

Ironically – or maybe not – Filiz, a Turk, knew only too well the doctor who many years before had performed a tubal ligation procedure on me in Sydney. 'Doctor Vardar', also a Turk, was a leading authority on a new form of keyhole surgery that specialised in permanent tubal ligation. It was Rhys's sister, who appeared to know all and sundry within the medical world because of her chronic endometriosis, who referred me to Doctor Vardar. My brushes with so many Turkish people in recent years had prompted a need to place Istanbul and Gallipoli as number one destinations on our honeymoon itinerary. Eser spoke so fondly about his homeland, and now that I understood what it represented I wanted to experience Turkey more than anywhere else.

The Springton house had finally been sold to a buyer who caused us so much angst I almost wished I'd never put it on the market. Settlement would take place while we were on honeymoon, so in the seven days between the wedding and leaving for Europe, we had to dismantle and move a five-bedroom home into the three bedroom one we had purchased in tiny Tungkillo. Such a way to begin married life. At least I got my wish, to have Adam and I live in a house all our own and not just mine. 'The stubborn Gladiatorial Taurean with a Scorpio moon, and all those planets in Gemini deserved everything she put herself through,' I thought.

My bridesmaids were dreamy, with my three daughters painting a perfect picture in their purple and silver dresses and flowing dark locks. An added treat was seeing 'emo' Kristen wear a dress with a plunging neckline instead of the habitual black baggy pants and multiple layers. Sabrina my 'third daughter' was Alycia's best friend since Year 8. I began emotionally raising Sabrina when her exotic and gregarious face adorned our home in Gunn Place on a regular basis. Unfortunately, like me and to some extent my children, Sabrina came from a dysfunctional and broken home, but she had gumption and wisdom and so, just like us, she bravely survived.

I was to be escorted into the ceremonial garden in style too. Adam's shooting buddy Brian, a self-made millionaire, drove us in his midnight blue Rolls-Royce. It was going to be the fairy tale wedding I'd always dreamt of, a far cry from the el cheapo affair of 1987. Good things *do* come to those who wait but I also had Alan Brewer to thank, given it was his money that paid for this dream. I was also grateful to Jenny, Adam's mother and another no nonsense Aquarian, yet different again from Rhys's Aquarian mother. Like Louise though, Jenny made a concerted effort to welcome me into her life, despite a burning desire for grandchildren, something that still gives me the occasional pang of guilt. Jenny's open warmth was a far cry from the frosty reception Adam's father and friends had afforded me. Given Gilda's narcissism and Louise's passing, I so needed another mother in my life. A crafts virtuoso, Jenny also handmade the place cards, again in purple and silver.

Gilda and Piero flew in from Sydney for our wedding, sans Alfonso. His damaged body had finally given up the ghost in March and I'd returned to Bonnyrigg not to farewell one of my tormentors but to save face with Gilda and her friends and, to *appear* to support my mother like the dutiful daughter I was expected to be. The stupid emotional blackmail I carried from Mother still hung around like a millstone round my neck. I hadn't attended Letitia's funeral out of principle yet here I was pandering to the greatest villain of my life once more. Why? I continued to feel hopelessly powerless in Gilda's hands but at least I succeeded in refusing to read an obituary Gilda had asked me to. For the most part, gone were the days I'd go against my moral compass to appease others; in my heart I knew I owed Alfonso nothing.

Feigning bravado, I also told Gilda she would not be singing at my wedding. This marriage would *not* resemble my first in any way, and by stopping Mother from singing I exercised a degree of revenge for the years of her neglect of me in favour of obsessive pursuit of a career that had failed to eventuate.

The thirty-minute drive from Springton to Lyndoch was filled with the most concentrated excitement and anticipation I'd ever felt. I could not wait to see my angel waiting for me on those chateau steps. I should have savoured the luxury of the beautiful car I was travelling in and contributed to the giggly repartee from my bridesmaids in the back seat, but all I wanted now was to see my future husband and the wonderful loving smile that intermittently lit up my life like a Christmas tree. I would soon be *Mrs Angelica Brewer*.

So many feelings. They sent the kind of sparks up my spine that had certainly not been there during the hour-long trip from Bonnyrigg to the Sydney CBD twentysix years before. And when finally, I arrived in Lyndoch there he was, standing on the elegant steps looking so impossibly handsome in his charcoal pinstriped suit and lilac cravat. Suddenly everyone and everything disappeared from view; all I focused on were the trickle of red rose petals that led me from Brian's Rolls-Royce to my future husband ... *Husband* ... how I loved the sound of that word now.

I call upon the people here present, to witness that I Angelica take you Adam to be my lawful wedded husband.

My beautiful husband, I am here today to pledge the rest of my life to you. Words cannot express how happy I am to be here standing next to you, knowing I am Mrs Brewer in only a few minutes.

Adam, you have saved me from myself. You have nurtured me. You have protected me. You have taught me to love again.

So many have said to me, 'You are strong Angelica, nothing can keep you down,' but had I not met you, I am not sure I would have got back up. Thank you for lifting me higher than I ever thought possible.

You are so patient with me, you never give up. You really see me as I am, not as I sometimes show you. You believe in me when I don't. For every one of my negatives, you have a positive. For every tear I shed, you have a warm hug. For every drama, you have a kind word. Who else would tickle someone to sleep each and every night? Who else would continue to love wholeheartedly under difficult circumstances that never seem to end? You are an Earth Angel Adam, and I am the luckiest woman in the world!

For me this is my FIRST marriage and today I know it will be my ONLY one. I promise to honour you, to care for you as you so generously care for me, to protect you from harm, to always listen to you and believe you, to love you as deeply and honestly as you love me.

I hope I am the kind of wife you so deserve. You are my best friend, and I've never known true happiness until I met you.

Lyndoch, 4 August 2013

On 9 August, the day before we left for our six-week honeymoon, Adam and I were moving and dumping our stuff from Springton to Tungkillo until 9 o'clock that night. I was in tears from sheer exhaustion. We had packed three of the most stressful situations a person goes through in life into the space of six days. Nonetheless, in ten hours' time we'd be kicking back inside our Singapore Airlines seats for a seventeen-hour flight to beautiful, exotic Istanbul.

* * *

The last few years had been tough, almost tougher than any previous times in my life. I was convinced this hallowed trip, one that ticked off so many items on my bucket list, was going to regenerate me and renew my faith in destiny.

We packed twelve countries into six weeks. Travel in Europe is not cheap so I figured we had to do absolutely *everything* in that time, including some of Adam's bucket list wishes too. First stop Turkey, following a brief stopover in Singapore.

To say I placed Turkey at the top of the list of our itinerary for no other reason than general interest would be a lie. Eser, and the intense relationship we'd shared, had aroused my curiosity. What I *will* insist on however, is that the moment Adam and I stepped foot in Istanbul, this location became all about *us* and the love affair we began there.

After settling into a quaint little hotel called the Basileus, situated near the *Ayasofya* (Hagia Sophia) Museum, just 300 metres from the Marmara Sea, we embarked on the fantastic journey that is *Türkiye*. On our way to the Hippodrome we were stopped by a young boy who spoke minimal English. As in Morocco it was virtually impossible to get away from him, but unlike Morocco he was not sleazy, dirty or rude. The young boy invited us into a little tavern that was richly adorned with what we thought must be national tapestries and artefacts. When he showed us the menu, Adam and I decided we were definitely ready for lunch and, as aficionados of Turkish cuisine back home, we couldn't wait for a course of genuine Turkish fare. Seeing us not recognising any of the dishes the smiling boy confirmed his 'uncle's tavern' was Kurdish, *with delicious authentic Kurdish cuisine just for you.* Being the only people inside and unable to disappoint the incredibly hospitable boy, we ordered away, and were delighted with our meal.

I smiled broadly as we toured the amazing sights of this ancient city, in complete wonderment as the locals appeared to smile back wherever we looked. At the Blue Mosque Adam and I were asked to follow religious courtesies by having him wash his feet, and me cover my hair with a hijab, which could be procured at certain entry points. This would possibly be the only time I'd wear a hijab, due to personal principles, but I just *had* to see the interior of this famous landmark. Also, I make a point never to disrespect national or religious requirements. This is perhaps why I get so fired up when other cultures disrespect mine.

I hold a great deal of respect for Turkish Muslims because generally speaking, they are non-fundamentalist and quite cosmopolitan. During the month prior to our departure, there were vast protests called the 'Taksim Square unrest' which challenged the government's encroachment of Turkey's secularism, along with their agenda on public assembly, freedom of expression and freedom of the press. This resistance filled my heart with added pride for a people I already loved for so many other reasons.

Our ferry ride over the rich blue and tranquil Bosporus was another inspirational treat. Eser had a photograph of himself with the Fatih Sultan Mehmet Bridge as its majestic backdrop, and when *my* breath was taken away by this scene I hugged my new husband tightly on the ferry's rear deck, instantly replacing that photograph with *real life* love.

Adam and I shared sunset filled dinners on Mediterranean terraces, catered with the type of service only a third world country offers. The food was lovingly created and served and Adam, as he enjoyed an *efes* or two, remarked on the congeniality of a people he'd only heard of during Anzac Day commemorations.

As devoted Australians, we could not come to Turkey and skip Gallipoli or *Gelibolu,* as it is known in Turkish. The five-hour trip to Çanakkale was well worth the journey. Here we included a day tour of Troy or *Truva,* where Adam climbed onto a makeshift Trojan horse. Gallipoli was everything I had imagined and much more. To call it beautiful seems inappropriate given its history, but I cannot describe the place in any other way.

Gallipoli had fascinated me since high school and the 1981 film of that name (starring a young Mel Gibson). Here I was today, standing on the hallowed ground too precious to ignore. Adam and I took a boat trip away from Anzac Cove to look at some sunken military wrecks and it was suggested by our polite guides that we take a swim in the pristine waters, waters once awash with teenage Australian blood. Adam jumped in and swam all the way to *Anzak Koyu* as a gesture of tribute to fallen compatriots.

Together we searched the many graves alongside Hill 60, Chunuk Bair, Lone Pine and Cape Helles. Along the Beach Cemetery we located the grave of John Simpson Kirkpatrick, the legendary soldier who, equipped with a faithful donkey, carried injured soldiers to safety and their beach evacuation. At Lone Pine Adam found the only Brewer serviceperson and attached a red poppy next to his name. A fellow traveller from Queensland broke down at the grave of a great uncle. His tears were heartbreaking and sad reminders of what this tranquil, spectacular panorama embodies.

Out of respect for our hosts and for the sake of holistic education, we visited the Turkish *Alay Şehitliği* (War Cemetery) containing the remains of the 85,000 Turkish soldiers who lost their precious lives. It was yet another humbling experience for us. I have never been racist as such but I *am* guilty – as are many – of generalised judgements. Each country has its heroes and villains, but when an opposition is viewed through *their* eyes, it becomes harder to crucify 'the enemy'. In wartime all sides are victims of social injustices.

Part of the *Alay Şehitliği* tour was the newly built Kabatepe Simulation Centre where an interactive IMAX-like film depicts the Great War from a Turkish point of view. Other Turkish tributes that evoked deep feelings of love and respect for Turkey and its people included a statue of a Turkish soldier carrying a wounded Australian, and the famous statement by Mustafa Kemal (also known as *Atatürk* or 'Father of the Turks') delivered in 1934 as a tribute to our fallen and their families:

Those heroes that shed their blood and lost their lives, you are now lying in the soil of a friendly country. Therefore, rest in peace. There is no difference between the Johnnies and the Mehmets to us where they lie side by side here in this country of ours. You, the mothers who sent their sons from faraway countries, wipe away your tears; your sons are now lying in our bosom and are in peace. After having lost their lives on this land they have become our sons as well.

One of Adam's fondest memories of Turkey involved our immersion in a tray of delicious *baklave* washed down with some refreshing *ayran* (a salted cold yogurt drink) as we sat dangling our feet over an expansive Marmara Sea embankment in Eceabat, a town and district of the Çanakkale Province in the Marmara region of Turkey, on the eastern shore of the *Gelibolu* Peninsula on the Dardanelles Strait. Earlier that day we had taken the ferry to Eceabat and back to Gallipoli. On a mountainside overseeing the harbour to the left of us, a large pictorial monument showing a soldier appearing to flee from a grenade stood grandiose. The poignant words, by Turkish poet Necmettin Halil Onan, are just one verse from a patriotic post-World War I poem.

> Stop wayfarer! Unbeknownst to you this ground
> You come and tread on, is where an epoch lies;
> Bend down and lend your ear, for this silent mound
> Is the place where the heart of a nation sighs.

Not far from our hotel in Çanakkale, stood another treat – the original Trojan horse built for the 2004 film, *Troy*. There was no doubt the Turkish experience had been an excellent start for our honeymoon. Alas, the broad smiles and sense of unity we acquired in Turkey were rather wiped away by the following locations on our itinerary: Bucharest and Braşov, two cities in Romania. Bucharest is also Romania's capital.

I just had to go to Transylvania. I had to fulfil my lifelong dream of seeing Dracula's castle with my own eyes, so imagine the disappointment when rather than stand in awe of some huge, frightening Bram Stoker style gothic castle, I was obliged to climb 1480 heart stopping concrete steps into a series of nondescript open air ruins. The view from Poenari Castle was well worth the effort though, and indeed completely gothic and medieval.

Poenari Castle stands invincibly on the plateau of Mount Cetatea, facing the west side of the Transfăgărăşan Highway atop a canyon formed on the Argeş River valley and close to the Făgăraş Mountains. The legendary Vlad the Impaler (the inspiration for the character of Count Dracula) had used this fortress until his death in 1476 (only four digits short of the steps built to get there). My knees were weak (from lack of fitness) but it was certainly an achievement getting there and I did not leave the fortress without a piece of my anti-hero's legend; terribly unethical of me I know, but ...

We did not stay long in Bucharest as we had a train to catch into Braşov, where we stayed two nights. Bucharest looked like it had just survived a war: dirty, abandoned, and unloved – even the McDonald's coffee was undrinkable. Our hotel in Braşov was terrible, as was the service along the Strada Republicii where most of the eateries and shops are located. There is no doubt in my mind Romania is one of the poorest of the former 'Eastern Bloc' countries; it is indelibly written on many of the faces we watched passing us by, colourless and expressionless. Not so with Eugene though, our hospitable taxi guide.

Eugene picked us up from the hotel right on time. Together we launched into the 180-kilometre drive along the Transfăgărăşan Highway to Wallachia, the site of Vlad's fortress. The rural landscapes peaked and dipped along the tallest sections of the Carpathian Mountains – this was a side of Europe I'd wanted to see all my life. Romania still seemed very medieval and unspoilt. It's the haystacks that remain branded in my mind, piled by hand they forlornly dotted the misty farmlands like crowds of Cousin Itts. When the highway traversed a high point, the landscape was so thick with fog the cows could barely be seen grazing in the deep valleys below us.

Eugene could not do enough for us, stopping whenever he sensed a photo opportunity. His English was good and his happy disposition even better. He dropped us at the foot of the Poenari Fortress and returned to his little taxi for a nap until we were done. On the way home, we stopped for lunch in a lovely township called Curtea de Argeş where Eugene made sightseeing recommendations and ordered food and drink on our behalf. We visited the Byzantine style Romanian Orthodox cathedral, where members of the Romanian royal family such as King Charles I and his wife Queen Elisabeth are buried.

My Count Dracula experience had not yet been fully satisfied, however, so on the way back to Braşov, Eugene parked his taxi near the Bran Castle markets and we purchased entry tickets for a Castelul Bran tour. The refurbished twelfth century castle, first built by the Teutonic Knights, seemed to be mainly a museum of artefacts collected by Queen Marie, the last queen of Romania. Still, it was a wonderful experience. One small section of the multi-chambered castle was indeed dedicated to Francis Ford Coppola's *Bram Stoker's Dracula* – the film I saw in Hawaii in 1992.

We then bid goodbye to sad but fabulous Romania and said hello to Hungary and its capital, Budapest.

The overnight train ride from Romania to Hungary was awful. I was reminded by my former Corrections friend Fred Harris – a lovably condescending Sagittarian – that to whine about a trip such as this was just short of sacrilegious … "Beautifully unspoilt Balkans countryside," Fred had mused. He was right of course. The countryside was so unspoilt I had to look twice when I saw a young mother and child bathing nude in a stream that traversed beneath the tracks.

Adam and I were booked into a luxury suite. If a rusty metal toilet and dripping shower head are considered 'luxury' items, then I do not envy the cattle cabins the poorer communist passengers were forced to endure. The train guards were dour and ominous, eerily similar to the stereotypes familiar from old spy films. At one point I had stood my ground when the guards refused to hand back our passports and travel documents; I won't deny I was a little fearful but hey, I had rights, and identity fraud is rampant in third world countries.

A short taxi drive from Budapest's Keleti station found us by the grandiose doors of the Sofitel Hotel and, given the last few days' accommodation, it was the best gift our travel agent could have bestowed on us. I dived straight into the plush, king-size bed and it took a lot of nudging by Adam to get me back out. Regrettably we were in Budapest only the one day and night. Travel propaganda is forever selling dream locations like Rome, Paris and London, yet they seem to ignore glorious Budapest – why?

Budapest is jaw dropping for its beauty. Adam and I wished we'd researched Hungary a lot more and placed it on our to-do list. Fortunately, we had a guided tour of the city booked, stopping in Szabadsag (Liberty) Square by a bronze statue of Ronald Reagan that had been placed there only two years before. The Heroes' Square, Budapest Opera House and Budapest Academy of Music followed. After a much needed coffee stopover in the city's oldest cafe, the Ruszwurm Cukraszda, where a couple from Oman bought us coffee, our quirky guide took us into the breathtaking Buda Castle district and Fisherman's Bastion, the kind of buildings fairy tales are based on. Relishing a dramatic view over the Széchenyi Chain Bridge, River Danube, and one-hundred-year-old palatial Hungarian Parliament House which boasts 691 rooms, Adam and I looked at each other and simultaneously uttered the same words: *why is Budapest such a well-kept secret?*

That night we walked along Széchenyi Chain Bridge with its giant sentinel lions, and were drawn to an eclectic night market, high in the distance. We boarded a funicular railway, one I recognised later in a film, *The Grand Budapest Hotel*. Walking hand in hand with my own fairy tale prince

I could not have been happier and yet, deep down inside something dark continued to stir.

Our next stop was Prague, a city described as Paris's equal, and one recommended to me by friends a dozen times. I was especially keen to visit the Sedlec *Kostnice* (Ossuary) church in the city of Kutná Hora, ever since a former colleague at Alastair and Marianne's had raved about it. Because I so love the macabre, the Ossuary was top of the list on our Czech adventure.

The *kostnice* was indeed macabre. It claimed to contain between 40,000 and 70,000 human skeletons, almost all of them arranged in decorative styles which include the House of Schwarzenberg coat of arms. On one display a sign reads.

The skulls of soldiers from the Hussite wars, 1421–1424. Fatal injuries caused by swords, flails, maces, and arrows. Scientific studies have proven survival of some injuries. (You can notice an apparent process of healing.)

Gothic is how I would describe Prague. It is certainly very beautiful, but I wouldn't quite put it up there with Paris. Prague embraces the sombreness of what the 'Eastern Bloc' became since World War II, so if you're an emo who enjoys a generous serve of melancholy mixed with smog covered cathedrals, this place is for you. Looking out from any rooftop at the sea of cupolas and terracotta tiled roofs, though, you'd be forgiven for thinking you were standing in Florence.

Wenceslas Square is a central point where I agreed to meet with Adam on a couple of fateful occasions. On the south-east end of the square stands the Czech National Museum, and to its right a pathway into the central railway and bus stations. As we ventured in the latter direction to catch a train from Prague to Nuremberg, we took an underground walkway. The second I saw what lay ahead of us, I gesticulated to Adam to get the hell out of there – and quickly. The area was teeming with drug users, either passed out or in the process of self-administration. Some of these living zombies had congregated in the square, eyeing passers-by for a chance of either solicitation or forcibly taking money for their next hit. I'd seen the horrible yellow tinge of their skin and eyeballs before, when Letitia contracted hepatitis from a dodgy mussel, but these people were beyond Letitia's condition and by their own hand.

Český Krumlov is possibly the stop in the South Bohemian Region that Adam and I enjoyed most. It is a medieval city built around the thirteenth century and known primarily for the Rosenberg Castle or Český Krumlov Castle. Once again the morbid element in my character was drawn to the torture chamber tour, which taught me a few more squeamish facts I had not been familiar with. In Český Krumlov we tasted our second good coffee since leaving Adelaide. Adam and I are both coffee lovers and, with great anticipation, we'd believed Europe would more than cater for our tastes. Not so.

Prague stands out in my book of honeymoon memories for reasons I am not proud of. It was here that Adam and I had our first 'honeymoon fight'; the reason was pitiful and in no way condoned the cruel attack my precious new husband endured from me. I was travel weary and not coping very well. Perhaps I was getting too old for such adventures, but once more I felt like a complete louse after the fact. Adam took my unbridled fury like he always did, with complete resignation, humility, and apology. A flood of tears would then follow. Adam deserved so much better than this. Who attacks their spouse on their honeymoon, anyway?

A fascination with Germany that stemmed from my early teens (for all the wrong reasons: simply because I wanted to transport myself as far away from my Latin roots as possible) finally found us in Beethoven's land. As an unsettled teen I endorsed everything Nordic and to a certain extent this included World War II German totalitarian ideology. I had read *Mein Kampf* and William L. Shirer's *The Rise and Fall of The Third Reich,* watched every Holocaust film and documentary made, and somehow developed a bizarre respect for Nazism. My perfect man was the typical Aryan blockhead, and I'd dreamt of the day I would visit Germany or Scandinavia and meet my Kraus, Fritz, Gustav or Lars. Reading Nancy Wake's autobiography *The White Mouse* changed my views on the Third Reich, and seeing *Schindler's List* cemented the change. Ironically both Nancy Wake and *Schindler's Ark*'s (to give the novel its original title) author, Thomas Keneally, are Australians.

The reason behind our visit to Nuremberg lay in an article I'd read a few years before about the Nuremberg Arena or Nazi party rally grounds. I'm no myth buster, but when I hear something that piques my interest in the supernatural I've got to check that bad boy out. The writer explained how a density of sound might impact our aural atmosphere. He used two examples: the first was a hotel room in the United States where newlywed lovers Clark Gable and Carole Lombard often spent steamy nights together, and the second involved the Nuremberg Arena. The writer claimed the fervour exuded by protagonists in both locations had broken through the sound barrier, penetrating the ether and crystallising as audible energy. The author further documented claims that the voices of 500,000 soldiers assembled in the Nuremburg Arena chanting

'Heil Hitler' could indeed be heard as if trapped inside air. I just had to test the claims for myself.

So off I went, standing like a loser in the middle of a park while random people walked by or threw balls for their dogs as I listened intently. I could not hear a thing but the sheer scale of this place was still worth seeing. The Luitpoldarena had been respectfully turned into a recreation park and the Zeppelinfeld used as a motor racing track or for music festivals. The giant swastika was blown off in 1945 and purposely left unrestored. I wasn't certain whether I felt disappointment standing among the ruins of a fabled empire or happy that an accountable Germany had refused to preserve its bloodied past. Answers came to me via a visit to the newly established Nazi Museum next to the uncompleted Congress Hall, a grandiose design envisioned by Hitler as a rival to the Roman Colosseum.

The museum was an assembly of Nazi history, completed by a first edition of *Mein Kampf* preserved beneath shatterproof glass. It concludes with the Nuremberg Trials and subsequent executions. In between these lie series after series of evidence of the carnage created and left behind by the Nazi regime. There was no Nazi glorification in this place and a photograph displaying naked and deceased Ukrainian women still clutching their slain children brought extreme shame to the teenage musings of a misguided girl determined to hurt her family at any cost.

Nuremberg was not an overly attractive city, with the only other piece of entertainment to cross our path a fat American tourist on our minibus who would not shut up, asking the kind of stupid questions that were clearly disrespectful to his host city.

When we alighted at the Berlin railway station a friendly and quick-off-the mark cab driver asked if we wanted to see parts of the Berlin Wall en route to our Best Western hotel. The portion he showed us was a rare one, as this double wall had held guard dogs that would chew absconders to death.

The hotel was the only one that inaugurated our honeymoon with a note and red balloons left on our bed, so well done Berlin's Great Western! Berlin was far more pleasant than Nuremberg but it still did not reflect the Germany I had anticipated all my life. As a lover of architecture and folklore I had been spoiled by London, Budapest, Rome and Paris. To be honest I didn't know *what* to expect but what I'd received in Germany so far was not very 'Nordic'. For starters I saw a lot more foreigners than Germans, or at least, my presupposed version of what German people look like. Then there was the unkempt environment and Bucharest-type atmosphere; I had been under the impression Germans were a proud and orderly nation. The various 'Berlin walls' around the place were political poster art that aptly depicted a revolutionary style of propaganda and this I did like, along with the many tribute icons that honoured the victims of Hitler's Holocaust. With them in mind, I then felt the need to visit the Jewish Museum in Lindenstraße.

Regret is sometimes short lived with me and, for yet another stupid reason I can't even recall, I brutally attacked Adam again. Like the beautiful puppy that he is, Adam followed me around the quirkily geometrical museum until I purposely lost him and then blamed him for not finding me. The sadness and dark energy of the museum evoked sudden feelings of desperation within my soul. I realised just how dependent I now was on Adam and how much I needed him by my side. I suffered a debilitating panic attack, darting in every direction sobbing, as I searched for my beloved puppy. Where was he?

I reported Adam as 'lost' to reception, a ridiculous move given my actions. With my ill-pronounced and sporadic German, I used stupid descriptive words like *grossen* and *hoch* and, coupled with the wild look in my eyes, I must have appeared like the proverbial dumb tourist of comic films.

Two days later we bid Berlin *auf wiedersehen* and caught a train to Ludwigslust where we met up with my cousin Valeria's former pen pal, Jens Lindemann, and his wife Solvig. Jens, who I had not seen since his visit to Sydney in 2001, greeted us at the station and kindly drove us back to his home in Parchim. No effort was too great for Jens and Solvig – including giving up their bedroom for us. The next day the couple took us on a tour of beautiful Schwerin, a town about 50 kilometres from Parchim in northern Germany, and it was here I finally encountered the Germany of my dreams.

Schwerin, with its majestic lakes, romantic palace, and neoclassical Alter Garten square, was like walking into another fairy tale. Walking up a narrow cobble stone *Straße*, a shop window caught my eye and I stopped Adam in his tracks. Thoughts returned to my 2008 Paris trip and how life sometimes gives you what you yearn for. I envisioned the two of us putting a padlock on the Pont de l'Archevêché in Paris as a tribute to our love. The little antiques shop beckoned and it was here we found our perfect 'love lock'. *Vielen Dank Herr Krämer Mr Shopkeeper, sealer of our precious union.*

Two days later it was time to bid a sad *bis später* to Jens and Solvig. Jens, an air traffic controller, was prolific in English, but conversations with Solvig were an exercise in gesticulation. I was very surprised to find that not many

Germans spoke English, given their schooling and a certain affinity between the two languages.

I was sad to leave the congenial hospitality of the Lindemann household; whatever the world thinks of Germany and its past, I have yet to meet a German who is not amiable, and certainly not the dour caricature the rest of the world likes to paint.

Next stop was Frankfurt, the banking capital of Europe and, like Nuremberg, not a lot to rave about.

Our accommodation in Frankfurt was actually worse than in Braşov, so much so that we dubbed it 'The Hooker Hotel'. The reception clerk was an older gentleman bearing an uncanny resemblance to Richard Griffiths playing Harry Potter's grandfather, and someone who candidly referred to himself as 'The Doctor' … *Just ask the Doctor*, he'd say in his 'Ya vol' accent.

The last leg of our Teutonic experience took place aboard a Rhine cruiser and we again experienced the idyllic Germany of my childhood expectations. The cruise left from a quaint Alpine village named Assmannshausen, famous for its Pinot Noir. We arrived at the village by chairlift. As we dangled above gullies and valleys, taking in the breathtaking views, there was nothing to keep me from breaking into a Julie Andrews song – everything the eye could see was just wow, wow, wow!

We enjoyed a lovely lunch and wine tasting experience inside a gorgeous little gem of a restaurant called Zum Anker. The exterior, interior, and the bathroom too, were beautifully decorated with interesting and unusual items collected from various German and European locations. Our eyes wandered in awe from nook to cranny to alcove, discovering something new each time. Our knowledgeable wine tasting hostess, Andrea, an American immigrant, was also highly entertaining. Overall, the wine tasting focused on the legendary *Eiswein* or ice wine, a dessert wine produced from grapes picked from the vine during the first freezing night of the year.

The guided cruise then took us from Assmannshausen to Loreley on the eastern bank of the Rhine, where the famous *Lorelei* sculpture beckons to all who view her. She is perched on a legendary rock that, according to legend, once served as a platform into her own death. We passed dozens of castles, sentinel towers, cathedrals and quaint villages, and the cliffside riverbanks were richly adorned with classic German historical flair.

We were allowed an hour in one of the villages – a place called Rüdesheim. I bought a much wanted cuckoo clock fridge magnet there, because I could not afford the real thing. Had I researched Germany properly I would not have wasted precious time in Berlin or Frankfurt, but never mind – a temporary bucket list had been ticked and I still had the rest of my life for further exploration.

Seeing Paris again with my new, darling husband was a must. When we placed the antique Schwerin lock on the Pont de l'Archevêché, the beauty and timelessness of that moment brought tears to my eyes. We both knew the lock would not last as it sat there among a thousand others, so instead of throwing the key into the Seine as is customary, we decided to keep it. It now sits on a rustic heart made from knotted tree branches that was given to us by our dear Mupulawangk friend Angela and her husband Joe, on our engagement day.

By the time we reached Paris, Adam and I were exhausted and took two of the eight days here to just sleep, eat, and lounge around our hotel room; a waste of precious sightseeing time, but we were seriously wrecked.

The highlights I shared with Adam in that city of lovers included the Paris Catacombs in Place Denfert-Rochereau, and if Kutná Hora felt even slightly surreal, the Catacombs were indescribably so. We entered via a nondescript crypt-like doorway descending 19 metres down a narrow spiral stone stairwell into what were once stone mines. Past an entrance that read *Arrête! C'est ici l'empire de la Mort* ('Stop! This is the Empire of the Dead'), were the remains of more than six million people exhumed from various resting places around the city, such as, in the 1780s, a medieval mass grave in the Holy Innocents cemetery.

Up on the Eiffel Tower I begged Adam to ask me to marry him again. I had dreamt of such a proposal and this was my only chance. It had been my plan to renew our vows one day anyway so why not three weeks after the wedding? Adam, my practical man, was reluctant, but agreed to indulge me all the same. Adam could never say no to me and that saddened me a little because I did not want Adam to trade in his identity for mine. Falling upon bended knee and holding in a visibly embarrassed chuckle, Adam proposed. Suddenly we heard excited gasps from the mezzanine above us.

"Oh look they're engaged!" came several voices, followed by celebratory applause. I immediately felt a little foolish but it was nevertheless an irreplaceable moment in my life. The trials this man has endured for the sake of female capriciousness …

We became familiar with the word *boulangerie* as we indulged ourselves with baguettes, croissants and, our favourite pastry, the *religieuse*, a kind of éclair. I was certain I had put on at least three more kilos. One night, desperately craving seafood, we stopped by a restaurant in Abbesses, not far from Montmartre, where we purchased a very expensive 'cold platter'. We were licking our lips for some juicy prawns and succulent shellfish, so what was placed before us was heartbreaking. The reason the platter was *cold* was because it was *raw* – raw escargots, raw clams, raw sea urchins, raw everything! I almost cried. Two gentlemen sitting next to us watched my reaction and were unable to contain their merriment.

"Ahhhh, French people! They *love* to eat everything raw!"

I wanted to know what the famous Moulin Rouge was all about so we booked a night there, and it was well worth it. A myriad of perky breasts flanked by multi-coloured feathers and sparkling rhinestones pranced about in perfect unison to cheesecake burlesque music. The best act of the night came from a lovely lady who jumped into a glass tank beneath the stage and writhed around with an enormous python. Jealousy would have eaten me alive, back in the day, but Adam had been so demure and nonplussed about the female forms on show that I didn't bat an eyelid. Besides, he'd been on a number of 'footy trips' with his mates that made all this look like Disneyland.

While on the subject of Disneyland, Euro Disney was a disappointment and did not hold a candle to its Anaheim forbear; but when in Paris do as an American might, even though you're Australian.

I did enjoy Les Invalides, a beautiful set of buildings I had seen only from afar on my previous Paris visit. Realising they were in fact a war museum I decided to walk past them, though I was all for Adam going in while I sipped a coffee nearby. What I did not realise was that Les Invalides is not only Napoleon Bonaparte's burial site, but a project commissioned by Louis XIV to appease angry builders on the verge of rebellion. Never allow preconceived notions to cheat you out of an exclusive experience.

And speaking of the Sun King, next stop Versailles – yet again.

I'd loved Versailles in 2008. It had been a dream come true, so naturally I was keen for Adam to see it too. Alas, the fountains were again inactive, it was raining for most of the day, and one of the sightseeing people-mover conductors was a total dick. There were some points of interest for him, but Adam was not as thrilled by Versailles as I was. Normandy on the other hand was *most* welcomed by my closet warmonger of a husband.

On the way to Normandy our tour guide was exasperating Adam with French inflections. She remains ingrained in our holiday memories like the tour guide at Kutná Hora who went ape at the two blokes sitting in front of us eating chips – only minutes after Adam and I had finished our own messy wraps.

"No chips! No eating on the bus!" he bellowed.

I can only imagine how difficult it must be to act as a tour guide, what with ignorant fat Americans asking about Hitler museums and their national unemployment rate and so on. Whilst in Budapest I infuriated the tour guide there by running off to do my own sightseeing while he spouted historical rhetoric for our listening pleasure. I want to *see* first and learn later!

Normandy was as beautifully melancholy as Gallipoli. The D-Day landing beaches still had several of the pill boxes and bunkers from World War II. Adam and I explored one of the bunkers overlooking the tranquil ocean in Longues-sur-Mer, between the *Omaha* and *Gold* landing beaches. Those initial *Saving Private Ryan* scenes became very real to me and I could not help thinking about all the mothers back home who'd lost sons before they had a chance to draw their weapons. It was the Gallipoli trenches all over again.

We ended a day of remembrance by visiting another poignant site: The Normandy American Cemetery and Memorial where 9387 American soldiers are buried, with a further 1557 commemorated because their precious bodies were never found. The countless rows of white crosses, many depicting a religious affiliation, brought home the futility and tragedy of war. I have never been a subscriber to war being 'romantic'; one needs to only look at the carnage of trench warfare to realise there's nothing idealistic about conscripted murder, whether instituted by greed or by misguided faith.

It was time to bid France *adieu* and head for the United Kingdom where my heart was stolen in 2008, but most certainly *not* before being wowed by the *Tour Eiffel* at night time. The light show was simply breathtaking. If only I were intrinsically romantic, I would have savoured this special moment alongside the most wonderful man on earth. I do have an appreciation for aesthetics but I simply do not know how to translate them into random acts of romance – this just happens to be Adam's domain, bless him.

I was privileged to cross the English Channel a second time via the Eurostar, then caught a hackney cab to Soho. The legendary London district of Soho is a melting pot for the pseudo-intellectual student seeking like-minded individuals. Sadly, we stayed in yet another awful hotel but greatly enjoyed the 'hop-on-hop-off' double decker tour buses, seeing much of London and saving our ruined limbs. I think I appreciated London more the second time around, and on this occasion I managed to visit the Tower of London *and* grab a lift on the London Eye – two more bucket list adventures ticked off!

Oxford Street, Windsor Castle, the Marble Arch, Westminster Abbey, Buckingham Palace, Piccadilly Circus and going past one of Jamie Oliver's 'Fifteen' restaurants, were just some of our London experiences. Westminster Abbey was closed for Sunday worship, so Adam missed out on the historic marvels locked inside.

Across from a cinema in Shaftesbury Avenue (where we watched *Pain and Gain*, a very funny film) I spotted an old man crouched over by the entrance of a tube station. Across the street from him stood a doughnut shop. Whenever possible I make a point of helping those less fortunate than myself, and on this occasion I bought the man a pink iced doughnut. When he lifted his head to me I noticed he was not old at all – the bluest eyes looked into mine and a smile of pure gratitude, underpinned by genuine surprise, spread across his dirty face. As I write this, I don't recall every detail of our London experience unless (as I'm doing now) I look over our photographs, but that face of someone not much older than twenty-five will never leave me. At what point in someone's life does one completely give up, and why? I then decided to make this the topic for a future book.

That night I could no longer sleep on the uncomfortable double bed, opting for the floor. Needless to say I caught a cold and missed most of Wales.

For the next leg of our UK tour Adam hired a car, and although I tried my best, with the help of a map, to direct him out of crazy, crowded London, I couldn't get us past Marble Arch, which we circumnavigated at least six times before deciding to exit anywhere. We ended up hopelessly lost. Thank goodness for my patient darling who never takes anything to heart. My hopeless attempts at navigation had been such traumatic experiences with Rhys and Jason that I still carry the scars of their abuse.

I was pleased to share the rustic delights of English bed and breakfast establishments (or B&Bs) with my husband, along with the historic musings of places like Bath, Sherwood Forest, the Cotswolds and Stonehenge. We so wanted to visit Dover but ran out of time; instead, we stopped by Stratford-upon-Avon where I entered the world of my literary hero, William Shakespeare. His sixteenth century childhood home on Henley Street was one of the most interesting edifices I have visited, more so than the relative luxury of the home he later enjoyed with wife, Anne Hathaway. This day was blissfully topped off by a visit to William's burial place inside the Holy Trinity Church's chancel where even in death Willy indulged those who'd visit with wicked mirth. His epitaph reads:

Good friend for Jesus' sake forbear,
To dig the dust enclosed here.
Blessed be the man that spares these stones,
And cursed be he that moves my bones.

The English countryside and townships are just as you see in TV programs like *Escape to the Country*. There simply is no other place I've visited so far that comes close to my idea of idyllic country living. I love the Tudor and Victorian styled cottages, the character plus of thatched roofed country pubs, the open medieval style markets, the stone churches and cathedrals, the worn cobblestones, the lush gardens overgrown by flowers I'd not found back home, and of course, the beautiful English hospitality. England was indeed my soul's sheath.

With Adam at the helm of our hire car, and me sick as a dog in the reclined passenger seat, we swung left from Stratford-upon-Avon towards Wales. Matt (or 'Welshy'), my former Corrections buddy, spoke highly of his homeland, offering us a couple of sightseeing lessons on the strict proviso we visit Castle Coch. Matt, you may recall, was the poor soul who like me got fucked up the ass by the Department, only harder.

"If you love castles," Matty said in his lilting Welsh accent, "Wales has more castles than England."

Boy did I love castles, and right there on our first stop was Cardiff Castle, or *Castell Caerdydd*. Twelve pounds was not a lot to pay for a famous castle tour but, given how unwell I was, I told Adam I couldn't bring myself to walk around it and, unwilling to leave me behind, Adam decided the entry fee was too much to pay anyway. By now we were running short on funds. The realisation that touring for six weeks on $4000 was too long had bitterly set in, but here we were; and regardless of our misguided vision we were living the experience of a lifetime and feeling grateful for it – snotty nosed and feverish to boot.

Wales, or *Cymru*, is mostly mountains with about 2700 kilometres of coastline. The wet, cloudy and windy weather did nothing for my cold, and I slept through the trip to Tongwynlais where the highly regarded Castell Coch was situated. The castle was as truly beautiful as Matty had described it but it was not an original building. The site dates from around 1081, but the castle is a nineteenth century Gothic Revival building, now controlled by a Welsh heritage agency. Wide eyed, I came to life as I explored the many turrets that adorn the tiny *castell*. My penchant for anything medieval was well served.

From Tongwynlais we drove north towards Scotland, staying in Monmouth, and ate the best fish and chips I'd had in a while by Soldier's Point House on Holy Island. I felt like a congested Cathy by the gloomy Yorkshire moors near Wuthering Heights, as I beseeched Heathcliff to release me from his vengeful grasp. Soldier's Point House was the perfect backdrop for such a tale of woe, especially at dusk. I'm certain it made my cold just that little bit worse too.

Re-entering England via Ross-on-Wye in Herefordshire, we passed Manchester and Liverpool on our way to York where we stayed in yet another picturesque B&B. Leaving traditional York behind us as we proceeded towards the Scottish border, we stumbled across the defensive Roman imperial boundary known as Hadrian's Wall. The countryside here was lush and spectacular; I could almost taste the freshly scooped cream born of happily fed cows. The wind was wild and sharp and my cold did not enjoy it.

I felt strangely excited about venturing into Scotland. Rhys was of Scottish descent and although our marriage brought me no joy, I was proud of the surname I carried for so many years – a surname my children would carry for a lifetime. A bucket list wish I needed to tick off here was to bring whatever history I could find regarding my children's lineage back to them. I was determined to locate the place their clan called home, Culcreuch Castle in Fintry, Stirlingshire. But first we were required to venture into the country's capital city *Dùn Èideann*, or Edinburgh, where again we got hopelessly lost.

The ambition of a comprehensive castle tour of the UK was sadly quashed as we arrived too late into the renowned home of the Military Tattoo, Edinburgh Castle. The icy Scottish wind cut through us like multiple knives which didn't endear us much to the city of festivals, coupled with the many construction blocks that derailed our designated routes. Once again I commended my husband for his patience. Personally I would have crashed the hired vehicle through those blasted construction fences.

The next day we left a dubious B&B which I decided was haunted, and made our next stop the domain of the legendary Scottish Independence hero, Sir William Wallace. His bronze tribute was visible from Stirling Castle situated nearby. Instead of the tartan scarf heralding my children's clan, I stumbled across something so bizarre I had to buy it at once: *haggis* crisps! Not bad tasting, either.

The wind on Castle Hill, where the majestic Stirling fortress sits, was so chilling, I had to buy a silly souvenir ushanka in order not to freeze my eardrums. One of the many historical figures I was obsessed with as a child was, in 1543, crowned in Stirling Castle: Mary Stuart, known as Mary, Queen of Scots. Only seven years before I had come across Mary's grave inside Westminster Abbey, the place I had so wanted to show Adam. I first became interested in Mary Stuart's unfortunate life when Mother took me to see *Mary, Queen of Scots* in 1971. A fascination with death meant the scenes involving the assassination of Mary's young French husband, and Mary's own beheading in that ominous red velvet gown, haunted me for years afterwards. Mary was Elizabeth I's cousin and for me, this heinous act by Elizabeth somehow mirrored the way Valeria had turned on me for no apparent reason.

Glasgow was another series of orientation mishaps; by now I was completely over navigating and not bothered about sightseeing. Aberdeen and Inverness are also a blur except for a rustic stop here and another there. What I *did* see of Scotland was spectacular, breathtaking, and a close competitor with England and everything I hold dear about her.

On the outskirts of Glasgow, we stayed in a most luxurious bed and breakfast with the kindliest of hostesses. Thirty kilometres away in Fintry I found my children's legacy, the one bestowed upon me by Rhys and his ancestors twentysix years ago via a misshapen marriage.

Culcreuch Castle was not the huge mausoleum I'd expected and the clan was a small and unpopular one. I had to chuckle. Many times I'd asked about the *Mac a' Bhreatannaich* castle and was looked at strangely; ironically the first three letters of Rhys's surname mean 'stranger' in Gaelic. Personal sentiments aside, Culcreuch Castle was a wonderful experience I will always treasure. The castle is nestled inside a small forest flanked by winding paths overlooking a small loch: pure fairy tale heaven. The friendly staff gave me as much information as they could muster so I could pass it on to my children, and when it was eventually handed over I had to wonder who was more enthused – them or me?

The beautiful two-day stay in the roomy B&B did wonders for my awful cold, as did the copious quantities of medicine Adam bought for me in Inverness, so by the time we reached my penultimate bucket list item, I was feeling 100 percent better.

From Inverness we drove to the infamous Loch Ness to see for ourselves whether 'Nessie' was indeed fact or fiction. The 'Loch Ness Monster' was another feature in Gilda's occult magazines that were ingrained in my mind. Real life would have it however that Loch Ness was more about extraordinary nature at its best than some obscure urban legend.

Ever since 1986, when I'd watched Christopher Lambert and Sean Connery in *Highlander*, I'd nursed the desire to visit the Scottish Highlands. Then, with Mel Gibson's *Braveheart* and the animated children's feature *Brave,* the desire intensified and I simply had to get there.

Loch Ness, situated in this magical part of Scotland, the Highlands, spans an enormous 56 square kilometres. The gorgeous properties that line the road on the left bank of the Loch literally took my breath away. I found myself playing the game I used to as a child called 'my house', daydreaming that someday I'd own such a home overlooking what has to be one of the many natural wonders of our world. The Loch is a perfectly still body of water inhabited by eels, sturgeon, minnow and trout, all species which feed on the plankton available. It seems obvious that the place could never sustain the enormous cryptid reported presumably by the kind of folk who also believe in banshees and Big Foot.

Back in the car and southbound via the Loch Lomond & The Trossachs National Park, we traversed the ominous and imposing mountains which left Adam and me spellbound – Glencoe or *A' Chàrnaich*. Glencoe has been utilised as a backdrop for a Harry Potter instalment and a recent James Bond film. It is a surreal place that leaves you feeling like you have melted through some time portal; this is due to a strange stillness that is almost tangible. Adam and I decided one day we would hire a caravan and resume a long trek into the Highlands in 'our time' and not life's; this type of spectacle should never be digested briskly.

We made our way to coastal Stranraer for the last leg of our UK tour, a much anticipated five nights in Eire. My musings with Ireland had nothing to do with leprechauns or Blarney Stones and everything to do with Enya, U2 and my own Celtic heritage.

We returned the hired car to the Stranraer ferry port only to discover we literally had minutes to check in and depart. By the time the ferry clerk booked us onto the vessel it was closing for departure. I asked one of the staff to ensure *we were damn well getting on that boat*; I wasn't waiting four hours for the next one! Fortunately for us the Scottish and Irish are lovely old fashioned folk, and we subsequently found ourselves running along a never-ending concourse behind ferry staff, with our heavy backpacks suddenly

light from anxious adrenalin, and with our guide blaring down his Motorola
– *hold that slipway!*

Once on board I pretty much passed out and forgot the reasons I was even
on this blasted six-week trip. I was completely spent. I felt every pound I had
put on and each pound weighed me down like an anchor. On a honeymoon
the bride is supposed to be pumping her groom virtually from morning till
night – I couldn't think of anything worse given all my ailments. Adam felt the
same thank God – not that my gallant knight would ever admit it or knock me
back if I'd jumped his bones.

Belfast, or *Béal Feirste,* is Northern Ireland's capital, a linen and tobacco
producing city and the land of the O'Neills. Because a majority of homo sapiens
are as morbid as I am, Belfast is today better known for the IRA bombings,
particulary the 'Bloody Friday' bombings in 1972. Due to fatigue we barely
looked at the place, moving right along to something I'd looked forward to
with all my heart: a two night stay at Cabra Castle in County Cavan. Cabra
Castle was my idea of heaven; here I was exhumed and resuscitated.

The castle had belonged to the O'Reilly family, until the murderous Oliver
Cromwell took it and gave it to an English immigrant, Colonel Thomas Cooch.
Handed down via marriage and progeny, the castle was bought in 1964 by the
Brennan family who converted it into a twenty-two room hotel (it now has
over one hundred bedrooms). It was our privilege to find accommodation
inside one of the luxury suites, which at long last afforded us the sense of being
real honeymooners.

Cabra Castle's manicured grounds were so sparse they encompassed a
golf course, an al fresco patio, a gallery terrace, a walled garden, a courtyard,
and majestic views of the Dun a Ri Forest Park. The interior was a visual
smorgasbord of everything one expects from a seventeenth century *caisteal:*
grand staircases, sweeping velvet drapes, four poster beds, baroque, Edwardian,
and art deco furnishings, enough oil portraits to rival the Louvre, and even a
lovable – albeit smelly – resident wolfhound called Oscar. Additionally, Cabra
Castle held four majestic silver service dining rooms and one 'Sherlock Holmes
bar'.

Rested and re-energised, we headed to Newgrange in the Boyne Valley,
County Meath. The Neolithic mound there was said to be a sacred religious
site designed to flood with light when the sun rose at the winter solstice. I
recognised the decorative rock carvings from the dozens of metaphysical texts
and magazines I'd read since that day in Petersham when Betty Shine's book

had found me, helping me to open my third eye. As with Stonehenge, I felt a part of Newgrange; whatever Celtic roots were once significant in my life, these mystic places and their tentacles reached over to me once more.

Our *very* Irish antenna man Kelvin, a Barossa neighbour who ironically returned to his homeland recently with his Asian bride, recommended we attend a medieval banquet in his hometown of Limerick. It had been firmly placed inside my head, from seeing so many film scenes of ancient feasts, that Adam and I partake in a medieval banquet. Almost out of money, though, we decided not to take in the banquet, opting instead for a night in at our Radisson Blu hotel and a quiet meal in the in-house restaurant. Provided I could don a hennin and embroidered tunic, I could enjoy a banquet and battling knights back home at the Gumeracha Medieval Fair.

Our last stop was Dublin, birthplace of that great Taurean muso and activist Paul David Hewson, aka Bono. We put on our cultural hats and visited the famous Temple Bar, the iconic Thunder Road Café (where Adam indulged in a genuine pint of Guinness), and the National Wax Museum. Sans Blarney Stone kiss or bowing before the Giant's Causeway, we bid *slán* to Ireland and flew out of *Aerfort Bhaile* Átha *Cliath* towards our penultimate destination: Stockholm, Sweden.

Without seeing *all* of Ireland, I do not wish to say I was somewhat disappointed with what I found here, yet what I *did* see held little of the rural romance depicted in films like *Silence* and *The Field*. Back home I could jump into my car and drive through the stunning Adelaide Hills for such stylised and romantic views. The Hills' forests, walking trails, vineyards, artisan shops, cafes and unique flora rival many a European landscape ... but perhaps I'd been relying too much on the movies? There were a few Irish people I knew back home I possibly should have consulted.

Adam and I stepped out of Stockholm's Arlanda Airport around four in the afternoon and jumped onto the Arlanda Express, an ultra-fast bullet train that travels at 200 kilometres an hour. We proceeded to our Ikea-style hotel room complete with a 'sexy' open access shower. There's no doubting the Swedes still know all there is to know about horizontal *delicto*.

Starved, we found a delicious Sizzlers-style place right across from the hotel. By the time we finished dining it was well and truly dark outside so, much to our regret we could see very little of what seemed like a magnificent city. Still, we walked a few kilometres in and around the archipelago on Riddarfjärden Bay where the Mälaren, Sweden's third largest lake, feeds. Even at night the

Stockholm Palace or *Kungliga slottet,* was a sight to behold. In this majestic manor reside the Swedish royal family.

The primary reason for our Swedish excursion was a former Hunter Connection workmate and friend, Lotta Thorner. Lotta and her family live in the southern city of Borås. Had I researched Stockholm a little better I would have stolen another day from Paris and allocated it to this spectacular location. Regardless and after twentyfive years of non-visual contact, I was so excited to see Lotta again that I decided that missing out on Sweden's capital just gave us a good reason to return there some day. So, off we flew to meet with Lars at Göteborg Landvetter Airport. Lars Olsson is Lotta's common-law husband of almost three decades.

Lars drove us the 56 kilometres to his hometown and pulled into his driveway in Bergdalsgatan, a street whose name I had mastered after years of letter writing. I held my breath for a moment ... what did I say to someone I had not seen since my eldest child was two? This question was resolved when Lotta ran out into her front yard with arms outstretched and a smile that would light a night sky. There was no mistaking those beautiful green eyes, and when she introduced me to her children, Anton and Jacob, I was taken aback by how equally beautiful both boys were.

Lotta wasted no time preparing dinner for us. As with Jens and Solvig, their hospitality was impeccable. Once more the marital bed was given up for us, despite vociferous objections from Adam and me. There's a lot to be said for European hospitality.

Stepping onto Viking soil finished my trip off perfectly. My bucket list was almost completed. Visiting the Göteborg City Museum where the Äskekärrsskeppet, the only Viking ship on exhibition in Sweden, lay, was another dream come true. As a teen in Mr Okell's class I'd built my very own longboat (scoring twenty out of twenty for my efforts) and now here I was in Sweden, about to view the real thing! Adam was excited for me too – when we entered the exhibition room his eyes would not leave mine. We looked around anticipating a grand vessel albeit in gross disrepair. We certainly didn't expect what met our eyes, and a curator perched on a mezzanine above us studied the look of dismay on my face with some amusement.

"Excuse me," I asked him, "Is this the only Viking ship on display?"

The curator nodded and I almost cried. The Äskekärrsskeppet on display was merely twothirds of the ship's hull, a shambolic display of driftwood. Adam hugged me, assuring me anything dating back to 930 AD had to be an extremely rare find and what a miracle it is that this portion even exists. I later read on Wikipedia that, yes, it was indeed a very rare find.

Moving right along from the residual Viking ship, I absorbed some interesting facts about my beloved Norsemen, for example that Viking women enjoyed a high level of respect in their communities, managing the home finances and farm whenever their husbands were away. Women also held the right to divorce if their husbands did not treat them fairly. Unwanted attention from other men was forbidden as was playful or suggested violence against them. The Vikings were not uncouth barbarians but orderly citizens who took great pride in their appearance. They were consummate artisans who created beautiful jewellery and mosaics and, as we already know, they were master ship builders.

Like most European caste systems, theirs was feudal with Kings at the top, followed by the Karls and the Jarls. At the very bottom of the caste system were the Thralls or slaves, but unlike other early European slaves they were able to buy their freedom. As a no nonsense hard worker, my admiration goes out to those whose simplicity and courage shine above ambition and who, unlike my Roman forebears, did not collapse as a society because of endemic vice or political corruption. Thus, in terms of admiration, the Vikings were at the top of the list as an ancient civilisation I could relate to.

Lotta and Lars took us on a tour of their hometown. Borås has a significant heritage in textiles and the arts, is typically Northern European and, unlike Ireland, exactly what I expected. My love of Northern Europe is visceral rather than acquired via study or a general interest. The words I would use to describe the little I saw of Sweden would include 'fresh' and 'wholesome', just like that old *Norska* commercial.

Lars took us to a roundabout where a giant bronze Pinocchio honoured Gustaf Tenggren, a Swedish illustrator who worked on the 1940 Disney film. Tenggren was once a nearby resident. We then visited the Olssen-Thorner summer house, a lifestyle extension for many Swedes. The summer house stood on the outskirts of a scenic conservation park and lake, not far from the Borås Zoo. The air in Borås, and in the Olssen-Thorner household, is one of tangible serenity so it did not take me long to trail into one of my idealistic relocation daydreams.

Our two beautiful days with exceptionally beautiful people came to an end all too soon. Lotta drove Adam and me back to Göteborg Landvetter Airport, and as a parting gift I gave her the only thing I had on me, Russell Brand's

My Booky Wook, which I'd managed to finish on the many train rides around Europe. I didn't know how Lotta would receive Russell's tales of drug-fuelled debauchery but hoped that like me, she'd see the jewel in a man who had bathed in all of that external muck.

"Let's hope it's not another twenty-five years before we see each other again Angelica." Lotta remarked as we embraced, her beautiful green eyes hiding a *Vikingar* tear.

I on the other hand allowed my tears to flow as freely as the *Göta* älv. I could never tolerate goodbyes.

In Copenhagen I crossed off the last entry on my European bucket list. By this stage Adam and I had had enough of travel. We discussed how in future we would never repeat such a feat, as we downed the last morsels of gluttonous foodstuffs at a Turkish restaurant close to our hotel. Exhausted, we retired for the night, looking forward to seeing the Little Mermaid the following morning.

When I was little, my Umberto Primo friend Alessandra – the one whose head I almost cracked open – bought me a children's storybook which I read from cover to cover more than once. *Den Lille Havfrue* (The Little Mermaid) was one of the stories I fell in love with, and not only with Copenhagen's most iconic landmark, but with *all* mermaids. Today on 27 September 2013 – my eldest daughter's twenty-fifth birthday – I stood in front of the Little Mermaid on her centenary and had my photograph taken. It was a phenomenal privilege. Adam urged me to step onto the stone platform for a closer shot but I was so scared of falling into the water before dozens of tourists who'd been clamouring on the adjacent rocks for their turn with the lady, I just opted for a forefront shot.

København, as it is pronounced in Danish, is pretty, clean, and makes you feel like there is nothing wrong with our world. Our walk along the Hans Christian Andersen Boulevard revealed a bronze sculpture of 'the father of fairy tales' and took us past the famous Tivoli Gardens as we searched for the last destination of the day, the National Museum for yet *another* Viking display. The museum is located inside the Prince's Palace which had a wonderfully interactive Viking section complete with 'dress up' opportunity which I urged Adam to utilise. The only thing that marred our efforts was that damned *spangenhelm* helmet which did not fit Adam's 'Hereford head', sitting on his gargantuan skull like a flat bottomed egg.

I would have given an arm and maybe a leg to visit the Viking Ship

Museum in Roskilde, but we ran out of time. Not all was lost however; I managed to bring home a few 'Thor's Hammer' pendants and keyrings for me, Adam and my co-Viking enthusiast pal, Fred Harris.

It was time to say *farvel* to two countries I had barely touched and head back to Adelaide. Outside the Copenhagen Central Station stood a sea of bicycles. Just how a person could identify their own was mystifying, but I discovered that 50 percent of Copenhageners commute by bicycle and this is an added reason Denmark is considered the happiest nation in the world: plenty of exercise and fresh air significantly lowers the physiological and emotional risk of illness.

Once home, where our little house was still in various stages of unpack and disarray, Adam and I collapsed into a week-long spell of jetlag and exhaustion. Within the course of planning a wedding, looking for a better job, getting married, trying to desperately sell one house, buy another, move out four days prior to our honeymoon, and *then* pack in twelve countries in six weeks, something snapped in both my physiology and my mental state.

We'd had without doubt the adventure of a lifetime, a dream come true, the opposite side of the rainbow, and something others might envy, but as blessed as I *did* feel, I could not help but crash harder than Dorothy Gale.

I returned to my hormones specialist feeling bloated and lethargic. Lindy took one look at me and declared me pre-diabetic. I weighed in at 106 kilos, the fattest I'd ever been – including at full-term gestation. Lindy suggested using a breakthrough diet technique I had ironically seen on an ABC TV program just two nights previously, the '5:2' regime developed by an English doctor, Michael Mosley. 'Why not?' I thought. What did I have to lose – only weight, right? After so many years of yoyo dieting, purging, and trying everything going around, how hard could it be? And did I really want to end up like Alfonso? Would *I* become *the slug* and a burden to my husband?

Emotionally I was *already* a burden to him – not that he'd ever admit to it or even see it that way. That thing that had snapped inside me, however, was irretrievable and things were about to get a whole lot worse.

The honeymoon was well and truly over.

CHAPTER TWENTY-NINE

TILL DEATH DO US PART AND OTHER DRUGS

———

2014 was a defining year for me. In January I honoured a pledge made to my daughters and took them to Vietnam. I also managed to obtain permanency at the disability organisation in Nurioopta and, therefore, much needed job security at last. Unfortunately, two of the clients allocated to me forced me to reconsider everything that was important to me right now, and so I returned to casual hours in order to pick and choose my shifts, as well as my clients. There were aspects of the disability field I still found difficult to accept and acclimatise to. The legacies left by Mother with Piero, by Jason with Sally, and Edan too, still haunted me and sometimes caused me to resent my work. I so wanted to return to basics and kick community service work to the kerb once and for all.

As a casual I was constantly chasing shifts in order to make ends meet, but also because I was not yet ready to become solely dependent on Adam, and with a mortgage I simply could not manage by myself financially. I began to realise that each time I took two steps forward in one area, I'd soon be taking at least one back in another. This rollercoaster that was my life never seemed to stop for me, and I wanted off. I was truly done … cooked to the bone in fact.

Even though guilt ate me up, in my mind being a disabled person was no excuse for poor behaviour. I wrote about Sally's calculated treachery on Yahoo

Answers, hoping to find someone who understood my point of view; instead, I was bombarded with fierce reprimands such as these:

Seems like you were mean to your little brother and God punished you by giving you a son with Mild Autism and a partner with a daughter with cerebral palsy. Live with it and be nice to these kids who are suffering. Stop being a nasty hoe.

And….

Your perspective on disability – calling your neurotypical daughters 'regular', i.e., implying that your son with autism cannot be, saying that disabled people are a burden … well, you disgust me just a little bit. I have nothing against abortion – because you don't have the money, time, or whatever to raise a child. I have everything against aborting a child you would otherwise want because they are disabled. We are not inferior beings. I'm Deafblind and neurodiverse.

But then this:

I feel for you very much Fire Dance With Me. Whether or not being traumatized by being made to take care of a severely handicapped person by your mother, it can be hard to overcome this. I too have an aversion such as this. I know that I will not have any great answer for you, but I agree with (other respondent), you have done nothing wrong. Keeping these feelings to one's self in this way is a self-defence mechanism. I fear that the only way to best overcome these feelings is by more exposure. In this way our resistance to it is lowered and we can manage. I say this because of your partner's daughter. It will be very hard for you not to be there for them, so you must try to overcome this for them. Now that you are older (than 10 years old) you have realized where this aversion stems from and therefore have put things in place so I feel that you will endure. My heart and prayers are out to you, and I do not believe that God is punishing you in anyway. (Other respondent), you should be ashamed of yourself for even suggesting that God would punish a mother by giving her an autistic child. I will ask God forgive you of your ignorance.

From the first two entries I can understand how people might very well keep their views to themselves in terms of 'loaded' topics. It's easy for the trolls and keyboard warriors of our world to condemn; for them pointing a mouse is just another form of warfare. It's so much harder to want to understand and heal someone, so a heartfelt THANK YOU to the last respondent for trying.

We all deserve and have the right to an opinion, it is the essence of the Freedom of Speech that democratic governments stand by, or appear to. When someone's prostrate feelings are insulted because they differ from others', or when their statement is misconstrued, it is none other than obstinate bullying and a sure fire way of creating war and separatism.

For the record I have *never* stated that disabled people have no rights, that they should be aborted, abused, ignored, or seen as lesser beings; I am the champion of the underdog and have always been. My question was about personal issues based on personal experience and how I might learn to handle them. I also attempted to explain how, like everyone else, some people with a disability abuse, hurt or disrespect those who do not have a disability, namely their carers, and why should society excuse or tolerate their bad behaviour *because* of their impairment?

My early entrapment in Catholicism had held me accountable on the topic of abortion, and at one point in life I was indeed an ardent 'pro-lifer'. My work with abused children, my spiritual belief system, and the dormant acknowledgement that relates to the familial abuse I suffered as a child, have clearly changed my attitude towards abortion. As with every other choice in life, abortion *is also* a choice. If you choose to try speed once – *only* the once and mean it – then that's your choice. If you then keep going with the drug, you'll run the risk of becoming an addict. If you abort once due to a mistake you realise will adversely impact your and the child's future, by all means abort, and we are truly grateful for your foresight, but when each 'mistake' you make ends up in countless abortions, you're an irresponsible ignominious dumb ass who needs a tubal ligation ASAP. Bringing a child into the world is not a right – it's a privilege.

Earlier, in 2012 Adam and Rod, a current Mupulawangk friend, flew to Chicago for a shot (pardon the pun) at a clay pigeon shooting world championship title. Adam was a natural at the sport and I fully supported this newfound ambition. When I met him, Adam was a radio controlled aeroplanes enthusiast, but Strathalbyn was so far from us now that he soon lost interest in the sport. The Southern Branch Field and Game club in Monarto was far more accessible. After everything Adam did for me on a daily basis, supporting his new sporting love was the least I could do for my husband.

I thought I'd be okay for two weeks alone in Springton without my angel, but instead, all the old insecurities and terrors resurfaced and I soon found myself in panic mode all day and every day Adam was gone.

Adam Brewer is the kind of man you could trust in a roomful of Playboy centrefolds, and yet my tortured mind began creating every scenario of covert debauchery that might exist. I was calling Adam daily and because of the time differences, usually at the most inopportune of times. I gave Adam no respect and displayed no regard for the fact he might be with important people who could further his sporting career, or that he might be driving on the wrong side of the road with Rod next to him. Nothing mattered except my emotional fix. I was completely pathetic and a hypocrite: when it was my turn to travel abroad without Adam in 2014, I did not expect to suffer the same repercussions I'd imposed on him.

The trip to Vietnam followed our whirlwind honeymoon a little too soon, with the $10,000 it cost us charged to our credit card as we had no savings left. A trait which defines me is my word so, money or not, I wasn't going to take my promise of Vietnam back. Perhaps a girls' trip with my daughters in a country I thought I'd love would cast fresh light into the murky waters that continued to waver within my psyche.

My love for Vietnam began in high school when the 'Asian Invasion' arrived in Cabramatta, around 1979. The Vietnamese kids in my year, although very conservative and private, were smart and polite, and even at a young age intelligence and manners were attributes I held in high regard. Vietnam itself is not a pretty country, but it is colourful, honest and historic. I appreciate forthcoming happy service when travelling, and this is what we received in Vietnam.

Each of us had to program a destination. Because Alycia and Kristen could often grow at odds with one another as is the norm among most siblings, I tried to ensure Vietnam would encompass everyone's needs and wants. Our first stop was Kristen's selection: The Củ Chi Tunnels in Southern Vietnam. This site comprised an elaborate network of connecting tunnels used by the Viet Cong during the Tết Offensive of 1968. Even though I'd lost some weight on the 5:2 diet, I had great difficulty squeezing my backside through the honeycomb of tiny doorways that comprised this incredible underground city. I would never have survived here and yet hundreds of Viet Cong and their families did just that, with malaria and intestinal problems being their second greatest killers, after combat.

The booby trap displays in Củ Chi were straight out of a Lara Croft adventure game and I found it unimaginable how those people conducted military campaigns in underground conference rooms, let alone cooked, slept, and even gave birth in them. My admiration for the Vietnamese grew instantly and, as with Gallipoli, I would never again view war the way it is portrayed by Hollywood.

Ho Chi Minh City, or *Thành phố Hồ Chí Minh*, was a throng of leftover Christmas colour, old and new shopfronts, eighteenth century French architecture, and a myriad of stalls, vendors, and of course those dreadful scooters that come at you from all sides in their hundreds.

The former trading port of Hội An was my and Alycia's favourite destination during our ten days in Vietnam, and where we did most of our shopping. There was a strong Japanese and Chinese presence by way of red glowing silk lanterns, altars to Buddha, Chinese temples, incense and, naturally, the famous Japanese Covered Bridge. In Hội An the shops and cafes are the predominant features – aside from the clamouring tourists along the *other* Japanese bridge that connects two old towns resting on the tranquil Thu Bon River. Ethereal Vietnamese girls reach up to the tourists from their little paddle boats asking them to light a lantern and make a wish. The lantern is then gently laid on the waters and left to drift upstream seeking fulfilment. Alycia urged me to light one and I did so, wishing for a job that was worthy of me, and I of it.

Kristen's highlight in Hội An presented itself at my expense. Looking for a comfortable pair of yoga pants that might get me through until the end of my miraculous weight loss on the 5:2 diet, we entered a typical express Tshirt shop where a mature Vietnamese lady greeted us with a toothy smile. Her English was minimal and in order to explain what I wanted, I pointed at the desired pants on a rack, then turned my back to her, stuck out my ample buttocks, and pointed to my derrière.

"Ahhhh!" the lady smiled again. "Many size for you!" And with that she pulled out a roomy pair, stretching the elasticised fabric to double the size of my butt.

"You fat, you pay!" she added.

Kristen was in stitches. More fabric meant additional cost. Weeks after our trip, Kristen presented me with a Tshirt she had made herself as the ingenious graphic designer that she is, commemorating the event with the slogan 'Many Size for You!'

Aside from water buffalo trotting along uneven roads, pagodas, rice paddies, baskets of raw fish, spices, bok choy sold on sidewalks, and rice paper merchants, other Vietnamese attractions included the Mỹ Sơn Hindu temple ruins in Duy Phú, one too many *phở* (rice noodle soup), delicious pork rolls, coconut smoothie splurges, and a 'cyclo' ride through Hanoi that neither I nor Alycia will ever forget. In Hanoi we saw Chairman Ho Chi Minh's embalmed body in the central hall of the Ho Chi Minh Mausoleum. We were asked to walk slowly, in two lines, and in complete silence as a corpus of perfectly still military honour guards guarded the famous body. Something that stood out for me was the number of military personnel you saw everywhere in Vietnam, some permanently posted in their communist regalia, machine-gun in hand, and ever vigilant in the little booths mounted alongside arterial roads and notable landmarks.

Another image I will never forget was when I peered down from the bus taking us to Hạ Long Bay. A cyclist next to us was heavily laden with a cage filled with dead or dying cats. Inside Juniperina Lenny had told me Vietnamese people ate cats and dogs and, on occasion, audited Vietnamese restaurants in Sydney were found to have the creatures in their freezers. As the avid lover of all animals that I am, and particularly regarding our domesticated brothers and sisters, I had decided it was just an unsavoury urban myth. When Kristen looked up the words for dog and cat in Vietnamese on her phone, sure enough the urban myth was validated and oh the horror! Several restaurants sporting pictures of Labradors and other cherished breeds, displaying signage with *thịt chó* for dog, and a few with *thịt mèo* for cat, left little to hope for.

In the township outside the Củ Chi tunnels I saw small dogs in cages, a breed I could not name. I learnt that the Vietnamese breed only certain types for consumption and that dogs and cats are not a free for all … you must want to try dog in order to eat it as it is served only in specified restaurants. Asian countries love their exotic food, but it wasn't until I saw Rat Stew and Snake Head Soup on a menu that I became convinced. One feature of Vietnamese alimentation that greatly surprised me, though, given I had expected better in Europe, was their coffee – it was fantastic.

Hạ Long Bay translates into 'Where the Dragon Enters the Sea', and it is as beautiful in reality as it appears on postcards. On this occasion the Bay was shrouded in fog, with the locals recommending a September visit for the full pristine aquamarine waters and green limestone island experience. We entered the Thien Cung grotto, which almost rivalled the Temple of Baal in the Blue Mountains in New South Wales for its space and beauty. The activities on board the junk boat were fun but especially the food making demonstrations. The cabins and sleeping cots, on the other hand, were hard and small.

Over the last two days spent in Hanoi my hoped for girls' trip unravelled, with me growing severely fed up with trying to cross the scooter crazy roads, and Alycia and Kristen coming to invisible blows over bitten nails. It was definitely time to go home. I spent one particularly angry morning and afternoon reading

Alycia's copy of Miranda Kerr's *Treasure Yourself* which breathed new life into my resolve to quit all forms of community service employment. I was worth a hell of a lot more than I was receiving, not so much from the clients as from the systems that ruled them.

I cherished Vietnam wholeheartedly. For me it was a wonderful and positive experience. I loved the beautiful smiling vendors, the numerous massages that cost less than an upsized fast food meal, the silent hard work its people produced, and an ambience of general peace despite obvious chaos. Poverty is not hidden in Vietnam and in comparison the West is so very spoilt and takes so much for granted. Having said this, I could possibly live there if I had to.

* * *

When I returned from Vietnam I immediately set Miranda's beautiful pink book into motion, determined to find a low stress job that would enable me to get back to basics and heal the nagging pain left by Juniperina, Mupulawangk and the Magill Training Centre. The disability organisation was a good and solid one and I was certainly not mistreated there, but a pair of clients had caused me to revisit a place I did not like to be in, and so I resigned my permanency and floated around as a casual for a further two years.

After decades of personal unrest, I was desperate for predictability and ease. I realised that the Angelica who gave and gave and gave was now spent, weak, and increasingly unable to regroup. Adam insisted I take three months off and finish this book instead of worrying about work, and although I greatly reduced my availability with Barossa Enterprises, a one wage household income was not enough for me to take time off completely. I began looking for the kind of work I believed I *could* do, without too many repercussions on my emotional wellbeing.

Around this time, I noticed some distinct distancing from people I held dear, with one of these Melissa from Corrections who had almost become my bridesmaid. The others were three of the childhood 'tried and true' friends from high school. In *Treasure Yourself*, Miranda Kerr speaks clearly about friendship:

> I have found that throughout my life as I have changed and grown from each experience, some of my friends around me have also changed. At first this used to bother me, as the people who I used to be close with were no

longer in my life. What I eventually realised was that as my values and beliefs evolved I began to attract like-minded people. Some of my friends are on a similar journey to me and I know they are the friends I will have for a lifetime. Others are markers on the road that point you in the right direction or travel with you for a while until you or they choose another path. I appreciate and value both kinds as all the people in my life have added to the person I am today. I was once told that if you wanted to see what type of person someone is, you just have to look at their friends. It's important to be around people who mirror the real you and not to change who you are to fit in with other people. In the end real friends accept you for who you are and walk in when others walk out.

Above all interpersonal traits, the two I cherish most are honesty and loyalty. I believed I personally applied both virtues to those I truly cared for and that being a *good* friend meant I only attracted other good friends to me. I'd probably watched one too many 'enduring friendship' films and had convinced myself that, just like marriage, friendship was for life. When my lifelong friendships disintegrated for no apparent reason, or at least none that made any real sense to me, I took it very poorly and, according to my survivor nature, I reacted badly and excessively.

Slowly I began to realise that my good friends were no longer those I'd believed in but a few new ones I'd met here in South Australia. Among these was Amanda Stewart, a colleague at the disabilities organisation. When I first met Amanda it was she who told me she preferred not to know her co-workers, keeping work separate from her private life. I was perfectly fine with this; I had been hurt so badly by 'friends' *and* family, and I was no longer putting my head on the chopping block for anyone either. Then one day I showed up for handover teary-eyed and unable to hold things together and it was Amanda who comforted me, and from there our friendship blossomed. Amanda is a genuine soul, this I could see, and given the experiences in my life, I was now learning to make accurate distinctions. Whereas people from my past looked to me for cheap laughs and physical or emotional favours, Amanda asked for nothing – only my company.

The other SA darling is Sue. Sue and I met on shift working in crisis care accommodation for child protection not long before I joined Corrections. On our hands we had a pair of extremely damaged brothers who had experienced maternal incest, just to name the worst of it. During a harrowing incident where it appeared the older brother was going to kill the younger one, Sue and I looked at one another, took a firm hold of the boy, and went against system protocol by restraining him for safety of self, of us, and his brother. It was an act of faith, trusting a complete stranger with a forbidden manoeuvre but Sue remained a faithful colleague throughout and a little later became a friend. Sue and I lost touch for some time after I joined Corrections but reunited when, new at Barossa Enterprises, I received this call:

"Hey you! Heard you're working with Lincoln!"

"Who's this?" I asked, clueless.

"Sue P! You and I dragged Travis and Brandon in Nuri years ago remember? I work at B.E. too."

Sue is a salt-of-the-earth, no nonsense 'mother hen' type. She embodies the two traits I mentioned earlier, honesty and loyalty, and I wish I could see more of her more often. Modern life has created a constant rush for us all, with people no longer connecting face to face like they used to. If it weren't for Facebook and text messages, I'd never hear from her. Sue is from a background that sometimes comes into sharp contrast with some of the principles I stand for, but it never comes between us; the respect we have for one another assures this.

What happened to me at Mupulawangk was traumatic in the highest order but for every bitter anecdote I reserve for the place, I need to remind myself of the very real friendships forged there: Lynda, Angela, Ruth, Kevin, Fred, Rod, and my husband, are all positive Mupulawangk legacies.

Sharon Schofield is a lady I was introduced to in 1990 by Annabella and her husband in Sydney. We spent many a day in each other's houses with our numerous littlies running around happily. Sharon and I had one thing in common: our husbands and their lack of respect for us. A few decades later, we'd both found Cancerian men worthy of us. Annabella, who must assume it is her mission in life to rescue discarded husbands regardless of the reasons for their disposal, cut Sharon off completely, and because of a quarrel with another 'tried and true', I was also dropped not long after. Sharon and I lost physical touch but yet again Facebook magic ensured we were never too far from reach. Ironically, Sharon found work in the disability field as well. She asked me to be her bridesmaid when she married her 'crab', the delightfully funny Phil Schofield, in 2015. This was the second time I've been bestowed such an honour. Unlike Maria, I take bridesmaid duties as a blessing and a privilege.

Today Sharon and I give each other strength throughout continuing personal trials and consider the other the sister we did not have. It's funny how we often ignore those who are a permanent and unwavering fixture in our lives because of misguided loyalty. Sharon and Sue never left me … it was I who left them to chase people and situations that flourished only in my imagination. These two grand ladies decided to bide their time and patiently waited for the prodigal friend's return, and for this I am truly grateful. My greatest regret today is to have invited Annabella to my wedding instead of Sharon (primarily because Annabella had been the first friend made in 1977 when we moved from Adelaide to Sydney).

Jan too is still by my side; she was my child protection offsider with the Harris children during a highly uncertain time as a newbie in South Australia. Jan has stated that she thinks of me like a daughter. I love Jan's warm Sagittarian wisdom which now replaces the hurt so many other Sagittarian women had injected me with.

A problem that has presented itself throughout my life is a desperate need for love, acceptance and sense of value. In order to secure and protect these needs, I have travelled through life collecting people. I'd nurture all of them spreading myself dangerously thin in the interim. I figured that if I pampered and served all of them well, they'd never stop loving me and would never leave me. In retrospect I expected far too much from people who were, in actuality, empty. I utilised a similar modus operandi within my jobs, giving my all to greedy bosses and colleagues. When it was time to reap any rewards, I suddenly became a nuisance, a threat, or a liability. One piece of valuable advice I was obviously not ready for at that time, was dispensed to me by my first unit co-ordinator at Juniperina:

"Just put your head down, ignore the idiots, work hard, and with time you'll get to where you need to be."

Had I followed this advice instead of giving everything to two vicious snakes, my career in Corrections may have continued. An incessant mourning of this period in my life created some detrimental psychological issues. I considered myself a conscientious and capable officer and to be prematurely pushed out of the job in such an unceremonious way haunted me, as did the tribunal fiasco with the Magill Training Centre. If the Universe did not want me working in these jobs, why did it present them to me in the first place? Had I lacked talent in those fields I may have overcome the pain more quickly, but I had a knack for this type of work – I communicated with people at risk in ways most cannot, and don't wish to. In this work I felt valued and needed, even loved. The same went with interpersonal relationships. What was I supposed to learn exactly? What was my lesson?

Denise consumed my thoughts. I tried everything – practical and metaphysical – to banish her from my being, but nothing seemed to work. I was simply not ready to let go. Valeria had the same effect. There was no reason for Valeria's cruel and intentional evasion, for her tacit derision. The snub I received from her regarding my wedding was hard to swallow. I extended a pleading hand to draw her back into my life by inviting her, and she turned it against me, slapping me hard with the pettiest of excuses; she may as well have told me to just *fuck off*. What then rubbed salt into a screaming wound was the way she maintained – even exalted – a relationship with my eldest daughter. I tried to discourage Alycia from staying in it but was met with strong vocal resistance and the possible loss of a far more important connection. Whether or not my cousin had been knowingly twisting the knife in, she certainly contributed to the speedy downward spiral that brought me several steps closer to a deep state of depression and neuro fatigue.

The way I saw things, Valeria had divided my already tiny family. Kristen remained by my side but Edan's disability meant he did not understand that going to 'Valeria's beach house' only plunged the knife in deeper. Rodolfo tried his best to have us both at family gatherings, but the invitations often were simply not relayed to me. It hurt like hell as I was not the antagonist in this story, but when Rodolfo's fiancée was diagnosed with secondary breast cancer not long after giving birth to their miracle child, I knew better than to kick up blinding red dust over personal calamities.

By September 2014 I had applied for so many 'basic' jobs, I lost count. I was either 'overqualified', or, as was my conviction, my many years in 'security work' impressed adversely on prospective employers looking for sweet, smiling, front of shop staff. Earlier on, in April, I managed to get a school cleaner's job in Birdwood, with a renowned Adelaide cleaning company. The job was crazy and it left an indelible physical disability but it was close to home, convenient, and sped up the weight loss the 5:2 regime had initiated. For the first time in ten years I was almost in the 80-kilos zone.

Sure, I still felt like a loser pulling paper rolls out of shit smeared toilets, or having to answer to snooty primary school teachers when I once negotiated with murderers, but I had a regular job with regular hours. Right now, right here in South Australia, I was unequivocally blacklisted from both both government departments I had worked for, and there wasn't a thing I could do about it. My career was gone, never to be retrieved, and I had to make peace with that. I tried returning to Corrections twice, and twice I was declared 'unsuitable'. When I sought assistance from the then present Corrections Minister, one who had successfully assisted friends of ours, he sent me a generic and rather condescending 'ministerial' reply stating:

'The fact that you were a former Correctional Officer, does not guarantee a re-entry into the department.'

This was untrue. Two people who opted out of Corrections from my course were re-employed, albeit having to redo the course. I then tried hard to convince myself a career was not important to a happy life. I needed to remain wary I didn't end up like the one person whose sole obsession I criticised and abhorred: my mother.

The monstrosity that was the vacuum cleaner the primary school employers expected me to use was putting my already fragile back out. My chiropractor wasn't happy but I wanted and needed to keep this job. Eventually, after five weeks, I informed the business I needed a new vacuum cleaner because my back could not take any more. The very next night my team leader informed me the business was letting me go; I'd used those dreaded WorkCover words – 'my back'. I was devastated but also somewhat relieved. My back could no longer take the systematic twisting of a mop, the full hour of nonstop vacuuming, or the unrealistic speed required in order to clean a ten room, five toilet, two kitchen, gym and library area in just *three* hours. The only consolation I leaned on came from the school principal after I'd rung him for a reference:

"But you're the best cleaner we've ever had! I'm going to lodge a complaint!"

I never did any job by halves. As with my personal relationships, I gave my all *all* the time. I worked to rule, respected my superiors, barely took 'sickies', was famously punctual, and tried to befriend and protect my colleagues. It was pointless; regardless of my effort I was always overlooked for promotion and was rarely treated with the respect and esteem I deserved and imparted on others.

My benign chiropractor took pity on my plight and offered me four hours on a Friday cleaning her huge house, as well as referring me to her mother-in-law for a further two hours clean on a Tuesday. As both my back and morale continued to decline, I withdrew from both positions and distributed fliers, searching for more suitable work. The postmistress at the Mount Pleasant Post Office, Anne, and her associate Rose, saw the flier on the Tungkillo Progress Club's notice board and brought me in to do some light cleaning on a Friday evening. Although I did not last there long, I forged two more beautiful and uncomplicated friendships with Anne and Rose, who coincidentally were also my direct neighbours.

Because of my past I am not a 'glass half-full' personality and I'd like to think I might be excused for it. Nevertheless, the way I now viewed my losses promptly led me into a state of mental illness I never imagined I'd fall into. With each rant of mine that was criticised, I'd delete my Facebook profile.

"Facebook is lighthearted fun Angelica. Stop being so negative and using it as a form of self-promotion," one person told me.

Going 'Facebook free' for four months did help me to feel better. I was able to bypass increasing feelings of isolation and paranoid anxiety by staying away, but Facebook was not the real problem. Facebook kept me connected with some beautiful people in Sydney and it brought me friendships with a couple of amiable strangers from abroad. Facebook is indeed lighthearted fun but I seemed to have lost that fun somewhere along the way. The rationale that social media isolates people is as flawed as the notion that violent films create serial killers. People have and *make* their own choices. I made my own choices based on a level of inner perception and then outward requirement.

My internal world was flawed but my reality was not. I have a husband who, for reasons I still don't see, adores me, who said nothing negative about my unemployment except to encourage and support me at every turn. My children suffer their own demons but they are loving, safe, and productive. Edan returned to me in March to remain in South Australia forever. I lived in a precious part of the countryside surrounded by sheep, lambs, cows, calves and rolling hills. I had a miniscule mortgage and future travel plans in the pipeline. As mentioned above I *had,* and was making, some lovely friends I obviously have not appreciated enough and the reason I haven't is because in spite of a deep understanding of spirituality and its myriad of modules, I have refused to believe people can change. Within my rationale people I grew up with, who knew me and my history and for whom *I* was there for *their* darkest moments – how could they suddenly turn around and deny, lie about, or condemn everything we once stood for? It simply did not make sense – not to me. Less than a handful of tried and true friends had motivated me into doubting and shutting out the rest of the world and this was *my* doing, not theirs. Noone can truly force you to be someone you are not and Miranda Kerr's simple wisdom had obviously not sunk in deeply enough.

But just as I was about to throw faith back into the Universe's face, I was successful in obtaining a sporadic job as a youth worker with the Department of Education and Child Development inside a residential program dedicated to secondary students from the Anangu Pitjantjatjara Yankunytjatjara Lands. This meant I had one foot back inside government work and with children, which I was always passionate about. Aside from the 'back to basics' work I believed I needed, working with our Indigenous people still rated favourably. When I received the 'successful applicant' call I was rather surprised, given that throughout the interview I'd bagged our government's stance on 'Aboriginal issues'. Never again would I offer gratuitous answers; from now on anything I earned I did so by speaking my own Truth. Could it be that this particular brand of *gubbas* weren't being paid to cover up bureaucratic chasms?

Unfortunately, the shifts with my little beauties were random and I could not rely on them. I supplemented my earnings by taking on another casual position cleaning 'holiday lets' in the Barossa Valley, which, to my surprise, I really enjoyed. The Aboriginal kids and particularly the junior girls, brightened my day with their cheeky purity and big white smiles. These kids *wanted* to be here and were altogether different from the Kooris and Nungas I had met in juve. I hoped that someday I might obtain a permanent part-time job here.

There was yet another reason to feel grateful, and it arrived in a little furry package we named Conan.

While still at Springton, Alycia artfully manipulated Adam and me into accepting in our home a gorgeous little Pomeranian cross Japanese Spitz princess she named Gogo. I'd never had a dog before and was not dog oriented so I had mixed feelings about Gogo from the get-go, but couldn't disappoint my daughter. As sure as the sun warms the earth, Gogo warmed our hearts and so when Alycia moved out into her own place taking Gogo with her, that sweet little soul left an empty spot in our lives. Enter Kristen and *her* big, well camouflaged heart.

In July Kristen finally relocated to South Australia which meant I had all three kids living here; yet another reason to feel grateful. Adam saw the sparkle re-ignite in my eyes whenever Gogo came to visit and suggested we buy a rescue dog from the Animal Welfare League. One visit to the shelter and I fled back outside in tears. How does one choose among the countless little faces clawing and yelping at their gate to take *them* home? Kristen solved the problem when she found a Pomeranian breeder in Salisbury, sending me a picture of the most adorable puppy … she'd even loan me the money without any pressure to pay it back. It was love at first sight.

Entering the smoke-filled premises where precious little souls were being raised, our eyes found the only mottled baby inside the pen, the very same one who last week stared back at me from my mobile screen. I didn't wait for Adam's decision, I didn't have to, as we both spoke simultaneously like we often do:

"We'll take this one!"

Cradling the tiny fur ball in my arms, I couldn't hand the money over fast enough to the dishevelled matriarch nursing a grandchild as its underage parents lounged by the TV set, oblivious to all but their bowl of crisps and litre of coke. My new baby needed clean air, and fast.

Conan, a Boxing Day baby, had his name before we knew he existed. I had asked Adam to name our future pet, not only because he had previously fathered a dog, but because I wanted Adam to have sole input in something of great importance for once. And so we christened our 'furry son' Conan; he would be the child we would never have together, and so, exactly as our son was Conan treated.

Although I've always been a lover of animals, I never fully understood the obsessive behaviour some people direct towards their dogs. Letitia had been like that with a dog called Stellina (a three-legged dog we had for a while in our Rome apartment) and I thought she was gross. There was no way I'd let a smelly, drooling dog lick my face like she had allowed hers. How rapidly my views changed when Conan came along: I not only let him lick my face, we exchanged great big kisses too. I lived for this little man, fretting about leaving him home alone and getting my lazy ass off the lounge to ensure he received his daily walk. Conan quickly replaced Adam as the first 'person' I needed to see when I got home. I babied Conan, I made every allowance for Conan, I fell head over heels in love with Conan, and Conan was the centre of my universe and my reason to smile, even in the grip of darkest despair.

My glass was still half empty, however. Instead of cherishing two added reasons for feeling incredibly fortunate, I mourned how these great joys had arrived so late in my life … the love of a good man, and the pure unconditional loyalty and undivided adulation only a dog knows how to give.

Regardless of a few small wins, searching for the elusive 'perfect-job-for-me' continued to consume me. Perfect also meant *reliable* and *permanent* even though I knew perfectly well life is fluid and variable and that absolutely nothing remains permanent. Was it my age? Where I lived? My karma? What exactly stopped it from happening?

I almost managed to place on hold the murderous feelings I harboured towards Denise and Fiona, but then just like that they resurfaced. Those two had been my curse and I blamed their evil and all that went with my relocation to South Australia for current failures. Adelaide, a giant country town full of tight lipped Lutherans and backwater free settlers … who did they think they were, refusing me the simplest of jobs?

I then cursed Valeria and Bianca. One of the principal reasons for moving to South Australia was to have my adopted sisters and brother around me. Now they ignored and avoided me like I did not exist, like I was some kind of filthy germ, and for what reason precisely? Apparently I had offended Bianca's husband. I apologised for something I may have said in jest, but when I asked to be reminded of what it was, I was given nothing. Prior to my wedding, when I asked Valeria why she had cut me off, she answered, "I don't know, and I don't know why you rub me the wrong way either. You just do."

Gratuitously and egotistically I forgot the many reasons for leaving Sydney and sanctioned ones for returning there, with the first being that I missed my friends – the ones who had *not* betrayed me, like Debra, Robbie, Sharon, Patricia, Karen and Sue. Secondly, I began to review the virtues of multicultural Sydney, a place I detested for its ghettos and petty crime. I decided Sydney was far more open minded and forthcoming than this conservative sewing circle I now lived in. Thirdly, I was never refused a working position in New South Wales; I was the one to leave a job, I was not ever made to.

I would have found more reasons to return there and they would have all been fabricated, because Sydney is an impractical hell-hole.

"Back in Sydney I'd have a job right now!" I seethed to Adam. "I *hate* Adelaide. Let's move to Tassie and apply for Risdon jail together."

Folly and madness were my middle names now and I was positively running from my problems yet again; I had learnt *nothing*. Did I truly expect my loyal, long suffering, darling husband, to say goodbye to all he knew and cherished just to follow the volatile musings of a woman he had, alas, fallen in love with? No, I would *not* make him do such a thing; it was all just inconsiderate mind chatter, using a good man's bountiful emotions as a crash test dummy to plug some nasty and nagging holes. My internal void was now an abyss that was devouring me piece by piece, moment by moment, but it would not drag Adam down with me, come what may.

A catalyst for deliverance finally presented itself. Sue P, my dear and well-meaning friend, was now working for an employment agency that assisted clients with physical or emotional impairment. I self-diagnosed as suffering from post-traumatic stress disorder and anxiety while seeking help from a US based internet support group and a psychotherapist. Suicidal ideation was also on the increase, as were tearful periods filled with blackest doom and despair. Getting out of bed to attend to responsibility was proving harder too, with Adam often having to wear the persistent angst and white hot rages. On days like these, and whenever I managed to catch lucidity, I would ask Adam to rethink our union and marriage.

"I told you *before* you committed yourself to me that I was damaged goods, Adam. You shouldn't have doubted me bubba – now look at where you are – trapped in a drowning pool with me pulling you down by the ankles. You can still leave Adam; I'll *never* get better. This is what life with me looks like, and is this what you *truly want?*"

I think even Adam's brother and father's deaths did not draw the flood of tears my words incited. Adam has great difficulty with self-expression and he'll just cry and cry in order to demonstrate hurt, and with each tear I'd hate myself more, dying inside another notch. I knew what *needed* to be done.

Sue arranged for me to have a Job Capacity Assessment done at Centrelink to be found eligible for employment assistance within her agency. Also, I needed a recommendation from my psychotherapist to further qualify. Just like that the enormity of my situation pounced on me like a rabid lion. I was once found capable for work with the most difficult, damaged, and sometimes dangerous people in our community, I acted in front line roles that covered most areas of community service work, and yet I was now too incompetent to sit in the seat of a checkout chick without receiving assistance from an employment agency for the disabled? And if I *did* register with this agency, was I signing myself over in blood as a confirmed lunatic? Is this how I would go out, aged forty-nine with a multitude of life experience and skills, having loved and assisted hundreds of people? Had work inside a factory alongside people with the IQ of a potato become the sum total of my existence?

No it was not. I was better than this.

On Wednesday 8 October 2014 I decided I *was* better than life's cruel epitaph. I took a sheet of Panadol capsules and another of Phenergan and swallowed them. I had no idea whether they'd take me out of this world, but as I started to feel drowsy I knew I had to tell Adam I loved him, and before it was too late.

CHAPTER THIRTY

SUCCUBUS NO MORE

———

T he night before my 'departure' I had put Adam through eight hours of cruelty. There was not a single sacred thing that I did not throw at this man, a man who'd blessed my life every day, my seventy MILLION camels, the reason I woke up most mornings wanting to give destiny another chance … my hero. I loved Adam so much that I swore on all that was of any importance to me that I would never again hurt him – not like that, not in *any* way. He deserved better than me.

I should have slipped away quietly. What possessed me to call my husband and say goodbye, knowing only too well he was acting up in a position of trust, was incorrigible. It was *I* who told Adam he was too smart for a key turner's job, I who pushed him to strive for more. Now he was doing just that, yet in a moment of perfect self-pity it was I who was now prepared to take it all away. Suicide is after all the most selfish of acts, is it not?

I could barely see the digits on my receiver but as I pressed on them, I felt myself becoming drowsier and drowsier. Adam's beautiful, familiar, warm voice, began talking to me at last:

"Adelaide Remand Centre, Adam speaking …"

"I just want to tell you I love you bubba …"

Adam knew immediately what I'd done. The little I remember about the call is his agonising screams and wretched, helpless tears. I then must have said "goodbye" to him with the last words I recall being, "Not like this bubba, not like this …"

The rest, except for some violent vomiting, remains a blur.

Irrespective of the mind's agenda or intent, I believe the body is overruled by our psyche. My physiology, at least, is governed by my emotions. If I am anxious I get diarrhoea, if I'm hysterical I'm out cold for days, and the only times I become an insomniac are when I'm eaten up by anger or resentment.

Louise L. Hay's beautiful and popular book *You Can Heal Your Life* has a large section which lists the correlation between illness, disease and the emotion(s) that instigate them. Another excellent, lesser known book I am currently reading goes even further, listing osteo-muscular areas affected by negative thinking. This is *The Body Is the Barometer of the Soul* by Annette Noontil, an Australian author. At this point in my life anxiety has been my worst enemy and *Louise L. Hay's highly successful book You Can Heal Your Life,* offers tangible affirmations that assist with the reversal or repetitive thought patterns.

Louise makes perfect sense. Hearing Adam's mortally wounded sobs created a physical shock such that waves of emotion forced the contents of my stomach to be catapulted from my body. With this, I failed to succumb to the eternal sleep I thought I longed for.

The fifty-minute drive from Adelaide to Tungkillo must have been the worst of Adam's life. Not knowing whether his wife would still be alive at the end of that journey must have been hell. Had I not felt so much love for Adam, I would not have called him, but then the physiological chain reaction would not have occurred and perhaps this story would end here. Once again Adam Heath Brewer saved my life – literally.

And no, suicide is rarely a selfish act, ladies and gentlemen, what it *is* – it's a horrible legacy to leave others to mourn and question.

A person wishing to end his or her life is ill – very ill. They need help and fast.

* * *

Wednesday 8 October 2014 marked my rebirth. From the ashes the phoenix *must* rise.

I thought I'd become a new Angelica once I'd moved back to South Australia, once I'd broken free from my marriage to Rhys, once I'd fled my home in Bonnyrigg. But with each change I was not renewed; I had simply made a few external alterations and the old Angelica remained – the same flawed, searching spirit.

The new Angelica emerged when she broke an angel's heart, when proof of just *one person's* incorruptible love kicked me wholly and solely in the face, full force, when at long last I felt more valued than any other human around me. On Thursday 9 October 2014 I made a vow to myself and my Adam … I vowed to *live* and live well – or at least, as well as I could muster.

In my case *Hoobastank* (the Californian music band), got it damn near perfect with their song's main chorus in 'The Reason'.

I took myself to a trusted local doctor and explained my suicidal ideation and subsequent attempt. I wept as I guiltily recounted the brutality I'd used towards my husband. She immediately prescribed antidepressants, 10 mg of Lexapro.

"My patients have experienced great results on this medication." She smiled, but memories of Prozac came flooding back and I was hesitant and afraid.

I hated medication. I believed, falsely, that a person should strive to triumph over their own demons. Additionally, I did not wish to profit the pharmaceutical companies who make trillions by keeping people zombified and subservient to corrupt governments and corporations. But, on Lexapro I did go, and I was also assisted by a psychotherapist, Chris Browning, who brought me to the realisation I had run out of fossil fuel, with Lexapro now the diesel needed to keep this old carriage running.

"But why now?" I asked Chris, perplexed. "Why now that I've finally found the one thing I was looking for since I can remember? Now that I no longer have to worry about infidelity, lies, or loneliness? Now that I've begun to feel safe and comforted?"

"It is exactly *now* that mental illness strikes Angelica," Chris explained. "When you've fought like a Spartan your whole life and been on your guard, the moment you drop that guard and the brain relaxes its hold on your emotions, your true vulnerability – the one you suppressed for so long, moves right back in. Fight and flight has closed its doors, with pain and regret left uncontrolled now, forcing other doors to open. Your emotional stores have been exhausted Angelica; your defences are down. You're going through withdrawal from a war-torn life. You now have triggers that bring you back into that war zone; this is what post-traumatic stress disorder looks like, and on top of it, I feel you suffer from adjustment disorder with a depressed mood."

Oh my God … my feelings were not all in my head after all – which is contradictory I know – but 'strength of character' could really do nothing to cure me now. I *needed* medication … I have a chemical imbalance … I *am* ill … people could stop telling me I was strong now for it simply was no longer the truth.

I was nonetheless determined *not* to wear my diagnoses like a badge of honour albeit the diagnoses being what I needed in order to begin anew; and anew I began – on *all* fronts. It was not easy. I'm still not an overnight success, but this is what Mindfulness, diplomatic assertion and self-love are about: daily practice.

Alongside Lexapro, my new best friend, Mindfulness and Adam's relentless and loving support are today offering me a new lease on life, a life force I *can* draw from. The only side effect of Lexapro is a mildly 'foggy' brain so that if I was easily distracted and forgetful before Lexapro, I'm now a little worse for it but I don't care, it's a minor glitch and so worth it. Since being on this medication I've not revisited the abyss once and this is how I like it. I'm back to a lighter shade of the Angelica I once was: conducive, playful, and mostly smiling. I am less trusting now and hypervigilant about bad behaviour and deceit, but after everything I've been through it's to be expected. This big mama Snake has been trodden on too many times, and right now I couldn't guarantee anyone *diplomatic assertion* … it's more a case of 'get out of my fucking way or I'll bite you!'

As I began to change in order to fit into the *real* me, outside circumstances and people also changed, starting with my tried and not so true Cabramatta High School friends. After years of listening to and helping *them* through their own personal traumas, I now forthrightly asked for support with mine. I was not only alienated for my 'audacity', I was actually accused of 'acting out' to gain attention. One 'friend' in particular emailed the following to me:

'I know you better than you know yourself Angelica. I know who you are and what you are. You cannot pull the wool over my eyes like you do with the others.'

Those self-assured words hit me like a sledgehammer. I will never forget them. I asked Leisl what she meant exactly, although I knew she was making reference to the nubile days in primary school where I had lied about this or that in order to fit in and give myself some worth as I tried to mask the decay and stench of my miserable home life. Naturally, Leisl refused to explain herself. She knew nothing more than what she had witnessed over the past thirty-seven years. It was not too difficult kicking her to the kerb, along with another 'friend' I had nurtured for years throughout her abusive marriage, one she vehemently denied when reminded. Although Leisl always gave out a congenial vibe she was self-absorbed and had rarely stuck her head out for anyone. Ironically, when I left Sydney I entrusted Leisl with my other 'friend'; I thought that in my absence they might grow stronger and wiser together instead of feeding each other's '*amour-propre*' egos.

When gauging a person's character, try to avoid their words and watch their actions. As the old adage says, *words are cheap*.

Annabella, the very first friend I'd made in New South Wales, decided to follow suit without much questioning on her part. Adam tried to have her 'see the light' but her answer to him was, "I guess I'm going to lose you too now." Unlike Leisl, Annabella's actions spoke for her innately kind heart, but her grey matter is even less dense than her misguided heart, and Annabella attempts to protect the 'hard done by' even when they are the perpetrators of the *hard doing*. Annabella lacks investigative ruthlessness and logic and so I can almost forgive her naivety, born as it is from ignorance and not malice.

It was a terrible time for me – not just because I felt horribly betrayed and abandoned by my peers, but because these three women had grown up with me and my dysfunctional family and knew my history inside out, or so I thought. How could they just leave me like this in my hour of need, and after I'd always been there for them? Disgusted and outraged I attempted to bring Leisl back to task, reminding her of the many times I had assisted her with her personal woes. Her reply was typical of those who lack honesty and intellectual acumen: "I know who my real friends are Angelica and they don't keep tally of what they do for me."

'What a fucking cop out!' I thought. We are souls having a human experience. We are actors on a global stage. Our interpersonal relationships are not 'unconditional'. Unconditional is an overly misused throwaway word, like that dreadful adage, *it is what it is*, which coincidentally Leisl used frequently to fob off unacceptable behaviour and circumstances. As for the third friend, someone I can't even bring myself to name under a pseudonym for she deserves nothing, well ... karma already has you in her clutches. My work here is done *ma cherie*.

Noone *truly* enters into a relationship expecting absolutely nothing. Noone gives and gives and is elated to never receive from a close bond – particularly when coming into dire need themselves. We homosapiens are two layers, the physical and the etheric, and as physical beings, we live a human life that is in sharp contrast with our etheric/spiritual one. Our Highest Purpose is to remember who we really are – a soul – but as we learn the earth lessons that ultimately better our spiritual condition, it also becomes a condition to follow the rules here on earth. The rules of Friendship and Romance allow for favours to be granted *and* taken, otherwise the friendship is no more than a host/parasite relationship. A host/parasite relationship teaches nothing except how to become greedy, co-dependent, hateful, or resentful. Physicality is dense, therefore the buoyancy of Spirit is trapped inside illusory webs of Earth logic, counteractivity and contingency.

When we believe the illusion and fallibility that *is* life, this is when we fall prey to all that is wrong with our world – suicide and a lack of 'available love'. Religious proselytising is particularly toxic to our journey – it robs us of our right to be, our unique individuality, *true* altruism, and sheer common sense. If you are born under a spiritual contract for good, you will follow that good irrespective of religious dogma. Personally I fail to see how a person who is governed by a set of ancient moral codes can function holistically in today's uncertain and confounding world. I have always gravitated towards the bohemian and 'alternative' because I find it dynamic and challenging, whereas a religious lifestyle is static and stifling. If nothing else remember this: WE ARE EXPRESSIONS OF LIFE.

When people I held close abandoned or betrayed me in my hour of need, I was suddenly given a blank canvas and asked to fill it regarding the nature and direction of human beings. I painted my canvas red with rage. I had spent my life trying to understand, care for, and listen to people, and now when I truly needed them, they threw me out like a broken toy. Family abandonment was particularly hard to swallow. I was born with a strong sense of familial obligation and loyalty. I began life without a father and only one flawed grandparent, but also no sibling I could relate to. My cousins were the only familial reference I could turn to, so when they too left without valid reason it was a terribly difficult thing to put into human perspective. With the exception of Rodolfo, who sporadically popped in and out of my life, I have taught myself to see Valeria and Bianca as people not worthy of my time or love for reasons that are obviously cosmically contractual. The only thing that still hurts is how these two go out of their way to be in my children's lives yet continue to display little regard for their mother. It seems hypocritical and almost intentionally cruel.

Rodolfo, too, has been hit with what I've labelled 'The [my maiden surname] Curse'. His wife of barely two years left our world in June 2016 after a threeyear battle with secondary breast cancer. Rodolfo is now their miracle daughter's only parent; little Giannina, named after my beautiful Auntie Gianna, is four years old. Rodolfo requires all the help he can get now and this will come from his sisters, so I am now resigned to the fact I will rarely see him – if ever. This now leaves me with one extended family member, Uncle Eduardo.

Another over used adage is *when one door closes another opens* but I can live with this one because it's true. I now believe 100 percent that the Universe hands out lessons until they are learnt, and only until then do we receive our prize. When I bid a difficult but decisive 'farewell and fuck off' to those three tried and *un*true friends, in walked Robbie Rogers, a beautiful soul I vaguely remembered from high school.

What do I say about an Earth Angel who cannot be described because of her blindingly radiant beauty? I know Robbie's heart and how unassuming she is, so I will keep her story and the fact we walked parallel lives a secret – *her* secret. This Earth Angel is nearly as instrumental in saving my life as Adam, and indeed it was Adam who sent me to Port Macquarie to be with Robbie shortly after my suicide attempt.

Robbie had been in my life for some time now but I did not 'see' her there. When a person is impeded by arrogance, pain and self-pity they tend to overlook the gems along the path for treading their own mud. Aside from 'talk' therapy and Lexapro, visiting Robbie and her surreal family was like manna from Heaven on my road to recovery. Entering the Rogers home was like entering a metaphysical temple nestled in the most blissful of forests … complete serenity and pure harmony.

Previously I had only felt such inner peace and freedom from external muck at the Brahma Kumaris retreat in Leura, a place I wanted to take my cherished Robbie to, and did. Robbie is today not only a great friend, she is another precious lifeline as well as my soul sister, and I love her with all my heart. With true love, however, comes fretting, and the fear of loss, not spiritual loss, only a physical one. I believe transcendental loss is impossible when dealing with Earth Angels. Robbie has taught me *acceptance* and I feel I may have taught her *protection*. When someone is as selfless and benign as Robbie, there are many predators waiting at their door.

Along with my emotional soul sister, others I overlooked for some time have now come to the forefront. I mentioned Sharon Schofield before, godmother to my son, and a lady I met through the aforementioned first school friend made in Sydney, around twentythree years ago. Sharon has been a valued reviewer of this book and along the way she has discovered uncanny similarities with my life. Sharon honoured and touched my sensibilities by stating I was the sister she never had. Since my Roman days I craved sisterhood, my sweet Sharon; did I know it would come, twentythree years ago? No. Do I feel it now? Yes. I have found my sister at long last and not a drop of Italian or Spanish blood runs through her veins.

There are many others I had not seen as true friends: Karen Drake, Sue Parmaxidis, Lee Casuscelli, Michael Sinemoglou and Cheryl Walker, people I brushed past in Years 7 to 10 but had not invited into my inner sanctum for reasons that seemed obvious at the time but irrelevant now. I credit Facebook for our reunification – a little late perhaps, but if unlike me you're a glass half-full type of person, we can change this to 'so early in our lives'. For me right now, *fifty* (years old) *is the new thirty.*

Facebook brought me to complete strangers, too. There were a couple of Americans, and a lovely Italo-Greek lady called Anna. A soul is a soul and it can transcend time and space; we don't need to touch in order to 'be touched'. Three years ago I finally met Anna and her husband Dom in the flesh and it was a beautiful, teary encounter, and although Anna lives in Sydney – ironically only two doors from the 'friend' who eventually alienated me from my 'tried and true' – I am not letting distance get in the way of a beautiful friendship. To the friends I have mentioned throughout this book, including my St Helens Park bestie, Debra, Lotta, and Lars (RIP) in Sweden, and Jens in Germany, I say *thank you* for your kindnesses, your ongoing presence, and for plugging the holes left by people I once held dear.

I don't know whether I've become *more* positive in my attitude now but whatever it is I'm doing, it's somehow attracting more positives into my life. A most important one arrived in the form of a job that suits my new lifestyle and mindset, and I didn't have to look far. Barossa Enterprises, the disabilities organisation I worked for after the Magill Training Centre fiasco, embarked on a significant reshuffle of titles and duties and offered me the right hours and conditions for a new lifestyle. I know you should never put all of your eggs into one basket but right now I view this job as my last; after forty jobs and eight career changes I think I can afford to remain optimistic.

Adam applied himself to the study that would take him where he wanted to go in Corrections, passing with flying colours. Adam had various aspirations he wished to fulfil in his current role, but with the prison awaiting a private takeover, his once secure job is now in question. The decision pending is whether Adam accepts an exit package and relocates into a completely different career, or simply transfers to another prison. A return to Mupulawangk is the most obvious answer, but this remains to be seen. As much as DCS hurt me, I cannot continue to condemn this department ot Mupulawangk, because it has treated my husband well which is what matters most in the grand scheme of things. With an early retirement planned for me, DCS is our bread and butter, so thank you.

The most important thing I need to do now is to work with the antidepressants, my Mindfulness, and my psychotherapist in order to avoid the deep low that almost took my life. I owe this to myself, to my children, my pets, but most of all to the man who taught me how to love again: Adam Brewer, my husband. I've also tried hard to keep up polite assertion but my chemical wiring still gets in the way and I do react a lot sooner on many occasions. People are opportunistic and I've had it with being an abused Good Samaritan. I do try and step back though, assessing carefully, allowing time to go by, and then act if still required to.

Regarding my reactive spirit my colleague and friend Amanda recently said, "You allow people to rope you in. You jump in too quickly and involve yourself in people's lives."

Amanda was correct … I say *was* because I'm learning quickly to stop doing this. Aside from the frail (I refrain from classifying them as 'the aged' for there are some highly toxic 'old' people out there who have learnt nothing), young children and most disabled individuals, there are three other types of needy people. There are those who have no determination to learn and just latch on for all they can receive, and there are those who wish to learn but are lost and afraid inside of themselves and are unable to recognise where or how to begin. The third type are bound by circumstances such as politics or climate and this is where the Red Cross, Amnesty International, and Médecins Sans Frontières are indispensable resources – so dig deep, if you can. In my current 'how to really live your life' books, the first type gets one chance and *only one*, and the second get one chance and a set of direction tools.

I believe this is as far as we are required to offer service although yes, it *is* spiritual fact that human beings find themselves on earth to offer service either as a healer or a teacher. However, please keep in mind that you cannot give what you don't have, and so, through self-love and polite assertion, be sure to fill your own stores first and *then* give to the world, lest you too become one of the world's needy or dangerous out of dire self-depletion.

Service does not always mean service to humans; we can serve our world by looking after the environment which ultimately sustains our people, and if you are a crazy animal lover like me and are often put off by humanity, there are our animal brothers and sisters who need us too. In Heaven we play and communicate with animals and do not eat them. Animals have a soul, an identity, a right to be, just like us.

I decided to adopt Kamrita, a Bengal tiger living in the Chitwan National Park, Nepal. Kamrita is one of approximately eightytwo breeding tigers living inside the conservation park which is still somewhat threatened by poachers and floods. Tigers are one of the world's most endangered species with as few as 3000 left in the wild. The threats driving the tiger population to the brink of extinction include a demand for parts as trophies, loss of habitat due to agriculture, and ingredients found in traditional Chinese medicine such as the tiger's penis, wrongly used as an aphrodisiac. Sadly Kamrita died of natural causes aged nine, but my sponsorship continues with another male tiger named Dalla.

I have perhaps gone a little too far in how I now view animal rights over human, but with seven billion of us devouring the earth's flora and fauna I feel it's our environment who is now the underdog. Education regarding population control and interpersonal relationships needs to begin inside the primary classroom, so as to bring future generations back to basics and a productive reality. The social ills that afflict us en masse today are threatening everyone and everything at an alarming rate, so that now I find myself advocating against multiple pregnancies more and more. What I've seen in my community service work is cringeworthy. Our children are not being honoured; they are being tortured to death on so many different levels. It would be absolutely wonderful if solid couples would adopt rather than conceive; there are so many abandoned kids out there, kids who without direction will only inhabit and propagate an already congested penal and welfare system.

But back to me now. I have to learn to leave politics and religion alone, hence getting off Facebook for a while again to reassess. Facebook is a friendship forum; I understand this, but because I am so passionate and outspoken about social and environmental issues, I can't help using it as a venting forum also. People are not interested in negativity or championing. They just want to share their happy snaps and empty calorie statuses. It's their right too, but for me there's too much going on in the world to mask it all with frivolity and ignorance.

Keyboard warriors and trolls have managed to find me via the accessibility of mutual Facebook friends, with the hot rages ensuing simply not worth my time and energy. Another old adage I appreciate is the evergreen *you can lead a horse to water but you can't make it drink*. People need to learn value systems on their own. Together with Facebook, a place I've cherished for bringing together me, Adam and so many known and unknown friends, I've seriously curtailed the amount of media current affairs consumption I devour. I cannot change the world on my own so why let 'edited' and sensationalised news govern my sensibilities and reactions.

I joined a writing group in Mount Pleasant that I'd had my eye on for almost a year. This group is headed by a young bisexual man suffering borderline personality disorder. I count Dwaine as one of my new and trusted friends and, yes, I still find myself oddly attracted to people who grapple with personal demons, but only ones who are nonetheless able to practise leadership, altruism, originality and authenticity. For me this is true testament of what dealing with life is truly all about. Suffering certain mental health issues is not immediate carte blanche for co-dependence and abusive behaviour. Even behind the dark veils of certain mental health issues lay a deep understanding of considerate accountability, of right and not so right.

Before joining Pleasant Prose and Poets I'd been a member of Barossa Writers for a year but found the admin side of things too boring, and decided to leave. A *writing* group should be all about writing, and Pleasant Prose and Poets fulfils this objective, and to a high standard. Our growing group is a blend of old, new, static and dynamic, and I just love it here.

I also decided to do something permanent about my weight. The idea of gastric sleeve surgery was sown into my head by Cheryl Walker, a former high school acquaintance who found great success with the procedure, having been preceded by her partner, Daniel. Adam joined me in this venture and together, on 7 September 2016, we had 90 percent of our stomachs removed.

Following the suicide attempt I fell off the 5:2 diet wagon and put the lost 16 kilos back on, plus another two. I overcame the purging side of bulimia a while ago but remained an emotional eater. As I write, I have lost 20 kilos and Adam a huge and transformative 43. As usual though I've taken a tool and run with it, hoping it will turn into a magic formula. I've stopped losing weight because although I still cannot sit down to a medium size meal, every half an hour or so I go and feed my face with cheese, crackers and biscuits, thus continuing to pile on excess calories. The Adelaide Bariatric Centre has placed me on a twoyear waiting list for a tummy tuck on the proviso I lose another 10 kilos ... time to rewire my subconscious if indeed I want to reach this goal. Very little in our lives comes to us via magick, although magick certainly does exist.

As we speak, life seems to be on track. Conan in particular gives me so much joy and love. One needs to observe animals for a short while to see how close to nature and 'God' they truly are, compared to us. Animals do not overthink anything, they just are, and if you gain their trust through charitable purity, they give back so much – and then some. For me animals are a salvation and children of the Universe ... even the brothers, sisters and family I so craved.

Where 'family' are concerned, this is yet another spoon-fed fable we are made to digest ad nauseam. *Blood is thicker than water* they say ... yet it is but another favourite cliché I find less than true.

As my family members fell by the roadside one by one they were replaced by complete strangers who showed me more love and good will with five sentences and two actions than my entire clan did in a lifetime. Choose your tribe wisely and don't allow your 'name clan' to force you into guilty servitude. You owe only to yourself and no other, unless deserving of your good will. We are free to choose who we want and do not want in our lives, toxic progeny included. Remember that other tired cliché: *you can choose your friends but not your family.* This one is slightly more accurate than the one above, although not on a metaphysical plane of course. But I'll let *you* look into that one.

With a renewed passion for our animal kingdom I can tell you this: over the decades I have given to people, and particularly the *wrong* people, enough of myself. So I have taken a leaf out of my own 'how-to' book and become highly discerning – even harsh – with anyone new that steps onto my turf, especially at work. The workplace can be the most distressing place of all if one allows it, with its pecking order, maniacal management teams, and competitive morality killers. Regardless of it being a personal or work-related relationship, I no longer jump in like a schoolgirl extending friendliness and a forthcoming nature to all and sundry. By holding back, assessing personalities and actions, I can now determine things much more clearly. I then dip one toe into the water and begin making a slow and well equipped approach. I no longer offer second chances because as *Dr. Phil wisely states: the best predictor of future behaviour is past behaviour.* Why waste time on recidivists?

Today the new Angelica commands people to *earn* her love and trust. I am no longer a free for all and I approach life holding up a huge neon warning sign.

Our tiny home in the Mid Murray one horse town of Tungkillo was originally designed to house Adam, me and Mango. Now we have Edan, Kristen, Mango, Conan, Caesar, Thor, Suzette and a visiting crow called Vincent, but, like Robbie's home, it's a small space filled with BIG love so my point here is all about *gratitude*. Dreams are compasses for ambition that need to be trialled, but don't go swapping this compass for the morality one. Take Mother for example: her obsession with a singing career and quest for fame robbed us both (and Piero too) of maternal bonding and protection. At eightyone years of age, Gilda is *still* 'undiscovered', she lives alone and away from family in Western Sydney, still in Housing Commission accommodation comprising an overflowing and cramped unit filled to the brim with soul destroying memorabilia. Had she abandoned something that was not for her for whatever reason, and had she embraced me and motherhood instead, just as I did with Alycia, Mother and I would be so much better off emotionally.

Gratitude is a terrific tool for good mental and spiritual health. Take stock of what you have and leave what is out of your reach … it wasn't meant for you this time around. Life has many fruits to choose from … just look at my own beginnings: I too wanted to be a singer and *Source* granted me a voice, and yet my voice was better suited to community services work where I'd talk people down and away from destructive behaviours. I wanted an older man, a father figure that would step into the shoes Ettore had vacated before my eyes could gaze upon his, but *Source* kept me waiting until at age fortyfour Adam, a younger man, was sent to teach me love. Had I met Adam before all of the trials and tribulations of life unfolded, I would not have appreciated him. The place I found myself in my youth required acknowledgement of kindness and surrender to love. I was controlling, tunnel visioned and wild. The love Adam and I share today is deep, kind, authentic and understanding, everything wedding vows attempt to be but often are not. With Adam there was no 'pre-nup' to abide by; we were both poor.

Adam and I don't need wild sex and varying scenarios to keep each other 'interested'. All those magazine clichés are directed at plastic relationships, often built on appearances and modern-day expectations. Adam and I feel completely harmonious just being inside the house together, yet doing our own thing or nothing at all. An occasional look in and *how are you doing bubba?* is enough for us. With Adam by my side or not, a great deal of the old anxieties and jealousies have left me. Adam is 100 percent trustworthy and reliable and I no longer seek further proof of his dedication to me.

Discovering the road to happiness yields many well-kept secrets, one of which entails keeping things simple and impersonal. My nature and extreme life experiences changed me from an inquisitive, artistic girl, to a combative, defensive justice seeker. I see clearly now that the fibre of humanity cannot be changed, and the reason for this is historical *and* metaphysical. *Carl Jung's 'what you resist persists' could ring no truer.

I spent aeons of time and precious energy trying to change those impacting my life, but all I succeeded in doing was force them to hurt or abandon me. When the due date is up, *it's up*. Shakespeare had known this all along when in his 1599 play *As You Like It* he wrote: 'All the world's a stage, And all the men and women merely players.' We are not this name, this body, this life, we are souls living many an existence on earth in order to atone karmic debt from a past life. We are here merely to learn and offer service through our learning and spiritual/emotional evolution. As already explained, 'service' does not mean wasting precious time and energy giving to those who are not yet ready to receive; become *a beacon* for obstinacy by setting examples and little more until they too come to their own realisations. One of my favourite Theosophical quotes is: *'When the pupil is ready, the Master appears.'

Lastly remember this: not everyone is meant to stay. As Shakespearean actors, some of us volunteer to play the villain, and he/she knows this before he descends onto the earth plane. The earth plane is the Universe's lowest vibrational sphere. The villain creates so much toxicity it will surely be at his detriment – or at best, as a vehicle for societal ostracising. How 'honestly' he plays his role will determine the screen billing he earns for his next incarnation. As for you, don't choose to become this villain's victim, so play your role well for if you concede you will surely be prompted to assume the role of victim next time around.

My own spiritual realisations arrived the day I found Betty Shine's book on that brick fence in Petersham in 1991. Nonetheless it took an attempt on my life and my husband's wails of pain to begin addressing them. Beware the 'Love and Light fairies'; some are as commercially bound to profiteering as pharmaceutical companies or fast food chains. They will preach this and that but rarely walk their talk because often the walk is a long one and can be dull and innocuous. Here's another adage … *not all that glitters is gold*.

Nothing worth having happens involuntarily. We often earn valuables through genuine intent and the careful navigation of personal experience. Our new toy – the 'New Age Movement' – is saturated with literature, paraphernalia and practicians who are no more conducive to our wellbeing than the purchase of a lottery ticket. Spirituality is *inside of us*, it's that tiny voice that comes from the gut and steers you like a compass to or away from self-fulfilment and self-effacement. Likewise, religion is another unnecessary moral barometer. If you require religion to act compassionately and be accountable, then you are *not* a compassionate or accountable being – at least not yet. Today you are perhaps that villain in order to teach others what they do not wish to become. 'Good' and 'bad' are only relative to an individual's karmic lesson; learn the lessons quickly and you'll beat karma while you are still young enough to enjoy some of the genuine beauty our earth plane can and does offer us.

I don't know what type of life student I've been. Personally I feel I've been stubborn and somewhat arrogant most of my time here, but then again I had to do a lot of it on my own because my formative role models were sorely lacking, and it was *I* who chose them up there in the astral – they were *my* karma. My greatest flaw has been a staunch determination to pursue what was not meant to be mine – just like Gilda. It's possibly the reason the shit continued and then created my mental illness. The physical body can only take so much before it begins to give up. For a tenacious character such as me, the Universe needed to become a boot camp tyrant.

Up until a few months ago I cried bitter and hateful tears for friends and family I loved, who misjudged and hurt me beyond explanation. The layers of injustice crushed me like a vice and I won't end this story proclaiming I've forgotten and forgiven all, for I certainly have not. The 'new Angelica' journey has only just begun and at fiftyone years of age, give a tired, stricken and fallible woman a little more time please.

To YOU my antagonists I say *thank you*; thank you for leaving, because by taking your exit from *my* stage you've vacated a precious place for those few who saw past the craziness, the violence, the profanities, the arrogance and stubbornness. These heroes and heroines have taken up the pain-body challenge, offering only their love, friendship, healing and understanding. Their gift of true humanity is everything this little illegitimate Italian girl Snake ever wanted or needed.

* * *

It is 15.59 on 27 December 2017. I've now finished my book and I'm overjoyed. I've been plodding along with this story for so long I don't remember when I first started. Thank you for reading it and I hope you can take something from it that might help you. I actually don't like clichés much (although I use them a lot) so I'll refuse to say: *if my book helps even one person, my job is done.* My job is *not* done because I'm still in the process of helping *me*, the most important person in the world. Our job is never done boys and girls, it continues on for eternity. I am as imperfect right now at 16.00 as I was at 16.00 back in 1982 or 2015. I am, today, merely a better version of those imperfections.

Living in the *now* is not easy. It is human predisposition to mourn the past and anticipate the future, but as we already know from all the esoteric books and teachings doing the rounds nowadays, the *now* is all we have and can control and an acknowledgement of the *now* is the fundamental principle for Mindfulness, something I can't talk enough about, the most important tool any mentally ill or hypersensitive person can use to regroup and self-regulate.

And, if life has given you a massive beating and depleted your brain of active chemicals, do not feel conspicuous about accepting adequate prescribed medication from a *genuine* doctor, not a pharmaceutical scout. Our soul is perfect and incorruptible, but once encased in dense matter that is fuelled by human desire, it is as vulnerable as a dwelling sitting in the path of a tornado.

Focus on the little things for they are your daily manna. Listen to how the different barks your dog makes to communicate with you lead you to a spiritual communion with him/her. Truly *taste* the love utilised in the meal your lover prepared for you. Appreciate the fact your child is a hard worker and does not indulge in drug taking, instead of wishing they had become a doctor or lawyer. And there is so much more to appreciate and celebrate: the productive way in which you spend your money, that kind post you found on your Facebook wall from a friend you don't see often, a sunny day to hang out your washing, the taste of a new flavoured Lindt ball, the bulb that popped up from nowhere in your garden. These are the simple joys that overshadow any major win in your life.

I've often been sought out for advice. I guess I've become a good teacher for others even though I've treated myself terribly. Various experiences have taught me 'street psychology' and I think I've become pretty cluey when it comes to *true character-and-intent-recognition*. Leisl said I could not pull the wool over *her* eyes like I had with 'everyone else', yet I reckon it's 'everyone else' who walks around wearing eyepatches made of thick wool as they await a perfect moment of ambush – Leisl included.

Offering unsolicited advice is not really my thing but if you were to ask me about my top eight lifestyle upset preventers, they'd look something like this:

Listen to your gut. Your gut is your Higher Self and it is never wrong. If you do not know what this feels like, it's the very first reaction you have when you meet someone or are about to embark in something new. Our heart is the voicebox for our human emotions, and our brain is the reactive or logical trigger. Our gut instinct, is *our Soul.*

Don't be pushed into any social norm, especially not marriage, religion or procreation. Too many children are born for a wrong reason. Don't be like my mother and have children because you happen to have fallen pregnant, your partner or inlaws want children/grandchildren, or because all your friends are doing it. Even less so if you are at risk of personal or interpersonal dangers, and definitely *not* in order to acquire welfare cheques. Who you have a child to is of paramount importance too. Remember that children require the guidance and love of *both* parents lest they later blame *you* for giving them only the one. Take your time getting to know your partner well before making this enormous and accountable decision. Abortion is not a sin, however in today's progressive age there is no excuse for not using reliable contraception. There are too many children suffering or in state care. Having a child is not a right, it is a privilege.

YOU FIRST! It sounds narcissistic and selfish but it is most certainly not so. When you are bountiful, satisfied and happy, you will automatically and naturally want to share these joys with others. Again, my muse Dr. Phil, often states that you can't give away what you don't have. Be discerning of who these 'others' are, for not everyone is honest or for your Highest Good. Cut off your losses quickly and defiantly and *never* look back because, and I repeat Dr. Phil's most influential statement, the *best predictor of future behaviour is past behaviour.* For humanitarian types like me or those who suffer 'rescuer syndrome', it is easy to fall into the empathy trap. Remember the aforementioned three needy types of people. Also, it is perfectly okay to aid those suffering from mental health issues, but beware the 'my love will make you whole' trap. Chances are your love will die of exhaustion or you'll acquire a mental health problem yourself. Always protect YOU FIRST!

Be truthful, and truthful does not mean tactless. The truth can hurt, yes, but it is not 'your stuff' if it does. People rarely want the truth because it forces them to take stock of their own bullshit and fakery. Truth is only relative to experience and upbringing, but there are Universal Truths that apply to us all. Stand proudly inside the power of your own Truth for it will set you free and bring to you the opportunities and people that will carry you forward in life.

Do not proselytise. Live by example. The haters will always hate, but those who want to improve themselves and return to their authenticity will come and ask for your help. Always put your trust in the Universe for it is always on your side – even when it sends you thunderbolts and brimstone. Believe wholeheartedly that if it is meant to be, it will. The Universe will not move an inch in your favour until you have understood and learnt its lessons. Don't keep the Universe and YOU waiting.

Don't worry too much about death; it is in fact another birth. Don't avoid situations in case you 'might be killed', you don't know when it will happen or how. It could be tragically or it could be quick and easy. It could be tomorrow or in fifty years' time, so why stress? It's out of your control. *Don't* take ridiculous risks in order to test out this theory, however. We choose our time and method of death when we sign our life contract before incarnating into our current role and 'physical overcoat'. Our past life memories are erased so that we can give our new life the best possible go, so *go* ahead and GIVE IT A BLOODY GOOD GO MATE!

If you are lonely or if people have let you down so much you fear getting close to someone again, get a rescue dog or cat. Each year in Australia alone 250,000 innocent cats and dogs are destroyed. If we did this to humans it would be labelled *genocide* and considered outrageous, and yet it seems perfectly okay to do it to them. Only arrogant religious zealots will tell you animals do not possess a soul. They do. They go to Heaven and either reincarnate into a new pet to console us from the loss of our departed one, or they simply wait for us to get there. An animal's heart is pure and his third eye is always open – unlike us. Animals in the wild act on instinct just like us, and yet 'we' are deemed the more intelligent species. Animals love unconditionally and are the best therapy for a broken mind and heart. Be a responsible pet owner and neuter your loved one so that his progeny will not risk forced euthanasia. There is no love warmer than that of a pet. I belong to a Pomeranian owners page on Facebook. There is a Texan lady here by the name of Judy Fletcher who posts her four adorable Poms regularly. These must be the most 'professional' Pomeranians on the face of the earth. She has them playing guitars, the piano, ringing bells for customer service, *cat*walking, sightseeing in their little motorised car, and their wardrobes surely rival anything even remotely close to a Lady Gaga entourage. The furbabies names are; Koji (aka Mr Whoopty-Woo), Keiko (aka KiKi), Kaija (aka Piggy Smalls), and my favourite, Kuma (aka the Angry Customer). I can be in the foulest of moods, or heartbroken or depressed, and Judy's beautiful, pampered, talented, and completely adored Poms just put that smile right back on my face. The power of animals and of those who love them.

As you have read, I am a music lover. To this day I find music far more therapeutic than talking about my problems. After all, you can only repeat things so many times before it begins to alienate others or, worse, this woe becomes a part of you through repetition. Unlike Mother I do not limit myself to one genre, but my predilection for progressive vocal trance stands. Surround yourself with music for music fills the void human contact sometimes creates. As you have read, this story of mine is filled with musical people and their contributions. I also find biographies and autobiographies helpful because they offer our pain perspective and dimension. Although we should never compare how pain affects us, it is encouraging to discover we're not swimming inside the abyss alone.

Exercise humour! Humour broke down barriers with difficult people, professional training couldn't. Don't chastise humorous people, learn from them. I can turn anything into a joke, and I can also take one. Too many are jumping on the 'offended' and 'precious' wagon nowadays, and slapstick, dark, and provocative humour has reached a level of censorship, disdain, and liability I find irreconciliable and pathetic. RIP the greatest, unbridled, most spontaneous and brilliant humourist of them all, the unabashed, undeterred, Sir Robin Williams.

* * *

So what am I looking forward to next? Not much. I think I've ticked off most bucket list items, including going to see my favourite anti-hero live on stage, the eclectic and enigmatic 'Sir' Russell Brand, and also his Gemini singing double, Boy George, in late November 2015. Would love to meet Dr. Phil though and maybe I will in 2020.

In July 2016 we returned from Italy, where Adam took part in another clay pigeon shooting world championship. I did not think I'd ever return to Italy after my Rome visit in 2008, but decided that Italy is not just Rome, and far from it.

We hired a car and began our pilgrimage, visiting Milan, then moved up to the picturesque Alpine region of Brescia staying in beautiful Lago di Garda, and paying the Perazzi gun factory in Botticino Mattina a prized visit, where a highly excitable Adam had his final fitting on a custom made $15,000 shotgun. Alas it was not ready to shoot at the competition held, on 14 July in Piancardato near Perugia.

In Venice we toured the watery city via *vaporetto,* declining the eighty euros required by the *gondolieri* for a half-hour trip. In legendary Murano I bought glass ornaments and jewellery for loved ones. The following day we found ourselves in Florence for Adam's forty-first birthday, then back onto the autostrada and its countless toll booths, on our way to Umbria.

For the shooting competition we stayed just outside of Assisi's medieval city centre. The shoot was held over four days, of which I decided to spend three doing my own thing. Following the hard labours that had been our honeymoon, I recognised that frequent rest and fewer destinations are the proper ways to travel. Besides, I had to dispel the bad memories that dormouse-skinning Paolo had created in 1974.

In Assisi I paid homage to my favourite saints, San Francesco Bernardone and his beautiful friend Santa Chiara Offreduccio, by visiting their respective cathedrals. I had already done this as a child but I'd lost those memories; Paolo's brutal ones had swallowed them up. I purchased a little San Damiano cross to atone for the loss of the one given to me forty-odd years ago. It now sits proudly with my collection of world travel memorabilia.

In Perugia we toured the famous *Baci* chocolate factory before setting out for an infamous part of *my* journey: Rome. When we'd landed at Milan airport, the customs officer supervising the arrival of Adam's Browning shotgun warned us Rome was a chaotic place. He wasn't wrong and the bad vibe I'd felt in 2008 had quadrupled. The single highlight in Rome – for me anyway – was a planned catch-up with Paigh, the 'juve' terror turned master's degree heroine and globetrotter. Paigh was nearing the end of a twoyear world trip, stopping in Rome to complete a course. Truth is sometimes stranger than fiction, no doubt.

Adam was interested in seeing Rome but corroborated my feelings regarding its negativity and disorganisation. Although he missed out on a few 'must do' items because of poor transport choices, Adam was equally glad to be out of the Circus Maximus. The 'eternally' chaotic Rome, the city where my own personal chaos began, can just go *a quel paese!* as the Italians would say. For me at least, there will never be another *Arrivederci Roma.*

The Amalfi Coast was not a planned destination but I am glad we went there – and Sorrento too, despite the white knuckled, teeth clenching drive up and down those tenuous hairpin bends. From the breathtaking coast we ventured into Naples and into the fabled, tragic, Pompeii – another childhood dream ticked off my extensive bucket list. Up north and once more on the autostrada to Pisa, and then hello again Milan airport, and homeward bound.

Italy is a beautiful country, and more so around the provinces and coastal towns. We were saddened by the recent spate of earthquakes that have destroyed ancient provinces like Amatrice and Pescara del Tronto, places we did not stop in but drove through. It was during this trip that I once and for all made my peace with my country of origin. I was also surprised when I realised how well I spoke Italian, given the many years away from 'home' and a lack of daily practice. So many locals congratulated my command of the language that I felt both elated and a little melancholy about possibly never again having the opportunity to converse like that. I now fully identify as an Australian of Southern European background and have dropped the 'Nordic' illusions of old.

All good things must come to an end, but at least I have wonderful memories I've shared with Adam and it felt good to have Adam savour his European wife in her original element.

In the meantime, I have Dr. Phil's show at noon on my days off, Conan's furry kisses, Alycia's thirty-first birthday in September 2019, Kristen's twenty-eighth, and Edan's twenty-third. I'll also be sleeping next to my husband tonight and most nights and this alone is a blessing. With a twenty plus kilo weight loss I've beaten my pre-diabetic symptoms and I'm wearing colourful and tailored clothes again for the first time in fifteen years. Hopefully in 2020 we'll visit Canada and Alaska and pop over to California so Edan can experience Disneyland and Warner Bros. Studios.

We had planned to stay in little Tungkillo for the rest of our lives but were flooded on Remembrance Day 2016, which then led us to seek out a new home and mortgage. On the 'eleventh hour', as is so very common for poor life students such as myself, we were approved for a bridging loan on a house in Flaxman Valley, an isolated part of the Barossa Valley I've loved so much. This beautiful colonial stone house with the bluestone frontage I'd always wanted became ours on 24 December 2016. It sits among the sprawling vineyards of an award winning South Australian Merlot (Irvine Wines) with a dam nearby, and five acres of land that accommodate the sheep I've always desired and hopefully an alpaca too some day. This home is Irvine Wines founder's former home, Mr Jim Irvine, so we are proud owners of a piece of historic Barossa Valley viticulture. This home is also my thirtieth move, but I will not die here; Adam and I have decided to retire to Abbruzzi or Tuscany. We fell in love with Italy's north on our 2016 trip, and I will honestly be able to say I came full circle in life once we get there.

A few months ago a breast screening organisation called to say they had found an abnormality. Struck dumb, as soon as I got off the phone I broke into bitter tears. I had witnessed how breast cancer had taken my cousin Rodolfo and little Giannina's beautiful wife and mother away, and it suddenly dawned on me I wasn't ready to go. Even though at this stage it was mainly presupposition on my part, I was not really surprised by the news. The years of angst and despair had ignited my cancer cells, no doubt, but hell, I WAS NOT READY TO GO! I had changed my mind about dying … I wanted to stay now, this was *not* my time!

And indeed it was not. After three horrible days of waiting and begging 'God' for forgiveness, my new scans and ultrasound returned a negative result. This scare was my last Universal warning, of this I'm certain. It's so easy to fall into old habits, folks …

I'm now actively learning to listen not only to my gut but also to my body, and because I *am* a little life ravaged I now recognise I require more rest, so the North American trip may be our last major one, but hey, I've also learnt to never say *never!* I have to learn to stop trying to control my future. I need to live for the NOW and just sit back and watch the magick unfold.

To continue reminding myself of uncelebrated good fortune, I've branded myself with two tattoos on the insides of my wrists. The first is a blend of my star sign, Taurus, and Adam's, Cancer. The second is the Wiccan symbol for spiritual protection, the pentagram, inside the symbol for the female gender.

I still have biweekly meltdowns because of feelings that overwhelm me – mostly due to PTSD, so the tattoos assist me to return to the 'reality base' and that all important *now*. Unfortunately, however, my life experiences have greatly changed my personal views on humanity. Whether my psyche shut down a great deal of emotional response in order to protect me or that 'earthbound' logic has hardened my heart, I cannot say, but one thing is certain: I have decided not everyone on earth is meant to – or deserves to – stay, and in order to make peace with this decision, I've had to separate the human *I* from the Spiritual *me*. The Spiritual 'me' knows we are all perfect souls adopting a momentary role but the human 'I' has had enough. I'm now here for a short time to live and learn about myself so humanity, get out of my goddamn way. I'm fiftyone years old and as I type this, I've *earned* the right to choose who or what I now give my energy to.

After decades of giving to mostly ungrateful people – my family included – today I am concentrating on God's most innocent of all creatures, our animal brothers and sisters. Species by species they are vanishing from our earth in their hundreds of thousands to make room for the real rodents, all seven billion of us. I understand the likes of Brigitte Bardot a lot better now, and not only for her involvement in animal protection.

During my 'black year' as I prefer to call it, my deep depression took me to the 'underworld' of the internet. I've certainly been curious and morbid my entire life, but as I began losing faith in everything and everyone, I needed to validate my core beliefs with a little research. With the exception of child porn (I did NOT need to see this as I knew it existed due to my work with children at risk), I left no stone unturned. What my computer found under these stones and threw at me nauseated and shocked me. I knew human beings were capable of immeasurable cruelty and amoral behaviour, I'd lived some of it and worked inside a lot more, but these images and videos … well, let me enlighten you.

The most graphic (for me), was the video of the beheading of an American aid worker that arrived under the banner of religious vindication (fundamentalist Islam). Aside from the fact this poor man had his head cut off slowly with a small, possibly blunt knife, the noises that came from him will remain ingrained in my mind forever. Second were the horrific revenge killings imposed on rivals by various South American drug cartels, with the worst depicting body parts grotesquely displayed in public places, to serve as warnings. I then watched actual footage of a man being dismembered as he hung upside down – ALIVE! In third place are various crime scene photographs ranging from serial killer cases to war zone ravages, and everything in between. There are also autopsy pictures (including ones where medical personnel have disrespected the corpse for their own sadistic pleasures), road traffic accident photographs that show horribly mutilated bodies, pictures of the ravages of drug abuse on the body (such as the famous Faces of Meth campaign in the US), 'crack whores' soliciting for drugs as they spread their infection onto men desperate for sex … Stills and footage involving gross self-mutilation such as the teen *'Coldnessinmyheart' pictures, extreme body modification, and suicide of every genre. Then there are the aborted foetuses, cultural horrors such as the misogynist trend in Pakistan, where acid is thrown in women's faces, and then sadly – and for me the most harrowing nowadays – animal cruelty. I cannot even stop and sign an animal abuse/anti-poaching petition on Facebook now because the images devour my soul and I cannot lay my soul bare a moment longer.

Porn. Anything and everything is available on the internet. Your children can access all of it with the click of a mouse, including all that I have described above. The most difficult for me to see, and I could not tell you why, was amputee porn, followed closely by (you guessed it) bestiality porn. Then you have the basest forms in scat, prolapse, gagging, and 'simulated' torture, rapes, and 'gangbangs'. I ask you to place firm child friendly filters on your computer sets.

Type anything you wish to see on your search engine and it will send it to you through the wantonness *sans frontières* of cyberspace. The only items I could not access, try as I might, were 'snuff films', but then these are far too lucrative on the black market to distribute for free, right?

This, ladies and gentlemen, is a great portion of humanity for you. Yes, you can choose to click on puppies and snowflakes, but surely the grossly ugly side could somehow be omitted? And with flash production 'progress' and insatiable consumption, gross overpopulation, and insidious political correctness, the ugly side is only getting uglier by the day.

Yet I do not see a shred of ugliness when I gaze into the eyes of an animal.

No, I'm sorry, I don't care too much about the populace anymore and I am convinced the zombie apocalypse is indeed upon us. Look around you … what do you see? Zombies everywhere, right? Drugged zombies, technology zombies, cultural zombies, frightened zombies, medical zombies (everyone identifies with one or more emotional/mental/behavioural illness now), commercial zombies, fashion zombies, religious zombies, work-bound zombies, sex zombies, reality TV zombies, crime zombies, terrorist zombies … and I'd better not say what I think lest I be labelled racist or prejudiced.

Again, I say that there *is* beauty left in our world if you get out of big cities and go your own way, but at what cost? Society is set up by the 'New World Order' to implode via frenzied production and frenzied consumerism. We need the mythical Biblical 'rapture' to take the righteous out before we are all dragged down the *S* bend – but are we ready? Could we abandon our jobs and illusory security borders called mortgages, to protest, Taksim Square style, against governments, religious factions, commercial wizards, nanny states, and taskmaster lawyers? *Rick Grimes we are not – I am not – not alone anyhow and certainly not today. I'm tired … so very tired.

Gilda, my selfish mother, was the first and last straw across my broken back and if you ask my wonderful chiropractor, Donna, she'll tell you how broken it is. I love my husband, my children, my clients, my animals, but I'm ready when my time comes, I'm completely ready for the Heavenly Spheres. Insofar as I do *not* wish to go now, I've set myself an exit age, eighty-four; to be asked to live longer than this inside this salacious chaos would be just downright cruel.

Just to top off my bizarre life, dear readers, my daughter Alycia was featured as one of the brides in last year's instalment (Season Five) of the reality television program, *Married at First Sight Australia*, and Kristen? She's moving to England for love. Edan has not been well, suffering major OCD and depressive mood escalation which is interfering with his supported employee work, and Adam is due for spinal surgery in May following a painful bulged disc mishap last March which refuses re-absorption.

I received a very unique gift for my fifty fourth birthday from my beloved husband. It unlocked one penultimate piece to this puzzle called 'my life'. A sample of my DNA revealed my geographic ancestral origins; I am 48% Italian, 44% Spanish, 7% French, and 1% Basque. So I was right in feeling more Italian than Spanish, my grandmother was right about my mother having *tainted* the virtual purity of our Spanish lineage by having me with a Roman, and I was wrong on all counts of feeling Northern European because 'I was certain' there were Anglos, Krauts, or Scandinavians involved *somewhere* at some point.

Life never stops giving aye? But remember Carl Jung's prophetic line: *What you resist persists*, so keep swimming 'cos if you don't, you drown! Bring on 2049 … I'm looking forward to my return Home.

I'd now like to end this chapter by reminding you all this is not a sob story … I do hope you realise this? I am a stubborn, slightly sanctimonious individual who carries a generous serve of oppositional defiant disorder and yes, it has taken me a long time to learn my lessons but *better late than never* as they say, right? I think I'm starting to learn them now, even if a little angrily. Anger in dedicated doses is good for you; unlike apathy, it keeps you going. Never, ever feel sorry for a determined individual in spite of their troubles. I only ever pity those who never find their way, for they remain too blind to see.

I don't know what genre to put this story into but I'm guessing it may belong to the 'Romance' sector, for it's a story about finding love, not just from an external human being, but from inside the self too.

EPILOGUE

———

I mention Facebook a lot. Facebook can be a curse or a blessing depending on how you choose to use it, but funnily enough I share a birthday with its creator, Mark Zuckerberg. Irrelevant perhaps, but I no longer hide how obsessed I am with astrology. I no longer hide *anything* about myself, and you either like me or you don't. I have now discovered Instagram which I much prefer because content here is far less conducive to combat and disagreement.

On Facebook a lovely woman called Amanda Ferguson 'added' me just because she liked a comment I made on my husband's friend's page. My husband's friend suffered, at age thirty-seven, a massive stroke which completely changed what appeared to be a charmed life. The same tragedy occurred with Amanda. Since then Amanda and I have become close and when finally I met her in person, I added her to my 'Sorella' soul group. Your true family can be anyone you resonate with and certainly not blood.

Just prior to ending my Facebook life for five months due to more meltdowns, Amanda sent me a meme that befits this epilogue. We are not certain who wrote it, so my apologies for any copyright breaches.

UNCONDITIONAL LOVE

The process of beginning to love yourself unconditionally means learning to enjoy spending time alone and getting to know your true self, heal your hurts and pain, and establish your own self-worth and value system. Once we achieve this, we take this value system and ground it within us so that we live our life according to this.

There is no room to be controlled, manipulated ... or used when we have established our true self-worth.

Therefore, we become responsive only to acts of kindness, respect and unconditional love.

Anything less than this fades away as an illusion

I have endured a lot; I won't say 'more than anyone else' but it's enough for me, I think. Noone can measure individual tolerance for pain. For one person their worst emotional pain might be as a victim of incest, and for another, not winning a beauty pageant. Everything in our lives is relative. If you don't like something or someone, stick with your tribe and let them be. Sure, defend yourself if you must, and darn well expect your tribe to support you, but if you are able to just walk away ... walk away. Karma isn't everyone's friend and it may bide its time, but be sure it will find them ... and you too!

* * *

Karma found Gilda.

Mother is now eighty-three years of age, and she just loves to play on her seniority to obtain clemency. In time, I managed to divest myself of the many villains who, for beneficial lessons or otherwise, had entered my life. The only one I could not seem to be rid of however was 'Mother'. Gilda has managed to keep a hold on me forever and a day, and this hold is called *filial emotional abuse.*

Filial emotional abuse is systematic, all pervasive and calculated. 'I brought you into this world, I can take you out of it.' ... that type of thing.

When I moved to South Australia I did not keep close contact with Gilda. Part of the reason for moving away was to be far from her and that is how I liked it. Hence, when she visited (three times, including once for my wedding) even an hour in the same room with her was enough to send me scratching at walls. Poor Adam had to take her out sightseeing so I could regroup. I'd lost all of my tolerance where she was concerned. I did not – and do not – love my mother ... I can't. Sometimes you love someone but you don't necessarily like them, but I also do not *like* Gilda, and I'm not sorry.

I did not end things with Mother many years before because I felt morally bound to her and because I believed my children needed a maternal grandmother. But just as Gilda lacked with me maternally, she sorely lacked as a grandmother too. It was Rhys's parents who filled that role.

Calling Gilda on the phone once a month or less proved a painstaking exercise. I used to find ways of putting this off until I felt forced to pick up that receiver, because the first three words to come out of Mother's mouth were usually accusatory and condescending, and she had done a good job keeping me filled with guilt.

Nevertheless, keeping my temper in check was proving harder these days, although Mother seemed happy for me and genuinely interested in my marriage. She would ask to talk to Adam and then force him to tell her he 'loved her'. Everyone was obliged to pay the diva homage and the stage had to be kept lit up for her.

Eventually I tried to explain my mental illnesses to Gilda. I could not find ways to translate – let alone relate – post-traumatic stress disorder or my special type of depression into Italian for her, and hoped my simple definitions might be enough … after all, Gilda was a (self-proclaimed) genius, so she'd understand.

Chris Browning, my psychotherapist, knew I needed to do something about Mother. Mother was a massive thorn that still festered in my side, but why couldn't I just say what I needed to? Filial emotional abuse, that's why.

Every situation holds within it a catalyst, and my surgery would be my way out. Gilda was once again staging one of her operatic productions and it coincided with our gastric sleeve surgery. I would seize this opportunity to test her 'maternal obligations' and see if she'd come to the party. When I called I was met with a speculative attitude. I explained to Gilda that I was pre-diabetic and did not wish to perish in the same miserable way Alfonso had, or like the many diabetes stricken patients I had met at Campbelltown Hospital. I suggested she consider the same procedure for Piero, who was in the vicinity of 130 kilos.

"No, I would never do *that* to him!" she snapped.

"Why?"

No reply.

Three months' post-op and not a word from Gilda. It was time to act on that catalyst. What *decent* mother does not pay her daughter a call to find out how a major operation went? All my mother was ever interested in was her goddamned productions! It was all she ever spoke of during our calls, even expecting me to make the journey across to New South Wales to sit through them.

Gilda had miserably failed my test and I now held carte blanche to say what I needed to – but how? I began by dipping one toe in – I sent her a simple Christmas card (with no gift) asking her why she had not yet contacted me about my surgery. Below is Gilda's return Christmas card reply (translated by me from the Italian language utilising all of Gilda's exclamations, capital letters, etc.):

> Dear Angelica,
>
> I have understood from your Christmas card that you are upset with me for not calling you regarding your surgery. I APOLOGISE FOR THAT! But I feel JUSTIFIED because the operation was not a dangerous one; had you been in any danger I would not only have called you, I would be in SA sitting by your bedside. I realise that for you and Adam, feeling healthy and ATTRACTIVE is very important, but in my opinion, this is simply a day-to-day preoccupation similar to shopping for groceries or washing the dishes. Over this side of the woods you need to realise I am now an eighty-year-old woman who is foolish enough to engage in activities that are too mentally and physically challenging. My memory fails me somewhat. You may gather evidence of which I am relating by asking your Uncle to show you the production video of the "Zarzuela Y Cancion"; here you'll clearly witness all of my miseries.
>
> There is something else I need to say to you, something rather ugly. You and I now live freely and independently from one another, correct? What I mean to say is that for many years you and I have not held mutual interests, including the management of your brother's future! I was born with a masculine character, one far more prone to career pursuits than family life. I realise this is a defect. So when you told me we would live completely separate from one another, I accepted it entirely. This was YOUR decision! I then decided to kill off my maternal instincts, but never MY SENTIMENTS.
>
> I care about you and admire your love of work and family life. These are indeed talents and qualities; I believe only in these areas are you better than I, but at my age I cannot change. I can only move forward, all the while grinding my teeth. I have decided to write two books; the first I have sent to a printer, but they have done nothing to get it published. It is a testament to humanity and transcendental in nature; a tool that could greatly aid humankind if it wasn't so mad and hell-bent on suicide. The second is an accumulation of personal experience and reflections that deal primarily with how I have been discriminated against throughout my life.
>
> I AM NOT A PERSON LIKE EVERY OTHER! I am filled with character flaws, some very serious, I know, but I can be excused for despising life, for it has well and truly massacred me. For a very long time I have also

despised God, and recently, I have even cursed my dead mother for bringing me into this world. I now realise however, that I was <u>CHOSEN</u> for a spiritual mission much greater than myself, and that my sufferings are the indirect sum total of this COSMIC destiny I must fulfil. In turn, your sufferings are also indirectly linked to this mission.

Forgive me for telling you these things, but there needs to be absolute clarity between us. Consider these disclosures an 'unusual' Christmas gift from me. And, if you still hold an ounce of trust in God, pray for me, because my soul is in mortal danger.

Your mother, Gilda.

I do not know what you, the reader, may see in this letter, but all I could see, was a distinct focus on 'I' and 'me', and a shitload of crazy bullshit and recrimination. As far as I was concerned, Gilda had flung open the door for a discussion I should have had with her decades ago.

I was particularly struck by the statement, 'You and I now live freely and independently from one another, correct? What I mean to say is that for many years you and I have not held mutual interests, including the management of your brother's future!' More than the rest, it was this portion of Gilda's letter that fuelled my rage.

Piero was *not* my responsibility! I paid my dues where my half-brother was concerned. My dislike of Piero brought me a failed marriage and a son with disabilities. Gilda had done absolutely *nothing* to improve Piero's life or that of future carers; why should I now be expected to pick up her slack? We'd already had this discussion – it was topic closed. I never once said I would not oversee his future or not ensure Piero lived in a place of integrity and trust, a place like the one I worked in, for example; but what Mother demanded of me was out of the question, and she had not accepted that.

While I lived with Piero I tried to teach him how to talk and a myriad of other skills. I'd also found a supported employee service close to Bonnyrigg that would offer Piero structure, purpose and self-worth, just as it now does with Edan at Barossa Enterprises, but Gilda would have none of that.

"It's human exploitation!" she snarled pompously, referring to the token wage Piero would receive, one offset by the lifetime disability pension he never got to keep.

Gilda believed Piero behaved 'almost' like a regular person and that 'her way' had made him more so. Gilda's 'way' included giving Piero permission to jump on a train – often without a ticket – to explore whichever locations he felt like, usually the Sydney CBD. Piero repeats what is said to him, does not know his address or phone number, and does not wear a medical ID bracelet or pendant. On one of his excursions, Piero decided to enter a random home, sat on the couch and turned on the owner's television. Enter the owner of the house from hanging out clothes in her backyard, and you can imagine the rest. Liverpool Police then took Piero to Liverpool Hospital where he was held overnight until his family could be located. It took the police almost seventytwo hours to track down his mother and stepfather.

On another occasion, my stepfather came to blows with a man at Cabramatta when he heard his young daughter's screams from inside a public toilet. The man rushed inside only to find Piero forcibly holding the frightened child by her arms. The man swung at Piero until Alfonso intervened.

"My son is handicapped! Can't you see this?" Alfonso yelled in the furious father's face.

Like it would matter to a loving and conscientious father!

It wouldn't be the first time an intellectually challenged individual has sexually assaulted someone ... but please, allow me to tell you why Piero *was* a good candidate for committing a sexual assault. In her infinite wisdom Gilda became convinced Piero needed sex and marriage just like any other regular person. In my opinion there are varying degrees of intellectual disability that enable individuals a right over such desires, and Piero is not one of them. Gilda would give Piero a designated time slot where he was encouraged to engage in masturbation.

"*Vai a fare la paja!*" she would direct Piero in half Spanish, half Italian.

Additionally, she'd ask me to look into mail-order brides for him.

"Surely there is a kindly, illiterate soul out there that would want him for a husband?"

When I refused to participate in such a ridiculous quest, Mother arranged a mock wedding for Piero in which she supplied a blow-up doll for his bride.

Piero became obsessed with a girl he'd met at respite. One night he left the house around midnight, walked to the girl's house, took off all his clothes on her porch, and banged on her door. The police were again called and the girl's parents took an Apprehended Violence Order out on Piero.

Piero himself became a victim of sexual assault. Piero spent most of his time loitering, eating, or watching DVDs. Mother would often send him to a nearby video shop to exchange his movies. On one occasion, he was set upon by a number of youths (Piero's version of events) who, not satisfied with stealing his videos and money, decided to sodomise him as well. Of course Gilda had no clue such an incident took place until Piero complained of a sore bottom, but by then it was too late for a rape kit sample.

Piero is also volatile and aggressive. He doesn't like being told 'no' and on several occasions has taken a knife or fists to Gilda and Alfonso. When my children were young, Piero was rough and excessive with them. He had covered four-year-old Kristen with as many blankets as he could find, then planted his enormous girth upon her. Fortunately, Letitia, who despised Piero and Alfonso equally, was on the ball and intervened in time. Piero has also pushed two-year-old Edan down the stairs and charged at my heavily pregnant stomach with a broom handle.

In spite of this 'regular' person's behaviour, Mother insisted that following her death, or before, Piero should be welcomed as a permanent fixture inside my home.

I sat at my desk and, with the assistance of Google Translate, I furiously began typing Gilda a long letter. My Italian is not strong enough to relate what I needed to, but forty pages later I'd said everything I should have thirty or so years ago – *all of it*!

Gilda's reply shook me to the core.

Adalgisa!

I cannot return a reply to your letter in the same tone you have used with yours. I shall tell you why; I do not possess a similar weapon as you, but before I disclose to you what type of weapon this is, I need to explain how it links to something you seem overly preoccupied with.

These practicians you speak of, the ones curing you, they can only see one part of the problem, the SCIENTIFIC PART; a part that only manifests externally (panic, anxiety, fear etc.) This part can be compared to a tree trunk and its branches. HOWEVER, WHAT THEY DO NOT SEE are the roots of the tree, buried deep into the ground. In your case, these "roots" have a name; HATRED! HATRED! Hatred consumes, destroys, and poisons the ENTIRE organism of those who house and fuel it! Organisms who are innately weak and do not possess the capability for hatred's annihilation within themselves.

Many times I have recognised my contribution to your sufferings, and I also begged for your forgiveness. This WEAPON that I have chosen for you, should have been enough to cure you of your emotive illnesses; it should have served you as true medication instead of resorting to "tablets", capsules, and the like. The ROOT of your PSYCHOSOMATIC illnesses is none other than SPIRITUAL, and no SCIENTIST (unless otherwise engaged in mysticism) can cure an external ailment that is entrenched in spiritual roots. These roots are also linked to your own willpower and a deep desire to end all physical and mental suffering.

This is all I am able to relate to you today. I have written a six-page letter (which translates into twelve as I have used both sides of the page), which you will receive as part of my will following my death. In this letter I have addressed many of the points you have raised in yours, a letter I consider a "succinct" document and information manual (or seminar) regarding hatred. I tell you this; you do not only HATE me (I who deserve your hatred), you also hold unfounded hatred for a naive and illiterate man who has wronged you only in that he wished to protect you from the perils that can befall a small child or teenager loitering outside her home. Yes, he was overprotective and he was wrong, but he was only looking out for you!

I don't know if this same HATRED forced you to break all ties with your cousins, but it is painfully obvious you have no love left for them either! Insofar as Letitia goes, I can't say you feel HATRED towards her; more so resentment (a lesser degree of the same sentiment). One thing is certain, you have alienated from your life others who would not "FUNCTION" as you wished them to, (because all human beings worthy of your "sanctuary" must be perfect). Have you asked yourself; "Am I perfect?" I'm pretty certain you have not asked it of yourself, because hateful people are completely lacking in auto critique.

Please, find yourself a practician with a high level of SPIRITUAL know how. It will prove a hard task because most medics suffer from scientific fanaticism, similar to religious fundamentalism when the religion is equally manufactured by ignorants. I am a religious person as well as an intellectual and I pray God does not punish me too severely for not setting foot inside a church. Truth be said, I find sermons boring, and I also don't want to hear provincial housewives demolish Beethoven's Ninth Symphony with their deformed voices. Yes, alas, I will always be a critical Operatic Soprano. MEA CULPA!

I now ask you to never write to me again; not during my entire life! What's left of it anyway. In order to continue living for as long as possible, I need to avoid added suffering. I HAVE responsibilities on many levels. I AM

EIGHTY YEARS OLD! And letters like this one which you have sent me, can only accelerate a journey towards the afterlife.

(No Signature supplied.)

Stubbornly, I replied to this letter. It was stupid of me, I know, but I had to. If I'd felt outraged before, now I felt mildly distraught. How does a mother disregard a daughter's pleas and full disclosures on heartbreaking topics like sexual and corporal abuse, suicide and mental illness, all the while proclaiming her own woes, without addressing a single one of mine? HOW?

Adam begged me to stop reading anything that might come back from Gilda. He had watched me move forward at great speed, and as a loving and conscientious husband – and human being – he wanted to keep me here.

"When the day arrives and you receive this six-page letter of hers, I'll check it for documents and we'll burn the rest unread together," Adam assured me.

A reply to my reply did arrive and Adam had bucket and matches ready. He took the letter from me but I snatched it back from him; what else could the monster say?

"It will be the last time bubba," I promised, "and I'll read it in front of you."

Same shit as above with a different smell. It began with (in capital letters): *WHY DID YOU WAIT SO LONG TO STICK YOUR KNIFE INTO MY BACK?* This was followed by further excuses, recriminations, and another request I stop writing.

By the end of this fiftyyear saga, I knew I had done the right thing *for me.* No matter the outcome, we need to liberate ourselves of what no longer serves us. *Everything* has consequences yet our predicament lies in the fact that some are harder to accept than others.

In order to feel 100 percent certain, I *had* done the right thing for me, I consulted my 'science fanatic, non-mystic' psychologist Chris Browning. Chris, who I now cherish and respect as a significant tool in my recovery, offered added advice that further compounded my decision not to give in to Gilda as I had throughout my life. She did not say to me that I was wrong or right; Chris, as the excellent practician that she is, had merely allowed me to see what already stood out in front of me, rather like Windex and a microfibre cloth might. Again it was a case of *you can take a horse to water but you can't make it drink.*

Additionally, there was my beloved Dr. Phil. So okay, this Texan retired psychologist is larger than life, a television sensation, but so what? His Truth is my Truth and that's all that matters.

One of Dr. Phil's segments dealt with parental abuse, and what Dr. Phil explained to the beseeching child occupying his studio, spoke to me on such a personal level I truly did not need to revisit guilt, ifs, buts, or second guesses ever again … Gilda was WRONG! She was unrepentant and I no longer needed her to fix what SHE'd broken!

I am now the only one for my Highest Good. *I* rewrite my life's script. *I* surround myself with people who genuinely love me. *I* am PROUD of ME.

* * *

Alongside my two daughters I chose Sabrina Gold as my third bridesmaid when I married Adam; a beautiful, soulful girl who walked a similar path as me during her childhood. I wasn't sure how I'd end this Epilogue let alone this entire story, so I looked at Adam's Facebook Newsfeeds and found Sabrina's latest post:

Once you learn how to be happy, you won't tolerate being around people who make you feel anything less.

Thank you Sabby. I *am* happy and I don't tolerate anyone who endeavours to make me feel anything less.

Yes, ladies and gentlemen, right now, right this moment *I am sooo happy* … whatever that word actually means.

Om Shanti Om)0(

CAST AND CREW

———

Because I am keeping the identity of many of this play's cast members confidential, perhaps you'd like to know where they are now.

Alessandra and Ileana (Umberto Primo school friends – Rome)
I located the two girls on Facebook (again, *thank you* Facebook). They are both successful women still living in Rome. Alessandra owns and runs a graphic design company and Ileana is a public servant for the Lazio region. Both girls remembered me but showed little interest in pursuing a long distance friendship.

Maria
Both Maria's family and Gilda were relocated by the NSW Housing Commission into new homes at Mount Pritchard, ironically ending up on the same street yet again. Maria devotes all her time to a handmade jewellery business (originally prompted by her boyfriend Con many years before). I located the business and Maria on Facebook. After exchanging a few inboxes, I discovered her father had passed away from advanced emphysema. Maria is still single and appears to have stopped dabbling in recreational drugs. Maria took twentyfive years of my life … longer than Rhys and some murder sentences.

Carla
I found Carla on Facebook. Carla suffers from debilitating multiple sclerosis. She is married with three children. We are no longer in touch.

Noel and Valerie
I reunited with Noel and Valerie via Facebook. Coincidentally the couple had moved out of their house in Rosemeadow only a few years before I moved into

mine. My house was only a couple of houses down the road from theirs. Sadly, and following three decades of marriage, Noel and Valerie split. Noel and I have maintained our long-term friendship, with him attending our wedding here in Adelaide. Noel is now married to Danielle and lives in Queensland. Adam and I attended *their* wedding.

Doug
I have seen Doug's profile on Facebook via Maria's page. I have written to him but received no response. Noel is also keen to reconnect with Doug.

Allira and Patrick
Allira and Patrick appear to be still happily married and live somewhere in South Australia. I inboxed Allira via Facebook but she declined a reply. I have not pursued either of them further. The couple are childless and successfully self-employed. Allira is also an active animal conservationist.

Alastair and Marianne
Alastair and Marianne continue to run their wedding cakes showroom. The business has featured in all the notable national bridal magazines and is established as Sydney's leading novelty and wedding cakes outlet. I recently discovered the showroom has been placed on the market due to falling sales. My source explained that Alastair is heartbroken and tired, and now just wants to save the family home and retire. I had kept in touch with Marianne but decided this part of my life has been exhausted and have deleted all relevant contacts.

Rhys
Rhys is remarried with a young child. Over the past few years Rhys and I have maintained civil contact in order to discuss our children, namely Edan. A year ago Rhys and his second family moved to South Australia, starting a new life here, and for proximity to Alycia, Kristen and Edan. Adam and I often congregate with Rhys and his family to celebrate our children's birthdays. I bear Rhys no ill will and have forgiven him his trespasses. I hope this book does not unravel all of the good work civility has sown between us to date.

Eser
I remained in touch with Eser via text for a few years following the dissolution of our relationship. Eser moved to Melbourne with a university student he

was romantically involved with, but insisted she return to Sydney with him. Eser cannot be found on any social media domain and I no longer seek him out.

Jason

Jason and the woman he cheated on me with (and on her with me) had a child together, a girl. Jason sold his beloved Rosemeadow Gardens home, the one he worked overtime to pay off throughout our two years together, in order to build a new home with Kyera. Kyera and Jason have since split and sold this home. Jason was stood down from Juniperina for quarrelsome behaviour, and had apparently tried to sue the Department for unfair dismissal. Jason made several attempts to contact me, confiding to a former colleague he was still in love with me. I have not fully forgiven Jason.

Denise and Fiona

Denise and Fiona continue working at Mupulawangk Prison. They are no longer allies, let alone friends; in fact, Fiona claims to detest Denise. Both foes are in the OPS3 acting up pool. My current Mupulawangk friends claim that officers at the prison now comprehend the kind of person Denise is; unfortunately, this 'realisation' has arrived too late and no longer offers me any comfort. I am still waiting for karma to tap their sorry asses.

Valeria

Valeria and her husband of twenty-two years have divorced. He has admitted cheating on her. In 2015 Valeria travelled to the United States with my eldest daughter and had, up to recently, maintained strong ties with her, which I dislike but was forced to accept. Valeria has made no attempt to reconcile with me and I no longer wait for her to. At Rodolfo's wedding, over a year ago, Valeria dropped a fleeting kiss onto my cheek and ran away. I do not know what it meant but I no longer care for an explanation, or for Valeria. When my Uncle Eduardo died recently, only two days after I visited him at a hospice he was placed in by his "nowhere to be seen children whilst he was alive", I finally laid my *inherited family* to rest once and for all. Valeria was instrumental in this final insult against my sensibilities; she who had not spoken to her father for four or more years until he was pronounced terminal. The letter I left below for her and her siblings is self explanatory:

Valeria, Rodolfo, Bianca,

Thank you so much for having kept me out of this sad situation by deliberately not disclosing my uncle's temperal lobe tumour biopsy results.

Please allow me to REMIND YOU ALL that whilst Biancawas interstate, Rodolfo a grieving single father, and Valeria a long term non contact, it was I and Adam who kept in constant contact with your father. WE were his lifelines. Alycia too was there whenever she could be, thank you also for not letting her know the results – possibly because you were so hellbent on my not getting them? Precious of you. What do you think I had planned? To attempt the taking over of his meagre possessions? Oh no my dear antagonists, I want nothing from my uncle just as I want nothing from your aunt Gilda when she passes. I am rich enough as I am with wonderful children, the greatest husband and my idyllic home and loving animals.

Today I've said my goodbyes to a man who was less than fair on me as well, Mr Eduardo (surname), but I pushed all that aside because intrinsically he was kind hearted and meant well. We (my maiden name) have gotten the wrong end of the stick because of our forefathers and mothers, and most of us are still suffering from what I have dubbed "The (maiden name) Curse"; but not I – not anymore. Today after kissing his brow, I close the door on everyone related to this clan of which I absolutely and categorically DO NOT BELONG TO!

Let me rue the day I am ever forced to cast my eyes on any of you again. You have unnecessarily and unfoundedly targeted a well meaning, innocent family member who once loved you all like the brothers and sisters she never had.

Please feel free to bury your aunt too and sort out her affairs – including the welfare of her son as there too I've been unfairly written out. You are all such resolute individuals, I'm sure you'll do a brilliant job. May karma continue to find you wherever you are.

Faithfully not part of your lives or family,

Angelica Brewer

ACKNOWLEDGEMENTS

Thank you to the following 'crew' for helping me throughout the arduous journey that is revisiting one's own difficult life. You were there when I needed you in one form or another:

Adam Brewer, Alycia, Kristen, Edan, Jenny Brewer, Yvon Wilson, Belinda and Daniel Longstaff, Nicole and Phil, Marie Nader (RIP), Mark and Lina, Yanek, Chad, and Melanie Rachwal, Sharon and Phil Schofield (Sharon – peer reviewer), Kiarnee and Billy Derksen, Jan Bomford, Sabrina Gold, Anna Cammareri, Amanda Ferguson, Danielle and Noel Wolfenden, Frederick Harris (peer reviewer), David Alston (Editor), Rachel Iasiello, Daniel Naüjoks, Robert Kelley (peer reviewer), Angela and Joe Marrone, Jens Lindemann, Lotta Thörner, Lars Olssen (RIP), Trish and Mark Kennedy Gilbert, Karen Drake, Robbie Rogers, Jonothan Milman, Jim and Leanne, Kim Shannon, Amanda Stewart, Ros Pursche, 'Eduardo' (RIP), 'Letitia' (RIP), 'Gianna' (RIP), 'Rhys', Lucy Fry, Dwaine Nethery and the gang at Pleasant Prose and Poets, Lynda Richards, Kerri C. (peer reviewer), Karen Healey, Kathryn Szyszka, Peter Hanns, and all my medical practitioners; 'Dr Ellie', Donna Palmer, BSc(Adel), MChiro(Macq), Tomatis (Level4) Consultant, Dr Natalie Payne, psychologists Chris Browning BA(Psych) HONS Grad Dip Ed, and Kirsty Moore BSc, Grad Dip Ed, MPsych (Clinical).

Now last but definitely not least, our best friends and furbabies, Conan, Frodo, Mango(RIP), Gogo, and Caesar, our five sheep, seven chickens, five fish, and six cockateils.

And a special thank you to Hannah, Fern, Alexa, Andrea, and Chelsea at Matador Publishing for their effortless work and patience getting this monumental job off the ground - finally!

I would like to dedicate this page to Robert Kelley. I met Robert through a mutual friend on Facebook. Robert lived in Colorado Springs, Colorado. Because Robert was a writer and literary editor, a member of a number of book clubs, and in his words, 'a voracious reader', I brazenly asked this virtual stranger if he'd mind being a peer reviewer for this book, and he generously agreed. On 1 May 2016, just after his eightieth birthday, Robert passed away following a battle with cancer. Before crossing over, our mutual friend asked Robert if I could identify him by name and photograph for the book's acknowledgements.

Robert feebly replied, "Anything."

Robert reached Chapter 14 of my story before departing for Heaven. Along the way, Robert sent me a few email comments and below is my most treasured:

Angelica … leave it to you to experience a phantom pregnancy. And of course later you come to the startling conclusion that 'If it isn't one thing, it's your mother'.

Completed Chapter 8 and thanks for your patience with me. As a rule, first person stories will not hold my attention. Yours is the exception and I keep expecting you to fall down in the narrative but you don't and this amazing story continues to unfold. Good job girl.

You've asked if it moves along and keeps the reader's attention. It does … and I am less than halfway through this saga and I know that you survived because I have seen you on Facebook. Lol

Also with the childhood you had and the abuse it's quite amazing that you are still with us and am I damned glad you are.

There is this strange counter-balance between the dark and the light, the life of and in an odd sense the privileges (travel, experience, fantasy), and the horrors of sexual abuse from both males and female and this mother of yours who shares the abuse spotlight with Joan Crawford. How awful for you but clearly your strength of character has prevailed. Perhaps in some weird way because of these horrors.

I feel privileged that you have allowed me to be a voyeur of your life and I thank you for it. Send me more soon as you have thoroughly hooked me even though I have a stack of books to be read and those I'm already reading.

Love to you my friend.

Robert

Robert Kelley

BIBLIOGRAPHY AND WORKS CITED

———

Opening Page - Split Enz Lyric (Copyright Tim Finn) courtesy of Mushroom Group (Mushroom Sync).

Pg XIV - "What you resist persists". Partial quote written by Swiss psychologist Carl Jung from his talk on 'the shadow self', circa 1913.

Pg XIV – "Where Attention goes Energy flows; Where Intention goes Energy flows!" Quote written by author James Redfield from his 1993 book 'The Celestine Prophecy' (Warner Books).

Pg 19 – "Now We Are Free". Song written by Hans Zimmer and Lisa Gerrard.

Pg 60 – "The Rose". Song written by Amanda McBroom.

Pg 65– "Lately". Song written by Stevie Wonder.

Pg 65 & 186 – "Evergreen". Song written by Barbra Streisand and Paul Williams.

Pg 66 – The words in this book are not the exact words written by Jon English. I had kept this note pasted inside a diary for a few years until such a day when during a fight with Patrick, I decided to put the entire diary into the trash, just to prove a point. A most regrettable action. Jonathan James "Jon" English, was an English born Australian singer, songwriter, musician, and actor. Jon died aged sixty-six on the 9th of March 2016 as a result of post-operative complications.

Pg 67 – Puberty Blues. A coming of age novel written by Gabrielle Carey and

Kathy Lette. Published in 1977 (McPhee Gribble). The film adaption for the book was released in 1981 and directed by Bruce Beresford.

Pg 75 – "I Ran". Song written by Mike Score, Ali Score, Frank Maudsley, and Paul Reynolds (A Flock of Seagulls).

Pg 76 – "Run Wild". Song written by Barry and Robin Gibb.

Pg 75 – Adel is the Christian name I go by. The one which appears in all of my documents. For this book I have chosen to write under my middle name of Angelica, I was however born Adalgisa.

Pg 78 – "Africa". Song written by David Paich and Jeff Porcaro (Toto).

Pg 96 – "Here Comes the Rain Again". Song written by Annie Lennox and Dave Stewart (The Eurythmics).

Pg 123 – Ginger Lynn Allen is an American pornographic actress and has made appearances as a mainstream actress also.

Pg 125 – "Separate Lives". Song written by Stephen Bishop.

Pg 145 – Fifty Shades of Grey. An erotic romance novel written by E.L. James. Published in 2011(Vintage Books).

Pg 156 – Mind to Mind. Autobiographical recount of a psychic healer by Betty Shine. 1990 (Corgi).

Pg 186 – "Wind Beneath My Wings". Song written by Jeff Silbar and Larry Henley.

Pg 190 – Dawn Hill is an Australian author living in the U.S. Her books have emerged around 1987 and published by Pan Books (Australia).

Pg 190 – Conversations with God (trilogy). A sequence of spirituality based books written by Neale Donald Walsch. First published in 1995 (Hodder & Stoughton).

Pg 209 – Extract taken from the novel, The Thornbirds by Colleen McCullough, 1977 (Harper & Row).

Pg 219 & 372 – "Pain Body" is a term written by Eckhart Tolle in his 1997 book, The Power of Now (Hachette).

Pg 232 – "Southern Sun". Trance vocal written and produced by Paul Oakenfold.

Pg 294 & 424 – You Can Heal Your Life. A self-help, New Age book by Louise L. Hay, 1984 (Hay House). Extract and title.

Pg 326 – Bernard Finnigan was an Australian politician who in 2011 was charged with child pornography offences. On November 10th 2015, Finnigan was then found guilty of one count of accessing child pornography.

Pg 335 - This is a fake prison Doc Number.

Pg 340 - This is a fake prison Doc Number.

Pg 341 - This is a fake prison Doc Number.

Pg 345 – Vince (Vinnie) Foccarelli is a high profile former Australian outlawed bikies gang member.

Pg 346 – "Screws" is a derogative name given to Correctional Officers by BrewerText_CT150819.indd 466 15/08/2019 11:58 bibliography and works cited 467 prison inmates.

Pg 348 – Bevan Spencer von Einem is a convicted child killer connected to a string of horrific murders dubbed by Police investigators as "The Family Murders".

Pg 352 – "It Started With A Kiss". Song written by Errol Brown.

Pg 372 – The Power of Now. A Guide to Spiritual Enlightenment. Self Help Text by Eckhart Tolle, 1997, (Hachette).

Pg 388 – The White Mouse. Historical autobiography by Nancy Wake, 1985, (Pan MacMillan).

Pg 412 & 413 – Title and extract taken from Treasure Yourself by Miranda Kerr, 2010 (Hay House).

Pg 424 – The Body is the Barometer of the Soul. Self-help, New Age book by Annette Noontil, 1994, (McPherson's Printing Group).

Pg 434 – Quote by Dr Phil McGraw often used on his American CBS talk show "Dr Phil".

Pg 436 – Proverb attributed to Buddha Siddhartha Guatama Shakyamuni.

Pg 445 – coldnessinmyheart is a profile found on Imgur, and posted by a member about "Joan" an extreme self-harmer who may be deceased.

Pg 446 – Rick Grimes is the protagonist in AMC's The Walking Dead series and created by writer Robert Kirkman and artist Tony Moore.